ADOPTION AND IMPACT OF

OER IN THE GLOBAL SOUTH

ADOPTION AND IMPACT OF

OER IN THE GLOBAL SOUTH

Edited by Cheryl Hodgkinson-Williams and Patricia B. Arinto

African Minds
Cape Town

International Development Research Centre
Ottawa • Cairo • Montevideo • Nairobi • New Delhi

Research on Open Educational Resources for Development
Cape Town

HOW TO CITE THIS VOLUME

Hodgkinson-Williams, C. & Arinto, P. B. (2017). *Adoption and impact of OER in the Global South*. Cape Town & Ottawa: African Minds, International Development Research Centre & Research on Open Educational Resources. DOI: 10.5281/zenodo.1005330

NOTE ABOUT THE PEER REVIEW PROCESS

This open access publication forms part of the African Minds peer reviewed, academic books list, the broad mission of which is to support the dissemination of African scholarship and to foster access, openness and debate in the pursuit of growing and deepening the African knowledge base. Chapters 2 to 15 in this volume have each been reviewed by at least two external reviewers. Chapters 1 and 16, which constitute the introduction and conclusion components of the volume, have not been peer reviewed. Copies of the reviews are available from the publisher on request.

First published in 2017 by African Minds, the International Development Research Centre (IDRC) and the Research on Open Educational Resources for Development (ROER4D) project.

African Minds
4 Eccleston Place
Somerset West 7130
Cape Town, South Africa
www.africanminds.org.za

A co-publication with
International Development Research Centre
PO Box 8500, Ottawa, ON, K1G 3H9, Canada
www.idrc.ca / info@idrc.ca

The research presented in this publication was carried out with the aid of a grant from the International Development Research Centre, Ottawa, Canada. The views expressed herein do not necessarily represent those of IDRC or its Board of Governors.

ISBNs:
Print edition 978-1-928331-48-3
eBook edition (IDRC): 978-1-55250-599-1
ePub edition: 978-1-928331-61-2

Orders:
African Minds
4 Eccleston Place, Somerset West 7130, Cape Town, South Africa
info@africanminds.org.za
www.africanminds.org.za

For orders outside Africa:
African Books Collective
PO Box 721, Oxford OX1 9EN, UK
orders@africanbookscollective.com

Contents

SECTION 4: SOUTH AND SOUTHEAST ASIA

SECTION 5: CONCLUSION AND RECOMMENDATIONS

Acknowledgements

The ROER4D Network Hub wishes to acknowledge the ongoing efforts of the ROER4D researchers and research associates in strengthening the Global South community of Open Education researchers, and for their commitment to the chapter development processes which resulted in the publication of this volume.

Sincere thanks to Tan Sri Emeritus Professor Gajaraj Dhanarajan and Maria Ng for sowing the seeds of the ROER4D project that now have come to fruition in this publication and the many other outputs on OER adoption in the Global South. Thanks also to the original planning group which contributed to the inception of the ROER4D project and provided much needed encouragement along the way: Laurent Elder, Phet Sayo and Matt Smith (all from the International Development Research Centre [IDRC]); Fred Mulder (former Rector of the Open Universiteit, Netherlands and UNESCO Chair in OER); Carolina Rossini (who at the time of her contribution to this project was the lead of REA Brazil, a project by Instituto Educadigital); Savithri Singh (Principal of Acharya Narendra Dev College, University of Delhi); and Stavros Xanthopoylos (former Associate Dean of the MBA program at Fundação Getúlio Vargas and Professor of the Production and Operations Management Department). Thanks to Marshall Smith for reviewing proposals and to Rob Farrow of the Open University OER Research Hub for his contribution at the inception phase.

The ROER4D Network Hub wishes to thank and acknowledge the contribution of the organisation representatives who provided invaluable support in the project's contractual processes: Keval Harie and Naseema Sonday at the University of Cape Town Research Contracts and Innovation office; and Lindsay Empey, Mano Buckshi and Kim Daley of the IDRC. Thanks also to Wawasan Open University, Universitas Terbuka Indonesia and Open University of Sri Lanka for hosting ROER4D workshops.

We also acknowledge the inputs and support of Dal Brodhead, Ricardo Ramirez, Julius Nyangaga and Charles Dhewa from the Developing Evaluation and Communication Capacity in Information Systems Networks (DECI-2) project.

The project owes a great debt to the supportive team of peer reviewers who assisted in the editorial development of this volume: Alan Cliff, Beck Pitt, Bea de los Arcos, Birgit Loch, Carolina Botero, Carolina Rossini, Catherine Cronin, Cher Ping Lim, George Sciadas, Ishan Abeywardena, Jophus Anamuah-Mensah, Kerry de Hart, Leslie Chan, Linda van Ryneveld, Mardu Parhar, Mary Burns, Megan Beckett, Mythili Ram, Patricia Watson, Rebecca Miller, Rajaram S. Sharma, Ryhana Raheem, Sacha Innes, Tel Amiel, Valerie Lopes and Venkaiah Vunnam.

Special thanks are due to the superb African Minds book production team: Simon Chislett, Glenn Jooste and Lee Smith; as well as to African Minds Director François van Schalkwyk for his partnership in the publishing process. The project is also greatly indebted to IDRC publisher Nola Haddadian for her tireless support in the publishing and editorial review process.

The project wishes to acknowledge the contribution of the ROER4D publishing team, comprised of Publishing Manager Michelle Willmers, Associate Editor Henry Trotter, Project

Curator Thomas King and Bibliographic Editor Ed Hart. Special thanks are also due to other Network Hub members: Project Manager Tess Cartmill, Communications Consultant Sukaina Walji and Evaluation Consultant Sarah Goodier.

Finally, the project wishes to thank the organisational hosts, the Centre for Innovation in Learning and Teaching at the University of Cape Town and Wawasan Open University; as well as the project funders: Canada's IDRC, the United Kingdom's Department for International Development and the Open Society Foundations.

About the editors

Cheryl Hodgkinson-Williams is an Associate Professor in the Centre for Innovation in Learning and Teaching (CILT) at the University of Cape Town (UCT), South Africa. She holds a PhD in computer-assisted learning and has taught and supervised in the field of information communication technologies (ICT) in education since 1994, first at the University of Pretoria, then at Rhodes University in Grahamstown and now at UCT. She teaches online learning design and research design in the Educational Technology postgraduate programme and is the coordinator of the Mellon-funded scholarships for this programme. She supervises PhD and masters students and is a supervisor for the Global OER Graduate Network (GO-GN). Her particular research interests include online learning design, electronic portfolios and the adoption and impact of OER. She is the Principal Investigator of the IDRC-funded Research on Open Educational Resources for Development in the Global South (ROER4D) project.

Patricia Brazil Arinto is a Professor and former Dean of the Faculty of Education at the University of the Philippines – Open University (UPOU). She has a Doctor in Education degree from the Institute of Education, University of London, and has designed training programmes on technology-supported teaching and learning for secondary school teachers, teacher educators and university faculty in the Philippines, Cambodia and Laos. She has also led several funded research programmes on ICT integration in Philippine schools, including a United States Agency for International Development (USAID)-funded blended teacher professional development program in early literacy instruction for K–3 teachers in 2015–2017, an Australian Government-funded study on use of tablet computers in nine public secondary schools in 2012–2014, and a USAID-funded national assessment of the state of ICT in Philippine basic education in 2012. She is the theme advisor for MOOC research in the Digital Learning for Development (DL4D) project and the Deputy Principal Investigator of the ROER4D project, both of which are funded by the IDRC.

Foreword by Tel Amiel
(UNESCO Chair in Open Education)

There was much to celebrate when The Year of Open activists and enthusiasts met in Ljubljana, Slovenia, as part of the 2nd World OER Congress in September 2017. The movement had gathered serious momentum and, as anyone in attendance could attest, there was no doubt that openness in education had become a global movement. Conferences are moments to celebrate and share, but, particularly at gatherings of this scale, they also provide an opportunity to reflect on gaps, limitations and biases. As a subset of educational technology and a child (or sibling) of the Free and Open Source Software and Open Access movements, it has has taken some time for the Open Educational Resources (OER) movement to recognise that the devil is in the detail. OER seems to be at the height of its hype cycle, and the field is now ripe for critical review, to counter a sometimes "Whig-like" narrative of inevitable progress.[1]

What do we mean by openness? How does openness actually materialise? Is more open always best? How is openness enacted? These fundamental questions have often been ignored, or worse, declared resolved by universal solutions. If these questions go unanswered, we leave room for other uncomfortable questions which are perennially brought up by more critical interlocutors: Who benefits from open? Who is defining what openness means? And more emphatically, does the mainstream view and current trajectory for OER necessarily lead to more emancipatory, democratic, egalitarian and inclusive education? These questions are (or should be) at the center of the debate in the Global South.[2] The work done by researchers in the Research on Open Educational Resources for Development (ROER4D) project, which is showcased in this volume, does much to shed light on some of these important issues.

Systemic aspects necessary for successful OER implementations are covered: culture and policy-setting at institutional and country-wide levels; connections to other open movements (such as Open Access); raising awareness and providing professional development and engagement opportunities — all of these are among the recurring factors discussed in the various studies in this volume.

Detailed and contextualised discussions are added to what, after 15 years, are just afterthoughts to many in the field. The lack of resources in multiple languages is highlighted in different studies. This issue is often emphasised, only to be repeatedly brushed aside both for widely spoken but not hegemonic languages, as well as for lesser spoken languages. The lack of appropriately adapted (or adaptable) resources to cultural contexts is given centre stage in discussions about localisation and access. In the context of professional development, light is shed on conditions, demands and the need for local production of resources. The clear connection between engagement with OER and access

---

1   This is perhaps most obvious in our over-emphasis on open licensing as the cornerstone (and for many, the only essential element) of the movement, as if new licensing practices alone would be enough to catalyse change.
2   I exercise, as one of the chapters in the book suggests, all the caveats of dividing the world along the equator, but rhetorical liberty is needed for this short foreword.

to material resources is discussed in light of the persistent digital divide. In this, examples include the challenges for professional development in different contexts and the issues faced by teachers in engaging with OER. Micro-politics, such as institutional demands, and technological momentum[3] are showcased in the research on faculty experiences with OER. More subtle aspects, including the ethics of openness and production, apathy to the idea of OER, and even negative experiences with OER, are presented. The seemingly naive educator who does not want to use a very liberal licence might just have good reasons to do so!

As the strong literature reviews in each chapter present, these discussions exist, scattered across the literature on OER. But here, and perhaps this is the volume's greatest contribution, we have these challenges laid out collectively, presenting detailed descriptions of initiatives and projects that showcase the activity around OER in regions which (if at all) are often presented in the aggregate,[4] and usually in negative (or barren) terms. What is also immensely relevant is that these works are presented in English, and are made available beyond the restricted audience that many scholars in these regions face when writing in their native language.

Discussions on who produces OER, under what conditions, and by whom they are made available should take centre stage. As OER gathers the attention of large corporations and institutions, and interfaces with industries and spheres with potentially conflicting interests,[5] knowing about and reflecting upon the experiences of multiple groups will be key to advance the principles of openness we hold dear.

Tel Amiel
Campinas, Brazil
November 2017

---

3   The notion that some aspects of technological development become locked-in so that changing them becomes a very complex task. An often used example is that of the format used for electricity sockets. Another might be institutional learning management systems.

4   Regions in the Global South are often the subject of generalisation – for example, one recent article discusses openness as "incipient" in Latin America and the Caribbean. The use of "developing nations" is common as well.

5   What should one do when OER (as well as Open Access and other movements) are promoted by traditional players, surveillance economy businesses (such as Google) and other actors which are, in principle, quite inimical to the ideals of OER?

Foreword by Matthew Smith
(IDRC)

The seeds of this book were planted a long time ago in the hearts and minds of my predecessor, Maria Ng, and wise educational minds like Gajaraj Dhanarajan of Wawasan Open University who supported a research network on Open and Digital Learning in Asia. Building on this earlier research, they helped conceive of the idea of a research network focused on the promise and challenges of Open Educational Resources (OER) in the Global South – which eventually became the Research on Open Educational Resources for Development (ROER4D) network. I am so grateful they did, because we are now reaping the benefits of those early seeds.

What ROER4D became and accomplished was much more than I think was envisioned in those early days – even with the very ambitious research agenda that was set out. The vision was to improve educational opportunities by supporting the production of influential, high quality research by researchers from the South and for the diverse contexts where the research was done. With the generous support of UKaid through the Information Networks in Asia and Sub-Saharan Africa programme, the project grew to reach over 100 researchers in 21 countries. ROER4D, the name of the network, has become synonymous with high quality OER research from a Southern perspective. Furthermore, the research and researchers within the network have gone on to have broader influence – such as helping to write OER policies for provincial education ministries in Sri Lanka and implementing state-sponsored OER portals for teacher professional development in three states in India.

The network didn't just research openness in education, it leveraged different openness practices strategically and to great effect. This volume being perhaps the most visible manifestation of that openness – an Open Access publication with associated micro-data where possible. But it ran deeper than that. The network embraced and experimented with the possibility of engaging openly throughout all of their work, from their highly inclusive decision-making processes to the degree of sharing and collaboration across the network.

Of course, none of this just happened – it took a lot of work. Often more than anticipated. While ROER4D was a collaborative effort involving many researchers across many time zones, at the centre of it all was the Network Hub, Cheryl Hodgkinson-Williams and her dynamic team within the Centre for Innovation in Learning and Teaching at the University of Cape Town. The successes of ROER4D would not have been possible without this dedicated and conscientious team who were truly open to learning, exploring new ideas, questioning assumptions, trying new things, and working very hard – and most of all, committed to improving educational opportunities around the world.

This Open Access book is a reflection of this diversity, collaboration, strategic application of openness and diligent work over the last five years. It is a rich tapestry of research, data and insights on the adoption and impact of OER from across a multitude of contexts. If you are interested in Open Education and OER, there is something in this book for you.

I would like to express my sincere gratitude to all those who worked hard to make it happen. It has been a real pleasure to have been a part of this ROER4D journey.

Matthew Smith
Ottawa, Canada
November, 2017

Section 1

Overview

Contents

Chapter 1

Research on Open Educational Resources for Development in the Global South: Project landscape

Patricia B. Arinto, Cheryl Hodgkinson-Williams, Thomas King,
Tess Cartmill and Michelle Willmers

Acronyms and abbreviations

DFID   Department for International Development
HEI   higher education institution
IDRC   International Development Research Centre
MOOCs   Massive Open Online Courses
OEP   Open Educational Practices
OER   Open Educational Resources
OSF   Open Society Foundations
PANdora   PAN Asia Networking Distance and Open Resources Access
ROER4D   Research on Open Educational Resources for Development
TESSA   Teacher Education in Sub Saharan Africa
UNESCO   United Nations Educational, Scientific and Cultural Organization
UCT   University of Cape Town
WOU   Wawasan Open University

Introduction

The Research on Open Educational Resources for Development (ROER4D) project was proposed to investigate in what ways and under what circumstances the adoption of Open Educational Resources (OER) could address the increasing demand for accessible, relevant, high-quality and affordable education in the Global South. The project was originally intended to focus on post-secondary education, but the scope was expanded to include basic education teachers and government funding when it launched in 2013. In 2014, the research agenda was further expanded to include the potential impact of OER adoption and associated Open Educational Practices (OEP).

ROER4D was funded by Canada's International Development Research Centre (IDRC), the UK's Department for International Development (DFID) and the Open Society Foundations (OFS), and built upon prior research undertaken by a previous IDRC-funded initiative, the PAN Asia Networking Distance and Open Resources Access (PANdora) project.

This chapter presents the overall context in which the ROER4D project was located and investigated, drawing attention to the key challenges confronting education in the Global South and citing related studies on how OER can help to address these issues. It provides an abbreviated history of the project and a snapshot of the geographic location of the studies it comprises, the constituent research agendas, the methodologies adopted and the research-participant profile. It also provides an overview of the other 15 chapters in this volume and explains the peer review process.

Open Educational Resources: Definitions and research

OER are "teaching, learning, and research resources that reside in the public domain or have been released under an intellectual property license that permits their free use and/

or re-purposing by others".[1] The term "Open Educational Resources" was coined during a United Nations Educational, Scientific and Cultural Organization (UNESCO) meeting in 2002 to optimise information sharing about what was then an emerging phenomenon (D'Antoni, 2008). Related terms used prior to 2002 include "open content",[2] "learning objects" (Downes, 2007; Hodgins, 2004), "reusable learning objects" (Boyle, 2003), "reusable learning content" (Duval et al., 2001) and "open courseware" (Malloy, Jensen, Regan & Reddick, 2002). After 2002, the terms "open eLearning content" (Geser, 2007), "digital learning resources" (Margaryan & Littlejohn, 2008) and "reusable digital learning resources" (Leacock & Nesbit, 2007) were also used to refer to OER. In the popular media, OER are also referred to as "open-source materials" or "open-source textbooks".[3] Equivalent terms for OER in other languages which need to be taken into account when researching this phenomenon across countries in the Global South include "*recursos educativos abiertos*" (REA) (Betancourt, Celaya & Ramírez, 2014) or "*recursos educativos digitales abiertos*" (REDA) (Sáenz, Hernandez & Hernández, Chapter 5[4]) in Spanish; "*recursos educacionais abertos*" (REA) in Portuguese (Amiel, Orey & West, 2011); "*sumber pendidikan terbuka*" (SPT) in Indonesian (Abeywardena, 2015); and "*Боловсролын нээлттэй нөөц (Bolovsroliin neelttei nuuts)*" in Mongolian (Zagdragchaa & Trotter, Chapter 11).

The most often-cited feature of OER is Wiley's "5Rs"[5] framework which defines the five rights afforded in the exchange of open content, namely: "the right to make, own, and control copies of the content (Retain); the right to use the content in a wide range of ways (Reuse); the right to adapt, adjust, modify, or alter the content itself (Revise); the right to combine the original or revised content with other open content to create something new (Remix); and the right to share copies of the original content, your revisions, or your remixes with others (Redistribute)".[6] Alternative descriptions of OER have been put forward by White and Manton (2011), more detailed reuse steps by Okada, Mikroyannidis, Meister and Little (2012), and a more practice-inclusive Open Education cycle by Hodgkinson-Williams (2014). All explanations of OER include a clause stipulating open licensing – that is, use of a licence that explicitly describes the ways in which a particular resource may be legally reused, shared, modified and curated. The most commonly used form of open licensing is Creative Commons,[7] although other forms of open licences (such as the GNU General Public Licence) offer similar functionality.

Since the early 2000s, there has been increasing interest in OER as a means of addressing key challenges in education and research in this area has grown significantly. Most OER research has, however, taken place in countries in the Global North. Within this context, the key educational issues raised by researchers centre around the rising costs of textbooks (Allen 2013; Hilton III, Robinson, Wiley & Ackerman, 2014; Levi, Hilton III, Robinson, Wiley & Ackerman, 2014; Wiley, Green & Soares, 2012) and, in some cases, the quality of student learning (Lovett, Meyer & Thille, 2008) or student outcomes (Feldstein et al., 2013).

---

1   Adapted from http://www.hewlett.org/programs/education-program/open-educational-resources.
2   https://web.archive.org/web/19990128224600/http://www.opencontent.org/home.shtml
3   http://abcnews.go.com/US/wireStory/open-source-textbooks-gain-push-college-affordability-36864005
4   Chapter cross-references in the in-text citations of Chapters 1, 2 and 16 refer to chapter numbers of the relevant chapters in this volume.
5   https://opencontent.org/blog/archives/3221
6   https://opencontent.org/blog/archives/3221
7   https://creativecommons.org/

In the Global South, unequal access to education, and more specifically to higher education, continues to be a major challenge (UNESCO, 2014). In better-resourced areas, universities often function in line with international standards, while in poorer regions educational systems tend to be dysfunctional on multiple levels. There are notable disparities in the level of access to the physical infrastructure and inputs needed for education (such as computer labs, classroom space and textbooks) as well as access to an enabling environment for educational innovation (such as policy and technical support). Digital interventions, including OER, risk reinforcing these inequalities. Hence the need for research that will provide a better understanding of the dynamics of OER use and its impact in the Global South.

Educational challenges facing the Global South

Education in the Global South faces several key interrelated challenges for which OER are seen to be part of the solution and against which use of OER might be evaluated. These challenges include: unequal access to education; variable quality of educational resources, teaching and student performance; and increasing cost and concern about the sustainability of education.

Unequal access to education

In contrast to the Global North, where student numbers are predicted to stagnate and even decrease as a result of demographic change (Vincent-Lancrin, 2008), student enrolments in the Global South have continued to grow, fuelled by population growth (World Bank, 2013). Many countries are reaching universal primary and secondary enrolment (Bold & Svensson, 2016; Kiamba, 2016), resulting in a massively increased demand for higher education (ADB, 2011; Teferra, 2013). In Sub-Saharan Africa, tertiary education enrolments increased by 8.7% every year from 1991 to 2005, which is double the global average (World Bank, 2009). In several countries in Asia, gross enrolment ratios in undergraduate programmes have increased more than tenfold over the last four decades, and the Asian region as a whole now accounts for almost half of higher education enrolment worldwide (UNESCO Institute for Statistics, 2014). Gross enrolment in tertiary education in Brazil has been rising steadily, but primarily amongst female students. In 2015, 59% of the enrolments were female.[8] A similar pattern of an increasing female student (94%) gross enrolment ratio is evident in Chile (compared to 83% male students). Likewise, in Colombia, gross enrolment ratios of female students (60%) surpass those of male students (52%).[9]

While participation rates have increased dramatically, funding for higher education has stagnated. University budgets in Asia have not kept up with the growth in enrolments (UNESCO Institute for Statistics, 2014) and in many countries in Africa funding for higher education has been falling in real terms (Newman & Duwiejua, 2016). This has adverse impacts on access to quality resources for education. In Sub-Saharan Africa, textbook

---

8   http://uis.unesco.org/en/country/br
9   http://uis.unesco.org/en/country/co

scarcity has been noted as a problem since the 1980s (Fredriksen, Brar & Trucano, 2015). Even when a country's economy is sufficiently developed to support a successful local publishing industry, such as in South Africa, not all students have textbooks (DBE, 2011) or textbooks are not always delivered on time. In many developing countries, there is a general lack of pedagogical materials – particularly instructional materials and teachers' guides (Kanwar, Kodhandaraman & Umar, 2010; Nazari et al., 2016). This is often coupled with and compounded by shortages in classroom space and computer labs, unreliable internet connectivity and irregular power provision (DBE, 2011; Mtebe & Raisamo, 2014).

The lack of educational resources is often exacerbated along spatial, gender and class lines. Rural communities generally have poorer physical infrastructure and internet connectivity (Hernandez & Benavides, 2012; Narváez & Calderón, 2016) and fewer schools and teachers.[10] Rural students also often face higher costs in accessing higher education opportunities due to their need to travel or relocate to urban areas where educational institutions are concentrated (Bray, Davaa, Spaulding & Weidman, 1994). By contrast, urban residents have better access to educational institutions and thus tend to have higher levels of educational attainment across all levels (primary, secondary and tertiary), which leads to improved socioeconomic outcomes over time (Xhang, Li & Xue, 2015). Teachers in urban areas also have more opportunities for teacher professional development (Robinson, 2008) and are thus better placed to develop new pedagogical knowledge and skills. They are also more likely to have access to personal digital devices and computer labs in which to practise technologically enabled educational innovation.

Gender remains a factor in access to education in the Global South. Despite significant gains in gender parity in primary and secondary education across the globe (UNESCO, 2016), female access to higher education remains constrained by traditional gender norms in Africa and Asia in particular. In Asia, while significant improvements in female participation in higher education over the last decade have led to females outnumbering and academically outperforming males in about a third of countries, there are proportionally fewer women in higher levels of education (UNESCO Institute for Statistics, 2014). Also, females are often still relatively disempowered within the education system due to a number of factors, such as sociocultural pressures placing women into more "feminine" but less prestigious and less economically rewarding fields of study (UNESCO, 2007). While primary and secondary teachers are more likely to be female (UNESCO, 2015), males hold the majority of academic posts in higher education, particularly in upper management.[11] In some contexts, the increased burden of childcare and housework may inhibit female teachers from accessing professional development opportunities, particularly if these opportunities incur time and travel costs.

Finally, in the Global South there is a wide disparity in terms of the educational opportunities afforded to the rich and the poor. In many countries in Asia, the disparity expands at each stage of schooling from primary to higher education (UNESCO Institute for Statistics, 2014). For example, in Vietnam 52% of young adults from the richest households have attended higher education institutions (HEIs), compared to only 4% of young adults from the poorest

---

10   https://www.brookings.edu/blog/techtank/2016/08/23/classroom-technologies-narrow-education-gap-in-developing-countries/
11   https://www.daad.de/veranstaltungen/en/52839-female-leadership-and-higher-education-management-in-developing-countries/

households. More generally, in middle- and low-income South and Southeast Asian countries, less than 7% of young adults from the poorest 20% of households have ever enrolled in higher education (UNESCO Institute for Statistics, 2014). In general, educational opportunities tend to favour young people from wealthier households – not only in terms of access to schooling, but also in terms of the types of schools that they attend and the quality of education they receive.

Variable quality of education

Aside from questions regarding adequacy of provision for rapidly increasing student numbers, education systems in the Global South face heightened concern about the quality of instruction, as increased access to education does not always result in improved learner performance. The results of international testing show that students in developing countries generally lag behind their peers in more developed countries, especially in science, mathematics and reading. Common problems across the Global South include poor skills development; persistent differences in urban–rural student attendance and performance; considerable inter- and intraregional variation in performance and outcomes (OREALC, 2008); low retention rates; and generally poor performance in key competencies (Dundar, Béteille, Riboud & Deolalikar, 2014; UNESCO–IICBA, 2016). For example, in Sub-Saharan Africa, deficiencies in primary education manifest in low levels of basic skills for large numbers of pupils after several years of schooling (Bold & Svensson, 2016). In India and Afghanistan, studies have found that students lack basic reading and comprehension skills (ACER, 2013; Magid, 2013).

One aspect of quality of instruction relates to instructional materials, which in the Global South are deficient not only in quantity, but also in quality. Teachers in developing countries often only have access to outdated, proprietary textbooks (Moon & Villet, 2016), and where textbooks have been updated they may be of low quality (Tani, 2014). Moreover, there is the problem of relevance and appropriateness of textbooks and instructional materials imported from the North, which are widely used in many developing countries. As Richter and McPherson (2012) have noted, uncertainty regarding the contextual appropriateness in developing countries of resources produced in the Global North is to be expected, particularly given that there are issues with adopting these resources even in their countries of origin where institutions have similar pedagogic strategies, curricular frameworks and cultural and linguistic norms.

As many OER are adapted from existing teaching and learning materials and contain specific sociocultural examples, users in developing contexts can experience dissatisfaction with topics, assumptions or illustrative examples designed for more developed or more resourced contexts. Language is also a key issue. Because the majority of currently available OER are in English (Krelja Kurelovic, 2016), speakers of less-used languages run the risk of being "linguistically and culturally marginalised" (Bradley & Vigmo, 2014, p.4). In addition to linguistic diversity, the presence of strong oral traditions, as is the case in Colombia (Sáenz et al., Chapter 5), can also hinder teachers' engagement with OER adaptation, as those teachers favour knowledge-sharing through personal interaction over formal and academic writing (Castro, Catebiel & Hernandez, 2005; Hernández, 2015).

The quality of teacher pedagogy is also a major concern in countries in the Global South. In resource-constrained areas, teachers may lack adequate qualifications and support – a situation compounded by poor physical infrastructure and overcrowding. In Asian HEIs, there are shortages of qualified instructors because staff recruitment has not kept pace with rapidly increasing enrolments (ADB, 2011). Teacher professional development is also in short supply in many parts of the Global South, such as India (PROBE, 1998) and Latin America (UNESCO, 2012b; 2012c). As noted by Burns and Lawrie (2015, p.7): "In many parts of the globe – particularly in the world's poorest and most fragile contexts where the need for quality teaching is greatest – the frequency of professional development is episodic, its quality variable, its duration limited and support or follow-up for teachers almost non-existent."

The need to meet increasing student demand places further pressure on educators and institutions to address the quality of education. Large numbers of enrolments in public institutions and the proliferation of private HEIs have drawn attention to the need for quality assurance in education in India (Varghese, 2015), Mongolia (ADB, 2011) and Chile (Fundación La Fuente/Adimark GFK, 2010), among others. There are considerable disparities in quality within single countries, resulting in low retention and throughput rates (MINEDC, 2012), which in turn gives rise to social problems for students and economic problems for institutions. Expansion occurring in conjunction with curricular reform and pedagogical change can result in a disordered educational system where practice is not supported by policy or is inhibited by an environment organised around a more traditional educational model.

Increasing costs and concerns about the sustainability of education

The expansion of the higher education system and increasing privatisation have resulted in increased higher education-related costs in many countries. Often these costs are borne by students, whether due to institutions beginning to charge fees where tuition had previously been free (such as in Mongolia), decreased public spending on higher education as a percentage of GDP (as in South Africa), or an increase in privatisation and for-profit tuition (as in Brazil and Chile). Even where tuition is free, students still need to cover the cost of textbooks and, where online resources are used to replace or supplement textbooks, fees for use of facilities to access these resources, such as devices and connectivity.

In many developing countries, college textbooks are sourced from the US and other Global North countries, which makes them expensive. In Brazil and other parts of South America, the average annual cost of textbooks to students is over 50% of the annual minimum wage (Frango, Ochoa, Pérez Casas & Rodés, 2013). In the Philippines, where the price of imported textbooks is prohibitive, there is widespread photocopying of textbooks by college students.[12] In public primary and secondary schools where textbooks are usually provided free of charge, the increasingly large numbers of students mean that the cost to government of providing textbooks sourced from proprietary publishers is substantial. In addition, there are costs incurred by problems associated with procurement and delivery, as has been reported in Afghanistan (Oates, Goger, Hashimi & Farahmand, Chapter 15), the Philippines[13] (Lontoc, 2007) and South Africa (SAHRC, 2014). In the Philippines, "[s]ustainability is also an issue as books may be lost, at times on a large scale, due to natural calamities" (Arinto & Cantada, 2013, p.144) and due to the destruction of schools in areas where there is armed conflict.

---

12   http://charles-tan.blogspot.co.za/2011/01/essay-ebook-piracy-and-copyright-in.html
13   http://www.gmanetwork.com/news/news/specialreports/98684/deped-adopts-textbook-walk/story/

OER as a response to educational challenges in the Global South

The adoption of OER as a response to educational challenges in the Global South has garnered support from intergovernmental agencies such as UNESCO and the Commonwealth of Learning, and attracted substantial funding from philanthropic organisations such as the Hewlett Foundation. Bliss and Smith (2017) estimate that the Hewlett Foundation has donated over USD 170 million to the Open Education movement over the past 15 years. UNESCO hosted the 1st World OER Congress in 2012, which issued the Paris OER Declaration (UNESCO, 2012a), and the 2nd World OER Congress in 2017, which produced the Ljubljana OER Action Plan (UNESCO, 2017). These calls to action build upon earlier initiatives such as the 2007 Cape Town Open Education Declaration.[14] This community- and funder-driven activity has recently been matched by initiatives in the private sector, as traditional publishers such as Cengage have announced that they are creating a new product line based on OER.[15] There has, therefore, been concrete, global support for OER as a potential response to pressing educational challenges. The three main value propositions that are raised in favour of OER adoption are that they can widen access to education, improve the quality of education and reduce the cost of education (Daniel, Kanwar & Uvalić-Trumbić, 2009).

Researchers have, however, cautioned that access to OER without the support structures and cultural practices that promote its use, is insufficient. Ehlers (2011) points out how the initial focus of the OER community on creating content and improving access to it through infrastructure, repositories and software tools has not resulted in the predicted increase in use, due largely to the lack of attention to practices supporting OER uptake, use and reuse. Similarly, Knox (2013, p.22) questions whether free access to information is sufficient to "realise the goals of universal education and economic prosperity often promised by the open education movement".

With regard to the potential of OER to improve the quality of education, at least three broad subsidiary categories can be distinguished, namely: how OER can improve the quality of learning materials; how OER can improve the quality of teaching practice; and how OER can influence student outcomes. In their seminal OER report, Atkins, Brown and Hammond (2007) posited that OER can foster high-quality content development. Kanwar et al. (2010) also highlight the potential of OER to improve the quality of education, particularly in developing countries where there is a dearth of quality materials. What constitutes OER quality has been the subject of a number of studies (Yuan & Becker, 2015) and reports (Camilleri, Ehlers & Pawlowski, 2014; Kawachi, 2014), and it continues to be a closely scrutinised topic, as evidenced by the current UNESCO project to determine a set of indicators to measure OER adoption and impact (Miao et al., 2017). The debates around OER as a "quality" product have included discussions around the value of a range of reuse activities, perhaps most comprehensively described by Okada et al. (2012), which include repurposing, contextualisation and translation, amongst others. The value of peer review

---

14 http://www.capetowndeclaration.org/
15 https://www.cengage.com/oer

and/or public scrutiny of OER (Weller, 2012) as well as trust in the organisations that produce OER (Clements & Pawlowski, 2012) are also aspects in the determination of OER quality.

Research on the role of OER in improving pedagogical practice (Casserly & Smith, 2009) points to collaborative development of materials and the shift in focus "from materials production to mentorship and facilitation" (Ossiannilsson & Creelman, 2012, p.3.) as enabling factors. There has been some research on how exposure to OER resources and tools can support collaboration among teachers and encourage new conversations about teaching practices (Petrides, Jimes, Middleton-Detzner & Howell, 2010). More recently, the role of OER adoption in improving the quality of teacher professional development has also been investigated (Wolfenden, Buckler & Keraro, 2012). In comparing two Global South teacher education programmes (Teacher Education in Sub Saharan Africa [TESSA] and Teacher Education through School-based Support in India [TESS-India]), Buckler, Perryman, Seal and Musafir (2014, p.221) highlight how these projects have prompted localisation of OER, "contribut[ing] to more equal knowledge partnerships in the pursuit of education quality". Studies in Zambia and South Africa have shown that use of OER within a school-based teacher professional development programme encouraged teachers to try out new pedagogical strategies, raised their expectations of their pupils, and helped them to adapt to their learners' level of understanding and adopt more learner-centred strategies (Hennessy, Haßler & Hofman, 2016).

The potential and/or actual influence of the use of OER on student outcomes has stimulated some research in this area (Feldstein et al., 2013; Fischer, Hilton III, Robinson & Wiley, 2015), despite the fact that it is very difficult to isolate OER as a single variable in educational settings, which are inherently complex and context-specific. In their study of the OER4Schools professional development programme, Hennessy et al. (2016, p.399) conclude that primary school students "built deeper understanding of subject matter, were actively engaged, worked collaboratively and used digital technologies for problem-solving". What needs to be taken into account in this finding is that this was a year-long programme with weekly teacher workshops; it is not clear whether this activity would be sustained when teachers are operating outside of the initiative. Students' perceptions of OER suggest that they like using open textbooks compared to traditional textbooks (Lindshield & Koushik, 2013), but it is not easy to ascertain whether this is a result of the format and design of the materials, rather than of the "openness" of the materials *per se*.

Finally, with regard to the proposition that OER can help to reduce cost and foster the sustainability of education, a great deal of attention has been paid to investigating cost savings arising from the use of OER, especially in the form of open textbooks (Allen, 2013; Wiley, Hilton III, Ellington & Hall, 2012). Other initiatives have explored the co-authoring (Okada et al., 2012) or collaborative development of OER in schools (Marcus-Quinn, Diggins, Griffin & Hinchion, 2012) and in higher education (Lane, 2012) as a way of lowering course development costs. Some researchers have pointed out that while there are obvious cost savings that accrue from use of learning resources that are "free", there are aspects of OER-based course development that could entail significant costs, such as the time spent on locating, evaluating and adapting OER, and the technical infrastructure required for production and dissemination of OER-based courses (Annand, 2015). The need for sustainable funding for institutional OER initiatives has also been pointed out (Annand, 2015; Annand & Jensen, 2017; de Langen, 2013; Mulder, 2013).

The ROER4D project

The ROER4D project sought to build on and contribute to the body of research on how OER can help to improve access, enhance quality and reduce the cost of education in the Global South. By examining various aspects of OER use and OER-related practices in secondary education, tertiary education and teacher training in a range of countries in South America, Sub-Saharan Africa and South and Southeast Asia, the ROER4D studies aim to help improve Open Education policy, practice and research in developing countries. The overarching research question that the studies as a group address is: In what ways and under what circumstances can the adoption of OER and OEP address the increasing demand for accessible, relevant, high-quality and affordable education in the Global South?

The next section provides a brief overview of the project's main activities, processes, participants and outputs.

Project formulation

Phase 0: Inception

Following on the IDRC-supported second phase of the PANdora project, which initiated mapping exercises to establish the nature, practice and challenges relating to the production and use of OER in Asia, it was proposed that a more extensive, long-term, multidimensional and multifaceted research project be developed to "explore the potential of OER for further educational development and to determine their value under present and forward practices in the 'Global South' (Asia, Sub-Saharan Africa, the Arab world and Latin America/Caribbean)" (Dhanarajan & Ng, 2011, p.8). To this end, a group of OER scholars was identified to form a Planning Group to devise a South–South collaborative OER research agenda (Dhanarajan & Ng, 2011) at a meeting in May 2012 in Chiang Mai, Thailand. It was at this roundtable meeting that the ROER4D project was conceived.

In July 2012, research proposals were solicited from those "who have already been developing OER so that they [can] focus on research generating evidence to motivate policy making" and from developing countries where assistance could serve to "influence educational policy change through applied research and development" (Dhanarajan & Ng, 2011, p.14). The independently-scoped proposals were evaluated by the Planning Group in October 2012 and those demonstrating high probability of research operationalisation were invited to present their proposals at a face-to-face meeting in Jakarta, Indonesia, in January 2013. A final set of 12 research proposals from all regions except the so-called Arab world[16] and a meta-synthesis proposal were submitted to the IDRC in May 2013.

Phase 1: Adoption studies

The main project grant was awarded by the IDRC to the University of Cape Town (UCT) as the ROER4D host institution in August 2013, with additional funding from the OSF for one project in Latin America. The first ROER4D workshop, held in Cape Town in December 2013, provided an opportunity for sub-project researchers to meet, refine their proposals

---

16   Political tensions precluded the involvement of the Middle East and North African regions at the time.

and participate in a gender-awareness workshop. Most of the ROER4D adoption studies, as this first cohort of 12 sub-projects was referred to, conducted their research from January 2014 until December 2015.

Phase 2: Impact studies

Funding from DFID through the Information and Networks in Asia and Sub-Saharan Africa programme made a second set of sub-projects possible and the proposal for a set of OER impact studies was submitted to the IDRC in January 2014. In April 2014, IDRC awarded the additional funds from DFID to Wawasan Open University (WOU), Malaysia, in its capacity as host of the second cohort of six impact studies – bringing the final number of ROER4D sub-projects to 18. The research proposals were solicited via an open call in August 2014, and between September and October 2014 these proposals were evaluated by a panel of jurors, including members from IDRC, the original Planning Group, an external expert and members of the ROER4D project management teams at UCT and WOU. In December 2014, shortlisted candidates were invited to present at a face-to-face meeting in Penang, Malaysia. Most of the ROER4D impact studies, which were independently scoped to suit their contexts, commenced their research in March 2015 and concluded in February 2017 (Figure 1).

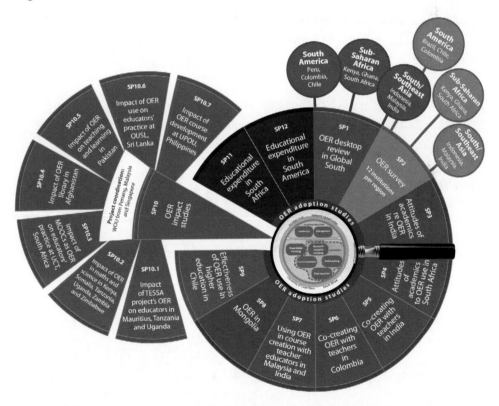

Figure 1: Snapshot summary of ROER4D adoption and impact studies

Figure 2 provides a global snapshot of the location of the 18 ROER4D sub-projects in 21 countries. A total of 103 research team members from 19 countries worked on these sub-projects: 18 lead researchers, 39 researchers, 27 local coordinators of a cross-regional survey, 14 research assistants and five meta-synthesis researchers from the Network Hub.[17]

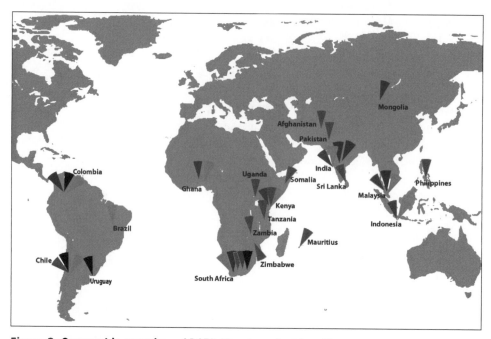

Figure 2: Geographic overview of ROER4D sub-project locations

The ROER4D researcher network was supported by a Network Hub of 12 people at two centres:
- UCT Network Hub, Cape Town, South Africa
  - Principal Investigator, Project Manager, Curation and Publishing Manager, Project Curator, Associate Editor, Communications Advisor and Evaluation Consultant
  - Deputy Principal Investigator from the University of the Philippines Open University
- WOU Network Hub, Penang, Malaysia
  - Project Leader/Coordinator and Research Assistant
  - Coordinator and Research Assistant

Methodological approach and participant profile

The ROER4D sub-projects employed a wide variety of data collection methods: survey questionnaires, interviews, focus group discussions, document analysis, workshops,

---

17   http://dx.doi.org/10.5281/zenodo.1036247

observations, logs and desktop reviews. In the course of conducting the studies, researchers produced chat records, concept maps, a database of student data, a lesson plan assessment tool, literature reviews, narratives, online interactions and self-reflections.[18] Ten sub-projects generated both quantitative and qualitative data in their research, six generated only qualitative data and two generated only quantitative data.

The sub-projects mainly focused on education in general, with mathematics (in five sub-projects) and science (in four sub-projects) being more prominent than other sub-disciplines.[19] Sub-projects also investigated OER use in a variety of disciplines, including educational research methodology, health and management, Islamiyat and Pakistan studies, languages, social science and teaching with technology. Nine sub-projects covered the higher education or university sector, six focused on in-service teacher education, one on pre-service teacher education, and two examined OER-related activity at governmental level.

The number of participants across the sub-projects reported on in the edited volume is as follows:

- **396 school teachers** from four countries: Afghanistan (51), Colombia (48), India (62) and Sri Lanka (230)
- **69 teacher educators** from four countries: Colombia (11), India (5), Mauritius (9), Tanzania (18) and Uganda (31)
- **701 university lecturers** from 15 countries: Brazil (17), Chile (33), Colombia (9), Ghana (38), India (250), Indonesia (44), Kenya (53), Malaysia (54), Malaysia and India (49), Mongolia (42), Somalia (1), South Africa (96), Tanzania (6), Uganda (5), Zambia (3) and Zimbabwe (1)
- **4 985 university students** from nine countries: Brazil (287), Chile (451), Colombia (170), Ghana (817), India (437), Indonesia (645), Kenya (798), Malaysia (716), Malaysia and India (43) and South Africa (621)[20]

Edited volume overview

The ROER4D project builds on previous Open Education research in the Global South, but is the first project of its kind in terms of the scope and scale of the study. The aim of this research endeavour has been to generate an empirical baseline upon which further OER research, advocacy and uptake work can be built.

Apart from this 16-chapter edited volume and the companion datasets for six sub-project studies,[21] ROER4D outputs[22] to date include at least 10 journal articles, three book chapters, two monographs, five keynote addresses, 10 conference papers, 75 conference presentations, 64 blogs and a number of teaching sessions with postgraduate students and staff. Further communication and dissemination activities are planned to leverage the work conducted in the project.

---

18   http://dx.doi.org/10.5281/zenodo.1036247
19   http://dx.doi.org/10.5281/zenodo.1036247
20   http://dx.doi.org/10.5281/zenodo.1036247
21   https://www.datafirst.uct.ac.za/dataportal/index.php/catalog/ROER4D
22   For a full list of ROER4D outputs, see goo.gl/r4PQfE.

In order to capture synthesised contributions of the various sub-projects and promote access to the Global South empirical contribution on Open Education research, the ROER4D Network Hub has published this edited volume in collaboration with the IDRC and African Minds Open Access publishers. The Network Hub decision to function as a co-publisher of the research produced was largely informed by the project's Open Research agenda, which enables a more self-determined approach in terms of advance online release and peer-review strategy. The peer-review process was administered by ROER4D in collaboration with African Minds publishers, with each chapter being reviewed by at least two external peer reviewers in an open and collaborative peer-review model.

The edited volume is composed of 16 chapters – 13 are based on the research reports of 13 ROER4D sub-projects, and three (Chapters 1, 2 and 16) are synthesis and overview chapters. The chapters are organised into five main sections: Overview, South America, Sub-Saharan Africa, South and Southeast Asia, and Conclusion. Within these broader sections, chapters are presented in sequence according to whether the research addresses basic or higher education.

Section 1 – Overview – includes this introduction and a meta-synthesis chapter, "**Factors influencing Open Educational Practices and OER in the Global South: Meta-synthesis of the ROER4D project**" by Cheryl Hodgkinson-Williams, Patricia Arinto, Tess Cartmill and Thomas King, as well as the chapter "**OER use in the Global South: A baseline survey of higher education instructors**" by José Dutra de Oliveira Neto, Judith Pete, Daryono and Tess Cartmill on the findings from the cross-regional quantitative survey of 295 instructors at 28 HEIs in nine countries (Brazil, Chile, Colombia; Ghana, Kenya, South Africa; India, Indonesia and Malaysia).

Section 2 – South America – presents research from Chile, Colombia and Uruguay. The first chapter in this section, "**Open Access and OER in Latin America: A survey of the policy landscape in Chile, Colombia and Uruguay**" by Amalia Toledo, provides valuable insight into the South American "open" policy landscape. It is followed by a chapter addressing "**Collaborative co-creation of OER by teachers and teacher educators in Colombia**", written by María del Pilar Sáenz Rodríguez, Ulises Hernandez Pino and Yoli Marcela Hernández, which describes a study conducted with public school teachers in southwestern Colombia by members of the Collaborative Co-Creation of Open Educational Resources by Teachers and Teacher Educators in Colombia (coKREA) project. The final chapter in this section, by Werner Westermann Juárez and Juan Ignacio Venegas Muggli, is an investigation into the impact of OER on learning outcomes in a Chilean university, titled "**Effectiveness of OER use in first-year higher education students' mathematical course performance: A case study**".

Section 3 – Sub-Saharan Africa – features research from South Africa, Mauritius, Uganda and Tanzania. The first of the chapters in this section, "**Tracking the money for Open Educational Resources in South African basic education: What we don't know**", is a desk review and document analysis of publicly available information on expenditure in South African basic education by Sarah Goodier which aims to better understand government influence on the cost-saving dimension of OER. It is followed by the chapter "**Teacher educators and OER in East Africa: Interrogating pedagogic change**" by Freda Wolfenden, Pritee Auckloo and Jane Cullen, which examines the use of OER in six teacher education institutions in three contrasting East African settings. The fourth chapter in this section,

"**Factors shaping lecturers' adoption of OER at three South African universities**" by Glenda Cox and Henry Trotter, focuses on understanding the obstacles, opportunities and practices associated with OER adoption. South Africa is also the focus of the final chapter in this section, "**OER in and as MOOCs**" by Laura Czerniewicz, Andrew Deacon, Sukaina Walji and Michael Glover. It reports on an investigation into the production and rollout of four Massive Open Online Courses (MOOCs) at UCT, and on how MOOC-making with OER influences educators' OEP.

Section 4 – South and Southeast Asia – presents research from Mongolia, India, Sri Lanka and Afghanistan. The first of the chapters in this section, "**Cultural-historical factors influencing OER adoption in Mongolia's higher education sector**" by Batbold Zagdragchaa and Henry Trotter, is a landmark study in terms of Open Education in the Mongolian context, investigating the strategies and practices of educators from six Mongolian HEIs in order to understand the role of OER in their work. The focus on use of OER by higher education faculty is also a central theme in the next chapter, "**Higher education faculty attitude, motivation, perception of quality and barriers towards OER in India**" by Sanjaya Mishra and Alka Singh, which compares data across four institutions in order to identify the issues that influence OER uptake in India. The next chapter, "**Impact of integrating OER in teacher education at the Open University of Sri Lanka**" by Shironica P. Karunanayaka and Som Naidu, reports on a research project implemented among secondary school teachers enrolled in a postgraduate programme at the Open University of Sri Lanka in order to investigate the impact of integrating OER in the teaching-learning process. This is followed by a chapter examining enabling and constraining techno-social, techno-pedagogical and sociocultural factors surrounding OER adoption in a teacher professional development context by Gurumurthy Kasinathan and Sriranjani Ranganathan titled, "**Teacher professional learning communities: A collaborative OER adoption approach in Karnataka, India**". The final chapter in this section, "**An early-stage impact study of localised OER in Afghanistan**" by Lauryn Oates, Letha Kay Goger, Jamshid Hashimi and Mubaraka Farahmand, evaluates a group of Afghan school teachers' use of OER from the digital Darakht-e Danesh Library, and is also a landmark study in terms of investigation into Open Education in the Afghan context.

Section 5 – "**OER and OEP in the Global South: Implications and recommendations for social inclusion**" by Patricia Arinto, Cheryl Hodgkinson-Williams and Henry Trotter – provides a summary statement on the findings from the ROER4D project and reflects on the extent to which the use of OER by educators and students is contributing to social inclusion in the Global South.

Conclusion

Each of the chapters in this edited volume seeks to identify the key educational challenges in specific contexts in the Global South to which OER and educators' associated OEP may be a useful response. Although these challenges are often similar to those experienced in the Global North, additional or more nuanced perspectives have surfaced in the ROER4D studies. These include the need to support teachers in war-torn countries such as Afghanistan (Oates et al., Chapter 15) or in post-war areas such as northern Sri Lanka (Karunanayaka & Naidu, Chapter 13); support equity of student access to higher education in a largely privatised system in Chile (Westermann Juárez & Venegas Muggli, Chapter 6);

and enhance the quality of educational materials for basic education in India (Kasinathan & Ranganathan, Chapter 14). Each chapter presented explores the degree to which OER and the underlying OEP have emerged as ways to address context-specific educational problems, and which factors might account for their variable adoption and nascent impact. The hope is that these empirical studies establish a baseline of Global South OER and OEP adoption and impact research that will stimulate more targeted advocacy, implementation and research.

References

Abeywardena, I. S. (2015). *Faceted search of Open Educational Resources using the Desirability Index*. Ph.D Thesis. University of Malaya, Malaysia. Retrieved from http://studentsrepo.um.edu.my/6097/1/Full_Thesis_(corrected_print_ready_3).pdf

ACER (Australian Council for Educational Research). (2013). *Monitoring Educational Development in Afghanistan: Technical proposal to extend development and implementation of MED program to grade 3 trial phase in 2014*. Sydney: Australian Council for Educational Research.

ADB (Asian Development Bank). (2011). *Higher education across Asia: An overview of issues and strategies*. Mandaluyong: Asian Development Bank. Retrieved from https://www.adb.org/sites/default/files/publication/29407/higher-education-across-asia.pdf

Allen, N. (2013). *Affordable textbooks for Washington students: An updated cost analysis of the Open Course Library*. Boston, MA: Student Public Interest Research Groups. Retrieved from http://www.studentpirgs.org/sites/student/files/resources/PIRG%20OCL.pdf

Amiel, T., Orey, M. & West, R. (2011). Recursos Educacionais Abertos (REA): Modelos para localização e adaptação. *ETD Campinas, 12*, 112–125. Retrieved from https://periodicos.sbu.unicamp.br/ojs/index.php/etd/article/view/1206

Annand, D. (2015). Developing a sustainable financial model in higher education for Open Educational Resources. *International Review of Research in Open and Distributed Learning, 16(5)*, 1–15. Retrieved from http://www.irrodl.org/index.php/irrodl/article/view/2133/3419

Annand, D. & Jensen, T. (2017). Incentivizing the production and use of Open Educational Resources in higher education institutions. *International Review of Research in Open and Distributed Learning, 18(4)*, 1–15. Retrieved from http://www.irrodl.org/index.php/irrodl/article/view/3009/4226

Arinto, P. B. & Cantada, R. (2013). OER in Philippine higher education: A preliminary study. In G. Dhanarajan & D. Porter (Eds.), *Open Educational Resources: An Asian perspective*. Vancouver: Commonwealth of Learning & OER Asia. Retrieved from http://oasis.col.org/handle/11599/23

Atkins, D. E., Brown, J. S. & Hammond, A. L. (2007). *A review of the Open Educational Resources (OER) movement: Achievements, challenges, and new opportunities*. Menlo Park, CA: The William and Flora Hewlett Foundation. Retrieved from http://cohesion.rice.edu/Conferences/Hewlett/emplibrary/A%20Review%20of%20the%20Open%20Educational%20Resources%20(OER)%20Movement_BlogLink.pdf

Betancourt, M. C., Celaya, R. & Ramírez, M. S. (2014). Open Educational Practices and technology appropriation: The case of the Regional Open Latin American Community for Social and Educational Research (CLARISE). *Revista de Universidad y Sociedad del Conocimiento (RUSC), 11(1)*, 4–17. Retrieved from http://dx.doi.org/10.7238/rusc.v11i1.1794

Bliss, T. J. & Smith, M. (2017). A brief history of Open Educational Resources. In R. S. Jhangiani & R. Biswas-Diener (Eds.), *Open: The philosophy and practices that are revolutionizing education and science* (pp. 9–27). London: Ubiquity Press. Retrieved from https://doi.org/10.5334/bbc.b

Bold, T. & Svensson, J. (2016). *Education, institutions and economic development.* The Hague: Economic Development and Institutions project. Retrieved from https://edi.opml.co.uk/wpcms/wp-content/uploads/2016/08/EDI-PF-PAPER-8.2-Svensson.pdf

Boyle, T. (2003). Design principles for authoring dynamic, reusable learning objects. *Australian Journal of Educational Technology, 19(1)*, 46–58. Retrieved from http://ajet.org.au/index.php/AJET/article/view/1690

Bradley, L. & Vigmo, S. (2014). *Open Educational Resources (OER) in less used languages: A state of the art report.* Brussels: LangOER project. Retrieved from http://files.eun.org/langoer/10%20WP2%20study.compressed%20(1).pdf

Bray, M., Davaa, S., Spaulding, S. & Weidman, J. C. (1994). Transition from socialism and the financing of higher education: The case of Mongolia. *Higher Education Policy, 7(4)*, 36–42. Retrieved from https://www.researchgate.net/publication/264348021_Mongolia

Buckler, A., Perryman, L., Seal, T. & Musafir, S. (2014). The role of OER localisation in building a knowledge partnership for development: Insights from the TESSA and TESS-India teacher education projects. *Open Praxis, 6(3)*, 221–233. Retrieved from http://dx.doi.org/10.5944/openpraxis.6.3.136

Burns, M. & Lawrie, J. (Eds.). (2015). *Where it's needed most: Quality professional development for all teachers.* New York, NY: Inter-Agency Network for Education in Emergencies. Retrieved from http://toolkit.ineesite.org/resources/ineecms/uploads/1162/Teacher_Professional_Development_v1.0_LowRes.pdf

Camilleri, A. F., Ehlers, U-D. & Pawlowski, J. (2014). *State of the art review of quality issues related to Open Educational Resources (OER).* Seville: Joint Research Centre, European Commission. Retrieved from http://is.jrc.ec.europa.eu/pages/EAP/documents/201405JRC88304.pdf

Casserly, C. & Smith, M. (2009). Revolutionizing education through innovation: Can openness transform teaching and learning? In T. Iiyoshi & M. S. V. Kumar (Eds.), *Opening up education: The collective advancement of education through open technology, content, and open knowledge* (pp. 261–276). Retrieved from https://mitpress.mit.edu/sites/default/files/9780262515016_Open_Access_Edition.pdf

Castro, G., Catebiel, V. & Hernandez, U. (2005). La Red de Investigación Educativa: hacia una construcción curricular alternativa en procesos de formación avanzada. *Revista ieRed, 1(3)*. Retrieved from http://revista.iered.org/v1n3/pdf/gcvcuh.pdfhttp://revista.iered.org/v1n3/pdf/gcvcuh.pdf

Clements, K. I. & Pawlowski, J. M. (2012). User-oriented quality for OER: Understanding teachers' views on re-use, quality, and trust. *Journal of Computer Assisted Learning, 28(1)*, 4–14. Retrieved from http://onlinelibrary.wiley.com/doi/10.1111/j.1365-2729.2011.00450.x/abstract

D'Antoni, S. (2008). *Open Educational Resources: The way forward: Deliberations of an international community of interest.* Paris: United Nations Educational, Scientific and Cultural Organization. Retrieved from https://oerknowledgecloud.org/content/open-educational-resources-way-forward-deliberations-international-community-interest

Daniel, J., Kanwar, A. & Uvalić-Trumbić, S. (2009). Breaking higher education's iron triangle: Access, cost, and quality. *Change: The Magazine of Higher Learning, 41(2)*, 30–35. Retrieved from https://www.researchgate.net/publication/225084031_Breaking_Higher_Education%27s_Iron_Triangle_Access_Cost_and_Quality

DBE (Department of Basic Education). (2011). *Action plan 2014: Towards the realisation of schooling 2025.* Pretoria: Department of Basic Education. Retrieved from http://www. education.gov.za/LinkClick.aspx?fileticket=jrxCOXJALPU%3d&tabid=418&mid=1211

de Langen, F. (2013). Strategies for sustainable business models for Open Educational Resources. *International Review of Research in Open and Distributed Learning, 14(2).* Retrieved from http://www.irrodl.org/index.php/irrodl/article/view/1533/2485

Dhanarajan, G. & Ng, M. (2011). Planning southern research on Open Educational Resources (OER). *Presented to the International Development Research Centre, 18–21 November.* Ottawa, Canada. Retrieved from http://dx.doi.org/10.5281/zenodo.1035167

Downes, S. (2007). Models for sustainable Open Educational Resources. *Interdisciplinary Journal of Knowledge and Learning Objects, 3,* 29–44. Retrieved from http://ijklo.org/ Volume3/IJKLOv3p029-044Downes.pdf

Duval, E., Forte, E., Cardinaels, K., Verhoeven, B., Van Durm, R., Hendrikx, K., Forte, M. W., Ebel, N., Macowicz, M., Warkentyne, K. & Haenni, F. (2001). The ARIADNE knowledge pool system. *Communications of the ACM, 44(5),* 73–78. Retrieved from https://www. researchgate.net/publication/220426316_The_Ariadne_knowledge_pool_system

Dundar, H., Béteille, T., Riboud, M. & Deolalikar, A. (2014). *Student learning in South Asia: Challenges, opportunities, and policy priorities.* Washington, D.C.: International Bank for Reconstruction and Development. Retrieved from http://documents.worldbank.org/curated/ en/554381468294334286/pdf/882670PUB0978100Box385205B00PUBLIC0.pdf

Ehlers, U-D. (2011). Extending the territory: From Open Educational Resources to Open Educational Practices. *Journal of Open, Flexible and Distance Learning, 15(2),* 1–10. Retrieved from http://www.jofdl.nz/index.php/JOFDL/article/view/64

Feldstein, A., Martin, M., Hudson, A., Warren, K., Hilton III, J. & Wiley, D. (2013). Open textbooks and increased student outcomes. *European Journal of Open, Distance and E-Learning, 2(1).* Retrieved from http://www.eurodl.org/?p=current&sp=full&article=533

Fischer, L., Hilton III, J., Robinson, T. J. & Wiley, D. (2015). A multi-institutional study of the impact of open textbook adoption on the learning outcomes of post-secondary students. *Journal of Computing in Higher Education, 27(3),* 159–172. Retrieved from http://link. springer.com/article/10.1007%2Fs12528-015-9101-x

Frango, S. I., Ochoa, X., Pérez Casas, A. & Rodés, V. (2013). *Percepciones, actitudes y prácticas respecto a los libros de texto, digitales y en formatos abiertos por parte de estudiantes de universidades de América Latina.* Ecuador: LATin Project. Retrieved from http://www.br-ie.org/pub/index.php/wcbie/article/download/1893/1656

Fredriksen, B., Brar, S. & Trucano, M. (2015). *Getting textbooks to every child in Sub-Saharan Africa: Strategies for addressing the high cost and low availability problem.* Washington, D.C.: World Bank. Retrieved from http://dx.doi.org/10.1596/978-1-4648-0540-0

Fundación La Fuente/Adimark GFK. (2010). *Chile y los libros 2010.* Santiago: Fundación Educacional y Cultural La Fuente. Retrieved from http://www.fundacionlafuente.cl/wp-content/uploads/2010/11/Chile-y-los-libros-2010_FINAL-liviano.pdf

Geser, G. (Ed.). (2007). *Open Educational Practices and Resources: OLCOS Roadmap 2012.* Salzburg: Open eLearning Content Observatory Services. Retrieved from http://www.olcos. org/cms/upload/docs/olcos_roadmap.pdf

Hennessy, S., Haßler, B. & Hofman, R. (2016). Pedagogic change by Zambian primary school teachers participating in the OER4Schools professional development programme for one year. *Research Papers in Education, 31(4),* 399–427. Retrieved from http://dx.doi.org/10.1 080/02671522.2015.1073343

Hernández, Y. M. (2015). Factores que favorecen la innovación educativa con el uso de la tecnología: una perspectiva desde el proyecto coKREA. *Revista Virtual UCN, (45)*. Retrieved from http://revistavirtual.ucn.edu.co/index.php/RevistaUCN/article/view/654

Hernandez, U. & Benavides, P. (2012). Para qué las TIC en la Educación Básica y Media: Reflexiones a partir de la cualificación de maestros en ejercicio en el suroccidente colombiano. In G. Castro & U. Hernandez (Eds.), *Saber pedagógico en el Cauca: Miradas de maestros en contextos de diversidad* (pp. 183–200). Popayán: Universidad del Cauca. Retrieved from http://openlibrary.org/books/OL25267478M/

Hilton III, J., Robinson, T. J., Wiley, D. & Ackerman, J. D. (2014). Cost-savings achieved in two semesters through the adoption of Open Educational Resources. *The International Review of Research in Open and Distributed Learning, 15(2)*, 68–84. Retrieved from http://www.irrodl.org/index.php/irrodl/article/view/1700

Hodgins, W. (2004). The future of learning objects. In *ECI Conference on e-Technologies in Engineering Education: Learning Outcomes Providing Future Possibilities, 11–16 August 2002*. Davos, Switzerland. Retrieved from http://dc.engconfintl.org/etechnologies/11

Hodgkinson-Williams, C. (2014). Degrees of ease: Adoption of OER, open textbooks and MOOCs in the Global South. *Keynote presentation at OER Asia Symposium, 24–27 June 2014*. Penang, Malaysia. Retrieved from https://www.slideshare.net/ROER4D/hodgkinson-williams-2014-oer-asia

Kanwar, A., Kodhandaraman, B. & Umar, A. (2010). Toward sustainable Open Education Resources: A perspective from the Global South. *The American Journal of Distance Education, 24(2)*, 65–80. Retrieved from http://dx.doi.org/10.1080/08923641003696588

Karunanayaka, S. & Naidu, S. (2017). Impact of integrating OER in teacher education at the Open University of Sri Lanka. In C. Hodgkinson-Williams & P. B. Arinto (Eds.), *Adoption and impact of OER in the Global South* (pp. 459–498). Retrieved from https://doi.org/10.5281/zenodo.600398

Kasinathan, G. & Ranganathan, R. (2017). Teacher professional learning communities: A collaborative OER adoption approach in Karnataka, India. In C. Hodgkinson-Williams & P. B. Arinto (Eds.), *Adoption and impact of OER in the Global South* (pp. 499–548). Retrieved from https://doi.org/10.5281/zenodo.601180

Kawachi, P. (2014). *The TIPS framework version 2.0: Quality assurance guidelines for teachers and creators of Open Educational Resources*. New Delhi: Commonwealth Educational Media Centre for Asia. Retrieved from http://cemca.org.in/publicationhome/quality-assurance-guidelines-open-educational-resources-tips-framework-version-20-pa#.VhkTEhOqqko

Kiamba, C. (2016). An innovative model of funding higher education in Kenya: The universities fund. In P. A. Okebukola (Ed.), *Towards innovative models for funding higher education in Africa* (pp. 25–38). Retrieved from http://www.adeanet.org/en/system/files/resources/aau-funding-book.pdf

Knox, J. (2013). The limitations of access alone: Moving towards open processes in education technology. *Open Praxis, 5(1)*, 21–29. Retrieved from http://www.openpraxis.org/~openprax/index.php/OpenPraxis/article/view/36

Krelja Kurelovic, E. (2016). Advantages and limitations of usage of Open Educational Resources in small countries. *International Journal of Research in Education and Science, 2(1)*, 136–142. Retrieved from https://oerknowledgecloud.org/sites/oerknowledgecloud.org/files/5000123134-5000259500-1-PB.pdfhttps://oerknowledgecloud.org/sites/oerknowledgecloud.org/files/5000123134-5000259500-1-PB.pdf

Lane, A. (2012). A review of the role of national policy and institutional mission in European distance teaching universities with respect to widening participation in higher education study through Open Educational Resources. *Distance Education, 33(2)*, 136–150.

Leacock, T. L. & Nesbit, J. C. (2007). A framework for evaluating the quality of multimedia learning resources. *Journal of Educational Technology & Society, 10(2)*, 44–59. Retrieved from http://www.ifets.info/journals/10_2/5.pdf

Levi, J., Hilton III, J., Robinson, T. J., Wiley, D. & Ackerman, J. D. (2014). Cost-savings achieved in two semesters through the adoption of Open Educational Resources. *The International Review of Research in Open and Distributed Learning, 15(2)*, 67–84. Retrieved from http://www.irrodl.org/index.php/irrodl/article/view/1700/2883

Lindshield, B. & Koushik, A. (2013). Online and campus college students like using an Open Educational Resource instead of a traditional textbook. *MERLOT Journal of Online Learning and Teaching, 9(1)*. Retrieved from http://jolt.merlot.org/vol9no1/lindshield_0313.htm

Lontoc, J. F. B. (2007). Straightening out the kinks: A look into the DepEd's textbook policy. *The UP Forum, 8(4)*.

Lovett, M., Meyer, O. & Thille, C. (2008). The Open Learning Initiative: Measuring the effectiveness of the OLI statistics course in accelerating student learning. *Journal of Interactive Media Education, 2008(1)*. Retrieved from https://www-jime.open.ac.uk/articles/10.5334/2008-14/#published

Magid, B. (2013). *Early Grade Reading Assessment (EGRA) and Early Grade Mathematics Assessment (EGMA) Afghanistan baseline report*. Kabul: Basic Education for Afghanistan Consortium/International Rescue Committee.

Malloy, T. E., Jensen, G. C., Regan, A. & Reddick, M. (2002). Open courseware and shared knowledge in higher education. *Behavior Research Methods, Instruments, & Computers, 34(2)*, 200–203. Retrieved from https://collections.lib.utah.edu/details?id=703558&q=Open+courseware+and+shared+knowledge+in+higher+education

Marcus-Quinn, A., Diggins, Y., Griffin, M. & Hinchion, C. (2012). Open Educational Resources for digital natives. Presented at *Edtech 2012, 31 May–1 June 2012*. Maynooth, Ireland.

Margaryan, A. & Littlejohn, A. (2008). Repositories and communities at cross-purposes: Issues in sharing and reuse of digital learning resources. *Journal of Computer Assisted Learning, 24(4)*, 333–347. Retrieved from https://isd-resource-space.wikispaces.com/file/view/Repositories+%26+Communities+at+Cross-Purposes.pdf

Miao, F., Petrides, L., Jimes, C., Mulder, F., Orr, D. & Janssen, B. (2017). OER indicators for national adoption and impact. Presented at the *2nd World OER Congress, 18–20 September 2017*. Ljubljana, Slovenia. Retrieved from http://www.oercongress.org/event/indicators/

MINEDC (Ministry of Education of Chile). (2012). *Deserción en la educación superior en Chile: Serie evidencias año 1, No. 9*. Santiago: Ministry of Education of Chile. Retrieved from http://portales.mineduc.cl/usuarios/bmineduc/doc/201209281737360.EVIDENCIASCEM9.pdf

Moon, B. & Villet, C. (2016). *Digital learning: Reforming teacher education to promote access, equity and quality in sub-Saharan Africa*. Vancouver: Commonwealth of Learning. Retrieved from http://oasis.col.org/handle/11599/2443

Mtebe, J. S. & Raisamo, R. (2014). Challenges and instructors' intention to adopt and use Open Educational Resources in higher education in Tanzania. *The International Review of Research in Open and Distributed Education, 15(1)*, 249–271. Retrieved from http://www.irrodl.org/index.php/irrodl/article/view/1687

Mulder, F. (2013). The LOGIC of national policies and strategies for Open Educational Resources. *International Review of Research in Open and Distributed Learning, 14(2)*. Retrieved from http://www.irrodl.org/index.php/irrodl/article/view/1536/2505

Narváez, A. & Calderón, L. (2016). Modelo tecnológico para la apropiación de Software Libre en sedes educativas públicas del Departamento del Cauca. *Revista*

Colombiana de Computación, 17(2). Retrieved from http://revistas.unab.edu.co/index. php?journal=rcc&page=article&op=view&path%5B%5D=2715

Nazari, N., Rose, A., Oates, L., Hashimi, J., Shakir, O. & Siddiqi, B. (2016). *Technical assessment of selected offices within the Afghan Ministry of Education for textbook development and distribution.* Kabul: United States Agency for International Development (USAID). Retrieved from http://pdf.usaid.gov/pdf_docs/PA00M4W5.pdf

Newman, E. & Duwiejua, M. (2016). Models for innovative funding for higher education in Africa – The case of Ghana. In P. A. Okebukola (Ed.), *Towards innovative models for funding higher education in Africa* (pp. 1–19). Retrieved from http://www.adeanet.org/en/ system/files/resources/aau-funding-book.pdf

Oates, L., Goger, L. K., Hashimi, J. & Farahmand, M. (2017). An early stage impact study of localised OER in Afghanistan. In C. Hodgkinson-Williams & P. B. Arinto (Eds.), *Adoption and impact of OER in the Global South* (pp. 549–573). Retrieved from https://doi. org/10.5281/zenodo.600441

Okada, A., Mikroyannidis, A., Meister, I. & Little, S. (2012). "Colearning" – collaborative networks for creating, sharing and reusing OER through social media. In *Cambridge 2012: Innovation and Impact – Openly Collaborating to Enhance Education, 16–18 April 2012.* Cambridge, UK. Retrieved from http://oro.open.ac.uk/33750/2/59B2E252.pdf

OREALC (Regional Bureau for Education in Latin America and the Caribbean). (2008). *Student achievement in Latin America and the Caribbean: Results of the Second Regional Comparative and Explanatory Study (SERC).* Santiago: Regional Bureau for Education in Latin America and the Caribbean. Retrieved from http://unesdoc.unesco.org/ images/0016/001610/161045e.pdf

Ossiannilsson, E. & Creelman, A. (2012). OER, resources for learning – Experiences from an OER project in Sweden. *European Journal of Open, Distance and E-Learning.* Retrieved from http://www.eurodl.org/materials/contrib/2012/Ossiannilsson_Creelman.pdf

Petrides, L., Jimes, C., Middleton-Detzner, C. & Howell, H. (2010). OER as a model for enhanced teaching and learning. In *Open Ed 2010 Proceedings, Proceedings of the Seventh Open Education Conference, 2–4 November 2010.* Barcelona: Universitat Oberta de Catalunya, The Open University (UK), Brigham Young University. Retrieved from http:// openaccess.uoc.edu/webapps/o2/bitstream/10609/4995/6/Jimes_editat.pdf

PROBE (Public Report on Basic Education). (1998). *Public report on basic education.* New Delhi: Oxford University Press. Retrieved from http://www.educationforallinindia.com/ public_report_basic_education_india-1998_probe.pdf

Richter, T. & McPherson, M. (2012). Open Educational Resources: Education for the world? *Distance Education, 33(2),* 201–219. Retrieved from http://dx.doi.org/10.1080/01587919. 2012.692068

Robinson, B. (2008). Using distance education and ICT to improve access, equity and the quality in rural teachers' professional development in Western China. *International Review of Research in Open and Distributed Learning, 9(1),* 1–17. Retrieved from http://www.irrodl. org/index.php/irrodl/article/view/486/1015

Sáenz, M. P., Hernandez, U. & Hernández, Y. M. (2017). Co-creation of OER by teachers and teacher educators in Colombia. In C. Hodgkinson-Williams & P. B. Arinto (Eds.), *Adoption and impact of OER in the Global South* (pp. 143–185). Retrieved from https://doi. org/10.5281/zenodo.604384

SAHRC (South African Human Rights Commission). (2014). *Report: Delivery of primary learning materials to schools.* Pretoria: South African Human Rights Commission. Retrieved from https://www.sahrc.org.za/home/21/files/Delivery%20of%20Learning%20Material%20 Report%20Final%20.pdf

Tani, W. B. (2014). *Textbook analysis in Afghanistan: Comparison of mathematics' textbooks of grades 7–9*. M.Phil in Education dissertation. Karlstads: Karlstads University.

Teferra, D. (2013). *Funding higher education in Sub-Saharan Africa*. Basingstoke: Palgrave Macmillan. Retrieved from https://link.springer.com/chapter/10.1057/9781137345783_1

UNESCO (United Nations Educational, Scientific and Cultural Organization). (2007). *Gender and empowerment: Perspectives from South Asia*. New Delhi: United Nations Educational, Scientific and Cultural Organization. Retrieved from http://unesdoc.unesco.org/images/0015/001561/156196e.pdf

UNESCO (United Nations Educational, Scientific and Cultural Organization). (2012a). *2012 Paris OER Declaration*. Paris: United Nations Educational, Scientific and Cultural Organization. Retrieved from http://www.unesco.org/fileadmin/MULTIMEDIA/HQ/CI/CI/pdf/Events/Paris%20OER%20Declaration_01.pdf

UNESCO (United Nations Educational, Scientific and Cultural Organization). (2012b). *UNESCO strategy on teachers 2012–2015*. Paris: United Nations Educational, Scientific and Cultural Organization. Retrieved from http://unesdoc.unesco.org/images/0021/002177/217775E.pdf

UNESCO (United Nations Educational, Scientific and Cultural Organization). (2012c). *Background and criteria for teachers' policies development in Latin America and the Caribbean*. Paris: United Nations Educational, Scientific and Cultural Organization. Retrieved from http://www.unesco.org/fileadmin/MULTIMEDIA/FIELD/Santiago/pdf/Background-mexico.pdf

UNESCO (United Nations Educational, Scientific and Cultural Organization). (2014). *Position paper on education post-2015*. Paris: United Nations Educational, Scientific and Cultural Organization. Retrieved from http://unesdoc.unesco.org/images/0022/002273/227336E.pdf

UNESCO (United Nations Educational, Scientific and Cultural Organization). (2015). *A guide for gender equality in teacher education: Policy and practices*. Paris: United Nations Educational, Scientific and Cultural Organization. Retrieved from http://unesdoc.unesco.org/images/0023/002316/231646e.pdf

UNESCO (United Nations Educational, Scientific and Cultural Organization). (2016). *Global education monitoring report 2016: Education for people and planet, creating sustainable futures for all*. Paris: United Nations Educational, Scientific and Cultural Organization.

UNESCO (United Nations Educational, Scientific and Cultural Organization). (2017). *Ljubljana OER action plan*. Paris: United Nations Educational, Scientific and Cultural Organization. Retrieved from https://en.unesco.org/sites/default/files/ljubljana_oer_action_plan_2017.pdf

UNESCO–IICBA (United Nations Educational, Scientific and Cultural Organization–International Institute for Capacity Building in Africa). (2016). *Teaching policies and learning outcomes in Sub-Saharan Africa: Issues and options*. Addis Ababa: United Nations Educational, Scientific and Cultural Organization. Retrieved from http://unesdoc.unesco.org/images/0024/002465/246501e.pdf

UNESCO Institute for Statistics. (2014). *Higher education in Asia: Expanding out, expanding up. The rise of graduate education and university research*. Montreal: UNESCO Institute for Statistics. Retrieved from http://unesdoc.unesco.org/images/0022/002275/227516e.pdf

Varghese, N. V. (2006). Growth and expansion of private higher education in Africa. In N. V. Varghese (Ed.), *Growth and expansion of private higher education in Africa* (pp. 25–54). Paris: International Institute for Educational Planning. Retrieved from http://unesdoc.unesco.org/images/0015/001502/150255e.pdf

Varghese, N. V. (2015). *Challenges of massification of higher education in India*. New Delhi: National University of Educational Planning and Administration. Retrieved from http://www.nuepa.org/new/download/Publications/CPRHE/March_2016/CPRHE_Research%20_%20Paper-1.pdf

Vincent-Lancrin, S. (2008). What is the impact of demography on higher education systems? A forward-looking approach for OECD countries. In OECD (Ed.), *Higher education to 2030 (Vol. 1): Demography* (pp. 41–103). Paris: Organisation for Economic Co-operation and Development. Retrieved from https://www.oecd.org/edu/ceri/41939423.pdf

Weller, M. (2012). The openness-creativity cycle in education. *Journal of Interactive Media in Education, 2.* Retrieved from http://jime.open.ac.uk/articles/10.5334/2012-02/

Westermann Juárez, W. & Venegas Muggli, J. I. (2017). Effectiveness of OER use in first-year higher education students' mathematical course performance: A case study. In C. Hodgkinson-Williams & P. B. Arinto (Eds.), *Adoption and impact of OER in the Global South* (pp. 187–229). Retrieved from https://doi.org/10.5281/zenodo.601203

White, D. & Manton, M. (2011). *Open Educational Resources: The value of reuse in higher education.* Oxford: University of Oxford. Retrieved from https://oerknowledgecloud.org/content/open-educational-resources-value-reuse-higher-education

Wiley, D., Hilton III, J., Ellington, S. & Hall, T. (2012). A preliminary examination of the cost savings and learning impacts of using open textbooks in middle and high school science classes. *The International Review of Research in Open and Distributed Learning, 13(3).* Retrieved from http://www.irrodl.org/index.php/irrodl/article/view/1153/2256

Wiley, D., Green, C. & Soares, L. (2012). *Dramatically bringing down the cost of education with OER: How Open Education Resources unlock the door to free learning.* Washington D.C.: Center for American Progress. Retrieved from http://files.eric.ed.gov/fulltext/ED535639.pdf

Wolfenden, F., Buckler, A. & Keraro, F. (2012). OER adaptation and reuse across cultural contexts in Sub Saharan Africa: Lessons from TESSA (Teacher Education in Sub Saharan Africa). *Journal of Interactive Media in Education, 1.* Retrieved from http://doi.org/10.5334/2012-03

World Bank. (2009). Accelerating catch-up: Tertiary education for growth in Sub-Saharan Africa. Washington, D.C.: World Bank. Retrieved from http://siteresources.worldbank.org/INTAFRICA/Resources/e-book_ACU.pdf

World Bank. (2013). *2013 world development indicators.* Washington, D.C.: World Bank. Retrieved from http://databank.worldbank.org/data/download/WDI-2013-ebook.pdf

Yuan, M. & Becker, M. (2015). Not all rubrics are equal: A review of rubrics for evaluating the quality of Open Educational Resources. *The International Review of Research in Open and Distributed Learning, 16(5).* Retrieved from http://www.irrodl.org/index.php/irrodl/article/view/2389/3412

Xhang, D., Li, X. & Xue, J. (2015). Education inequality between rural and urban areas of the People's Republic of China, migrants' children education, and some implications. *Asian Development Review, 32(1),* 196–224. Retrieved from http://www.mitpressjournals.org/doi/pdf/10.1162/ADEV_a_00042

Zagdragchaa, B. & Trotter, H. (2017). Cultural-historical factors influencing OER adoption in Mongolia's higher education sector. In C. Hodgkinson-Williams & P. B. Arinto (Eds.), *Adoption and impact of OER in the Global South* (pp. 389–424). Retrieved from https://doi.org/10.5281/zenodo.599609

How to cite this chapter

Arinto, P. B., Hodgkinson-Williams, C., King, T., Cartmill, T. & Willmers, M. (2017). Research on Open Educational Resources for Development in the Global South: Project landscape. In C. Hodgkinson-Williams & P. B. Arinto (Eds.), *Adoption and impact of OER in the Global South* (pp. 3–26). Retrieved from https://doi.org/10.5281/zenodo.1038980

Corresponding author: Patricia B. Arinto <patricia.arinto@gmail.com>

Chapter 2

Factors influencing Open Educational Practices and OER in the Global South: Meta-synthesis of the ROER4D project

Cheryl Hodgkinson-Williams, Patricia B. Arinto, Tess Cartmill and Thomas King

Summary

This chapter provides a meta-synthesis of the findings from the Research on Open Educational Resources for Development (ROER4D) empirical studies based on the 13 sub-project chapters in this volume as well as other sub-project research reports. It does so by analysing how three phases of Open Educational Resources (OER) adoption – OER creation, use and adaptation – are observed in the studies as forms of Open Educational Practices (OEP), identifying where there are most likely to be disjunctures that inhibit optimal OER adoption processes and their longer-term sustainability. It compares the open practices reported in the ROER4D sub-project studies to an idealised or maximal set of open processes, modelled as the Open Education cycle framework. It draws upon social realist theory to uncover agential decision-making about OER creation, use and adaptation in relation to structural and cultural environments, and seeks to answer the ROER4D project's overarching research question: Whether, how, for whom and under what circumstances can engagement with OEP and OER provide equitable access to relevant, high-quality, affordable and sustainable education in the Global South?

This chapter interrogates findings from the ROER4D empirical studies using a meta-synthesis approach. Following a review of sub-project research reports (including, in some cases, primary micro data), the authors used a literature-informed set of themes to create the meta-level conceptual framework for claims about OER and OEP in relation to access, quality and affordability; the Open Education cycle; and structural, cultural and agential influences on the potential impact on access, quality and affordability. ▶

Nvivo software was used to help reveal literature-informed and emergent themes in the studies, identifying the most frequently occurring themes to provide a more comprehensive and classified interpretation of the findings across the empirical studies. Insights and recommendations were then distilled according to Archer's (2003; 2014) social realist theoretical framework which assesses social change – and its counterpart, stasis – according to dynamically interactive structural, cultural and agential factors. The authors used these three factors to guide their analysis of the ROER4D findings, as understood in relation to the three broad phases of OER adoption (creation, use and adaptation) proposed in the Open Education cycle.

Findings show that in the Global South contexts studied, the ideal or maximal Open Education cycle is incomplete in terms of optimising the benefits of OER adoption. There are five key points of disjuncture: (1) the dependence on copying of existing OER and the corollary failure to localise; (2) the adaptation of OER, but with inconsistent curation and rehosting of derivative works on publicly available platforms or in repositories, limiting access to the derivative OER; (3) limited circulation of derivative OER due, in part, to the absence of a communication strategy; (4) inconsistent quality assurance processes; and (5) a weak feedback loop for continuous improvement of the original or derivative work.

The chapter concludes with a critical exploration of the range of influences of OER and associated practices on access to educational materials, the quality of educational resources, educators' pedagogical perspectives and practices, and student performance as well as the overall affordability and sustainability of education in the Global South. It argues that full participation in the OER movement in the Global South requires that certain structural factors be put in place – including a minimum level of infrastructural support, legal permission to share materials and OER curation platforms – to curate curriculum-aligned OER in local languages. However, these structural adjustments alone are insufficient for the full value proposition of OER to be realised. While individual educators and some institutions are sharing OER, this willingness needs to be bolstered by a much stronger cultural change where communities of educators and students are given technical and pedagogical support to enable OER uptake – especially the creation and adaptation of OER produced in the Global South.

Acronyms and abbreviations

AVU	African Virtual University
CC	Creative Commons
CC BY-SA	CC Attribution-ShareAlike licence
CILT	Centre for Innovation in Learning and Teaching
CW4WAfghan	Canadian Women for Women in Afghanistan
DDL	Darakht-e Danesh Library
DIETs	District Institutes of Education and Training
FOSS	Free and Open Source Software
HEI	higher education institution

ICT	information and communication technologies
KOER	Karnataka Open Educational Resources
LMS	learning management system
MIT	Massachusetts Institute of Technology
MOOCs	Massive Open Online Courses
NGO	non-governmental organisation
OEP	Open Educational Practices
OER	Open Educational Resources
QA	quality assurance
ROER4D	Research on Open Educational Resources for Development
TESSA	Teacher Education in Sub-Saharan Africa
UCT	University of Cape Town
UNESCO	United Nations Educational, Scientific and Cultural Organization
UNISA	University of South Africa
WOU	Wawasan Open University

Introduction

From the late 1990s, there has been a concerted effort by a number of higher education institutions (HEIs), intergovernmental organisations and non-governmental organisations (NGOs) located predominantly in the Global North to intentionally create and share educational materials that are legally open for reuse and free to any user. Often referred to as "Open Educational Resources" (OER) or "open content", these materials are seen as a mechanism to address some of the formidable educational challenges in the Global South. These challenges include unequal access to education (UNESCO, 2014a); variable quality of educational resources, teaching and student performance (UNESCO, 2014b); and increasing cost and concern about the sustainability of education (UNESCO, 2017).[1] Although OER are not culturally neutral, as both the content and language are inherently value-laden and embedded within the pedagogical context in which they originate, the value proposition of OER is that these materials can be legally adapted for reuse in other educational environments.

There have been a number of OER research and implementation initiatives, but the extent and impact of OER adoption[2] in the Global South are not fully understood. The Research on Open Educational Resources for Development (ROER4D) project has sought to address this gap through 17 empirical studies undertaken in 21 countries across South America, Sub-Saharan Africa, and South and Southeast Asia (sometimes referred to as "developing countries" or "least developed countries"[3]). This chapter provides a meta-synthesis of 15 of these independent studies, drawing upon sub-project research reports and the chapters in this volume. The studies include one cross-regional survey of higher education students and university staff across nine countries; three studies on university

---

1   See Chapter 1 of this volume by Arinto, Hodgkinson-Williams, King, Cartmill and Willmers for a more detailed discussion of the Global South context and how it shapes OERs' potential.
2   The term "adoption" in this context refers to the activities in each of the three broad OER adoption phases: creation, use and adaptation.
3   https://unstats.un.org/unsd/methodology/m49/

academics' adoption of OER in India, Mongolia and South Africa; three studies on teacher professional development in Colombia, India and Sri Lanka; one study of a Malaysian open university's use of OER as the basis for a postgraduate course; one on the influence of OER on students' performance in Chile; one on the use of an existing OER collection in Africa; one on teacher educators in four countries in East Africa; and one on the use of OER as component elements of Massive Open Online Courses (MOOCs).

This chapter analyses OER creation, use and adaptation in these studies, comparing the open practices reported to an "idealised" or maximal set of open practices, as elucidated in Hodgkinson-Williams' (2014) Open Education framework. This is done to help identify where disjunctures may inhibit optimal OER adoption processes and their longer-term sustainability. It draws upon Archer's (2003; 2014) social realist theory to uncover the structural and cultural factors most likely to influence the agential practices of OER creation, use and adaptation. The chapter concludes with a critical exploration of the range of influences of OER adoption and associated practices on access to educational materials, quality of educational resources, educators' pedagogical perspectives and practices, student performance, and the overall affordability and sustainability of education in the Global South.

OER and Open Educational Practices

This section provides a brief overview of how OER and their inherent Open Educational Practices (OEP) are understood in the existing literature, how they have been understood by the ROER4D researchers, and how the concepts are deployed in this meta-synthesis.

As discussed in more detail by Arinto et al. (Chapter 1), the term "OER" has been defined in a variety of ways by international agencies, philanthropic organisations and educational institutions as well as by researchers trying to describe the concept. The United Nations Educational, Scientific and Cultural Organization (UNESCO) originally defined OER as "any type of educational materials that are in the public domain or introduced with an open license. The nature of these open materials means that anyone can legally and freely copy, use, adapt and re-share them. OER range from textbooks to curricula, syllabi, lecture notes, assignments, tests, projects, audio, video and animation".[4] According to the Hewlett Foundation, OER are "teaching, learning, and research resources that reside in the public domain or have been released under an intellectual property license that permits their free use and re-purposing by others".[5] In 2012, the Paris OER Declaration adapted the original UNESCO version and defined OER as "teaching, learning and research materials in any medium, digital or otherwise, that reside in the public domain or have been released under an open license that permits no-cost access, use, adaptation and redistribution by others with no or limited restrictions".[6] The concept of open sharing of educational content was further entrenched in 2007 following Wiley's articulation of the "4Rs"[7] (revise, reuse, remix and redistribute) to describe the rights associated with OER (in 2014 he extended this to the "5Rs"[8] to include retention of resources). Each of these "Rs" essentially describes a

---

4   http://www.unesco.org/new/en/communication-and-information/access-to-knowledge/open-educational-resources/what-are-open-educational-resources-oers/
5   http://www.hewlett.org/programs/education/open-educational-resources
6   http://www.unesco.org/new/fileadmin/MULTIMEDIA/HQ/CI/WPFD2009/English_Declaration.html
7   https://opencontent.org/blog/archives/355
8   https://opencontent.org/blog/archives/3221

practice or set of practices an educator would employ in the course of their teaching when creating, using or adapting OER.

ROER4D researchers were invited to participate in a research concepts harmonisation process which led to a reasonable level of consensus on the phenomenon under scrutiny, but slightly different tacit understandings remained, due in part to linguistic norms and socially situated meanings. Most drew explicitly upon the UNESCO, Hewlett or Paris Declaration definitions, while some drew on slightly different sources to formulate their own working definitions of OER (Westermann Juárez & Venegas Muggli, Chapter 6) or used the more encompassing concept of "Open Education" to cover both OER and Open Access (Toledo, Chapter 4). For the purposes of this chapter, the term "OER" is seen as a component of Open Education and is understood to refer to teaching, learning and research resources that reside in the public domain or which have been released under an intellectual property licence that permits activities enabled by different degrees of openness.

Since at least 2007, researchers have included "practices" as a constituent aspect of the OER movement (Andrade et al., 2011). The term "OEP" primarily refers to the practices involved in planning, creating, adapting, curating, sharing and reviewing OER. Masterman (2016, p.41) argues that developing an OEP conceptual framework "involves disparate sources", as there is a lack of a "holistic repertoire of practices currently observable in the field". Originally, Conole and Ehlers (2010, p.2) defined OEP as "the practice of creating the educational environment in which OER are created or used". Subsequently, other practitioners and researchers have elaborated upon these definitions to include a more deliberate focus on "collaboration" (Karunanayaka, Naidu, Rajendra & Ratnayake, 2015), "open/public pedagogies in teaching practice" (Beetham, Falconer, McGill & Littlejohn, 2012), "crowdsourcing" (Weller, 2013), "open peer review" (Hegarty, 2015) and "using open technologies" (Beetham et al., 2012). The concept of OEP is more fluid and understood in a range of ways in the ROER4D studies. Teasing out what is "open" in an educational practice in different sociocultural settings and exactly how it differs from locally determined "good" pedagogical practice is sometimes very subtle.

In the ROER4D project, OEP are construed as individual or collaborative use, adaptation, creation, curation (retention) and circulation (distribution) processes of OER for others to locate, copy (reuse in its unaltered form), and/or adapt (customise or combine) and subsequently re-curate and re-circulate as teaching materials (Hodgkinson-Williams, 2014). OEP also include collaboration between educators, co-creation of materials by educators and students, crowdsourcing of ideas and/or materials among educators and members of the public, open peer review of materials, and use of open technologies to optimise sharing and reuse. It is posited that for OER to exist, there must of necessity be prior OEP, in the same way that Cronin relates OEP and OER more deliberately in her most recent definition: "[OEP] is a broad descriptor of practices that include the creation, use and reuse of [OER] as well as open pedagogies and open sharing of teaching practices" (2017, p.15). In other words, to optimise the use of OER to achieve equitable, good-quality and sustainable education, educators and students need to engage in OEP.

Although much of the production of and research on OER and OEP has taken place in the Global North (Andrade et al., 2011; Ehlers, 2011; Porter, 2013), a growing number of studies in the Global South are charting the shift from OER to OEP (Czerniewicz, Deacon, Glover & Walji, 2016; Perryman & Seal, 2016). Most ROER4D researchers initially focused on the phenomenon of OER, rather than OEP, except for two (Czerniewicz, Deacon, Walji & Glover, Chapter 10; Wolfenden, Auckloo, Buckler & Cullen, Chapter 8). However, as studies progressed, it became clear that adoption of OER automatically involves some type of OEP (e.g. Karunanayaka & Naidu, Chapter 13; Kasinathan & Ranganathan, Chapter 14).

OER and OEP as components of an Open Education cycle

In 2014, Hodgkinson-Williams proposed an elaboration of the practices associated with OER[9] (Okada, Mikroyannidis, Meister & Little, 2012; White & Manton, 2011), framing them within a more comprehensive set of OEP encompassing 10 distinct activities of an Open Education cycle (originally called the "10Cs" – creation, curation, circulation, certification, etc.) posited to optimise the key value proposition of OER, namely access to affordable, high-quality education. This model has evolved over the course of the ROER4D research process (Walji & Hodgkinson-Williams 2017a; 2017b) and been refined into an Open Education cycle which is based around a common conceptualisation activity, followed by three distinct phases: a creation phase, a use phase and an adaptation phase (Figure 1).

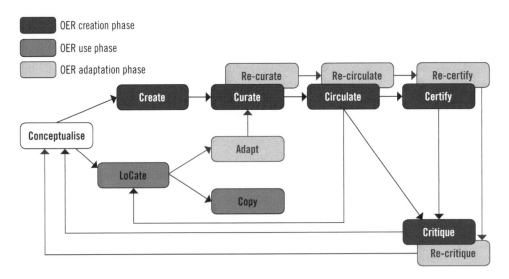

Figure 1: **Proposed "optimal" Open Education cycle (Adapted from Hodgkinson-Williams, 2014; Walji & Hodgkinson-Williams, 2017a)**

The **conceptualisation** activity includes planning what OER and which pedagogical strategies might be most suitable in a specific context; it is implicit in the OER creation, use or adaptation phases.

The **creation** phase refers to the development of original materials and/or tuition by the author or institution, either as a "self-use" of existing materials or as "born open" OER (i.e. developed with the view of being shared freely and openly). In order for these materials to be made publicly available, they need to be **curated**; that is, they need to be hosted on

9   https://opencontent.org/blog/archives/3221

a publicly accessible platform with sufficient descriptive information (i.e. metadata) and appropriate open licensing (e.g. Creative Commons [CC])[10] for them to be easily found through internet search tools and legally reusable. Further **circulation** amongst potential users of the OER is required to raise awareness of the existence of the OER (e.g. via social media, OER portals), which are then ideally **certified** through some type of quality assurance mechanism, either by the OER creator, their peers, an educational body or the hosting organisation. Best practice also requires that the OER can be **critiqued** to ensure that user feedback informs subsequent phases of conceptualisation regarding the OER.

The **use** phase refers to finding OER (artificially referred to as "**loCate**" in this phase) so that it can be used in its original form (i.e. **copied**) in other contexts. This use phase, where OER are used "as is", implies a finite path as no subsequent OER are created from this activity.

The **adaptation** phase refers to OER being customised (e.g. revised, modified) or combined (e.g. remixed with more than one set of OER) in order for these derivative OER to be re-curated, re-circulated, re-certified and re-critiqued.

Factors influencing OEP and OER

To understand the adoption of OER and the OEP that are entailed in their creation and optimisation, as well as the impact of OER and OEP on increasing access to educational materials, improving learner performance, enhancing teacher pedagogy and improving the quality and reducing the costs of the materials themselves, some type of social theory needs to be advanced. In this meta-synthesis, we adopt Archer's social realist perspective that "for any process to merit consideration as a generator of social change it must necessarily incorporate structured human relations (context-dependence), human actions (activity-dependence) and human ideas (concept-dependence)" (Archer, 2013, p.4). In other words, "every theory about the social order necessarily has to incorporate SAC: structure, agency and culture" (Archer, 2013, p.4).

Porpora elaborates upon Archer's conception and suggests that "social change involves a dialectical relation between human agency and the contexts in which those agents find themselves, contexts that include culture, structure, and physical things" (2013, p.29). He includes "things, both natural and humanly made, since … new or transformed things also play a role in social change" (2013, p.29) and mentions the invention of computers and the internet as prominent examples.

Structural factors

Broadly speaking, structural conditions can refer to government and/or institutional policies, systems and infrastructure. Archer describes social "structure" as the "objective features of society" (2003, p.i) or the "material … aspects of social life" (1988, p.xi), as evidenced in "roles, organisations, or institutions" (2003, p.5). She maintains that "the identification of structures is possible because of their irreducible character, autonomous influence and relatively enduring character, but above all because this means that they pre-date any particular cohort of occupants" (1995, p.168). In Archer's theory, social structure also refers

---

10   https://creativecommons.org/

to "human relations among human actors – relations like power, competition, exploitation, and dependency [or more precisely the] relations among social positions that human actors occupy" (Porpora, 2013, p.25).

In the ROER4D meta-synthesis, the concept of structure is understood to denote relatively enduring relations among human actors, the social positions they occupy, and things made by humans. These can include infrastructure, such as power supply, hardware, software, connectivity and information and communication technologies (ICT); the availability of OER in various repositories and portals as well as support of OEP on collaborative platforms; open licensing (such as CC); government or institutional policies, strategies, programmes and procedures; and funding from donors, governments and/or institutions. Structure also refers to the socioeconomic and geographic context in which students and educators are located (Table 1).

Table 1: Structural factors potentially influencing OER adoption

Structural factors	
Physical factors	**Relations and social positions**
Infrastructure – power supply, hardware (devices and printing facilities), software, connectivity	Policies, strategies, programmes and/or procedures at government, national, provincial and/or institutional level with respect to: – Initial teacher training, teacher professional development, academic staff development in HEIs – Intellectual property, copyright and CC licensing – Free and Open Source Software (FOSS), Open Access, OER
OER repositories, aggregators, collaborative platforms and learning management systems (LMS)	Funding – Donor – Government – Institutional – Self-funding Institutional support
Geographic contexts (urban and rural)	– Technical support – Curriculum and learning design support – Library services

Cultural factors

Archer describes "culture" as "ideational aspects of social life" (1988, p.xi) that are manifest in "beliefs, theories, value systems, mathematical theorems, and novels etc" (2014, p.97). In order to undertake cultural analysis, Archer distinguishes more specifically between cultural "products" as the "cultural system" and "ideas" as the "socio-cultural" domain. The former has "an objective existence and autonomous relations among its components (theories, belief, values, arguments, or more strictly between the propositional formulation of them) in the sense that these are independent of anyone's claim to know, to believe, to assert or to assent to them" (Archer, 1996, p.107).

In this ROER4D meta-synthesis, OER are seen as the "products" that form the "cultural systems", whereas the "socio-cultural domain" is seen as the prevailing social, institutional and/or disciplinary values, norms, conventions, expectations and practices that may encourage or deter educator and student engagement in the adoption of OER. These norms include perceptions of what counts as "valuable knowledge" and, consequently, how the "quality" of OER and OEP is determined (Table 2).

Table 2: Cultural factors potentially influencing OER adoption

Cultural factors	
Cultural system (relations between ideas)	**Sociocultural domain (differences in ideas among people)**

OER as a product
   – Cultural content
   – Language
	Institutional/disciplinary norms or conventions
	Epistemic stance
	Perceptions of quality
	Pedagogic practices

Agential factors

As a number of individuals, institutions, government agencies and/or NGOs are involved in the need for and provision of formal education, this meta-synthesis endeavours to identify the agents who can influence and who are influenced by a range of factors in the process of adopting OER and/or engaging with OEP. The term "agent" (Archer, 2000) is used deliberately to indicate intentional agency exhibited by stakeholders, and their uptake (or not) of OEP and OER in response to the "structural and cultural" (Archer, 2003) conditions they face. In relation to Open Education, individuals and/or institutions are accorded the choice of whether (or not) to engage in OEP and/or adopt OER (Table 3).

Table 3: Agential factors potentially influencing OER adoption

Agential factors	
Institutional	**Individuals or groups of individuals**

Intergovernmental agencies
 	
Government – national and/or provincial (e.g. ministries of education)
   – Educational institutions
   – Schools
   – Teacher training colleges
   – Universities
   – NGOs
	Students (primary, secondary and university students)
	Educators (school teachers, teacher educators and university lecturers)
	Formal communities of practice or informal networks
	And their:
	   – Digital proficiency
	   – Curriculum and learning design skills
	   – OER awareness (including knowledge of copyright and open licensing)
	   – Professional identity (including reputation)
	   – Motivation and beliefs
	   – Priorities (including time constraints)

In the ROER4D project, Archer's theoretical perspective is used to understand under what conditions (structural and cultural) individuals', and/or institutions' decision-making (agential) result in change or constancy in OEP associated with OER adoption that may in turn influence access to affordable and good-quality education.

Methodological approach

In order to provide insights into the relationship between engagement with OER and OEP, and change or stasis with respect to equitable access to relevant, high-quality, affordable and sustainable education, findings from 15 of the 17 ROER4D empirical studies have been interrogated using a meta-synthesis approach. Scruggs, Mastropieri and McDuffie (2007, p.395) explain that:

> Unlike quantitative synthesis (meta-analysis) of group experimental research reports, qualitative metasynthesis is not concerned with summarizing or reducing findings to a common, standardized metric, such as a mean effect size. Rather, the purpose is to integrate themes and insights gained from individual qualitative research into a higher order synthesis that promotes broad understandings of the entire body of research, while still respecting the integrity of the individual reports.

This is a useful methodology to adopt when, as is the case with the ROER4D studies, researchers used a variety of methodologies, included a range of participants and conducted their research over different time periods (Arinto et al., Chapter 1). This meta-synthesis therefore does not set out to compare the findings of each of the independent studies, but rather endeavours to engage more broadly with the key issues that may help to better understand what structural and cultural circumstances influence institutional and/or individual (agential) adoption of OER. It also seeks to understand whether and how the adoption of OER can improve access to educational materials, the quality of educational resources, educators' pedagogical perspectives and practices and student performance, as well as the overall affordability and sustainability of education in the Global South.

This meta-synthesis included the following stages:

1. Reading through draft and final versions of sub-project research reports (including, in some cases, primary micro data) and noting similarities and/or differences in terms of key themes in their findings.
2. Engaging with the researchers to clarify concepts, data and/or findings to aid in the comparison of key themes.
3. Using a literature-informed set of themes to create the meta-level conceptual framework for the claims about OER and OEP in relation to the cycle of Open Education; and for the structural, cultural and agential influences on the potential impact on access, quality and affordability.
4. Ingesting pre-peer-reviewed research reports into the qualitative software analysis tool Nvivo to assist in the analysis of the literature-informed and emergent themes.
5. Using the meta-level conceptual framework to code the themes in the findings of each of the studies and then adjust the framework to include unanticipated themes emerging from the findings.
6. Identifying the most frequently occurring themes to provide a more comprehensive and classified interpretation of the findings across the empirical studies.
7. Distilling insights according to the theoretical framework proposed above.

Findings

The findings draw on the sub-project studies (Chapters 4–15) as well as the cross-regional study (Chapter 3) to understand the various types of educational practices related to or involving OER, and to identify structural, cultural and/or agential factors that might account for these in various countries. The findings are analysed and discussed according to the Open Education cycle (Figure 1) highlighting the three key OER adoption phases in the order in which they appear most frequently in ROER4D studies, namely use, creation and adaptation.

Factors influencing stages of the Open Education cycle

Before examining practices, two key constraining and/or enabling factors that influence open practices are foregrounded. Firstly, agents' awareness of OER is key to both the adoption of OER and research on the phenomenon, and, secondly, the necessary infrastructure required to engage in OER-related practices.

Variable awareness of OER amongst educators and students

One of the key challenges in the ROER4D studies was knowing precisely what respondents considered "Open Educational Resources" to be, given the various terms[11] used to describe similar free and openly licensed materials. Most ROER4D respondents conflated OER with digital materials that are freely available on the internet, and they were generally not aware of copyright regulations that restrict use of online materials or alternative open licensing mechanisms that make freely available resources "legally open" (de Oliveira Neto, Pete, Daryono & Cartmill, Chapter 3; Oates, Goger, Hashimi & Farahmand, Chapter 15; Wolfenden et al., Chapter 8). Wolfenden et al. articulate the general sentiment in the ROER4D studies that "[l]ack of awareness of the licence did not preclude educators from adapting resources (even in cases where this may not have been permissible in terms of the resource licence), and there was much reported sharing of articles and videos directly with students through multiple channels, such as email, print, and posts on Facebook and other social media platforms" (Chapter 8, p.273). Thus, all data presented and inferences drawn need to be treated with some caution as the phenomenon being studied was imprecisely understood and/or implemented by participants.

Better access to infrastructure for educators than for students

Educators and students require access to particular infrastructure to adopt digital OER. A prerequisite for accessing digital OER is some form of power supply. In the Global South, access to uninterrupted electricity cannot be taken for granted, as reported by a number of ROER4D researchers. In Afghanistan, Oates et al. (Chapter 15) highlight the lack of a reliable power supply in the rural Parwan province, where their study was located. In East Africa, Wolfenden et al. (Chapter 8) and Adala (2017) both report the lack of a reliable power supply as a structural constraint to OER access. In India (Kasinathan & Ranganathan, Chapter 14) and South Africa (Cox & Trotter, Chapter 9), power outages can be quite common, although urban areas typically have fewer power disruptions than rural areas. In Mongolia (Zagdragchaa & Trotter, Chapter 11) and South Africa (Cox & Trotter, Chapter 9), higher education educators were more likely to enjoy a more robust power supply than university students, with school educators and students in rural environments having the least reliable power supply (Kasinathan & Ranganathan, Chapter 14).

---

11   See Chapter 1 for a more extended discussion on the various definitions and terms associated with OER.

Access to, although not necessarily ownership of, digital devices is also a prerequisite for OER adoption. In the ROER4D project, the discernible trend was that educators had more ready access to such devices (sometimes owning more than one) than students. In Afghanistan, it was found that "almost all of the teachers in the study owned at least one digital device ... However, of those who did own a digital device, less than half ... had internet access on their device" (Oates et al., Chapter 15, p.562). In Mongolia, Zagdragchaa and Trotter (Chapter 11, p.407) report that of 42 higher education staff surveyed, "57% ... own their own laptops, though many also use the desktop computers provided by their HEIs". Wolfenden et al. (Chapter 8) elaborate that even in cases where HEIs in East Africa provided computers, teacher educators often complemented these with personal mobile phones. Although access to mobile devices was quite common amongst students and educators alike, students were less able to access computers as these were often insufficient for the large number of students (Adala, 2017) or the computers available were dysfunctional (Kasinathan & Ranganathan, Chapter 14). Kasinathan and Ranganathan point out that District Institutes of Education and Training (DIETs) in the provinces in India are making a special effort to replace dysfunctional computer labs in schools in order to advance the OER agenda.

In Sub-Saharan Africa, the availability, stability, speed, cost and limitations on internet connectivity were major factors in the extent to which educators engaged in digitally based OEP, including downloading and uploading OER. In their East Africa study, Wolfenden et al. (Chapter 8, p.269) accentuate the fact that "an absence of fast, consistent internet connectivity; and limited access to laptops and desktop computers were all reported to limit teacher educators' exploration of and familiarity with OER, most acutely [at a rural higher education institution] in Uganda". A similar situation was reported at the University of South Africa (UNISA), where adequate internet access was available only to educators as "many students did not have reliable access because they live in poor, rural areas with weak infrastructural support, or in urban townships far from the UNISA satellite centres" (Cox & Trotter, Chapter 9, p.306). The consequence is that "all teaching materials must be printable and deliverable by post so that every student gets the same educational experience"; should an academic wish to use OER in their teaching, "these resources [can] only be offered as 'additional' or 'optional' materials for the online students" (Cox & Trotter, Chapter 9, p.309).

In Asia, there is a more mixed picture of the availability and quality of connectivity. In Mongolia, most of the higher educators in this study "connect to the internet at work (81%) and/or home (76%) at speeds that they describe primarily as 'medium' (52%) or 'fast' (29–33%)" (Zagdragchaa & Trotter, Chapter 11, p.407). By contrast, restricted or slow internet access among educators is reported in Afghanistan (Oates et al., Chapter 15), and limited internet access and connectivity issues inhibited the work of teacher educators and pre-service teachers in Sri Lanka (Karunanayaka & Naidu, Chapter 13). In India, Kasinathan and Ranganathan (Chapter 14) report that connectivity was "patchy" and that this poor connectivity could have inhibited school teachers from uploading OER to the Karnataka Open Educational Resources (KOER) portal.[12]

In Chile, Westermann Juárez and Venegas Muggli (Chapter 6) report that more than 50% of higher education students felt that the institutional infrastructure supported the

---

12   http://karnatakaeducation.org.in/KOER/en/index.php/Main_Page

optimal use of OER, although the educators saw the lack of infrastructure and connectivity as a barrier to student internet access. Poor internet connectivity was also reported by teachers in rural areas in Colombia (Sáenz, Hernandez & Hernández, Chapter 5).

It is worth noting that, while this discussion has been premised on OER being digitally mediated, it is not the case that all OER are digital. For example, Wolfenden et al. (Chapter 8) point out that printed copies of the Teacher Education in Sub-Saharan Africa (TESSA) materials are available from the libraries at the participating HEIs. In her study of five African countries, Adala (2017) also confirms that teacher educators accessed materials from the African Virtual University (AVU) collection online and via print copies. Similarly, Goodier (Chapter 7) reports that printed open textbooks were distributed to students in publicly funded schools in South Africa, whilst in Chile, according to Westermann Juárez and Venegas Muggli (Chapter 6), printed versions of a teacher-adapted Wikibook were given to higher education students. However, Wolfenden et al. note the inadequacy of print OER over the long term and compellingly argue that "[a]ccess to the internet is central; without this, individual use of OER is static" (Chapter 8, p.266).

Having laid out these agential and structural prerequisites for engagement with OER and associated open practices, we now turn to an analysis of the use, creation and adaptation of OER reported most frequently in the ROER4D studies. Baseline data on OER use by higher educators (de Oliveira Neto et al., Chapter 3) and students[13] are drawn from the cross-regional survey to provide a quantitative benchmark of OER use. Findings from the other sub-projects are also scrutinised in an attempt to explain the extent of OER uptake. However, it must be noted that these are not exact comparisons and at best might indicate trends and factors influencing these trends. Referring to examples from the ROER4D studies, the next section highlights the uneven uptake or relative absence of some of the practices that would optimise the adoption of OER. The discussion begins with findings regarding conceptualisation, which is the first step in each of the three phases of OER use, creation or adaptation. This is followed by a description of the most frequently occurring "use" phase (conceptualising, locating, copying), followed by the "creation" phase (creating, curating, circulating, certifying and critiquing), and finally the less commonly reported "adaptation" phase (conceptualising, locating, adapting, re-curating, re-circulating, re-certifying and re-critiquing). For each step within these phases, the key enabling and/or constraining structural, cultural and/or agential factors are identified in an attempt to explain the degree of the variable uptake of OER and the associated OEP.

The conceptualisation stage in the use, creation and adaptation of OER

The ROER4D studies revealed different degrees of explicitness in conceptualising the search for existing OER, production of new OER or adaptation of existing OER. More specifically, it was found that conceptualisation may take place anywhere along a continuum of intentionality, from being completely subconscious to being part of a formal curriculum planning process at the institutional level.

---

13   http://roer4d.org/3305

Overt planning of OER more easily discernible in institutional or project-based settings

Lesson planning is often implicit in the process of searching for OER (or any materials on the internet) by individual educators; it is seldom made explicit unless there is a specific requirement to do so. In the East African institutions studied by Wolfenden et al. (Chapter 8), the normally opaque activity of finding and copying OER verbatim by individual educators became visible as they were required to create lesson plans. In Afghanistan, lesson plans were also analysed to identify changes in pedagogic practice (Oates et al., Chapter 15). A similar requirement, although in the context of shared lesson planning, was stipulated by the in-service teacher education programme at the Open University of Sri Lanka where student teachers were required to reflect on and write up their experiences in planning and implementing their OER-based lessons (Karunanayaka & Naidu, Chapter 13). In Colombia, the planning process was made visible in the oral presentations that the educators gave about their experience in developing OER, although writing up these processes was an unusual practice for these educators (Sáenz et al., Chapter 5).

Moreover, the ROER4D studies suggest that implicit planning to use materials "as is" by individual educators and students is driven more by the relevance of materials than by their "openness" *per se*. As Cox and Trotter summarise: "the 'openness' of an OER is rarely more important than the practical, pedagogical concerns surrounding the relevance, utility and quality of *any* educational material" (Chapter 9, p.293). In their study, one of the respondents from a South African institution remarked: "there's a lot of stuff that's just not applicable. Some of the stuff has snippets that are nice. [But] I seldom find things that I want to use as a whole" (Cox & Trotter, Chapter 9, p.315). This sentiment is shared by educators in Mongolia whose key concern was local relevance, irrespective of whether the material was openly licensed (Zagdragchaa & Trotter, Chapter 11). More generally, because the criteria used are often not made explicit, much of the reasoning around the selection of OER is still not well understood.

By contrast, in institutional or project-supported settings where the organisational reputation risks are high, planning and support, especially in the OER creation phase, are more deliberate and elaborate. For example, in the institutionally funded University of Cape Town (UCT) MOOC Project involving lecturers, learning designers and video production experts, formal planning processes were needed to produce the MOOCs (which included original OER as constituent elements) (Czerniewicz et al., Chapter 10). At Wawasan Open University (WOU) in Malaysia, an official curriculum committee conceptualised the structure of a formal distance learning course prior to identifying existing OER to be used in the course instead of proprietary textbooks to reduce the cost of course development (Menon, Palachandra, Emmanuel & Kee, 2017). A team of writers, editors, librarians and learning designers put together the OER-based course package and offered it in both Malaysia and India (Menon et al., 2017). Similarly, a full-time multilingual editor organises and manages teams of volunteer translators from around the world to translate English-language OER into Dari and Pashto for the digital Darakht-e Danesh Library (DDL) in Afghanistan (Oates et al., Chapter 15).

Overall, analysis of the ROER4D sub-projects suggests that the more institution-, programme- or project-driven the OER development process is, the more likely it is for the curriculum or resource planning activities to be made overt, shared with others and/or formally documented. The latter provides a framework for how others might use the original or adapted versions, especially within a formal teaching environment.

The OER use phase

For the purposes of this analysis, the concept of "OER use" is deployed in the first instance to mean reuse of the resource in its original form (also referred to as use "as is", verbatim or in an unaltered form) in various contexts (e.g. in a class, in a study group, on a website, in a video) following Wiley's definition.[14] The ROER4D studies also employed the term "use" in a broad sense to distinguish between "creation" (Cox & Trotter, Chapter 9) and the more overarching concept of OER uptake in general. In a number of the sub-projects, the term "use" was employed to refer to copying original OER as well as adapting OER through some form of customising (revising) or combining (remixing). Where it was possible to disaggregate these practices, they are reported separately.

Use of existing OER reported more frequently by educators than students

The ROER4D cross-regional survey (de Oliveira Neto et al., Chapter 3) provides an overall sense of the use of OER by educators in the Global South (Figure 2). The survey was administered to 295 randomly selected educators at 28 HEIs in nine countries across South America, Sub-Saharan Africa, and South and Southeast Asia. Slightly more than half (51%) of the educators surveyed stated that they had used OER at least once; one-quarter (25%) said they had never used OER; and slightly fewer than a quarter (24%) said they were not sure whether they had used OER. This suggests that while a small majority have used OER and have some familiarity with it, a sizeable minority have never used OER and/or are not aware of the concept. As Figure 2 illustrates, the level of OER use appears to be slightly differentiated by region: 50% in South America, 46% in Sub-Saharan Africa, and 56% in South and Southeast Asia.

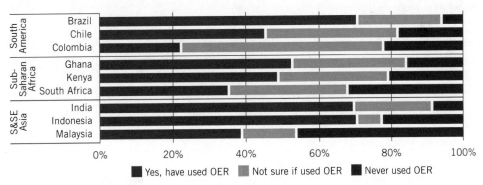

Figure 2: OER use by educators (Source: de Oliveira Neto et al., Chapter 3)

By contrast, far fewer students reported using OER compared to the educators. Of the 4 784 randomly selected students surveyed in the same study, only 39% reported having used

---

14   https://opencontent.org/blog/archives/3221

OER at least once; more than a third (35%) were not sure whether they had used OER; and slightly over a quarter (26%) had never used OER before[15] (Figure 3).

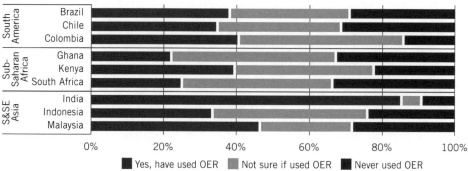

Figure 3: OER use by students[16]

Compared to the other countries, student use of OER in India (85%) is exceptionally high, and considerably higher than use of OER by the educators in the same study. Apart from the cross-regional survey, the majority of the ROER4D studies focused primarily on OER adoption by educators, so probing student adoption of OER presents an opportunity for further research.

Selecting OER challenging for educators given the volume of online resources

In order to use OER, educators must first find and select them. Some participants found this quite challenging. Wolfenden et al. (Chapter 8, p.269) note: "Many respondents found the sheer volume of available online resources daunting and were anxious for quality guidelines; without these they doubted whether they had sufficient expertise to judge whether a resource was of appropriate quality." Karunanayaka and Naidu (Chapter 13) report that the pre-service teachers in Sri Lanka who participated in their study found the workshop activities that specifically taught them how to identify suitable OER especially valuable. Amongst university educators in South Africa, workshops on locating OER highlighted that: "This process was a revelation for many, as most had never searched for OER via a dedicated OER repository, meaning that they had previously struggled to determine which materials were legally open for reuse and which were closed" (Cox & Trotter, Chapter 9, p.314).

Educators valued having a repository of materials relevant to their context

The OER platforms or repositories mentioned by participants in the ROER4D studies varied and included a few that are OER-friendly (e.g. Wikipedia, Google Scholar, Khan Academy, AVU, TESSA, TED Talks, Massachusetts Institute of Technology (MIT) OpenCourseWare, Commonwealth of Learning and Wikimedia Commons). However, not all participants were

---

15   http://roer4d.org/3305
16   http://roer4d.org/3305

aware that materials on these sites are in fact OER. Some participants reported looking for resources by searching Google and YouTube, but without filtering for materials with an open licence even though this functionality exists. In the study on Mongolia, of the educators who reported using OER, "the majority (50%) stated that they find resources through Google Scholar searches, followed by institutional repositories (33%) and personal websites or blogs (25%)" (Zagdragchaa & Trotter, Chapter 11, p.413). In Sri Lanka (Karunanayaka & Naidu, Chapter 13), India (Kasinathan & Ranganathan, Chapter 14) and Afghanistan (Oates et al., Chapter 15), and in partner institutions of the AVU (Adala, 2017), some respondents said they really valued having a specific repository of materials that they felt was relevant to their context. These resource collections were hosted on an institutional LMS (Karunanayaka & Naidu, Chapter 13), a provincial OER portal (Kasinathan & Ranganathan, Chapter 14), a project website (Sáenz et al., Chapter 5) and a local-language digital library (Oates et al., Chapter 15).

Locating OER a time-consuming process for educators

Those searching specifically for OER, such as the curriculum development team at WOU in Malaysia, confirmed that there was a sufficient number of materials for them to use, even though they took some time to find, and few video and audio materials were available (i.e. they were mostly text-based materials in HTML or PDF format) (Menon et al., 2017). The researchers noted that knowing how to identify OER and good internet searching skills might have reduced the time spent locating suitable OER (Menon et al., 2017). Similarly, educators in Sri Lanka observed that finding OER is a time-consuming process, specifically because so many OER exist (Karunanayaka & Naidu, Chapter 13).

Use of OER in its original form or not at all

With regard to type of OER use, merely copying the original seemed to be a common practice amongst educators. In Mongolia, respondents reported being more likely to use resources "as is" in their original form (Zagdragchaa & Trotter, Chapter 11). In East Africa, educators accessed the TESSA materials in print form from the library or from CDs to provide ideas for teaching, which is in line with the activity-based TESSA approach where "when you actually read these materials you should be able to actually copy and then you are able to do in your teaching" (Wolfenden et al., Chapter 8, p.272). One of the East African respondents "spoke eloquently about how many staff had a binary approach to OER: they either use OER in their original form or reject it outright as inappropriate" (Wolfenden et al., Chapter 8, p.271).

In Afghanistan, Oates et al. report that "[w]hile 20 teachers reported that they used both OER and the textbook, and eight said they mainly used OER from the DDL to design their lesson plan effectively, 23 said they did not use any OER and relied solely on a textbook when preparing their lesson plan" (Chapter 15, p.561). This pattern is similar in the five African countries in Adala's (2017, p.21) study:

> [One respondent noted] that the AVU OER was used as a primary resource, also [stating] that "the modules are heavily supplemented and complemented by other OER sources, sometimes to the extent that they may not necessarily take a primary position".

Educators' lack of awareness that they are using OER

There were a number of reports of general "use" of OER, but educators did not necessarily know that they had been using OER. For example, at one university in South Africa, Cox and Trotter (Chapter 9, p.318) report that: "All six interviewees we spoke to at UCT said that they had used OER, but only three had done so deliberately (seeking out materials from the Khan Academy, TED Talks and MIT OpenCourseWare)." At another South African university: "When asked who had used OER, five interviewees said yes and one said no, though two of the five admitted that they had done so inadvertently, not knowing that the materials were OER at the time (it only became apparent to them during the workshop that they had used OER before)" (Cox & Trotter, Chapter 9, p.323).

Table 4 provides a summary overview of the structural, cultural and agential factors influencing the use of OER at the ROER4D research sites.

Table 4: Structural, cultural and agential factors influencing use of OER in the ROER4D studies

	Structural factors	Cultural factors	Agential factors
LoCate (find)	**Enablers** – Global, national, provincial or institutional repositories – Institutional or project support and guidance **Constraints** – Volume of online resources	**Enablers** – OER relevant to context hosted locally **Constraints** – Searching for OER not the norm – Need for quality guidelines	**Enablers** – Skills to search for online materials **Constraints** – OER awareness and open licensing awareness – Time to find materials – Lack of skills to filter by open licences
Copy (use in original form, "as is")	**Enablers** – Institutional or project support and guidance – OER available in print **Constraints** – Mostly text-based, while video and audio sought	**Enablers** – Copying a common practice – Some relevance of materials **Constraints** – OER not aligned to curriculum – OER not applicable to context	**Enablers** – Expertise to judge quality **Constraints** – Anxiety about ability to judge quality

The OER creation phase

Hodgkinson-Williams (2014, p.9) describes the OER creation phase as "the development of original materials and/or tuition by the author or institution either as a 'self-use' of existing materials or [as] 'born open' OER, i.e. developed with the view of being shared freely and openly". In the ROER4D project, this definition was extended to include collaborative creation as well as individual and/or institutional development and co-creation with students (Walji & Hodgkinson-Williams, 2017a; 2017b).

Limited creation of OER, especially by students

Trying to ascertain the practice of OER creation when participants were not always clear about the concept of OER posed a real challenge to researchers in the ROER4D project. To estimate OER creation, de Oliveira Neto et al. (Chapter 3) in their cross-regional study asked whether individual educators had shared educational materials with an open licence. They found that 23% of the 295 randomly selected higher education educators surveyed reported that they had openly licensed their teaching materials (Figure 4). In the sub-project in Mongolia, 76% of the higher education educators surveyed said that they had never created and shared OER (Zagdragchaa & Trotter, Chapter 11).

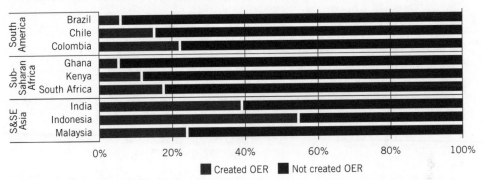

Figure 4: OER creation by higher education educators as indicated by applying open licensing on teaching materials (Source: de Oliveira Neto et al., Chapter 3)

Still, in general, OER creation was the second most likely OEP undertaken by educators in the ROER4D studies – on par with informally sharing materials found on the internet, but less frequent than "as is" use of existing OER. The study of 117 higher education educators in India found that they were more likely to create materials than customise or combine OER (Mishra & Singh, Chapter 12).

With respect to higher education students, the cross-regional survey revealed that only 9% of the 4 784 randomly selected students reported that they had openly licensed their own materials in some fashion, thereby creating OER[17] (Figure 5).

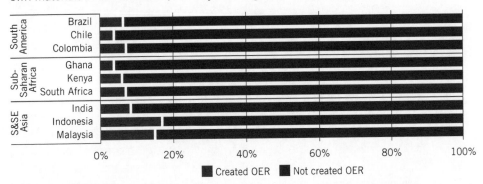

Figure 5: OER creation by higher education students as indicated by open licensing of shared materials[18]

---

17   http://roer4d.org/3305
18   http://roer4d.org/3305

As Figure 5 illustrates, there appears to be more OER creation by higher education students in South and Southeast Asia (9%) than in South America (5%) and Sub-Saharan Africa (5%). Both tertiary educators (41%) and students (16%) in Indonesia reported creating OER more frequently than the educators and students in the other countries.

Lack of legal permission for educators to share the OER they create

Among the structural and agential factors that specifically influence OER creation, the most important is whether educators actually have the requisite permission to share materials they create while working at an institution. In their study of three South African HEIs, Cox and Trotter (Chapter 9, p.301) highlighted the importance of determining "whether it is the lecturers (the actual developers of the teaching materials) or the institution itself which holds copyright over the teaching materials". They established that at UCT, "lecturers possess copyright on their teaching and learning materials, allowing them to transform any of their teaching resources into OER" (Cox & Trotter, Chapter 9, p.307) if they choose to do so. This practice stands in contrast to the other two institutions they studied (Cox & Trotter, Chapter 9). They explored the extent to which other universities in South Africa hold copyright over materials produced by their educators and found that lecturers hold copyright on their teaching materials in only five of the country's 26 universities.[19] This is in line with South Africa's Copyright Act of 2008 which grants employers default copyright ownership over employees' work-based creations.

A ROER4D (2017) briefing document on OER policy reports that intellectual property laws in some other countries have different provisions. An OER-friendly arrangement is in place in Mongolia where the Copyright Law of 2006 states that: "The author of a work created in the course of execution of his/her duties shall enjoy non-economic intangible rights; the employer may have the exclusive rights over the exploitation of the work created as part of the exercise of official duties if not otherwise stipulated in the contract."[20] This suggests that educators should be able to share their teaching materials as OER as long as they do not profit financially from the process.

Low digital proficiency inhibits OER creation by educators and students

A number of the ROER4D studies focused on OER creation by educators (Cox & Trotter, Chapter 9; Czerniewicz et al., Chapter 10; Kasinathan & Ranganathan, Chapter 14; Menon et al., 2017; Sáenz et al., Chapter 5; Westermann Juárez & Venegas Muggli, Chapter 6); only one included OER creation by students (Westermann Juárez & Venegas Muggli, Chapter 6). These studies raised digital proficiency as an agential factor in educators' and students' ability to create OER. At UCT, where researchers interviewed the academics who had worked with the Centre for Innovation in Learning and Teaching (CILT) team to collaboratively create MOOCs, the individual creators were relatively skilled in the use of various digital technologies and the CILT team included technically skilled pedagogical support staff (Czerniewicz et al., Chapter 10). In India, by contrast, the educators in the teacher professional development group were observed to have "nascent digital literacy skills and limited time to gain technical proficiency" (Kasinathan & Ranganathan, Chapter

---

19   http://roer4d.org/2298
20   http://www.wipo.int/wipolex/en/text.jsp?file_id=203958

14, p.527). In both the Indian and Colombian studies, researchers actively supported participants' acquisition of digital skills by teaching them how to use FOSS. According to Sáenz et al. (Chapter 5, p.163), "free and/or open software … was encouraged to promote greater coherence between the technologies used and the open licensing approach to promote social values within an open culture framework". Lack of digital proficiency as a barrier to OER creation also emerged in the sub-project in Chile, where students who were required to contribute to Wikibooks found the editing quite complicated and were therefore reluctant to contribute (Westermann Juárez & Venegas Muggli, Chapter 6).

Participation in professional development networks aids collaborative OER creation

In Karnataka province in India, 88% of school teachers who were part of a professional development network produced 25 original video resources in the local Kannada language for demonstration of various science concepts, which formed the core resource material for a statewide training programme (Kasinathan & Ranganathan, Chapter 14). Collaborative OER creation was also reported by groups of pre-service teachers in nine provinces in Sri Lanka (Karunanayaka & Naidu, Chapter 13). In Colombia, 22 teachers from six schools created 16 OER, of which 10 were created individually and six collaboratively. The researchers noted that this was a new practice for the school teachers, who did not usually create materials, either on their own or collaboratively (Sáenz et al., Chapter 5).

Like school teachers, higher education faculty do not often create materials collaboratively unless there is a specific institutional policy or project (usually accompanied by funding) which requires them to do so. An example is the MOOC Project at UCT that was undertaken by academics in collaboration with an institutional learning design and materials production unit (Czerniewicz et al., Chapter 10). The creation of these MOOCs "inspired careful consideration of licensing options for the MOOC as well as discussion about the kind of licensing in the educators' future formal courses" (Czerniewicz et al., Chapter 10, p.370).

Co-creation among students and educators still a nascent activity

Co-creation of materials among students and educators is likewise still in a nascent phase at the ROER4D research sites. In Chile, Westermann Juárez and Venegas Muggli (Chapter 6) report that even though their project provided opportunities for co-creation with students, not many students took up this offer. In the East African institutions they studied, Wolfenden et al. (Chapter 8) also mention some educators sharing student work with the next cohort of students. In Afghanistan, after undergoing OER training, 78% of the participating Afghan teachers said that OER helped them initiate collaboration among students (Oates et al., Chapter 15).

Curating original OER more likely with government, institutional or project support

Hodgkinson-Williams (2014) describes the curation phase of the Open Education cycle as the hosting of materials and/or tuition on a publicly accessible platform with sufficient descriptive information (i.e. metadata) and appropriate open licensing (e.g. CC) for these resources to be easily found with search engines on the internet and aggregation platforms.

The term "curation" is more often used by librarians, but it is gradually becoming a familiar term amongst educators.

In the Karnataka study, the KOER portal began as an initiative to publish the resources shared by school teachers participating in the Subject Teacher Forum mailing lists (Kasinathan & Ranganathan, Chapter 14). The overt curation strategy was the creation of a MediaWiki-based portal, maintained by the NGO IT for Change[21] where all content created by the teachers is uploaded and assigned a CC Attribution-ShareAlike (CC BY-SA) licence. Some of the teachers reported difficulties uploading their materials to the KOER portal, primarily due to a lack of technical competence, sometimes reverting to sharing materials via email instead (Kasinathan & Ranganathan, Chapter 14). However, IT for Change, with some support from the provincial government, has been able to act as curator and assist teachers in sharing materials, particularly those in the Kannada language (Chapter 14). This model is being implemented by the government in two other states in India.

In Afghanistan, the DDL[22] was established by the NGO Canadian Women for Women in Afghanistan (CW4WAfghan) to serve as an independent source of knowledge, information and pedagogical tools for Afghan school teachers (Oates et al., Chapter 15). Like IT for Change, CW4WAfghan takes responsibility for the curation and ongoing maintenance of OER uploaded to the DDL. While the teachers are able to upload materials to the DDL and choose a relevant open licence, it seems that this is still an incipient practice (Oates et al., Chapter 15).

In the Colombian project, as mentioned, the participating school teachers created 16 OER in Spanish and thus faced the challenge of where to curate these materials and how to describe them so that they would be found through a Google search. With the support of the ROER4D researchers in Colombia, the teachers were able to upload their materials to third-party platforms (in most cases YouTube) and publish on the Collaborative Co-Creation of Open Educational Resources by Teachers and Teacher Educators in Colombia project website[23] to make clear the attributed author and copyright holder of the materials, the open licence used (in this case, CC BY-SA), and other descriptive data such as subject area, grade level, institution and its location, and the email details of the author. Sáenz et al. (Chapter 5, p.174) note that:

> Addressing copyright and open licensing in the activities of adaptation, curation and creation with teachers and students … and identifying the possibilities offered by ICT in schools … resulted in deep reflection by the participant teachers in this study on their practices and their teaching models, driven by a realisation that they and their students can have a more active role in the creation and co-creation of knowledge.

There were other ROER4D studies that alluded to an open curation strategy. For example, the MOOC production team at UCT used third-party MOOC platforms (FutureLearn and Coursera) to host their MOOCs (Czerniewicz et al., Chapter 10). At least two of the MOOCs were curated well enough to be reused by the MOOC educators in their regular campus-

---

21   http://karnatakaeducation.org.in/KOER/en/index.php/Main_Page
22   https://www.darakhtdanesh.org/en
23   https://karisma.org.co/cokrea/

based classes, and one was used at a university in Maryland, USA (Czerniewicz et al., Chapter 10). Cox and Trotter (Chapter 9) report that creators of OER at UCT curated their original materials on the OpenUCT[24] institutional repository, where uploading the materials and attributing metadata is the responsibility of the individual lecturer. Although this strategy recognises the agency of the lecturers and bolsters autonomy, there is a risk that the OER will not be described adequately to make them easy to find online.

The lack of an open curation strategy is evident in many of the other ROER4D sub-projects where educators report using and storing OER, very likely without metadata, on a password-protected LMS (Adala, 2017; Karunanayaka & Naidu, Chapter 13; Wolfenden et al., Chapter 8). In this case, even if the original OER have a CC licence, the adapted OER, which may include more up-to-date material, more relevant examples and/or more creative activities, may never be shared or used by others, even within the institution.

Based on the foregoing, the structural and agential factors that seem to enhance the curation of original OER include the availability of a suitable platform with ongoing technical support, as well as knowledge of open licensing and digital fluency on the part of the participants. The establishment and sustainability of a content-curation platform is more likely if it is supported by government, an institution or a NGO.

Informal sharing of materials more frequent than sharing via formal OER distribution channels

"Circulating" is a term used to describe dissemination of OER through informal sharing and formal distribution mechanisms to aid discoverability. It follows very closely on the heels of curation, and is undertaken in order to share content more widely via email or a formal platform, as merely curating materials on an institutional or third-party platform is insufficient for optimal visibility and reusability.

The ROER4D studies confirm that educators are generally willing to share their materials informally (Karunanayaka & Naidu, Chapter 13; Oates et al., Chapter 15). Mishra and Singh (Chapter 12) report that their respondents in Indian HEIs felt that it is a teacher's inherent responsibility to share. Several of the respondents in East Africa described how they shared their own resources as well as those of their students under CC licensing (Wolfenden et al., Chapter 8). However, while many educators were keen to share their own materials and those of others, this often seemed to take place irrespective of licensing conditions. In Chapter 14, Kasinathan and Ranganathan observe that educators seldom openly licensed their materials and it "appeared that teachers treated the resources created by them and shared on mailing-lists as self-evidently open" (Chapter 14, p.538) – what these authors termed "implicit OER". They go on to explain that "during the focus group discussions, it emerged that teachers found the default copyright approach counter-intuitive, especially in the context of online digital resources, since these were usually easy to download and re-use, and were mostly gratis" (Kasinathan & Ranganathan, Chapter 14, p.537).

However, not all educators were willing to share, mostly citing concerns about quality and contextual and pedagogical appropriateness (Cox & Trotter, Chapter 9; Wolfenden et al., Chapter 8). One of the respondents in Wolfenden et al.'s study said that she would not share her materials if she was unsure about the quality or if someone might not find them useful.

---

24 https://open.uct.ac.za/

In terms of communication about the OER, even in MOOCs which are formally curated on a third-party platform, Czerniewicz et al. (Chapter 10) report that lecturers adopted strategies to extend the reach of OER beyond the MOOC platform (e.g. the "Ask Mark" collection on YouTube that was developed in the "What is a Mind?" MOOC).[25] The dissemination of these materials and other MOOC offerings was supported through active Twitter and Facebook campaigns to alert potential students. Although some of these "OER communication" activities emerged as a result of the learning design and production team supporting the lecturers, at least one of the lecturers had previously produced his own videos on a dedicated YouTube channel.

Factors inhibiting sharing seem to be more agential in nature, with educators not fully understanding copyright and open licensing and having to make sense of the paradox of being able to find and download both fully copyrighted and openly licensed materials, but being legally restricted from sharing the former and not the latter. On the other hand, factors encouraging communication about OER seem to be related to the imagination and technical skills of educators and support teams.

Quality assurance more likely within institutional or project initiatives

The "certify" and "critique" steps in the Open Education cycle, which represent the quality assurance and feedback activities that ideally link back to further integration of OER, were deemed important by the participants in the ROER4D studies, but were seldom reported as personal practices. Individual educators frequently expressed their concern about the quality of their teaching materials. In their South African study, Cox and Trotter (Chapter 9, p.316) report that educators were not confident about sharing their work "as OER just yet [or] would have to reassess their work with an eye to making it public before doing so".

In cross-country, institutional or project initiatives, quality assurance processes are often included in the original development of OER. For example, with respect to the AVU materials, Adala (2017) mentions the quality assurance and accreditation processes followed and how these processes included ministries of education and organisations such as the Teachers Service Commission. At an institutional level, Menon et al. (2017, p.32) report that the quality framework adopted at WOU was a "very robust one involving a number of systematically sequenced standard operational practices, including feedback loops at relevant stages of curriculum formulation, OER selection, material development and draft material trials". By contrast, from a project perspective in India, Kasinathan and Ranganathan (Chapter 14, p.536) acknowledge that the:

> ... large volume of materials shared on mailing lists and the KOER platform means that only a very small sample has been formally checked for quality assurance purposes. One of the expectations of the Education Department was that teachers would peer review the resources uploaded to the KOER platform, and use MediaWiki functionality to continually edit and revise the content. Such continuous peer editing and revision of resources is a higher-order skill not yet seen in the KOER context. Acknowledging that more formal structures are required for review processes, [the Directorate of School

---

25 https://www.futurelearn.com/courses/what-is-a-mind

Educational, Research and Training] is considering setting up state and district resource groups of teachers and teacher educators to play the role of peer reviewing and revising OER.

An unexpected finding was that individual educators reported using OER to check the quality of the materials they create but which they do not necessarily share. In their study in East Africa, Wolfenden et al. (Chapter 8, p.271) highlight the perspective of an educator who suggested that the benefit of exploring OER was that it "gave them a quality benchmark which sometimes caused them to feel they were doing a 'substandard' job compared to their international peers and that they were using 'old' methods". Similarly, Cox and Trotter (Chapter 9, p.320) report that an educator had "used OER to check the quality of her own teaching materials, not to incorporate them into her teaching practice".

Formal critique or feedback more easily actionable in institutional initiatives

Although, in principle, educators felt that "sharing education resources helped them obtain feedback … if [they were] seeking to improve their materials" (Mishra & Singh, Chapter 12, p.436), this ambition was more easily discernible in institutional initiatives than in cross-country, project-based or individual initiatives. For example, with regard to the UCT MOOC Project, Czerniewicz et al. (Chapter 10, p.372) reflect that:

> … the experience of making a MOOC not only exposed educators to new open pedagogical strategies, but also to feedback from MOOC participants. The feedback in the form of completed assessments, peer review, comments, discussion threads and assignments enabled the educators to witness the effect of the pedagogical strategies they employed as they taught in a distributed network and as part of a diverse community.

The feedback led to educators designing additional online activities, such as video recordings of the lecturer responding to questions from students.

Table 5 provides a summary overview of the structural, cultural and agential factors influencing the creation of OER in the ROER4D research sites.

Table 5: Structural, cultural and agential factors influencing OER creation in ROER4D studies

	Structural factors	Cultural factors	Agential factors
Creation	**Enablers** – Government support for OER portal – OER creation part of teacher development programme – School-based OER support programme – Institutional funding for OER – Institutional, technical and/or learning design support – Project activity supporting OER creation in local languages – Permission to use open licences **Constraints** – Variable government support for infrastructure – Lack of institutional permission to share created works, including OER	**Enablers** – Professional teacher development network – Input from students **Constraints** – Unfamiliar practice amongst educators	**Enablers** – Digital proficiency – Consideration for future reuse in formal courses **Constraints** – Lack of digital proficiency – Lack of awareness of OER and open licensing – Lack of time to gain digital proficiency
Curation	**Enablers** – Public but local (language, curriculum) OER platform – Ongoing technical support **Constraints** – Password-protected LMS	**Constraints** – Curation not a common practice amongst educators	**Enablers** – Prospect of reuse **Constraints** – Digital proficiency – Lack of knowledge of licensing and how to assign metadata
Circulation	**Enablers** – Formal platform – Technical support **Constraints** – Default copyright clause	**Enablers** – Informal network	**Enablers** – Willingness to share – Responsibility to share – Adopting strategy to share on a range of platforms **Constraints** – Concern about quality
Certify and Critique (quality assurance) [QA]	**Enablers** – QA built into institutionally created OER – Feedback loop – Availability of continuous revision loop **Constraints** – Formal structures required for QA	**Enablers** – Using OER to check quality of own teaching materials **Constraints** – Quality not always checked in community of informal sharing	**Enablers** – Feedback enabled review of pedagogical strategies **Constraints** – QA not usually part of individual practice

The OER adaptation phase

Hodgkinson-Williams (2014, p.9) originally described the adaptation phase as consisting of two separate actions, namely: "customise", equivalent to Wiley's concept of "revise", and "combine" as a simpler way of describing what Wiley refers to as "remix".[26] It should be noted that the latter concept does not necessarily have a ready translation in other languages. During the course of the ROER4D project these two processes were deliberately collapsed into "adaptation" (Walji & Hodgkinson-Williams, 2017b), as it became clear that respondents in the ROER4D studies could not easily discern the subtle differences between revising a single OER and remixing multiple OER. In the meta-synthesis it became apparent that respondents and researchers alike used a range of other terms to describe the adaptation process, including modify, change, translate, contextualise, localise, refine, repurpose, rewrite, edit, add, reduce, delete, resequence and improve, mirroring the reuse processes described by Okada et al. (2012) quite closely.

Limited adaptation of OER by educators and students

The cross-regional survey shows that only 18% of the 295 randomly selected educators surveyed reported having adapted (modified) OER at least once (de Oliveira Neto et al., Chapter 3) (Figure 6).

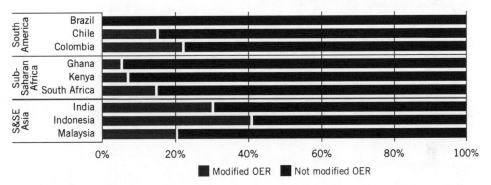

Figure 6: OER adaptation by higher education educators (Source: de Oliveira Neto et al., Chapter 3)

As Figure 6 illustrates, the level of OER adaptation by higher education educators appears to be greater in South and Southeast Asia (30%) than in South America (12%) and Sub-Saharan Africa (9%). Moreover, none of the nine educators surveyed in Brazil reported adapting OER; in contrast, 15% and 22% of the educators surveyed in Chile and Colombia, respectively, reported that they had adapted OER (de Oliveira Neto et al., Chapter 3). Conversely, Kasinathan and Ranganathan (Chapter 14) provide an indication of high levels of adaptation by the "Collaborative OER Adoption" cohort of teachers in their study.

The adaptation of OER by tertiary students is very limited, with only 6% of the 4 784 randomly selected students surveyed reporting that they have modified OER at least once[27] (Figure 7).

---

26   https://opencontent.org/blog/archives/355
27   http://roer4d.org/3305

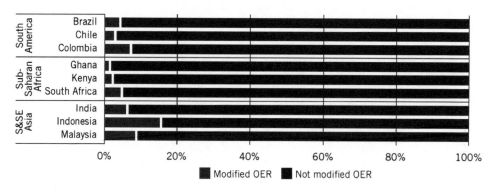

Figure 7: OER adaptation by tertiary students[28]

As Figure 7 illustrates, there appears to be more OER adaptation by tertiary students in South and Southeast Asia (11%) than in South America (4%) and Sub-Saharan Africa (3%), which mirrors the regional differentiation for educators. Both tertiary educators (41%) and students (16%) in Indonesia reported adapting OER more frequently than the educators and students in the other countries in the three regions surveyed. As no ROER4D case study was undertaken in Indonesia, further research is needed to explain this trend, which may have to do with the initiative by Universitas Terbuka (one of the institutions where educators and students were surveyed) to use OER in their open and distance courses.

OER more readily adapted by institutions if coherent collections of OER are available

Where institutions aim to use OER as the basis for entire courses, having collections of OER might support their adoption. With regard to the OER-based courses at WOU, Menon et al. (2017) highlight the value of having a large coherent collection of OER materials in reducing the time needed for adapting and weaving resources together. Their study also highlights the level of knowledge of the discipline required for a curriculum development team to be able to integrate existing OER into a course.

Predominance of English-based OER requires a level of fluency in English

Both Adala (2017) and Wolfenden et al. (Chapter 8) mention the need for fluency in English for educators to be able to accurately translate OER into their language of choice. The educators in Wolfenden et al.'s study (Chapter 8, p.273) pointed out that "sometimes the use of OER made considerable demands on their students – for example, students accessed resources in English, but were then expected to use them in their practice in Swahili". Zagdragchaa and Trotter (Chapter 11) refer to the conundrum facing educators in Mongolia who would like to translate English-language OER into Mongolian to aid optimal comprehension by their students, but who have to consider the time investment of doing so if the students are sufficiently fluent in English to understand the materials in the original. The CW4WAfghan group responsible for the DDL in Afghanistan makes no such assumptions of English fluency and has volunteers from around the world undertaking the translation of English-language OER into Afghan languages (Oates et al., Chapter 15).

---

28 http://roer4d.org/3305

Workshops needed to model and provide experience in OER adaptation

The ROER4D studies in India (Kasinathan & Ranganathan, Chapter 14; Mishra & Singh, Chapter 12), Sri Lanka (Karunanayaka & Naidu, Chapter 13) and Malaysia (Menon et al., 2017) all report the value of conducting workshops for school teachers and course writers to demonstrate and provide practice in OER adaptation. A teacher in the Sri Lankan study explained that "workshop activities helped us to identify relevant OER and identify the nature of their licences ... it helped us to gain some knowledge and practice of the '4R' concept through practical activities organised during the workshop" (Karunanayaka & Naidu, Chapter 13, p.483).

Workshops can also provide educators with opportunities to use FOSS to create or adapt materials (Kasinathan & Ranganathan, Chapter 14; Sáenz et al., Chapter 5). In the ROER4D study context, they also helped educators learn how to upload materials to a public platform for sharing local curricula in local languages, as in the case of the KOER portal in India (Kasinathan & Ranganathan, Chapter 14), or to an institutional OER repository hosted on the LMS, such as the Open University of Sri Lanka's Moodle-based LMS (Karunanayaka & Naidu, Chapter 13). Post-workshop technical support was mentioned as a necessary function to assist the Indian school teachers in uploading or directly linking OER on the KOER portal (Kasinathan & Ranganathan, Chapter 14), but the researchers noted that even with ongoing technical support the teachers contributed more material to the portal during the workshop period than afterwards.

Adapted OER not always re-curated by educators and seldom by students

Where public and locally relevant OER portals and/or institutional repositories were available, OER adaptation could be observed and tracked in the ROER4D studies. The challenge was that not all educators had access to such repositories, or if they were available, they did not always know about them. For example, even if they had access to the original AVU materials, the educators in Adala's (2017) study did not know where or how to re-curate adapted versions. One of the educators mentioned that the majority of the educators and students were unaware of the materials and that his institution rarely created different versions of the AVU materials. While some of the educators interviewed said that they had been using AVU OER as supplementary material, the overall impression was that the adaptations of these materials were not publicly shared for readaptation. Thus, the original AVU materials are now considered outdated, inadequate and misaligned with the current curricula (Adala, 2017). Although there are a few reports of educators including OER in their courses, these versions are not accessible to other educators or students.

Need for ongoing support from institutional policy-makers and OER champions

Both Adala (2017) and Wolfenden et al. (Chapter 8) point to the valuable influence of institutional or project OER champions in building a culture of sharing. Provision of institutional support for OER adoption at WOU (Menon et al., 2017) and departmental support at UCT (Czerniewicz at al., Chapter 10) is noteworthy. Similarly, the ongoing support for OER adoption that is provided by IT for Change in India (Kasinathan & Ranganathan, Chapter 14), by CW4WAfghan in Afghanistan (Oates et al., Chapter 15) and by the Karisma Foundation in Colombia (Sáenz et al., Chapter 5) demonstrates the value of projects and/

or strategies to optimise the adaptation of OER. Without a formal strategy for continuous development, OER are likely to become outdated, which means that one of the key value propositions of OER will remain unrealised.

Table 6 provides a summary overview of the structural, cultural and agential factors influencing the adaptation of OER in the ROER4D research sites.

Table 6: Structural, cultural and agential factors influencing OER adaptation in ROER4D studies

Structural factors	Cultural factors	Agential factors
Enablers – Availability of "generic" and coherent body of OER for adaptation – Formal workshops to model and provide experience of adapting OER – Public but local (language, curriculum) OER platform to curate adapted OER – Public platforms on which educators and students can host and edit OER (e.g. Wikibooks, MediaWiki) – Technical support for re-curating post-workshop activities **Constraints** – Lack of locally relevant OER portals, repository or even institutionally driven OER repository hosted on an LMS – Lack of a strategy for continuous development of OER to avoid materials becoming out of date	**Enablers** – Presence and advocacy of local OER champions to build culture of sharing – Use of FOSS to promote open social values – Repurposed for different contexts **Constraints** – Adapted OER not always shared within community	**Enablers** – Sufficient knowledge of the discipline to combine congruent OER – Learning design skills – Ability to write materials – Fluency in English sufficient to be able to accurately translate OER **Constraints** – Lack of fluency in English sufficient to be able to accurately translate OER – Time to translate OER into local languages may outweigh benefits if students are already sufficiently fluent in English – Lack of time – Lack of knowledge of copyright and licensing

Discussion

The discussion section discusses the disjunctures within the Open Education cycle that are apparent from the patterns of OER adoption described in the previous section. The factors that account for these disjunctures are summarised, and their impact on OER as a means for widening access to educational materials, improving the quality of educational materials, enhancing the quality of teaching and learning and improving the affordability and sustainability of Open Education are explored. The discussion also touches upon the power dynamics around OER adoption in the Global South that are apparent in the ROER4D studies.

The incomplete Open Education cycle

What is clear from the findings of the ROER4D project is that in the Global South contexts studied, the ideal Open Education cycle is incomplete, resulting in the benefits of OER adoption not being fully optimised. There are five key points of disjuncture: (1) the dependence on copying of existing OER and the corollary reluctance to localise; (2) in the adaptation of OER, inconsistent curation and rehosting of derivative works on a publicly available platform or repository, which limits access to the derivative OER; (3) limited circulation of derivative OER due, in part, to the absence of a specific dissemination strategy; (4) inconsistent quality assurance processes; and (5) a weak feedback loop for continuous improvement of original or derivative OER (Figure 8). There is also one unexpected enactment of the use phase, namely the emergence of the use of existing OER to prompt ideas for pedagogic practice (Oates et al., Chapter 15; Wolfenden et al., Chapter 8).

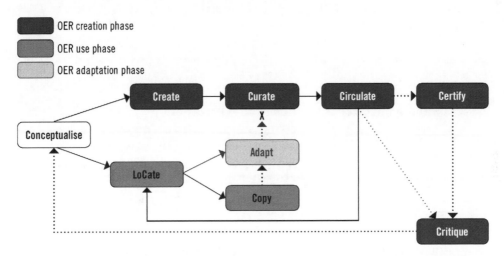

Figure 8: Enactment and disjunctures of the Open Education cycle in ROER4D studies

These disjunctures in the Open Education cycle indicate that educators in the Global South seem to be relying heavily on OER created in the Global North for use in their original form, thereby unwittingly reinforcing Northern epistemic hegemony. In addition, because most of the current OER are available in English, the reuse of OER "as is" and even the translation of OER, which requires a certain level of English fluency, sustains Anglo-linguistic preeminence. The latter seems to be more problematic in countries in South America, some countries in Sub-Saharan Africa and specific countries in Asia, for example Afghanistan.

More positively, it is clear that educators, and to a lesser extent students, are starting to create, curate and circulate local-language OER, albeit informally. While the formal quality assurance mechanisms are still nascent in individually developed OER, these are more well developed in OER creation that is supported by institutions or NGOs. The feedback loop, which ideally allows for critique to inform the next conceptualisation of OER, seems to be quite weak across the studies undertaken in the ROER4D project, with the exception of institutionally funded projects, such as the UCT MOOC Project. The value of this incipient OER creation phase is that countries in the Global South are taking the opportunity to showcase, at a global level, diverse perspectives and expertise through locally relevant resources and socially situated practices.

The major disjuncture is in the adaptation phase where the studies report not only limited revising and remixing of OER, but also virtually no re-curation, re-circulation, re-certification or re-critique. The consequence is that an opportunity to include adapted OER in the global collection of culturally and linguistically diverse OER is being missed.

The factors that might influence this incomplete Open Education cycle are summarised in the following section in terms of their consequences for access to affordable, good-quality education in the Global South.

Structural, cultural and agential factors influencing OER adoption for access to affordable, good-quality education

This section synthesises the structural, cultural and agential factors influencing OER adoption and associated practices to improve access to educational materials, the quality of educational resources, educators' pedagogical perspectives and practices, and student performance as well as the overall affordability and sustainability of education in the Global South.

Factors influencing access to educational materials

The ROER4D studies suggest that, overall, the availability of OER is increasing access to educational materials in the Global South, even though they are mostly in English. Awareness of OER is, however, not ubiquitous and many educators and students cannot easily differentiate OER from other resources on the internet. Structural factors enabling access include provision of requisite infrastructure, which appears to be better in HEIs than in schools and better in urban than in rural areas – although this is not uniformly so across the countries studied in the ROER4D project. Provision of an uninterrupted power supply, access to functioning computers, especially in schools, and affordable internet connectivity cannot be assumed.

Despite these infrastructural challenges, it would seem that, in general, educators and students are sufficiently digitally fluent to use OER in the most limited sense of copying and reusing them for other purposes. The bigger challenge is where to curate and host adapted OER to provide continued access to updated materials. The emergence of local-language and curriculum-aligned OER platforms such as the KOER portal in India and the DDL digital library in Afghanistan helps in the provision of contextually relevant educational materials. Moreover, government support for the KOER portal and others like it in two other Indian states points to the value of locally relevant OER. However, the practice of hosting original and adapted OER on password-protected LMSs was also evident in some of the research sites, which, even with more encompassing open licensing provisions (such as CC BY), restricts rather than opens up access to educational materials. What seems to aid access to adapted materials is the provision of technical support to license and upload OER and an institutional or project-based strategy for continuous development of OER to avoid materials becoming dated.

Broadly speaking, the power over access to OER is mainly vested in provincial or state arms of government with respect to the schooling sectors and in institutions for the higher education sector. Where governments or institutions are unable or unwilling to invest in the infrastructure required to enable access, NGOs can provide temporary infrastructural support; the burden of access otherwise falls to the individual educator and student. What seems equally important is individual educators' and students' "epistemological access"

(Lotz-Sisitka, 2009), which reveals the educators' and students' ability to understand the OER in its original form as well as the linguistic fluency to be able to use or adapt it for their own sociocultural setting. In the ROER4D studies, educators and students reveal differing levels of epistemological access, as well as what van Dijk (2005) refers to as "skills access" to undertake the technical activities required to create, use and/or adapt OER.

Factors influencing the quality of educational materials

The influence of OER adoption on the quality of the educational materials themselves remains uncertain, as suggested by the range of articulated and unarticulated quality assurance mechanisms evident in the ROER4D studies. For example, although WOU has a quality assurance process which specifies quality checks at a number of points along the curriculum development process, the derivative OER remain behind a password-protected LMS. This means that they are not available for others to critique and adapt, and the adaptation process does not feed back into the Open Education cycle to encourage the ongoing refinement so valuable for the production of good-quality OER. The UCT MOOCs fare a little better as they have been subjected to quality assurance processes and are publicly available on a MOOC platform, but it is still not easy for others to access all of the constituent open materials for reuse, adaptation, re-curation and ongoing quality assurance. The quality of the OER in the DDL digital library in Afghanistan fares even better as there is a process for quality assurance of translations of existing OER.

The key influencing factors seem to be structural in nature, as institutions and/or projects have implemented or still need to implement strategies for continuous development and quality assurance of adapted OER. On the positive side, the lack of such strategies does not prevent educators from exercising agency – not only in selecting OER (and other materials) that they perceive to be relevant for their context (e.g. cultural, linguistic, geographic), but also in adapting these OER to meet specific pedagogic purposes. However, for individuals adapting existing OER, there is the complicating requirement of basic competency in English, which cannot always be assumed.

Overall, the ROER4D studies reveal that although the individual educators and students have power over searching for the OER they deem to be of a quality that is "fit-for-purpose" (Biggs, 2001) for their sociocultural context, they are dependent on the perceived reputation of the institutions or organisations from which the OER originates as a benchmark of quality assurance. This implies that the reputation of well-known and well-respected institutions or organisations indirectly holds a great deal of power over which OER are used.

Factors influencing the quality of pedagogy

The ROER4D studies seem to confirm the influence of OER on educators' pedagogical perspectives and practices, prompted by professional training and/or learning design support. For example, in the study in Afghanistan, Oates et al. (Chapter 15, p.565) suggest that a combination of "exposure to OER lesson models in the DDL, the general benefit of the DDL professional training, [and] review or the use of the lesson plan template in creating lesson plans" led to improved lesson design and instructional practice. The lecturers who were part of the UCT MOOC Project likewise attributed their adoption of more learner-centred pedagogical strategies to their involvement in MOOC-making – this was enacted not only within the MOOC, but also in their formal university teaching. It was noted that this learner-centred pedagogical practice was "more enthusiastically enacted ... when they were supported by learning designers" (Czerniewicz et al., Chapter 10, p.381). In the Mongolian study, one of the primary motivating factors identified for creating OER was that it "improved educators' own teaching materials because they knew that other educators might use them" (Zagdragchaa & Trotter, Chapter 11, p.416). However, some caution is needed when interpreting the relationship between OER use and improved teaching practice, especially over short periods of time, as the ROER4D studies also observed the persistence of entrenched practices, such as using the textbook exclusively as the basis for lesson planning and delivery (Oates et al., Chapter 15).

In general, the educators in the ROER4D studies exhibit quite strong agency over their pedagogical practices in terms of whether and how to engage with OER and whether or not to work in groups or individually. However, the power over their pedagogical choices is not absolute, as local institutional norms still hold sway – sometimes quite explicitly (such as in a school principal's lack of support) and at other times more implicitly (in relation to social expectations and unwritten codes of behaviour). For example, it is still common that educators at schools and in HEIs act autonomously, and collaboration is unusual unless there is a specific funded project which calls for it. Nevertheless, the greatest impact of OER adoption reported in the ROER4D studies centres around changes in teacher pedagogy and surfaces some shifts towards more learner-centred approaches, some collaborative work and embryonic co-creation with students.

Factors influencing student performance

Only one of the ROER4D studies specifically investigated the possible influence of the use of OER on student performance (Westermann Juárez & Venegas Muggli, Chapter 6). While circumspection is required in any attempt to draw causal relationships, this is particularly so in this case due to the many variables that could have accounted for the results, despite the fact that the researchers made every effort to isolate these variables in their quasi-experimental approach. An expected result was that students using video-intensive OER, such as a Khan Academy collection, were less likely to attend face-to-face classes than those using a teacher-adapted resource or the traditional textbook. Less expected was the fact that students using the Khan Academy collection did significantly better in their examinations, although not in the course as a whole. A different group of students using a similar set of video-intensive OER in a blended course fared no better than students using the proprietary resources provided by the institution. What is perhaps most surprising is that student results did not improve significantly when using a teacher-adapted OER in Wikibooks that enabled the students to contribute their own examples, despite the fact that the teacher and students alike said they preferred the Wikibooks resource. Overall, the results of the influence of OER on student performance are therefore slightly contradictory in this instance and may have more to do with the overall learning design and medium of delivery than the openness of the resources *per se.*

The ROER4D studies had a very limited focus on the influence of OER on student performance, so generalisations are not possible. A key issue raised in terms of further research is the need for more explicit and subtle discrimination between the learning design of resources, their digital nature and the features of the open practices involved in order to make claims about the influence of OER on student performance.

Factors influencing the affordability and sustainability of Open Education

While OER may be "free" for any user, there are "costs of access" that need to be considered in economically stressed environments, particularly the cost of internet connectivity. There may also be costs associated with certification, as mentioned by the MOOC researchers (Czerniewicz et al., Chapter 10). Nevertheless, based on findings from MOOC development at UCT (Czerniewicz et al., Chapter 10) and OER-based course development at WOU (Menon et al., 2017), it would seem that while there are initial costs in the creation and/ or adaptation of OER, especially in terms of technical and pedagogic competencies, there are longer-term cost and time efficiencies to be gained. While these efficiencies are yet to be determined in the WOU course studied, they are apparent from the reuse of the UCT MOOCs, which include re-runs of the same MOOC for external audiences, reuse of MOOC resources by lecturers within their own classes and reuse of MOOC resources by other lecturers in other institutions (although full cost-recovery models have not yet emerged in this case).

The key to achieving cost-effectiveness in education through OER adoption seems to be the development of the core materials and curating them carefully enough for both the original creator and others to adapt and re-curate. However, in the ROER4D sites in general, the most significant disjuncture in the ideal Open Education cycle is in the re-curation of OER, since all subsequent processes are dependent upon easy access to well-described and appropriately licensed materials. Having a specialised technical and learning design team to assist with this is more likely in HEIs than in schools, so a different configuration of support has to be envisaged. Kasinathan and Ranganathan (Chapter 14, p.531) provide just such a vision, as follows:

> For sustained OER creation, [the Collaborative OER Adoption cohort of] teachers suggested a decentralised model, comprising district-level resource groups which could regularly contribute to KOER, facilitated by the DIETs in each district. They also suggested increasing the core group of resource creators through the decentralised district-level groups. The teachers further emphasised that in order to allow teachers to continue this OER process in a sustainable way, it was important for the Education Department to make resource creation a formal responsibility of teachers and to incorporate a mechanism for reviewing the quality of resources.

Overall, the ROER4D studies suggest that the power to achieve cost-efficiency with OER lies with government and institutions, either in direct support of OER development or support for more formal communities of practice. An important caveat to this statement is that governments and institutions need to be more accurate and transparent about the costs of developing or procuring other educational materials in order to make credible evidence-based claims for the cost reduction that can be directly attributed to OER.

Conclusion

In sum, the ROER4D studies show that educators and students are not always aware of the legal distinctions between OER and copyrighted online resources, but the practice of searching for supplementary resources is growing. Use of OER is reported more frequently by educators than students and more readily in South and Southeast Asia by both groups than in South America and Sub-Saharan Africa. A key barrier to OER adoption in all three regions is a lack of the necessary technical infrastructure, including internet connectivity. This is more of a drawback for schools than for HEIs, and it is a notable constraint in rural environments.

Creation of local OER is the second most frequently reported activity in the ROER4D studies. An enabling policy environment is key in OER creation, as most school teachers and university lecturers do not have the legal permission to share the materials they produce in the course of their employment. Creation of OER by educators is enhanced with technical support and access to OER platforms, repositories, portals or websites. Educators are otherwise inclined to share created materials informally (e.g. via email), increasing the risk that these materials will not become part of locally relevant resources that others could draw upon. Support from government, institutions and NGOs is pivotal within this context, as the ROER4D studies show that quality assurance and ongoing development are more likely if OER creation is part of an institutional or project initiative.

One of the most compelling value propositions of OER is that they can be regularly updated and localised, thus reducing the cost of producing educational materials. However, the ROER4D studies show limited adaptation of OER by educators and students. A number of explanations for this are advanced, including the fact that most of the currently available OER are in English and a certain level of fluency in this language is required to understand and translate these materials. In addition, adaptation takes time, which can be reduced if more coherent collections of OER are available, rather than many quite granular OER. A disjuncture in the ideal Open Education cycle is noted in the adaptation phase where educators and students seldom re-curate their adapted OER, thus limiting peer review, quality assurance and redistribution. This gap needs to be systematically addressed if materials from countries in the Global South are to become part of the global knowledge resource collection.

What seems clear is that full participation in the OER movement in the Global South requires that certain structural factors be put in place, including a minimum level of infrastructural support, permission to share materials and OER platforms to curate curriculum-aligned OER in local languages. However, these structural adjustments alone are insufficient for the full value proposition of OER to be realised and for social change to occur. While individual educators and some institutions are sharing OER, this willingness needs to be bolstered by a more profound cultural change where communities of educators and students are given governmental and institutional support to enable OER uptake – especially the creation and adaptation of OER produced in the Global South.

Acknowledgements

The authors wish to thank Henry Trotter and Michelle Willmers for their editorial support, as well as fellow members of the ROER4D Network Hub team for their assistance in the chapter development process. Special thanks also to Freda Wolfenden and Gurumurthy Kasinathan, who provided valuable input in the chapter drafting process, and to Alan Cliff and Leslie Chan, who acted as superb peer reviewers of this chapter.

References

Adala, A. (2017). Assessing the impact of OER availability on the emergence of Open Educational Practices in Sub-Saharan Africa: The case of an ICT-integrated multinational teacher education programme in mathematics and science. Unpublished ROER4D report to the International Development Research Centre.

Andrade, A., Ehlers, U-D., Caine, A., Carneiro, R., Conole, G., Kairamo, A-K., Koskinen, T., Kretschmer, T., Moe-Pryce, N., Mundin, P., Nozes, J., Reinhardt, R., Richter, T., Silva, G. & Holmberg, C. (2011). *Beyond OER: Shifting focus to Open Educational Practices*. Essen: Due-Publico. Retrieved from https://oerknowledgecloud.org/sites/oerknowledgecloud.org/files/OPAL2011.pdf

Archer, M. S. (1988). *Culture and agency: The place of culture in social theory* (1st ed.). Cambridge: Cambridge University Press.

Archer, M. S. (1995). *Realist social theory: The Morphogenetic approach*. Cambridge: Cambridge University Press.

Archer, M. S. (1996). *Culture and agency: The place of culture in social theory* (2nd ed.). Cambridge: Cambridge University Press.

Archer, M. S. (2000). *Being human: The problem of agency*. Cambridge: Cambridge University Press.

Archer, M. S. (2003). *Structure, agency and the internal conversation*. Cambridge: Cambridge University Press.

Archer, M. S. (2013). Social Morphogenesis and the prospects of Morphogenic society. In M. S. Archer (Ed.), *Social Morphogenesis*. Dordrecht: Springer Science+Business Media.

Archer, M. S. (2014). Introduction: Other conceptions of generative mechanisms and ours. In M. S. Archer (Ed.), *Late modernity: Trajectories towards Morphogenic society*. Switzerland: Springer International Publishing.

Arinto, P. B., Hodgkinson-Williams, C., King, T., Cartmill, T. & Willmers, M. (2017). Research on Open Educational Resources for Development in the Global South: Project landscape. In C. Hodgkinson-Williams & P. B. Arinto (Eds.), *Adoption and impact of OER in the Global South*. Chapter 1 advance publication. DOI 10.5281/zenodo.1038981

Beetham, H., Falconer, I., McGill, L. & Littlejohn, A. (2012). *Open practices: Briefing paper*. Oxford: Jisc. Retrieved from https://oersynth.pbworks.com/w/page/51668352/OpenPracticesBriefing

Biggs, J. (2001). The reflective institution: Assuring and enhancing the quality of teaching and learning. *Higher Education, 41(3)*, 221–238. Retrieved from https://doi.org/10.1023/A:1004181331049

Conole, G. & Ehlers, U–D. (2010). Open Educational Practices: Unleashing the power of OER. *Paper presented to UNESCO Workshop on OER*, May 2010. Windhoek, Namibia. Retrieved from https://oerknowledgecloud.org/sites/oerknowledgecloud.org/files/OEP_Unleashing-the-power-of-OER.pdf

Cox, G. & Trotter, H. (2017). Factors shaping lecturers' adoption of OER at three South African universities. In C. Hodgkinson-Williams & P. B. Arinto (Eds.), *Adoption and impact of OER in the Global South* (pp. 287–347). Retrieved from https://doi.org/10.5281/zenodo.601935

Cronin, C. (2017). Openness and praxis: Exploring the use of Open Educational Practices in higher education. *International Review of Research in Open and Distance Learning, 18(5)*, 15–34. Retrieved from http://www.irrodl.org/index.php/irrodl/article/view/3096/4301

Czerniewicz, L., Deacon, A., Glover, M. & Walji, S. (2016). MOOC-making and Open Educational Practices. *Journal of Computing in Higher Education, 29*, 81–97. Retrieved from http://rdcu.be/nzlw

Czerniewicz, L., Deacon, A., Walji, S. & Glover, M. (2017). OER in and as MOOCs. In C. Hodgkinson-Williams & P. B. Arinto (Eds.), *Adoption and impact of OER in the Global South* (pp. 349–386). Retrieved from https://doi.org/10.5281/zenodo.604414

de Oliveira Neto, J. D., Pete, J., Daryono & Cartmill, T. (2017). OER use in the Global South: A baseline survey of higher education instructors. In C. Hodgkinson-Williams & P. B. Arinto (Eds.), *Adoption and impact of OER in the Global South* (pp. 69–118). Retrieved from https://doi.org/10.5281/zenodo.599535

Ehlers, U–D. (2011). From Open Educational Resources to Open Educational Practices. *E-learning papers, 23*, 1–8. Retrieved from http://www.openeducationeuropa.eu/en/article/From-Open-Educational-Resources-to-Open-Educational-Practices

Goodier, S. (2017). Tracking the money for Open Educational Resources in South African basic education: What we don't know. *The International Review of Research in Open and Distributed Learning, 18(4)*. Retrieved from http://dx.doi.org/10.19173/irrodl.v18i4.2990

Hegarty, B. (2015). Attributes of open pedagogy: A model for using Open Educational Resources. *Educational Technology, July-August*, 3–13. Retrieved from https://upload.wikimedia.org/wikipedia/commons/c/ca/Ed_Tech_Hegarty_2015_article_attributes_of_open_pedagogy.pdf

Hodgkinson-Williams, C. (2014). Degrees of ease: Adoption of OER, open textbooks and MOOCs in the Global South. *Keynote address at the OER Asia Symposium 2014, 24–27 June 2014*. Penang, Malaysia. Retrieved from https://open.uct.ac.za/handle/11427/1188

Karunanayaka, S. & Naidu, S. (2017). Impact of integrating OER in teacher education at the Open University of Sri Lanka. In C. Hodgkinson-Williams & P. B. Arinto (Eds.), *Adoption and impact of OER in the Global South* (pp. 459–498). Retrieved from https://doi.org/10.5281/zenodo.600398

Karunanayaka, S., Naidu, S., Rajendra, J. & Ratnayake, H. (2015). From OER to OEP: Shifting practitioner perspectives and practices with innovative learning experience design. *Open Praxis, 7(4)*, 339–350.

Kasinathan, G. & Ranganathan, S. (2017). Teacher professional learning communities: A collaborative OER adoption approach in Karnataka, India. In C. Hodgkinson-Williams & P. B. Arinto (Eds.), *Adoption and impact of OER in the Global South* (pp. 499–548). Retrieved from https://doi.org/10.5281/zenodo.601180

Lotz-Sisitka, H. B. (2009). Epistemological access as an open question in education. *Journal of Education, 46*, 57–79. Retrieved from http://joe.ukzn.ac.za/Libraries/No_46_June_2009/Completeissue_No_46.sflb.ashx#page=61

Masterman, E. (2016). Bringing Open Educational Practice to a research-intensive university: Prospects and challenges. *The Electronic Journal of e-Learning, 14(1)*, 31–42. Retrieved from http://www.ejel.org/issue/download.html?idArticle=483

Menon, M., Palachandra, B., Emmanuel, J. & Kee, C. L. (2017). A study on the processes of OER integration for course development. Unpublished ROER4D Report to the International Development Research Centre.

Mishra, S. & Singh, A. (2017). Higher education faculty attitude, motivation and perception of quality and barriers towards OER in India. In C. Hodgkinson-Williams & P. B. Arinto (Eds.), *Adoption and impact of OER in the Global South* (pp. 425–458). Retrieved from https://doi.org/10.5281/zenodo.602784

Oates, L., Goger, L. K., Hashimi, J. & Farahmand, M. (2017). An early stage impact study of localised OER in Afghanistan. In C. Hodgkinson-Williams & P. B. Arinto (Eds.), *Adoption and impact of OER in the Global South* (pp. 549–573). Retrieved from https://doi.org/10.5281/zenodo.600441

Okada, A., Mikroyannidis, A., Meister, I. & Little, S. (2012). "Colearning" – collaborative networks for creating, sharing and reusing OER through social media. In *Cambridge 2012: Innovation and Impact – Openly Collaborating to Enhance Education, 16–18 April 2012*. Cambridge, UK. Retrieved from http://oro.open.ac.uk/33750/2/59B2E252.pdf

Perryman, L-A. & Seal, T. (2016). Open Educational Practices and attitudes to openness across India: Reporting the findings of the Open Education Research Hub Pan-India Survey. *Journal of Interactive Media in Education, (1)*, 1–17. Retrieved from http://jime.open.ac.uk/articles/10.5334/jime.416/

Porpora, D. V. (2013). Morphogenesis and social change. In M. S. Archer (Ed.), *Social morphogenesis* (pp. 25–37). Amsterdam: Springer.

Porter, D. A. (2013). *Exploring the practices of educators using Open Educational Resources (OER) in the British Columbia higher education system*. Burnaby: Simon Fraser University. Retrieved from http://summit.sfu.ca/item/13663

ROER4D (Research on Open Educational Resources for Development). (2017). *Spotlight on OER policy in the Global South: Case studies from the Research on Open Educational Resources for Development (ROER4D) project*. Cape Town & Ottawa: African Minds, International Development Research Centre & Research on Open Educational Resources for Development. Retrieved from http://dx.doi.org/10.5281/zenodo.844695

Sáenz, M. P., Hernandez, U. & Hernández, Y. M. (2017). Co-creation of OER by teachers and teacher educators in Colombia. In C. Hodgkinson-Williams & P. B. Arinto (Eds.), *Adoption and impact of OER in the Global South* (pp. 143–185). Retrieved from https://doi.org/10.5281/zenodo.604384

Scruggs, T. E., Mastropieri, N. A. & McDuffie, K. A. (2007). Co-teaching in inclusive classrooms: A metasynthesis of qualitative research. *Exceptional Children, 73(4)*, 392–416. Retrieved from http://www.schoolturnaroundsupport.org/sites/default/files/resources/Scrugg_2007.pdf

Toledo, A. (2017). Open Access and OER in Latin America: A survey of the policy landscape in Chile, Colombia and Uruguay. In C. Hodgkinson-Williams & P. B. Arinto (Eds.), *Adoption and impact of OER in the Global South* (pp. 121–141). Retrieved from https://doi.org/10.5281/zenodo.602781

UNESCO (United Nations Educational, Scientific and Cultural Organization). (2014a). *Position paper on education post-2015*. Paris: United Nations Educational, Scientific and Cultural Organization. Retrieved from http://unesdoc.unesco.org/images/0022/002273/227336E.pdf

UNESCO (United Nations Educational, Scientific and Cultural Organization). (2014b). *EFA global monitoring report: Teaching and learning – Achieving quality for all*. Paris: United Nations Educational, Scientific and Cultural Organization. Retrieved from http://unesdoc.unesco.org/images/0022/002256/225660e.pdf

UNESCO (United Nations Educational, Scientific and Cultural Organization). (2017). *Policy paper 30: Six ways to ensure higher education leaves no one behind.* Paris: United Nations Educational, Scientific and Cultural Organization. Retrieved from http://unesdoc.unesco.org/images/0024/002478/247862E.pdf

van Dijk, J. (2005). *The deepening divide: Inequality in the information society.* Thousand Oaks, CA: Sage Publications.

Walji, S. & Hodgkinson-Williams, C. (2017a). Understanding the nature of OEP for OER adoption in Global South contexts: Emerging lessons from the ROER4D project. Presented at *OER17, 5–6 April 2017.* London, UK. Retrieved from https://www.slideshare.net/ROER4D/understanding-the-nature-of-oep-for-oer-adoption-in-global-south-contexts-emerging-lessons-from-the-roer4d-project

Walji, S. & Hodgkinson-Williams, C. (2017b). Factors enabling and constraining OER adoption and Open Education Practices: Lessons from the ROER4D project. Presentation at *World Conference for Online Learning, 15–19 October 2017.* Toronto, Canada. Retrieved from https://www.slideshare.net/ROER4D/factors-enabling-and-constraining-oer-adoption-and-open-education-practices-lessons-from-the-roer4d-project

Weller, M. (2013). The battle for open – A perspective. *Journal of Interactive Media in Education, 2013(3).* Retrieved from http://jime.open.ac.uk/articles/10.5334/2013-15/

Westermann Juárez, W. & Venegas Muggli, J. I. (2017). Effectiveness of OER use in first-year higher education students' mathematical course performance: A case study. In C. Hodgkinson-Williams & P. B. Arinto (Eds.), *Adoption and impact of OER in the Global South* (pp. 187–229). Retrieved from https://doi.org/10.5281/zenodo.601203

White, D. & Manton, M. (2011). *Open Educational Resources: The value of reuse in higher education.* Oxford: University of Oxford. Retrieved from https://oerknowledgecloud.org/content/open-educational-resources-value-reuse-higher-education

Wolfenden, F., Auckloo, P., Buckler, A. & Cullen, J. (2017). Teacher educators and OER in East Africa: Interrogating pedagogic change. In C. Hodgkinson-Williams & P. B. Arinto (Eds.), *Adoption and impact of OER in the Global South* (pp. 251–286). Retrieved from https://doi.org/10.5281/zenodo.600424

Zagdragchaa, B. & Trotter, H. (2017). Cultural-historical factors influencing OER adoption in Mongolia's higher education sector. In C. Hodgkinson-Williams & P. B. Arinto (Eds.), *Adoption and impact of OER in the Global South* (pp. 389–424). Retrieved from https://doi.org/10.5281/zenodo.599609

How to cite this chapter

Hodgkinson-Williams, C., Arinto, P. B., Cartmill, T. & King, T. (2017). Factors influencing Open Educational Practices and OER in the Global South: Meta-synthesis of the ROER4D project. In C. Hodgkinson-Williams & P. B. Arinto (Eds.), *Adoption and impact of OER in the Global South* (pp. 27–67). Retrieved from https://doi.org/10.5281/zenodo.1037088

Corresponding author: Cheryl Hodgkinson-Williams
                                <cheryl.hodgkinson-williams@uct.ac.za>

Chapter 3

OER use in the Global South: A baseline survey of higher education instructors

José Dutra de Oliveira Neto, Judith Pete, Daryono and Tess Cartmill

Summary

The research presented here provides baseline data regarding the use of Open Educational Resources (OER) by higher education instructors in the Global South (South America, Sub-Saharan Africa, and South and Southeast Asia). It does so while attending to how such activity (or inactivity) is differentiated across continental regions and associated countries. The chapter addresses two questions: what proportion of instructors in the Global South have used OER, and which variables may account for different OER usage rates between respondents? This is done by examining which variables – such as gender, age, technological access and digital proficiency – seem to influence OER use rates, thereby allowing the authors to gauge which are the most important for instructors in their respective contexts.

This study is based on a quantitative research survey taken by 295 randomly selected instructors at 28 higher education institutions in nine countries (Brazil, Chile, Colombia; Ghana, Kenya, South Africa; India, Indonesia, Malaysia). The 30-question survey addressed the following themes: personal demographics, infrastructure access, institutional environment, instructor attitudes and open licensing. Survey responses were correlated for analysis with respondents' answers to the key question of the survey: whether they had ever used OER or not.

Findings indicate that 51% of respondents have used OER, a rate slightly differentiated by region: 49% in South America, 46% in Sub-Saharan Africa and 56% in South and Southeast Asia. A number of variables were associated with varying levels of OER use rates – such as instructors' country of habitation (and its gross domestic product per capita), level of digital proficiency, educational qualification, institutional position and attitude to education – while many others were not, such as instructors' gender, age or perception of their institutions' OER-related policies. ▶

For these respondents in the Global South, OER use is predicated upon instructors enjoying a certain minimum level of access to information and communication technologies infrastructure – especially hardware (computers, mobile devices, etc.) and internet connectivity (broadband, Wi-Fi, etc.) – which, once achieved, can be described as an enabling factor for OER engagement, but not a motivating factor. Beyond that minimum, increased internet speeds, lower internet costs and greater diversity of technical devices do not seem to lead to ever-increasing OER use rates. Similarly, while OER-related policies would likely be a crucial factor in OER creation, they did not seem to be important regarding OER use. Lastly, it was instructors in the comparatively less-developed countries who were using OER at a markedly higher rate than those from the more developed countries (at least intra-regionally). This suggests that instructors from the relatively lesser-developed countries may find greater utility in OER because it serves to overcome some of the pressing educational challenges associated with their nations' contexts' lower economic development.

The dataset arising from this study can be accessed at:
https://www.datafirst.uct.ac.za/dataportal/index.php/catalog/609

Acronyms and abbreviations

CC	Creative Commons
COL	Commonwealth of Learning
GC	global coordinator
GDP	gross domestic product
GNU GPL	GNU General Public Licence
HEI	higher education institution
ICT	information and communication technologies
LC	local coordinator
MOOCs	Massive Open Online Courses
OER	Open Educational Resources
RC	regional coordinator
ROER4D	Research on Open Educational Resources for Development
USD	United States dollars
VBA	Visual Basic for Applications (Excel programming function)

Introduction

Despite the many useful studies on the use of Open Educational Resources (OER) in higher education, most are focused on the activity of instructors located in the Global North who enjoy comparatively higher levels of economic development, educational provision, policy elaboration, and technological access than those in the Global South (Allen & Seaman, 2014; CERI/OECD, 2007; Clements & Pawlowski, 2012; Pegler, 2012; Reed, 2012; Rolfe,

2012). This means that less is known about educators' OER-related practices in the region where OER is touted as having its potentially greatest impact (Butcher, 2011; COL, 2016; Kanwar, Kodhandaraman & Umar, 2010). This is an imbalance which recent studies have started to address (Dhanarajan & Porter, 2013; Kanwar et al., 2010) and which this study seeks to make a contribution in mitigating.

Within this context, one of the most challenging questions that has emerged in the literature concerns how the deployment of OER – as a largely digital innovation – may in fact reinforce global, regional and national economic and social inequalities through a "digital divide" (Friemel, 2016; Kruger & Gilroy, 2013; Lopez, Gonzalez-Barrera & Patten, 2013; Velaga, Beecroft, Nelson, Corsar & Edwards, 2012) that benefits those with educational and technological access and skills, while bypassing those without (Lane, 2009). This goes against the ethic driving the Open Education movement, which in large part aspires to get more educational resources into the hands of those who have not been able to access educational content through traditional channels. Many OER advocates hope that such materials will provide greater educational accessibility and reduce social division (Hassani, 2006) because of the cost advantages associated with "free" materials. However, as Lane (2009) cautions, these "free" resources rely on a rather expensive foundation of infrastructural, technological and intellectual capacities that many do not enjoy, especially in the Global South, by which we mean "developing countries, which are located primarily in the Southern Hemisphere" (UNDP, 2012, p.1), especially in Latin America, Africa and Asia.

While it is possible to broadly distinguish between a relatively wealthier and more developed "Global North" and a comparatively poorer and less developed "Global South", we remain mindful of the fact – as revealed in the cumulative evidence of the Northern-based OER studies – that the Global North is, within itself, highly differentiated, with pockets that resemble the stereotype of the Global South – i.e. characterised by relatively low economic development, political instability and uneven technological accessibility. This recognition prompts us to also pay attention to differentiation within the Southern context under investigation, seeking to understand it in all of its nuance and idiosyncrasy. Thus, while it is useful to marshal the Global South as an analytical construct – since we tend to know less about the OER activities here than elsewhere – it is also crucial to embrace the diversity and contradictions it contains.

This study focuses on higher education instructors in the Global South, concentrating on those located in South America, Sub-Saharan Africa, and South and Southeast Asia. Based on a survey of 295 instructors at 28 higher education institutions (HEIs) in nine countries (Brazil, Chile, Colombia; Ghana, Kenya, South Africa; India, Indonesia, Malaysia), this research seeks to establish a baseline set of data for assessing OER use in these regions while attending to how such activity is differentiated across continental areas and associated countries. This is done by examining which variables – such as gender, age, technological access, digital literacy, etc. – seem to influence OER use rates, thereby allowing us to gauge which are the most important for instructors in their respective contexts.

The two research questions that drive this study are:
1. What proportion of instructors in the Global South have ever used OER?
2. Which variables may account for different OER usage rates between respondents in the Global South?

The study's survey compares respondents' OER use against a variety of demographic, contextual and pedagogical variables in order to understand which factors seem to have the greatest influence on whether instructors in the Global South have used OER. This is the first study of its kind to focus solely on OER use amongst higher education practitioners across the Global South, though it draws inspiration from surveys that have been conducted in the Global North (CERI/OECD, 2007; Masterman & Wild, 2011; OER Hub, 2014; ORIOLE, 2013) as well as portions of the Global South (OERAsia, 2010; UNESCO/COL, 2012). Ultimately, we hope that this will assist educational researchers, advocates and policy-makers to better understand the current OER landscape, while at the same time inspiring further studies to yield additional insights on this issue.

Literature review

In order to address the research questions posed by this study, the growing body of OER literature was consulted so as to grasp which factors or variables were key to determining OER activity by instructors in the Global South. This informed the choice of survey questions that were asked of respondents, allowing us to see whether the variables identified in the literature were relevant for understanding OER use in the Global South context.

Demographics

The first set of variables noted in a number of studies was demographic in nature. Respondents' geographical context, primarily their region or country, was considered a potential factor in some studies (Kanwar et al., 2010). Gender was listed by others as a potential differentiator for educational praxis (Takeda & Homberg, 2013). Such personal, identity-related characteristics were also seen as extending to age (Friemel, 2016), as well as to instructors' first language (Conole, 2012) and the educational language context in which they worked (Amiel, 2013; Clements & Pawlowski, 2012).

Extending these demographic considerations to instructors' experiential characteristics, studies also suggest that OER use could be influenced by level of digital proficiency (ECDL, 2011), level of academic qualification (Lane, 2009), disciplinary area (Coughlan & Perryman, 2011) and employment position (Oyelaran-Oyeyinka & Adeya, 2004a).

Infrastructure

The second set of variables centred on respondents' infrastructural context, one of the most commonly assumed differentiating factors between people in the Global North and South. Numerous studies discuss the potential impact of technological accessibility (to hardware, internet, etc.) on OER engagement (Dhanarajan & Porter, 2013; Teixeira et al., 2012).

Investigations into technological accessibility are nuanced by other studies dealing with internet affordability (Watson, Clouser & Domizi, 2013), availability (Lane, 2009), cost (Herrera, 2010), speed (Hassani, 2006), stability (Oyelaran-Oyeyinka & Adeya, 2004b), quality (Hassani, 2006), place of access (Jackson et al., 2006) and types of devices used to access the internet (Ericsson, 2014).

Institutional environment

A third set of variables focused on the institutional environment in which instructors work – particularly the OER-related policies, strategies and structures that are, or are not, in place. A number of studies look at the relationship between OER use and whether an institution has an OER repository (McGreal, 2012), OER-related training or support for instructors (Nonyongo, 2013), OER-related support for learners (Simpson, 2013), OER policies (Harley & Lawrence, 2007), an OER-related promotion or rewards system for instructors (Allen & Seaman, 2012), and an intellectual property policy that is favourable for the adoption of OER by instructors (Rhoten & Powell, 2007).

Instructor attitudes

A fourth set of variables identified in the literature relates to the personal attitudes of instructors towards openness and OER (van der Merwe, 2015), which includes their level of awareness around the concept (Mtebe & Raisamo, 2014), their intention to use OER (Lee, Yoon & Lee, 2009) and their perception on OER's ease of use and pedagogical utility (Lee et al., 2009). These studies address the question of personal volition and agency in the decision to use (or not use) OER.

Pedagogical practices

Lastly, the literature consulted focused on variables centring on OER use and creation practices, which are valuable for examining OER-specific practices as well as those pertaining to other types of (fully copyright-protected) educational resources. Studies covered such practices as OER reuse (Clements & Pawlowski, 2012; Pegler, 2012), creation (McGreal, Kinuthia & Marshall, 2013), revision (McGreal et al., 2013), remixing (Amiel, 2013; McGreal et al., 2013), redistribution (Lansu, Cillessen & Bukowski, 2013; McGreal et al., 2013) and curation (Mihailidis & Cohen, 2013).

These five thematic areas shaped the decisions made about key areas of focus to be investigated in the survey questionnaire, discussed in further detail in the Methodology section.

Methodology

This study employed a quantitative research approach in which a survey acted as the principal means of data collection. This section discusses the many facets comprising the survey effort and some of the challenges faced in terms of site selection, operations, instrument design, random sampling (including validation), survey administration and data analysis.

Site selection

The target respondents for the survey were instructors at HEIs from the three major regions that are referred to collectively as comprising the Global South: South America, Sub-Saharan Africa, and South and Southeast Asia. Within each region, selection efforts focused on three countries, identified through a convenience sampling method based on areas where other studies in the Research on Open Educational Resources for Development (ROER4D) project were being undertaken, and where collaborators who could help administer the survey were most easily found. The following countries, grouped by region, were chosen: Brazil, Chile and Colombia; Ghana, Kenya and South Africa; India, Indonesia and Malaysia.

Within these countries, the collaborators – called local coordinators (LCs) – were recruited based on their access to HEIs that were potential research sites. Often, they were members of staff at those institutions, or scholars who were able to petition and gain permission from an institution to conduct surveys there. This selection process took many months to finalise due to the fact that it was not always easy to identify collaborators who were free to work during the specified time period, or because the chosen institutions had privacy policies precluding outsiders from conducting research among their staff. Additionally, even within institutions that allowed such external research, there were often extensive ethics clearance processes that took many months to complete, making the initial institutional selection process quite time consuming.

In each of the nine countries, four HEIs were identified and targeted for participation in the study. With the help of the LCs, institutions were selected that, collectively, would possess most of the characteristics making up the national higher education landscape, based on variables such as rural/urban, large/small, residential/distance, public/private, and so forth. This was done so that the survey would adequately represent the diverse and complex national education systems under study. In most cases, this was achieved at a satisfactory level.

The initial proposal for the study called for the participation of 36 HEIs across the nine countries, but we were unable to gather data at eight of those HEIs due to data restrictions enforced by the institutions that were approached. (This was also the case at alternative institutions which were selected as second choices.) Ultimately, because of time constraints, the selection and solicitation process could not go on indefinitely, which resulted in a sample of 28 institutions, as listed in Table 1.

As can be seen from Table 1, the project's greatest challenge in terms of institutional participation was in South America, where institutions were hesitant to participate in a survey led by non-institutional, external researchers which might expose their instructors' practices to scrutiny. Given that the subject of the study was OER, a field that deals with intellectual property (i.e. legal) issues, some institutions feared that the survey might reveal practices that could negatively impact their reputations. Though the final version of the survey did not focus extensively on that element of educational practice, meaning that it is doubtful the questionnaire would have unduly exposed an institution to embarrassing revelations, we respected the concerns of the different institutions.

Table 1: HEIs participating in the study

Region	Country	Institution
South America	Brazil	Claretiano – Centro Universitário, Batatais
		Universidade de São Paulo
	Chile	Universidad de Chile
		Universidad Santo Tomás
		Universidad de Tarapacá
	Colombia	Universidad Nacional de Colombia
Sub-Saharan Africa	Kenya	Great Lakes University
		Jomo Kenyatta University of Agriculture and Technology
		Maseno University
		Tangaza University College
	Ghana	Catholic Institute of Business and Technology
		Kwame Nkrumah University of Science and Technology
		University of Cape Coast
		University of Ghana
	South Africa	University of Cape Town
		University of Fort Hare
		University of Pretoria
		University of South Africa
South and Southeast Asia	India	Gauhati University
		University of Delhi
	Indonesia	Universitas Mercu Buana
		Universitas Nasional
		Universitas Pancasila
		Universitas Terbuka
	Malaysia	Disted College
		Kolej Damansara Utama
		University of Malaya
		Wawasan Open University

Operations

The key members involved in this research project were the global coordinator (GC), the regional coordinators (RCs), the LCs, a project mentor, a statistician, a research assistant and a journalist. Project team members were also assisted more broadly by the ROER4D Network Hub team.

The lead researcher of the project (José Dutra de Oliveira Neto) acted as the GC for all survey-related activities, overseeing the activities of the RCs from Sub-Saharan Africa (Judith Pete) and South and Southeast Asia (Daryono), and acting as the RC for South America himself. A member of the ROER4D Network Hub (Tess Cartmill) also came on board in the final writing and analysis phase to assist with data preparation and analysis.

The RCs were tasked with appointing and supporting the LCs, who collected data from the various institutions. The GC was further supported by a project mentor who provided assistance and advice regarding OER research; a statistician to help with the particular issues involved in quantitative statistical methods and analysis; a research assistant to assist with both operational and analytical matters; and a journalist to keep project stakeholders aware of the process and the findings via social media.

The LCs took responsibility for collecting data from respondents in the HEIs surveyed. They helped gather the information necessary for allowing the GC and the statistician to randomly select which instructors would be targeted for surveying. The GC typically emailed the survey invitations to respondents via SurveyMonkey. However, in contexts where respondents lacked easy access to computers or the internet, the LCs printed out and administered the survey manually, then uploaded the responses into SurveyMonkey themselves. They delivered survey completion incentives (such as USB flash drives, free lunches on campus, etc.) to respondents who stated that they were interested in being considered for the incentives (which were typically determined through a random "draw" process after completion of the surveys). Incentives for respondents were provided to promote increased participation and boost the quality of responses (Hogan & LaForce, 2008; Tambor et al., 1993). After collecting all the responses, the LCs wrote brief reports about their institutional contexts and their data collection experiences in order to assist the RCs in the data analysis process.

Instrument design

In order to reduce the threats to validity in the instrument design, a strategy was adopted based on previous studies by Burton and Mazerolle (2011) and Messick (1989) to define the constructs, develop and assess the questions, and pilot the survey. This yielded a survey instrument that had 24–28 questions (depending on the skip pattern and how respondents answered certain questions) and took 15–20 minutes to complete.

Step 1: Define the constructs

In order to define the primary constructs of the study, a comprehensive review of the OER literature was conducted and a series of focus group discussions with OER experts was initiated. The construct definitions were centred on the factors influencing the adoption of OER, in line with the primary focus of the research questions.

A comprehensive review of the OER literature was conducted using bibliometric analysis to identify variables within the literature that addressed issues affecting OER adoption. To do this, data were collected from the Web of Science Collection and a tool called Histicite was used for conducting historical reviews while allowing for data-mining and citation analysis from the sample of papers generated (Garfield, Pudovkin & Istomin, 2003). The search terms used were "OER", "Open Education Resources" and "education resources".

Additionally, several focus group discussions occurred with members of the ROER4D researcher network to discuss variables for inclusion in the survey. This was done in conjunction with a broader ROER4D survey question harmonisation experiment (Trotter, 2015), facilitated by the project Network Hub. Through this process, 71 variables – most of which are mentioned in the Literature Review – were identified that were seen as potentially shaping OER adoption activity amongst higher education instructors. Based on these variables, questions for a draft pilot survey were formulated.

Step 2: Develop and assess the questions

To increase the validity of the survey – and to reduce the number of variables involved so as to focus only on the most relevant ones – "investigator triangulation" was used. This is a process more commonly used by qualitative researchers to check and establish validity in studies by incorporating several viewpoints (Yeasmin, 2012).

Invitations were sent to 34 researchers in the ROER4D researcher network (of which 76% had six or more years of research and educational experience) to assess the draft instrument's content and validity. This was followed by a questionnaire comprising 62 questions – each associated with a particular variable and rated according to a Likert scale from 1 (extremely low) to 7 (extremely high) – administered with the SurveyMonkey tool. Respondents had to answer questions based largely on the following formulation: "To what extent does [variable X] have an effect on the adoption of OER?" In the questionnaire, OER "adoption" was defined as OER "use and/or adaptation".

Based on the responses of these OER specialists, the survey was streamlined to a set of 30 questions, some of which utilised skip logic, meaning that if respondents answered certain questions in certain ways, they would either continue with further questions or skip to the next section. There were four different language versions of the questionnaire: English, Bahasa Indonesia, Portuguese and Spanish. All translation was done by a native translator from the main English version.

Step 3: Pilot the survey

The pilot survey was delivered to a sample of 63 English-speaking students and instructors, 10 Bahasa Indonesia-speaking instructors, eight Portuguese-speaking students and instructors, and three Spanish-speaking students and instructors from the education institutions in our sample. This cognitive test was done so as to identify potential problems with the survey (Postlethwaite, 2005) and to understand respondents' experience in completing it (Creswell, 2012).

A number of challenging issues surfaced from the pilot. First, many respondents did not understand the meaning of the term "Open Educational Resources". Most had never used any form of open licence for sharing their own educational materials, nor had they been exposed to the concept. The final survey therefore needed to include explicit definitions of the concept throughout.

Second, because the level of awareness of the OER concept was low for pilot respondents (meaning that they were perhaps exposed to the concept for the first time during the survey), it was clear that it would be difficult to compare the study's findings to other surveys, at least as regards actual OER practices. In many cases, for respondents who were encountering the concept for the first time, their responses to certain questions were hypothetical rather than based on actual experience. Thus, a number of questions in the survey were revised and the term "Open Educational Resources" was replaced with the broader "educational resources" so that it would be possible to establish some baseline data on respondents' practices with the usual educational materials they dealt with. In other words, the survey approach shifted to look more at general practices than at just open practices, in case there was a relationship between the two. (Within this context "educational resources" included OER.) The responses to these general questions about educational materials were later correlated with question 26 that asked about OER use and open licensing.

Third, to test the new version of the questionnaire, a second pilot test (in English and Spanish) was conducted with 34 instructors from the sample of HEIs to be surveyed based on a convenience sampling method. Minor revisions were made after this second pilot phase and the 30-item questionnaire was finalised.

Random sampling

To identify the most representative group of respondents possible at each research site, a random sampling method was used to eliminate potential selection biases by giving all individuals an equal chance to participate.[1] The process required a series of steps to be completed at each institution, which generally proceeded in the following fashion:

1. The LC obtains a list of all courses being taught at the institution during the appropriate semester.
2. The GC and the statistician randomly select 30 courses from those lists at each institution using the Excel VBA function, order them in a hierarchical sequence, then share the results with the LCs.
3. The LCs approach the instructors of the courses, starting with the first course on the list and proceeding in numerical order to: (1) ascertain whether that course has more than 30 students enrolled and, if so, (2) ask the instructor whether they would then be willing to participate in the survey, along with some of their students. Randomly selected courses that did not have 30 students were de-selected and the LC went to the next one on the list. This process continued until 10 instructors of courses with 30 or more students agreed to participate in the survey. (As noted, we carried out a similar survey with students at these same institutions, assessing their level of OER awareness and use. For the purposes of this chapter, however, we focus on the instructors' survey. We anticipate publishing the results of the student survey in the future.)

Survey administration

With the email addresses of the selected instructors provided by the LC, the GC initiated the survey process by sending them emails with links to the online SurveyMonkey-generated surveys. In many cases, the GC had to send follow-up invitations to remind respondents to complete the survey.

Because each HEI had a target sample of 10 instructors, the process described continued until these numbers were reached (relying on the ordered lists generated through the random sampling process). As can be seen in Table 2, this process entailed a certain level of variation from the description above, with some LCs obtaining more than the necessary respondents, and others less. This speaks to the unique circumstances that each LC faced at their respective institutions. However, despite the unevenness of the response

---

1   https://www.ma.utexas.edu/users/mks/statmistakes/RandomSampleImportance.html

rates at the different institutions, we believe that we obtained a truly random – and therefore representative – sample of instructors as survey respondents.

In total, questionnaires were distributed to 390 instructors, of whom 379 consented to complete the survey and 11 declined to give consent. Of those who consented, 346 began to answer the initial questions, with numbers gradually declining to 295 respondents who answered the key question (number 26 in the survey) concerning whether they had ever used OER. For the purposes of the analysis in the Findings section, the 295 respondents are those of most interest as their data can be correlated to their responses regarding OER use.

Table 2: Survey response numbers by country (fully completed)

Region	Country	Number of institutions	Number of instructors
South America	Brazil	2	17
	Chile	3	33
	Colombia	1	9
Regional total		6	59
Sub-Saharan Africa	Ghana	4	38
	Kenya	4	43
	South Africa	4	34
Regional total		12	115
South and Southeast Asia	India	2	23
	Indonesia	4	44
	Malaysia	4	54
Regional total		10	121
Total		28	295

Data analysis

The survey comprised 30 questions: 24 for respondents who had never used OER before, an additional four questions for those who had used OER, and two opening questions that were not of analytical relevance, dealing with the respondents' consent to take the survey and the name of their institution.

For the purposes of this chapter, the thousands of potential data points that the survey yielded are reduced to only those that will help us answer the two key research questions. To answer these, the majority of the questions have not only been analysed in and of themselves but, more importantly, have been correlated with the responses given to the key question of the survey: whether a respondent has used OER or not. Thus, the following variables are compared with OER use responses to understand whether they affect OER engagement:

Demographics
- Country
- Region
- Gender
- Age
- Level of digital proficiency
- Highest educational qualification
- Teaching areas
- Position at HEI

Infrastructure
- Location/s of internet access
- Device/s used to access internet
- Internet cost, speed and stability

Institutional environment
- Institutional policy/perspective on OER

Instructor attitudes
- Perspective on which educational materials are "free" to use
- Willingness to use OER again

Open licensing
- Use of licences on educational materials in teaching approach (copyright, Creative Commons [CC], etc.)

By combining and graphing these variables with respondents' answers to whether they had ever used OER, we generated the necessary data to attempt to answer our key research questions, as discussed in the Findings section.

Data sharing

The instructor data from the administered survey (n = 295) and the accompanying English-language questionnaire were published on the DataFirst Data Portal after undergoing a multiphased quality assurance and de-identification process. The authors and the ROER4D Curation and Dissemination team checked data files for consistency and correctness, whereafter a de-identification process was undertaken utilising an omission and abstraction strategy.

The resulting dataset, published under a Creative Commons Attribution (CC BY) licence, comprised the instructor survey questionnaire in PDF; the instructor survey microdata shared in CSV, STATA, SAS and SPSS formats; and accompanying metadata.

Findings

This section presents the findings of this multi-country OER survey, focusing first on the instructors' demographic variables, followed by those related to infrastructure, institutional environment, instructor attitudes and pedagogical practices. Before assessing OER use according to these factors, it is useful to start by revealing the baseline OER use established by the survey, which answers our first research question: What proportion of instructors in the Global South have ever used OER? These percentages will need to be kept in mind as we discuss the influence that the different factors have on OER use. Thus, Table 3 reveals instructors' responses to the question: Have you ever used OER that are available in the public domain or that have an open (e.g. CC) licence that allows it to be used and/or adapted by others? (This was asked after instructors had been given a definition of OER.)

Table 3: Instructors' use of OER

Region	Country	Yes (%)	Not sure (%)	No (%)
South America	Brazil (n = 17)	71	24	6
	Chile (n = 33)	45	36	18
	Colombia (n = 9)	22	56	22
Regional total	**n = 59**	**49**	**36**	**15**
Sub-Saharan Africa	Ghana (n = 38)	53	32	16
	Kenya (n = 43)	49	30	21
	South Africa (n = 34)	35	32	32
Regional total	**n = 115**	**46**	**31**	**23**
South and Southeast Asia	India (n = 23)	70	22	9
	Indonesia (n = 44)	70	7	23
	Malaysia (n = 54)	39	15	46
Regional total	**n = 121**	**56**	**13**	**31**
Totals	**n = 295**	**51**	**25**	**24**

Note: Some rows do not add up to 100% due to rounding.

Table 3 reveals that, in total, just over half (51%) of all instructors surveyed in the Global South have used OER (at least once). Roughly one-quarter have never used OER, and a quarter were not sure whether or not they had used OER.

These numbers are difficult to assess because they are not directly comparable to similar studies. For instance, if we compare these to the results of a recent Commonwealth of Learning (COL) study of OER use amongst school teachers, higher education instructors and other education practitioners across the Commonwealth, a similar use rate of 47% emerges (COL, 2016). When the COL survey is disaggregated by region, however, 67% of Asian respondents and 63% of African respondents said that they had used OER, which is appreciably higher than the results revealed here. Yet it is difficult to make too much of this difference because COL's study surveyed a much broader array of educators (at all levels, not just higher education) and did not appear to use a random sampling methodology similar to this one (which has implications for the likelihood of obtaining a representative sample of respondents).

The analysis in the rest of the chapter focuses largely on the data on instructors' OER use with the many variables that the survey covers, allowing for a better understanding of which factors are truly important for influencing OER use. For each variable, we start by sharing the assumption that guided our decision to highlight it as a variable. We then analyse the findings that are revealed by correlating the variable with the use responses. In most cases, figures or tables are provided to show the relevant responses by both country and region.

Instructors' demographics

The first set of variables to correlate with instructors' use of OER concerns demographic ones, including instructors' region, country, gender, age, digital proficiency, years of teaching experience, highest educational qualification, teaching discipline and position at their HEI.

Region and country

The assumption examined is that, based on the various economic and political differences that characterise the three regions studied, instructors' OER use should be positively correlated with higher levels of economic development, as such development provides opportunities for accessing and engaging with online educational platforms in greater depth and breadth (Lane, 2009). Essentially, the presumption is that the region or country that instructors live in should have an influence on OER use.

Figure 1 shows the percentage of instructors who said that they had used OER, were not sure if they had used OER or had not used OER, based on the region where they are located.

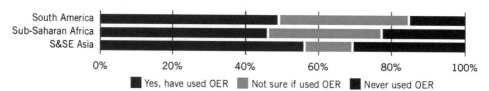

Figure 1: Instructor OER use by region

The data show that instructors from the South and Southeast Asian region had the highest comparative OER use rates, with 56% asserting that they had used OER before. South American instructors were modestly behind at 49%, and Sub-Saharan Africans at 46%. This means that there was only a 10% difference between the highest and lowest instructor OER use response rates; the three regions therefore show similarities in this regard.

However, a slightly different pattern of OER use amongst instructors emerges in individual countries (Figure 2).

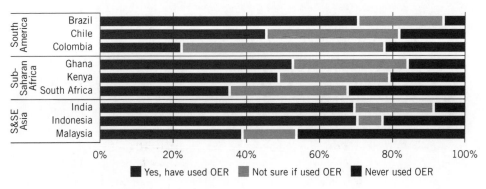

Figure 2: Instructor OER use by country

At the national level, Figure 2 shows that the Brazilian, Indian and Indonesian instructors surveyed claimed the highest levels of use, at around 70% each. These positive rates were quite high compared to those of other regional countries, which tended to be below 50%. Thus, while 71% of Brazilian instructors surveyed said they had used OER, only 45% said the same in Chile and 22% in Colombia. It is important to note, however, that due to the low absolute response rates from Brazil (n = 17), Colombia (n = 9) and Chile (n = 23), these percentages must be treated with some caution compared to those from the other countries where there were more than 30 respondents each.

African instructors surveyed revealed a range of 35–53% OER use by country, with "unsure" rates at about 30% each. South Africa – the most economically developed country by GDP per capita (see Table 4) – had the lowest rate of instructor OER use compared to Ghana and Kenya. In this instance, it does not appear that national GDP per capita rates played a positive role in promoting OER use amongst instructors, comparatively speaking. In fact, an opposite phenomenon may be at play. Perhaps it is precisely the relative lack of "development" (as expressed through GDP per capita) – and all this might entail, such as less local educational publishing, etc. – that may have encouraged more Ghanaian and Kenyan instructors to consider the use of OER.

Table 4: Gross domestic product (GDP) per country

Country	GDP per capita (USD)	GDP per capita world ranking
Brazil	15 600	103
Chile	23 500	80
Colombia	13 800	115
Ghana	4 300	175
Kenya	3 200	186
South Africa	13 200	108
India	6 200	158
Indonesia	11 100	132
Malaysia	26 300	69

(Source: CIA, 2016)

A similar pattern is clear amongst the Asian countries. While Malaysia enjoys the highest GDP per capita (USD 26 300) compared to India (USD 6 200) and Indonesia (USD 11 100), it also has the lowest OER use rates (39%) of the instructor group. The other two countries boast markedly higher OER use rates of 70% each (with the caveat that only two Indian institutions were surveyed compared to four in the other two Asian countries).

Thus, based on the data provided here, we cannot sustain our assumption that instructors' OER use rates can be positively correlated to higher levels of economic or political development. Indeed, the data suggest the opposite – that it is instructors from countries that are less economically developed who have sought out more OER for use. A similar trend is apparent in the COL (2016) study, in which respondents from the regions of Africa (63%), Asia (67%), the Caribbean (70%) and the Pacific (64%) all claimed higher OER use rates than those in Europe (16%). This perhaps suggests that instructors from these countries or regions have had to be more resourceful than their colleagues in more developed countries and regions in seeking out non-traditional educational materials that suit their needs from a cost and accessibility perspective. However, our data cannot confirm this with certainty, but it raises important questions about how and where OER is being used in the Global South, nuancing our understanding of educational practices across the regions.

Gender

The assumption tested here is that gender is often a differentiating factor in people's access to education and technology (Takeda & Homberg, 2013). Because of this, we would expect that there might be a mild association between greater gender privilege (e.g. for males in relatively patriarchal contexts) and higher OER use because OER is a pedagogical innovation that sits at the intersection of education and technology.

Figure 3 shows the percentage of instructors surveyed who said that they had used OER, were not sure if they had used OER or had not used OER, based on their gender and distinguished by region.

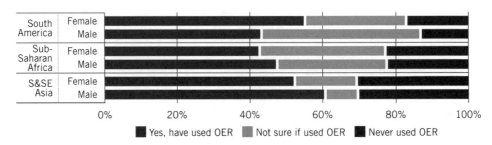

Figure 3: Instructor OER use by gender per region

Among the instructors who said that they had used OER, in South America the male/female rate was 43%/55%, in Africa it was 48%/43%, and in South and Southeast Asia it was 61%/52%. Thus males had slightly higher "yes" rates in Africa and Asia, but lower in South America. These findings suggest that there weren't major differences between gender responses to OER use amongst instructors in the three regions. In fact, the differences between regional responses tended to be mirrored in the gendered results of those regions, meaning that regional trends about instructor OER use tended to be stronger than gender trends about OER use.

This argument is further reinforced at the national level (Figure 4), but in a nuanced manner. In Africa, there was a great discrepancy in Ghana between female instructors who appeared to be less certain of their OER use (71% said they were "not sure") compared to their male counterparts (21%). This corresponded to the large difference in OER use response, with 29% of females reporting having used OER compared to 58% of males. These gendered differences appear to be substantial and may emanate from a cultural or economic distinction within Ghanaian society, but without further information it is impossible to discern from the data why OER use in particular would be gendered in this way. Caution is further warranted by the fact that this gender distinction is reversed in Kenya, with greater female use (60%) compared to male (43%), though in less extreme terms.

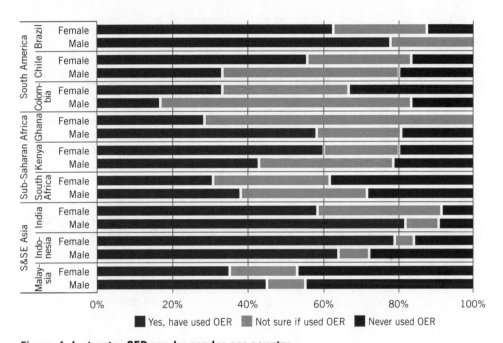

Figure 4: Instructor OER use by gender per country

In general, these data do not support the assumption about gendered OER use amongst instructors. In certain countries, there might be some mild gender differences, but they are just as likely to show greater female instructor use than male. This apparent randomness is likely due to the fact that, since all of the survey respondents worked in higher education contexts with some degree of access to the internet and OER platforms, respondents' gender would probably not have been the key variable in whether they used OER or not. Gender would certainly shape numerous elements of the respondents' lives, but it is not clear that it does so with regard to OER use.

Age

The assumption is that the age of instructors can have an impact on the pedagogical traditions and commitments that they hold, stemming both from the values that shape their actions at different points of their lives, and the types of technologies to which they are exposed at critical moments of their teaching-style development (Friemel, 2016). In this case, we imagine that one of two possible contrasting outcomes will occur with OER use based on age: that older instructors who are secure in their identities and positions as instructors will feel more open to new pedagogical innovations such as OER; or that younger instructors will be more likely to be "early adopters" of OER because they emerge from a digital ecosystem in which younger people feel more comfortable.

Figure 5 shows the percentage of respondents who said that they had used OER, were not sure if they had used OER or had never used OER, by age and region.

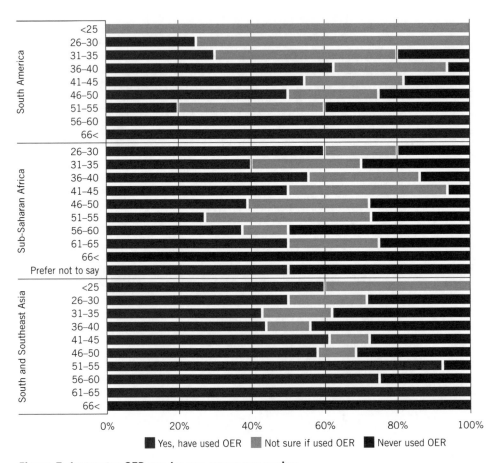

Figure 5: Instructor OER use by age group per region

For South America, the younger age brackets of instructors show a relatively greater OER use uncertainty, with "not sure" being the highest response for the first three age brackets (i.e. 25–35). The middle three age brackets (36–50) show the "yes" response as the highest, corresponding with greater certainty about use or non-use. The next bracket (51–55) shows an equal number of "not sure" and "no" responses, while the final two brackets (56+) show only "yes" responses. (Note that in the case of South America there were no respondents in the 61–65 age category; there were also no respondents in Sub-Saharan Africa younger than 25.) These numbers suggest that younger instructors are less certain whether they have used OER than older instructors. Middle-aged instructors are more likely to have used OER, while the older instructors show a mixture of positive and negative responses. (However, it is worth noting the relatively small absolute numbers involved for the South American data, as the total number of regional respondents [n = 59] is spread across nine age categories.)

In Africa, it was harder to discern any patterns with regard to age, as there are high levels of non-use amongst instructors across all the age categories, and relatively low levels of certainty. Only in a few of the age categories was OER use higher than both uncertainty and non-use, but with no apparent reason.

In Asia, respondents in six of the 10 age categories said that they had used OER. Only those between 31–40 years old (n = 47) were less likely to have used OER, as well as those over 66 (n = 1). The data confirm the impression established above about the general regional profile, where certainty of OER use or non-use is relatively high across the age categories.

When it comes to the activities of younger instructors, they did not reveal "early adopter" approaches to OER in their responses. In fact, younger instructors were more likely to reveal a lack of certainty about whether they had ever used OER, as indicated by the yellow bars in Figure 5.

The quantitative research approach taken here has not revealed a strong association between the age of instructors and their OER use, but qualitative research could be employed in future to better understand the ways in which age might shape instructor OER use, even if unevenly and idiosyncratically.

Digital proficiency

The assumption assessed here is that OER use requires some level of digital literacy, thus the levels of OER use for instructors should be higher for those who are more digitally proficient (ECDL, 2011). Figure 6 shows the percentage of instructors who said that they had basic, intermediate or advanced digital literacy, distinguished by country and region.

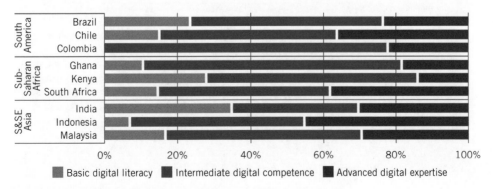

Figure 6: Instructor self-reported digital proficiency by country

These findings are based on self-reporting, meaning that respondents assessed themselves subjectively according to these three categories, but they show that – if the numbers are aggregated and viewed as a whole – the majority of instructors viewed themselves as having intermediate digital competence (54%), followed by advanced digital expertise (29%) and, more rarely, basic digital literacy (17%).

Figure 7 shows how these self-reported digital proficiency claims align with instructors' OER use. It suggests that, at a national level, self-reported digital literacy levels do not have a consistent upward impact on OER use. That is, there is no consistent increase in OER rates moving from the basic digital literacy category to the intermediate to the advanced. In reality, while instructors with basic digital literacy had the lowest levels of OER use (as expected), the majority of instructors stating that they had used OER identified themselves as having intermediate, not advanced, levels of digital competence.

While the Kenyan and Indonesian instructors claiming to have advanced digital proficiency were more likely to be OER users than the other categories, it was the opposite in Chile. The responses elsewhere showed mixed results, making it impossible to state strongly that there is a definite association between instructor digital proficiency and OER use.

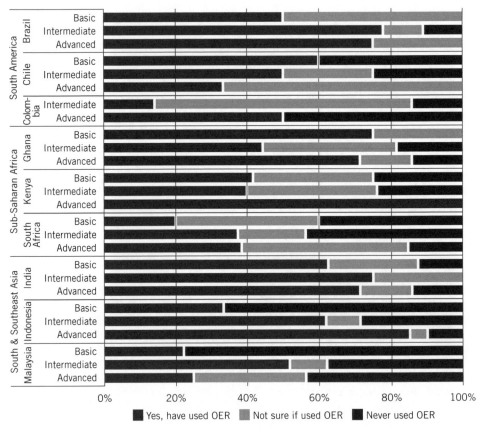

Figure 7: Instructor OER use by self-reported digital proficiency per country

In fact, the profile of basic, intermediate and advanced self-identifiers is essentially the same for OER users as it is for non-users and those who don't know, as shown in Table 5.

Table 5: Instructors' digital literacy profiles according to region and OER use response

Region	Basic digital literacy (%)	Intermediate digital competence (%)	Advanced digital expertise (%)
South America	15	54	31
Sub-Saharan Africa	18	59	23
South and Southeast Asia	17	48	36
Global South (totals)	17	54	29
Global South (OER users)	14	53	33

If it is the case that self-reported digital proficiency is not highly correlated with OER use patterns, then it means that the digital proficiency required to engage in OER use might be quite low. The fact that OER use is a very broad category of activity makes it difficult to interrogate this in detail because there are many types of OER that are easily available for quick and immediate use and insertion in one's own teaching materials, such as YouTube videos (for "as is" use) and Wikimedia images. Instructors do not necessarily need high levels of digital proficiency to engage with these sites, although they may require more sophisticated skills for engagement with other types of OER-specific teaching platforms.

The assumption of a correlation between instructor digital proficiency and OER use is not convincingly proved, but neither is it disproved. There is a mild potential relationship, though not a strong one. It appears that OER use is enhanced by instructors possessing *a certain minimum level* of digital proficiency – somewhere between basic and intermediate – that allows them to engage with OER with some confidence. The low levels of OER use amongst instructors with basic literacy skills confirm this, while the relatively high rates amongst those with intermediate skills do so as well, pointing to some level between those categories that allows for greater OER use. Having advanced digital proficiency, however, did not seem to increase the likelihood of OER use above that of instructors with intermediate skills.

Highest educational qualification

Our underlying assumption was that OER use rates should increase relative to instructors' higher levels of qualification (Lane, 2009), based on their exposure to a more extensive range of disciplinary materials through their academic studies. Figure 8 shows the percentage of instructors who said that they had used OER, were not sure if they had used OER or had not used OER, based on their highest educational qualification and distinguished by country and region.

In South America, instructors of each country surveyed were more likely to have used OER if they did not have PhDs. There was a mild association with OER use and comparatively lower educational qualifications. The same was also true in three other countries, with only Kenya, India and Indonesia showing responses suggesting that possession of a PhD was associated with higher OER use than was the case for lower qualifications.

This outcome contradicts the assumption of a correlation between OER use rates and level of qualification. This might be because instructors without a PhD are more likely to look to other providers of educational materials for their teaching than to develop everything from scratch themselves. They may not consider themselves full "experts" on a subject and thus are happy to look to other educators' materials for support. Additionally, these instructors may have earned diplomas, bachelor's or master's degrees with the express aim of focusing on teaching – rather than research, as might be the case for those with PhDs – and thus have spent more time and energy seeking out innovative materials for their teaching. More evidence is required for advancing this supposition but we can ascertain that, at least according to these data, the assumption that educational qualifications are positively related to OER use does not hold.

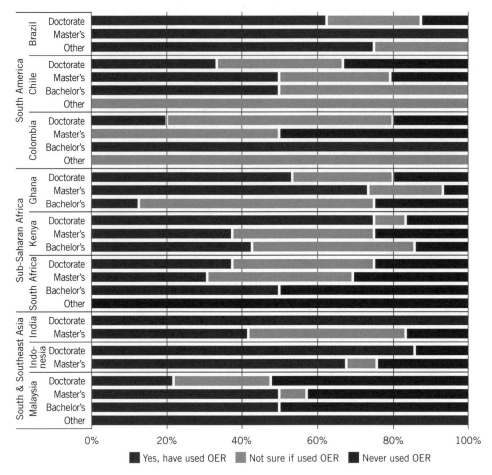

Figure 8: Instructor OER use by highest educational qualification per country

Teaching discipline

The assumption being tested here is that every academic discipline has different norms and expectations around sharing materials openly or even collegially (between colleagues, not openly). They also have different types of materials that would be shared, with some being easier or more pertinent and useful than others. Based especially on the insights of Coughlan and Perryman (2011), we assume that disciplinary norms around sharing would influence the number of OER generally available, and whether one engages in the use of OER.

Table 6: Disciplinary area of teaching associated with OER use across all three regions (more than one answer allowed)

Discipline	Number of instructors	OER users (%)
Humanities and Arts	54	44
Social Sciences (including Education and Law)	95	54
Management and Commerce	43	47
Natural Sciences	70	64
Engineering and Technology	89	55
Agriculture and Veterinary Sciences	3	0
Medical and Health Sciences	34	50
Other	9	56

The numbers of respondents per discipline are too small to make any convincing arguments about each discipline's influence on OER use at a country or regional level. However, at the Global South level, Table 6 shows that discipline may have a mild effect on OER use rates. Most disciplines reported an OER use rate of 44–56%, hovering around the 50% mark. Only Natural Sciences showed a substantially higher use rate at 64% (the 0% of Agriculture and Veterinary Sciences can be discounted for having too few respondents to be meaningful). This might be due to a greater culture of sharing educational materials within Natural Sciences – or as Coughlan and Perryman (2011) argue, within the "hard pure" and "hard applied" sciences versus the "soft pure" disciplines of the Humanities – or perhaps there is greater pedagogical utility for using OER in this discipline versus others. The survey did not seek to identify why such a situation might be the case in any particular discipline, but simply to determine whether any differences existed.[2]

Given the similarity in OER use rates across most of the disciplines, the assumption around disciplinary differentiation is not well supported by the survey data. However, the slight outlier of the Natural Sciences and the general higher percentages of the hard sciences over the Humanities suggest that more research would be valuable in this area.

Position at HEI

The assumption being examined here is that the position instructors hold at an HEI will influence their teaching practices (Oyelaran-Oyeyinka & Adeya, 2004a), including whether or not they are exposed to OER and use it. We assume that position matters for OER use and will have a telling effect on instructor OER use response rates.

Table 7 shows that the range of OER use responses is quite narrow (52–55%) amongst junior, mid-level and senior instructors. This largely matches the total use rate of 51% across the Global South. The two outlier categories – those of "administrator" and "teacher" – have relatively small respondent numbers. It is thus difficult to make broad generalisations about why administrators appear to use OER far more than the average instructors, or why teachers appear to use OER far less than them.

---

2   No significance tests have been performed to substantiate statements in this regard.

Table 7: Instructors' position at institution associated with OER use (more than one answer allowed)

Position	Respondents (total)	OER users (%)
Administrator	16	69
Manager	17	53
Teacher	10	40
Junior academic (lecturer, etc.)	128	52
Mid-level academic (senior lecturer, etc.)	100	55
Senior academic (associate/full prof.)	67	52
Other (researcher, etc.)	43	53

It is worth stating that the question did not require respondents to choose only one category for describing themselves. They could choose more than one, such as senior academic and manager – a description that would fit many respondents who fill multiple roles at their institutions. Thus, the relatively high OER use rates of the administrators are not exclusive of the academic responses, though they may suggest that academics with multiple roles – especially where they facilitate the work of other instructors – may encourage higher OER use. They may be placed in a position to have a pedagogical influence on others and thus take an interest in gaining exposure to the current trends shaping teaching practice, which would include OER. This is speculation, begging further research.

Based on the data from the survey, the assumption of a clear relationship between position held at an HEI and OER use is not well supported. There is no strong indication that academic rank or institutional position has an influence on OER use. While each institution's prevailing culture (Cox & Trotter, 2016) might shape this relationship differently, the three levels of academic positions showed similar OER use rates, thus reducing the likelihood that such hierarchical considerations are key to understanding different OER use rates in the Global South. However, the outlying responses of the "administrators" (an admittedly small group here) suggest that more in-depth research would be useful on this question.

Infrastructure

The second set of variables for comparison with respondents' use of OER concerns infrastructure, including instructors' location of internet access, devices to access the internet, and internet cost, speed and stability.

Location of internet access

The underlying assumption is that as engagement with OER is largely an optional activity for instructors, one would expect to find higher levels of OER use in contexts where respondents access the internet in locations where they enjoy higher levels of comfort, ease and privacy (such as at home or at work rather than in a public setting) (Jackson et al., 2006).

Figure 9 shows instructors' OER use rates by location of internet access per country.

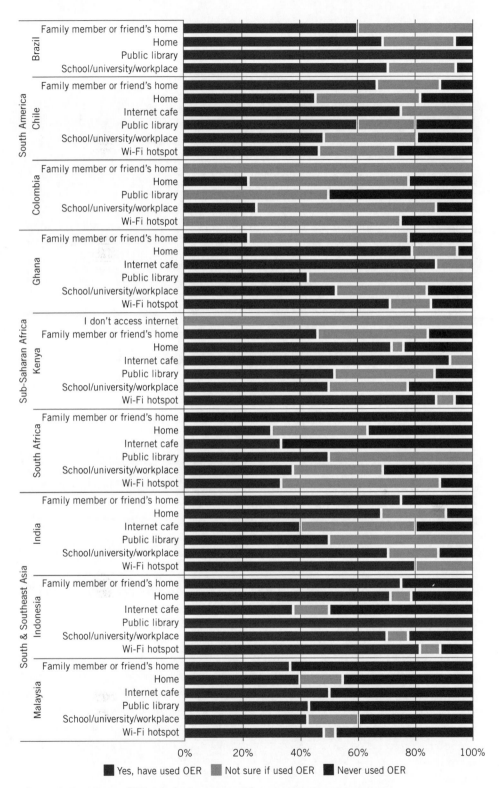

Figure 9: Instructor OER use by location of internet access per country

The data revealed no discernible pattern nationally regarding where instructors access the internet and whether they have used OER or not. For instance, in South America, Chilean responses suggested that all locations were positively correlated with using OER, while in Colombia all places were negatively correlated. In Africa, Ghanaians and Kenyans were more likely to use OER if they frequented internet cafes, but this was not so in South Africa.

In Asia, respondents using Wi-Fi hotspots were more likely to use OER than those who accessed the web from internet cafes. In fact, the data show that the response rates tend to resemble those of the respective countries and regions in general in this dataset. Thus, the positive response by Indonesians at all internet locations is relatively high compared to Malaysian respondents, who, as a country, already showed a low OER use rate.

Part of the challenge with interpreting the responses to this question is that the answer possibilities are not exclusive, meaning that respondents could list multiple places in which they engaged with the internet, such as at home and at an internet café. Moreover, the characteristics of these different locations can be quite different nationally. Public libraries in some countries may be better equipped for accessing the internet than in other countries, making them difficult to compare.

Thus, the assumption that the location of internet access should influence OER use does not appear to hold, at least not in any obvious way. There are definitely national and regional differences regarding OER use rates, but they do not appear to be highly influenced by the types of locations that respondents use to access the internet. For instructors who most likely enjoy a general level of internet access at work by virtue of their employment at an HEI (though internet stability and speed might be variable), the simple ability to access the internet from different locations may not be a defining feature of whether they use OER or not.

Devices used to connect to the internet

Another related assumption is that the types of devices that instructors use to access the internet affect their OER use (Ericsson, 2014).

Respondents were asked whether they used the following devices to access the internet: desktop computer, laptop computer, mobile phone, tablet. They could choose more than one device. Figure 10 shows instructors' OER use rates according to the devices they use to access the internet.

Figure 10 reveals that in South America the instructor OER use rates were basically the same for each device per country. There was also no marked difference in OER use rates between the different devices used in each country. This suggests that the particular type of hardware that instructors have access to does not make much difference as to whether they use OER or not. However, the fact that this is not an exclusive question also makes it difficult to see which type of device would actually make a difference.

In Africa, instructors who had tablets in Ghana and Kenya reported a noticeably higher level of OER use than those using other devices. In these contexts, it might be that the tablet is a relatively rare, high-tech device (compared to the ubiquity of mobile phones and computers) that reveals a certain level of technological investment and interest. Thus tablet owners may be more likely to use the pedagogical offerings available on the internet, including OER.

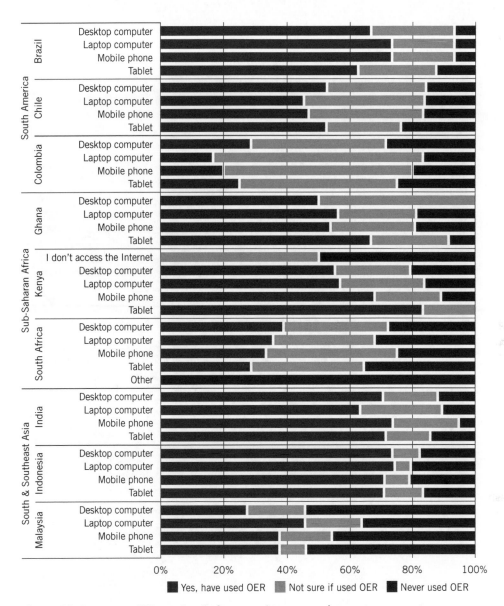

Figure 10: Instructor OER use by devices used to access internet per country

In Asia, there was very little variation of OER use within a country based on the type of device that instructors used to access the internet.

Thus, the type of device used to access the internet may not make as big a difference for HEI instructors and their likelihood of OER use as was assumed. These are people who likely have multiple devices, such as laptops and mobiles, and perhaps even desktops and tablets. In most countries, OER use rates were similar across devices, suggesting that the national character of OER use was not highly influenced by the particular device used to access the internet.

Internet cost

The assumption being scrutinised is that internet costs (as expressed through levels of satisfaction) should affect OER use, in that they influence the amount of time users spend on the internet, and the type of activities they engage in (Herrera, 2010). We assume that higher satisfaction would mean that internet access is cheaper and therefore more available for potential users.

Respondents were asked to rate their satisfaction with their internet costs according to the following prompts: satisfied, unsure and dissatisfied. Figure 11 shows instructors' OER use rates according to their perception of the costs.

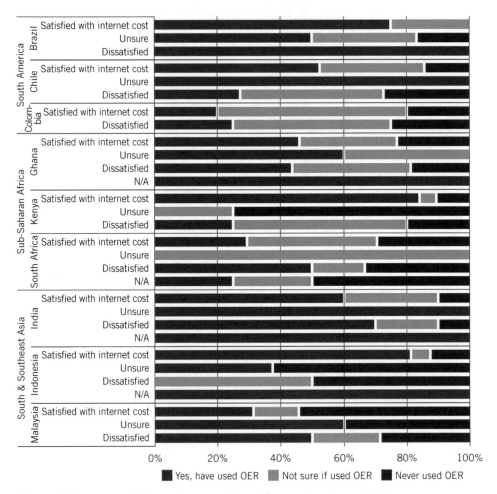

Figure 11: Instructor OER use by perception of internet cost per country

This question seeks to tease out a subjective element of the internet access experience, that of instructors' perception of the costs associated with accessing it, and to tie it to OER use practices. This subjective approach has a number of challenges, especially because the perceptions invoked can be based on quite idiosyncratic criteria for respondents. For instance, wealthier respondents might feel more satisfied with the costs than poorer respondents, or vice versa, but it is impossible to know based on the data yielded by the question. But this subjective approach was preferred over a more "objective" measure, such as the literal, numerical cost of internet bundles per megabyte. Given the massive differentials between exchange rates, purchasing power per currency unit and an ever-fluctuating currency market environment, it would not have made this issue any clearer by determining that the price of a megabyte was cheaper or more expensive in one country than another, given all the factors that influence the impact of that megabyte price on respondents. Thus we preferred to simply ask for respondents' perceptions on connectivity costs with the hope of determining whether this subjective experience of an otherwise objective reality influences OER use.

Only instructors in Kenya and Indonesia showed our expected trend of higher satisfaction being associated with higher OER use. In other countries, this trend was either reversed or non-existent. Indeed, because the Kenyan and Indonesian experience was not the case anywhere else, it is impossible to make any broad generalisations about instructors' level of cost satisfaction in accessing the internet and their level of OER use. Thus the assumption that internet costs affect OER use cannot be sustained.

Internet speed

An associated assumption is that higher levels of satisfaction with internet speed affect levels of OER use, as speed should influence the quality and effectiveness of instructors' engagement with the internet in general (Hassani, 2006).

Figure 12 show instructors' OER use rates according to their perception of their internet speeds. As was the case with internet costs, satisfaction with speed does not appear to have an important influence on whether instructors use OER. It was only associated marginally in Indonesia. This might be explained by the fact that the OER question does not refer to general repeated use of OER, but rather at "any time in one's life", which would not necessarily be related to a general sense of satisfaction with internet speed.

Thus, we would need a more precise type of data (rather than general speed satisfaction versus possible one-time use) to understand the role of internet speeds on OER use. Moreover, for instructors who may enjoy fast internet speeds at home but not at work, or vice versa, this question does not differentiate between them. Further research would need to be far more detailed to draw specific conclusions.

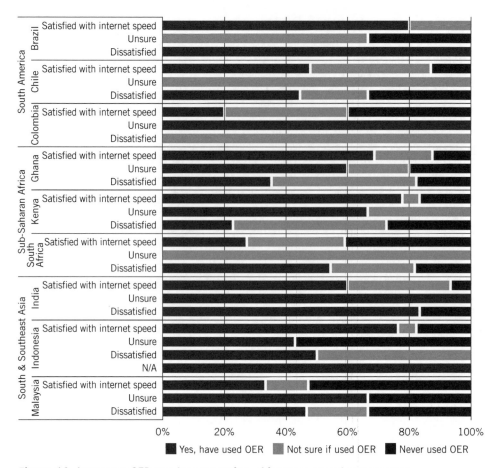

Figure 12: Instructor OER use by perception of internet speed per country

Internet stability

The assumption under scrutiny here is that higher levels of satisfaction with internet stability affect levels of OER use (Oyelaran-Oyeyinka & Adeya, 2004b), as stability is likely to influence the quality and effectiveness of instructors' engagement with the internet in general.

Figure 13 shows instructors' OER use rates acccording to their perception of their internet stability. Though one would reasonably assume that the stability of instructors' internet connection would influence their internet use at the OER use level, only in Kenya do instructors suggest that their level of internet stability satisfaction is related to their OER use. Again, there may be many reasons for this, but it appears that most instructors enjoy at least some level of minimum internet stability to be able to achieve their online goals, whether related to OER use or not. Thus, while stability may impact internet use at a general level, it does not appear to impact whether instructors have "ever" used OER or not.

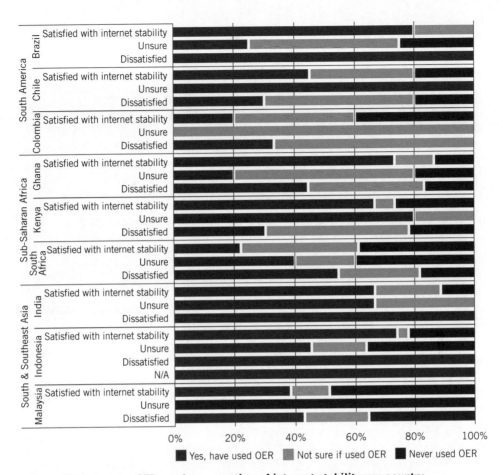

Figure 13: Instructor OER use by perception of internet stability per country

Institutional environment

The third factor related to instructors' use of OER concerns institutional variables, specifically the institutional perspective on OER.

Institutional perspective on OER

The underlying assumption is that OER-related institutional policies influence whether instructors use OER or not (Allen & Seaman, 2012; Harley & Lawrence, 2007; Nonyongo, 2013).

Respondents were asked to rate their degree of awareness of whether institutional policies support OER according to the following prompts: agree, neutral, disagree and not available/not aware.

Figure 14 shows respondents' assessment of whether their institutions have policies that support the adoption of OER, distinguished by country and region.

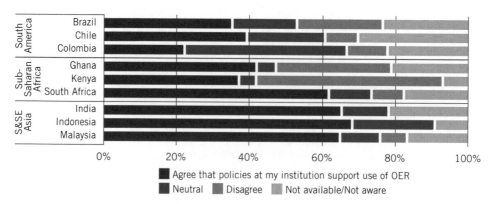

Figure 14: Instructor perceptions of whether their institutions have policies that support OER

The data show that the majority of respondents in four countries – South Africa and the three Asian countries – believe that their institutions have policies that support OER, while only a minority in the other five believe the same about their institutions. Indeed, the sizeable difference in the positive response rates for these two groups of countries would suggest that, if this is the case, the OER use rates in the different countries would also be comparably affected.

In reality, we do not see a clear alignment of OER use rates by the instructors and their perception of OER-related institutional policies. If we compare the OER use response percentages from Table 3 with the responses in Figure 14, we see a mixed result. For instance, the OER use rates for instructors (drawn from Table 3) from Chile (45%) and Colombia (22%) are low, which conforms to the low-level agreement regarding pro-OER institutional policies. In addition, 70% of Indonesian instructors said they had used OER, which corresponds well with the 68% of respondents who said that their institutions had positive OER support policies. However, a minority of Brazilians (35%) say that their institutions have pro-OER policies, but a majority (71%) say that they have used OER. Most South Africans (63%) say their institutional policies support OER, but only a minority (37%) have used them. These contradictory results suggest that some responses appear to support the assumption while others do not.

Part of the challenge in interpreting this question is that we did not define the characteristics of a pro-OER policy for respondents, which means that they were free to determine this in their own minds. This reduces the comparability of their responses. However, it was difficult to impose any strict definition of what a pro-OER policy entails as it would never be able to account for the myriad ways in which different institutional policies might influence OER adoption. Thus, we wanted to leave this for respondents to decide for themselves, even if it meant that we did not learn what exactly those policies entailed and why the respondents perceived them in the way that they did.

In fact, given that many of the respondents from the same institutions held different perceptions about the OER-related merits of their institutional policies, this suggests that either the policies were open to interpretation (especially if they did not refer to OER explicitly) or the respondents had differentiated expertise in understanding the details of their policies as they relate to OER.

In either case, the assumption that OER-related institutional policies influence whether instructors use OER or not is neither proven nor disproven based on these data. Thus we continue to assume that institutional policy remains a salient factor in OER use, though not necessarily the most important one for many instructors who have engaged with OER for other reasons.

Instructor attitudes

The fourth set of variables related to respondents' use of OER concerns their perspectives on the legal issues relating to use of teaching materials available on the internet, and users' willingness to use OER again in the future.

Perspective on legal use of materials on the internet

The underlying assumption is that instructors' perceptions of which online materials they feel free to use will affect their use of OER, either reducing their likelihood of seeking them out (such as those who feel free to use "anything on the internet") or increasing their likelihood (such as those who feel that they should only use openly licensed materials).

Figure 15 shows the comparative responses given to the prompt of which online materials instructors feel free to use for their teaching, distinguished by country and region. They are raw numbers, and respondents could answer more than one field.

The purpose of this question was to get an idea of instructors' understanding of the legal dimensions of online digital materials and its impact on their OER use. It was asked to assess their awareness of the distinctions between OER and other online materials and to establish which concepts guided their activity. The results revealed many instructors' relative lack of awareness surrounding OER, and also hinted at why there may not be much of an incentive to learn more about it.

As Figure 15 shows, one of the top responses in most countries was that instructors felt free to use materials "covered by 'fair use' regulations". "Fair use" (also referred to as "fair dealing" in certain contexts) refers to the right instructors have to freely use a portion of copyrighted materials for educational purposes without requesting permission from the copyright holder, usually for illustrative purposes in a teaching setting (Band & Gerafi, 2013). This may amount to a small sample of the copyrighted materials, though the precise amount may differ according to jurisdiction. Not all countries make provision for "fair use" regulations in their copyright regimes, but many instructors nevertheless feel they are covered by this provision in their use of online materials. Such claims of "fair use" may also refer to instructors' traditional practices of "borrowing" that are rarely, if ever, legally challenged.

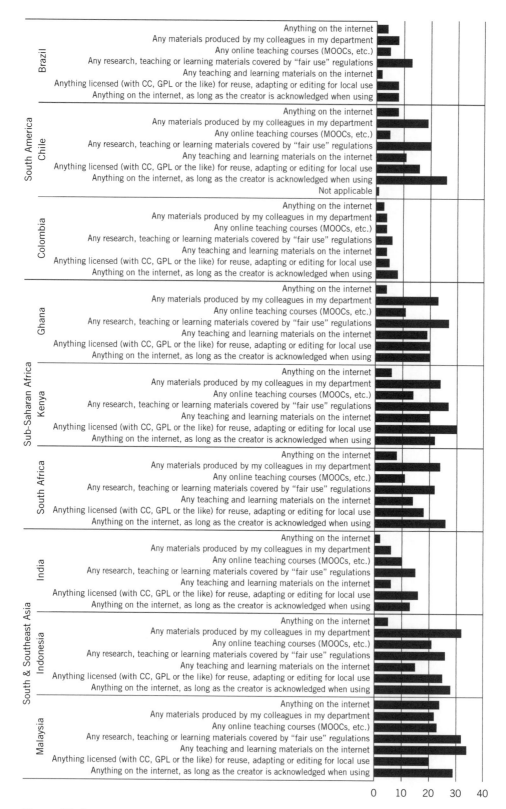

Figure 15: Instructor responses to prompt "Materials you feel free to use for teaching" (raw numbers)

The "fair use" principle could arguably be applied to almost any type of material found online. That is, for the respondents who said that they felt comfortable using "anything on the internet", they may not necessarily hold this position because they have no regard for copyright or the law. Rather, they may feel that anything on the internet can be used for educational purposes because of the fact that "fair use" conventions shaping educational practice can be vague and very challenging to interpret. However, such a response may also reveal a more activist defiance of copyright regimes, in which instructors use anything they like on the internet because they want to offer the best possible education to their students regardless of copyright legalities. It may also suggest that the defining feature of an online resource for most instructors is not its *legal status* ("anything licensed for reuse, adapting or editing"), but rather its *purpose* ("any teaching and learning materials on the internet", especially for Malaysians), *provenance* ("any materials produced by my colleagues in my department", especially for Indonesians), *acknowledgeability* ("anything on the internet, as long as the creator is acknowledged when using", especially for South Africans), or, less so, *formality* ("any online teaching courses").

These responses reveal a variety of approaches to online materials and instructors' comfort in using them, but what do they say about the likelihood of instructors' OER use?

Figure 16 shows the percentage of respondents who said that they had used OER, were not sure if they had used OER or had not used OER, based on their response to the prompt of which online materials they felt free to use for their teaching, distinguished by country and region.

The figure shows a strong association between the likelihood of OER use and feeling comfortable using "anything licensed openly". In South Africa and Indonesia, this was the top response; it was also a top-three response in Chile, Colombia, Ghana, Kenya, India and Malaysia. This suggests that those who have an understanding of the legal implications of open licensing are also more likely to have used materials that are specifically licensed as such. It also shows a low association between OER use and respondents feeling free to use "anything on the internet", suggesting that those who do not care about the legal distinctions of online materials also do not make any special effort to use OER – they just use whatever they find (which may not, in many cases, be legally open).

Interestingly, only in Ghana and Kenya was "fair use" associated with OER use. Elsewhere there was more of a middling response. This may suggest that those who are comfortable using materials under "fair use" provisions do not go out of their way to seek OER, as essentially any type of material – whether open or closed – can be used for teaching purposes (again, within the limits established in their jurisdictions). Such a sensibility may in fact reduce the attraction of OER because they comprise just a small subset of all possible materials found on the internet, which, according to instructors' perception of the "fair use" principle, are useable within a particular educational context.

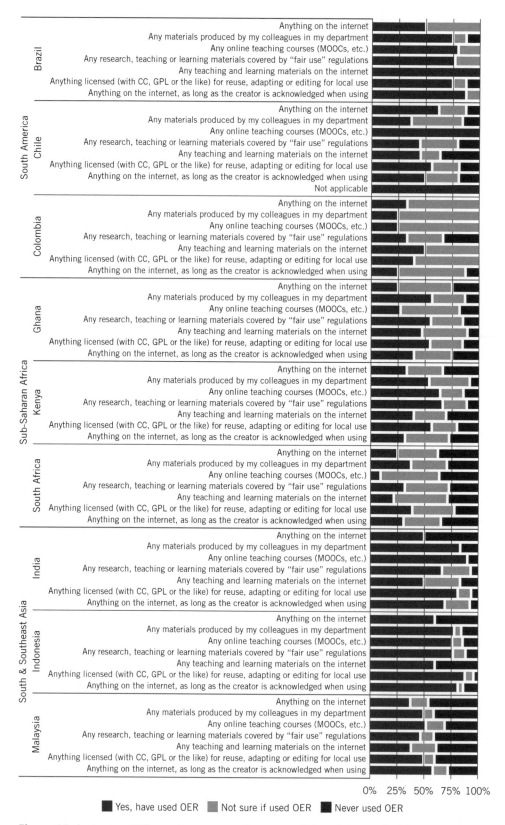

Figure 16: Instructor OER use by response to prompt "Materials you feel free to use for teaching" per country

Willingness to use OER again

An associated assumption tested is that the prior use of OER positively influences whether respondents feel interested in using them again in the future (Lee et al., 2009).

Figure 17 shows OER users' (n = 150) responses to the statement "I am willing to participate in other OER opportunities", distinguished by country and region.

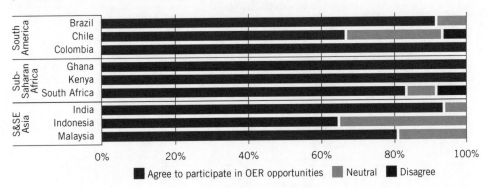

Figure 17: OER-using instructors' willingness to participate in OER opportunities again

This question was designed to discover whether those who had already used OER were interested in doing so again. As Figure 17 shows, the vast majority of respondents said that they were willing to do so. This is not the same as stating that they planned to use OER in the future, just that they were open to the possibility. It appears that their experiences with OER in the past were positive enough for them to remain willing to engage with OER again. Only a small percentage of respondents from Chile and South Africa (each less than 10%) said that they would not be willing to do so.

Thus, the assumption is sustained, as the data suggest that prior OER use by instructors is associated positively with their willingness to use OER in the future.

Open licensing

The final set of variables surveyed pertained to instructors' experience with applying open licences to their educational materials.

The assumption is that instructors' familiarity with and use of particular types of licences to share their teaching materials – primarily open licences, such as CC – will influence the likelihood of their using OER (McGreal et al., 2013).

Figure 18 shows the number of respondents who said that they used a licence to share their own teaching materials, distinguished by country and region.

The figure shows that in seven of the nine countries – including all sites in South America – the majority of instructors stated that they had never applied any type of licence to their teaching materials for sharing purposes. This suggests that they either have typically not shared their teaching materials with other instructors or, if they have done so, they have done it informally, perhaps with colleagues in their own departments.

This question illuminates the comparative rarity of instructors formally sharing teaching materials under legal open licensing provisions in the Global South. While 23% of instructors have shared their materials with a CC licence, GNU GPL licence or "other open content licences" (n = 67),[3] the majority (77%) revealed that they had either not applied any open licence to their materials (n = 228), meaning that they had not applied any type of licence to their materials (n = 162), or that they retained full copyright on their work, implying that the materials were not open (n = 66).[4]

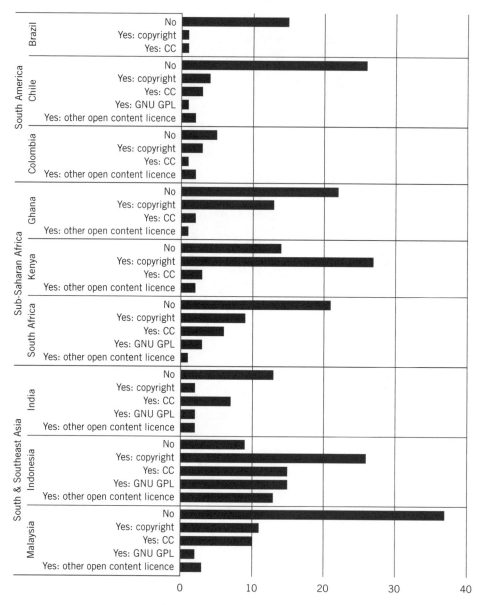

Figure 18: Instructors' use of licences (raw numbers)

3   There are 97 instances of open licensing noted in Figure 18, the result of 67 respondents answering yes to multiple open licence fields.
4   There are 96 instances of copyright licensing noted in Figure 18, though 30 of these responses were from respondents who had licensed some of their other materials with an open licence (thus we counted them in the "OER creator" numbers). Thus the tally of respondents who have only used copyright, and none of the open licences, is 66.

These data demonstrate that more respondents say that they have *used* OER (n = 150, Table 3) than have *created* OER (n = 67), which is precisely what would be expected given the relatively low barriers to OER use compared to OER creation. While it is comparatively simple to source and use OER for educational purposes, it takes greater technical and legal knowledge to share one's work as OER.

Thus, OER use is likely to be more prominent than OER creation in virtually all contexts. Does this pattern of licensing activity suggest anything about respondents' OER use patterns? Figure 19 shows instructors' OER use rates according to their previous experience with copyright licensing.

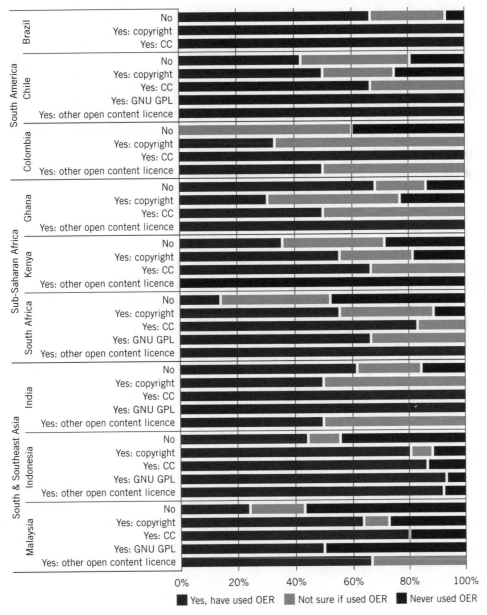

Figure 19: Instructor OER use by previous experience with copyright licences per country

These data suggest that those who have shared their materials openly are more likely to have also used OER than those who have not shared their materials openly. Thus, the assumption stands as there is a positive association between open licensing practices and OER use.

Discussion

In this section, we discuss the meaning of the findings as they relate to the research questions driving this study:
1. What proportion of instructors in the Global South has used OER?
2. Which variables may account for different OER usage rates among respondents in the Global South?

OER use rates

The key survey question used to answer this study's first research question was, "Have you ever used OER that are available in the public domain or has an open licence (e.g. Creative Commons) that allows it to be used and/or adapted by others?" The possible responses were: yes, not sure or no.

The survey data reveal that 51% of instructor respondents have used OER (Table 3). This is a small majority of respondents, and may in fact understate the use rate because 24% of respondents were "not sure" if they had ever used OER. Some may have done so without knowing. However, for the purposes of this study, we will stay with the 51% OER use rate. This is a baseline number that is useful for comparison purposes in other studies, and one that is slightly differentiated between the three regions, with use rates slightly lower in South America (49%) and Sub-Saharan Africa (46%), and a little higher in South and Southeast Asia (56%).

Because this is the first study to attempt to determine the OER use rate for higher education instructors across (and solely in) the Global South, it is impossible to determine whether the slim majority of users represents a high or low use rate. As noted, other potentially comparable surveys (COL, 2016) include respondents outside of higher education, outside of the Global South or who may not have been recruited through a random sampling methodology, as was the case in this study.

What these numbers do show, however, is that there is plenty of room for greater OER engagement. It is anticipated that OER use rates will gradually increase over time, but probably not to the extent that the practice becomes ubiquitous. Just as there are many reasons to consider using OER, instructors may also feel that there are reasons to avoid using them, especially if the OER content that they find is not of the requisite quality, relevance, level (undergraduate vs graduate), language or format they require. As more OER are shared openly by OER creators, there is a greater likelihood that some of these concerns will be allayed as the density and diversity of materials start to meet more instructors' needs.

Variables affecting OER use

The second question guiding this study sought to discover which variables might account for different OER usage rates between respondents in the Global South. In the Findings section, we looked at how a number of variables covered in the survey either influenced OER use or did not appear to do so. The survey attempted to identify variables relevant to instructors in the Global South in terms of influencing their OER choices, grouped under the following themes and discussed below: demographics, infrastructure, institutional environment, instructor attitudes and pedagogical practices.

Demographics

The survey results showed that a number of demographic variables influenced OER use. First of all, the country in which instructors worked and lived appeared to have a sizeable influence on OER use, but not in the way that was expected. While we assumed that OER use would be higher in countries that enjoyed greater economic development – as expressed by GDP per capita – we found that it was largely the opposite in that respondents in the lesser-developed countries of a particular region were more likely to be OER users than those in the more developed nations within that region. Thus, in Africa, Ghanaian and Kenyan instructors had a higher OER use rate than South Africans; in South and Southeast Asia, Indians and Indonesians had a higher use rate than Malaysians. (The low number of respondents from Brazil and Colombia makes the South American use rates more difficult to compare.)

While this trend from the data does not prove that OER use rates are universally associated with lower economic development, it suggests that OER may be more useful for instructors in countries that lack certain resources compared to instructors in more developed countries, precisely because it overcomes some of the challenges associated with lower economic development, such as lower access to quality teaching materials that are affordable and flexible. This does not mean that we would therefore expect to find the highest rates of OER use in a country such as Somalia (which has the lowest GDP per capita in the world), but it may suggest that, *above a certain level of economic development*, it might be the instructors from the countries that arguably "need" OER the most that actually use them the most. OER may be more of an optional luxury in more developed countries, and are thus treated as such, while in less developed countries they may be treated as crucial "free" resources in resource-constrained environments.

Second, a similar logic applies to the association between instructors' digital proficiency and their use of OER. While we assumed that higher (self-declared) proficiency would translate into higher OER use, we found that while it was true that those who rated their proficiency as "basic" had the lowest OER use rates, those with "advanced" proficiency did not have the highest. It was those in the "intermediate" category who had the highest. Thus, it appears that, regarding OER use, once instructors reach *a certain level of digital proficiency* – somewhere between basic and intermediate – they have the necessary technical skills to engage with OER. Below that level, their lack of skills is a barrier to OER use. However, once the appropriate level is reached, then further skills development does not lead to ever-greater OER use.

Third, the survey found a counter-intuitive relationship between instructors' highest level of educational qualification and OER use. While we had assumed that OER use rates would increase relative to educational qualification – following the logic of the exposure effect – the results showed an opposite trend. Instructors with PhDs were less likely to use OER than those with lower qualifications. This may be due to the possibility that PhD holders are more confident in their own ideas and thus more likely to develop their own teaching materials from scratch, thereby not engaging with OER. Or they may feel that OER do not have the requisite quality for the courses that they teach. By contrast, instructors with diplomas, bachelor's or master's degrees may have entered the profession with the express desire to teach (not research) and thus taken more time to acquaint themselves with the full array of teaching materials available for use. They may also not feel that they are expert enough in their field to create educational materials from scratch and thus rely on external OER for support. Whatever the reasons, it appears that OER fulfil a useful role for instructors without PhDs.

Lastly, there was a curious, albeit mild, association between instructors' positions at their HEIs and their OER use. While there was no association based on hierarchical ranking – from junior to mid-level to senior positions – there was a greater likelihood of OER use if respondents said that they were administrators or managers. These respondents were all instructors as well, but they also noted that they played administrative or managerial roles – a fact that appeared to boost their rate of OER use. This may be due to the fact that these roles create an incentive for them to be aware of the variety of pedagogical innovations available, so as to provide better stewardship or leadership to fellow instructors. Further research is required to probe this relationship, but it appears that OER is an innovation that HEI administrators and managers are likely to be familiar with in the Global South.

The above variables were the only ones in the demographic category to show some sort of association with OER use. The many other variables did not. For example, we found no discernible pattern in the relationship between gender and OER use. The same was true regarding instructors' years of teaching experience and their teaching areas. While these variables influence a variety of aspects of instructors' lives, the survey data did not show that they affected OER use.

Thus, for instructors, demographic variables do not appear to determine OER use, though some variables seem to influence it. Part of the reason for this is that OER use requires a certain minimum threshold of access to ICT infrastructure, which the HEIs we surveyed provide. Beyond that key infrastructural factor, demographic variables would appear to play only a mild role in shaping OER use by instructors.

ICT infrastructure

The preceding insights help clarify the otherwise surprising result that suggests that infrastructure variables – location of internet access, device/s used to access internet, and the cost, speed and stability of internet provision – do not have a determining influence on OER use. Though many areas in the Global South face ICT challenges, the data provided by the survey respondents (all of whom worked in HEIs) did not suggest that ICT infrastructure influenced their personal level of OER use. The reason for this is that they worked or studied in contexts that provided at least the minimum level of ICT access for them to engage with

OER. Once that condition was met, infrastructure issues no longer acted as a defining set of variables for OER use.

This outcome is a surprise because the concern about ICT infrastructure and access is prevalent in studies about education in the Global South (Teixeira et al., 2012). However, it appears that most HEIs in the Global South – or at least the ones surveyed in this study – are able to meet the minimum level of access required for instructors to engage with OER, making it less of an issue with regards to OER use. This is heartening for OER proponents, as it allows them to focus their advocacy on less intractable or large-scale challenges than ICT infrastructure (which entails heavy costs) in higher education settings. It also suggests that once a country or HEI is able to achieve a certain standard of ICT provision, OER use rates should not be determined by infrastructure concerns, but by other variables.

Institutional environment

The institutional environment – the place where instructors teach, access the internet and interact with colleagues – has a crucial influence on educational practices, including engaging with OER. For most instructors, it provides the necessary infrastructure and opportunity for using OER. Another key variable within that environment is whether the institution has policies that support the use of OER. In the survey, respondents were asked to say whether they believed that their institutions had policies that were supportive of OER (thus making the question subjective to an extent). Our assumption was that those who worked in more "pro-OER" environments would also be more likely to have used OER.

However, that was not the case. There was no discernible association between respondents' perceptions of their institutions' OER-related policies and their use of OER. Indeed, respondents from the same institutions often had differing perceptions of their policy environment, thus making it difficult to know for certain whether the policies were indeed pro-OER, or what element of those policies was deemed to be pro-OER.

While we continue to assume that policy remains a crucial variable in OER engagement – more on the OER creation side, however, than in OER use – this survey did not establish a relationship between policy perception and use rates as the data were inconclusive.

Attitudes

Beyond institutional variables, there are also broader national policies and pedagogical norms that appear to influence instructor decisions regarding OER. This is evident in the responses to the question in the survey concerning which materials instructors feel free to use in their teaching. Many feel free to use anything on the internet regardless of legal licence, which negatively related to OER use. Since they felt this way, they did not treat OER as a special or better type of educational content. It was not the key consideration in how they made pedagogical decisions. This agnosticism towards OER was also shown by respondents who declared that they felt they could use anything as long as it conformed to "fair use" provisions – a broad, vague category of activity. The fact that instructors feel covered by fair use in their "borrowing" of materials for teaching suggests that they do not feel restricted to search only for materials that are explicitly licensed for open use.

However, those who stated that they were comfortable using "anything licensed openly" (especially in Colombia, Ghana, South Africa and Indonesia) and who understood the legal implications of open licensing, were also more likely to use materials that were specifically licensed as such. This implies that there is an association between respondents' open ethic and OER use. When instructors agree with the principles of the Open movement, they are more likely to also use the products of that movement, such as OER. This should not be a surprise, but it reveals the central role that personal attitudes and values play in pedagogical decision-making.

For the 51% of instructors who said that they had used OER, more than 90% said that they would be willing to use OER again. This suggests that instructors' experiences with OER were positive enough to allow them to imagine future use opportunities. This is a highly positive result for OER as a category of educational materials, suggesting that such use will spur further engagement with it.

Pedagogical practices

Lastly, the survey attempted to ascertain whether there was an association between OER use and whether instructors had ever created OER themselves. When asked whether they had ever applied any type of licence to their teaching materials, those who said that they had applied a CC, GNU GPL or other form of open licence to their work were much more likely to have used OER than others who had never applied such licences to their work or who had retained full copyright restrictions on their work.

This suggests that OER creation is associated with OER use (though not necessarily the other way around). The level of awareness around OER is often quite high for an OER creator as it requires a level of legal and technical knowledge that is greater than for OER use. That is why the rate for OER creation was lower than for OER use.

Conclusion

The key insight from this research is that, for our survey respondents in the Global South, OER use is predicated upon instructors enjoying a certain minimum level of access to ICT infrastructure – especially hardware (computers, mobile devices, etc.) and internet connectivity (broadband, Wi-Fi, etc.) – which, once achieved, can only be described as an enabling factor for OER engagement, but not a motivating factor. Beyond that minimum, increased internet speeds, lower internet costs and greater diversity of technical devices do not lead to ever-increasing OER use rates. Once the minimum is met, the infrastructure issues that are often seen as the defining contextual factors of the Global South, no longer have much influence on OER usage, as other variables shape instructors' decisions around such practices. As has been demonstrated, in the higher education context focused on in this study, the minimum standard for ICT infrastructure was met for virtually all instructors working at HEIs, thus access issues were not key to whether they used OER or not.

Additionally, demographic variables played only a minor role in influencing respondents' OER use. The social or employment status of instructors did not appear to have much of an impact on usage rates. This is likely due to the fact that all of these instructors share similar educational missions; they possess a similarity of purpose that more profoundly shapes their OER use than does their gender, age, position and so forth. Thus, just as respondents shared a certain standard of access to ICT infrastructure (thereby decreasing it as a differentiating variable between them for OER use), they also shared a common educational interest which, for the most part, made their personal, identity-related characteristics less important for influencing whether or not they would use OER.

Similarly, while policy would likely be a crucial factor in OER creation, it did not seem to be important regarding OER use. This appears to be due to the conventions and traditions around teaching materials development, where notions of "fair use" remain prevalent, meaning that instructors feel relatively free to include what they like in their materials as long as it conforms to the needs of the curriculum. Whether those inclusions are OER or not would have less to do with the institutions' policies on OER per se, and more on their policies regarding copyrighted materials, which may be either borrowed under "fair use" principles or paid for through a licensing agreement with the publisher. Thus, for OER *use*, policy did not appear to be a key differentiator for the respondents in the institutions surveyed.

Instructors' national economic development contexts do, however, appear to have played an important role in determining OER use trends. In contrast to the assumption that higher economic development (as expressed in GDP per capita figures) would be associated with higher OER use rates, the data suggest the opposite. Instructors in the comparatively less developed countries were using OER at a markedly higher rate than those from the more developed countries (at least intra-regionally). This suggests that instructors from the relatively lesser-developed countries may find greater utility in OER because they serve to overcome some of the educational challenges associated with their national contexts' lower economic development, such as less funding for expensive copyrighted teaching materials, less student capacity to buy textbooks and fewer materials emanating from a local publishing industry. Such instructors may feel structurally compelled to seek out viable solutions to these challenges through free OER. This is a tentative conclusion requiring further research, but it opens up interesting questions about how OER are being used, and by whom.

With this in mind, it appears that the two key motivating factors of OER use (though not creation) in the Global South revolve around the national economic context in which instructors and their students live, and the ethics and values that instructors have in approaching their pedagogical practices. In essence, the national development aspect acts as a broad structural motivator, encouraging instructors to seek out alternatives to the expensive textbook and teaching materials market. That, in turn, helps shape individual instructors' beliefs about good educational practice, encouraging them to explore OER as one type of innovation in the field that may answer their particular needs. The fact that more than 90% of respondents who had used OER in the past said that they would be open to using them again suggests that these materials had some utility for them, and indeed coincided with their values.

Acknowledgements

The authors wish to thank Ishan Abeywardena and George Sciadas for valuable input received in the peer review process.

References

Allen, I. E. & Seaman, J. (2014). *Growing the curriculum: Open Education Resources in U.S. higher education.* Babson Park, MA: Babson Survey Research Group. Retrieved from http://www.onlinelearningsurvey.com/reports/growingthecurriculum.pdf

Amiel, T. (2013). Identifying barriers to the remix of translated open educational resources. *International Review of Research in Open and Distributed Learning, 14(1),* 126–144. Retrieved from http://www.irrodl.org/index.php/irrodl/article/view/1351/2428

Band, J. & Gerafi, J. (2013). *The fair use/fair dealing handbook.* Washington, D.C.: American University Program on Information Justice and Intellectual Property. Retrieved from http://infojustice.org/wp-content/uploads/2013/03/band-and-gerafi-2013.pdf

Burton, L. & Mazerolle, S. M. (2011). Survey instrument validity part II: Validation of a survey instrument examining athletic trainers' knowledge and practice beliefs regarding exertional heat stroke. *Athletic Training Education Journal, 6(1),* 36–45. Retrieved from http://natajournals.org/doi/pdf/10.4085/1947-380X-6.1.27

Butcher, N. (2011). *A basic guide to Open Educational Resources (OER).* Vancouver: Commonwealth of Learning. Retrieved from http://unesdoc.unesco.org/images/0021/002158/215804e.pdf

CERI/OECD (Centre for Educational Research and Innovation/Organisation for Economic Cooperation and Development). (2007). *Giving knowledge for free: The emergence of Open Educational Resources.* Paris: Centre for Educational Research and Innovation & Organisation for Economic Co-operation and Development. Retrieved from http://www.oecd.org/edu/ceri/38654317.pdf

CIA (Central Intelligence Agency). (2016). *CIA world factbook.* Langely, VA: Central Intelligence Agency. Retrieved from https://www.cia.gov/library/publications/the-world-factbook/rankorder/2004rank.html

Clements, K. I. & Pawlowski, J. M. (2012). User-oriented quality for OER: Understanding teachers' views on re-use, quality, and trust. *Journal of Computer Assisted Learning, 28(1),* 4–14. Retrieved from http://onlinelibrary.wiley.com/doi/10.1111/j.1365-2729.2011.00450.x/abstract

COL (Commonwealth of Learning). (2016). *Open Educational Resources in the Commonwealth 2016.* Vancouver: Commonwealth of Learning. Retrieved from http://oasis.col.org/bitstream/handle/11599/2441/2016_Phalachandra-Abeywardena_OER-in-Commonwealth-2016.pdf?sequence=4

Conole, G. (2012). Fostering social inclusion through open educational resources (OER). *Distance Education, 33(2),* 131–134. Retrieved from http://www.tandfonline.com/doi/abs/10.1080/01587919.2012.700563

Coughlan, T. & Perryman, L.-A. (2011). Something for everyone? The different approaches of academic disciplines to Open Educational Resources and the effect on widening participation. *Journal of Open, Flexible and Distance Learning, 15(2),* 11–27. Retrieved from http://oro.open.ac.uk/31071/1/42-239-1-PB.pdf

Cox, G. & Trotter, H. (2016). Institutional culture and OER policy: How structure, culture, and agency mediate OER policy potential in South African universities. *The International Review of Research in Open and Distributed Learning, 17(5).* Retrieved from http://www.irrodl.org/index.php/irrodl/article/view/2523/3877

Creswell, J. W. (2012). *Educational research: Planning, conducting, and evaluating quantitative and qualitative research.* Boston, MA: Pearson.

Dhanarajan, G. & Porter, D. (Eds.). (2013). *Open Educational Resources: An Asian perspective*. Vancouver: Commonwealth of Learning. Retrieved from https://oerknowledgecloud.org/sites/oerknowledgecloud.org/files/pub_PS_OER_Asia_web.pdf

ECDL (European Computer Driving Licence). (2011). *Identifying essential ICT skills and building digital proficiency through appropriate certification*. Brussels: European Computer Driving Licence. Retrieved from http://www.ecdl.org/media/White%20Paper%20-%20 Digital%20Literacy%20and%20ECDL%20Foundation%20Certifications.pdf

Ericsson. (2014). *South East Asia and Oceania: Ericsson mobility report appendix*. Stockholm: Ericsson. Retrieved from https://www.ericsson.com/res/docs/2014/emr-november2014-regional-appendices-raso.pdf

Friemel, T. N. (2016). The digital divide has grown old: Determinants of a digital divide among seniors. *New Media & Society, 18(2),* 313–331. Retrieved from http://www.friemel.com/docs/Friemel_2016_NMS_Digital_Divide.pdf

Garfield, E., Pudovkin, A. I. & Istomin, V. S. (2003). Mapping the output of topical searches in the Web of Knowledge and the case of Watson-Crick. *Information Technology and Libraries, 22(4),* 183–187. Retrieved from http://garfield.library.upenn.edu/papers/casewatsoncrick2003.pdf

Harley, D. & Lawrence, S. (2007). *The regulation of e-learning: New national and international policy perspectives*. University of California, Berkeley: Center for Studies in Higher Education. Retrieved from http://escholarship.org/uc/item/74q6c70t

Hassani, S. N. (2006). Locating digital divides at home, work, and everywhere else. *Poetics, 34(4–5),* 250–272. Retrieved from http://www.sciencedirect.com/science/article/pii/S0304422X06000209

Herrera, S. (2010). Open educational resources: How can open education programs be sustainable? *Access to Knowledge, 2(1),* 1–11. Retrieved from http://web.stanford.edu/group/ojs3/cgi-bin/ojs/index.php/a2k/article/view/425/251

Hogan, S. O. & LaForce, M. (2008). Incentives in physician surveys: An experiment using gift cards and checks. *Presented to the American Association for Public Opinion Research, May 2008*. New Orleans, USA. Retrieved from https://www.rti.org/sites/default/files/resources/hogan_aapor08_pres.pdf

Jackson, L. A., von Eye, A., Biocca, F. A., Barbatsis, G., Zhao, Y. & Fitzgerald, H. E. (2006). Does home internet use influence the academic performance of low-income children? *Developmental Psychology, 42(3),* 429–435. Retrieved from https://pdfs.semanticscholar.org/c18e/65f2798cc25c04d2c47a30d49dcbaa614bae.pdf

Kanwar, A., Kodhandaraman, B. & Umar A. (2010). Toward sustainable Open Education Resources: A perspective from the Global South. *The American Journal of Distance Education, 24(2),* 65–80. Retrieved from http://dx.doi.org/10.1080/08923641003696588

Kruger, L. & Gilroy, A. (2013). *Broadband internet access and the digital divide: Federal assistance programs*. Washington, D.C.: Congressional Research Service. Retrieved from https://www.fas.org/sgp/crs/misc/RL30719.pdf

Lane, A. (2009). The impact of openness on bridging educational digital divides. *International Review of Research in Open and Distributed Learning, 10(5),* 1–12. Retrieved from http://www.irrodl.org/index.php/irrodl/article/view/637

Lansu, T. A. M., Cillessen, A. H. N. & Bukowski, W. M. (2013). Implicit and explicit peer evaluation: Associations with early adolescents' prosociality, aggression, and bullying. *Journal of Research on Adolescence, 23(4),* 762–771. Retrieved from http://onlinelibrary.wiley.com/doi/10.1111/jora.12028/abstract

Lee, B. C., Yoon, J. O. & Lee, I. (2009). Learners' acceptance of e-learning in South Korea: Theories and results. *Computers and Education, 53(4)*, 1320–1329. Retrieved from http://www.sciencedirect.com/science/article/pii/S0360131509001614

Lopez, M. H., Gonzalez-Barrera, A. & Patten, E. (2013). *Closing the digital divide: Latinos and technology adoption*. Washington, D.C.: Pew Research Center. Retrieved from http://www.pewhispanic.org/2013/03/07/closing-the-digital-divide-latinos-and-technology-adoption/

Masterman, L. & Wild, J. (2011). *OER impact study: Research report*. Oxford: Jisc. Retrieved from https://www.webarchive.org.uk/wayback/archive/20140614114910/http://www.jisc.ac.uk/media/documents/programmes/elearning/oer/JISCOERImpactStudyResearchReportv1-0.pdf

McGreal, R. (2012). Open Educational Resource repositories: An analysis. In *HBMeU Annual Congress, 30 January–2 February 2012*. Dubai, United Arab Emirates. Retrieved from http://elexforum.hbmeu.ac.ae/Proceeding/PDF/Open Educational Resource.pdf

McGreal, R., Kinuthia, W. & Marshall, S. (Eds.). (2013). *Open Educational Resources: Innovation, research and practice*. Vancouver: Commonwealth of Learning & Athabasca University. Retrieved from https://oerknowledgecloud.org/sites/oerknowledgecloud.org/files/pub_PS_OER-IRP_web.pdf

Messick, S. (1989). Validity. In R. L. Linn (Ed.), *Educational measurement* (3rd ed., pp.13–103). Washington, D.C.: The American Council on Education & the National Council on Measurement in Education.

Mihailidis, P. & Cohen, J. M. (2013). Exploring curation as a core competency in digital and media literacy education. *Journal of Interactive Media in Education, 13(1)*, 1–19. Retrieved from http://files.eric.ed.gov/fulltext/EJ1007224.pdf

Mtebe, J. S. & Raisamo, R. (2014). Challenges and instructors' intention to adopt and use Open Educational Resources in higher education in Tanzania. *The International Review of Research in Open and Distributed Education, 15(1)*, 249–271. Retrieved from http://www.irrodl.org/index.php/irrodl/article/view/1687

Nonyongo, E. P. (2013). Training course team members and supporting OER development: The instructional designer's perspective. In *Seventh Pan-Commonwealth Forum on Open Learning* (PCF7), *2–6 December 2013*. Abuja, Nigeria. Retrieved from http://oasis.col.org/handle/11599/1829

OERAsia. (2010). *A study of the current state of play in the use of Open Educational Resources (OER) in the Asian region (survey instrument)*. Penang: Wawasan Open University. Retrieved from https://oerasia.org/images/files/OERAsia%20Survey%20Instrument.pdf

OER Hub. (2014). *OER Hub survey questions*. Milton Keynes: The Open University. Retrieved from https://docs.google.com/spreadsheets/d/1fL_yf-O7OZjvH67Ue8LlfidjEXwtDQ5T0TBe-Z1GYaI/edit#gid=0

ORIOLE (Open Resources: Influence on Learners and Educators). (2013). *ORIOLE survey 2013*. Milton Keynes: The Open University. Retrieved from https://docs.google.com/file/d/0B77aM81pfNQ5MmdCTzRFNFJXWnM/edit

Oyelaran-Oyeyinka, B. & Adeya, C. N. (2004a). Dynamics of adoption and usage of ICTs in African universities: A study of Kenya and Nigeria. *Technovation, 24(10)*, 841–851. Retrieved from http://isiarticles.com/bundles/Article/pre/pdf/16530.pdf

Oyelaran-Oyeyinka, B. & Adeya, C. N. (2004b). Internet access in Africa: Empirical evidence from Kenya and Nigeria. *Telematics and Informatics, 21(1)*, 67–81. Retrieved from http://www.sciencedirect.com/science/article/pii/S0736585303000236

Pegler, C. (2012). Herzberg, hygiene and the motivation to reuse: Towards a three-factor theory to explain motivation to share and use OER. *Journal of Interactive Media in Education, 2012(1)*. Retrieved from http://doi.org/10.5334/2012-04

Postlethwaite, T. N. (2005). *Educational research: Some basic concepts and terminology.* Paris: International Institute for Educational Planning/United Nations Education, Science and Cultural Organisation. Retrieved from http://unesdoc.unesco.org/images/0018/001824/182459e.pdf

Reed, P. (2012). Awareness, attitudes and participation of teaching staff towards the open content movement in one university. *Research in Learning Technology, 20(4).* Retrieved from http://dx.doi.org/10.3402/rlt.v20i0.18520

Rhoten, D. & Powell, W. W. (2007). The frontiers of intellectual property: Expanded protection versus new models of open science. *Annual Review of Law and Social Science, 3(1)*, 345–373. Retrieved from https://web.stanford.edu/group/song/papers/ScienceandPropertyARLSS.pdf

Rolfe, V. (2012). Open educational resources: Staff attitudes and awareness. *Research in Learning Technology, 20(14395).* Retrieved from https://www.dora.dmu.ac.uk/handle/2086/6188

Simpson, O. (2013). *Supporting students in online, open & distance learning.* New York: Routledge.

Takeda, S. & Homberg, F. (2013). The effects of gender on group work process and achievement: An analysis through self- and peer-assessment. *British Educational Research Journal, 40(2)*, 373–396. Retrieved from http://onlinelibrary.wiley.com/doi/10.1002/berj.3088/abstract

Tambor, E. S., Chase, G. A., Faden, R. R., Geller, G., Hofman, K. J. & Holtzman, N. A. (1993). Improving response rates through incentive and follow-up: The effect on a survey of physicians' knowledge of genetics. *American Journal of Public Health, 83(11)*, 1599–1603. Retrieved from https://www.ncbi.nlm.nih.gov/pmc/articles/PMC1694880/

Teixeira, A., Correia, C. J., Afonso, F., Cabot, A. G., López, E. G., Tortosa, S. O, Piedra, N., Canuti, L., Guzmán, J. & Solís, M. A. C. (2012). Inclusive open educational practices: How the use and reuse of OER can support virtual higher education for all. In *Proceedings of the 7th EDEN Research Workshop* (pp.56–65), *22–23 October 2012.* Leuven, Belgium. Retrieved from http://www.esvial.org/?dl_id=43

Trotter, H. (2015). Harmonising research between south and north: Results from ROER4D's question harmonisation experiment (ROER4D). In *Open Education Global Conference 2015, 22–24 April 2015.* Banff, Canada. Retrieved from http://conference.oeconsortium.org/2015/presentation/harmonising-research-between-south-and-north-results-from-roer4ds-question-harmonisation-experiment-roer4d/

UNDP (United Nations Development Program). (2012). South-South Cooperation. *Poster for the Special Unit for South-South Cooperation, United Nations Development Program.* Retrieved from http://ssc.undp.org/content/dam/ssc/documents/exhibition_triangular/SSCExPoster1.pdf

UNESCO/COL (United Nations Education, Science and Culture Organisation/Commonwealth of Learning). (2012). *2012 World Open Educational Resources Congress (OER) Questionnaire.* Paris: United Nations Educational, Scientific and Cultural Organization & Commonwealth of Learning. Retrieved from http://www.unesco.org/new/fileadmin/MULTIMEDIA/HQ/CI/CI/pdf/themes/HewlettQuestionnaire_English.pdf

van der Merwe, A. (2015). The attitudes of high school teachers to open education resources: A case study of selected South African schools. *Paper presented at Open Education Global Conference, 22–24 April 2015.* Banff, Canada. Retrieved from http://conference.oeconsortium.org/2015/wp-content/uploads/2015/01/Alex-van-der-Merwe.Open-education-conference-paper.pdf

Velaga, N. R., Beecroft, M., Nelson, J. D., Corsar, D. & Edwards, P. (2012). Transport poverty meets the digital divide: Accessibility and connectivity in rural communities. *Journal of Transport Geography, 21*, 102–112. Retrieved from http://www.sciencedirect.com/science/article/pii/S0966692312000026

Watson, C. E., Clouser, S. & Domizi, D. (2013). Improving the quality of instruction and increasing the affordability of higher education through the adoption of Open Education Resources (OERs), 2011–2012. *Paper presented at the Conference on Higher Education Pedagogy, 5–7 February 2014.* Blacksburg, USA. Retrieved from http://www.cideronline.org/conference/presentation1.cfm?pid=1652

Yeasmin, S. (2012). "Triangulation" research method as the tool of social science research. *BUP Journal, 1(1),* 154–163. Retrieved from http://www.bup.edu.bd/journal/154-163.pdf

How to cite this chapter

de Oliveira Neto, J. D., Pete, J., Daryono & Cartmill, T. (2017). OER use in the Global South: A baseline survey of higher education instructors. In C. Hodgkinson-Williams & P. B. Arinto (Eds.), *Adoption and impact of OER in the Global South* (pp. 69–118). Retrieved from https://doi.org/10.5281/zenodo.599535

Corresponding author: José Dutra de Oliveira Neto <dutrausp@gmail.com>

Section 2

South America

Contents

Chapter 4

Open Access and OER in Latin America: A survey of the policy landscape in Chile, Colombia and Uruguay

Amalia Toledo

Summary

This chapter presents an overview of the mechanisms (funding, policy, legislative and procedural) adopted by Latin American governments with respect to Open Access and Open Educational Resources (OER) initiatives in the higher education sector. It addresses three questions: How do the higher education systems of Chile, Colombia and Uruguay operate and fund their activities in general? How do existing policies and processes incorporating Open Access and/or OER influence student access to learning and research materials in these countries? What policy, advocacy and community-building interventions might be useful for promoting Open Education activities in these contexts?

This study employed a descriptive, case study approach to examine whether and how Open Access and OER policies have been applied at national and institutional levels. It first engaged in an Open Education policy country-mapping exercise, then conducted a comparative analysis, and concluded the research process with a workshop conducted with 10 regional education experts and activists to validate findings.

Findings indicate that while each country has its own approach to funding higher education, there are few or no specific national and/or institutional policies aimed at promoting Open Education in the higher education sectors. Low OER awareness and a commercialised model of higher education appear to account for the lack of any OER policies in Chile, while in Colombia various national and institutional strategies reveal a country at a nascent stage of Open Education policy development. By contrast, the nature of OER management and extent of policy implementation in Uruguay suggests that it is an enabling environment for current and future open policy development. ▶

All of these countries are making investments in science, technology and innovation programmes and projects, making this the most fruitful field for potential Open Education advocacy.

Based on the outcomes of this study, a number of recommendations are proposed, including: fostering and strengthening networks among Latin American civil society organisations promoting Open Education; engaging with higher education stakeholders on how to develop open policies; promoting open policies and mandates for publicly funded research; developing bottom-up and top-down strategies for greater engagement with OER; and providing greater visibility to existing Open Education projects in the region.

Acronyms and abbreviations

BVS-LILACS	*Biblioteca Virtual em Saúde* (Virtual Library on Health)
BVSDE-REPIDISCA	*Biblioteca Virtual Desarrollo Sostenible y Salud Ambiental – Red Panamericana de Información en Salud Ambiental* (Virtual Library of Sustainable Development and Environmental Health – Pan American Network for Environmental Health)
CLACSO	*El Consejo Latinoamericano de Ciencias Sociales* (Network of Virtual Libraries of Latin American Council of Social Sciences)
Colciencias	Administrative Department of Science, Technology and Innovation
CONICYT	*Consejo Nacional de Ciencia y Tecnología* (National Commission for Scientific and Technological Research)
CRUCH	*Consejo de Rectores de las Universidades Chilenas* (Principals Council of Chilean Universities)
EIC	educational innovation centre
FOSS	Free and Open Source Software
GDP	gross domestic product
HEI	higher education institution
ICT	information and communication technologies
MECESUP2	*El Programa de Mejoramiento de la Calidad y Equidad de la Educación* (Programme for Improvement of Quality and Equity in Higher Education)
MoECo	*Ministerio de Educación* (Ministry of Education)
OER	Open Educational Resources
PISA	Programme for International Student Assessment
REDA	*Recursos Educativos Digitales Abiertos* (National Strategy for Digital Open Educational Resources)
Redalyc	*Red de Revistas Científicas de América Latina y el Caribe, España y Portugal* (Network of Scientific Journals from Latin America and the Caribbean, Spain and Portugal)

REMAR	*Red Mercosur para la Accesibilidad y la Generación Colaborativa de Recursos Educativos Abiertos* (Mercosur Network for Accessibility and Collaborative Creation of Open Educational Resources)
SIDALC	*Alianza de Servicios de Información Agropecuaria* (Alliance of Agricultural Information Services)
SciELO	Scientific Electronic Library Online
STI	science, technology and innovation
UdelaR	*Universidad de la República Uruguay* (University of the Republic of Uruguay)
UTEC	*Universidad Tecnológica* (Technological University)

Introduction

It is undeniable that the provision of equitable access to quality education is one of the greatest challenges facing Latin America. Within this context, increased investment in and focus upon higher education is a key element in the pursuit of more equitable societies.

Latin American countries are currently spending billions of dollars on education every year. In many of these countries, public spending on education has been increasing.[1] This has, however, not always translated into an improvement in the quality of education. For example, the 2012 Programme for International Student Assessment (PISA) reveals that Latin American countries have a low performance and high inequality level compared with other countries. It is noteworthy that all eight Latin American countries that participated in the 2012 PISA evaluation were located in the lower third of the ranking among the 65 countries analysed (OECD, 2014). According to the Inter-American Development Bank's analysis[2] of the 2012 PISA results, the participating Latin American countries are among the lowest-performing countries. Chile, which achieved the highest score among all participating Latin American countries, is ranked 50 out of 65, while Colombia and Peru are ranked 62 and 65, respectively (OECD, 2014). Latin America has consistently received worse educational results than its level of per capita expenditure on education suggests it should (OECD, 2014).

Open Education encompasses a set of enabling policies, practices, resources and tools that are freely shared with the intent to improve the accessibility, relevance, quality and effectiveness of education. This global movement seeks to encourage opportunities for participatory – and in some cases, personalised – learning through affordable teaching and learning materials, and to limit the barriers that hinder students and teachers from taking advantage of free and legally shareable materials. Open Education is grounded in the principle of the open exchange of knowledge and resources, and takes advantage of information and communication technologies (ICT), especially the internet, for digital publication and dissemination to widen access to knowledge.

Aspects of openness in education are evidenced in the use of Open Access research articles as educational resources for students, and in the creation and use of Open

---

Educational Resources (OER). The Open Access publishing model promotes immediate, unrestricted access to digital academic and scientific materials, particularly as relates to peer-reviewed journal articles. These articles are not only important in the context of promoting the global research agenda, but also constitute a valuable source of information in the teaching and learning context. The principles of Open Access have been enshrined in a number of international declarations[3] and promote the elimination of economic, legal and technological barriers to accessing knowledge.

OER are teaching, learning and research materials that are in the public domain or have been published with a licence that allows free use or repurposing by others (Atkins, Brown & Hammond, 2007). The principles of Open Education and/or OER have been promoted in key international declarations, specifically the Cape Town Open Education Declaration[4] and the Paris OER Declaration.[5]

The international community that supports the adoption of OER has become an organised social movement over the years. This Open Education movement seeks, among other things, the development and implementation of concrete policies that promote Open Access and OER at state and institutional levels, and operates on the foundational principle that research and educational resources are common goods that should be available for the benefit of all citizens. While education is understood as the process in which knowledge, ideas and information are shared with others, speaking about Open Education denotes an expanded educational approach. The adjective "open" not only refers to accessing materials, resources, tools, processes, practices and information, but also to the ability to reuse, modify and redistribute them to respond to individual, group and institutional needs. The adjective "open" also goes beyond to inform new methodological practices based on ideas of flipping the classroom and using modern methodologies, such as design thinking, to empower students, teachers and the school community to participate in building the knowledge they find locally appropriate.

Within this context, it is essential to move beyond thinking that more investment and expenditure on education is needed, to a critical reflection on how funds are spent on education, how the results of education expenditure can be made readily available to a broader public, and how the Open Education movement can contribute to meaningful responses or alternatives to the challenges of education accessibility and quality.

The aim of this chapter is to map, from the academic literature, policy documents and previous research undertaken by the Karisma Foundation,[6] the current mechanisms (expenditure, relevant policy, legislation and processes) employed by three Latin American governments – Chile, Colombia and Uruguay – in Open Education initiatives in the higher education sector in order to identify possible policy, advocacy and community-building efforts. This chapter will explore the higher education systems of these three countries in

---

3   See, for example:
    - Budapest Open Access Initiative (2002) – http://www.budapestopenaccessinitiative.org/boai-10-recommendations
    - Bethesda Statement on Open Access Publishing (2003) – http://legacy.earlham.edu/~peters/fos/bethesda.htm
    - Berlin Declaration on Open Access to Knowledge in the Sciences and Humanities (2003) – https://openaccess.mpg.de/Berlin-Declaration
4   http://www.capetowndeclaration.org/
5   http://www.unesco.org/new/fileadmin/MULTIMEDIA/HQ/CI/WPFD2009/English_Declaration.html
6   The Karisma Foundation, based in Bogota, Colombia, was the organisational host for this study.

order to gain a better understanding of how they operate and are funded, and to identify the existing policies, legislation and processes incorporating open principles, either through Open Access and/or through OER. With the analysis of the data and the knowledge gained in the process of mapping the available information, the authors identify areas for action and opportunities for transformation and capacity-building at national and institutional level.

Brief overview of Open Access and OER initiatives in Latin America

The information available on the higher education sector in Latin America demonstrates various scenarios in relation to the affordability, quality and accessibility of education. In a region characterised by inequality, higher education can be a huge burden for low-income families. The acquisition of textbooks in Latin American universities represents an additional non-trivial financial burden for poor students. For example, as reported in 2013, the average annual cost of textbooks at the University of São Paulo (Brazil's largest public university) was 1 900 euros (approximately 2 420 USD) – 67% of the annual minimum wage in the country (2 820 euros, or approximately 3 590 USD, per annum) (Frango, Ochoa, Pérez Casas & Rodés, 2013). A similar situation occurs in Argentina, and the picture worsens in other Latin American countries (Frango et al., 2013).

University libraries in the region have tried to address the lack of textbooks by offering services for photocopying copyrighted material free of charge, but the resources allocated for this have been insufficient to meet demand. In many cases these initiatives were also shut down by multinational publishers which felt these practices negatively impacted upon their market share. As a result of the high cost of textbooks and the lack of alternatives, there is currently a ratio of 50 students per textbook in the most well-attended courses (Frango et al., 2013). Thus, some students end up sourcing illegal copies of textbooks, while others do not have any access at all. In the study conducted by Frango et al. in Argentina, Chile, Brazil, Ecuador, Mexico, Peru, Uruguay and Venezuela in 2013, just over 40% of survey respondents stated that they did not have access to the required textbooks; the type of material most (43% of respondents) used was photocopies of textbook chapters (Frango et al., 2013).

In this context, open access to educational and academic resources in higher education could be part of the strategy to close the gaps in educational provision and to support strategies of lowering the economic cost (for both households and universities) of teaching and learning materials (Babini, 2011). The implementation of Open Access initiatives in the region has, however, faced a number of challenges. A study on access to scientific production in Latin America and the Caribbean found minimal presence of scientific journal articles published with Open Access permissions (Babini, 2011). Nevertheless, while Open Access uptake remains restricted, there have been a number of service offerings aimed at promoting open access to academic publications in the region. These include: (1) multidisciplinary portals for accessing scientific journal articles, such as the Scientific Electronic Library

Online (SciELO)[7] and Redalyc;[8] (2) a directory of portals called Latindex journals;[9] (3) the Cybertesis portal;[10] and (4) the thematic digital repositories, such as SIDALC,[11] CLACSO,[12] BVS-LILACS,[13] and BVSDE-REPIDISCA.[14] This minimal Open Access content offering in the region is in stark contrast to the extensive scientific production "which remains within the circuit of international commercial distribution of journals, invisible and inaccessible to those who do not subscribe to those services" (Babini, 2011, p.35). This is not a minor issue, and more research is needed to understand the dissemination of journals and how libraries provide this access to students in the region. It is likely that the situation would be different for public and private institutions, rural and urban students, contact and distance programmes, and may be related to income.

Despite the challenges around Open Access implementation, there have been a number of noteworthy Latin American initiatives aimed at increasing access to educational and scientific content that has the potential to become an important educational resource for students. First, SciELO, initiated in 1997, aims to give visibility and universal access to scientific literature produced in developing countries, particularly in Latin America and the Caribbean. Initially, the SciELO project stemmed from a collaboration between the Foundation for Research Support in the state of São Paulo, the Latin American and Caribbean Centre on Health Sciences Information, and national and international institutions related to scientific communication. Currently, the project has expanded its network to include Argentina, Bolivia, Brazil, Chile, Colombia, Costa Rica, Cuba, Spain, Mexico, Peru, Portugal, South Africa, Uruguay and Venezuela.

The SciELO model comprises three components. The first is the SciELO methodology, which facilitates the interoperability of electronic publication of scientific journals, bibliographic and full-text databases, text retrieval, preservation of the electronic record, and the production of statistical indicators of impact and use of scientific literature. The methodology also includes "a set of policies, standards, guidelines, procedures, and tools regarding electronic publishing as well as evaluation and admission of journals for indexing and permanence in the collections".[15] The second component is the application of the methodology, that is, the website of the SciELO collection that profiles the electronic journal collections. The final component is the development of an ongoing partnership between national and international scientific communication stakeholders, the aim of which is to promote dissemination and improve the sustainability of the SciELO project.

Another initiative that should be highlighted in the context of promoting Open Access in the region is the Network of Scientific Journals from Latin America and the Caribbean, Spain and Portugal (*Red de Revistas Científicas de América Latina y el Caribe, España y Portugal*, or Redalyc),[16] a bibliographic database and a digital library of Open Access journals. The project was initiated in 2002 by the *Universidad Autónoma del Estado de México* with the

---

7   http://scielo.org/php/index.php?lang=en
8   http://www.redalyc.org/
9   http://www.latindex.org/latindex/inicio
10   http://www.tesislatinoamericanas.info
11   http://www.sidalc.net
12   http://biblioteca.clacso.edu.ar
13   http://lilacs.bvsalud.org
14   http://www.bvsde.paho.org/sde/ops-sde/ingles/repidisca.shtml
15   http://www.scielo.org/php/level.php?lang=en&component=42&item=3
16   http://www.redalyc.org/info.oa?page=/acerca-de/faqredalyc.html#tab3

overall goal of building a multidisciplinary scientific information system comprised of leading journals published in and about Latin America. Today, Redalyc also evaluates the scientific and editorial quality of knowledge outputs in Ibero-America.

Redalyc offers an online journal library that enables reading, downloading and redistribution by adopting open licensing of scientific articles. It also generates indicators to assess quantitatively and qualitatively the way science is undertaken and reported in Latin America. Thus, it supports efforts to make scientific findings available for greater discussion among experts and visible to the broader public, including students.

Additionally, in 2012, the science and technology bodies of eight Latin American countries signed a commitment to setting up an Open Access network known as the Federated Network of Institutional Repositories of Scientific Publications (LA Referencia).[17] The objective of LA Referencia is "to share and give visibility to the scientific production of higher education institutions (HEIs) and scientific research in Latin America" and it has worked as a boost to the Open Access movement in Latin American countries.[18] Since its inception, the LA Referencia strategy has focused on creating a framework of technical and organisational arrangements in order to build a federated network of institutional repositories. This initiative currently has a search engine for scientific articles from nearly 100 universities in Latin America, which has been made possible by the commitment of country institutions.

The outcome of the efforts driven by LA Referencia can be seen in the shaping of national policies to ensure open access to publicly funded research. Argentina, Mexico and Peru are three of the LA Referencia member countries with Open Access legislation in place.

In Argentina, Law No. 26.889 of 3 December 2013[19] legislated that, with state funding, the institutions of the National System of Science and Technology must create open, digital institutional repositories, in which national outputs from scientific–technological production are deposited (e.g. technical and scientific papers, academic theses and journal articles). In addition, the law provides for the mandatory publication of primary research data five years after collection in order to facilitate reuse and verification.

In 2013, Peru passed the Law on National Digital Repository of Science, Technology and Innovation Open Access,[20] which establishes the obligation to publish the results of all scientific research funded (as a whole or in part) by public sources in the national digital repository, which is interoperable with other regional and global repositories. In 2015, the Peruvian government passed a decree[21] regulating the application of the 2013 law.

In 2014, Mexico amended the Law on Science and Technology, the General Education Law and the Organic Law of the National Council of Science and Technology[22] to promote open access to all knowledge generated with public funding. The Mexican legislation also

17 http://lareferencia.redclara.net/rfr/sites/default/files/LAReferenciaTresPaginas.pdf
18 http://lareferencia.redclara.net/rfr/sites/default/files/edicion-especial12.pdf. The science and technology bodies in Argentina, Brazil, Chile, Colombia, Ecuador, El Salvador, Mexico, Peru and Venezuela are part of this project. In 2015, Costa Rica's science and technology body became a new LA Referencia observer country. The status of observer is transitory and involves interoperability testing on the status of the repositories through a first harvest test.
19 http://www.casi.com.ar/sites/default/files/ley26899- repositorios digitales.pdf
20 http://www.leyes.congreso.gob.pe/Documentos/Leyes/30035.pdf
21 http://portal.concytec.gob.pe/images/stories/images2013/portal/areas-institucion/dsic/reglamento_repositorio_nacional_alicia.pdf
22 http://www.dof.gob.mx/nota_detalle.php?codigo=5345503&fecha=20%2F05%2F2014

expanded the powers of the *Consejo Nacional de Ciencia y Tecnología* (CONICYT), the Mexican federal body responsible for developing national policies on science and technology, to develop a national strategy for the democratisation of scientific information and to develop quality criteria and technical standards to establish digital repositories. Additionally, it established the foundation for the creation of a national Open Access repository, operated by CONICYT.

The Open Education and OER movement in Latin America – a movement manifested globally through initiatives such as the Open Policy Network[23] and Open Education Week[24] – has mainly emerged in the wake of preceding Open Access activity. Compared to the Open Access landscape, however, the picture related to the Open Education movement is less encouraging. The debate around the adoption of OER is still incipient in Latin America, with the exception of Brazil and some small pockets of activity driven by local institutions. In Brazil, noticeable strides have been made in the OER debate and the community is growing in strength (Amiel, 2012; Amiel & Santos, 2013; Dos Santos, 2011; Rossini, 2012). It currently serves as an example of an enabling environment for creating public policies that foster the promotion and development of OER.[25]

Another milestone example of OER development in Latin America is the National Strategy for Digital Open Educational Resources (*Recursos Educativos Digitales Abiertos*, or REDA) of Colombia, adopted in 2012 (Ministerio de Educación Nacional, 2012). This strategy is unique in the region and focuses on higher education by establishing the roadmap for creating a national OER system. A Ministry of Education (MoECo) official defines REDA as an investment project that is only possible with the technical collaboration of HEIs. The participation of HEIs has therefore been paramount to its implementation.[26]

In Colombia, the REDA strategy is materialising through technical committees formed by HEIs engaged in the ministry-led process. In this way, the MoECo ensures the participation of key stakeholders in the process of developing the national system. REDA recognises three types of resources: learning objects, virtual courses and education applications. At the time of writing, 13 learning objects had been approved in the external quality assessment process and could be found on the REDA portal.[27] Although the 13 resources are openly licensed materials, the system has been designed so that publicly funded resources that are not open can also be shared there.

The Colombian strategy provides a good example of how to engage educational institutions and government in a joint project to promote, strengthen and enhance the production, management and use of OER. It is too early to assess the process, but it is a government commitment that is worth following closely.

Open Education in Latin America is still in its infancy. Mapping what is already happening in terms of Open Access and/or OER in the region may help to "inspire the creation and implementation of new OER initiatives in Latin America, enabling the sharing of content and pedagogical practices both regionally and internationally" (Inamorato, Cobo & Costa, 2012, p.17) and determine further opportunities for policy development.

---

23 https://openpolicynetwork.org
24 http://www.openeducationweek.org
25 http://www.rea.net.br
26 Presentation during a workshop, conducted during Phase 3 of this project, with Open Education experts and activists from Latin America, held in Bogota, Colombia, 4 September 2014.
27 http://186.113.12.159/web/rn/inicio

Methodology

A descriptive, case study approach to national and institutional policies around OER and Open Access was applied and developed in three phases: first, a country-mapping exercise was undertaken, followed by comparative analysis, and, finally, a workshop was conducted with education experts and activists to validate the research findings.

Phase 1 mapped Open Access and OER initiatives in five countries of the region: Chile, Colombia, Costa Rica, Ecuador and Uruguay. These countries were chosen based on ease of access from Colombia (where the research team was based), the presence of potential partners for further engagement, and public data availability. The lack of previous deep research into these countries also presented itself as an opportunity for the authors to understand new trends emerging from these less studied countries. After identifying study-site countries and defining measurement variables, a mapping exercise was undertaken to identify the three countries (Colombia, Uruguay and Chile) with the most enabling environments for undertaking advocacy activity regarding the development of Open Education policy. The mapping process utilised the following general and specific measurement variables:

- General variables: (1) civil society organisations working on Open Access and Open Education; (2) state policies on Open Access and/or OER; and (3) institutional policies on Open Access and/or OER.
- Specific variables: (1) plans and/or strategies regarding the processes identified in the general variables through which OER could be developed or acquired; (2) type of resource for cases where information showed the existence of OER or development plans; and (3) policies and/or legislation, including OER funding processes.

Phase 2 was comprised of a study of the higher education systems of the three countries identified in Phase 1. The result of this phase was three country reports[28] containing context-specific data, information on specific initiatives identified and interviews with key stakeholders. The three countries all had at least one civil society organisation working on developing and/or fostering Open Access and/or OER, as well as Open Education strategies and policies at the state or institutional level. The country reports were used as an additional source of information for analysis in this study.

Each country report includes the identification of the organisation or institution implementing some sort of Open Access and/or OER policy advocacy or activity, funding sources, quality assurance methodologies, and programmes for innovation and ICT. In addition, national copyright regimes were examined in order to identify legal frameworks that were conducive to openness in the education and research sectors. In order to gain a more concrete example of Open Education policies and programmes, eight universities (four public and four private from capital cities and the departments/provinces) in Colombia and Chile were examined. In Uruguay, only two universities (one public university that covers the vast majority of student enrolment in the country and one private university, which is the second-largest tertiary institution in terms of enrolment) located in the capital city of

---

28   https://docs.google.com/document/d/1NFGR4jidenlmI1Orbm1bfkIDnemuge-s6GWdQr35iAQ/edit#

Montevideo were reviewed. The university selection was based on the results of the 2013 Quacquarelli Symonds Latin American University Rankings.[29] Each country report was produced from collected and analysed data that are available in public and in bibliographic databases. Whenever possible, a series of interviews with relevant stakeholders was undertaken (four interviewees were approached, half of whom responded).

Finally, the comparative analysis in Phase 3 was undertaken through a workshop process in which Open Education experts and activists from Chile, Colombia and Uruguay, in addition to representatives from Argentina and Brazil, were presented with the information gathered and invited to review the country reports generated in Phase 2. During the workshop, the 10 participants had the opportunity to comment, criticise and provide supplementary data in order to improve the country report data. The workshop also provided a forum to discuss the latest developments in Open Education and possible approaches to strengthening practice. This information was gathered from October 2013 to September 2014, and formed the basis for the final mapping process of analysing all the information gathered in order to articulate the findings and recommendations presented in this chapter.

Overall, some challenges were encountered in conducting the study, which had an influence on the depth of findings and their validity. These included:

- Lack of transparency in educational resources acquisition and development budgets in the HEI analysis conducted in Phase 2.
- Low response rates on the part of some stakeholders approached with requests for information.
- High variability of publicly available information, hindering the comparative analysis between countries and within a single country.
- A dearth of studies on higher education in the region.

Findings

Latin America is a region of great similarities and disparities. In the higher education sector, the situation is no different. The diversity of systems poses a challenge for comparative analysis, but it is still possible to extract and examine emerging themes and trends.

Variety of funding streams demonstrating the level of state support in public higher education

The three countries analysed reveal differences within their social, economic, political and cultural contexts. This section presents findings on the funding streams for higher education in Colombia, Uruguay and Chile.

Colombia's higher education system consists of a total of 288 universities, professional technological institutions and technical-vocational schools, with a coverage rate of 45.5%

---

29 http://www.topuniversities.com/university-rankings/latin-american-university-rankings/2013#sorting=rank+regi
    on=+country=+faculty=+stars=false+search=

of a total population of 47 662 000 (Ministerio de Educación Nacional, 2014).[30] According to data from the National System of Higher Education Information (*Sistema Nacional de Información de la Educación Superior*), there were about 2.2 million students registered at tertiary institutions in 2014, which shows a growth of about 950 000 places in the last 10 years. Of the total number of enrolments, about 57% are in public HEIs and 43% in private institutions (Ministerio de Educación Nacional, 2015).

Expenditure within public HEIs is part of public social expenditure in that it is aimed at covering unsatisfied basic needs (specifically education), tends to the general welfare of the state, and improves the quality of life of the population (Presidente de la República de Colombia, 1996). Since 2010, the government has carried out a public finance strengthening programme in Colombian public HEIs in order to increase student enrolment and retention, bolster human resources, and improve physical and technological infrastructure and research. In 2013, the public expenditure on public higher education as a percentage of gross domestic product (GDP) was 0.82%. This figure does, however, represent a decline in terms of the resources allocated as a percentage of GDP in 2001, which reached 1.04% (Ministerio de Educación Nacional, 2014).

Public higher education funding in Colombia is undertaken through subsidies generated through supply and demand mechanisms for programmes at higher education level (Ministerio de Educación Nacional, 2010). The funding stream established to finance the supply mechanism is comprised of: direct contributions from national and territorial entities; resources that each institution generates through training courses, continuing education and research; the university's revenue stamp;[31] support from the Administrative Department of Science, Technology and Innovation (Colciencias); and resources granted by the Ministry of National Education for development projects (for instance, projects funded by the World Bank or any other international cooperation agency). In funding mechanisms designed to address the demand for higher education programmes, resources are assigned in order to ensure the entry and retention of high-school graduates in higher education. In this context, the Colombian Institute for Student Loans and Study Abroad (*Crédito Educativo y Becas en el Exterior*) offers loans and scholarships to encourage the retention of students in the system (Ministerio de Educación Nacional, 2010).

The University of the Republic of Uruguay (*Universidad de la República Uruguay*, or UdelaR) monopolised public higher education until 2013. A 2004 study by Collazo and Pebé demonstrated that UdelaR accounted for 90% of the total student enrolment in the country (80 000 students), as opposed to the private sector, which covered the remaining 10% (Collazo & Pebé, 2004). The latest data available on student enrolment show that 131 015 students out of 157 674 are registered in public universities, while the rest are in private institutions (Ministerio de Educación, 2014). In 2013, Law No. 19.043 of 28 December 2012 (Republica Oriental del Uruguay, 2012) mandated the establishment

---

30   According to articles 17–19 of Colombian Law No. 30 of 28 December 1992, technical-vocational schools offer vocational training programmes; professional technical institutions advance vocational training programmes, academic training programmes in professions or disciplines, and specialisation programmes; and universities are recognised as such and credited with their performance in the following activities: scientific or technological research, academic training in professions or disciplines, and the production, development and transmission of knowledge.

31   The university's revenue stamp, or *estampilla Pro-Universidad*, is a para-fiscal levy earmarked for strengthening state universities managed directly by those universities, on whose behalf the tax is imposed. Law No. 1697 of 20 December 2013 established this tax.

of a Technological University (*Universidad Tecnológica*, or UTEC) to bring public tertiary education to the interior of the country through the establishment of Regional Technical Institutes and to provide tertiary and vocational technical education according to the needs of the regional context. Public higher education in Uruguay has therefore been more evenly distributed between UdelaR and UTEC since 2013.

The private higher education sector does not, in general, receive funding from the state. Uruguay's public expenditure on higher education from 2002–2004 was less than 3% of GDP. Until 2004, UdelaR steadily received a low budget allocation from government, while the cost of tuition rose by 40%. From 2006–2009, the government approved a 50% increase in the university budget – a milestone that reaffirmed the government's commitment to free public education (Contrera, 2008). By 2010, public expenditure on higher education as a percentage of GDP was 4.5%. Although it exceeded the lag of less than 3% from 2002–2004, 2010 saw public expenditure decrease in comparison to the 2004–2009 recovery period. In 2011, the incremental GDP investment trend on education recovered (Ministerio de Educación Nacionale, 2015).

Certainly, Uruguay's context is unique in terms of the coverage of public versus private higher education. By contrast, Chilean higher education is one of the most unequal landscapes, regionally and internationally, and is known for being one of the most expensive and private systems worldwide. The higher education funding system is of a mixed nature, including public ownership and management by the state and its organs, as well as private, whether subsidised or paid for. In Chile, there are 59 universities, 25 of which are part of the Principals Council of Chilean Universities (*Consejo de Rectores de las Universidades Chilenas*, or CRUCH) – 16 of which are state universities and nine are private. All of them receive contributions from the state of Chile. The remaining 34 are private universities that do not receive state funding (Espinoza, 2012).

Higher education in Chile is founded on a self-funding system. Thus, at the time of writing, HEIs were funded through the payment of tuition and other fees by the students themselves, combined with the generation of resources through consulting and services, tuition increases, private bank loans, private entity donations, research funding, and investment projects funded by the Ministry of Education, among others (Espinoza, 2012).

The average annual fees of Chilean universities correspond to 41% of per capita income of the country. When compared with other countries – for instance, in the USA 28%, Australia 12% and Canada 10% – this turns out to be one of the highest fee structures in the world (Rodríguez Ponce, 2012). Chile's self-funding system does allow those institutions that wish to do so to develop their own financial markets, largely due to the absence of state regulation in this regard (Rodríguez Ponce, 2012). This provides institutions with an opportunity to explore alternative business models, sometimes for commercial ends, for educational provision.

The most important funding instrument for traditional Chilean universities belonging to CRUCH is the Direct Fiscal Contribution, a freely available subsidy. In total, 95% of the CRUCH funding budget is allocated according to historical criteria (that is, according to a formula that considers the basis of the total amount allocated to HEIs in the previous year), while the remaining 5% is distributed according to annual performance indicators (Ministerio de Educación, n.d.). There is also an Indirect Fiscal Contribution, granted annually by the state to all universities, professional institutes and technical training centres that: (1) are recognised as HEIs by the Ministry of Education; and (2) admit the 27 500 best scores of the University Selection Examination (Ministerio de Educación, n.d.).

Additionally, the Chilean government has created other funding channels that categorise HEIs by various levels – universities which place an emphasis on teaching, research and doctoral programmes; universities with an emphasis on teaching and targeted research; and universities with an emphasis on teaching – and are intended to support students, infrastructure development, and the operation of institutions in order to enhance education quality and equity, and strengthen teaching. There are also special funds designated to promote the accreditation of technical and vocational training institutions. Other mechanisms that play a unique role in financing Chilean higher education are private donations, as well as student loans and grants.

Following far-reaching social unrest in which Chileans demanded an end to the commercialisation of higher education in 2014, the Chilean government has allocated 34 billion pesos (approximately 55 million USD) to the higher education sector (Centro de Estudios Consorcio de Universidades del Estado de Chile, 2014). Many have expressed their dissatisfaction with the actual budget increase announced by the government as part of the education reform that seeks progressive change to improve education quality, provide free education and put an end to admission inequalities. One of the central objections to the budget increase was that it was merely a subsidising policy for the demand component in higher education or state support to students, rather than one aimed at strengthening HEIs. This is premised on the fact that the predominant area of investment was in grants and loans to individual students rather than bailing out HEIs.[32]

Against this background, it is not unreasonable to conclude that, despite the upcoming implementation of the new education reform that seeks free education at all levels, Chile will face a major challenge in higher education provision in the near future. The higher education system that prevails in the country is one where education is conceived of as a market and not as a public good, with objectives aligned with public purposes, such as training of technicians and professionals, research, innovation and artistic creation.

Evidence of development and implementation of strengthening programmes in science, technology and innovation

The three countries examined are undertaking substantial efforts to strengthen science, technology and innovation (STI) in order to participate in the international arena of knowledge generation. It did, however, appear that knowledge management of Open Education in the fields of STI is fairly weak, presenting an opportunity for transformation. This section provides an overview of what is happening in each of the three countries examined with regards to STI development and implementation, with the aim of highlighting key areas for advocacy as well as Open Education opportunities.

In Colombia, MoECo is running several programmes to strengthen the National System of Educational Innovation, focusing on: teacher training in the pedagogical use of ICT; digital educational content management for K-12 via the educational portal *Colombia Aprende*;[33]

---

32 http://www.latercera.com/noticia/las-razones-del-rechazo-transversal-al-presupuesto-de-educacion-superior/
33 http://aprende.colombiaaprende.edu.co/

promotion of virtual programmes in the context of higher education; fostering of research in educational innovation utilising ICT by funding STI research projects; provision of equipment and connectivity to K-12 educational institutions; enhancement in the use, management and appropriation of ICT in the subnational authorities of educational administration; and the creation of educational innovation centres (EICs).

The EIC programme is progressive in its objectives and strategy implementation. The aim is to strengthen capacity for the modernisation of education by promoting innovation, research development and use of digital educational content (Centro de Innovación Educativa, n.d.). The strategy to achieve this goal is supported by the collaboration and participation of HEIs located in four different regions of Colombia, as well as government entities and the commercial sector.

It should be noted that within the framework of strengthening the current research agenda, MoECo, Colciencias, the national government and the commercial sector have worked together to bring new sources of funding from the Colombian Budget General's Office, the private sector, international partners, as well as domestic and foreign donors, in order to finance STI projects and activities. There is, therefore, evidence of strong interest in the country in terms of supporting scientific production, innovation projects and technology development – all areas in which advocacy is paramount in order to ensure open access to publicly funded outputs.

In Uruguay, national scientific research takes place almost exclusively within the University of the Republic, which is entirely funded by the state, as described above. Private HEIs are focused exclusively on teaching, with very little research activity taking place. Substantial challenges therefore remain in terms of addressing the STI agenda.

In Chile, it is worth noting the second phase (2006–2011) of the Programme for Improvement of Quality and Equity in Higher Education (MECESUP2), established by Resolution No. 6138/2013 (Ministerio de Educación Nacional, 2013) and facilitated by research funds managed by CONICYT, which funded actions for the improvement of academic innovation in accredited public universities. In terms of the arrangements around calls for participation and agreements concluded by the state through the MECESUP2, the intellectual property policy adopted was that the copyright on project outputs should be transferred to implementing institutions. That is, the default intellectual property approach adopted by this programme is to limit access to the knowledge produced (through restrictive, full copyright provisions), unless the implementing institution assumes a different stance and decides to adopt an open licensing strategy. In this regard, it is worth noting that the MECESUP2 funded a project implemented by the Universidad Austral de Chile, which has a focus on the design, creation and management of OER among students in the Health Sciences. This project is being implemented in collaboration with Brazilian technologists who are experts in OER and distance education and national scholars with expertise in technologies for learning and distance education. In this case, the decision has been taken to openly license the OER produced. Initiatives of this kind provide an opportunity to promote OER within programmes that aim to support academic and curricular innovation (Beltrán Delgado & Lehmann Preisler, 2014).

CONICYT has programmes promoting human capital formation and the strengthening of scientific and technological bases in Chile. Their commitment to this area is evidenced in the fact that its budget increased by 227% from 2006–2013 (CONICYT, 2014). This has enabled it to double the sponsorship of projects dedicated to basic research. It has funded more than 40 research centres to develop their work in association with other institutions, provided financial aid to around 3 500 doctoral students, enhanced equipment and scientific infrastructure, and promoted international scientific cooperation (CONICYT, 2014).

While there has been substantial investment in scientific and technological research in Chilean higher education, CONICYT has adopted the MECESUP2 approach to intellectual property policy on investigation outcomes, in that the intellectual property becomes an asset of the implementing institutions. There are opportunities to promote openness in Chilean higher education in the context of this increased funding. Funding mechanisms and lines of action have been defined, but there is a need for more awareness about openness in the context of knowledge management and intellectual property.

Variety of manifestations of Open Education policies originating from HEIs or state funding agencies

Phase 1 of the investigation revealed that there are few or no specific national and/or institutional policies aimed at promoting Open Education in the higher education sectors of the countries surveyed. The Colombian National Strategy for Open Educational Resources (REDA), approved in 2012 by MoECo, does play a role and is aimed at promoting OER in higher education in Colombia, but the commitments adopted by the science and technology body as part of LA Referencia are yet to materialise in the form of policy or legislation on Open Access or OER.

According to information shared by MoECo[34] in 2014, there was an initiative within Colombia to publish a national framework on open access to knowledge, which could be an additional boost to the national REDA approach. In addition, MoECo has been working on an Open Access Bill. This activity suggests that Open Education policy development at state level in Colombia holds promise, but is still in a nascent stage of development as there had been no development in this regard at the time of writing.

While Colombia has the REDA framework, there is still much work to be done in the policy development sphere, particularly at the institutional level. None of the four Colombian universities examined showed evidence of a uniform policy framework for addressing the creation and reuse of educational resources. The Centre for Innovation in Technology and Education at the University of the Andes runs the Conecta-TE[35] portal that aims to connect professors with the university community in order to guide educational practices and provide a repository of educational resources developed by different faculties. This repository operates a variable licensing strategy, determined by the faculty or course for which the materials were created, suggesting that there is no university-defined strategy to promote Open Education policy, particularly in OER.

In contrast to the situation in Colombia and Chile, Uruguay actually seems to present an enabling environment for Open Education. The University of the Republic, which, as mentioned earlier, accounts for the vast majority of the country's total student enrolment, is the main site for the promotion of Open Access and the development of OER. The Central

---

34 Presentation during a workshop with Open Education experts and activists from Latin America, held in Bogota, Colombia, 4 September 2014.
35 http://conectate.uniandes.edu.co/index.php/conecta-te/el-portal

Board Council, the university's governing body, is internally promoting the adoption of policies intended to implement more open use of virtual resources, the use of Free and Open Source Software (FOSS), the creation of an Open Access repository, and the development of a proposal to foster Open Access in academic production.[36]

From a policy perspective, the Academic Technical Support Department of the University of the Republic's Sectorial Commission on Teaching, which is responsible for implementing the Programme for the Development of Virtual Learning Environments, operates under a notably broad definition of Open Education. In their approach, the Open Education ecosystem of the university consists of: (1) the use of OER; (2) the development of Open Educational Practices; (3) the use of FOSS; and (4) openly licensed publications.[37] The institution is currently engaged in two European Union-funded OER projects: LATin Project[38] and the Mercosur Network for Accessibility and Collaborative Creation of Open Educational Resources (*Red Mercosur para la Accesibilidad y la generación Colaborativa de Recursos Educativos Abiertos*, or REMAR),[39] both aimed at higher education. LATin Project focuses on creating textbooks that can be copied, printed, modified and distributed freely and legally over the internet. It also seeks to facilitate the cultural and linguistic adaptation of texts according to the region where they are used. REMAR aims to offer Latin American teachers a virtual communication space to share experiences and tools that facilitate the use of accessible educational content.

While the country does not appear to have a centralised policy for all HEIs, other "grassroot"-type OER programmes are appearing in Uruguay. These include the Wikipedia Project[40] and the OER Network[41] established as part of *Plan Ceibal*.[42] The Wikipedia Project in Education began in November 2012. It has been developed by the Uruguayan Education Training Board and *Plan Ceibal* in partnership with the Wikimedia Foundation and is supported by the National Administration of Public Education. Its goal is to "create spaces for appropriation of technology in the field of teacher education",[43] using Wikipedia in teaching and learning processes.

The Uruguayan OER Network "aims to promote the building of a Network of Centres for Teacher Education to create, share and reuse Digital Educational Resources"[44] that are part of a shared national repository. This initiative is part of *Plan Ceibal*'s renewed strategy, which aims to reposition teacher training centres with a focus on the creation of open educational content. These initiatives are implemented with the support of state education entities and are aimed at establishing Open Education principles in initial teacher education. Thus the nature of OER management and extent of implementation in Uruguay is very encouraging, suggesting an enabling environment for any future activity.

---

36 See the institutional policy documents: Resolution No. 4 of 2013 of *Consejo Directivo Central of UdelaR*, Resolution No. 5 of 2013 of *Consejo Directivo Central*, and the University of the Republic Institutional Repository website (https://www.colibri.udelar.edu.uy).

37 Presentation during a workshop, conducted during the second phase of the project, with Open Education experts and activists from Latin America, held in Bogota, Colombia, 4 September 2014.

38 http://latinproject.org/

39 https://proyectoremar.wordpress.com/

40 https://outreach.wikimedia.org/wiki/Education/Countries/Uruguay

41 http://www.ceibal.edu.uy/art%C3%ADculo/noticias/docentes/Lanzamiento-Formacion-Educativa

42 http://www.ceibal.edu.uy/

43 https://outreach.wikimedia.org/wiki/Education/Newsletter/June_2014/Wikipedia_Education_Project_in_Uruguay

44 http://www.ceibal.edu.uy/

The Chilean case stands in stark contrast to the contexts in Colombia and Uruguay. According to the Centre for Research in Education report, investment in libraries and resources in this country is low (Espinoza, 2012). Added to this, the national knowledge generation and management system is built upon a competitive, market-driven approach aimed at private profit. None of the four HEIs examined had specific and articulated guidelines on OER and/or open access to educational, scientific and academic production.

It does therefore appear that the absence of Open Access and/or OER policies in Chilean universities may be linked to the commercialisation model of higher education. The current educational reform provides opportunities to enact openness within collaborative production and knowledge management models. An advocacy plan focused on funding structures, such as the National Commission for Scientific and Technological Research (CONICYT), could be useful in promoting the open agenda.

Raising awareness of Open Access and OER amongst the key stakeholders in Chilean higher education is an essential first step towards providing equitable access to affordable learning and teaching resources. Chile's commitment to LA Referencia can also be leveraged, since there has not been much progress in developing state policies on open access to publicly funded scientific publications. As the LA Referencia structure relies on government commitment, it may be an advisable strategy to explore in order to push the government to comply with the commitments made as part of this regional initiative.

Conclusion and recommendations

The Latin American context is complex and extremely diverse, but it is hoped that the analysis undertaken in Colombia, Uruguay and Chile can help to foster a better understanding of the Open Education movement in the region and provide suggestions for possible ways forward. These three countries all provide Open Education advocacy opportunities that have the potential to make a positive impact on higher education research, teaching and learning in those countries in the medium and long term.

In Colombia, the REDA framework provides a good starting point to boost transformation. Uruguay has an exceptionally enabling environment, conducive to the promotion of national Open Education policy. Chile, despite its well-established private higher education system, has started seeing a resurgence in the public approach to education in the context of its forthcoming educational reform, which also provides opportunities for advocacy. In each of these countries, the LA Referencia initiative provides a vehicle for the articulation of open policies at both institutional and national level, particularly as relates to scientific production derived from public investment. The countries will undoubtedly be enriched if there is a comprehensive action plan to raise awareness about Open Education and the potential benefits it can bring to society.

After more than a decade of Open Education initiatives around the world, there is now an imperative to develop a roadmap to drive the development of policy to support Open Education. Based on the outcomes of this study, the following recommendations are proposed:

1. Foster and strengthen networks among Latin American civil society organisations[45] promoting Open Education in order to enhance regional dialogue, make experiences visible, collect data and boost processes and initiatives addressing Open Education. Networks of this kind could build on and strengthen international initiatives such as the Open Policy Network, localising efforts and entering into more direct dialogue with partners.

2. Engage higher education stakeholders – government entities for education administration and financing, HEIs, teacher groups and unions, research groups, student movements, etc. – by undertaking academic research that demonstrates what is needed to develop open policies within HEIs, implement support networks, and create synergies for the development and implementation of OER and Open Access.

3. Articulate public expenditure indicators and make requisite data openly available in order to evaluate the impact of public expenditure on educational, academic and scientific production. This will help to facilitate the evaluation of investment and dissemination policies regulating access to affordable and good-quality learning and research materials.

4. Promote open policies and mandates in public-funded calls for projects on STI, so that their outputs are shared on an Open Access and OER basis.

5. Designate bottom-up mobilisation strategies with the aim of establishing the need to include a discussion on Open Education in the public agenda. These strategies could be associated with international initiatives such as Open Access Week,[46] Open Education Week[47] and the Open Government Partnership,[48] which articulates stakeholder relationships and has oversight mechanisms for civil society.

6. Articulate a strategy to promote top-down policies where local stakeholders can collaborate on the agenda promoted by local civil society groups and LA Referencia management in order to understand local commitments and develop action plans to promote LA Referencia.

7. Develop a visibility and communication strategy for existing initiatives in the region through education forums in which different stakeholders showcase their Open Education projects. In this context, opportunities would be created for sharing lessons learned, challenges and success stories of local Open Education initiatives with a large number of educational institutions, government entities and teachers.

8. Undertake economic studies in the region to provide insight into the economic benefits of using OER and implementing Open Access practice.

These recommendations present possible pathways for providing equitable access to affordable and locally relevant research, teaching and learning resources.

---

45 During Phase 1 of this study, the existence of a few civil society organisations working on the issue was identified, which is a starting point to promote a Latin American network.
46 http://openaccessweek.org/
47 http://www.openeducationweek.org/
48 http://www.opengovpartnership.org/

Acknowledgements

Thanks are due to Natalia Duarte, who was instrumental in the initiation of the research, particularly during Phases 1 and 2 of this study. Thanks are also due to Carolina Botero for her unconditional support, constant guidance and thorough review throughout the development of this analysis. Special thanks are extended to the experts and activists from the region who participated in Phase 3 of the project, contributing with their input, validations and recommendations: Pilar Sáenz, Ulises Hernández, Marcela Hernández, Juan Carlos Bernal, Patricia Díaz, Werner Westermann, Silvia Nakano, Débora Sebriam and Carolina Rossini. Finally, thank you to the Research on Open Educational Resources for Development Network Hub team, particularly Cheryl Hodgkinson-Williams and Michelle Willmers, for their input and review. Special thanks are also due to Carolina Botero, Carolina Rossini and Werner Westerman for providing final peer-review commentary.

References

Amiel, T. (2012). Educação aberta: configurando ambientes, práticas e recursos educacionais. In B. Santana, C. Rossini & N. L. Pretto (Eds.), *REA: Práticas colaborativas e políticas públicas*. São Paulo: Casa da Cultura Digital. Retrieved from http://aberta.org.br/livrorea/artigos/wp-content/uploads/2012/05/REA-amiel.pdf

Amiel, T. & Santos, K. (2013). Uma análise dos termos de uso de repositórios de recursos educacionais digitais no Brasil. *Trilha Digital, 1*, 118–133.

Atkins, D. E., Brown, J. S. & Hammond, A. L. (2007). *A review of the Open Educational Resources (OER) movement: Achievements, challenges, and new opportunities*. Menlo Park, CA: The William and Flora Hewlett Foundation. Retrieved from http://cohesion.rice.edu/Conferences/Hewlett/emplibrary/A%20Review%20of%20the%20Open%20Educational%20Resources%20(OER)%20Movement_BlogLink.pdf

Babini, D. (2011). Acceso abierto a la producción científica de América Latina y el Caribe. Identificación de principales instituciones para estrategias de integración regional. *Revista CTS, 6(17)*, 31–56. Retrieved from http://eprints.rclis.org/15574/1/babini_EDITADO_FINAL.pdf

Beltrán Delgado, A. & Lehmann Preisler, P. (2014). UACh construirá Recursos Educativos Abiertos en Salud a través del Fondo de Innovación Académica. *Noticias UACh*. Retrieved from https://protect-za.mimecast.com/s/19b5BnH45noGuM, http://noticias.uach.cl/principal.php?pag=noticia-externo&cod=77936

Centro de Estudios Consorcio de Universidades del Estado de Chile. (2014). *Análisis Ley de Presupuesto de educación Superior*. Santiago, Chile: Centro de Estudios. Retrieved from http://uestatales.cl/cue/sites/default/files/documentacion/Análisis%20Ley%20de%20Presupuesto%20Educación%20Superior%202015.pdf

Centro de Innovación Educativa. (n.d.). *Colombia avanza con la implementación de los Centros de Innovación Educativa*. Bogotá, Colombia: Actualidad. Retrieved from http://www.colombiaaprende.edu.co/html/micrositios/1752/w3-article-337962.html

Collazo, M. & Pebé, P. (2004). *Sistema Nacional de Educación Superior de la República Oriental del Uruguay*. Montevideo, Uruguay: Proyecto Tuning – América Latina 2004–2005. Retrieved from http://tuning.unideusto.org/tuningal/images/stories/presentaciones/uruguay_doc.pdf

CONICYT (Consejo Nacional de Ciencia y Tecnología). (2014). *Memoria de Gestión 2010-2013*. Santiago, Chile: Comisión Nacional de Investigación Científica y Tecnológica. Retrieved from http://www.conicyt.cl/wp-content/uploads/2012/07/MEMORIA-CONICYT-2010-2013.pdf

Contrera, C. (2008). La educación superior en Uruguay. *Revista da Avaliação da Educação Superior, 13(2)*, 533–554. Retrieved from http://www.SciELO.br/pdf/aval/v13n2/13.pdf

Dos Santos, A. I. (2011). *Open Educational Resources in Brazil: State-of-the-art, challenges and prospects for development and innovation*. Paris: UNESCO Institute for Information Technologies in Education. Retrieved from https://oerknowledgecloud.org/sites/oerknowledgecloud.org/files/3214695.pdf

Espinoza, O. (2012). *Fortalezas y debilidades del sistema educacional chileno: una mirada crítica*. Santiago, Chile: Centro de Investigación en Educación. Retrieved from http://www.cie-ucinf.cl/download/position_papers_del_cie/El%20Sistema%20Educacional%20Chileno%20Una%20Mirada%20Critica%20Final%20OE.pdf

Frango, S. I., Ochoa, X., Pérez Casas, A. & Rodés, V. (2013). *Percepciones, actitudes y prácticas respecto a los libros de texto, digitales y en formatos abiertos por parte de estudiantes de universidades de América Latina*. Ecuador: LATin Project. Retrieved from http://www.br-ie.org/pub/index.php/wcbie/article/download/1893/1656

Inamorato, A., Cobo, C. & Costa, C. (2012). *Open Educational Resources: Cases from European and Latin American higher education*. Oxford: Proyecto OportUnidad. Retrieved from http://www.oportunidadproject.eu/COMPENDIO_REA_TRILINGUE.pdf

Ministerio de Educación. (n.d.). *Financiamiento institucional*. Santiago, Chile: Ministerio de Educación. Retrieved from http://www.mecesup.cl/index2.php?id_seccion=4963&id_portal=59&id_contenido=28082

Ministerio de Educación. (2014). *Panorama de la Educación 2014*. Montevideo, Uruguay: Ministerio de Educación de Uruguay. Retrieved from http://www.mec.gub.uy/innovaportal/file/11078/1/mec-panorama-educacion-2014.pdf

Ministerio de Educación Nacional. (2010). *Financiación de la educación superior*. Bogotá, Colombia: Ministerio de Educación Nacional. Retrieved from http://www.mineducacion.gov.co/1621/w3-article-235797.html

Ministerio de Educación Nacional. (2012). *Estrategia Nacional de Recursos Educativos Digitales Abiertos*. Bogotá, Colombia: Graficando Servicios Integrados. Retrieved from http://www.colombiaaprende.edu.co/html/home/1592/articles-313597_reda.pdf

Ministerio de Educación Nacional. (2013). *Resolution No. 6138*. Santiago, Chile: Ministerio de Educación. Retrieved from http://www.mineduc.cl/usuarios/MECESUP/File/2013/convocatoria2013/rex6138_bases-CDPM.pdf

Ministerio de Educación Nacional. (2014). *Estadísticas de educación superior*. Bogotá, Colombia: Ministerio de Educación Nacional. Retrieved from http://www.mineducacion.gov.co/sistemasdeinformacion/1735/articles-212350_Estadisticas_de_Educacion_Superior_.pdf

Ministerio de Educación Nacional (2015). Colombia, un país que avanza hacia el mejoramiento de las oportunidades de acceso a educación superior. *Boletín educación superior en cifras, 5*. Retrieved from http://www.mineducacion.gov.co/1759/articles-350451_recurso_4.pdf

OECD (Organisation for Economic Co-operation and Development). (2014). *PISA 2012 results in focus. What 15-year-olds know and what they can do with what they know*. Paris: Organisation for Economic Co-operation and Development. Retrieved from http://www.oecd.org/pisa/keyfindings/pisa-2012-results-overview.pdf

Republica Oriental del Uruguay. (2012). *Ley No. 19.043: Universidad Technológica Creación*. Montevideo, Uruguay: Republica Oriental del Uruguay. Retrieved from https://legislativo.parlamento.gub.uy/temporales/leytemp6682891.htm

Rodríguez Ponce, E. (2012). La educación superior en Chile y el rol del mercado: ¿culpable o inocente? Ingeniare. *Revista chilena de Ingeniería, 20(1)*, 126–135. Retrieved from http://dx.doi.org/10.4067/S0718-33052012000100013

Rossini, C. (2012). Brazilian policy on digital inclusion and access to digital creative contents. *Global Congress on Open Educational Resources, 2012*, 1–15. Retrieved from https://oerknowledgecloud.org/sites/oerknowledgecloud.org/files/Position%20paper%20ingl%C3%AAs%20(1).pdf

---

How to cite this chapter

Toledo, A. (2017). Open Access and OER in Latin America: A survey of the policy landscape in Chile, Colombia and Uruguay. In C. Hodgkinson-Williams & P. B. Arinto (Eds.), *Adoption and impact of OER in the Global South* (pp. 121–141). Retrieved from https://doi.org/10.5281/zenodo.602781

Corresponding author: Amalia Toledo <adharra222@gmail.com>

Chapter 5

Co-creation of OER by teachers and teacher educators in Colombia

María del Pilar Sáenz Rodríguez, Ulises Hernandez Pino and Yoli Marcela Hernández

Summary

This chapter, based on research conducted by members of the Collaborative Co-Creation of Open Educational Resources by Teachers and Teacher Educators in Colombia (coKREA) project, assesses whether and how a contextually based, bottom-up approach to the promotion and advocacy of Open Educational Resources (OER) – in which teachers are encouraged to collaboratively co-create resources – supports the adoption of OER in Colombian schools.

The study, conducted with public school teachers in southwestern Colombia, used a Participatory Action Research approach, in which the object of study is not external to the researchers, as the social practices under study are performed by the same subjects who are conducting the investigation. This allows teachers to identify possibilities of OER in their own educational practices, as well as the conditions required for their adoption, based on collective thinking processes immersed in their own sociocultural contexts.

A call for research participation was issued to teachers who were experienced in using information and communication technologies (ICT) in their teaching. The data collection process was undertaken through administration of a series of online questionnaires (completed by 19 teachers), a survey (completed by 248 teachers), webinars (in which 28 teachers connected and 14 participated actively), unstructured telephone interviews (with 30 teachers) and a series of focus group discussions (with a cohort of 49 teacher educators, teachers and students). A face-to-face workshop was also conducted with teachers to provide an introduction to OER, after which they identified challenges to incorporating OER into their pedagogical practices and discussed their own OER-related activities. ▶

> Data analysis followed a rigorous Grounded Theory process and involved an "approach stage" to identify key teacher practices; a "deepening stage" to uncover relationships and affinities; and a "condensation phase" to surface a theory of change.
>
> The main finding in this study is that teachers create and use OER more effectively when they receive flexible and continuous pedagogical support that: (1) fosters pedagogical practices drawing upon constructivist models, so that teachers and students have an active role in the creation and recreation of knowledge; (2) promotes open licensing that respects authors' rights, but allows for legal reuse and adaptation; and (3) facilitates the use of ICT available in schools and at home to access, create and share OER. Similarly, it was found that this pedagogical support generated better outcomes when teacher teams work around a project in their schools instead of attending general training sessions on OER.
>
> The key recommendation is that pedagogical support be provided to encourage team-based teacher OER development projects within schools.

Acronyms and abbreviations

CA	Axial Category (from Spanish acronym)
CN	Core Category (from Spanish acronym)
coKREA	Collaborative Co-Creation of Open Educational Resources by Teachers and Teacher Educators in Colombia
CS	Selective Category (from Spanish acronym)
FOSS	Free and Open Source Software
ieRed	Educational Research Network comprised of schoolteachers, university professors and others professionals related to the education sector. Teacher educators associated with this study belonged to this network.
ICT	information and communication technologies (*Tecnologías de la Información y las Comunicaciones* [TIC] in Spanish)
OEP	Open Educational Practices (*Prácticas Educativas Abiertas* [PEA] in Spanish)
OER	Open Educational Resources (*Recursos Educativos Abiertos* [REA] or *Recursos Educativos Digitales Abiertos* [REDA] in Spanish)
PAR	Participatory Action Research (*Investigación – Acción Participación* [IAP] in Spanish)
ROER4D	Research on Open Educational Resources for Development project
UNESCO	United Nations Educational, Scientific and Cultural Organization

Introduction

The 21st century has been marked by deep social changes associated with the rise of a new knowledge-based economy which requires that individuals and organisations be capable of mastering technologies in order to innovate and constantly adapt to a rapidly changing global environment (Castells, 2000). There is a global commitment to develop these new social skills in order to achieve effective and efficient management of knowledge through information and communication technologies (ICT).

In the field of education, particularly in Latin America, ICT-related policies have been proposed from three perspectives: (1) economic: to be competitive as a nation to achieve greater prosperity and quality of life; (2) social: closing digital gaps to reduce social divides, and expanding the possibilities of participation in an interconnected world; and (3) educational: changing teaching practices to help students develop skills in line with the needs of emerging markets (Sunkel, Trucco & Möller, 2011; Valdivia, 2008).

The Colombian case has not been different. Since 2000, economic and social policies have promoted access to ICT and quality education as strategic priorities for national development (Colombia Departamento Nacional de Planeación, 2000). In fact, the government's projection is that by 2019, "all Colombians [will be] connected and informed, making efficient use of ICTs to improve social inclusion and competitiveness" [author translation] (Colombia Ministerio de Comunicaciones, 2008, p.4). Thus, activities in the education sector have focused on providing technological infrastructure; digital literacy and the appropriation of ICT for teaching and school management; and the creation of educational content and access thereto through online portals (Colombia Ministerio de Educación Nacional, 2013). In terms of the challenges that have been experienced in Colombia, Open Educational Resources (OER) are also recognised as an important part of addressing the access and quality challenges in education experienced by countries transitioning from developing to developed status, as reflected in Daniel, Kanwar and Uvalić-Trumbić's (2006) analysis of the future of higher education.

By opening access to resources created globally, as well as providing opportunities for revision and reuse of those resources, OER are seen as a potential mechanism to address existing quality concerns. Apart from impacting the quality of learning materials, it is claimed that the quality of teaching practices and the quality of learning outcomes can also be improved by opening up the content creation process for formal peer review and informal public scrutiny (Petrides, Jimes, Middleton-Detzner & Howell, 2010). Moreover, Wiley, Hilton III, Ellington and Hall (2012) suggest that the utilisation of open textbooks can reduce the overall cost of curricular resources by over 50% in middle and high school sectors. The development and use of OER and their potential to expand access, decrease costs and improve the quality of education is therefore one of the emerging issues in educational discourse today, particularly in developing countries where there is a dearth of quality materials (Kanwar, Kodhandaraman & Umar, 2010).

Current adoption of OER by teachers and institutions in the Global South does, however, seem to be marginal. Hatakka comments that while "OER initiatives are very commendable and needed, open content is not being used by educational organizations in developing countries (or rather the usage of the free resources is low)" (2009, p.1). There is therefore a need to understand the factors that impact upon the adoption of OER in the Global South along sociocultural, educational and technosocial dimensions.

Sociocultural context

The global OER movement is located predominantly in the geopolitical North and most OER programmes, as well as OER websites, portals and delivery channels, are located in Northern institutions (Zancanaro, Todesco & Ramos, 2015). Given that educational systems in the North have an advantage in terms of institutional maturity and the methods and processes employed in curricular resource design and development, their resources may *prima facie* appear superior. OER-based educational approaches have the potential to further strengthen the hegemony of the North in the global educational sphere by expanding the diffusion and reach of Northern OER (Cobo, 2013).

Another important consideration for local content stems from the diverse backgrounds of learners. Learner characteristics in the Global South are likely to be quite different from those of learners in the North, reflecting, among other things, the diversity in their prior learning contexts and learning experiences as well as their sociocultural backgrounds (Gun, 2003). This situation is reinforced in the Colombian context – a country with wide cultural diversity, which creates considerable challenges for the recognition and strengthening of local ethnic identities from a content and methodological perspective.

Most openly licensed educational resources are in English (Krelja Kurelovic, 2016), but only 1% of the Colombian population is considered bilingual, and only 6.5% of higher education students have a good level of oral and written English comprehension (Sánchez, 2013). In the case of Colombia, the dearth of Spanish-language OER may therefore hinder the adoption of OER.

Furthermore, previous research in the Global South has noted the existence of socioeconomic, cultural, institutional and national issues that inhibit the realisation of OER (Ngimwa, 2010). Hence, there is a need to explore how these issues could be addressed to overcome the challenges inherent in the adoption of OER in Southern contexts in general and in Colombia in particular.

Educational context

The relatively modern educational philosophy of constructivism argues that learning is social in nature, so it is appropriate for teaching processes to promote constant interaction among individuals. The goal is to seek methodologies that promote learning through social exchange and use teaching content strongly related to the local culture (Coll et al., 2007). This perspective argues that curricular resources need to be revised for local needs and contexts, as there are no universal benchmarks of quality (Moreno, Anaya, Benavides, Hernandez & Hernández, 2011).

In a South African study, Sapire and Reed (2011) explored whether collaborative design and redesign of materials can enhance quality while containing time and resource costs, and whether such collaboration encourages uptake of OER as well as further redesign to accommodate the needs of particular teachers and students. They concluded that effective collaborative design and redesign of existing materials contributes to solving these challenges, while allowing these materials to be used in a wide range of contexts (Sapire & Reed, 2011).

In their study of the Community College Open Textbook Project, Petrides, Jimes, Middleton-Detzner, Walling and Weiss (2011) found that access to OER and the possibility of collaborative creation using these resources encourages teachers to interact with each other and improve their educational practices. Furthermore, these interactions between teachers and students contribute to breaking existing educational paradigms in which teaching is done in a class to transmit the knowledge of the teacher to the students, learning is achieved through memorisation of data by the student, and the validity of the knowledge is determined by the hierarchy of the teacher. In light of these results, there is a need to examine the factors and processes that would determine whether a similar impact could be obtained in a Global South country such as Colombia, given the differences in overall institutional and learning contexts.

In Colombia there is a long-standing tradition in education that the use of existing resources – as opposed to the production or creation of resources by teachers – is paramount, resulting in ongoing requests that students purchase textbooks (Torres & Moreno, 2008). Until recently, neither the government nor educational institutions had thought of utilising incentives to encourage teachers to create and share their own materials. In this regard, it is worth noting that in 2014 and 2015 a national initiative was developed to involve teachers in the creation of digital educational resources for public access.[1]

Within this context, it is an important consideration that Colombia is a country with a strong oral tradition which favours knowledge-sharing through personal interaction over formal and academic writing (Hernandez, 2015). This predominance of oral culture can hinder teachers' processes of planning, structuring and producing educational resources (Castro, Catebiel & Hernandez, 2005a; Lieberman, 2013).

Another noteworthy feature of the Colombian environment is that educational policies (or any new innovation, such as OER) are generally received with suspicion, resulting in multiple forms of resistance to prevent or delay their implementation. An example of this is the pronouncement against the policies of the Ministry of National Education presented in July 2016 by ASOINCA, one of the teacher unions in the region, in which ideas such as "ICT are a tool that the State comes implementing to displace teachers with programs such as *telesecundaria* where a teacher is no longer needed but a system operator" [author translation] (p.2) are being used as an argument for teachers to "not attend meetings and trainings that are initiated [by the state] to impose these programmes when we clearly know that they threaten public education, our acquired rights and job stability" [author translation] (p.3).

Traditionally, educational policies are not developed in consultation with stakeholders in the schooling system, meaning that teachers' expectations, needs and knowledge of local realities are largely ignored (Fullan, 2002). This lack of recognition of the teachers' role in decision-making processes, among other things, keeps them tied to their traditional forms of instruction, even when they engage in training and other processes of professional development led by the government (Benavides, 2015). It is therefore important to promote bottom-up approaches for the adoption of OER in schools through projects that take into account local realities as well as teachers' expectations and contextual needs.

Technosocial context

Since 2000, there have been a series of government programmes providing Colombian schools with computers, digital devices and teacher training. Impact studies of these programmes evaluating their influence on education quality have yielded conflicting results (Barrera & Linden, 2009; Rodríguez, Sánchez & Márquez, 2011). For example,

---

1   http://www.colombiaaprende.edu.co/html/micrositios/1752/w3-propertyname-3020.html

the Colombian teacher training programmes in ICT, though important in terms of teacher exposure to multiple approaches towards utilising technology in the classroom, have failed to make an impact on teaching practices (Hernández, 2015; Hernandez & Benavides, 2012; Narváez & Calderón, 2016) This results in a situation in which ICT is reserved exclusively for information transmission in the classroom rather than stimulating information-creation processes and fostering student creativity (Sáenz, Hernandez & Hernández, 2014).

The situation suggests that a complex set of techno-pedagogic skills (Harris, Mishra & Koehler, 2009) are needed to advance teaching practice and that there is a need for research to understand the influence of ICT in the adoption of OER by teachers. Within this context, there is not only an imperative to ensure availability and access to technological infrastructure and educational content, but also a need for teachers to identify the advantages and learning possibilities of new platforms and open resources (Kaplún, 2005; Moreno et al., 2011; Watson, 2001).

With regards to connectivity, public government reports reveal positive internet access statistics,[2] but different parts of the country are still struggling to receive optimal, continuous service. This is particularly a factor in rural areas, which may also suffer from unreliable electricity supply (Hernandez & Benavides, 2012; Narváez & Calderón, 2016). In this respect, even though an increasing number of users are connecting to the internet using mobile devices, this does not necessarily mean that sufficient infrastructure is in place in schools to ensure uninterrupted access to virtual environments and online platforms for accessing educational resources.

Conceptual and theoretical framework

This study draws upon the United Nations Educational, Scientific and Cultural Organization (UNESCO) definition of OER as "teaching, learning and research materials in any medium, digital or otherwise, that reside in the public domain or have been released under an open license that permits no-cost access, use, adaptation and distribution by others with no or limited restrictions" (UNESCO, 2012, p.1). Within the context of this definition, it is important to emphasise two aspects that differentiate OER from other resources: (1) the explicit permission of use and redistribution at no cost (Lozano, Ramírez & Celaya, 2010); and (2) the ability to use or adapt them as components of other resources (Gértrudix, Álvarez, Galisteo del Valle, Gálvez de la Cuesta & Gértrudix, 2007; Moreno et al., 2011).

While content published on the internet may be publicly available, meaning that anyone has the right to see or hear the information (Botero, 2011; Butcher, 2015), copyright restrictions impose limitations in terms of third-party copying, adaptation and distribution. In order to conduct activities of this kind without the express permission of the author or copyright holder, an open licence is required – the terms of which will determine the extent and nature of possible reuse (Schmitz, 2009).

The ability to adapt resources is central to the idea of OER. When teachers take an OER and modify it, they compare the content, methodologies and cultural aspects implicit in the resource, appraising it in light of their educational needs. This process allows teachers

---

2   http://www.mintic.gov.co/portal/604/w3-article-11345.html

to analyse and improve their pedagogical practices (de los Arcos, Farrow, Pitt, Weller & McAndrew, 2016; Petrides et al., 2011). OER are also, in some instances, adapted and distributed by students (Grinsztajn, Steiznberg, Córdoba & Miguez, 2015). We thus see a move towards an educational paradigm in which teachers and students can both operate as agents in creating knowledge in a more equal fashion – a principle which forms the basis of Open Educational Practices (OEP) (Hegarty, 2015; Stagg, 2014).

A review of approximately 150 academic journal articles on the subject[3] shows that most teachers working on OER in the Latin American context are located in Spanish and Mexican universities, and few resources are being produced for the basic (K–12) education sector. In this review, it is noteworthy that users assume OER to be any publicly available online educational resources, usually without being explicit or clear about the concept of legal or technical openness (Cedillo, Romero, Peralta, Toledo & Reyes, 2010; Pinzón, Poveda & Pérez, 2015; Rodríguez, Tellez & Vértiz, 2010). The word "open" is used as a synonym for "free access", ignoring the legal permission for others to adapt, remix and share these resources through open licensing provisions, even though this is the key aspect of UNESCO's definition of OER.

Key issues of concern raised in the OER research studies reviewed include: search and selection criteria, quality assessment criteria, technical compatibility and financial sustainability associated with the production of these type of resources (Contreras, 2010; Glasserman & Ramírez, 2014). The issue of public access to OER through repositories and the creation of indexing mechanisms is also a matter of keen interest (Gértrudix et al., 2007; Sanz, Sánchez & Dodero, 2011).

In Colombia, two government initiatives to promote OER uptake have been implemented. The first was a programme called *Recursos Educativos Digitales Abiertos* (REDA) (Open Educational Digital Resources) which was active until 2016 and which aimed to strengthen and bolster the production, management and use of OER in higher education institutions. For this purpose, a platform was created to support institutional repositories and a metadata standard was adapted for OER publication (Colombia Ministerio de Educación Nacional, 2012). Secondly, between 2014 and 2016, national government financed the development of digital OER for K–12 through Regional Educational Innovation Centers.[4] However, the idea of openness in these cases is limited to producing resources which are free to the user rather than integrating open licensing and, by extension, promoting other characteristics of OER such as modifying or remixing.

Despite these efforts on the part of government, it is unusual to find Colombian teachers integrating OER in their educational practices. In cases where OER are used, it is generally only as an additional information source and not as a medium to generate new interactions in the classroom in terms of content selection, revision and creation (Anaya, Hernandez & Hernández, 2010). In this sense, teachers' use of any supplementary resources seems to be replicating the usual instructivist mode they adopt when using school textbooks (Glasserman & Ramírez, 2014).

It must be taken into account that the relevance of OER for education goes beyond the ability to legally access, share and distribute content. Its principal value lies in the affordance

---

3   Articles were retrieved from the following repositories: http://redalyc.org, https://dialnet.unirioja.es and http://www.scielo.org.
4   http://www.colombiaaprende.edu.co/html/micrositios/1752/w3-propertyname-3020.html

for anyone to take advantage of open licensing characteristics – encapsulated in Wiley's 5Rs (retain, reuse, revise, remix and redistribute)[5] – to stimulate learning processes through collaboratively creating and recreating information in the classroom. Within this context, OER can become a mechanism for engaging with and recording the traditions and characteristics of a local context, and are not merely closed, unidirectional products for delivering information (Sáenz et al., 2014). As such, pedagogical practices that create, reuse, revise, remix, retain and redistribute OER are understood in the context of this study as OEP.

The Open Educational Quality Initiative, an international network in which UNESCO was a participant, defined OEP and its relation with OER as "practices which support the (re) use and production of OER through institutional policies, promote innovative pedagogical models, and respect and empower learners as co-producers on their lifelong learning path" (OPAL, 2011, p.12). Accordingly, DeRosa and Robison (2017) argue that in addition to free access to content, one of the affordances provided by OER is that students can assume the role of producers of the ideas which are circulating around the world. Therefore, in the context of this study, the adoption of OER is seen as part of a more encompassing set of OEP, as it enables reflection and transformation of teachers' pedagogical practices.

OER adoption and the new kinds of pedagogical approaches it enables rely on a complex set of legal mechanisms that facilitate open content sharing. In Colombia, copyright legislation is framed in the tradition of European continental law, meaning that legal protection in intellectual creation lies with the author. There is also no legal doctrine of "fair use" – a feature of the American legal system which makes provision for educational use of copyrighted materials – making provision for use of copyright-protected content in a classroom setting. Domestic copyright law does establish a list of limitations and exceptions to copyright under certain conditions pertaining to time, manner and specific place (usually associated with non-profit use), but few exceptions refer to the educational process (Colombia Congreso de la República, 1982). The exceptions allowed currently refer to quoting fragments of a work; photocopying elements of a work for teaching or evaluation; or communicating a work in an educational institution to the educational community (Comunidad Andina de Naciones, 1993).

Current copyright exceptions in Colombian copyright law do not address scenarios such as downloading images or videos from the internet and incorporating these into educational resources which are designed to be freely reused and redistributed. Neither do they address everyday practices such as electronic document sharing through online platforms such as blogs, or the modification and publication of a work as part of a learning exercise. Strengthening and promoting the global knowledge commons through alternative copyright approaches such as Creative Commons licensing is, therefore, essential (Lessig, 2004), particularly in the promotion of educational models focused on collaboration and the use of new technologies for the creation and recreation of contextualised knowledge (Hernández, Hernandez & Sáenz, 2014).

Studies like the ones conducted by Antúnez (1999), Castro, Catebiel and Hernandez (2005b) and Montero (2011) have found that daily teaching work is usually performed individually, showing that collaboration with other teachers in materials production is very unusual and that the engagement of teachers in communities of practice is rare.

---

5   https://opencontent.org/blog/archives/3221

Although multiple factors shape the nature of the teaching process, it is important to recognise that the isolated approach is promoted by an education system with a hierarchical and rigid organisational structure that does not give space, time or incentive to develop collaborative teaching practices (Castro et al., 2005b). Moreover, some teachers may also utilise the isolation factor to avoid questions about their knowledge, pedagogical approaches and teaching methods (Antúnez, 1999; Montero, 2011).

Learning and collaborative work among teachers commonly generates difficulties and resistance. However, when it is possible for teachers to work with others, conditions can be improved in order to ensure the continuity of any transformation processes affecting their teaching practices. According to Antúnez (1999), this occurs when a group provides emotional support and collective recognition, and contributes to the resolution of questions and problems in a timely fashion, providing an incentive to persist with the collaboration despite the difficulties encountered.

According to the literature review by Collazos, Muñoz and Hernández (2014), the essential components required for successful collaborative work are: positive interdependence, meaning that what affects one member also affects the rest of the group; personal responsibility, in which everyone in the group knows what their role is; interpersonal skills necessary to negotiate and resolve conflicts; and ongoing group evaluation.

This collaborative way of working is underpinned by Coll et al.'s (2007) constructivist conception of learning and teaching, based on the ideas of Vygotsky, Piaget and Ausubel. From this perspective, it is clear that learning is not an individual action, limited to the act of copying or reproducing concepts; teaching should therefore not focus on transmitting information, but on developing activities to enable people to reconstruct concepts through their previous knowledge and interaction with others. In this sense, learning leads to the creation of personal conceptions of knowledge, which makes it meaningful.

Developing pedagogical practices from a constructivist approach raises the need for educational resources with a licence that allows for adaptation and use with other resources, and which does not discriminate in terms of teacher or student activity. Therefore, OER can be seen as mediation tools aligned with the constructivist approach, facilitating the processes of creation and recreation of knowledge amongst multiple individuals.

Despite an increased focus on collaboration in the learning process, the existence of pedagogical perspectives such as constructivism, and government programmes in Colombia supporting the production of OER, most everyday educational processes focus on the idea of the unidirectional transmission of information. In the process of teacher training, it is actually quite typical that the curriculum is centred on developing individual competences rather than collaborative strategies, even though this procedure generates a lesser impact (Barrera & Linden, 2009; Benavides, 2015).

Getting teachers to align themselves with this constructivist approach implies not only providing training on technological, pedagogical and legal aspects, but also on offering continuous pedagogical support based on teachers' personal interests and promoting collaborative work between colleagues (Benavides, 2015). Pedagogical support constitutes a mentoring methodology in which a teacher or a professional with teaching experience undertakes a series of in-school meetings with other teachers or with a small group of teachers around a project or particular experience (Mogollón & Solano, 2011). The meetings are intended to provide advice on the design, planning, execution and recording of teaching and learning activities to be conducted by a teacher or group, so that the project or teaching experience not only achieves the expected outcome, but also constitutes a source of learning for other teachers (Huayta, Gómez, Atencio & Arias, 2008).

When working with teachers from the perspective of pedagogical support, there is mutual recognition and dialogue, providing possibilities for the exchange of views, experiences, beliefs, expectations and aspirations that come into play in educational practices, even though they are not necessarily consciously acknowledged by teachers (Restrepo, 2004). This approach implies that teacher facilitators need to acknowledge that teachers have tacit knowledge arising from their own experiences, which is valuable in the educational context in which they work and which may not directly match codified educational theories and methodologies. It also requires a dialogical encounter, which is the recognition from teachers that teacher facilitators can contribute to their teaching practices based on their knowledge and experiences (Martínez & González, 2010).

Pedagogical support is intended to broaden the perspective of teachers' pedagogical practice, offering theoretical and methodological perspectives through which to recognise the limits of their current teaching practices and identify possible ways to enhance them. In order to achieve this, the support process should consider the following activities, as proposed by Huayta et al. (2008): design and development together with teaching practices; design instruments for collecting and analysing information to assess outcomes and impacts achieved; provide emotional and educational support for teachers in order to assist them in persevering despite difficulties; and encourage review of their progress, outcomes and lessons learned through teaching events or academic publications.

The provision of pedagogical support to foster collaborative work among teachers and to promote teaching and learning from a constructivist approach using OER constituted the methodological basis of this research study. Therefore, the assumed principles are:

1. All content (both educational and other) contains in itself the values and ideologies of the society in which it is created. Therefore, in order to minimise the cultural influence of the North where the production of OER is currently focused, it is necessary that teachers in the Global South transform themselves from being educational content consumers to creators of these resources, incorporating the particularities of their sociocultural context.

2. Production of educational content is commonly carried out by teams of experts, which is not only insufficient to meet the demands of the education sector, but also means that resources typically have a universal perspective, which usually does not respond to the requirements and educational needs of teachers in particular local contexts. Therefore, in order to achieve a model of continuous, relevant and sustainable production of OER, teachers need to be introduced to collaborative processes of co-creation and publication.

3. To take optimal advantage of the potential of OER in education requires that teachers not only use these resources, but also undertake processes of contextualising, curating and co-creating educational resources as part of their usual pedagogical practice.

Bearing in mind the problems and context of the Colombian education system, as well as the general assumptions raised above, the broad objectives of this study are:

1. To study how a collaborative and local OER model can be embedded within the ecosystem of a teacher community in Colombia.
2. To understand how an "adaptation-curation-creation" OER model can contribute to effective use of OER for teacher development.

The primary research question that guided the study is: Whether and how does a contextual, bottom-up approach, in which teachers collaboratively and actively co-create resources, support the adoption of OER in Colombian schools?

In order to deepen and analyse the key dimensions raised in this study, the following research sub-questions were identified as key points of study and analysis:

1. What kind of processes would support a community of teachers in actively engaging with the creation and adaptation of a contextually situated and collaborative OER model?
2. What enabling conditions would encourage wider adoption by peers of contextually created OER within the community?
3. What new skills are required among teachers and teacher educators to adopt a new learning culture with OER?
4. How do local needs and contexts (local language, local culture, social issues, geographies, ecology, needs, aspirations, priorities, etc.) impact upon the universal (mostly defined through normative systems of the Global North) versus local notions of meaningfulness/quality of OER?
5. How do institutional and systemic factors in a public system, which are perceived as compartmentalised and hierarchical, interact with and influence the building of a participatory OER model within the government/public system?

The research presented in this study was undertaken under the auspices of the Collaborative Co-Creation of Open Educational Resources by Teachers and Teacher Educators in Colombia (coKREA) project,[6] hosted by the Karisma Foundation of Colombia. The name "coKREA" combines "co" (the Colombian country code which also functions as an abbreviation for "collaboration"), while the "K" stands for the Karisma Foundation, and the "REA" represents the Spanish acronym for OER. The project name was also chosen because "KREA" references the term "to create".

Methodology

Given the primary aim of establishing whether and how a contextual, bottom-up approach, in which teachers collaboratively and actively co-create resources, supports the adoption of OER in Colombian schools, it was necessary to adopt a methodology which supported a "bottom-up" investigation process that took place alongside teachers, rather than them being mere subjects of the research process (Restrepo, 2002). Participatory Action Research (PAR) (Kemmis & McTaggart, 2005) was therefore deemed to be the most appropriate methodology.

---

6   CoKREA project website: http://karisma.org.co/cokrea

The object of study in PAR focuses on human actions that are considered problematic or unacceptable for a social group, and which require a practical solution (Kemmis & McTaggart, 2005). Unlike other research methodologies, the object of study is not external to the researchers because the social practices under study are performed by the same subjects who are conducting the investigation (Elliott, 2000). Kemmis and McTaggart argue that "Three particular attributes are often used to distinguish participatory research from conventional research: shared ownership of research projects, community-based analysis of social problems, and an orientation toward community action" (2005, p.273). In other words, PAR provides "opportunities for co-developing processes *with* people rather than *for* people" (McIntyre, 2008, p.xii).

According to Elliott (2000), the theoretical construction of PAR implies that the participants involved in the research process deepen their understanding of the common sense guiding their actions. Elliott acknowledges that common sense is imprecise and vague when confronted with scientific theories, but the apparent imprecision is favourable in that it allows participants to identify the contradictions and complexities of the social practices under investigation, allowing them to make decisions conducive to more coherent action, which is the aim of this research process.

In PAR, the aim is not to produce models that can objectively predict the behavioural characteristics of the phenomena studied, as many scientific theories do. PAR is instead a substantive or a human action theory that is validated in conversation with participants and not directed to the deduction and verification of theoretical categories (Elliott, 2000).

PAR proposes a model of reflection and action iteratively determined with the participants, through the following phases (Elliott, 2000; Kemmis & McTaggart, 2005):

1. Diagnosis of the problem situation in the educational practice.
2. Formulation of action strategies to solve the problem.
3. Implementation and evaluation of strategies.
4. Diagnosis of new problem situations.

Finally, this methodology is founded on the recognition that collaborative work has more impact on human actions than individual work (Kemmis & McTaggart, 2005).

Addressing this research study through a PAR approach allowed teachers to identify possibilities of OER in their own educational practices, as well as the conditions required for their adoption, based on collective thinking processes immersed in their own contexts. In this way, it was intended that teachers approach and adopt OER-related concepts based on personal interest – not as a means to fulfil the requirement of a possible Colombian government policy or other in-house school policies. It is important to consider that, as proposed by Fullan (2002), processes of educational change require a deep commitment from people, which can be achieved by involving them in the definition and implementation of policies and programmes designed to achieve this objective.

Involving teachers as researchers of their own practices did, however, pose a challenge for the study design. First of all, because the rules governing a school teacher's work in Colombia do not include the allocation of time for research activities or strong incentives to be included in this type of process, it was difficult to find teacher-researchers at this education level. On the other hand, as evidenced by previous research on training processes for pedagogical appropriation of ICTs in southwest Colombia (Hernandez & Benavides,

2012), teachers are more interested in receiving training on ICT usage than pondering pedagogical views regarding these technologies. However, in this same research study it was also found that offering ICT training contributes to engaging teachers in reflexive processes relating to their own practice. This perspective, also proposed by Kaplún (2005), informed the processes adopted in this study.

Research site

This study was conducted with a group of teachers from public schools in southwestern Colombia, which includes the departments[7] of Valle del Cauca, Cauca, Nariño and Putumayo. This is a region of great geographical, cultural and socioeconomic diversity, where there are few cities, high levels of unsatisfied basic needs, and the main focus of economic activity is agriculture, livestock farming and mining.

The region was selected as the site for this study for the following reasons:

1. It is representative of the socioeconomic, cultural and technological conditions in large parts of Latin America.
2. It had the support of the Educational Research Network (ieRed) – a network of school and university teachers, researchers and teacher trainers involved in various teacher training programmes and projects in ICT – which facilitated the call for participation amongst teachers who are leaders in incorporating ICT in K–12 education.

Research participant selection process

As noted, subjects in a PAR process are the same individuals who are conducting the study to address their own practice. For this reason, the call for research participation was undertaken among school teachers in southwestern Colombia who were experienced in using ICT in their teaching practice. The call for participation was made through ieRed and was directed at teachers who had already attended government ICT training processes, thereby ensuring that they had some expertise in computer use and classroom teaching experience with technology.

To participate, teachers had to form groups of at least three individuals from the same school. In order to minimise resistance to teamwork, there were no restrictions placed on the collaborative teacher groups in terms of subject area or level of ICT expertise. However, some teachers opted not to participate in the study due to the condition of collaborative work.

Research process

The phases of the research process were as follows:

Phase 0: Call for participation and establishment of teacher teams.

---

7   Colombia is divided into 32 departments. These are in turn divided into municipalities.

Phase 1: Implementation of seven virtual seminars and a workshop with teacher educators in the city of Popayán aimed at providing an introduction to OER for the adoption, curation and development of these types of resources within educational practices; the objective of the PAR study; pedagogical approaches; Creative Commons licensing and Free and Open Source Software (FOSS).

Phase 2: Identification, along with the teachers, of the educational problems related to their pedagogical practices in response to which they could adopt, curate and create OER collaboratively and configure OEP with each group of teachers.

Phase 3: Collection of information (with teachers) about their own OER-related activities from the beginning and analysis thereof in light of the study's sub-questions. This phase occurred alongside each of the other phases and included meetings at the end of the research process to analyse and determine the conclusions drawn throughout the investigation.

Finally, another way in which teachers' reflections and learnings were collected throughout the research process was through coKREA's Audiovisual Memory sharing strategy, conceived to highlight ideas regarding processes, results and learnings through the voices of the teachers themselves, making it possible to expand the dialogue around Open Education. This strategy includes a series of videos that were circulated via social networks in the second half of 2016.[8]

Data collection

Considering the non-allocation of time for research activities of school teachers and the low initial interest in being researchers of their own pedagogical practice, the project coordination team developed and applied data collection instruments and carried out their initial processing. The intention was to reduce the number of meetings dedicated to reflection upon the actions taken to appropriate OER, and to optimise the short time that teachers voluntarily dedicated to this study; this was done in an attempt to sustain their interest in the process.

The following data collection instruments were used:

- Questionnaires: While questionnaires are commonly seen as an instrument administered to a sample of people to collect information on a specific topic and to analyse it in a quantitative way (Corral, 2010), in this research study questionnaires were designed with open questions to inquire about previous ideas from the virtual seminars and analyse this information in a qualitative way.
- Chat records: Chats allow one to examine what people say in written form during informal conversations. The recording of these conversations generates texts through which one can analyse the ideas expressed by people and the relationship they establish with others (Orellana & Sánchez, 2006).
- Interviews: Interviews are intentional conversations of limited duration which are specialised or focused on an issue of common interest (Deslauriers, 2004). In this

---

8   The audiovisual memory of the coKREA project can be found at https://karisma.org.co/cokrea/?p=1290.

study, interviews were used as a means to uncover the relationship between teachers' initial expectations about the project and their perceptions after their participation in the first research phase.

- Focus groups: Focus groups are interviews with a group of people. Their value lies in the fact that collective dialogue helps people to remember their actions, specify their judgements and identify shared behaviours and social values (Deslauriers, 2004). In this study, focus groups were undertaken to explore activities associated with the research and comment on the analysis of the data.

Table 1 provides an overview of the data collection instruments and the research phase with which each is associated.

Table 1: Overview of instruments used in data collection process

Instrument	Description	Phase
Questionnaires	Seven questionnaires: Teachers' responses to a set of online questionnaires with open questions about their ideas and opinions gathered from the topics of virtual sessions. Questionnaires were completed voluntarily by an average of 19 teachers before each session. These data are available in Spanish: https://goo.gl/9zpWOV https://goo.gl/9zpWOV https://goo.gl/9zpWOV	1
	One survey: Teachers' responses to the online survey on access to ICT and access to and creation of OER. This questionnaire was a Spanish translation of the instrument designed collectively by the ROER4D researcher network. It was completed by 248 school teachers, 16 of whom were part of the coKREA project. These data are available in Spanish: https://goo.gl/Sm3TXd	3
Chat record	Seven webinars: An Internet Relay Chat session was established as an interactive channel during the "Introduction to OER" webinar, through which teachers' comments, questions and concerns were collected. On average, 28 teachers were connected per session, of whom 14 on average participated actively throughout with comments, opinions and questions. These data are available in Spanish: https://goo.gl/3QnGFK https://goo.gl/3QnGFK https://goo.gl/3QnGFK	1
Interview	Thirty unstructured telephone interviews: Notes were taken by the research team on telephone conversations conducted with teachers to assess Phase 1. Phone calls were made to 30 teachers associated with the project. These data are available in Spanish: https://goo.gl/O758r4https://goo.gl/O758r4https://goo.gl/O758r4	1

Focus groups	One focus group with teacher teams: Discussion to establish how teachers were engaging with the coKREA project and their views on the "Introduction to OER" phase. A face-to-face focus group with five teacher educators and a virtual interview with one additional teacher was undertaken. These data are available in Spanish: https://goo.gl/IbY92Zhttps://goo.gl/IbY92Zhttps://goo.gl/IbY92Z	1
	Two focus groups with team leader teachers: Meetings with teachers to discuss data analysis and the experience of creating OER. The first meeting was held virtually to discuss preliminary findings from data collected in Phase 1 of the project (nine teachers participated). The second meeting was conducted in person with a teacher educator living near Popayán in order to assess her experience. These data are available in Spanish: https://goo.gl/aHYyZnhttps://goo.gl/aHYyZnhttps://goo.gl/aHYyZn	2
	Six focus groups with teacher teams: Interviews with teams to share their views and experiences regarding the adoption of OER (four on average per focus group). These data are available in Spanish: https://goo.gl/X72qHW https://goo.gl/X72qHW https://goo.gl/X72qHW	3
	Two focus groups with students: Meetings with groups of students who participated in teacher-led activities on the use and creation of OER, aimed at better understanding their opinions and experiences (10 students participated). These data are available in Spanish: https://goo.gl/HXytfahttps://goo.gl/HXytfahttps://goo.gl/HXytfa	3

Data collected at each phase of the investigation were de-identified and published via the coKREA website under Creative Commons Attribution (CC BY) licences so that any interested parties (particularly teachers participating in the project) could undertake their own analysis of the data.[9] The dataset is comprised of eight separate files, seven of which contain interview transcripts, and answers to open questions in questionnaires or chat logs; the other file is a spreadsheet with statistics from a survey with closed questions about OER. All data are in Spanish, the mother tongue of the participants. The collected data, the form of processing and its publication have the consent of the participants.

The data de-identification process entailed assigning codes for each instrument and establishing an encryption system for teachers' names (Table 2).

Table 2: Explanation of codes used in the data de-identification process

Explanation of codes	Options (In parentheses, the word in Spanish)	Example	
Research phase	E1: Phase 1 *(Etapa 1)* E2: Phase 2 *(Etapa 2)* E3: Phase 3 *(Etapa 3)*	E3	E3.2ED.R2.59.ALS
Number of data collection instruments	The number at the beginning of each phase	2	
Instrument type	C: Questionnaire *(Cuestionario)* R: Chat record *(Registro)* E: Interviews and focus groups *(Entrevista)*	E	

---

9   The open data arising from this study are available (in Spanish) at https://karisma.org.co/cokrea/?p=1007.

Person with whom the instrument is associated	D: Teacher *(Docente)* E: Student *(Estudiante)*	D	
Type of activity and sequence	R: Meeting *(Reunión)* S: Session *(Sesión)* P: Question *(Pregunta)*	R2	
Number assigned to the paragraph of the transcript	The sequence restarts in each file	59	
Initial assigned to each teacher	A random combination of unique letters assigned for each teacher	ALS	

When referring to an instrument, it is identified by its code (for instance, E3.2ED), and when transcript fragments are used to illustrate a concept or category of analysis, an alphanumeric sequence is associated with them (as in the case of E3.2ED.R2.59.ALS). This coding system means that the instrument can be identified, as well as the associated session, meeting or specific question and paragraph from where it was extracted.

Data analysis

Collaborative reflection and action processes on the studied phenomenon are an important feature of data analysis in the PAR approach (Elliott, 2000). PAR does not, however, specify methods for analysing the reflection process. For this reason, it was decided to use Grounded Theory, which provides a series of procedures and techniques for analysing unstructured information, enabling the extraction of elements to understand and act on the social realities of research interest (Strauss & Corbin, 2002).

In the development of each of the phases, the project coordination team compiled and coded the records. This prior organisation of the information was undertaken to facilitate and expedite the process of analysis with the teachers in the small amount of time they had for this work. The information was processed utilising LibreOffice and CmapTools concept mapping software, both FOSS products. These activities were beneficial to the participant teachers, in that they facilitated the establishment of a collective analysis process in just a few meetings. This provided a means of circumventing the challenges associated with the limited amount of time available and the teachers' low levels of willingness to engage with research activities.

The Grounded Theory approach was undertaken in three principal stages, allowing for progressive data analysis developed in line with the research:

1. **Approach stage (research phases 1 and 2):** The initial stage was focused on creating various opportunities for conversation in order to identify, through teachers' observation of their own actions and those of others, the differences between ICT-supported teaching practices in general and teaching practices utilising OER through webinars, virtual meetings, interviews and focus groups. Open coding was used to group teachers' ideas into Open Categories.

2. **Deepening stage (research phases 2 and 3):** The Open Categories were then organised and classified according to their relationships and affinity with the research sub-questions, using axial coding to synthesise recurring themes. Later, these Axial

Categories were validated in conversation with teachers, establishing how these themes resonated with their experience and grouping them through Selective Categories, which constituted the substantive research theory.

3. **Condensation stage (research phase 3):** This is the stage in which the conversation between substantive theory and formal theory occurs. This was carried out with teachers, allowing the emergence of the Core Category (CN in Spanish), which provides an explanation of the social phenomenon studied.

Figure 1 provides a graphic representation of the data analysis process.

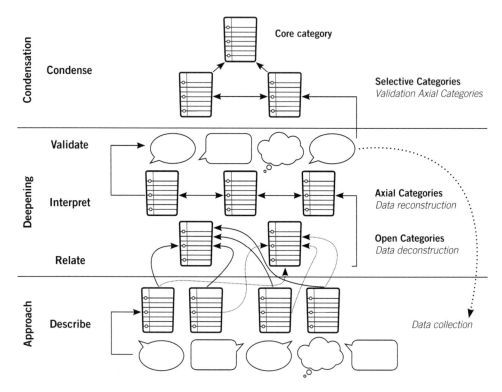

Figure 1: Qualitative data analysis process based on the Grounded Theory approach

In the Findings section, the categories are coded for easy tracking. In the case of Axial Categories, this code has four elements: the first two letters indicate the Axial Categories (CA in Spanish), followed by the question associated with it, and finally a letter listing the different dimensions of the answer to the question (e.g. CA1A, CA1B).

In the case of the Selective Categories, the code has only two parts: the first two letters indicate that it is a Selective Category (CS in Spanish) and then a sequential number (e.g. CS1, CS2).

Findings

In keeping with the PAR approach, research stages included some activities aimed at the adaptation-curation-creation of OER by teachers, while other activities were specifically designed to respond to the research question and sub-questions.

In Phase 0 (comprising the call for participation and establishment of teacher teams), 11 groups, comprised of 48 teachers, were formed in 11 schools in four departments of southwest Colombia: one in Risaralda, two in Valle del Cauca, seven in Cauca and one in Putumayo.[10] Of the 48 teachers participating in the study, 20 were women and 28 were men.

Of the 11 groups, 10 were comprised of high school teachers and one was composed of primary school teachers. Ten of the groups included teachers from different disciplines working on cross-cutting projects, and one group consisted of mathematics teachers only. The groups' composition showed that teachers decided to team up with people with whom they had a personal affinity based on their work style, rather than with colleagues with whom they shared the same disciplinary area.

Not all groups were involved in the entire investigation. Of the 11 groups, six developed OER under an OEP framework. The remaining five groups withdrew their participation at different stages of the investigation. The study coordination team noted that the dropout was due in large part to the teachers' lack of interest in moving from oral discourse to written production, which is necessary for the development, adaptation and curation of OER. Likewise, there was a greater willingness to participate in workshops on the use of technological tools than in the activities of pedagogical reflection on Open Education. Another factor that discouraged involvement was the difficulty teachers experienced with group work, since project activities were group oriented. Ultimately, 22 teachers from six groups actively participated in the project.

In Phase 1, seven virtual seminars were held, which were offered openly so that others could contribute to topics under discussion. Sessions were recorded and published on the project's website.[11] In the seven virtual seminars, there was an average attendance of 17 teachers involved with the project and 14 unrelated participants.

In the course of conducting these online introductions to OER seminars, the research team was able to identify three consecutive reactions that each teacher had in order to recognise the implications of the Colombian copyright regime and the application of open licensing in their daily practice of accessing, producing and exchanging content in the classroom (described in more detail in Sáenz et al., 2014):

1. Resistance and anger at copyright limitations in terms of reproducing and adapting works, where the general feeling expressed by teachers can be summarised in two phrases: "It's not fair" and "I have my hands tied in terms of trying to do my work".

2. Interest in understanding the alternatives provided by open licensing, beginning to express statements like: "What if ...?" and "How do I search with open licences?"

3. The decision to share. In all cases, teachers expressed the importance of conveying issues around copyright limitation to principals, students and colleagues. In several cases, this became a direct action or invitation to support activities in their educational institutions or to incorporate the subject of Creative Commons licensing in their curriculum.

---

10 A map with the location of schools is available at https://karisma.org.co/cokrea/?page_id=622.
11 https://karisma.org.co/cokrea/?page_id=46

Phase 2 focused on the design and development of experiences around the adaptation-curation-creation of OER in relation to various kinds of OEP. A total of 16 OER were published, three of which were blogs, one was a workshop exercise and 12 were virtual learning objects. Of the 16 OER, six were created by several authors together to be used transversally in their respective school areas, and 10 were created by individual authors.[12] Regardless of whether OER were generated individually or collectively, the teachers in each group supported each other in the design, revision and evaluation of their resources, with the assistance of the research team.

In analysing the OER created by teachers, the research team identified five dimensions regarding the advantages of these types of resources in education:

1. **OER as content-systematising teaching strategies.**[13] This finding is consistent with other research which found that innovations in teaching strategies by school teachers generally have a limited range because there is no practice of documenting or publishing them (Castro et al., 2005b; Lieberman, 2013). Similar to the findings of Anaya and Hernandez (2008), this study found that the learning objects published as OER not only contain the content taught, but also reflect how teachers were conducting their classroom work.

2. **Content creation and experiences related to the local sociocultural context.**[14] Events in small towns or rural areas are rarely reported upon in the media. It is also uncommon to find information such as photos and videos about local news on the internet, and even less common to find openly licensed content. Consistent with the findings of Anaya and Hernandez (2008), this study found that the ability to create and adapt OER informed by teachers' own classroom realities serves as a recognition of the importance of local context, fostering the creation and publication of information based on their environment. This not only serves to make the region more visible, but also influences the way it is perceived by teachers and students, which is vital in the process of identity construction.

3. **Adaptation and reuse of openly licensed content.**[15] Being able to modify or adapt a work was one of the most exciting benefits of open content mentioned by the teachers. It was also found that it helps in that it saves time and money because it leverages content produced by other authors. This supports findings from a study by Wiley et al. (2012) in the United States. Most of the openly licensed content reused by the teachers in this study was comprised of Wikipedia articles, as well as photos and videos obtained from Flickr, YouTube and Wikimedia Commons.

4. **Incorporation of Creative Commons licensing in the curricula.**[16] Several teachers began to engage peers and students on issues around copyright and open

---

12 The OER created by teachers are available at https://karisma.org.co/cokrea/?page_id=1079.

13 An example of the OER dimension as content-systematising teaching strategies is the OER "*Conociendo la dinámica de mi ciudad*" ("Knowing the dynamics of my city"): https://karisma.org.co/cokrea/?page_id=1130

14 An example of the dimension of "Content creation and experiences related to the local sociocultural context" is the OER "*La minería ¿Una enfermedad o solución para el Quilichagüeño?*" ("Mining: A disease or solution for the Quilichagüeño?"): https://karisma.org.co/cokrea/?p=724

15 An example of the dimension "Adaptation and reuse of openly licensed content" is the OER "*Estadística en contexto*" ("Statistics in context"): https://karisma.org.co/cokrea/?p=716

16 An example of the dimension "Incorporation of Creative Commons licensing in the curricula" is the OER "*Aprendiendo sobre licencias Creative Commons*" ("Learning about Creative Commons licenses"): https://karisma.org.co/cokrea/?p=711

licensing based on their experience in this research process. They explained this action based on the fact that recognising the rights and duties to their own works and those of others is part of the comprehensive training that should be provided by the school, and that teachers have a responsibility to know and set a good example on the subject. They also had an interest in spreading open licensing practice, recognising that licensing content in this way promotes an atmosphere of cooperation and interaction underpinned by mutual recognition, as well as more conscious participation in content creation from a legal perspective (see further detail in Hernández et al., 2014).

5. **FOSS to support educational processes.**[17] In the adaptation, curation and creation of OER produced by the teachers, the use of free and/or open software (eXeLearning, LibreOffice, Audacity) was encouraged to promote greater coherence between the technologies used and the open licensing approach to promote social values within an open culture framework, as suggested by Lessig (2004). The use of these types of tools also facilitated expansion of the functionality of teachers' computers with programmes intended to offer web services in the school's local network environment (Moodle, Etherpad, MediaWiki). These strategies were particularly important in order to avoid the usual issues associated with limited internet bandwidth (as reported in more detail in Ortiz, Caldón & Hernandez, 2015).

These dimensions demonstrate the study's influence in terms of supporting a group of teachers in identifying the potential of OER for their educational practice, as well as generating an interest in copyright and Creative Commons licensing as a cross-cutting issue, implicit in all aspects of their work with their students as well as their fellow teachers. Some educators have become Open Education ambassadors within and outside of their educational institutions, not only by setting an example through publishing their OER, but also through implementing changes to their curricula, incorporating open licensing as a criterion for the delivery of school assignments, organising lectures and institutional workshops, and sharing their experiences at local academic events.[18]

Phase 3 was comprised of both the collection and processing of data, which was done alongside the activities in Phases 1 and 2, as well as the collective analysis and reflection based on the main question and sub-questions of this research. The findings of the study are presented according to the three stages associated with Grounded Theory: approach, deepening and condensation.

It is noteworthy that as part of the PAR process, teachers were encouraged to share the results of the analysis of their pedagogical experiences with OER at different events. Consequently, when teachers communicated their reflections on their classroom practices, they could learn from their own pedagogical experiences, teach others and improve their teaching and learning processes with OER. Specifically, participant teachers developed 22 presentations and two posters for academic events in 2015 and 2016, and six groups of teachers produced reflection texts about their experience with OER. The outcome of this

---

17 An example of FOSS to support educational processes is the OER "*Taller no. 1: Razonamiento lógico*" ("Workshop no. 1: Logical reasoning"): https://karisma.org.co/cokrea/?page_id=1132

18 A list of the academic events in which the teachers presented their experience around OER is available at https://karisma.org.co/cokrea/?page_id=997.

written production was considered a particular achievement, as school teachers in Colombia largely subscribe to an oral tradition from which it is difficult to undertake systematisation and writing processes (even when based on their own experiences).

Approach stage: Opening the reality of creation, adoption and curation of OER in Colombian schools

In order to relate the Open Categories to the five sub-questions that support the primary research question, the Axial Categories occur as dimensions of the answers given to each sub-question. The analysis of the relationships and hierarchies found between Axial Categories is synthesised in the Selective Categories. In the tables and figures which follow, the abbreviation CA is used for the axial categories and CS for the selective categories (based on the Spanish acronym).

As an extension of this analysis, this section shows only the Axial Categories with a representative quotation from all the categories. Each quotation is presented as an excerpt with the Axial Category it represents. It is presented in this way to facilitate reading in Spanish (the mother tongue of the teachers and researchers in this study) and translation into English. At the end of the section, a table summarising the relationships between these categories and the Selective Categories is shared.

Sub-question 1: What kinds of processes would support a community of teachers in actively engaging with the creation and adaptation of a contextually situated and collaborative OER model?

The study revealed that any teacher training process conceived to promote the appropriation of OER should consider the following four principles:

Principle 1: Teacher training should be focused on continuous pedagogical support rather than just training (CA1A).[19]

Spanish (original)	English (translation)
"Yo lo que recomiendo es que las próximas capacitaciones que nos de la Secretaría de Educación pues sean así como la que ustedes nos están haciendo. Que no es venir y dar una charla e irse, es con seguimiento, nos están acompañando, nos corrigen, nos dan alternativas de solución a las problemáticas que nosotros planteamos, y pues nos ha parecido muy interesante. Yo pienso que el resto de compañeros, si tienen ese mismo acompañamiento que ustedes nos están brindando a nosotros, pues van a sentir más interés por capacitarse y cambiar la forma como están trabajando actualmente." (E3-2ED.R2.63.ANI)	*"I hope that the next training undertaken by the Secretariat of Education will be like the one you're doing. It is not to come and give a lecture and leave, but also to follow up what we do; to accompany us, correct us, give us alternative solutions to [educational] issues that we raised, as that was very interesting. I think if other teachers have that same kind of support, they will be more interested in receiving training and change how they are currently working."* (E3-2ED.R2.63.ANI)

---

19 In Colombia, the Education Secretariats are administrative offices attached to the municipal authorities or departmental governments. They aim to coordinate and verify compliance with national policies in the educational institutions under their charge. One of their duties is to offer teacher training courses.

Principle 2: OER should be created and used within constructivist pedagogical models (CA1B).

Spanish (original)	English (translation)
"Pienso que los REA son herramientas necesarias para que los niños construyan, modifiquen y compartan conocimientos. Además de fomentar la comunicación." (E1-2RD.S6.20.AUA)	*"I think OER are necessary tools for kids to build, modify and share knowledge, in addition to fostering communication."* (E1-2RD.S6.20.AUA)

Principle 3: Collaboration among teachers for creating OER should be promoted (CA1C).

Spanish (original)	English (translation)
"Los maestros trabajamos muy aislados, como que cada quien hace lo suyo y ya. Nos falta eso de saber trabajar en equipo, de planear cosas juntos. Porque uno sí se colabora, pero en cosas puntuales, no es una colaboración en el sentido de trabajar las clases de forma articulada ... hacer proyectos interdisciplinares o esto, es complejo por eso." (E3-2ED.R1.5.ALI)	*"Teachers work in a very isolated manner, and everyone does his/her thing and that's all. We lack that knowledge of how to undertake teamwork, planning things together. Because we collaborate but in specific things; it is not a partnership in the sense of teaching together ... doing interdisciplinary projects. It is so complex."* (E3-2ED.R1.5.ALI)

Principle 4: Opportunities to share and publish educational experiences as OER should be encouraged (CA1D).

Spanish (original)	English (translation)
"Estoy muy emocionado con el tema ... las personas se asustan al principio porque no saben cómo es, pero es de explicar. Yo quiero hablarle a todo el mundo de esto." (E2-1RD.S1.16.LRE)	*"I am excited about the subject ... people are scared at first because they do not know what OER are, but it is easy to do, they only need someone to explain it. That's why I want to tell everyone about this."* (E2-1RD.S1.16.LRE)

Sub-question 2: What enabling conditions would encourage wider adoption by peers of contextually created OER within the community?

The findings of this research indicate that the following three conditions are required to foster greater contextualisation and creation of OER by teachers in Colombia:

Condition 1: The existence of policy and programmes, nationally and locally, to foster the adaptation, curation and creation of OER (CA2A).

Spanish (original)	English (translation)
"Incluso [en] los mismos libros para las instituciones se debería también propender por recursos abiertos, son cambios que pueden empezar desde la Secretaría, pero lastimosamente a eso se le da tan poca importancia." (E3-2ED.45.R3.UAR)	*"Even the same textbooks should be open resources. These are changes that can start from the Secretariat, but unfortunately this is given so little importance."* (E3-2ED.45.R3.UAR)

Condition 2: Greater respect of copyright on all intellectual production conducted on the part of teachers and school managers (CA2B).

Spanish (original)	English (translation)
"Realmente para generar un impacto grande también se tienen que empezar a formar [al] otro. Porque no se puede que tres estemos hablando un idioma y el resto estén aceptando cosas que no se deben. Entonces se genera un choque y en el proceso se generan rupturas ahí." (E3-2ED.R3.43.UAR)	*"To really create a big impact, there is a need to begin to train other [teachers]. Because it is unfair that only three [teachers] are speaking one language and the rest are accepting things that are wrong. A collision is then generated and in the process there are ruptures."* (E3-2ED.R3.43.UAR)

Condition 3: Existence of a national, government-supported platform where teachers can find OER and publish their own resources (CA2C).

Spanish (original)	English (translation)
"La idea es que con este tipo de ejercicio que estamos haciendo nosotros, se genere una comunidad académica y empecemos a generar nuestros propios repositorios... y que todos y cada uno de los maestros podamos utilizarlos, aprovecharlos y adecuarlos." (E1-2RD.S6.30.OEL)	*"The idea is that with this type of exercise we are doing, an academic community is generating and we start producing our own repositories ... and every teacher can use and adapt them."* (E1-2RD.S6.30.OEL)

Sub-question 3: What new skills are required among teachers and teacher educators to adopt a new learning culture with OER?

The skills that teachers need today are not only technical, but should also incorporate teaching skills in the framework of a global society. This study has identified five key skills required by teachers and teacher educators to develop a culture of learning with OER.

Skill 1: An interest in exploring and learning to use existing ICT, particularly tools and services enabling the search, creation and adaptation of audiovisual, image and text resources (CA3A).

Spanish (original)	English (translation)
"Los maestros se han encontrado con que cuentan con los recursos tecnológicos, portátiles, tabletas, móviles, pero no los saben utilizar. O no tienen esa conexión de cómo a partir de ese equipo yo puedo realizar este objeto o ese recurso para llevarlos a la clase. No sé en otras partes de Colombia, pero acá es mínimo y en primaria casi es cero." (E1-3RD.R1.37.ALA)	*"Teachers have found that they have the technology resources, laptops, tablets, mobiles, but do not know how to use them. Or do not have that connection to use them to make this object or resource, and take it to the class."* (E1-3RD.R1.37.ALA)

Skill 2: In addition to ICT literacies, teachers need to have a working knowledge of copyright and open licensing (CA3B) so that they can indicate the permissions under which their work can be shared.

Spanish (original)	English (translation)
"El trabajo de licenciamiento es bien apasionante. En primera instancia porque hay total ignorancia, yo lo reconozco, total ignorancia ... había escuchado a lo lejos "Derecho de Autor" y eso en la música, que lo de los CD piratas, pero de las cosas que uno por allá a lo lejos escucho y nada más. Pero ya cuando uno se empieza a meter y a leer y a hallarle la razón de ser... ¡Dios mío! Empieza uno como a evaluarse y por Dios Santísimo todas las metidas de patas que yo he realizado en mi vida profesional han sido bárbaras. Entonces es como ir metiéndolo a uno y de una manera indirecta ir metiendo a los muchachos [estudiantes] en un concepto que es el concepto de la legalidad, del reconocimiento del valor del otro, de que los aportes que se hacen se tienen que valorar y respetar en todo su concepto. Me parece eso un aporte para el proceso educativo grandísimo, porque yo le cuento que yo llevo ya 24 años de docente y esto para miíme ha significado un cambio total en mi forma de trabajo, en mi forma de ver cómo utilizo mis clases y los elementos de otros, cómo los reconozco, cómo los puedo reutilizar, cómo los puedo aplicar y al mismo tiempo los chicos empezar a ver que los trabajos son valorados y respetados por los demás, pienso que ése es el aporte más grande que puede haber en mi área." (E3-2ED.R2.2.ALS)	*"The licensing work is very exciting. In the first instance because there is a total ignorance. I admit ... I had heard somewhere about copyright and that in music it relates to pirated CDs, but these are things one hears in the distance and nothing else. But when one begins to read and see the rationale ... My God! One begins to self-evaluate, and oh my God! All gaffes that I have made in my professional life have been barbaric. So it's like going and getting the kids [students] indirectly into the legality concept, recognising the value of the other, that their contributions have to be valued and respected. I think that's a great contribution to the educational process, because, let me tell you, I have been teaching for 24 years and this for me has meant a total change in my way of working, the way I see how I use in my classes elements created by others, how to recognise them, how I can reuse them, how I can apply them at the same time, the kids begin to see that works are valued and respected by others. I think that might be the biggest contribution in my area."* (E3-2ED.R2.2.ALS)

Skill 3: Teachers need to strengthen their use of constructivist educational models in using ICT in order to engage in OEP and to create and use OER optimally (CA3C).

Spanish (original)	English (translation)
"Los estudiantes pueden ser protagonistas y los profesores orientar mediante recursos, pero esto sólo se dará si logran modificar las prácticas educativas. Lo digo porque lo que yo veo es que se hace uso de tecnología en una clase, en ocasiones, sólo para acceder a los repositorios de contenidos del profesor." (E1-2RD.S6.25.ABA)	*"Students can be protagonists in the classroom and the teachers counsellors, using resources, [open or not], but this will only occur if educational practices are changed. I say that because what I see is that using technology in the classroom sometimes is just to access teacher's content repositories."* (E1-2RD.S6.25.ABA)

Skill 4: Teachers need to develop an interest in and an ability to share and work within communities of teachers and teacher educators (CA3D).

Spanish (original)	English (translation)
"Yo creo que ha dificultado el hecho de trabajar en equipo. Primero, porque no tenemos el espacio para reunirnos durante la jornada, y por fuera es muy complicado por el trabajo de otros. Así, la verdad hubiera sido mejor solos, pero no tendría el mismo impacto que el obligarnos a trabajar en equipo, sobre todo porque nos obligamos a trabajar involucrando ideas y áreas entre todos." (E2-1RD.S1.40.OEL)	*"I would have been better off alone, because it is very difficult to have the time to work together. But it would not have the same impact if we were not forced into teamwork, especially because we compel ourselves to work by connecting ideas and areas together."* (E2-1RD.S1.40.OEL)

Skill 5: Teachers need to be supported to reflect on their teaching practice and document their pedagogical experiences (CA3E).

Spanish (original)	English (translation)
"Interesante [en la sistematización lo de] la retroalimentación, así la experiencia se vuelve cada vez más enriquecedora. Muchos docentes realizamos trabajos en las instituciones que no damos a conocer, tal vez por falta de conocimiento en herramientas informáticas, o por no pensar que pueden servir de guía para alguien más." (E1-2RD.S4.39.ALE)	*"It was interesting getting feedback to make the experience become increasingly richer. Many teachers create works in the institutions that go unknown, perhaps because we do not think they can serve as a guideline for someone else."* (E1-2RD.S4.39.ALE)

Sub-question 4: How do local needs and contexts impact upon the universal (mostly defined through the normative system of the Global North) versus local notions of meaningfulness/quality of OER?

In considering OER as a way to meet local needs and contexts (local language, local culture, social issues, geographies, ecology, needs, aspirations, priorities, etc.), teachers highlighted two key issues.

Issue 1: Teachers acknowledged the need for good-quality, universal disciplinary resources that can be adapted to their local sociocultural realities (CA4A).

Spanish (original)	English (translation)
"Yo buscaba antes una página sobre el tema que estaba trabajando de ciencias naturales, y luego ahí llegaban y miraban. Les servía como para que ellos vayan fortaleciendo sus conocimientos y los que no entendían resolvían sus dudas." (E3.2ED.R6.1.AIA)	*"I used to look at web pages on the subject that I was working on in the natural sciences, and then showed them to the students. It helped them to strengthen their knowledge and for those who did not understand, as a way to resolve their doubts."* (E3.2ED.R6.1.AIA)

Issue 2: Teachers recognised that if they want local, contextualised resources for their students they will need to start creating their own materials (CA4B).

Spanish (original)	English (translation)
"(…) a veces nos limitamos mucho. Cuando el maestro se va a los textos como tal, como en matemáticas, los ejercicios están desde una perspectiva… por ejemplo desde escenarios netamente matemáticos, escenarios subreales para el contexto, donde está el avión, la represa tal, pero eso no pertenece a la realidad del estudiante. Entonces si uno quiere generar procesos desde la realidad del estudiante en la asignatura correspondiente, pues necesita empezar a crear ciertas cosas uno mismo." (E3-2ED.R3.5.UAR)	*"We simply use the texts as we receive them. As in mathematics, the exercises are from one perspective … for example, from purely mathematical scenarios, or with elements that do not relate to the reality of the student, like talking about planes, trains, or dams. So, if I want to produce processes considering the reality of the student in the corresponding subject matter, I need to start creating some things myself."* (E3-2ED.R3.5.UAR)

Sub-question 5: How do institutional and systemic factors in a public system, which are perceived as compartmentalised and hierarchical, interact with and influence the building of a participatory OER model within the government/public system?

The study identified three key institutional policy and systemic factors that negatively influence the building of a participatory OER model within government schools in Colombia.

Factor 1: Systemic factors within the public schooling sector were unfavourable in terms of building an OER participatory model, as policies do not promote the creation of OER by teachers or provide the time for them to do so (CA5A).

Spanish (original)	English (translation)
"Cuando llevamos la carta para poder trabajar como equipo [Carta o formulario para vincularse formalmente al proyecto], ella [La directora] fue muy enfática en decir que si y solo sí nos reuníamos por fuera de clase, por fuera del horario académico, firmaba. Así que buscamos espacios entre los tiempos libres que tenemos para reunirnos y avanzar en el proceso." (E2-1RD.S2.32.OEL)	*"When we took the letter [application form to the principal to work as an institution in the project] to work as a team, she [the principal] was very emphatic in saying that she signed it if and only if we met outside class, outside of school hours. So we found some free time to come together and advance the process."* (E2-1RD.S2.32.OEL)

Factor 2: Institutional policies and practice seem to reinforce traditional ideas about the classroom being a space for the transmission of information (CA5B).

Spanish (original)	English (translation)
"Yo también tuve la intención de trabajar en 10 y 11 con aplicaciones, materiales educativos que servían para los niños de primaria. Llegaron padres de familia y me dijeron: "profesora, pero de qué le sirve a los niños pequeños que trabajen en eso. Enséñeles otra clase de cosas, por ejemplo a hacer una carta, o hacer un acta" y bueno... listo, eso se puede hacer, pero lo que yo estaba planteando les está aportando a los jóvenes, y no sólo a ellos sino también a otros. Pero les cuento que eso ha sido complejo, porque mi intención es una y lo que ellos quieren es otra." (E1-3RD.R2.17.NOA)	*"I had the intention to work on 10 and 11 applications to create educational materials to be used for primary school students, but parents came and said, 'Mrs Teacher, what is the value for the children to do this? You should teach other kinds of things, for example, to write a letter or give a correct quote' ... And this can be done, but what I was asking them to do is to contribute to the youth, and not only them but also to others. But, let me tell you, this has been difficult because my intention is one thing and what they want is another."* (E1-3RD.R2.17.NOA)

Factor 3: The current teaching culture is rooted in individual work schemes rather than in collaborative work (CA5C).

Spanish (original)	English (translation)
"Yo no había trabajado con ellos antes... en grupo... no. Es que en las instituciones lo que pasa es que somos grupo pero para reuniones y para recocha, pero ya como de sentarse a trabajar yo creo que es la primera vez, yo llevo seis años en el colegio y es la primera vez que nos sentamos a ver qué íbamos a hacer." (E3-2ED.R2.48.ALS)	*"I had not worked in a group with them. The thing is that in the institutions we are a group just for meetings and hanging out, but like coming together to work, I think this is the first time. I have been at the school for six years and it is the first time we sat down together to see what we would do."* (E3-2ED.R2.48.ALS)

Deepening stage: Establishing the foundation to promote the adoption of OER in Colombian schools

Once the Axial Categories were established, the next step was to establish the relationships between them in order to obtain the Selective Categories, bearing in mind the primary research question. The categories and the relationship between them were discussed and reviewed with teachers through virtual and face-to-face meetings.

As a result of this analysis, the Selective Categories emerged. For the purposes of this study, these are statements about what should be considered in order to foster a pattern of OER adoption amongst a community of Colombian teachers:

- CS1: Teachers implement pedagogical models based on constructivist theory.
- CS2: Teachers learn to use ICT to create and express (not only access) information.
- CS3: Teachers use open licences to promote collaborative creation by teachers and students.
- CS4: Teachers receive pedagogical support rather than mass standardised training.

- CS5: Policies, programmes and infrastructure are in place to promote the adoption, curation and creation of OER at institutional and national levels.

Table 3 outlines the relationship between Axial and Selective Categories in the data analysis approach, mapped against research sub-questions.

Table 3: Relationship between Axial and Selective Categories in data analysis approach

Research questions	Code	Axial Categories	Code	Selective Categories
1. What kind of processes would support a community of teachers in actively engaging with the creation and adaptation of a contextually situated and collaborative OER model?	CA1A	Teacher training should be focused on continuous pedagogical support rather than just training.	CS4	Teachers receive pedagogical support rather than mass, standardised training.
	CA1B	OER should be created and used within constructivist pedagogical models.	CS1	Teachers implement pedagogical models based on constructivist theory.
	CA1C	Collaboration among fellow teachers for creating OER should be promoted.	CS4	Teachers receive pedagogical support rather than mass, standardised training.
	CA1D	Opportunities to share and publish educational experiences with OER should be encouraged.	CS5	Policies, programmes and infrastructure are in place to promote the adoption, curation and creation of OER at institutional and national level.
2. What enabling conditions would encourage wider adoption by peers of contextually created OER within the community?	CA2A	The existence of policy and programmes, nationally and locally, would foster the adaptation, curation and creation of OER.	CS5	Policies, programmes and infrastructure are in place to promote the adoption, curation and creation of OER at institutional and national level.
	CA2B	Need for greater respect of copyright on all intellectual production conducted on the part of teachers and school managers.	CS3	Teachers use open licences to promote collaborative creation by teachers and students.
	CA2C	The existence of a national, government-supported platform where teachers can find OER and publish their own resources.	CS5	Policies, programmes and infrastructure are in place to promote the adoption, curation and creation of OER at institutional and national level.

3. What new skills are required among teachers and teacher educators to adopt a new learning culture with OER?	CA3A	Interest in exploring and learning to use existing ICT, particularly tools and services enabling the search, creation and adaptation of audiovisual, image and text resources.	CS2	Teachers learn to use ICT to create and express (not only access) information.
	CA3B	Copyright knowledge and use of open licences.	CS3	Teachers use the open licences to promote collaborative creation by teachers and students.
	CA3C	Strengthening of constructivist educational models based on the use of new technologies.	CS1	Teachers implement pedagogical models based on constructivist theory.
	CA3D	Ability to share and work within communities of teachers and teacher educators.	CS4	Teachers receive pedagogical support rather than mass, standardised training.
	CA3E	Systematic reflection to transform teaching practices.	CS4	Teachers receive pedagogical support rather than mass, standardised training.
4. How do local needs and contexts (local language, local culture, social issues, geographies, ecology, needs, aspirations, priorities, etc.) impact upon the universal (mostly defined through normative system of the Global North) versus local notions of meaningfulness/ quality of OER?	CA4A	Teachers need universal, disciplinary, quality content that can be reused.	CS5	Policies, programmes and infrastructure are in place to promote the adoption, curation and creation of OER at institutional and national level.
	CA4B	Importance of local and contextualised resources for student learning.	CS2	Teachers learn to use ICT to create and express (not only access) information.
5. How do institutional and systemic factors in a public system that is perceived as compartmentalised and hierarchical interact with and influence the building of a participatory OER model within the government/public system?	CA5A	Education policy does not promote or provide time for the creation of educational resources by teachers.	CS5	Policies, programmes and infrastructure are in place to promote the adoption, curation and creation of OER at institutional and national level.
	CA5B	Traditionally, education has the primary function of transmitting information.	CS5	Policies, programmes and infrastructure are in place to promote the adoption, curation and creation of OER at institutional and national level.
	CA5C	Current teaching culture is rooted in individual work schemes rather than collaborative work.	CS4	Teachers receive pedagogical support rather than mass, standardised training.

Condensation stage: Collaborating in context for the adoption of OER in Colombian schools

The analysis of the relationship between the Selective Categories and the research question led to the establishment of a Core Category: *The adoption of OER is more effective when teachers adopt pedagogical models focused on collaboratively creating and recreating contextually relevant knowledge.* The Core Category (CN based on Spanish acronym) is the synthesis of the substantive theory, which emerges from data processing using the Grounded Theory technique, and collaborative data analysis conducted with teachers through the reflection and action spiral of the PAR process.

Analysis of Selective Categories around specific objectives allowed clarification of the relationships related to the aim of the research, culminating in a concept map of the Core Category (Figure 2).

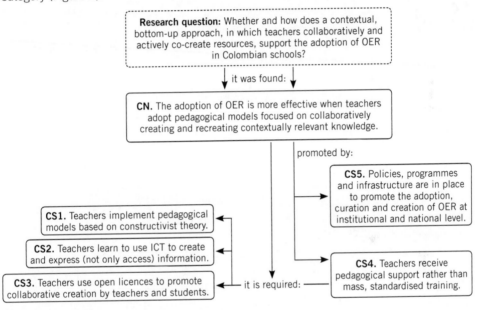

Figure 2: Concept map of the Core Category

In relation to Objective 1 of the study – to study how a collaborative and local OER model can be embedded within the ecosystem of a community of teachers in Colombia – it emerged that this is possible under two general conditions:

Condition 1: Pedagogical support that encourages long-term participation of teachers (linked to CS4), where teachers participate in reflection and actions (linked to three axes):

1. Pedagogical practices where teachers see themselves and their students in an active role in generating knowledge, which is connected to constructivist models based on a deep understanding of the realities of the sociocultural context (linked to CS1).

2. An approach to the use of ICT that favours not only access, but also creation and expression, incorporating ICT infrastructure available to teachers and students (linked to CS2).

3. The adoption of open licensing as a base structure to promote the collaborative creation of resources and sharing in the classroom (linked to CS3).

This pedagogical support involves providing ongoing, flexible and personalised follow-up with teachers about their OER projects. This means identifying and working according to subjects of interest, expectation and the learning needs of teachers and the school where they teach. It also entails this process not taking place according to a uniform and rigid schedule of sequentially developed topics. To this end, training strategies should promote feedback and support among teachers, as well as an interest in sharing ideas, knowledge and learning – in other words, encouraging teamwork and participation in Open Education networks and communities. In order to achieve this, it is important for the advisor to carry out processes of adaptation, curation and creation of OER in pedagogical practice in order to become a role-model for teachers.

Condition 2: Formulation of policies and programmes at institutional and national level to promote the adoption, curation and creation of OER (linked to CS5). In this regard, it was recognised that changes in classroom practices are more responsive to actions and reflections emerging from a bottom-up approach than to external directives. At the same time, the need arose for institutional conditions (particularly from the perspective of educational policies) to assist in decreasing the resistance of teachers and principals to participating in OER activity. This fosters the sustainability of initiatives beyond the efforts of just a few teachers who have an intrinsic motivation for the development of pedagogical innovation with ICT.

Concerning Objective 2 of the study – to understand how a model of adaptation-curation-creation of OER can contribute to effective use of OER for teacher development – it was established that the participation of teachers in a process of using and adapting OER that takes into account teacher needs as well as the sociocultural realities of their students, encourages uptake of OEP that revolve around the use of OER.

Addressing copyright and open licensing in the activities of adaptation, curation and creation with teachers and students (linked to CS3), and identifying the possibilities offered by ICT in schools (linked to CS2), resulted in deep reflection by the participant teachers in this study on their practices and their teaching models, driven by a realisation that they and their students can have a more active role in the creation and co-creation of knowledge (linked to CS1). In this sense, the activities and reflections developed in this study allowed the participant teachers to recognise the predominance of information transmission in their pedagogical practices – which is set by the schools' curricular structure where emphasis is placed on the content rather than on skills development.

The participation of teachers in an experience that served as an example of pedagogical support secured long-term teacher engagement going beyond training (linked to CS4), enabling them to articulate concerns and thoughts about how to replicate this type of learning scenario with their own students. Therefore, teachers were not limited to the co-creation of OER, but developed pedagogical practices with their students where learning revolved around the creation and collaborative employment of information, using and publishing openly licensed content. Thus the main results or outcomes of this research are not the published OER, but the OEP that developed around these resources.

Finally as proposed in the Core Category (Figure 2), it was identified that it was possible to foster the adoption of OER when teachers are recognised and supported as content creators in collaboration with other teachers and students. This finding indicates that a bottom-up, contextually situated approach effectively supports the adoption of OER.

Discussion

The literature on OER suggests that this kind of resource has the potential to address current education challenges, such as the high cost of accessing information, the cultural homogenisation of the North, lack of cultural contextualisation and lack of customisation of educational content, among others. A central question is how to encourage OER adoption by teachers and schools in the Global South in order to take advantage of their benefits and establish efficacy in the sphere of education.

Most OER initiatives have focused on access and free distribution of content to achieve true democratisation of knowledge, as seen in the Colombian government programmes such as *Recursos Educativos Digitales Abiertos* (Open Educational Digital Resources) (Colombia Ministerio de Educación Nacional, 2012) and *Centros de Innovación Educativa Regional* (Regional Educational Innovation Centers).[20] In this sense, some studies show that it is common for teachers to adopt OER because of the possibility of using them without modification in their classroom activities (Lozano et al., 2010). However, other authors such as Gértrudix et al. (2007) and Moreno et al. (2011) have stated that OER have a tremendous value – not only in terms of these resources being a finished product that promotes access to knowledge, but above all for being a means to transform classroom relationships with respect to the creation and recreation of knowledge.

In light of the activities and collective reflection processes carried out with teachers in this study, the authors suggest that OER can be a means to transform pedagogical practices when adopted through collaborative processes of adaptation, curation and creation of content that takes advantage of open licensing. This concurs with findings expressed by Anaya and Hernandez (2008) in previous research undertaken in southwestern Colombia.

In this sense, phrases like "resistance and anger", "interest to understand" and "desire to share" expressed by teachers in the course of this study were learning situations that encouraged them to be creators (and not merely consumers or content users) by getting to know the limitations of a traditional conception of copyright and the possibilities of open licensing (Hernández et al., 2014). The importance of moving from information access to information creation is an essential aspect for some authors when referring to processes of pedagogical appropriation of ICT, such as Kaplún (2005) and Moreno et al. (2011).

The findings mentioned in the context of Phase 1 of this research showed that working with open licences became a way to get teachers interested in the pedagogical implications of their decisions when choosing types of material to circulate in the classroom. This interest helped teachers to move quite naturally to OEP. This study was therefore about more than just the experience of co-creating OER, but served as a means to provide examples of OEP where creating and sharing content with open licensing was key in the training process.

---

20 http://www.colombiaaprende.edu.co/html/micrositios/1752/w3-propertyname-3020.html

This resonates with prior research undertaken by Grinsztajn et al. (2015), Hegarty (2015) and Stagg (2014).

Despite this enabling context, OER adoption did not happen automatically. Teachers expressed that receiving information on OER, open licensing and copyright issues allowed them to engage with the concepts superficially, but that adoption and true understanding took place only in the production of resources and the continuous review and feedback processes. It was found that the way to appropriate these concepts was learning by doing, particularly when doing so with others, as pointed out by Sapire and Reed (2011) regarding OER, as well as by Antúnez (1999) and Huayta et al. (2008) in their studies on teaching practice. This is correlated with the perspective of social learning that Coll et al. (2007) present in their studies on constructivism.

It was thanks to the OER creation process that teachers' concerns emerged and were clarified, particularly when working on topics such as what to consider when using Creative Commons licensing, how to find compatible resources depending on each licence, and how to assign licences correctly. Through this process, teachers also learned about the implications of taking a decision to create resources for sharing, how to exploit the works of other authors and the value of collaborative creation.

This process was relevant because teachers compared what they were previously doing in the classroom with the new aspects that the use of OER makes possible, encouraging reflection which led to changes in their ways of teaching. It provided further support to the idea that – as suggested by some authors, such as Elliott (2000) and Petrides et al. (2010) – collective reflection and understanding of one's own actions stimulates change. This was not an easy transition and required flexible and permanent support around action in the classroom. This pedagogical support model was a decisive factor in promoting changes inside the classroom, as established by two previous studies conducted by Benavides (2015) and Hernández (2015) in southwestern Colombia.

By assuming the adoption of OER as a way to transform classroom practices, it was possible to confirm Lessig's (2004) ideas on the value of open licensing to enrich and expand cultural expressions through collaborative work. In this particular study, it was found that the retention, reuse, revision, remixing and redistribution of existing OER[21] facilitated the development of collaborative experiences in at least two dimensions: when a teacher contributes to the work of others through the publication of his or her own work, and when teachers gather to create materials together.

With respect to this first dimension, creating and publishing any work using open licensing is a way in which authors invite others to take their work as a starting point for developing their own ideas. Although this relationship does not involve direct interaction between people, it does represent a form of collaboration, according to the characteristics identified by Collazos et al. (2014). First of all, interdependence is present because every personal creation depends on the extant works and licences chosen by other authors when they originally published these works. Secondly, it is a type of collaboration that meets the following responsibilities: respect for the author's will expressed through the chosen licence, the work's attributions and the commitment to publish and share using open licensing. Finally, it constitutes a social agreement achieved through this type of licensing where

---

21   https://opencontent.org/blog/archives/3221

authors favour free access to cultural expressions over the personal benefits of their work (Lessig, 2004).

The second dimension refers to experiences where a group of teachers interact in order to create resources, utilising open licensing as a guideline. In this scenario, teachers have a common goal to which they have committed individually, marking the beginning of collaborative work. However, by using open licensing as a legal platform to collaborate, they adhere to a system of ideas and practices related to retention, reuse, revision, remixing and redistribution of content – actions that reinforce collaboration in terms of positive interaction, individual responsibility and the development of social skills for negotiation and co-evaluation (Collazos et al., 2014).

Even though the above-mentioned dimensions of collaboration were observed in the teacher teams participating in this study, teachers revealed that it was not easy to work in groups. Castro et al. (2005b) point out that these difficulties derive from an educational system that is focused on the individual work of teachers and on the individual outcomes that their students achieve. This leads to conceiving the curriculum as a form of "subjectification" (treating subjects as individuals and apart from one another), which promotes a teaching practice that fragments knowledge into academic disciplines and usually perpetuates the gap between theory and practice. The result is that teachers operate in isolation, disconnected from knowledge communities, and privileged pedagogic practices encourage students to respond to narrowly defined, competitive and individualistic evaluation systems.

Collaboration does not come naturally; there are no policies that encourage it in the educational sector, a factor which was confirmed by the teachers who participated until the end of this study. They admitted that the proposed collaborative work was not easy to achieve and that this was perhaps the reason some groups and teachers ended up withdrawing from the process. At the same time, the teachers revealed that their personal learning and the collective results obtained would not have been possible if they had worked individually.

Teachers acknowledged that group work helped them to stay motivated to continue the process. Moreover, thanks to mutual support, teachers were able to co-evaluate not only their OER but also practices surrounding these resources, and solve concerns about technological, pedagogical and legal aspects related to their teaching. Results are evidenced in the use of OER elaborated by the teachers themselves, in papers accepted and presented at different academic events, and in pedagogical reports that they wrote to account for the developed OEP – production processes in which teachers usually do not participate.

Conclusion

This study demonstrated that recognising the restrictive use of works that traditional interpretation of copyright imposes confronts teachers with uncomfortable realities because it does not correspond with the traditional dynamics of access, production and information exchange that occurs in schools. This reaction generates in teachers a greater interest to know more about open licensing and how to take advantage of the possibilities of adaptation, curation and creation of OER.

This initial finding revealed that any change in the attitudes and practices of teachers is enhanced when they are involved in guided experiences that prompt them to question and reflect on what they do from a different perspective. In this case, the questioning and reflection emerged when addressing copyright and open licensing in a process of examining pedagogical practices when using OER.

On reflection, the research team felt that they were correct to focus on the process of implementing OER by addressing the affordances of retention, reuse, revision, remixing and redistribution which are provided by open licensing. This made it possible for teachers to understand that the importance of OER is not merely the final output, but rather their capacity to serve as a mediation tool in a pedagogical process where active and collaborative work among students and teachers is recognised and encouraged, as well as the importance of referring to a sociocultural context to achieve deeper learning. In conclusion, the purpose of OER is to use these resources as a way of learning through adaptation, curation and collaborative creation of contextually appropriate content – not only as a free-access resource.

We also found that the adoption of OER in Colombian schools may be more effective if capacity-building efforts go beyond standardised, mass-training courses and are focused on pedagogical support for the development of OEP with an emphasis on the following aspects:

1. Promoting the adoption of constructivist pedagogical models where teachers and students have a more active role in the educational process.
2. Fostering the use of available ICT in schools, as well as the use of personal devices to not only access information and entertainment, but also create and capture ways of thinking and responding.
3. Harnessing Creative Commons licensing to find, adapt, create and publish content collaboratively with fellow teachers and students, as well as fostering alternative copyright management in schools. This implies rethinking the role and production of conventional textbooks.

Additionally, although this research was based on the interests, dynamics and needs of the participants to define a collaborative model of OER implementation, the teachers stated that the existence of government policies and programmes can help to create the necessary conditions to encourage a greater number of colleagues to include OER in their educational practices. As a result, teachers identified two kinds of actions which are required: first, specific initiatives by teachers and schools on Open Education; and second, to promote the adoption of OER as a means for implementing and consolidating OEP.

It is not always easy to permeate the pedagogical practices of teachers with these ideas. In this study, clues were found regarding the conditions that led to the distancing of some teachers from the proposed activities, the most important ones being: an idea of education centred on the transmission of information from a teacher or expert to a passive subject; low levels of ICT capacity; interest in learning practical aspects rather than being involved in pedagogical reflections on ICT; the difficulty of moving from an oral discourse to a formal written production that accounts for learning about practices themselves; and a culture where individual work predominates over collaboration. It was not possible to delve more deeply into these aspects because there was a reluctance on the part of teachers who stopped participating to continue interaction with the research team.

By contrast, it was found that teachers who see themselves, their peers and their students as social actors who can create and recreate knowledge are more inclined to explore the implications of permissions and conditions behind content sharing in the classroom by utilising open licensing. In this sense, they understand and favour the development of OEP which responds to the specific sociocultural context of the classroom. It is by recognising teachers as valid interlocutors and actors in generating educational resources and in open pedagogical and educational initiatives that we work towards addressing the educational challenges in Colombia.

Acknowledgements

The coordination team of the coKREA project acknowledges the dedication and collaboration of the school teachers who made developing this PAR process possible through their continuous participation. These co-researcher participants were: Alid Armando Mera Mosquera, Blanca Elsa Beltrán Quinayás, Edy Yaneth Martínez Torres and Nidia Lucía Girón Bucheli (School Normal Superior de Popayán – Cauca); Andrés Enrique Noguera Fuentes and Leonardo Ordoñez Gómez (School John F. Kennedy – Cauca); Yorlani Sáenz Montilla (School Liceo Alejandro de Humboltd – Cauca); Luisa Fernanda Hernández Barbosa, Magaly Astrid Henao Mosquera, Mariana Elizabeth Pérez and Martha Elizabeth Pizo Ocoró (School Técnico Agropecuario Margarita Legarda – Cauca); Lady Clementine Castro Arias, Marco Antonio Mina and Yilver Enrique Polanco Marin (School Límbania Velasco – Cauca); Margoth Loaiza Jaramillo, José Nelson Álvarez Carvajal, Jose Aldemar Yate Galvis, Julián Bedoya Giraldo and Libardo Antonio Corrales (School INEM Felipe Pérez – Risaralda); Carlos Abel Martínez Valencia, Dumas Manzano Franco and Martha Viviana Vélez (School Corazón del Valle, Valle del Cauca).

In addition, the project team would like to thank ieRed for its support in the calls for participation of teachers and the social-oriented events of the project, as well as the management and advisory team of the Research on Open Educational Resources for Development project and the International Development Research Centre which made this study possible.

References

Anaya, S. & Hernandez, U. (2008). Construcción de un referente metodológico para la realización de Materiales Educativos Computarizados (MEC) a partir del enfoque CTS, las pedagogías críticas y el Software Libre. *Presentation at IV Encuentro en Línea de Educación y Software Libre EDUSOL.* Tlalnepantla, México. Retrieved from http://www.iered.org/archivos/Grupo_GEC/Ponencias/2008-11_Referente-MEC_presentacion.pdf

Anaya, S., Hernandez, M. & Hernández, U. (2010). Crear y publicar con las TIC en la escuela: una propuesta educativa desde la Cultura Libre. *Presentation at VI Encuentro en Línea de Educación y Software Libre EDUSOL.* Tlalnepantla, México. Retrieved from https://vimeo.com/49250298

Antúnez, S. (1999). El trabajo en equipo de los profesores y profesoras: factor de calidad, necesidad y problema. *Educar, 24*, 89–110. Retrieved from http://www.raco.cat/index.

php/Educar/article/view/20705/20545http://educar.uab.cat/article/view/v24-antunezhttp://
educar.uab.cat/article/view/v24-antunez

ASOINCA (Asosiación de institutores y tabajadores de le educación del Cauca Asoinca).
(2016). *Circular 249 de 2016: Programas del MEN que atentan contra la educación y los
derechos laborales.* Popayán: Asosiación de institutores y tabajadores de le educación del
Cauca Asoinca. Retrieved from http://www.asoinca.com/circulares/324-circular-249

Barrera, F. & Linden, L. (2009). *The use and misuse of computers in education: Evidence
from a randomized experiment in Colombia.* Washington, D.C.: World Bank. Retrieved from
http://documents.worldbank.org/curated/en/346301468022433230/pdf/WPS4836.pdf

Benavides, P. (2015). *Causalidad de la formación para la apropiación de las TIC en las
prácticas pedagógicas de docentes de Educación Básica y Media del suroccidente
colombiano.* Unpublished M.Phil thesis, Universidad del Cauca, Cauca, Colombia.

Botero, C. (2011). *Guías legales: Editores Colombia.* Santiago: ONG Derechos Digitales.
Retrieved from https://www.derechosdigitales.org/wp-content/uploads/Guia_Editores_
Colombia.pdf

Butcher, N. (2015). *A basic guide to Open Educational Resources (OER).* Paris:
Commonwealth of Learning & United Nations Educational, Scientific and Cultural
Organization. Retrieved from http://unesdoc.unesco.org/images/0021/002158/215804e.pdf

Castells, M. (2000). *La sociedad red.* Madrid: Alianza.

Castro, G., Catebiel, V. & Hernandez, U. (2005a). La cultura digital en el aula de clase:
¿Estamos los maestros preparados para asumirla? *Nodos y Nudos, 2(18),* 85–93. Retrieved
from http://revistas.pedagogica.edu.co/index.php/NYN/article/view/1259http://revistas.
pedagogica.edu.co/index.php/NYN/article/view/1259

Castro, G., Catebiel, V. & Hernandez, U. (2005b). La Red de Investigación Educativa: hacia
una construcción curricular alternativa en procesos de formación avanzada. *Revista ieRed,
1(3).* Retrieved from http://revista.iered.org/v1n3/pdf/gcvcuh.pdf

Cedillo, M., Romero, D., Peralta, M., Toledo, M. & Reyes, P. (2010). Aplicación de Recursos
Educativos (REAs) en cinco prácticas educativas con niños mexicanos de 6 a 12 años.
Revista Iberoamericana sobre Calidad, Eficacia y Cambio en Educación, 8(1). Retrieved
from http://www.redalyc.org/pdf/551/55113489007.pdf

Cobo, C. (2013). Exploration of open educational resources in non-English speaking
communities. *The International Review of Research in Open and Distributed Learning, 14(2),*
106–128. Retrieved from http://www.irrodl.org/index.php/irrodl/article/view/1493

Coll, C., Martín, E., Mauri, T., Miras, M., Onrubia, J., Solé, I. & Zabala, A. (2007). *El
constructivismo en el aula* (17th edn.). México: Graó. Retrieved from http://www.terras.edu.
ar/biblioteca/3/3Disponibilidad-del-aprendizaje.pdf

Collazos, C., Muñoz, J. & Hernández, Y. (2014). *Aprendizaje colaborativo apoyado por
computador.* Guayaquil: Proyecto LATIn. Retrieved from http://www.proyectolatin.org/books/
Aprendizaje_colaborativo_apoyado_por_computador_CC_BY-SA_3.0.pdf

Colombia Congreso de la República. (1982). *Ley 23 de 1982: sobre derechos de autor.* Diario
Oficial. Bogotá: Colombia Congreso de la República. Retrieved from http://derechodeautor.
gov.co/documents/10181/182597/23.pdf/a97b8750-8451-4529-ab87-bb82160dd226

Colombia Departamento Nacional de Planeación. (2000). *Documento conpes 3072: Agenda
de conectividad.* Bogotá: Colombia Departamento Nacional de Planeación. Retrieved from
https://www.mintic.gov.co/portal/604/articles-3498_documento.pdf

Colombia Ministerio de Comunicaciones. (2008). *Plan nacional de tecnologías de la
información y las comunicaciones.* Bogotá: Colombia Ministerio de Educación Nacional.
Retrieved from http://eduteka.icesi.edu.co/pdfdir/ColombiaPlanNacionalTIC.pdf

Colombia Ministerio de Educación Nacional. (2012). *Recursos Educativos Digitales Abiertos: Colombia*. Bogotá: Colombia Ministerio de Educación Nacional. Retrieved from http://www. colombiaaprende.edu.co/html/home/1592/articles-313597_reda.pdf

Colombia Ministerio de Educación Nacional. (2013). *Competencias TIC para el desarrollo profesional docente*. Bogotá: Colombia Ministerio de Educación Nacional. Retrieved from http://www.mineducacion.gov.co/1759/articles-339097_archivo_pdf_competencias_tic.pdf

Comunidad Andina de Naciones. (1993). *Decisión 351: Régimen común sobre derecho de autor y derechos conexos*. Lima: Comunidad Andina de Naciones. Retrieved from http:// www.uninorte.edu.co/documents/72553/12744051/R%C3%A9gimen+Com%C3%BAn+so bre+Derecho+%281%29.pdf/5b8aabc5-55fa-443c-8811-449334d1680e

Contreras, R. (2010). Recursos educativos abiertos: Una iniciativa con barreras aún por superar. *Apertura, 2(2)*. Retrieved from http://www.redalyc.org/articulo.oa?id=68820827009

Corral, Y. (2010). Diseño de cuestionarios para recolección de datos. *Revista Ciencias de la Educación, 20(36)*. Retrieved from http://servicio.bc.uc.edu.ve/educacion/revista/n36/ art08.pdf

Daniel, J., Kanwar, A. & Uvalić-Trumbić, S. (2006). A tectonic shift in global higher education. *Change: The Magazine of Higher Learning, 38(4)*, 16–23. Retrieved from http://www. learntechlib.org/p/98724

de los Arcos, B., Farrow, R., Pitt, R., Weller, M. & McAndrew, P. (2016). Adapting the curriculum: How K-12 teachers perceive the role of Open Educational Resources. *Journal of Online Learning Research, 2(1)*, 23–40. Retrieved from http://oro.open.ac.uk/id/ eprint/46145

Deslauriers, J. P. (2004). *Investigación cualitativa: Guía práctica*. M.Phil thesis. Pereira: Universidad Tecnológica de Pereira. Retrieved from http://repositorio.utp.edu.co/dspace/ handle/11059/3365

DeRosa, R. & Robison, S. (2017). From OER to open pedagogy: Harnessing the power of open. In R. S. Jhangiani & R. Biswas-Diener (Eds.), *Open: The philosophy and practices that are revolutionizing education and science* (pp. 115–124). London: Ubiquity Press. Retrieved from https://doi.org/10.5334/bbc.i

Elliott, J. (2000). *La investigación-acción en educación* (4th edn.). Madrid: Morata.

Fullan, M. (2002). El significado del cambio educativo: un cuarto de siglo de aprendizaje. *Profesorado: Revista de currículum y formación del profesorado, 6*. Retrieved from http://www.ugr.es/~recfpro/rev61ART1.pdf

Gértrudix, M., Álvarez, S., Galisteo del Valle, A., Gálvez de la Cuesta, M. C. & Gértrudix, F. (2007). Acciones de diseño y desarrollo de objetos educativos digitales: Programas institucionales. *Revista de la Universidad y Sociedad del Conocimiento, 4(1)*, 14–25. Retrieved from http://www.redalyc.org/articulo.oa?id=78040107

Glasserman, L. D. & Ramírez, M. S. (2014). Uso de Recursos Educativos Abiertos (REA) y Objetos de Aprendizaje (OA) en educación básica. *Teoría de la Educación: Educación y Cultura en la Sociedad de la Información, 15(2)*. Retrieved from http://www.redalyc.org/ articulo.oa?id=201031409005

Grinsztajn, F., Steizmberg, R., Córdoba, M. & Miguez, M. (2015). Construcción de saber pedagógico y recursos educativos abiertos en la formación de profesionales para la docencia universitaria. *REDU: Revista de Docencia Universitaria, 13(3)*, 237–254. Retrieved from https://polipapers.upv.es/index.php/REDU/article/view/5457

Gun, M. (2003). Opportunity for literacy? Preliterate learners in the AMEP. *Prospect, 18(2)*. Retrieved from http://www.ameprc.mq.edu.au/docs/prospect_journal/volume_18_ no_2/18_2_3_Gunn.pdf

Harris J., Mishra, P. & Koehler, M. (2009). Teachers' technological pedagogical content knowledge and learning activity types: Curriculum-based technology integration reframed. *Journal of Research on Technology in Education, 41(4)*, 393–416. Retrieved from http://files.eric.ed.gov/fulltext/EJ844273.pdf

Hatakka, M. (2009). Build it and they will come?: Inhibiting factors for reuse of open content in developing countries. *The Electronic Journal on Information Systems in Developing Countries, 37(5)*, 1–16. Retrieved from http://www.is.cityu.edu.hk/staff/isrobert/ejisdc/37-5.pdf

Hegarty, B. (2015). Attributes of Open pedagogy: A model for using Open Educational Resources. *Educational Technology, July–August 2015*, 3–13. Retrieved from https://upload.wikimedia.org/wikipedia/commons/c/ca/Ed_Tech_Hegarty_2015_article_attributes_of_open_pedagogy.pdf

Hernandez, U. & Benavides, P. (2012). Para qué las TIC en la Educación Básica y Media: Reflexiones a partir de la cualificación de maestros en ejercicio en el suroccidente colombiano. In G. Castro & U. Hernandez (Eds.), *Saber pedagógico en el Cauca: Miradas de maestros en contextos de diversidad* (pp. 183–200). Popayán: Universidad del Cauca. Retrieved from http://www.iered.org/archivos/Publicaciones_Libres/2012_Saber_Pedagogico_Cauca/SaberPedagogicoCauca_3-5-UlisesHernandez-y-PastorBenavides.pdf

Hernández, Y. M. (2015). Factores que favorecen la innovación educativa con el uso de la tecnología: Una perspectiva desde el proyecto coKREA. *Revista Virtual UCN, 45*. Retrieved from http://revistavirtual.ucn.edu.co/index.php/RevistaUCN/article/view/654http://revistavirtual.ucn.edu.co/index.php/RevistaUCN/article/view/654

Hernández, Y. M., Hernandez, U. & Sáenz, M. P. (2014). Creative Commons como respuesta a las restricciones que el derecho de autor genera en las prácticas docentes. *Perspectivas, 6*. Retrieved from http://www.iered.org/archivos/Proyecto_coKREA/Publicaciones/2014-07_CC-Practica-Docente_MHernandez-UHernandez-y-MPSaenz.pdf

Huayta, E., Gómez, M. L., Atencio, L. L. & Arias, W. R. (2008). *Guía para el acompañamiento pedagógico de proyectos de innovación en las regiones*. Lima: Fondo Nacional de Desarrollo de la Educación Peruana. Retrieved from https://www.scribd.com/document/162122218/Guia-de-Acompanamiento-Pedagogico

Kanwar, A., Kodhandaraman, B. & Umar A. (2010). Toward sustainable Open Education Resources: A perspective from the Global South. *The American Journal of Distance Education, 24(2)*, 65–80. Retrieved from http://dx.doi.org/10.1080/08923641003696588

Kaplún, G. (2005). *Aprender y enseñar en tiempos de Internet: Formación profesional a distancia y nuevas tecnologías*. Montevideo: Centro Interamericano para el Desarrollo del Conocimiento en la Formación Profesional. Retrieved from http://www.oitcinterfor.org/node/6185

Kemmis, S. & McTaggart, R. (2005). Participatory action research: Communicative action and public sphere. In N. K. Denzin & Y. S. Lincoln (Eds.), *SAGE handbook of qualitative research*. Thousand Oaks, CA: Sage.

Krelja Kurelovic, E. (2016). Advantages and limitations of usage of Open Educational Resources in small countries. *International Journal of Research in Education and Science (IJRES), 2(1)*, 136–142. Retrieved from https://oerknowledgecloud.org/sites/oerknowledgecloud.org/files/5000123134-5000259500-1-PB.pdf

Lessig, L. (2004). *Free culture: How big media uses technology and the law to lock down culture and control creativity*. New York: Penguin. Retrieved from http://www.free-culture.cc/freeculture.pdf

Lieberman, A. (2013). Cuando se tiene una experiencia de aula y no se escribe, esta se va: Si la escribes, puedes mantenerla y conceptualizarla. *Profesión Docente, 51*, 78–83. Retrieved from http://www.revistadocencia.cl/new/wp-content/pdf/20131205182411.pdf

Lozano, F., Ramírez, M. S. & Celaya, R. (2010). Apropiación tecnológica en profesores que incorporan Recursos Educativas Abiertos en educación media superior. *Revista Mexicana de Investigación Educativa, 15*, 487–513. Retrieved from http://www.redalyc.org/articulo. oa?id=14012507007

Martínez, H. A. & González, S. (2010). Acompañamiento pedagógico y profesionalización docente: Sentido y perspectiva. *Ciencia y Sociedad, XXXV*, 521–541. Retrieved from http:// www.redalyc.org/articulo.oa?id=87020009007

McIntyre, A. (2008). *Participatory action research: Qualitative research methods series, Vol. 52.* Thousand Oaks, CA: Sage.

Mogollón, S. & Solano, M. (2011). *Active schools: Our convictions for improving the quality of education.* Durham: FHI 360. Retrieved from https://www.fhi360.org/resource/active-schools-our-convictions-improving-quality-education

Montero, L. (2011). El trabajo colaborativo del profesorado como oportunidad formativa. CEE *Participación Educativa, 16*, 69–88. Retrieved from https://dialnet.unirioja.es/servlet/ articulo?codigo=4942213

Moreno, J. J., Anaya, S., Benavides, P., Hernandez, U. & Hernández, Y. M. (2011). *Los Proyectos Pedagógicos de Aula para la integración de las TIC: Como sistematización de la experiencia docente* (2nd edn.). Popayán: Universidad del Cauca. Retrieved from http:// openlibrary.org/books/OL25415251M//

Narváez, A. & Calderón, L. (2016). Modelo tecnológico para la apropiación de Software Libre en sedes educativas públicas del Departamento del Cauca. *Revista Colombiana de Computación, 17(2)*, 50–56.

Ngimwa, P. (2010). *OER readiness in Africa: A report submitted to the OLnet Project, August 2010.* Barcelona: OLnet. Retrieved from https://oerknowledgecloud.org/sites/ oerknowledgecloud.org/files/37994804-OER-Readiness-in-Africa.pdf

OPAL (Open Educational Quality Initiative). (2011). *Beyond OER: Shifting focus to Open Educational Practices – The OPAL Report 2011.* Essen: University of Duisburg-Essen. Retrieved from https://oerknowledgecloud.org/content/beyond-oer-shifting-focus-open-educational-practices

Orellana, D. & Sánchez, M. (2006) Técnicas de recolección de datos en entornos virtuales más usadas en la investigación cualitativa. *Revista de Investigación Educativa, 24(1)*, 205–222. Retrieved from http://revistas.um.es/rie/article/view/97661

Ortiz, W., Caldón, E. & Hernandez, U. (2015). Potenciar la Infraestructura TIC de las Instituciones Educativas para generar espacios pedagógicos de trabajo colaborativo. *Presentation at III Encuentro de Experiencias Pedagógicas e Investigativas del Departamento del Cauca, 8 May 2015.* Popayán, Colombia.

Petrides, L., Jimes, C., Middleton-Detzner, C. & Howell, H. (2010). OER as a model for enhanced teaching and learning. In *Open Ed 2010 Proceedings, 2–4 November 2010.* Barcelona, Spain. Retrieved from http://openaccess.uoc.edu/webapps/o2/ bitstream/10609/4995/6/Jimes_editat.pdf

Petrides, L., Jimes, C., Middleton-Detzner, C., Walling, J. & Weiss, S. (2011). Open textbook adoption and use: Implications for teachers and learners. *Open Learning, 26(1)*, 39–49. Retrieved from http://www.tandfonline.com/doi/abs/10.1080/02680513.2011.538563

Pinzón, Y. P., Poveda, O. & Pérez, A. (2015). Un estudio sobre el desarrollo del pensamiento aleatorio usando Recursos Educativos Abiertos. *Apertura, 7(1)*. Retrieved from http://www. redalyc.org/articulo.oa?id=68838021003

Restrepo, B. (2002). Una variante pedagógica de la investigación-acción educativa. *Revista Iberoamericana de Educación de la OEI.* Retrieved from http://www.rieoei.org/ deloslectores/370Restrepo.PDF

Restrepo, B. (2004). La investigación-acción educativa y la construcción de saber pedagógico. *Educación y Educadores, 7*, 45–55. Retrieved from http://educacionyeducadores. unisabana.edu.co/index.php/eye/article/view/548

Rodríguez, C., Sánchez, F. & Márquez, J. (2011). *Impacto del programa "Computadores para Educar" en la deserción estudiantil, el logro escolar y el ingreso a la educación superior. Documentos CEDE, 15.* Bogotá: Universidad de los Andes. Retrieved from https:// economia.uniandes.edu.co/components/com_booklibrary/ebooks/dcede2011-15.pdf

Rodríguez, N., Tellez, A. C. & Vértiz, M. P. (2010). Estudio de casos: REA (Recursos Educativos Abiertos) en clases de Historia de México. *Magis: Revista Internacional de Investigación en Educación, 3(5)*. Retrieved from http://www.redalyc.org/articulo.oa?id=281023476009

Sáenz, M. P., Hernandez, U. & Hernández, Y. M. (2014). Contenidos y tecnologías abiertas: Un enfoque para repensar la formación del sujeto cognoscente. In L. C. Certuche (Ed.), *Constructivismo, competencias y escuela.* Almaguer: Normal Santa Clara. Retrieved from https://openlibrary.org/books/OL25636699M/

Sánchez, A. (2013). *Bilingüismo en Colombia.* Cartagena de Indias: Banco de la República. Retrieved from http://www.banrep.gov.co/es/dtser-191

Sanz, J., Sánchez, S. & Dodero, J. M. (2011). Determinando la relevancia de los Recursos Educativos Abiertos a través de la integración de diferentes indicadores de calidad. *RUSC: Universities and Knowledge Society Journal, 8(2)*. Retrieved from http://www.redalyc.org/ articulo.oa?id=78018793005

Sapire, I. & Reed, Y. (2011). Collaborative design and use of Open Educational Resources: A case study of a mathematics teacher education project in South Africa. *Distance Education for Empowerment and Development in Africa, 32(2)*, 195–211. Retrieved from http://dx.doi. org/10.1080/01587919.2011.584847

Schmitz, C. (2009). Propiedad Intelectual, Dominio Público y equilibrio de intereses. *Revista Chilena de Derecho, 36(2)*, 343–367. Retrieved from http://www.redalyc.org/articulo. oa?id=177014523006

Stagg, A. (2014). La adopción de los recursos educativos abiertos: Un continuo de práctica abierta. *RUSC: Universities and Knowledge Society Journal, 11(3)*, 160–175. Retrieved from http://www.redalyc.org/articulo.oa?id=78031423012

Strauss A. & Corbin J. (2002*). Bases de la investigación cualitativa: Técnicas y procedimientos para desarrollar la teoría fundamentada.* Medellín: Universidad de Antioquía.

Sunkel, G., Trucco, D. & Möller, S. (2011). *Aprender y enseñar con las Tecnologías de la información y las Comunicaciones en América Latina: Potenciales beneficios.* Santiago: Comisión Económica para América Latina y el Caribe. Retrieved from http://www.cepal.org/ cgi-bin/getProd.asp?xml=/publicaciones/xml/9/42669/P42669.xml

Torres, Y. & Moreno, R. (2008). El texto escolar, evolución e influencia. *Revista Laurus, 14(27)*. Retrieved from http://www.redalyc.org/articulo.oa?id=76111892004

UNESCO (United Nations Educational, Scientific and Cultural Organization). (2012). *2012 OER Paris Declaration.* Paris: United Nations Educational, Scientific and Cultural Organization. Retrieved from http://www.unesco.org/new/fileadmin/MULTIMEDIA/HQ/CI/CI/pdf/Events/ Paris%20OER%20Declaration_01.pdf

Valdivia, I. (2008). *Las políticas de tecnología para escuelas en América Latina y el mundo: Visiones y lecciones.* Santiago: Comisión Económica para América Latina y el Caribe. Retrieved from http://www.cepal.org/es/publicaciones/4006-politicas-tecnologia-escuelas- america-latina-mundo-visiones-lecciones

Watson, D. (2001). Pedagogy before technology: Re-thinking the relationship between ICT and teaching. *Education and Information Technology, 6(4)*, 251–266. Retrieved from https:// pdfs.semanticscholar.org/8716/a18fc92e7aef2ce58990490f58f89d22c535.pdf

Wiley, D., Hilton III, J. L., Ellington, S. & Hall, T. (2012). A preliminary examination of the cost savings and learning impacts of using open textbooks in middle and high school science classes. *The International Review of Research in Open and Distributed Learning, 13(3)*. Retrieved from http://www.irrodl.org/index.php/irrodl/article/view/1153/2256

Zancanaro, A., Todesco, J. & Ramos, F. (2015). A bibliometric mapping of open educational resources. *The International Review of Research in Open and Distributed Learning, 16(1)*. Retrieved from http://dx.doi.org/10.19173/irrodl.v16i1.1960

How to cite this chapter

Sáenz, M. P., Hernandez, U. & Hernández, Y. M. (2017). Co-creation of OER by teachers and teacher educators in Colombia. In C. Hodgkinson-Williams & P. B. Arinto (Eds.), *Adoption and impact of OER in the Global South* (pp. 143–185). Retrieved from https://doi.org/10.5281/zenodo.604384

Corresponding author: María del Pilar Sáenz Rodríguez <mpsaenz@karisma.org.co>

This work is licensed under a Creative Commons Attribution 4.0 International (CC BY 4.0) licence. It was carried out with the aid of a grant from the International Development Research Centre, Ottawa, Canada.

Chapter 6

Effectiveness of OER use in first-year higher education students' mathematical course performance: A case study

Werner Westermann Juárez and Juan Ignacio Venegas Muggli

Summary

This chapter aims to understand the impact of Open Educational Resources (OER) on first-year mathematics students at the Instituto Profesional Providencia (IPP) in Santiago, Chile, where more than half (52%) of first-year students typically drop out of their studies. In order to address this, the institution established an innovation fund and a project to profile, assess and monitor student performance through an early warning system. IPP stakeholders envisioned that a strategy to promote OER uptake could complement these efforts. By looking at an OER intervention amongst first-year students, this study seeks to identify ways in which OER can provide new tools, opportunities, and contexts to improve student performance and lower dropout rates by answering the following research questions: What is the effect of OER use on first-year students' mathematics course performance? In face-to-face instruction, what is the effect of OER use on first-year students' class attendance? What are teachers' and students' perceptions of the OER adoption process?

To answer questions one and two, this study used a quantitative method to estimate the effect of OER use on students' mathematical course performance and class attendance. Five groups of first-year students were compared based on the analysis of two scenarios. In Scenario 1, a control group and two treatment groups were in a traditional face-to-face classroom setting. The control group relied on a proprietary textbook; the first treatment group was taught with the help of a Khan Academy OER collection; and the second treatment group was taught by means of a custom-designed Open Textbook. Scenario 2 compared two classes in blended-mode Algebra and Calculus courses. The control group relied on a proprietary resource, ▶

and the treatment group used a Khan Academy collection of OER in addition to the proprietary resource. In order to estimate the effectiveness of OER use on students' mathematical performance, the impact analysis focused on three result variables: (1) students' marks before the final exam, (2) students' final exam marks, and (3) students' final course marks after the exam.

To answer research question three, a mixed-methods approach was applied in the form of a series of semi-structured interviews, a focus group discussion and a student survey. The students who used the Khan Academy OER collections or the Open Textbook were asked to participate in this study in order to better comprehend learners' and teachers' perceptions of OER.

Students in Scenario 1 who used Khan Academy resources obtained statistically significantly better exam grades than those who used the proprietary resource or the Open Textbook, suggesting that not all kinds of OER have the same effect on student performance. In Scenario 2, there was no improvement in mathematical course performance amongst students using OER. In terms of student attendance, face-to-face mode students who used Khan Academy OER had significantly lower attendance levels than those who relied on the proprietary textbook, which may be due to the fact that when students have access to the infrastructure required to access OER remotely they tend to work more from home.

With regard to student and teacher perceptions of the OER adoption process, the qualitative and quantitative data confirmed the assumption that OER can be relevant and useful to Chilean students.

The chapter concludes with the insight that "openness" does not necessarily produce an impact in and of itself, but is instead part of a greater set of tools and practices in which many variables exert an influence. Neither the intrinsic nature of information and communication technologies nor openness are tools or instruments that can be said to result in a specific outcome.

The dataset arising from this study can be accessed at:
https://www.datafirst.uct.ac.za/dataportal/index.php/catalog/577

Acronyms and abbreviations

ESD	Education for Sustainable Development
ICT	information and communication technologies
IPP	Instituto Profesional Providencia
LMS	learning management system
OER	Open Educational Resources
PSM	Propensity Score Matching
US	United States

Introduction

Education is a pivotal means of promoting development in every developing country. As countries seek to develop their human capital to participate in the global knowledge society and address the challenges of the new global economy, there is increasing pressure on educational systems, particularly those in higher education, to meet the increasing demand for equal educational opportunities and supply high-quality, relevant and efficient formal and informal educational processes.

Both equity and quality are major challenges for national educational systems in terms of the level of innovation and transformation required. The United Nations Educational, Scientific and Cultural Organization coined the phrase "Education for Sustainable Development" (ESD)[1] as an umbrella term for the many forms of educational practice that promote efforts to rethink educational systems (both in terms of curriculum and pedagogy) in countries facing extreme educational challenges. ESD requires participatory teaching and learning approaches in order to motivate teachers and empower learners to change their behaviour and take action to achieve sustainable development. It promotes competencies such as critical thinking, imagining future scenarios, making decisions and solving problems in a collaborative way.

As a reimagined education system is required to create a new set of skills and competencies for the burgeoning number of new learners, there appears to be widespread consensus that new forms of educational provision need to be online and free of cost to the learner. The European Commission (2012, p.9) states that digital technology "offers unprecedented opportunities to improve quality, access and equity in education and training", and that it is a "key lever for more effective learning and for reducing barriers to education, in particular social barriers". It recognises, however, that technology on its own does not assure innovation; it is instead the level of openness in the use of technology, in the context of an open learning environment (European Commission, 2013), that enables capacity development in order to stay current, promote innovation and exploit the potential of new learning technologies and digital content.

Recent trends in the use of Open Educational Resources (OER), also referred to as "open content"[2] or "*Recursos Educativos Abiertos*" in Spanish (Betancourt, Celaya & Ramírez, 2014), are enabling fundamental changes and innovation in educational provision. New ways of learning, characterised by personalisation, engagement, use of digital media, collaboration, bottom-up practices and an approach where the learner or teacher is a creator as well as consumer of learning content, have been facilitated by the exponential growth of OER in recent years. OER are important for stimulating innovative learning environments where content can be adapted by users according to their needs (Keegan & Bell, 2011). The European Commission has asserted that "stimulating supply and demand for high-quality OERs is essential for modernizing education" (European Commission, 2013, p.8). In the current global educational environment, OER are recognised as having the potential to make an impact in the following areas (Orr, Rimini & Van Damme, 2015):

---

1   http://en.unesco.org/themes/education-sustainable-development
2   https://web.archive.org/web/19990128224600/http://www.opencontent.org/home.shtml

- Harnessing the possibilities afforded by digital technology in order to address common educational challenges.
- Acting as a catalyst for social innovation and new forms of interaction between teachers and learners in the knowledge-generation process.
- Promoting the idea of an extended lifecycle beyond original design and purpose, where the process of distribution, adaptation and iteration can improve access to high-quality, context-appropriate educational materials for all.

In the case of Chile, the educational system has been challenged by the demands of civil society to access quality education. Following a series of ongoing student-led protests across the country that set the foundation for a national social reform movement, the second presidential term of Michelle Bachelet's government (2014–2018) has embraced the challenge through complex and structural educational reform.[3] An ambitious legislative agenda seeks equal accessibility to quality education as a civil right, more direct state participation in primary and secondary education, the end of for-profit education, an increase in state support for public universities, the creation of a government agency to apply the law against for-profit activities in higher education, and an improvement in quality accreditation processes (Brunner, 2008). In short, it is a system of reform based on strengthening the public supply of education.

Although educational resources are considered in the various strategies of multi-dimensional educational reform in Chile, there is no reference to openly licensed resources as part of a strategy for equitable access to quality educational services and increasing the affordability of education to address wider and constantly growing demand. The issue of how to leverage legal and technical openness to improve the quality of education therefore remains a central challenge.

Professional institutes (*Institutos profesionales*), which address around 60% of national, post-secondary education supply, typically accommodate many underprivileged and disadvantaged students with low levels of basic knowledge and cognitive skills. However, a recent study stated that nearly three out of four professional institute graduates lacked basic reading comprehension skills (Fundación La Fuente/Adimark GFK, 2011). Conducting research on how innovative open approaches to learning can impact upon and improve student performance is particularly important in the context of first- and second-year students with deficits in knowledge and skills who enrol in higher education courses. Along with the need to improve student performance, retention rates in first- and second-year students, alongside poor throughput (graduation) rates, are the main problems in higher education (MINEDC, 2012). When considering the tertiary education sector in Chile,[4] the dropout rate is a substantial challenge, as many institutions have retention rates of less than 40%. This places a heavy burden on institutions and on society, particularly as relates to the loss of tuition revenue from the students who drop out or transfer to other institutions (MINEDC, 2012).

---

3   http://www.gob.cl/la-reforma-educacional-esta-marcha/
4   The Chilean higher education system is formed by three types of institutions: universities, technical training centres and professional institutes (known as a technical colleges), which can also award some professional or bachelor's degrees.

At the Instituto Profesional Providencia (IPP),[5] the higher education institute where this study was situated, more than half (52%) of first-year students drop out of their studies. In order to address this situation, the institution has established an innovation fund and project to profile, assess and monitor student performance through an early warning information management system. IPP stakeholders envisioned that a strategy to promote OER uptake could complement these efforts, but there was little on-the-ground institutional awareness of OER or Open Education at the time of the study.

The lack of awareness and level of indifference towards OER is not restricted to IPP, and can be seen in most higher education institutions in Chile. This study attempts to aid advocacy initiatives by addressing the need for empirical evidence on the impact of OER adoption. Specifically, the study is concerned with identifying ways in which OER can provide new tools, opportunities and contexts to address student performance challenges and dropout rates. In line with these ambitions, the study asks the following research questions:

1. What is the effect of OER use on first-year students' mathematics course performance?
2. In face-to-face instruction, what is the effect of OER use on first-year students' class attendance?
3. What are teachers' and students' perceptions of the OER adoption process?

It is hoped that findings of this study will not only contribute to the emerging field of impact studies in OER research, but also raise awareness amongst IPP stakeholders on how OER can contribute to addressing institutional challenges for accessible and quality higher education.

Literature review and conceptual framework

Literature review

OER, and Open Education more broadly, have become a major trend in public educational policy-making. A series of initiatives have demonstrated how momentum in the OER movement has led to numerous institutional, local, regional and national policies supporting OER throughout the world, such as Policies for OER Uptake,[6] the European Open Education Policy Project,[7] and the Creative Commons OER Policy Registry.[8] These have been mapped by projects such as the OER Impact Map[9] and promoted by initiatives such as the Institute for Open Leadership.[10] Coinciding with the growth of the OER movement, the OER research agenda has also matured considerably. As the first phase of global OER initiatives was focused on providing infrastructure and delivery mechanisms for OER, initial OER research was mainly focused on measuring the deployment, access and use of these resources. The

---

5   http://ipp.cl
6   http://www.poerup.info
7   http://oerpolicy.eu/
8   https://wiki.creativecommons.org/wiki/OER_Policy_Registry
9   http://oermap.org/policy-map/
10   https://openpolicynetwork.org/iol

first objectives in this field were to investigate and develop solutions in terms of access to knowledge in the context of key OER repository projects (e.g. Merlot, OpenCourseWare, Curriki, OER Commons and Temoa),[11] and to address challenges related to copyright management (UNESCO–IITE, 2011). As the OER movement evolved, a new wave of research studies manifested in order to assess the efficacy and impact of OER adoption and deployment[12] (Santos-Hermosa, Ferran-Ferrer & Abadal, 2013). A nationally representative survey of over 2 100 faculty members in the United States (US) recently rated "proven efficacy" and "trusted quality" as the two most important criteria for selecting teaching resources among a wide variety of factors (Allen & Seaman, 2014). In order for OER to gain traction in the higher education sector, it is important to gather empirical evidence demonstrating the efficacy and quality dimensions of OER adoption. In line with this principle, there is an overarching need for rigorous, controlled impact studies in a variety of settings to establish the impact of OER on learning outcomes and the cost of education in comparison with other digital or more traditional materials (Shear, Means & Lundh, 2015).

This research study was scoped in 2012, at a time when the OER impact field was relatively nascent, and utilised the JISC 2011 OER Impact report[13] as its main frame of reference. The OER research landscape has since evolved quite rapidly, shifting its focus to effectiveness and impact issues as OER initiatives are increasingly deployed and scaled.

OER effectiveness and impact studies have principally focused on whether and how adoption at the institutional level brings about financial benefit for students and institutions. Within this context, most impact research has been focused on the cost-effectiveness of "packaging" OER into courseware or textbooks (Bliss, Hilton III, Wiley & Thanos, 2013; Wiley, Hilton III, Ellington & Hall, 2012). While cost savings represent a major feature of OER advocacy for OER adoption in the Global North, this does not seem to be as much of a critical factor in developing countries as digital "piracy" and reproduction through photocopying appear to persist and are often overlooked at the institutional level.[14] This research study therefore focuses on the effectiveness of OER as relates to the teaching and learning process, rather than its efficacy in matters such as cost-saving.

Prior studies have attempted to investigate the impact of the use of OER on educational processes. The OER Research Hub[15] defined 11 hypotheses which represent some commonly stated beliefs and motivations regarding OER (Weller, de los Arcos, Farrow, Pitt & McAndrew, 2015). Three of those hypotheses are particularly pertinent to this study:

- Performance: Use of OER leads to improvement in student performance and satisfaction.
- Openness: The "open aspect" of OER creates different usage and adoption patterns.
- Reflection: Use of OER leads to critical reflection by educators, with evidence of improvement in their practice.

---

11 Merlot (https://www.merlot.org/merlot/index.htm), OCW (http://ocw.mit.edu/index.htm), Curriki (http://www. curriki.org/), OER Commons (https://www.oercommons.org/) and Temoa (http://www.temoa.info/es)
12 http://www.hewlett.org/library/ruminations-on-research-on-open-educational-resources/
13 http://www.webarchive.org.uk/wayback/archive/20140614114910 and http://www.jisc.ac.uk/media/ documents/programmes/elearning/oer/JISCOERImpactStudyResearchReportv1-0.pdf
14 http://blogs.lse.ac.uk/impactofsocialsciences/2016/04/07/how-do-students-access-the-resources-they-need/
15 http://oerresearchhub.org/

Previous research has also helped to shape this study with regards to the specific type of OER selected, namely, open textbooks and their relationship to learning outcomes. Hilton and Laman (2012) compared the performance of 690 students from Houston Community College in the US using an open textbook in an introductory psychology class of 370 students who had used a traditional commercial textbook in a previous semester. They concluded that students who used the open textbook achieved better grades in the course, had a lower withdrawal rate and scored better on the final examination. Feldstein et al. (2012) found that, in a sample of 991 students in nine core courses at the Virginia State University's School of Business, those using open textbooks typically had higher grades and lower failure and withdrawal rates than those in courses with traditional commercial textbooks.

Fischer, Hilton III, Robinson and Wiley (2015) recently published a multi-institutional study examining the academic outcomes of more than 16 000 students from 10 higher education institutions in the US who were assigned open textbooks, versus those assigned traditionally published textbooks. The main finding was that conventional, expensive textbooks were not superior to open ones, and that students assigned to work with open textbooks did as well as or better than their peers in terms of grades, course completion and other measures of academic success. Overall, students in more than half of the courses that used open textbooks improved according to at least one academic measure used in the study, and students in 93% of these courses did at least as well on all other measures (Fischer et al., 2015).

In terms of concern about whether OER might in some way negatively affect the learning endeavour, Allen, Guzman-Alvarez, Molinaro and Larsen (2015) studied a class of 478 students at the University of California, Davis, who used an OER known as ChemWiki as their primary textbook while a control class of 448 utilised a traditional textbook. These two classes were taught in the same semester at consecutive hours by the same faculty member and teaching assistants in order to control for potential bias. Students in the classes also took the same exams. No substantial differences were found between the two groups in terms of performance. Beginning of the semester pre-tests combined with final exams showed no noteworthy differences in individual learning gains between the two groups, indicating that OER could be substituted without any negative impact on learning.

There is great diversity in the kinds of educational resources currently referred to as OER, and many factors influence the ultimate "success" of a teaching resource, making it difficult to isolate the "openness" dimension and draw meaningful conclusions about use and value based on the open nature of a resource. This issue, which the OER Research Hub refers to as the "level of openness" dimension (Shear et al., 2015), is pertinent in that we need to investigate more deeply specific types of openness as enablers for educational quality, innovation and sustainability.

Conceptual framework

To estimate the effectiveness of OER use in improving the academic performance of first-year IPP students, the OER selected had to cover the curriculum comprehensively so that they could be used with high frequency throughout the course.

The first type of OER employed in this study was Khan Academy collections. Khan Academy is a not-for-profit organisation whose main goal is to "change education for the better by providing free world-class education for anyone anywhere".[16] This is achieved through sharing thousands of openly licensed resources, including an extensive library of video content (more than 4 500 video lessons and growing), complemented by a modular and interactive assessment process that incorporates practice exercises. It also offers a personalised learning dashboard that empowers learners to study at their own pace in and outside of the classroom. Unlike many other open content platforms, Khan Academy has translated its web platform, and the resources contained therein, into Spanish,[17] enabling broader global reach.

Khan Academy has organised its numerous resources by subject, K–12 educational level and different standardised test categories arranged in "courses", which are a suggested sequence of learning resources. Khan Academy has enhanced features for teaching, enabling a "coach" to build "courses" by selecting and sequencing (in a sense, remixing) Khan's resources for delivery to subscribed users in the "course". The coaches can be educators or parents; in fact, anyone who can mentor or follow a learner through detailed analytics in order to track the learning process. Both teachers participating in this study utilised the Khan Academy platform to curate (or "bundle") "courses" designed to fit their specific teaching challenges and needs. Students were provided with access to the content via the online platform, under the teachers' attentive monitoring, which is made possible through platform analytics. In order to avoid confusion with formal institutional courses, the specific "courses" curated in the Spanish Khan Academy website for this intervention will be referred to as "**Khan Academy Collection 1**" and "**Khan Academy Collection 2**".

To avoid exclusive focus on the potential efficacy of a specific digital educational resource, a second OER was incorporated in order to better analyse the characteristics of the resource in the learning process, rather than their digital nature. In the absence of any OER similar to the Khan Academy in terms of focus and, most of all, extensive coverage of the course syllabus, an open textbook crafted by the Arithmetic teacher involved was developed for the purposes of this study. Based mainly on teachers' materials, notes and resources, the open textbook was published on Wikibooks – a wiki platform which enables easy, participatory editing of the content, exports material to a wide range of formats and supports LaTex (a coding language for generating mathematical formulas). For a face-to-face course, the Arithmetic open textbook adapted and published in Spanish on the Wikibooks platform was *Numeros y Operaciones* ("Numbers and Operations")[18] (Figure 1). It was delivered in both print and digital format and is referred to as the "**Open Textbook**" in the context of this study.

---

16   http://khanacademy.org
17   http://es.khanacademy.org
18   https://es.wikibooks.org/wiki/Matem%C3%A1ticas/N%C3%BAmeros_y_Operaciones

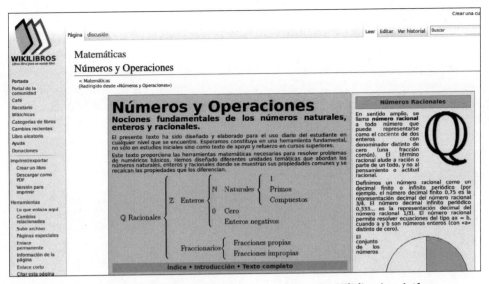

Figure 1: Screenshot of the Open Textbook homepage on the Wikibooks platform

The Khan Academy collections and the Open Textbook sought to replace (in the case of Scenario 1) or supplement (in the case of Scenario 2) the traditional, proprietary textbooks which serve as the usual mandatory resources in the formal course syllabus. There are issues relating to resource access because of a limited number of printed volumes or copies of e-books in the institutional library. The usual procedure students adopt to get around this access challenge is to make photocopies; this is, however, much more difficult with the e-books.

In Scenario 1, the two proprietary textbooks were e-books,[19] which have a low cost (USD 16) but are only accessible to five students, who can each only access the book for a limited time period through the library.

In Scenario 2, the proprietary textbook was a printed volume,[20] which cost USD 45. There were only six printed copies in the library, which had to be shared across three different IPP campuses. In addition to the mandatory printed textbook, there was also an online version of proprietary course notes made available by the institution, which was used as a supplementary resource.

The Open Textbook developed by the Arithmetic teacher for this study is licensed with a Creative Commons Attribution (CC BY) 4.0 International license, one of the more permissive forms of open licences in terms of facilitating reuse. The Khan Academy Terms of Use[21] state that all its educational content and resources are licensed under a more restrictive Creative Commons Attribution Non-Commercial ShareAlike (CC BY-NC-SA) United States 3.0 licence. It is recognised that the OER selected and developed in the context of this study have different properties in terms of their degrees of openness, where the legal openness is just one of the key attributes of OER, along with technical and social attributes (Hodgkinson-

---

19 The two e-books are: Goñi, J. M. (2011) *Didáctica de las matemáticas*; and Goñi, J. M. (2011) *Matemáticas, Complemento de la formación disciplinar*.

20 Zill, D. (2011). *Álgebra y Trigonometría*.

21 https://www.khanacademy.org/about/tos

Williams & Gray, 2009). In that sense, the Open Textbook treated in this study would be "more open", while the Khan Academy resource is "less open".

The Khan Academy collections had some limitations in terms of their technical openness, in that they could not be integrated into IPP's learning management system (LMS). A javascript function prevented presentation/duplication of the resources on another web-based system or platform, with the exception of the video lessons that were accessible via YouTube. This meant that a second or parallel environment (in addition to the IPP LMS) had to be accessed (via a link from the LMS) by students utilising the Khan Academy collections (Figure 2).

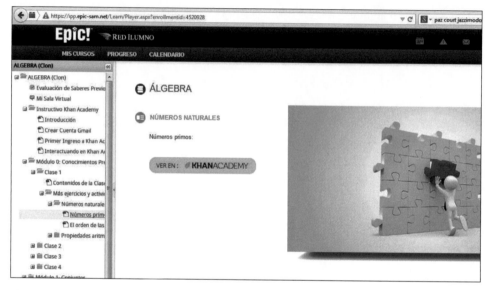

Figure 2: Screenshot of Khan Academy Collection 2 linked from courseware in the IPP LMS

From a legal perspective, the Khan Academy was also more restrictive in terms of reuse, as it is "impermissible [...] to provide training, support, or editorial services that use or reference the Licensed Educational Content in exchange for a fee".[22]

In the face-to-face mode classroom, the Open Textbook was available via the Wikibooks platform. The wiki functionality of this platform, combined with the affordances of the CC BY licence, enabled a different degree of participation in terms of content creation on the part of students, who could add and revise exercises as well as contribute other notes complementing existing material. In order to overcome constraints in internet access, each student in the class utilising the Open Textbook was also given a low-cost printed version of the textbook at the start of the course (Figure 3).

---

22 https://www.khanacademy.org/about/tos#7

Figure 3: Students in Treatment Group 2 received printed copies of the Open Textbook on day one of their course

Methodology

This study employs a mixed-methods approach. The first part of this methodological overview outlines the quantitative methods used to estimate the effect of OER use on students' mathematical course performance and class attendance. The mixed methods used to understand student and teacher perceptions are then described. The two components of the study are complementary in that the mixed-methods component attempts to expand upon and cross-check the quantitative results.

Quantitative method to address research questions 1 and 2: What is the effect of OER use on first-year students' mathematics course performance and class attendance?

In order to answer research questions 1 and 2, a quasi-experiment with non-equivalent control groups was undertaken. Five groups of first-year students in courses in the School of Education and School of Engineering were compared based on the analysis of two scenarios (Figure 4). The three courses were chosen in consultation with IPP academic authorities in order to ensure that each scenario was filled randomly with students pursuing different degrees within each school (Education has four degree streams and Engineering has 12 degree streams).

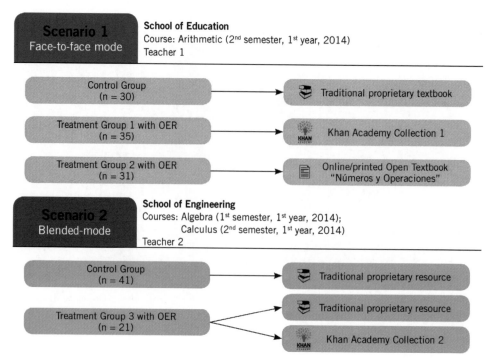

Figure 4: Overview of scenarios comprising the study

In Scenario 1, there were three classes in an Arithmetic course in the School of Education offered in a traditional classroom setting (face-to-face mode). The first class (Control Group, n = 30) relied on a traditional proprietary textbook. The second class (Treatment Group 1, n = 35) was taught with the help of Khan Academy Collection 1. And, finally, a third class (Treatment Group 2, n = 31) was taught by means of a custom-designed Arithmetic Open Textbook, *Números y Operaciones* ("Numbers and Operations"). This scenario was enacted during the second term of 2014 over a period of four months. In this scenario, the OER were the sole mandatory resources used by students (as opposed to the proprietary textbook).

Scenario 2 compared two classes in blended-mode Algebra and Calculus courses, delivered across two "bimesters", in the School of Engineering. Students met physically only for tests and the final exam. The first class (Control Group, n = 41 students) relied on a traditional proprietary (institutionally produced) resource. The second class (Treatment Group 3, n = 21 students) used Khan Academy Collection 2. This scenario was implemented during the first and second terms of 2014. In this scenario, the OER was complementary and used in addition to the traditional proprietary resource.

In order to estimate the effectiveness of OER use on students' mathematical performance, an impact analysis database was established, comprising two different datasets. It was envisioned that these data components could provide baseline information against which students' overall progress could be measured.

The first dataset contained information about students in the three student cohorts which comprised Scenario 1. This dataset contained information on which resource grouping each student was associated with (i.e. traditional proprietary, Khan Academy Collection 1 or Open

Textbook), students' course attendance during the term and three specific result variables: (1) students' marks before the final exam, (2) students' final exam marks, and (3) students' final course marks after the exam. This information was provided by the Arithmetic teacher, and was complemented with sociodemographic data on the students (income, mother's education level, age and geographical region of origin) which were sourced in a survey designed for this purpose.

The second dataset contained information regarding students in Scenario 2. The information contained in this dataset was the same as the data captured in the first dataset, the only difference being that in this case there were only two resource groupings (traditional proprietary and Khan Academy Collection 2).

All classes in each course were taught by the same teacher in order to counter potential bias factors arising from different teacher practices.

Mixed methods to address research question 3: What are teachers' and students' perceptions of the OER adoption process?

In order to answer research question 3, a mixed-methods approach was applied in the form of a series of semi-structured interviews, a focus group discussion and a student survey. Specifically, the students who used the Khan Academy collections or an Open Textbook (in face-to-face as well as blended mode) were asked to participate, in light of the fact that they were the groups with direct exposure to OER.

This component of the study provided an opportunity to gain a better understanding of the association between OER and improved mathematics course performance, and to better comprehend end-user (learners' and teachers') perceptions of the benefits and challenges related to their experience of using OER. It involved the implementation of the following research processes over the three-month period between June and August 2015:

- One semi-structured interview with a student from Scenario 1, Treatment Group 1 (n = 1).
- Two semi-structured interviews with students from Scenario 1, Treatment Group 2 (n = 2).
- One focus group discussion with students from Scenario 1, Treatment Group 2 (n = 5).
- Two semi-structured interviews with Teachers 1 and 2 (n = 2).

Given that students participating in the blended-mode course were spread throughout the country, it was not possible to conduct a focus group discussion with students in Scenario 2.

Based on the data provided by participants in this initial qualitative phase (n = 10), an online survey was designed in order to gauge student perceptions regarding their use of OER. The categories utilised in the survey were drawn from the interviews and focus group discussion with students and teachers. A total of 49 students from Scenarios 1 and 2 were surveyed following an open call for survey participation. The low number of respondents was largely due to the high dropout rate in the course, resulting in a relatively small pool of students who could be drawn upon.

The survey probed students' perceptions of OER use, focusing specifically on their evaluation of a number of resource characteristics, problems identified and recommendations for better use of these resources in the future. Lime Survey,[23] an online open source survey tool, was used to administer the survey.

Quantitative data analysis

With the various comparison groups and scenarios now defined, it is necessary to demonstrate if and how these groups can be compared in order to estimate the effect of OER use on student mathematical course performance.

The effect of OER use was estimated for each of the two scenarios through two separate processes. The first compared performance results between students of the three classes in Scenario 1 to establish whether students of the two Treatment Groups obtained different results to those of the Control Group. The second process conducted the same comparison between the two classes of the blended mode (Scenario 2) to ascertain whether students who used Khan Academy Collection 2 obtained better results than those who used the traditional textbook.

In all comparison processes, the effect of the use of OER among the first-year students was measured as the difference of a result variable of students having used OER (or not) during their studies. This can be represented as follows:

$$\Delta_i = Y_{i,D=1} - Y_{i,D=0}$$

Where $Y_{i,D=1}$ is the result of the student if he/she received the treatment[24] and $Y_{i,D=0}$ is the result of the student if he/she did not receive the treatment.

The problem with this formula is that it is not possible to know, in the same time period, the result that the student would have had in both situations (of receiving the treatment and not). Based on this limitation, it is necessary to make inferences about the results that a treatment student obtained. Even though it is not possible to know this for only one student, the average impact for a group of students can be estimated as far as two statistically equal groups are compared. In this case, the average effect is the average result in a result variable of those students who used OER, minus the average of those students who did not use OER in their courses. However, as this is a quasi-experiment with non-equivalent control groups, the group of people who received the treatment is not statistically equal to the group of students who did not receive the treatment.

When comparing both groups there is a possibility that they may have observable and unobservable differences, making them incomparable. One way to address this problem is to randomly assign students to the Treatment and Control groups. This means that from the 100% of students who participated in the study, we randomly selected those students who would use OER in their courses and those who would not use them. Because it is not always possible to randomly assign people to Treatment and Control groups, one sometimes has to look for alternative methodologies that assure the comparability of both groups.

---

23   https://www.limesurvey.org
24   In the context of this study, to be "treated" means that a student took a course that included the use of OER as a compulsory element of the learning process.

In the case of this research study, students were pseudo-randomly assigned[25] to the comparison groups; therefore, in order to estimate the effect of the treatment, one merely has to compare means of the result variables of both groups through mean difference tests. In order to be more certain that groups are statistically identical, the study also applied a quasi-experimental methodology known as Propensity Score Matching (PSM) (Dehejia & Wahba, 1999; Heckman, Ichimura, Smith & Todd, 1998; Rosenbaum & Rubin, 1983).

PSM is a technique used for impact evaluation studies, and is based on the estimation of the probability of receiving a specific treatment. In this sense, the PSM takes cognisance of the selection bias by comparing Treated and Control groups with the same probability of being treated. The fact of having been taught with the use of OER is first modelled using a set of observable variables that could affect the situation and influence the result. The probability of being treated is then predicted, the outcome of which is used to match students that received and did not receive the treatment in order to define two groups with the same probability of having participated in a course that included the use of OER. Finally, the effect is calculated as the difference in the results of both groups.

In order to estimate the effect of the use of OER on mathematical course performance, once the probability of being treated was calculated, it was necessary to define the mechanisms through which Treated and Control students would be compared. There are different ways to do so. This study used the Inverse Probability Weight matching algorithm, which compares the results of individuals from the Control Group that are most similar compared with Treated individuals, giving a greater weight in the estimations to those Control individuals who have a higher probability of being Treated and less weight to those Control individuals with a lower probability of being Treated (Imbens & Hirano, 2002).

In sum, when comparing students' results in the two scenarios, this study examined result variable means of the Treatment and Control groups through both mean difference tests that directly compare group means and tests that consider PSM in their estimations.

The last elements that had to be defined regarding these estimations were the results variables. These are the measures that were used to compare the Treatment and Control groups regarding the subject upon which the use of OER is supposed to have an effect. The result variables used in this study were:

- Student results in the final exam of the evaluated course.[26]
- Student final grades in the evaluated course.
- Percentage of student attendance (in the case of Scenario 1).

Each of these result variables was used as a dependent variable in ordinary least squares models that have as an independent variable a dummy variable that indicates whether the student was part of Treatment or Control groups, and several variables about students' sociodemographic characteristics that were used as control variables.[27] Moreover, in order

---

25 The process of allocating students to comparison groups is considered "pseudo-random" in that there was not a rigorous group allocation process, taking into account specific variables that could have influenced the study. Administrative staff were asked to assign students in each class according to their date of registration – in the sense that the first student who registered was assigned to the first class, the second student to the second class, and so on. This process had a random element, but it cannot be stated that students were rigorously distributed among the different classes of each course.

26 This exam is exactly the same for every student in each of the examined scenarios.

27 These control variables included age, family income and number of education years of the mother.

to have more comparable results, all result variables were standardised so that analyses of OER effects could be conducted in terms of standard deviations.

Mixed-methods data analysis

Once transcribed, qualitative data from interviews and focus group discussion were analysed using a content analysis technique, whereby the more recurrent ideas presented in the analysis were identified and grouped. Content analysis is a research technique that aims to be an objective, systematic and quantitative study of the manifest content of communication (Berelson, 1952).

Information was therefore organised according to the questions posed to the students and teachers who used both sets of OER in Scenario 1. In each of the investigated aspects, first responses or key ideas shared by the two profiles and refer to the two types of OER were pooled; then, in the second stage, the most relevant and specific points regarding use of the Open Textbook or Khan Academy Collection 1 were identified and disaggregated.

Data sharing

The data utilised to assess performance in the first phase of this study, as well as Spanish-language instruments and transcripts of the student focus group discussion and teacher interviews, have been published on the DataFirst Data Portal[28] after undergoing a multi-phased quality assurance and de-identification process. The author and the Research on Open Educational Resources for Development Curation and Dissemination team checked data files for consistency and correctness, whereafter a de-identification process was undertaken utilising an omission and revision strategy.

The resulting dataset, published under a Creative Commons Attribution (CC BY) licence, is comprised of the interview transcripts shared in Rich Text (.rtf) and Excel (.xlsx) formats, survey data shared in CSV, SAS, SPSS and STATA formats, as well as data collection instruments, a dataset description, a project description and a de-identification overview in PDF format.

Findings

Estimation of the effect of OER use on student mathematical course performance

OER effect in School of Education face-to-face Arithmetic course (Scenario 1)

The first approach analyses students' mathematical course performance considering only academic results of first-year undergraduate students enrolled in the face-to-face mode Arithmetic course offered by the IPP School of Education in the second term of 2014 (Scenario 1).

---

28 https://www.datafirst.uct.ac.za/dataportal/index.php/catalog/577

Table 1 shows the effect of OER use when comparing the Treatment Group 1 (n = 35) and the Control Group (n = 30). It estimates the effect of the use of OER (in this case, Khan Academy Collection 1) in comparison with the use of a traditional textbook, considering the three result variables previously described.

Each coefficient shown in the first row of Tables 1 to 6 describes the effect of the use of Khan Academy Collection 1 in relation to the Control Group in terms of standard deviation, while the second row specifies the standard deviation of these effects. In simpler terms, these coefficients indicate the average difference between Treatment Group 1 and the Control Croup regarding three result variables when controlled for other variables, namely age, family income and number of education years of the mother.

Table 1: Estimation of the effect of using Khan Academy Collection 1 versus the traditional textbook

Attendance	Final exam	Final course score
-0.90**	0.66**	0.15
(0.28)	(0.29)	(0.30)

*** = $p < 0.01$; ** = $p < 0.05$; * = $p < 0.1$; $n = 65$

All tables represent the effect of a dummy variable, where 1 = use of OER and 0 = no use of OER, in several regression models that separately used each of the result variables as the dependent variables.

The first coefficient indicates that the use of Khan Academy Collection 1 had a negative effect of 0.9 standard deviations on student attendance levels, which is significant at the 5% level. This means that students in the Control Group have significantly higher levels of attendance than those who used OER. Table 1 also shows that the effect of OER on students' final exam marks was positive and significant at the 5% level of significance. These results indicate that students who used the Khan Academy Collection 1 had significantly better examination results than those who did not use it. However, when we consider students' final grades in their courses (tests and final exam, in which the final exam constitutes 40% of the final grade), there is no significant difference between the comparison groups.

Table 2 shows the same estimations as in Table 1 (Scenario 1: Treatment Group 1 versus Control Group), but in this instance each effect was estimated with the PSM method to make both groups more comparable.

Table 2: Estimation of the effect of using Khan Academy Collection 1 versus the traditional textbook (using PSM)

Attendance	Final exam	Final course score
-0.86**	0.54*	0.13
(0.36)	(0.30)	(0.33)

*** = $p < 0.01$; ** = $p < 0.05$; * = $p < 0.1$; $n = 65$

In this estimation, and all others done with the PSM method, sample size is reduced due to the fact that PSM only considered students with a specific probability of being treated.

It can be observed that results are very similar to what was found without the use of PSM.[29] The use of Khan Academy Collection 1 had a negative effect on attendance (-0.86) and a positive effect on final exam grades (0.54), but no effect regarding students' final course scores. This reaffirms the suggestion that OER appear to improve students' examination performance, but decrease their attendance levels. The second exercise compared Treatment Groups 1 and 2 of Scenario 1 (i.e. the class that used Khan Academy Collection 1 and the class that used the Open Textbook as the sole resource). Table 3 shows the effect of using Khan Academy Collection 1 versus the Open Textbook (n = 66). The data indicate that those students who used Khan Academy Collection 1 had significantly lower attendance levels than those who used the Open Textbook.

Table 3: Estimation of the effect of using Khan Academy Collection 1 versus the Open Textbook

Attendance	Final exam	Final course score
-1.38***	1.49***	0.21
(0.21)	(0.18)	(0.25)

*** = $p < 0.01$; ** = $p < 0.05$; * = $p < 0.1$; n = 66

The use of Khan Academy Collection 1 had a negative effect on attendance of -1.38 standard deviations. Moreover, it was also observed that students who completed their courses with the help of this resource obtained better results in their final exam when compared with students who used the Open Textbook as the sole resource. The magnitude of this effect is 1.49 standard deviations, which means the Khan Academy Collection 1 OER had a strong effect on students' final exam results when compared with the results of students who used the traditional textbook. However, the results also indicate that OER use had no effect on students' final scores (tests and final exam) in their courses.

Table 4 compares students who used Khan Academy Collection 1 with students who used the Open Textbook (Scenario 1), but through the PSM estimation method.

Table 4: Estimation of the effect of using Khan Academy Collection 1 versus the Open Textbook (using PSM)

Attendance	Final exam	Final course score
-1.24***	1.55***	0.28
(0.25)	(0.20)	(0.24)

*** = $p < 0.01$; ** = $p < 0.05$; * = $p < 0.1$; n = 66

As in the first examined comparisons, similar results are obtained when the estimation method is changed. It can be seen that the effect of the use of OER on attendance is negative and significant at the 1% level of significance (-1.24). Moreover, it is observed that students who used Khan Academy Collection 1 had significantly higher exam results than

---

29 This was expected due to the fact that students were assigned to each group in a pseudo-random way, which made both groups comparable without the use of PSM.

those who used the Open Textbook, and that there was no effect with respect to final course scores. This result reaffirms that use of Khan Academy Collection 1 had a more positive effect on students' final exam performance than the traditional proprietary textbook (Control Group) or the Open Textbook (Treatment Group 2).

Table 5 presents the final analysis concerning Scenario 1, evaluating whether those students who were taught through the use of the Open Textbook obtained better results than those who were taught with the traditional textbook (n = 61). It shows that the only result variable where significant differences were found was the final exam score. This difference does not, however, have the expected direction as it is observed that the use of the Open Textbook has a negative effect of -0.88 standard deviations on students' final exam grades, which is significant at the 1% level of significance. This means that students who were taught with the traditional textbook have higher exam grades than students who were taught with the help of the Open Textbook. Regarding attendance levels and final course scores, Table 5 shows that it did not make any difference whether students were taught with the help of the Open Textbook or with the traditional textbook.

Table 5: Estimation of the effect of using the Open Textbook versus the traditional textbook

Attendance	Final exam	Final course score
0.51	-0.88***	-0.10
(0.29)	(0.25)	(0.30)

*** = $p < 0.01$; ** = $p < 0.05$; * = $p < 0.1$; n = 61

Table 6 shows that when the same comparisons are made using the PSM method, similar results are obtained to those in Table 5.

Table 6: Estimation of the effect of using the Open Textbook versus the traditional textbook (using PSM)

Attendance	Final exam	Final course score
0.11	-0.80***	-0.14
(0.33)	(0.25)	(0.27)

*** = $p < 0.01$; ** = $p < 0.05$; * = $p < 0.1$; n = 61

The exam score is again the only result variable where significant differences are found and the direction of this association is negative. These results appear to confirm that the use of the Open Textbook in this examined course did not improve students' academic performance.

OER effect in School of Engineering blended Algebra and Calculus courses (Scenario 2)

This section analyses the effect of OER on student performance in Scenario 2. In this case, the examined course was a blended-mode course on Algebra and Calculus offered by the School of Engineering in the first and second semesters of 2014. In this scenario, a Control Group (n = 41) relied on a traditional proprietary resource, while Treatment Group 3 (n = 21) utilised Khan Academy Collection 2.

The data presented in Table 7 show that there were no significant differences in either of the two results variables analysed in this scenario. There was no significant difference between those who used Khan Academy Collection 2 and those who used the traditional resource in terms of improved final exam grades or final course scores. As this was a mostly online course, attendance levels were not used as a result variable.

Table 7: Estimation of the effect of using Khan Academy Collection 2 versus traditional resource

Final exam	Final course score
-0.22	0.12
(0.30)	(0.31)

*** = $p < 0.01$; ** = $p < 0.05$; * = $p < 0.1$; n = 62*

When the same two estimations are calculated with the PSM method in order to make both groups more comparable, similar results are obtained (Table 8). Neither of the effects is statistically significant, which means that the use of OER did not result in a discernible improvement in students' mathematical performance in the blended course.

Table 8: Estimation of the effect of using Khan Academy Collection 2 versus traditional resource (PSM method)

Final exam	Final course score
-0.26	0.04
(0.29)	(0.28)

*** = $p < 0.01$; ** = $p < 0.05$; * = $p < 0.1$; n = 62*

In sum, analysis of the effect of OER (Khan Academy Collections 1 and 2 and the Open Textbook) on students' mathematical performance in the two scenarios shows that only in Scenario 1 can it be observed that some students who used OER obtained significantly better academic results than students who relied on the traditional textbook (i.e. when students were taught with the help of the Khan Academy Collection 1). In this same scenario it was also observed that students who were taught with the traditional textbook obtained better results than those who were taught with the Open Textbook. In relation to Scenario 2, non-significant effects were found.

Student and teacher perceptions of the use of OER

In this section, findings regarding teacher and student perceptions of the experience of using OER are examined.

Data are presented according to the different themes that informed the questions posed to students and teachers who used OER during the initial qualitative phase. The views of students and teachers are presented for each of these aspects. In addition, where possible, qualitative data are complemented with information obtained from the student survey that was developed based on the qualitative initial-phase results.

Student and teacher experience of using OER

Overall, students and teachers in the study felt satisfied about the use of OER. They pointed out that OER were important tools in supporting the deployment of the courses, and their use was therefore beneficial to both students and teachers.

Khan Academy collections

In the case where Khan Academy Collection 1 was used (Scenario 1), teachers and students pointed out that these resources provided them with vital support, contributing to the achievement of different types of learning outcomes in the face-to-face classroom mode, as well as in the home environment. In both scenarios, teachers positively highlighted the characteristics of the Khan Academy collections as having appropriate theoretical content and corresponding practical exercises that allow students to easily comprehend the content. Students considered the resources to be user friendly and felt that the various mechanisms of the platform enabled them to learn easily.

Regarding use of Khan Academy Collection 2 (Scenario 2), the evaluation of the experience was also positive for both classes that utilised OER. It was considered a very good support mechanism in terms of providing complementary material, and was also reported to be dynamic. From the point of view of the students, it provided a way to support learning more comfortably, in a more visually appealing manner – and even sometimes, for some students, more effectively – than was the case when using the traditional textbook.

> It is complementary, because it replaces a teacher more efficiently, because I can repeat, repeat, repeat and I see the result and I can move forward ... Because sometimes the texts are not as motivating when you're tired ... Sometimes, it is as if very pedagogical things make you go to the next step, they get you excited. (Student, Treatment Group 1, Scenario 1)

> It was very pedagogical, didactic. I liked it better, because other Algebra classes I had had – or related to mathematics – included very little support material other than documents, texts, it was not enough. (Student, Treatment Group 3, Scenario 2)

Open Textbook

Teachers and students also spoke of the experience of using the Open Textbook as beneficial. Students indicated that they used the Open Textbook instead of the traditional proprietary textbook in Scenario 1 in order to engage with content covered in the course syllabus, and as a means to continue their exercises at home. As a positive factor, they emphasised that the use of the resource was voluntary and was never positioned as being obligatory by the teacher.

In terms of the Wikibooks platform on which the Open Textbook was hosted, the teacher highlighted the positive aspect of being able to intervene and directly edit the resource, as well as the fact that she could access information regarding how often and what type of exercises were being used by the students.

> It was personal, in fact, the teacher gave it to us and everyone decided what they wanted to do ... Sometimes he also recommended the book, saying that in certain page there were exercises about what we had seen that day ... Yes, but it was not as an obligation, she made us see that it was a kind of help. (Student, Treatment Group 2, Scenario 1)

With respect to the use of OER, the survey (n = 49) provided a means to examine levels of use. Students were asked to indicate their approximate frequency of use based on an ordinal variable with six categories, ranging from "no use" to "use it every day". Based on these data, the frequency of use was shown to be dissimilar: while 12% did not use it, or did so sporadically, a similar percentage reported daily use of this resource. The most frequently cited use of the resource was once a week (35%).

We can also compare levels of use by student attributes. Given the small sample size (n = 49), the six original categories of the variable frequency of use were captured in two categories: one that included students who used it once a week or less, and another that included those who used it more than once a week. In this regard, the data in Table 9 suggest that the Khan Academy collections were used far more frequently than the Open Textbook: 62% of those who used the Khan Academy collections declared that they used these more than once a week, while 30% of Open Textbook users reported this frequency.

Table 9: Frequency of use by resource type, age group and income category (n = 49)

		Once a week or less (%)	More than once a week (%)
Resource type	Khan Academy collections	38	62
	Open Textbook	70	30
Age group	19–24 years	62	38
	25 years and over	43	57
Monthly household income	USD 400 and below	62	39
	Over USD 400	39	61
Total		**51**	**48**

These data show that OER as a joint category was most frequently used by older students (57%) and those from higher-income families (61%). The latter could be explained hypothetically by the greater likelihood of higher-income students having access to these resources in their own households on personal computers or electronic devices.

Student and teacher perceptions of platform functionality

The second general aspect examined in terms of student and teacher perception is the overall assessment of Khan Academy and Wikibook web platform functionality. Both scenarios highlighted certain characteristics or applications as positive or negative (depending on the resource in question).

Khan Academy

In the case of the Khan Academy, teachers in Scenarios 1 and 2 provided specific opinions about the differing learning mechanisms the platform provides. They highlighted the following positive features: the fact that levels of difficulty increase according to student progress; the fact that the use of video is more appealing to students than text-based resources (and may therefore improve their learning levels); and the fact that when students perform an exercise poorly, the hint system offered by the platform motivates them to keep trying until they achieve the correct result.

From the teacher perspective, the only thing that did not work well was the Khan Academy reward system, which was perceived as a "childish" mechanism for higher education students.

> The use of Khan was very didactic, because it has different areas, in the preparation part, application and theory, giving students enough explanations if they do not understand an exercise. So I found Khan very useful, not for the whole class, but certainly for several parts of it. (Teacher 1, Scenario 1)

Students in Scenarios 1 and 2 provided positive feedback on the functionality of the Khan Academy platform. They emphasised the speed of connection to the site and ease of use as features that contributed to good performance.

> It was a good experience because when you were completing an exercise, for example if there was something you did not understand you had the possibility of using YouTube to understand through videos or online with other teachers. You can understand it, it is easy to understand. (Student, Treatment Group 1, Scenario 1)

Wikibooks

The general functionality of the Wikibooks platform, as well as the ancillary resources and applications it contains, were evaluated by teachers and students in Scenario 1. Both cohorts highlighted how useful the printed version of the book was, in that it served as a supportive, complementary resource that allowed students to learn about alternative ways to create exercises and solve problems. Also positively highlighted were the fact that the platform allowed students to undertake exercises at their own pace; the level of interaction provided by the application; and the coherence between the functionality of the digital media and the printed book.

The ability to edit content was highlighted by Teacher 1, who could modify the language of the exercises, and by students, who also used the language editing function.

> It allowed me to edit it and be constantly checking it. My students also liked it for that matter. They liked being able to edit it, to be participants of their own book. (Teacher 1)

> We created the Wikibooks account and we could see the same subject matter we were studying in class there. We could also find it in the account. And besides, we could improve ourselves by making up exercises and uploading them to the account and support ourselves with the book. (Student, Treatment Group 2, Scenario 1)

Student survey responses relating to the use of OER

Evaluating the functionality of the OER used was an important element of the student survey, which complemented initial information obtained in the qualitative phase. Results from student perceptions represented in the survey are presented in three different ways: first, the distribution of student responses is analysed at different levels according to 39 statements in the student survey about different aspects relating to the use of OER; second, an evaluation index of OER is generated from the 39 statements, analysing the average of this index as a number of respondents' attributes; and third, responses to evaluation questions that inquired directly into how students rated different aspects of the OER on a scale of 1 to 7 are examined.

Figure 5 presents statements of the survey that reflect a positive view of the OER used. From these data we can see that a large majority of students from Scenarios 1 and 2 agreed with all the positive statements about OER. In most cases, the responses "agree" or "strongly agree" reach 80% or more. In particular, those aspects for which there is greatest consensus are related to the use of video as a medium which stimulates teaching, feedback delivery and ease of study – all with more than 90% of answers as "agree" or "strongly agree".

Figure 6, by contrast, presents statements where agreement implied a negative view of OER in general. In this instance, the percentage of cases where students expressed their agreement around issues of usability of the resources and platforms led to confusion and a less positive sense of OER.

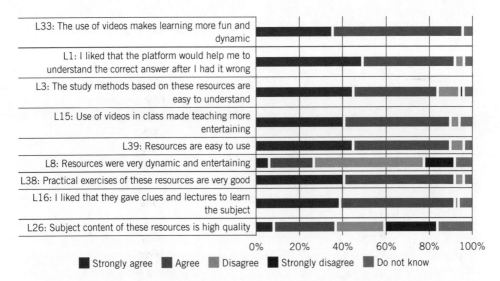

Figure 5: Level to which students agreed with statements regarding positive aspects of OER (n = 49)

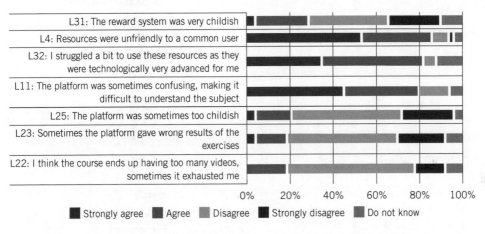

Figure 6: Level to which students agreed with negative statements regarding the use of OER (n = 49)

Figures 7 and 8 present views on the use of OER in specific educational contexts. In terms of the main positive features of OER (Figure 7), the majority of respondents thought that these "resources were a good complement to the course" (86%) and allowed for better understanding of the content (84%). Likewise, up to 83% of respondents felt that the IPP technological infrastructure allowed for good use of these resources. In contrast, only 38% of respondents said their teacher had adequate knowledge to use the tools required.

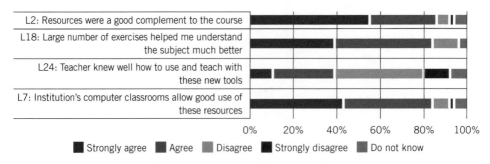

Figure 7: Level to which students agreed with positive statements regarding the general use of OER in a specific context (n = 49)

Figure 8 presents negative aspects associated with the use of OER in Scenarios 1 and 2. Just over 40% of students identified problems associated with inconsistency between content presented in the classroom and the OER. They also pointed out the challenge of slow internet connectivity in terms of accessing OER online via IPP infrastructure (40%), and the lack of information provided at the beginning of the course on the evaluation mechanisms used (67%). Moreover, only 20% expressed that the use of OER affected attendance.

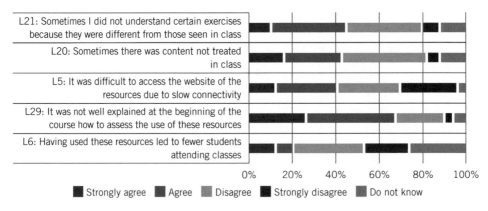

Figure 8: Level to which students agreed with negative statements regarding the general use of OER in a specific context (n = 49)

Figure 9 presents an evaluation of the personal experience of using OER, which was generally positive. In this regard, around 90% of respondents said that the resources helped them study, they enjoyed the experience, they preferred these resources and the OER improved their learning outcomes.

Also positive was the fact that between 70% and 80% of respondents liked the resources as they could be used at home, were fun to engage with and helped with personal mathematical problems. Over 60% also said that they would not have performed as well without these resources.

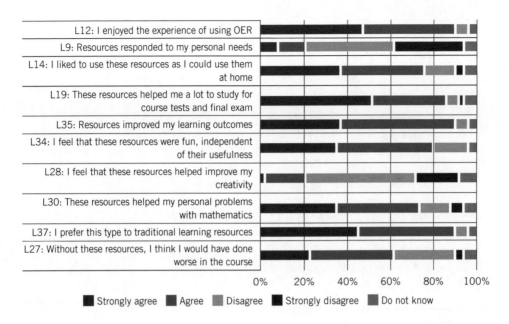

Figure 9: Level to which students agreed with statements regarding their personal experience of using OER (n = 49)

Figure 10 contains various statements that relate to recommendations for general use of OER. In this regard, 84% would recommend these resources to other students, and 84% were in favour of extending their use to all subjects. Almost half of the respondents (47%) said that their use should be optional, not mandatory. A total of 61% were in favour of being evaluated on their use of these resources, while 35% rejected it.

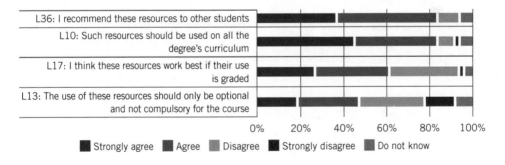

Figure 10: Level to which students agreed with recommendations regarding OER use

Following analysis of the perception of the resource in its various dimensions for the total sample, the next step is to review some of the statements made about OER by users of the different resources. Even though the evaluation of OER by the students of both Scenarios 1 and 2 is similar in most of the dimensions studied, some differences can be highlighted.

"The resources led to fewer students attending contact-mode classes"

Figure 11 shows that while 70% of Open Textbook users argued that its use did not affect attendance, only 41% of the Khan Academy collection users held this opinion, while a high percentage (38%) answered that they did not know.

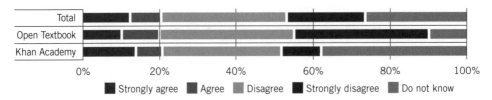

Figure 11: Level to which students agreed with the statement that OER led to lower attendance in Scenario 1 (n = 49)

"The use of these resources should be optional and not compulsory"

Another important difference can be seen in Figure 12: almost 65% of Open Textbook users agreed with the statement that the use of this resource should be optional, while only 34% of Khan Academy collection users thought so.

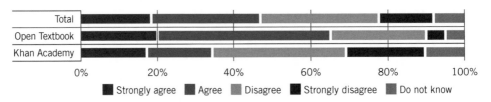

Figure 12: Level to which students agreed with the statement that the use of OER should be optional and not obligatory (n = 49)

"My teacher taught us well on how to use these resources"

Figure 13 shows that 45% of students using the Khan Academy OER thought their teachers were able to teach them how to use the resources effectively, while only 30% of the Open Textbook users agreed that their teacher knew how to use the resource.

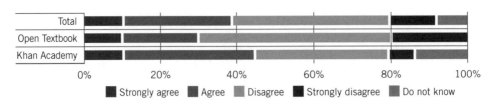

Figure 13: Level to which students agreed with the statement that teachers taught them well on how to use resources (n = 49)

"I think the course ends up having too many videos, sometimes it exhausted me"

Another important difference relates to the belief that both types of OER contained too many videos. In this regard, Figure 14 shows that although only a minority in both groups believed that the use of video was excessive, this view was held by a discernibly lower number of Open Textbook users (10%) than Khan Academy collection users (24%). No respondents indicated that they "strongly agree" with the assertion.

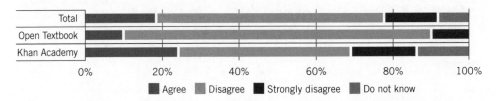

Figure 14: Level to which students agreed with the statement that the course ends up exhausting them because there is too much video in the OER (n = 49)

"The platform was sometimes too childish"

A final observable difference, presented in Figure 15, relates to the level of agreement that the Khan Academy and the Open Textbook platform were too simplistic, or "childish". Only 20% of both Khan Academy and Open Textbook users agreed that the resources were too simplistic or "childish", while 80% of Open Textbook users and 72% of Khan Academy users disagreed.

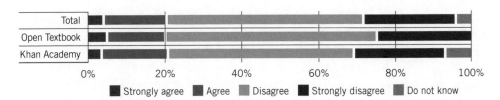

Figure 15: Level to which students agreed with statements about a negative "childish" characteristic of OER (n = 49)

The second level of analysis for evaluating student survey responses relating to the use of OER involved the generation of an index. For this purpose, an index value was calculated for each respondent based on information from 37 of the 39 survey items developed using a Likert scale, noting that agreement with two of these items does not imply positive or negative evaluation of the resource. To develop this index, affirmations where agreement implied a negative evaluation of the resource were recorded to allow that the highest score in each item entailed a higher evaluation. In other words, index ranges between 1 and 10 were established from the information of the 37 items, with 10 being the highest rating. This scale was also tested regarding its internal consistency, with a Cronbach Alpha reliability coefficient of 0.93 being established (implying that the scale has good internal consistency).

Table 10 shows the average of this index as a number of characteristics of respondents. It is noted that, although averages of the groups being compared are fairly similar, there may be some differences. First, we see that Open Textbook users had a slightly more positive evaluation than the Khan Academy collection users (7.17 versus 6.97). At the same time, the younger respondents had a greater appreciation of the use of OER, as the group aged 19–24 had an average of 7.25, while the group aged over 25 had an average of 6.91.

Table 10: OER use evaluation index mean by resource type, age group and income category (n = 47)

		Mean
Resource type	Khan Academy collections	6.97
	Open Textbook	7.17
Age group	19–24	7.25
	25 and over	6.91
Household monthly income	USD 580 and under	6.91
	Over USD 580	7.24
Level of use	Once a week or less	6.95
	More than once a week	7.17
Total		**7.06**

Table 10 also shows that students with higher incomes and those with a higher level of use revealed a more positive evaluation of OER. This could be explained by the previously described phenomenon in which those who declared having higher incomes used OER more frequently.

Evaluation questions inquiring how students rated different aspects of OER

The final analysis of student survey responses relating to the use of OER involves analysing how students evaluated different elements of the two kinds of OER. Specifically, respondents were asked to rate, on a scale from 1 to 7, different aspects involved in the use of OER, with 7 being the best possible score. Figure 16 shows that in all evaluated aspects the majority of respondents assigned 6 or 7 points, and 90% or more assigned at least 4 points. The exception was the rating of infrastructure and equipment at IPP.

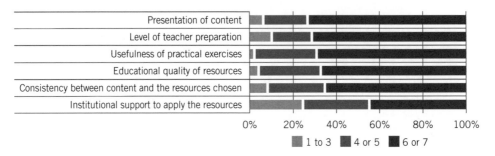

Figure 16: Level (scale of 1 to 7) to which students agreed with statements about how they evaluate the use of OER (n = 49)

This analysis of the various aspects related to the use of both OER can also be examined against the particular resource in question. Table 11 shows the averages obtained in each area according to the type of resource used by students. The comparison shows that higher averages are obtained in all aspects by Open Textbook users.

Table 11: Evaluation of different aspects of the use of OER on a scale from 1 to 7 (mean) by resource type and age group (n = 49)

Aspect of OER use	Resource type			Age group	
	Total	Khan Academy collections	Open Textbook	19–24	25+
Educational quality of resources	5.82	5.72	5.95	5.86	5.79
Usefulness of delivering practical exercises	5.90	5.69	6.20	6.23	5.64
Presentation of subject content	5.98	5.66	6.45	6.23	5.79
Consistency between content covered in the class and content covered in the resources	5.80	5.59	6.10	6.20	5.50
Level of teacher preparation	5.90	5.52	6.45	6.40	5.50
Institutional support to apply resources	4.76	4.17	5.60	4.95	4.61

Table 11 also shows evaluation by age group. In all aspects the group aged 19–24 gave better evaluations of the different dimensions of OER use. The biggest differences are in the level of teacher preparation and consistency between the subjects of the classes and those treated in the resource, where younger students provided a more favourable evaluation.

Table 12 presents an evaluation of the same dimensions, but according to income group and level of use. Regarding the former, lower-income students provided a more positive evaluation of the different dimensions, particularly as relates to level of teacher preparation and quality of resources. Regarding the latter, those who used the resource most frequently were more positive about the usefulness of the practical exercises.

Table 12: Evaluation of different aspects of OER use on a scale from 1 to 7 (mean) by income group and level of use (n = 49)

Aspect of OER use	Income group			Level of use
	Total	USD 400 000 and under	Over USD 400 000	Once a week or less
Educational quality of resources	5.82	5.96	5.65	5.68
Usefulness of delivering practical exercises	5.90	6.04	5.74	5.72
Presentation of the subject content	5.98	6.03	5.91	5.92
Consistency between content covered in the class and content covered in the resources	5.80	5.92	5.65	5.76
Level of teacher preparation	5.90	6.08	5.70	5.88
Institutional support to apply resources	4.76	4.92	4.57	4.68

Based on the data presented in this section, it can be observed that both forms of OER were positively evaluated by students and teachers. Moreover, the Open Textbook appeared to be more beneficial than the Khan Academy collections. These results could appear contradictory in terms of the data presented in the first part of the Findings section, which suggested that students who used the Khan Academy collections obtained better academic results than those who used the Open Textbook. Moreover, even those students who used the traditional textbook obtained better results than those who used the Open Textbook. This apparent inconsistency can, however, be understood in light of the fact that perceptions about a process do not always concur with the specific results of that process. For example, Open Textbook users highly valued the use of this kind of resource in terms of improving mathematical performance, despite the fact that use of the Open Textbook did not appear to improve their actual grades.

Positive aspects of resource use

The data presented in this section pertain to the most positive aspects perceived by students and teachers regarding use of the two kinds of OER. The qualitative section data reflect that responses vary depending on the resource, with a wider variety of comments being made in reference to Open Textbook use.

Khan Academy collections

Regardless of the study mode (face-to-face or blended), teachers and students highlighted the high level of accessibility of the Khan Academy collections as what they liked most about this platform, with use being possible at IPP, at home or on mobile devices. Blended-mode students also pointed out that the accessibility and stability of the page display was good.

> As I say, it was always available and did not fail. It would have been terrible to be in the middle of an exercise and have the page fail. So that was important to me. (Student, Treatment Group 3, Scenario 2)

Open Textbook

Students and teachers typically agreed on which aspects of the Open Textbook resources they liked most. Among the positive features mentioned, and one of the most frequently cited factors, was the ability to edit content. For teachers, this was a positive factor in that they could adapt content and language to better suit the needs of the class. Consistent with this view, students reported that the aspects they liked most included the ability to edit and upload exercises they created, the fact that the printed book provided valuable support, and the fact that there were many practical exercises.

> It allowed us to edit. Because, for example, I didn't write this book, someone else did. So the language that I use, and the one someone else uses were relatively different, so in some cases, I simplified a few things, I added some exercises or changed some definitions or missing content. (Teacher 1, Scenario 1)

Having identified the most positive aspects of OER use perceived by students and teachers through the qualitative phase, the survey complemented examination of this issue by asking students to select the top three positive aspects of OER from a list of 12. The results are presented in Figure 17, which highlights the contribution of OER to understanding course content, an aspect mentioned by 65% of the students. Other positive features highlighted included explanations being delivered in a more didactic and entertaining way, and the presence of practical exercises.

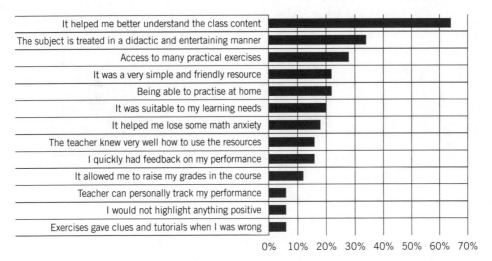

Figure 17: Level to which students agreed with statements about the contribution of OER to understanding course content (n = 49)

The benefits presented in Figure 17 can also be examined according to what kind of resource was used. Some notable differences were observed (Table 13). While didactic, entertaining teaching and the fact that exercises could be conducted at home were more prominent features for Khan Academy users, the access to practical exercises and the level of teacher preparation were more important for users of the Open Textbook.

Table 13: Positive aspects highlighted regarding the use of OER by resource type (n = 49)

Aspect of OER use	Khan Academy collections (%)	Open Textbook (%)
Helped better understanding of class content	62.1	70.0
Subject treated in a didactic and entertaining manner	44.8	20.0
Access to many practical exercises	20.7	40.0
Ability to practise at home	31.0	10.0
Simple and friendly resource	20.7	25.0
Suitable to learning needs	17.2	25.0
Reduced mathematics anxiety	20.7	15.0
Rapid feedback on performance	10.3	25.0

Teacher proficient in use of resources	6.0	30.0
Facilitated improved grades	13.8	10.0
Teacher can personally track performance	10.3	0
Exercises provide clues and tutorials in cases of error	10.3	0
Nothing particularly positive	6.9	5.0

Main problems in resource use

Another topic analysed was the main problems relating to OER use identified by the study participants. The main problem identified by teachers and students in the qualitative phase was lack of time to use the resource. For both types of OER, teachers identified a longer list of inconveniences. A problem expressed by teachers in both scenarios was that some older students were not familiar with computers, and did not know how to create or use the resources.

> Not everyone used it. I was able to check directly the movements each student did on Khan [Academy]. ... In fact I talked to the kids in a friendly way and at some point I also had to get angry, and ask why. And it was because there was no time; it was mainly because there was no time. (Teacher 1, Scenario 1)

With regards to infrastructure and equipment, Teacher 1 identified infrastructure problems such as a lack of computers and the fact that computers were in poor condition, as negatively influencing optimal use of OER by students. By contrast, students did not generally observe any major problems, although when comparing the two types of resources, more difficulties were perceived by Khan Academy users.

Khan Academy collections

From the point of view of face-to-face mode Teacher 1 (Scenario 1), the most discernible difficulties identified were: slow uptake on the part of the cohort that was supposed to be using the resource (utilising their personal notes instead); the fact that certain aspects of the content covered in the class were not included in the resource; and that some students struggled to understand exercises posed in a different manner to how they would have been presented by their class teacher.

Teacher 2 of the blended-mode courses (Scenario 2) pointed out that some students believed that this mode of delivery was easier and required less commitment than the traditional face-to-face mode. Students therefore tended to put in less effort and sometimes became frustrated and discouraged when they found more complex content or activities that they struggled to solve and did not have a teacher at hand to consult. The low level of student participation was noted as a problem, and, given the fact that the Khan Academy Collection 2 had many videos and educational activities, it was felt that the resource was not used to its full potential benefit.

From the point of view of the face-to-face mode students in Scenario 1, the only problem observed was that the right answer in the case of a particular exercise in Khan Academy Collection 1 was not listed among the answer options, which was communicated to the corresponding Teacher 1.

The blended-mode students in Scenario 2 pointed out that they were initially not adequately informed that the use of the platform was to be assessed, which resulted in a lack of interest at the start of the course.

> I had not understood that it was another grade ... so at first I didn't take it into consideration. So, then I got behind, so I tell you that, at the end I quickly absorbed it, I used it all, but I wasn't really aware what the final goal was. (Student, Treatment Group 3, Scenario 2)

Open Textbook

In terms of Open Textbook use, the level of difficulty in understanding the Wikibooks editing platform (built with the Latex programming language) was identified as a problem by some students, particularly the older ones.

> I had students in that section that were a little older, that in some way had a little reluctance to the Wikibook. Then, in the editing part when they uploaded their exercise, they refused a little, because it was complicated. (Teacher 1, Scenario 1)

The principle difficulties of OER use were also explored in the survey administered to students. Figure 18 shows that 30.6% of respondents reported no particular problem. The main difficulties identified by the rest of the class included the time lag in loading resources, IPP's technological infrastructure, and, to a lesser extent, the lack of time for student use. Only 2% of respondents declared that OER use required a level of knowledge that they did not have.

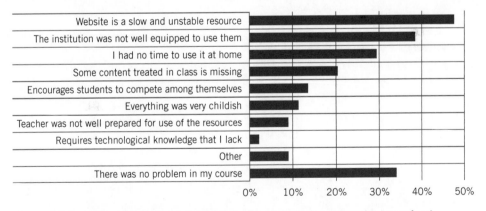

Figure 18: Level to which students agreed with statements about the perceived difficulties of OER use (n = 49)

Table 14 presents the difficulties associated with OER use expressed by resource type. Issues related to IPP infrastructure were more prevalent for users of the Khan Academy collections, while difficulties associated with bandwidth and the lack of certain kinds of content were identified by Open Textbook users.

Table 14: Main perceived difficulties of OER use by resource type (n = 49)

Difficulties of OER use	Khan Academy collections (%)	Open Textbook (%)
Internet connectivity	37.9	50.0
Institutional infrastructure	37.9	30.0
No time for use at home	24.1	30.0
Some content covered in class not represented	13.8	25.0
Encourages students to compete among themselves	6.9	20.0
Lack of sophistication	10.3	10.0
Teacher not adequately prepared	10.3	5.0
Required restrictive level of technological knowledge	0	5.0
Other	13.8	0
None	31.0	30

Suggestions to improve OER use

The final topic examined with regard to student and teacher perceptions of OER deals with suggestions to improve OER use. The main suggestion of teachers and students engaged in the qualitative phase was to extend OER use to more subjects. Concerning the observed problems, another shared suggestion mentioned by Teacher 1 was that computer labs should be in working condition in order to optimise the use of learning tools by students.

> For example, starting with computer labs, they must be in good condition so I do not need someone else to help me do my classes. Because it happened to me many times that I took them to the computer lab and half of the computers were inoperable. (Teacher 1)

> It should be used in all sessions for a larger use in mathematics, to complement more, everyone should use it constantly. It should be used by a lot of people. (Student, Treatment Group 2, Scenario 1)

Khan Academy collections

Teachers 1 and 2, who both used the Khan Academy collections, made two suggestions for improvement. First, they suggested changing the reward system, as the current system was seen to lack sophistication. Second, and specifically in the case of Teacher 2, they suggested that the content of the courses should be more coherent with different topics covered in the resources.

Scenario 1 students considered the fact that teachers used competition as an incentive as a negative factor, in the sense that they felt that the environment should be more collaborative. Scenario 2 students suggested that the details of resource use and implications should be better explained earlier in the course.

> I think it would work well if you didn't have to compete. Because teachers tend to do that ... She projected the platform on a screen and showed who

had logged on, who had the highest score, who had less ... It was graded, they gave it a grade. (Student, Treatment Group 1, Scenario 1)

Open Textbook

Students who used the Open Textbook made very specific recommendations. First, they suggested that the printed book should contain more exercises. They also suggested that, since the use of the platform was somewhat complex, it would be a good idea to provide training for teachers before the course.

> Yes, because that way we could be told how to use it ... How to do the exercises, because there were definitions of what it was about or how it was done. But without the guidance of a teacher we could not have done it. (Student, Treatment Group 1, Scenario 1)

The student survey helped to deepen findings regarding the main recommendations for improving OER use. In a similar way as was done with the questions about positive and negative aspects of OER use, students were asked in the survey to select up to three recommendations for improving the use of OER from a list of predefined alternatives. According to the results (Figure 19), the most frequently identified recommendations relate to implementing strategies to encourage participation in the use of OER (43%), allocating more time in class to use OER (39%), improving institutional infrastructure for OER use (37%) and expanding OER use to other courses (35%).

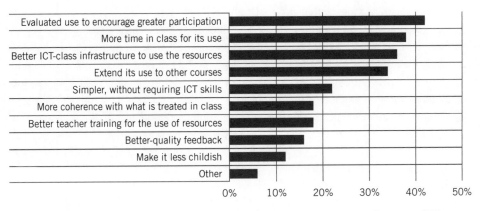

Figure 19: Level to which students agreed with recommendations to improve OER use (n = 49)

Table 15, which highlights recommendations for improving OER use based on resource type, reflects that users of the Open Textbook stated that the OER approach should be expanded to other courses, and that the resource should be easier to implement in the classroom. Khan Academy users recommended that there be more consistency between the content that is taught in the class and what is presented in the resource.

Table 15: Recommendations to improve OER use by resource type (n = 49)

Suggestions for improving OER use	Khan Academy collections (%)	Open Textbook (%)
Evaluate use of the resource in order to encourage greater participation	44.8	40.0
Make more time in class for use	34.5	45.0
Establish better ICT infrastructure	37.9	35.0
Extend use to other courses	27.6	45.0
Less ICT skills required	17.2	30.0
More coherence with what is covered in class	24.1	10.0
Better teacher training	20.7	15.0
Better-quality feedback	13.8	20.0
More sophisticated interface	17.2	5.0
Other	6.9	5.0

Discussion

Research question 1 of this study asked: "What is the effect of OER use on first-year higher education students' mathematics course performance?" The most noteworthy result appears to be that students who used Khan Academy Collection 1 (Treatment Group 1) obtained significantly better exam grades than students who used the traditional proprietary resource ($p < 0.05$) or those who used the Open Textbook ($p < 0.01$).

In Scenario 1, results were consistent in terms of showing that the Open Textbook did not enhance student performance, and that students who were taught with the help of this resource sometimes obtained poorer results than students who used the traditional proprietary textbook. This finding leads to the conclusion that not all kinds of OER have the same effect and that differences regarding types of OER always have to be considered when analysing the impact or efficacy of these resources. Other factors, such as the design of the materials and teachers' expertise in using the platform, also need to be considered.

In Scenario 2, it was found that there was no improvement in mathematical course performance amongst students using OER. This finding should not, however, be considered categorical with regards to the utility of OER in blended-mode course delivery, and should be tested in a larger sample. It may be the case that, in order to take full advantage of OER, there needs to be a teacher who insists on the importance of these resources within the course.

With regard to research question 2, relating to the effect of OER use on class attendance, another important finding was that face-to-face mode students (Scenario 1) who used one of the two types of OER had significantly lower attendance levels than students who relied on the traditional proprietary textbook. This situation might be explained by the fact that when students have access to the infrastructure required to access OER remotely, they tend to work more from home.

With respect to research question 3, related to student and teacher perceptions of the OER adoption process, the qualitative and quantitative material examined reconfirmed the assumption that OER can be a relevant asset to Chilean students. Qualitative data demonstrated that both teachers and students had a positive experience of using the two types of OER. These positive views were reinforced by the survey results, which demonstrated a positive evaluation of OER. The majority of respondents in the student survey indicated that teaching with OER was more dynamic, resources were easier to use, there was good explanatory and support material, and practical exercises were available. A positive evaluation of the personal experience of using these resources was also observed, as most students declared that they liked using both types of OER, which led to improved learning, and that they would recommend OER use in other subjects as well as in their same degree. Finally, the survey also highlighted the fact that teachers were well prepared in terms of integrating OER into the teaching process.

This positive evaluation of OER contrasts somewhat with findings relating to the first research question on whether the use of OER led to an improvement in student performance. In this first component of the research it was found that only one of the studied groups (Treatment Group 1) performed significantly better in the exam than the group of students who did not use OER. It was also found that the use of the Open Textbook did not improve mathematical performance.

This discrepancy does not have to be understood as an inconsistency in the context of the examined data, since results and perceptions of the learning experience are not necessarily always in accordance. Simply because OER was not found to have a positive effect on the specified result variables, it does not mean that these resources were not seen as useful by students. The data merely suggest that in several considered cases, course averages and exam grades were not significantly higher amongst students using OER versus those who did not use OER. This means that the positive effect perceived by students may not be reflected in higher grades, but could manifest in other ways, such as increased motivation or improved ICT skills. It is also possible that students' increased skills or capabilities may not necessarily be reflected by the tests used here.

Beyond general results about the effect of OER and how these resources are valued, the second, mixed-methods component of the research (which was aimed at addressing research question 3) shows that there were also negative perceptions about specific problems that emerged from the use of OER. The data highlight the fact that OER implementation did not work well when students lacked adequate time and the appropriate infrastructure in which to interact with these resources. With regard to this, the qualitative component of the research highlighted that one of the main reasons for not using OER was that there was not enough time to do so. Furthermore, the fact that optimal utilisation of resources relied on IPP providing computer labs in appropriate working condition was also highlighted. These findings were supported by the quantitative data, which identified areas for improvement. These data highlight the institutional infrastructure challenge in learning how to properly use and interact with OER, problems associated with OER platforms and websites, and lack of time. All of the suggestions for improvement were aimed at enhancing conditions in which OER strategies could be implemented rather than criticising the utility of these resources, reconfirming that students had a positive overall evaluation of their OER experience.

Finally, another important point addressed in the second component of the research process relates to student perceptions observed in the survey. The survey showed some differences by income level, age group and levels of student use. Although significant differences were not found among the groups, it is possible to highlight some general trends. Younger students and those with higher levels of resource use valued the experience of using OER more. Income group, on the other hand, does not appear to generate discernible differences. When considering the Impact Analysis Database, students with higher income achieved higher scores, but when considering the specific evaluation of certain aspects of OER use, students with lower income had a more positive perspective.

However, these results about the effects of OER need to be treated with caution as they were obtained from a small not completely random sample, representing only a very specific cohort of Chilean students. In terms of their representativeness, these findings do not mean that OER cannot have a positive effect amongst other student cohorts. Nevertheless, these findings have little external validity and more research on the effect of OER is required in order to justify the use of these resources in a broader context.

Conclusion

Although there is more evidence today on how the "free" aspect of digital resources has a measurable educational impact, we are only at the beginning of assessing how the "open" aspect might contribute to accessible, high-quality education. In the same way that consensus has not been achieved in terms of measuring the impact of ICTs in education (despite the fact that there is widespread agreement regarding their importance), "openness" does not necessarily produce an impact in itself, but is instead part of a greater set of tools and practices in which many variables exert an influence. ICTs and openness are not tools or instruments that intrinsically cause a specific outcome.

This factor aside, they are surely game-changers and enablers of many uses and practices which draw on the power of human cooperation and that contain some combination of the aspects inherent to "digitally enabled openness": sharing ideas and knowledge; the ability to reuse, revise and repurpose content; increasing transparency of processes; expanding participation; and collaborative production (Smith & Reilly, 2013).

As the road to a global knowledge society and a new global economy can be either smooth or rocky, a short- or long-run effort, and more or less inclusive, the concept of "openness" reminds us that we inhabit a world rapidly on its way to becoming a networked society, which poses substantial opportunities and threats for international development. Capitalising upon the opportunities and diminishing the threats of openness is a major challenge, particularly for countries that need to make the transition towards openness in order to aid development.

Acknowledgements

The authors wish to thank Ana Elena Schalk, former IPP Academic Vice-Rector and Substitute Rector, for the institutional support received in conducting this study. Thanks are also due to Daniela Cerón for her mathematical expertise and to Patricio Acevedo for his support selecting and bundling Khan Academy resources for the courses. Rebeca Parra and Celso Soto, the IPP teachers that accepted the challenge to work with their students in utilising these new resources, made a great contribution to the study. Finally, special thanks are due to George Sciadas and Birgit Loch for valuable comments received in the peer-review process.

References

Allen, I. E. & Seaman, J. (2014). *Opening the curriculum: Open Education Resources in U.S. higher education, 2014.* Babson Park, MA: Babson Survey Research Group & The William and Flora Hewlett Foundation. Retrieved from http://www.onlinelearningsurvey.com/reports/openingthecurriculum2014.pdf

Allen, G., Guzman-Alvarez, A., Molinaro, M. & Larsen, D. (2015). *Assessing the impact and efficacy of the Open-Access ChemWiki textbook project.* New York: EDUCAUSE. Retrieved from https://library.educause.edu/resources/2015/1/assessing-the-impact-and-efficacy-of-the-openaccess-chemwiki-textbook-project

Berelson, B. (1952). *Content analysis in communication research.* New York: Free Press.

Betancourt, M. C., Celaya, R. & Ramírez, M. S. (2014). Open Educational Practices and technology appropriation: The case of the Regional Open Latin American Community for Social and Educational Research (CLARISE). *Revista de Universidad y Sociedad del Conocimiento, 11(1),* 4–17. Retrieved from http://dx.doi.org/10.7238/rusc.v11i1.1794

Bliss, T. J., Hilton III, J., Wiley, D. & Thanos, K. (2013). The cost and quality of online open textbooks: Perceptions of community college faculty and students. *First Monday, 18(1–7).* Retrieved from http://firstmonday.org/ojs/index.php/fm/article/view/3972

Brunner, J. J. (2008). El sistema de educación superior en Chile: Un enfoque de economía política comparada. *Revista da Avaliação da Educação Superior (Campinas), Edición Especial, 13(2),* 451–486. Retrieved from http://www.scielo.br/scielo.php?pid=S1414-40772008000200010&script=sci_arttext&tlng=es

Dehejia, R. H. & Wahba, S. (1999). Causal effects in nonexperimental studies: Reevaluating the evaluation of training programs. *Journal of American Statistical Association, 94(448),* 1053–1062. Retrieved from http://users.nber.org/~rdehejia/papers/dehejia_wahba_jasa.pdf

EC (European Commission). (2012). *Rethinking education: Investing in skills for better socio-economic outcomes.* Brussels: European Commission. Retrieved from http://eur-lex.europa.eu/procedure/EN/202132

EC (European Commission). (2013). *"Opening up education": Innovative teaching and learning for all through new technologies and Open Educational Resources.* Brussels: European Commission. Retrieved from http://ec.europa.eu/education/news/doc/openingcom_en.pdf

Feldstein, A., Martin, M., Hudson, A., Warren, K., Hilton III, J. & Wiley, D. (2012). Open textbooks and increased student access and outcomes. *European Journal of Open, Distance and E-Learning, 2(1).* Retrieved from http://www.eurodl.org/materials/contrib/2012/Feldsteint_et_al.pdf

Fischer, L., Hilton III, J., Robinson, T. J. & Wiley, D. (2015). A multi-institutional study of the impact of open textbook adoption on the learning outcomes of post-secondary students. *Journal of Computing in Higher Education, 27(3),* 159–172. Retrieved from http://link.springer.com/article/10.1007%2Fs12528-015-9101-x

Fundación La Fuente/Adimark GFK. (2011). *Chile y los libros 2010.* Santiago de Chile: Fundación Educacional y Cultural La Fuente. Retrieved from http://www.fundacionlafuente.cl/wp-content/uploads/2010/11/Chile-y-los-libros-2010_FINAL-liviano.pdf

Heckman, J. J., Ichimura, H., Smith, J. A. & Todd, P. E. (1998). Characterizing selection bias using experimental data. *Econometrica, 66(5)*, 1017–1098. Retrieved from http://jenni. uchicago.edu/papers/Heckman_Ichimura_etal_1998_Econometrica_v66_n5_r.pdf

Hilton III, J. & Laman, C. (2012). One college's use of an open psychology textbook. *Open Learning, 27(3)*, 265–272. Retrieved from http://scholarsarchive.byu.edu/cgi/viewcontent. cgi?article=1069&context=facpub

Hodgkinson-Williams, C. & Gray, E. (2009). Degrees of openness: The emergence of Open Educational Resources at the University of Cape Town. *International Journal of Education and Development using Information and Communication Technology, 5(5)*, 101–116. Retrieved from https://open.uct.ac.za/handle/11427/8860

Imbens, G. W. & Hirano, K. (2002). Estimation of causal effects using propensity score weighting: An application to data on right heart catheterization. *Health Services and Outcomes Research Methodology, 2(1)*, 259–278. Retrieved from https://scholar.harvard. edu/imbens/publications/estimation-causal-effects-using-propensity-score-weighting-application-data-righ

Keegan, H. & Bell, F. (2011). YouTube as a repository: The creative practice of students as producers of Open Educational Resources. *European Journal of Open, Distance and E-learning*. Retrieved from http://www.eurodl.org/materials/special/2011/Keegan_Bell.pdf

MINEDC (Ministry of Education of Chile). (2012). *Deserción en la educación superior en Chile. Serie Evidencias Año, 1(9)*. Santiago: Ministry of Education. Retrieved from http://portales. mineduc.cl/usuarios/bmineduc/doc/201209281737360.EVIDENCIASCEM9.pdf

Orr, D., Rimini, M. & Van Damme, D. (2015). *Open Educational Resources: A catalyst for innovation, educational research and innovation*. Paris: OECD Publishing. Retrieved from http://dx.doi.org/10.1787/9789264247543-en

Rosenbaum, P. & Rubin, D. B. (1983). The central role of propensity score in observational studies for causal effects. *Biometrika, 70(1)*, 41–55. Retrieved from http://www.stat.cmu. edu/~ryantibs/journalclub/rosenbaum_1983.pdf

Santos-Hermosa, G., Ferran-Ferrer, N. & Abadal, E. (2013). Recursos educativos abiertos: repositorios y uso. *El profesional de la información, 21(2)*, 136–145. Retrieved from http:// www.accesoabierto.net/sites/accesoabierto.net/files/Santos-Ferran-Abadal-EPI.pdf

Shear, L., Means, B. & Lundh, P. (2015). *Research on open: OER Research Hub review and futures for research on OER*. Menlo Park, CA: SRI Education. Retrieved from http://www. hewlett.org/wp-content/uploads/2016/08/OERRH%20Evaluation%20Final%20Report%20 June%202015.pdf

Smith, M. L. & Reilly, K. M. A. (Eds.). (2013). *Open development: Networked innovations in international development*. Cambridge, MA: MIT Press. Retrieved from https://www.idrc.ca/ en/book/open-development-networked-innovations-international-development

UNESCO–IITE (United Nations Educational, Scientific and Cultural Organization–Institute for Information Technologies in Education). (2011). *Activity report 2010–2011*. Paris: United Nations Educational, Scientific and Cultural Organization. Retrieved from http://iite.unesco. org/publications/3214690/

Weller, M., de los Arcos, B., Farrow, R., Pitt, B. & McAndrew, P. (2015). The impact of OER on teaching and learning practice. *Open Praxis, 7(4)*. Retrieved from http://openpraxis.org/ index.php/OpenPraxis/article/view/227

Wiley, D., Hilton III, J. L., Ellington, S. & Hall, T. (2012). A preliminary examination of the cost savings and learning impacts of using open textbooks in middle and high school science classes. *The International Review of Research in Open and Distributed Learning, 13(3)*. Retrieved from http://www.irrodl.org/index.php/irrodl/article/view/1153/2256

How to cite this chapter

Westermann Juárez, W. & Venegas Muggli, J. I. (2017). Effectiveness of OER use in first-year higher education students' mathematical course performance: A case study. In C. Hodgkinson-Williams & P. B. Arinto (Eds.), *Adoption and impact of OER in the Global South* (pp. 187–229). Retrieved from https://doi.org/10.5281/zenodo.601203

Corresponding author: Werner Westermann Juárez < wernerwestermannj@gmail.com>

Section 3
Sub-Saharan Africa

Contents

Chapter 7

Tracking the money for Open Educational Resources in South African basic education: What we don't know[1]

Sarah Goodier

Summary

This study aims to develop an understanding of government funding allocated to educational resources in basic education in South Africa. Linked to claims about potential cost savings associated with using Open Educational Resources (OER), the main intention was to establish a benchmark of public spending on educational resources in order to be able to ascertain the economic benefits of using OER. As such, the following research questions are considered: How much public money is currently being spent on educational materials in basic education in South Africa? How much public money is currently being spent on OER in basic education in South Africa? Do OER represent a cost reduction with regard to educational resource acquisition in basic education in South Africa?

The study is comprised of a desk review and document analysis of publicly available information on expenditure in South African basic education. This approach was adopted in order to develop a conceptual understanding of South African government funding allocation for general educational resources as well as OER.

The findings highlight the fact that individual provinces, rather than central government, have the authority to determine budget allocations for the procurement and delivery of what are termed Learning and Teaching Support Materials (LTSM). ▶

---

1   This chapter has been reproduced from the *International Review of Research in Open and Distributed Learning* (IRRODL) Volume 18, Issue 4, using a Creative Commons Attribution International 4.0 licence. © 2017 Sarah Goodier.

Although each provincial Department of Education budget includes a line item for LTSM, these are not sufficiently disaggregated to determine the actual expenditure on specific categories, such as textbooks, in order to establish a benchmark for potential cost savings of OER. The findings also illustrate a possible cost-recovery model based on the local Siyavula open textbook initiative.

In order to make claims about OER and their cost-saving potential in the South African education system, national and provincial government budgets will need to be disaggregated to a more granular level and made more readily available for in-depth investigation of budgetary allocations.

Acronyms and abbreviations

DBE   South African Department of Basic Education
DHET   Department of Higher Education and Training
LTSM   learning and teaching support materials
MEC   Member of the Executive Council
OER   Open Educational Resources
PASA   Publishers' Association of South Africa
PDEs   Provincial Departments of Education
SACMEQ   Southern and Eastern African Consortium for Monitoring Educational Quality
ZAR   South African rands

Introduction

In terms of potential cost-saving mechanisms, Open Educational Resources (OER) have been claimed, as well as found in some cases, to be a cost-effective mechanism for providing educational materials to students and educators in the USA (e.g. Allen & Student PIRGs, 2010; Hilton III, Robinson, Wiley & Ackerman, 2014; Wiley, Hilton III, Ellington & Hall, 2012). However, OER cost saving has not been investigated with regard to public funding of OER in South African basic education (K-12 equivalent) to date.

This study utilises the definition of OER laid out in the 2012 Paris OER Declaration, namely that OER are

> teaching, learning and research materials in any medium, digital or otherwise,
> that reside in the public domain or have been released under an open licence
> that permits no-cost access, use, adaptation and redistribution by others with
> no or limited restrictions. (UNESCO, 2012, p.1)

This study focuses on the use of public funding, defined here as money allocated by the South African National Treasury through the annual budget and appropriation process.

The aims of this study are to investigate whether any public funding is being channelled specifically into OER, and, if so, whether it is possible to calculate any potential cost savings that have been realised thus far. The backdrop of the study, including the high costs of education in the region, the importance of easy access to learning materials and the potential for OER to reduce costs, is described below.

Background

The key role of education in societal and economic development is recognised in the right to primary education forming part of many international statements on human rights. This important right is also enshrined in the Constitution of the Republic of South Africa (Republic of South Africa, 1996), which makes provision for receiving education in any one of the country's 11 official languages. South Africa achieved the Millennium Development Goal of universal primary education ahead of the 2015 target year[2] (UNECA, 2015), demonstrating that access to primary education has increased. This broad-based access is, however, not cheap.

Currently, substantial amounts of money are spent on education by governments across the African continent, with average public expenditure on education in the region as a percentage of gross domestic product increasing from 4.2% to 4.9% between 2000 and 2012 (UNECA, 2015). In South Africa, education expenditure has been on the increase for decades, from ZAR 31.1 billion in 1995, to ZAR 59.6 billion in 2002, and to ZAR 105.5 billion in 2007 (OECD, 2008). In the current global climate of austerity, there is a pressing need to maximise outcomes from increasingly limited resources.

Despite financial pressures within the education system, teaching and learning materials are recognised as foundational to learning. A Development Bank of Southern Africa (DBSA, 2012) review highlights adequate resources and "instructional materials, such as textbooks, supplementary teachers' guides and materials, library books, and the like" (p.196) as the basic inputs necessary in education, and among those that improve student achievement. In the South African context, such materials are referred to as learning and teaching support materials (LTSM) and this term will be used in this chapter. LTSM, formerly called learning support materials, refers to "a variety of learning and teaching materials used in classroom. These range from teacher and learner created resources to commercially produced classroom resources such as wall charts, workbooks, textbooks, e-books, readers, stationery, science kits, dictionaries, encyclopaedias, etc." (DBE, 2014, p.3).

Textbooks have increasingly been seen as an important part of South African basic education following the 2009 Review of the Implementation of the National Curriculum Statement (DBE, 2009; 2011). The minister, in her 2009 Curriculum Review speech indicated that "the textbook is the most effective tool to ensure consistency, coverage, appropriate pacing and better quality instruction" (DBE, 2009, p.1). This was because the textbook was considered to be the primary delivery mechanism in providing both teachers and learners with the curriculum requirements (OECD, 2008), and served as a key tool in helping students to understand relationships between topics and concepts within topics, as well as being critical in enabling students to do homework (DBE, 2011). In developing countries, it has been found that children who have access to LTSM, such as textbooks,

---

2   http://www.za.undp.org/content/south_africa/en/home/post-2015/mdgoverview/overview/mdg2/

learn more relative to those without (DBSA, 2012). Therefore, increasing expenditure on LTSM, despite the climate of austerity, to enable access to learning materials has been seen as a valid strategy (OECD, 2008).

In its Action Plan 2014, the Department of Basic Education (DBE) recognises the need for improved access to learning materials in South Africa. Two of the 27 goals listed in the Action Plan 2014 relate directly to learning materials:

> Goal 19: Ensure that every learner has access to the minimum set of textbooks and workbooks required according to national policy.

> Goal 20: Increase access amongst learners to a wide range of media, including computers, which enrich their education. (DBE, 2011, p.6)

These goals originate from a historical legacy of a lack of access to required LTSM such as textbooks and other materials in South African schools (OECD, 2008). The Southern and Eastern African Consortium for Monitoring Educational Quality (SACMEQ) II and III results show no substantial change in South Africa for the percentage of sole-use access to Grade 6 reading textbooks (46% and 45%, respectively) (Spaull, 2012). This level of access is only approximately 3% above the SACMEQ average (UNESCO IIEP, 2010), and varies widely among provinces. A 2005 survey of 20 schools in three South African provinces found that in allocating the required learner support materials, schools gave preference to Grade 12 as well as other secondary-school grades (Financial and Fiscal Commission, 2005). Despite this, the survey also found that delivery of the minimum number of textbooks required for Grades 8 to 11 was often not met (Financial and Fiscal Commission, 2005). In 2008, only 64% of Grade 4 to 7 learners were in classes where every student had a mathematics textbook (DBE, 2011). These textbook access problems, especially in poorer schools, are a recognised obstacle to learning (DBE, 2011). Goal 19 stated above was therefore listed as a priority goal to be reached in 2014 (DBE, 2011).

Performance indicators in the 2015 Budget (National Treasury, 2015) indicate a high level of coverage in terms of learners' access to the required workbooks and textbooks. For example, the percentage of learners with access to the required textbooks in all school grades and in all subjects per year was 97% in 2011/12, 98% in 2012/13, and 91.8% in 2013/14. It is, however, not stated whether this is individual access to the books or whether they are shared among learners. Therefore, while access has improved, Goal 19 was not reached. There have been reported instances of non-delivery and late delivery of textbooks to schools indicated by educators (DBE, 2013b), as well as serious under-allocation of budget to provide the required textbooks.[3] In December 2015, the Supreme Court of Appeal ruled that every child has a right to start off the school year with their textbooks, increasing the pressure on the DBE to deliver on providing timely access across the country (Supreme Court of Appeal of South Africa, 2015).

---

3   http://mg.co.za/article/2013-08-23-00-south-africas-hidden-textbook-crisis

Schools and OER: Evidence for reduced cost

OER has been suggested by several stakeholders as a possible solution to both cost and access issues in education. Studies conducted in the United States, with a particular focus on tertiary education, have examined the cost of OER and the savings they can potentially facilitate. Allen and Student PIRGs (2010) calculated potential savings for students by analysing the cost of textbooks from ten US college-level courses which had an open textbook available for that subject. An average annual saving of 80% was found (Allen & Student PIRGs, 2010). Hilton III et al. (2014) found that the average cost of the standard textbook used for these same classes was USD 90.61. Using a cost of zero for the OER, a potential saving of over USD 200 000 was found for all students (n = 2 642) enrolled in classes that used OER as textbooks in the Kaleidoscope Open Course Initiative (Hilton III et al., 2014).

What has been proposed is that using OER could potentially help to decrease the cost of educational resource acquisition in the long term, allowing countries to better meet the growing demand for education, while also potentially improving outcomes. Jimes, Weiss and Keep (2013) draw attention to the potential of OER to contribute "high-quality teaching and learning resources that can be freely used, shared, and modified by educators to suit local instructional needs" (p.74). Governments that recognise this potential and its asserted link to reducing their costs have been shown to favour open textbooks (Frydenberg & Matkin, 2007). The DBE has printed and issued several OER textbooks to high school science and maths students since 2012 in partnership with OER publisher Siyavula (DBE, 2013a; Jimes et al., 2013).[4,5,6] This presents an opportunity to potentially investigate whether OER has reduced costs. Comparing open textbook costs to those associated with traditional textbooks is an important step in producing evidence for or against cost reduction. For example, if an open and traditional textbook cost the same to produce, the open textbook could still represent a longer-term cost advantage as it could be revised and the relevant sections printed and combined with the original instead of an entirely new book being produced and printed. Establishing whether these textbooks can or already do result in reduced costs would provide vital information to government and other stakeholders in guiding the way forward.

Context of the present study

This study is aimed at understanding whether the utilisation of OER would result in cost savings in the South African basic education context. As such, the specific objectives of this study have been to:

- Review information sources on basic education provision and policy in South Africa in order to understand and establish a baseline for the allocation of funds used by government to develop and/or buy educational resources for basic education.

---

4   http://arthurattwell.com/2012/01/05/a-sea-change-in-south-african-schoolbook-publishing/
5   http://www.gov.za/statement-during-announcement-2011-national-senior-certificate-grade-12-examination-results-mrs
6   http://ventureburn.com/2012/10/is-siyavula-the-answer-to-south-africas-textbook-crisis/

- Ascertain whether any public funding has been channelled specifically into OER production and/or acquisition in South Africa.
- Determine whether and to what extent, from the established baseline, OER represent a cost reduction with regards to educational resource acquisition in basic education in South Africa.

These ambitions are embodied in the following research questions:

1. How much public money is currently spent on the production and acquisition of educational materials in basic education in South Africa?
2. How much public money is currently being spent on OER production and acquisition in basic education in South Africa?
3. To what extent do OER represent a cost reduction with regards to educational resource acquisition in basic education in South Africa?

Method

Data on expenditure regarding education "are essential for effectively addressing critical education policy questions" (UNESCO IS, 2011, p.11). These kinds of data can provide insight into where it may be possible to lower costs. However, information on the allocation of funds from public sources specifically around educational resource acquisition and development (including digital objects, textbooks, learning platforms, scientific books and publications) is not necessarily readily available beyond publicly available government budgets and expenditure reports. To track the allocation of funds it was necessary to develop an understanding of the structure of education departments and how they acquired and distributed their funding.

An extensive desktop review surveying studies, reports and other literature on cost in education was undertaken in order to identify, access and review official information sources on South African education in order to understand the government allocation of funds into the production and acquisition of LTSM. Information on any funding contributing to the production and acquisition of OER was also reviewed. The sources of information used are summarised in Table 1.

Table 1: Primary document analysis sources by research question

Research question	Information source (organisation type)	Document/data type
1. How much public money is currently being spent on the production and acquisition of educational materials in basic education in South Africa?	Government information sources International and regional organisations tracking educational systems and expenditure Media	National budgets Provincial budgets Government policy documents Government reports Government websites Organisation reports Organisation data News reports

Research question	Information source (organisation type)	Document/data type
2. How much public money is currently being spent on OER production and acquisition in basic education in South Africa?	Government information sources International and regional organisations that track educational systems and expenditures Media	National budgets Provincial budgets Government policy documents Government reports Government websites Organisation reports Organisation data News reports
3. To what extent do OER represent a cost reduction with regard to educational resource acquisition in basic education in South Africa?	Government information sources International and regional organisations that track educational systems and expenditures OER publishers	National budgets Provincial budgets Government policy documents Government reports Government websites Organisation reports Organisation data Documentation from Siyavula

As this is an exploratory review of a topic that is documented in both academic as well as public and government literature, online searches were conducted in both general search engines (Google and Yahoo) as well as in academic databases (Google Scholar, EBSCOHost) and a repository (CSIR ResearchSpace). The search terms used, in various combinations, were "educational expenditure", "South Africa", "textbook", "DBE", "procurement process", "public funding", "National Norms and Standards for School Funding", "quintile system", "government budgeting", "department of basic education", "provincial departments of education", "OER", "open educational resources", "primary education", "OER cost", "cost", "Africa", "basic education", "secondary education" and "Siyavula open textbook". Specific websites, such as the DBE's website,[7] the National Treasury site[8] and newspaper websites were also searched. Sources of information were included if they carried information relevant to educational expenditure funding allocation in South African basic education, or had any particular reference to OER.

Findings

The key findings from the desk review and document analysis of official information sources on South African basic education are presented in a narrative below.

Provincial versus national budget allocation in the South African basic education system

Since the bifurcation of the South African National Department of Education in 2009, the responsibility for education has been shared by the DBE and the Department of Higher Education and Training (DHET).[9] DHET is responsible for universities as well as other post-

---

7   http://www.education.gov.za/
8   http://www.treasury.gov.za/
9   http://www.dhet.gov.za/

school education and training, while schools, from Grade R (the Reception year in the South African school system, similar to kindergarten) to Grade 12, and adult basic education are the responsibility of the DBE (Government Communications and Information Systems Department, 2014). Schooling is compulsory from age seven to 15 or up to the end of Grade 9, whichever occurs first, and the majority of students do in fact complete Grade 9 (OECD, 2008; van Wyk, 2015). One of the drivers for compulsory education is the historical context of restricted access to education in South Africa under the apartheid system. It is, as such, designed to address the need to "make education structurally accessible to all who were previously denied, or had limited access to it" (OECD, 2008, p.38).

Under the National Education Policy Act No. 27, the DBE (1996a) is responsible for determining national education policy and monitoring its implementation by the Provincial Departments of Education (PDEs). It is, however, the PDEs that are responsible for implementing policies aligned with national government goals and allocating their own budgets (determined by provincial allocations) based on the number of schools and students in their areas. As with all government departments, the DBE and DHET are funded through the annual national budget allocation and appropriation process. The same process also applies to the provinces, which in turn provide the funds for their PDEs. These processes are described below.

The Public Finance Management Act No. 1 of 1999 regulates national and provincial government financial management and outlines the responsibilities of those in charge, while the National Treasury manages the country's budget preparation process and its implementation. All money received by the national government, for example taxes collected by the South African Revenue Service, is deposited into the National Revenue Fund, and there are provincial treasuries which prepare and implement the budget for each province. Parliament and the provincial legislatures must devote money for specific purposes for each financial year that fulfil the requirements of the state and the provinces, respectively. The annual budget is tabled in February in the National Assembly by the Minister of Finance preceding the start of the financial year, following which the Member of the Executive Council (MEC) for Finance in each province tables the annual provincial budget. The budget allocates money to the national, provincial and local spheres of government. Money from the national budget allocation funds government departments such as the DBE and DHET, while money from the provincial allocation funds the PDEs. Each province receives an equitable provincial share, which is the overall amount determined by the parliament of South Africa to fund the provision of provincial services. This equitable share is calculated by a formula taking into account various factors, such as the provincial population. The percentage allocation that goes to various provincial sectors (such as education) is determined by the Provincial Legislature – not national government or the DBE (DBE, 2011). This funding process is outlined in Figure 1.

The South African Schools Act No. 84 of 1996 provides for the establishment and administration of public schools from provincial legislature funds in the Provincial Treasury (DBE, 1996b). The responsibility for this provision rests with the MEC for Education. The PDEs receive the funds and distribute them in line with their budgeting process (DBE, 2011; DOE, 2006). Every PDE budget will contain a line item for teaching and learning materials, including textbooks that are prescribed for each grade. This makes tracking expenditure on a specific category of items possible, at least at PDE level.

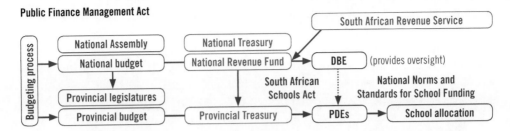

Figure 1: Simplified schematic of the national budgeting and allocation process for basic education

The National Norms and Standards for School Funding established public school allocations (DOE, 2006). As each province takes responsibility for its schools, and the school allocation budgets and expenditure priorities can be different, what is considered appropriate in terms of norms and standards can vary widely between the provinces.[10] School allocations are defined as "an amount allocated by the state to each public ordinary school in the country on an annual basis in order to finance non-personnel non-capital expenditure items" (DOE, 2006, p.24). The annual school allocations made include provision for expenditure on LTSM (DOE, 2006). The LTSM procurement and delivery process is described below.

Procurement and delivery of LTSM

The executive director of the Publishers' Association of South Africa (PASA), in his supporting affidavit to Section 27's legal action against the DBE regarding the 2012 textbook crisis in the South African province of Limpopo, described the textbook procurement and delivery process presented in Figure 2 below (Wafawarowa, 2012). Once the National Catalogue is produced by the DBE, PDEs liaise with schools around their requisition forms for these books and usually place consolidated orders in August/September of the year preceding the academic year for which the books are required. When orders are received, PASA members initiate the processes to supply the books, and orders placed by September are filled prior to the December school holidays. Later ordering results in later delivery, but even when orders are placed in December/January, books are usually still received early in the year. However, if books are not in stock and need to be printed, a time lag of eight weeks can pass before delivery. Books are usually delivered to the PDE's central warehouse rather than directly to the schools; the PDE then delivers the textbooks to the schools.

Figure 2: Simplified schematic of the South African basic education textbook procurement process

---

10 http://oerhub.net/collaboration-2/siyavula-educator-survey-results-educational-contexts-part-ii/

LTSM (including textbooks) form a large part of the South African publishing industry's print output, with the government as one of its largest consumers (PASA, 2004). The cost to government is substantial, as approximately ZAR 1.5 billion is paid to the publishing industry annually for orders of textbooks by the DBE (Butcher & Hoosen, 2012). In terms of LTSM, the National Catalogue of Textbooks (established in 2011) reflects the catalogue of textbooks reviewed and recommended by the DBE, enabling choice and, potentially, better value through negotiations and economy of scale (DBE, 2013a). The timing of the release of this list has implications for ordering and the DBE noted that releasing the list early in 2012 allowed the PDEs to order with sufficient time to ensure that delivery of the curriculum-aligned books could take place in time for the 2013 school year (DBE, 2013a).

While Figure 2 shows the process for book ordering from traditional publishers, there has been one case where OER textbooks have been supplied to schools through a partnership between an OER publisher and the DBE.

A South African OER initiative

Founded in South Africa in 2007, Siyavula is an education technology company and OER publisher that aims to make open textbooks and other content "available for all grades and subjects within South Africa".[11] Released under Creative Commons licences,[12] these resources are free for users to print and adapt as needed, depending on the licence chosen.

Siyavula has successfully partnered with the DBE[13] to review and endorse the open textbooks Siyavula produces, and to enable the printing and distribution of free-to-the-user copies of their textbooks, *Everything Maths* and *Everything Science*, and their Thunderbolt Kids workbooks for Grades 4 to 6 in natural science and technology to all government schools across the country (DBE, 2013a; Jimes et al., 2013).[14,15,16] In 2012, government printers printed both the Siyavula *Everything Maths* and *Everything Science* textbooks, teacher guides for Grades 10, 11 and 12, and the Grades 4–6 workbooks (DBE, 2013a).[17] It is, however, unclear exactly how many books were actually printed or which budget(s) the costs were recovered from. Shillington[18] cites approximately 2.5 million books being printed at a cost of ZAR 35 a copy, while the DBE (2013a) indicates that four million were printed. In January 2013, Grade 11 books were distributed again and there was a plan to distribute the books to Grade 12 learners in 2014 (DBE, 2013a). From 2012 to date, it is estimated that approximately 10 million Siyavula textbooks have been printed and distributed to schools all over the country by government.[19] As the total print numbers and costs, as well as distribution costs are not available, actual unit costs cannot be accurately calculated.

---

11 http://www.siyavulaeducation.com/about-history.html
12 http://creativecommons.org/licenses/
13 http://www.siyavulaeducation.com/work-partnered.html
14 http://arthurattwell.com/2012/01/05/a-sea-change-in-south-african-schoolbook-publishing/
15 http://www.gov.za/statement-during-announcement-2011-national-senior-certificate-grade-12-examination-results-mrs
16 http://ventureburn.com/2012/10/is-siyavula-the-answer-to-south-africas-textbook-crisis/
17 http://www.gov.za/statement-during-announcement-2011-national-senior-certificate-grade-12-examination-results-mrs
18 http://ventureburn.com/2012/10/is-siyavula-the-answer-to-south-africas-textbook-crisis/
19 http://oerhub.net/college/siyavula-educator-survey-results-sample-part-i/

In terms of internal content development costs, Siyavula produces textbooks as OER through a sponsorship model where a sponsor signs on to fund production costs in exchange for advertising in the books, which is one of the factors that makes the books cheaper for the government. A comparison between Siyavula's model and traditional textbook publishing, in terms of cost recovery, is shown in Figure 3.

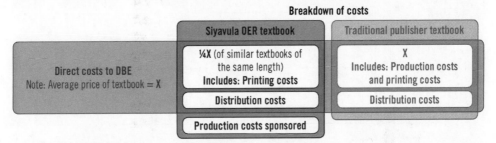

Figure 3: Siyavula textbook costing model versus traditional textbook publishing model highlighting basic cost information needed to calculate any savings from using OER: production, printing and distribution costs. This does not include additional factors such as profit margin or royalties.

As a cost-saving option to government, the Siyavula textbooks have been noted to be attractive as these books cost "a quarter of the unit price of similar textbooks of the same length" (DBE, 2013a, p.14). However, the data to substantiate this claim are not provided and no analysis of cost difference or the figure to conduct one were found during this study. Therefore, although the Siyavula case provides some evidence for the availability of mathematics and science OER in the form of textbooks in South African basic education, there is little and conflicting available information on their distribution and printing and the costs associated with these. This makes it difficult to even estimate cost to public sources or determine which budgets covered these costs.

Challenges in tracking LTSM-related expenditure

As illustrated above, tracking allocation of funds and expenditure on specific categories of items is difficult due to the complex nature of the funding structures, with expenditure spread across various budgets and levels of government. In terms of the National Norms and Standards for School Funding, funds for LTSM are allocated by provinces (DOE, 2006).

The actual and projected expenditure amounts on LTSM by PDE, as reported in the 2014 National Treasury provincial budget documentation (National Treasury, 2014a–i), are presented in Figure 4. Figure 4 shows the LTSM allocations from the annual 2010/11, 2011/12 and 2012/13 budgets, the adjusted appropriation from the 2013/14 budget, and the medium-term estimates for the 2014/15, 2015/16 and 2016/17 financial years for each province. In 2013/14, just over 3.8 billion ZAR was the total appropriation for all provinces, with an average of 0.424 billion ZAR per province. Most provinces, except for the Free State and Northern Cape, show a general upward trend in LTSM expenditure since 2010/11. The large differences in education expenditure and budget between provinces as well as between years reflect the different priorities from year to year in terms of educational budget expenditure and the relative need for LTSM acquisition, which can be affected by the number of learners and which books they require. Therefore, while the overall baseline of LTSM spend per year can be obtained, there is no detail available in these PDE budgets to separate the OER spend from the overall LTSM spend.

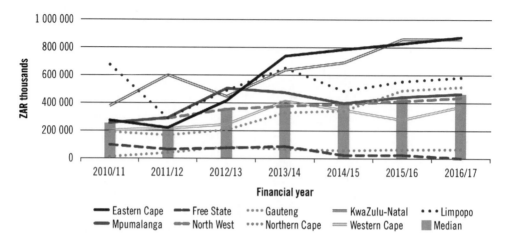

Figure 4: Budget allocations for LTSM by PDE (2010–2017). As these are from 2014 budget figures, 2014/15, 2015/16 and 2016/17 are projected figures. (Source National Treasury, 2014a–i).

In terms of the DBE's budget and expenditure on LTSM, it is not clear how much money was spent on LTSM-related purchases and, by extension, on OER. There is no line item for LTSM in the programme budget breakdowns in the national budgets and it is unclear where printing or distribution of these resources, for example in the Siyavula case, might fit into the budget categories.

Discussion and conclusion

In aiming to meet the constitutional obligation to be able to make provision for primary education to be received in any one of the country's 11 official languages (Republic of South Africa, 1996), as well as the DBE's Action Plan goals related to providing access to the minimum prescribed resources (DBE, 2011), OER has the potential to enable (legally translatable) resources that could potentially be cheaper than traditional textbooks over the longer term. These books could be printed and distributed as well as shared electronically. There has also been a growing focus on digital resources and access platforms, with both the Gauteng and Western Cape Education departments recently launching digital education initiatives.[20,21] This is in line with trends elsewhere around the globe where basic education continues to incorporate digital components (Brown & Green, 2015) as

---

20 http://www.timeslive.co.za/thetimes/2015/07/27/Paperless-classroom-a-reality
21 https://www.westerncape.gov.za/elearning

a strategy to maximise public spending and improve quality (Toledo, Botero & Guzmán, 2014). Having resources available on these platforms explicitly under an open licence would help to facilitate adoption and use as well as potentially reduce costs over time. In order to calculate any cost savings, however, cost benchmarks as well as OER spend data would need to be available.

While broad figures on LTSM expenditure by PDEs were available in government budgets, insufficient information is currently available to track any OER spend or to ascertain any possible cost savings that the adoption of OER might bring. The level of detail in the available government information does not provide a useable benchmark for a cost-saving analysis. The lack of this information has been found elsewhere in the Global South. Toledo et al. (2014) were similarly not able to gather such information in their Latin American study examining expenditure in Argentina, Chile, Paraguay, Uruguay and Colombia, as it was either not available from the government departments or not compiled in a useable state.

Further research into LTSM expenditure and allocation of funds for OER could inform better decision-making on where resources should be directed. Information on the allocation of funds from public sources into educational resource acquisition and development is, however, not necessarily readily available beyond government budgets and expenditure reports, and those reviewed do not provide the level of detail required to attempt a cost-benefit analysis regarding the introduction of OER. Filling these important information gaps would provide the data to begin to calculate how much public money is currently being spent on OER in basic education in South Africa and whether this has resulted in any savings. Examples of the information needed to establish a baseline and measure any potential cost savings are included in Figure 5.

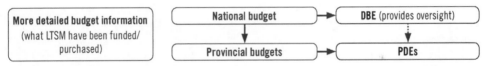

Examples of information needed to measure any cost savings:
− Categories/types of LTSM purchased/funded (including OER)
− Cost per LTSM unit
− Breakdown of cost, including production, printing and distribution

Figure 5: Information gaps identified in the national budgeting and allocation process for basic education

While the Siyavula OER initiative provides some indication of the categories of costs involved in producing OER (i.e. production, distribution, printing), this does not provide any information that can be used to assess potential savings against current LTSM costs incurred by government. The aggregated LTSM spend by province would need to be accompanied by detailed data regarding how many books and other resources were bought for how many learners and at what cost per unit. A breakdown of the cost as far as possible, indicating individual components such as procurement and distribution, would better enable a potential cost saving from OER to be calculated. While the absence of a LTSM line item in the DBE budget makes it impossible to calculate how much DBE money is being directed to LTSM production and distribution, this is not surprising due to the fact that it is the PDEs that are mandated to acquire and distribute LTSM. The DBE's role is one of primary oversight and policy formulation. However, providing accurate figures relating to any spend related to OER by the DBE (e.g. printing and distribution in the case of Siyavula) would assist in calculating if there is any cost benefit in using OER in the basic education system, which could inform policy decisions and textbook choices.

The question of how to source credible, authoritative data on financial resource allocation in the South African education system remains a challenge for all future research in this area. Targeted interviews conducted with authoritative sources could be a solution; however, as discovered when interviews were attempted during this research, officials are reluctant to share financial data that are not already publicly available. The concept of OER is in the very early stages of being incorporated into policy, which may ultimately assist in tracking any expenditure in this area in the future, which is encouraging. While this study has provided a foundation for future research on the extent of public funding of OER in South African basic education, certain data-sourcing challenges remain and it is still to be determined whether and to what extent OER represent a cost reduction with regard to educational resource acquisition in South African basic education.

References

Allen, N. & Student PIRGs. (2010). *A cover to cover solution: How open textbooks are the path to textbook affordability*. Washington: Center for Public Interest Research. Retrieved from http://www.hewlett.org/wp-content/uploads/2016/08/A-Cover-To-Cover-Solution.pdf

Brown, A. & Green, T. (2015). Issues and trends in instructional technology: Leveraging budgets to provide increased access to digital content and learning opportunities. In M. Orey & R. M. Branch (Eds.), *Educational media and technology yearbook* (pp. 11–21). Cham: Springer International. Retrieved from https://www.researchgate.net/publication/275581450_Issues_and_Trends_in_Instructional_Technology_Leveraging_Budgets_to_Provide_Increased_Access_to_Digital_Content_and_Learning_Opportunities

Butcher, N. & Hoosen, S. (2012). *Exploring the business case for Open Educational Resources*. Vancouver: Commonwealth of Learning. Retrieved from http://oasis.col.org/handle/11599/57

DBE (Department of Basic Education). (1996a). National education policy act No. 27 of 1996. *Government Gazette*, (Vol. 555, No. 34620). Retrieved from http://www.education.gov.za/Portals/0/Documents/Legislation/Acts/NATIONAL%20EDUCATION%20POLICY%20ACT,%20NO%2027%20OF%201996,%2028%2010%202011.pdf?ver=2015-01-30-102109-667

DBE (Department of Basic Education). (1996b). South African schools act, no. 84 of 1996. *Government Gazette*, (Vol 377, No. 17579). Retrieved from http://www.gov.za/sites/www.gov.za/files/Act84of1996.pdf

DBE (Department of Basic Education). (2009). *Statement to national assembly by the Minister of Basic Education on curriculum review process, 5 November 2009*. Pretoria: Department of Basic Education. Retrieved from http://www.education.gov.za/ArchivedDocuments/ArchivedSpeeches/tabid/459/ctl/Details/mid/954/ItemID/2937/Default.aspx

DBE (Department of Basic Education). (2011). *Action plan 2014: Towards the realisation of schooling 2025*. Pretoria: Department of Basic Education. Retrieved from http://www.education.gov.za/LinkClick.aspx?fileticket=jrxCOXJALPU%3d&tabid=418&mid=1211

DBE (Department of Basic Education). (2013a). *Annual performance plan 2013–2014.* Pretoria: Department of Basic Education. Retrieved from http://www.education.gov.za/LinkClick.aspx?fileticket=SA2WZvctNMM%3D&tabid=358&mid=1263

DBE (Department of Basic Education). (2013b). *Report on the national School Monitoring Survey (DBE013, conducted in 2011).* Pretoria: Department of Basic Education. Retrieved from http://www.education.gov.za/LinkClick.aspx?fileticket=nbaa%2Bhb1H%2Bw%3D&tabid=741&mid=3176

DBE (Department of Basic Education). (2014). *Draft national policy for the provision and management of Learning and Teaching Support Material (LTSM).* Pretoria: Department of Basic Education. Retrieved from http://www.education.gov.za/LinkClick.aspx?fileticket=MnCEAX7Qrac%3D&tabid=390&mid=1125

DBSA (Development Bank of Southern Africa). (2012). *Development report 2011: Prospects for South Africa's future.* Halfway House: Development Bank of Southern Africa. Retrieved from http://www.dbsa.org/EN/About-Us/Publications/General/DBSA%20Development%20Report%202011.pdf

DOE (Department of Education). (2006). *South African schools act, 1996 (act no 84 of 1996): Amended national norms and standards for school funding.* Pretoria: Government Printer. Retrieved from https://www.gdeadmissions.gov.za/Content/Files/SchoolsAct.pdf

Financial and Fiscal Commission. (2005). *Annual submission for the division of revenue 2006/07.* Halfway House: Financial and Fiscal Commission. Retrieved from http://www.ffc.co.za/docs/submissions/dor/2006/fullreport.pdf

Frydenberg, J. & Matkin, G. W. (2007). *Open textbooks: Why? What? How? When?* Menlo Park, CA: William and Flora Hewlett Foundation. Retrieved from http://www.hewlett.org/wp-content/uploads/2016/08/OpenTextbooks.pdf

Government Communications and Information Systems Department. (2014). *Education.* Pretoria: GCIS. Retrieved from http://www.gcis.gov.za/sites/www.gcis.gov.za/files/docs/resourcecentre/Education2015.pdf

Hilton III, J., Robinson T. J., Wiley, D. A. & Ackerman, J. (2014). Cost-savings achieved in two semesters through the adoption of Open Educational Resources. *International Review of Research on Distributed and Open Learning, 15(2).* Retrieved from http://www.irrodl.org/index.php/irrodl/article/view/1700/2833

Jimes, C., Weiss, S. & Keep, R. (2013). Addressing the local in localization: A case study of open textbook adoption by three South African teachers. *Journal of Asynchronous Learning Networks, 17(2),* 73–86. Retrieved from http://eric.ed.gov/?id=EJ1018301

National Treasury. (2014a). *Eastern Cape vote 06: Education provincial budget 2014. Estimates of provincial revenue and expenditure standardised tables in Excel format.* Pretoria: National Treasury of South Africa. Retrieved from http://www.treasury.gov.za/documents/provincial%20budget/2014/7.%20Estimates%20of%20Provincial%20Revenue%20and%20Expenditure%20standardised%20tables%20in%20Excel%20format/EC/EC%20-%20Education.xlsx

National Treasury. (2014b). *Free State vote 06: Education provincial budget 2014. Estimates of provincial revenue and expenditure standardised tables in Excel format.* Pretoria: National Treasury of South Africa. Retrieved from http://www.treasury.gov.za/documents/provincial%20budget/2014/7.%20Estimates%20of%20Provincial%20Revenue%20and%20Expenditure%20standardised%20tables%20in%20Excel%20format/FS/FS%20-%20Education.xlsx

National Treasury. (2014c). *Gauteng vote 05: Education provincial Budget 2014. Estimates of provincial revenue and expenditure standardised tables in Excel format.* Pretoria: National Treasury of South Africa. Retrieved from http://www.treasury.gov.za/documents/

provincial%20budget/2014/7.%20Estimates%20of%20Provincial%20Revenue%20
and%20Expenditure%20standardised%20tables%20in%20Excel%20format/GT/GT%20
-%20Education.xlsx

National Treasury. (2014d). *KwaZulu-Natal vote 05: Education provincial Budget 2014.*
Estimates of provincial revenue and expenditure standardised tables in Excel format.
Pretoria: National Treasury of South Africa. Retrieved from http://www.treasury.gov.
za/documents/provincial%20budget/2014/7.%20Estimates%20of%20Provincial%20
Revenue%20and%20Expenditure%20standardised%20tables%20in%20Excel%20format/
KZN/KZN%20-%20Education.xlsx

National Treasury. (2014e). *Limpopo vote 03: Education provincial budget 2014. Estimates*
of provincial revenue and expenditure standardised tables in Excel format. Pretoria:
National Treasury of South Africa. Retrieved from http://www.treasury.gov.za/documents/
provincial%20budget/2014/7.%20Estimates%20of%20Provincial%20Revenue%20
and%20Expenditure%20standardised%20tables%20in%20Excel%20format/LIM/LIM%20
-%20Education.xlsx

National Treasury. (2014f). *Mpumalanga vote 07: Education provincial budget 2014. Estimates*
of provincial revenue and expenditure standardised tables in Excel format. Pretoria:
National Treasury of South Africa. Retrieved from http://www.treasury.gov.za/documents/
provincial%20budget/2014/7.%20Estimates%20of%20Provincial%20Revenue%20
and%20Expenditure%20standardised%20tables%20in%20Excel%20format/MPU/
MPU%20-%20Education.xlsx

National Treasury. (2014g). *Northern Cape vote 04: Education provincial Budget 2014.*
Estimates of provincial revenue and expenditure standardised tables in Excel format.
Pretoria: National Treasury of South Africa. Retrieved from http://www.treasury.gov.
za/documents/provincial%20budget/2014/7.%20Estimates%20of%20Provincial%20
Revenue%20and%20Expenditure%20standardised%20tables%20in%20Excel%20format/
NC/NC%20-%20Education.xlsx

National Treasury. (2014h). *North West vote 08: Education provincial Budget 2014. Estimates*
of provincial revenue and expenditure standardised tables in Excel format. Pretoria:
National Treasury of South Africa. Retrieved from http://www.treasury.gov.za/documents/
provincial%20budget/2014/7.%20Estimates%20of%20Provincial%20Revenue%20
and%20Expenditure%20standardised%20tables%20in%20Excel%20format/NW/NW%20
-%20Education%20and%20Training.xls

National Treasury. (2014i). *Western Cape vote 05: Education provincial budget 2014. Estimates*
of provincial revenue and expenditure standardised tables in Excel format. Pretoria:
National Treasury of South Africa. Retrieved from http://www.treasury.gov.za/documents/
provincial%20budget/2014/7.%20Estimates%20of%20Provincial%20Revenue%20
and%20Expenditure%20standardised%20tables%20in%20Excel%20format/WC/WC%20
-%20Education.xls

National Treasury. (2015). *Budget 2015: Estimates of national expenditure (vote 14 Basic*
Education). Pretoria: South African National Treasury. Retrieved from http://www.treasury.
gov.za/documents/national%20budget/2015/enebooklets/Vote%2014%20Basic%20
Education.pdf

OECD (Organisation for Economic Co-operation and Development). (2008). *Reviews of*
national policies for education: South Africa. Paris: OECD Publishing. DOI: http://dx.doi.
org/10.1787/9789264053526-en

PASA (Publishers' Association of South Africa). (2004). *Print Industries Cluster Council report*
on intellectual property rights in the print industries sector. Cape Town: Print Industries

Cluster Council. Retrieved from http://www.publishsa.co.za/downloads/intellectual_property_report.pdf

Republic of South Africa. (1996). *Constitution of the Republic of South Africa, 1996.* Pretoria: Government of South Africa. Retrieved from http://www.gov.za/documents/constitution/chapter-2-bill-rights#29

Spaull, N. (2012). *South Africa at a glance: SACMEQ at a glance series.* Stellenbosch: Research on Socio-economic Policy (RESEP). Retrieved from http://resep.sun.ac.za/wp-content/uploads/2012/07/Spaull-2012-SACMEQ-at-a-Glance-10-countries.pdf

Supreme Court of Appeal of South Africa. (2015). *Minister of Basic Education v Basic Education for All* (20793/2014) [2015] ZASCA 198 (2 December 2015). Retrieved from http://www.justice.gov.za/sca/judgments/sca_2015/sca2015-198.pdf

Toledo, A., Botero, C. & Guzmán, L. (2014). Public expenditure in education in Latin America: Recommendations to serve the purposes of the Paris Open Educational Resources Declaration. *Open Praxis, 6(2),* 103–113. Retrieved from https://oerknowledgecloud.org/sites/oerknowledgecloud.org/files/119-547-2-PB.pdf

UNECA (United Nations Economic Commission for Africa). (2015). *MDG report 2015: Assessing progress in Africa toward the millennium development goals.* Addis Ababa: United Nations Economic Commission for Africa. Retrieved from https://www.uneca.org/publications/mdg-report-2015-assessing-progress-africa-toward-millennium-development-goals

UNESCO (United Nations Educational, Scientific and Cultural Organization). (2012). *2012 Paris OER Declaration.* Paris: United Nations Educational, Scientific and Cultural Organization. Retrieved from http://www.unesco.org/new/fileadmin/MULTIMEDIA/HQ/CI/CI/pdf/Events/Paris%20OER%20Declaration_01.pdf

UNESCO IIEP (United Nations Educational, Scientific and Cultural Organisation International Institute for Educational Planning). (2010). In search of quality: What the data tell us. *IIEP Newsletter, 28(3),* 1–16. Retrieved from http://www.iiep.unesco.org/sites/default/files/nl_2010-3_en.pdf

UNESCO IS (United Nations Educational, Scientific and Cultural Organisation Institute for Statistics). (2011). *Financing education in Sub-Saharan Africa: Meeting the challenges of expansion, equity and quality.* Canada: UNESCO Institute for Statistics. Retrieved from http://unesdoc.unesco.org/images/0019/001921/192186e.pdf

van Wyk, C. (2015). An overview of key data sets in education in South Africa. *South African Journal of Childhood Education, 5(2),* 146–170. Retrieved from http://www.scielo.org.za/scielo.php?script=sci_arttext&pid=S2223-76822015000200008&lng=en&tlng=en

Wafawarowa, B. (2012). Supporting affidavit in the matter between Section 27, Hanyani Thomo Secondary School and Condani Lydia Masiphephethu versus Minister of Basic Education and Member of the Executive Council: Limpopo Department of Education. Retrieved from http://www.section27.org.za/wp-content/uploads/2012/05/Supporting-affidavit.pdf

Wiley, D., Hilton III, J., Ellington, S. & Hall, T. (2012). A preliminary examination of the cost savings and learning impacts of using open textbooks in middle and high school science classes. *The International Review of Research in Open and Distributed Learning, 13(3),* 262–276. Retrieved from http://www.irrodl.org/index.php/irrodl/article/view/1153/2256

How to cite this chapter

Goodier, S. (2017). Tracking the money for Open Educational Resources in South African basic education: What we don't know. *The International Review of Research in Open and Distributed Learning, 18(4)*. DOI: http://dx.doi.org/10.19173/irrodl.v18i4.2990

Corresponding author: Sarah Goodier <sarah.goodier@uct.ac.za>

 It was carried out with the aid of a grant from the International Development Research Centre, Ottawa, Canada.

Chapter 8

Teacher educators and OER in East Africa: Interrogating pedagogic change

Freda Wolfenden, Pritee Auckloo, Alison Buckler and Jane Cullen

Summary

This study examines the use of Open Educational Resources (OER) in six teacher education institutions in three contrasting East African settings – Mauritius, Tanzania and Uganda – all of which had previous engagement with OER initiatives. Drawing primarily on interviews with teacher educators, the study examines how and when teacher educators engage with OER, the factors that support and constrain sustained OER engagement, and the influence of such engagement on their teaching practice. It seeks to answer the following three research questions: What kinds of OER are teacher educators aware of and how do they access them? How and for what purpose are they using the OER? What intended and enacted pedagogic practices are associated with OER use?

The study takes a sociocultural approach, paying attention to the practices of teacher educators and the context and culture of the teacher education institutions within which they work, as well as the national policies relevant to these institutions. Surveys were sent to academic staff at each of the participating institutions who were, or had been, involved in curriculum development work involving OER. Male and female educators from different disciplinary backgrounds and with varying roles and periods of service within the institutions were targeted. From the respondents, selected individuals were asked to participate in semi-structured interviews concerning OER and their pedagogical practices. A total of 58 surveys were completed by teacher educators along with 36 in-depth teacher educator interviews and six institutional stakeholder interviews. ▶

The results of the study indicate that teacher educators' understanding and use of OER is highly fragmented, with little traction at department or institutional level. At all the study sites there was dissonance between the ways in which individual educators are using OER and the dominant institutional values and discourse. There were also numerous structural and cultural factors acting to limit agency with regards to OER use. The demands of curriculum and assessment, professional identity, digital skills, provision of equipment and connectivity, values and weak cultures of collaboration all exerted an influence and enabled or constrained teacher educators' efforts to achieve agency with OER.

For a small number of teacher educators (OER "champions"), OER provides a tool for extending their agency to move towards more participatory practices. In their interviews, several of these educators spoke of the formative role of academic training and many were linked to external OER networks. These elements of historic identity formation influence how they respond to OER, and enhance their confidence to take risks in moving beyond conventional practice.

Enabling educators to act in an agentive way with OER is not easy. Moving forward, attention should be given to issues of access so that educators are able to locate and view OER relatively easily and experiment with their use. This study recommends that time be made available for educators to enhance their skills in working digitally and to become familiar with principles of learning design such that these become integral dimensions of their professional identity. It is also argued that extending and deepening engagement with OER requires opportunities for professional dialogue and collaboration to support the development of productive educator identities with OER and transformation of the community's field of practice.

Acronyms and abbreviations

COL   Commonwealth of Learning
HEI   higher education institution
ICT   information and communication technologies
MOOCs   Massive Open Online Courses
OER   Open Educational Resources
ORELT   Open Resources for English Language Teaching
TESSA   Teacher Education in Sub-Saharan Africa

Introduction

Across the world there is great concern about the quality of classroom teaching and learning processes. Research studies from Sub-Saharan Africa highlight disturbingly low levels of basic skills for large numbers of pupils after several years of schooling (Bold & Svensson, 2016). In recent years, national policies across the continent have advocated a shift towards "learner-centred" education to support improvements in student learning (Schwiesfurth, 2013). A set of teaching skills and practices that is congruent with such a learner-centred approach has been identified and reported to support improved learning outcomes (Muijs et al., 2014). However, as yet, such practices are only rarely observed in African classrooms and there is much attention being given to how pre-service teacher preparation and in-service programmes can work in cost-effective ways to help teachers develop these learner-centred practices (UNESCO, 2014).

Teacher educators are recognised as playing a critical role in the transformation of teachers' practice, but the dominant discourse positions them as a barrier to pedagogic change, chastising them for failing to model the enactment of learner-centred pedagogy in their own practice (Westbrook et al., 2014). Such characterisation, however, often fails to recognise the ways in which teacher educators' mediation of learner-centred education policy is influenced by multiple factors, including their own histories of participation in learning and teaching, their skills, the contexts in which they work, and the tools made available to them (for instance, teachers frequently only have ready access to limited, outdated proprietary teaching materials) (Moon & Villet, 2016). Their pedagogic choices are influenced by deeply embedded cultural scripts which act to authorise and reproduce ways of being as a teacher (Bruner, 1996).

Open Educational Resources (OER) are distinguished from other educational resources by their characteristics of being legally free to access, copy, distribute, use, adapt or modify (UNESCO, 2002). Like other educational resources, they can take multiple forms, and range from short videos or lesson plans to full courses. Over the last 10 years, there has been much rhetoric about the potential of OER to improve the quality of education, particularly in regions of the world such as Sub-Saharan Africa where access to high-quality resources is scarce. OER have been proposed as having a role to play in improving teacher education in these contexts (Moon & Villet, 2016), and they are increasingly being produced for and utilised in both in-service and pre-service teacher education programmes. Advocates outline how OER offer educators access to high-quality materials at low cost and, critically (because they are open, shareable, adaptable and promote co-construction of knowledge), how the overarching concept behind OER promotes the ethos of a learner-centred approach. Thus they also offer opportunities for participation in practices that are associated with such an approach (Brown & Adler, 2008; Hewlett Foundation, 2013; Umar, Kodhandaraman & Kanwar, 2013; Wolfenden, 2008). However, to date there is little documented evidence of OER supporting such transformational change in practice, whether in formal education institutions or informal learning episodes, in both high- and low-income contexts (Beetham, Falconer, McGill & Littlejohn, 2012; Ngugi, 2011; Scanlon, McAndrew & O'Shea, 2015).

This study attempts to examine teacher educators' practices with OER in three contrasting settings in East Africa – Mauritius, Tanzania and Uganda – all of which have national policies supporting the enactment of learner-centred education. The empirical work was situated in six teacher education institutions which had previously reported involvement with OER initiatives and different ways of using/adapting OER within educational provision. The study took a sociocultural approach, paying attention to the practices of the teacher educators and the context and culture of the teacher education institutions within which they work, as well as the national policies relevant to these institutions. No distinction was made between learning in informal, everyday situations and formal learning in programmes (Lave, 2008). This perspective encouraged us to focus on the opportunities for and constraints to participation in learning with OER in each context. In-depth interviews with teacher educators were utilised to better understand teacher educators' perceptions of the possibilities for action with OER that are available to them, and the impact of these actions in terms of shifts in their pedagogic practice.

Regional context

Throughout the East African region, national information and communication technologies (ICT) policies single out the importance of training teachers in ICT skills and the use of ICT for pedagogic purposes. They point to a belief that use of ICT in teaching and learning will improve standards in primary and secondary schools. However, implementation of these ambitious policies has been inconsistent and, in most countries, inhibited by slow progress with establishing ICT infrastructure (as well as, in some locations, the absence of reliable power supply). Whilst OER have yet to appear in the national policies of the countries studied here, over the last 10 years OER use in East Africa has been promoted by a number of institutions and initiatives, most notably OER Africa (an OER advocacy and policy initiative) through its work in various advocacy workshops and, most recently, in an action research project with four institutions, including one of the Tanzanian institutions included in this study (TU1) (Ngugi & Butcher, 2016).

Mauritius

Since 2011, the government of Mauritius has invested considerably in educational technologies. Primary schools have been given digital classrooms complete with projectors and interactive whiteboards, many through the Sankore Project (Bahadur & Oogarah, 2013). In secondary schools, the government has been purchasing thousands of tablets for students and teachers on an annual basis, whilst concurrently improving internet connectivity with fibre-optic connections. At present, internet connectivity is variable, although many teachers have internet access at home (Government of Mauritius, 2016).

At national level, government strategy makes explicit reference to the use of OER (MECHR, 2009). The adoption of OER and ICT was discussed at the Commonwealth Conference for Education Ministers held in Mauritius in 2012, which was followed up with support from the Commonwealth of Learning (COL) in 2014.[1] Following this engagement, the Mauritius Tertiary Education Commission proposed an OER policy for the country and a national OER repository. This government-level engagement with OER has influenced the policies and practices of higher education institutions (HEIs). The University of Mauritius, for example, has been involved in several OER initiatives, including hosting a mirror site of the Massachusetts Institute of Technology OpenCourseWare, making this open content available across the MU1 campus; contributing to the European Union SIDECAP[2] project, which focuses on the repurposing of OER for distance learning programmes; and participating in the Virtual University for Small States in the Commonwealth project.[3]

---

1   https://www.col.org/news/blog-posts/progress-oer-2014-stock-taking-commonwealth
2   http://sidecap.pbworks.com/w/page/33114051/Sidecap%20Home
3   http://www.vussc.info/

Tanzania

At national level, policy documentation such as *The Tanzania Development Vision 2025*, (URT, 2010a), the *National Strategy for Growth and Reduction of Poverty* (NSGRP II) (URT, 2010b) and the *Education Sector Development Programme 2008–2017* (URT, 2008) promote education as a key driver for socioeconomic development and for improving the quality of life of the citizens of Tanzania. The last 10 years have seen a rapid increase in total enrolment in primary schools, accompanied by a smaller increase in pupil numbers at secondary level. At both levels there is a shortage of qualified teachers, resulting in high pupil–teacher ratios and very low pass rates in national examinations (UNESCO, 2014). Teacher education is guided by the Teacher Development Management Strategy (2008–2013) (MoEVT, 2008), which sets targets for teacher education. These targets do not, however, include use of ICT or OER. The Tanzania Beyond Tomorrow initiative aims to integrate ICT into teaching and learning in basic education (Hooker, Mwiyeria & Verma, 2011), but the very recent *National Information and Communications Policy* (URT, 2016) recognises the inadequacy of ICT facilities in many educational institutions and the ineffectiveness of teacher training programmes with respect to ICT. This policy also addresses higher education. Activity in this sector has been taken forward previously in the *Higher Education Development Programme 2010–2015* (URT, 2010c, p.30), where there is a focus on "taking advantage of ICT enhanced approaches to improve teaching and learning", but again with no mention of OER. This use of ICT in higher education and teacher training reinforces earlier ambitions outlined in the *Education Sector Development Plan 2008–2017*, but recent research indicates low use of OER across the higher education sector in Tanzania, with a range of structural barriers inhibiting engagement and uptake (Mtebe & Raisamo, 2014; URT, 2016).

Uganda

Demographic pressure on the education system in Uganda is immense. The school-aged population is growing rapidly, constraining the ability of the education sector to support national development goals. Current education performance indicators are low, with national and international assessments indicating that many students do not acquire minimum standards, and there is a perceived need both for more teachers and for additional primary teachers' colleges to improve pedagogical training (UNESCO, 2015). The *National ICT Policy for Uganda 2013–2017* (Ministry of Information and Communications Technology, 2014), which was revised in 2014, points to the importance of ICT training and use in education, in particular that teachers should be trained in the use of computer skills and how to make use of ICT in lesson preparation and in producing teaching materials. The policy does not contain any reference to the use of open content, but it does indicate an aspiration for the sharing of educational resources and for digital content to be translated into local languages.

Literature review and theoretical framework

This literature review begins by briefly identifying the problems of practice in teacher education in developing-country contexts, and then examines contemporary evidence for shifts in practice with OER. It concludes with the theoretical positioning adopted in this study.

Teacher education: Problems of practice

Since the dawn of the new millennium, the pursuit of pedagogic change in classrooms to improve the quality of teaching and learning has been an education priority for governments in Sub-Saharan Africa (UNESCO, 2014). Such change is predominantly expressed as a movement from didactic, teacher-led classrooms characterised by rote memorisation, to a more participatory "learner-centred" pedagogy. "Pedagogy" as a term is much contested, with multiple definitions and realisations. The definition used in this study is congruent with a sociocultural approach: pedagogy is taken to be what people deem to be important, meaningful and relevant in conceptions of learning and knowledge as they engage in teaching-related activity (Nind, Curtin & Hall, 2016). A learner-centred pedagogy emphasises a view of learning as occurring through participation in social enterprises, and recognises learners as active, reflective agents engaged in the construction of knowledge (Murphy & Wolfenden, 2013; Schweisfurth, 2013).Thus, a participatory learner-centred pedagogy will be characterised by practices (see Figure 1) that enable interaction between learners as they work with others on problem-solving through dialogic inquiry, creating opportunities to exchange prior ideas and consider new ones drawing on the cultural and linguistic "funds of knowledge" they bring to the classroom (Gonzalez, Moll & Amanti, 2006), as well as the language and artefacts used and valued by their communities (James & Pollard, 2011; Lave & Wenger, 1991).

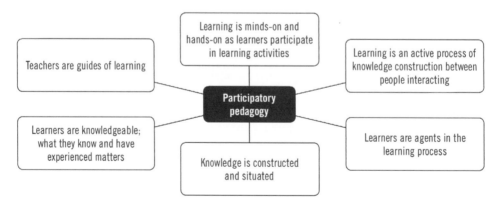

Figure 1: Characteristics of a participatory, learner-centred pedagogy

Enacting this participatory, learner-centred approach in classrooms requires a repositioning of teachers to a more facilitative role. However, across the globe, pre- and in-service teacher training is frequently identified as having failed to support teachers to move towards this new form of identity (UNESCO, 2014; Westbrook et al., 2014). Programmes and courses for teachers are reported to be predominantly theory-based and isolated from the context of the schools and local communities they serve. There is, for example, little recognition of the multilingual context of many classrooms or the presence of students with disabilities (Akyeampong, Lussier, Pryor & Westbrook, 2013). Teacher educators' practice within colleges of education and universities is usually described as lecture-based, positioning student teachers as passive receivers of transmitted knowledge, with little opportunity to argue or challenge (Dyer et al., 2004; Kunje, 2002). Thus, for trainee teachers there is a mismatch between the pedagogy that they hear being advocated in policy and lectures, and that which they experience. For most, there are few opportunities to engage with a more participatory, learner-centred pedagogy (Pryor, Akyeampong & Westbrook, 2012). This is critical: studies find that many early-career teachers draw mainly on knowledge and experiences gained through their training rather than on evidence from practice in their own classrooms (Akyeampong et al., 2013).

Teacher learning can be conceptualised as "learning to be" (Cook & Brown, 1999), occurring through participation in a community built around a particular practice (in this case, the practice of becoming a teacher). This shared endeavour involves both teachers and teacher educators building on the cultural practices of previous generations (Rogoff, 2003). Thus, for lasting classroom improvement, revision of the pedagogical practice of both teachers *and* teacher educators is required. Changing the practice of teacher educators requires a shift in their understanding of their learners (trainee teachers), learning and the nature of knowledge – i.e. a fundamental revisiting of what is valued as knowledge and how it is constructed (Tabulawa, 2003).

Making such ontological and epistemological shifts is not easy. Epistemological movement, for example, is frequently undermined by the hierarchical view of knowledge embedded within the specified curriculum, assessment policy and curriculum tasks in which local knowledge is given little status. Teacher educators therefore often negotiate tensions between different views of knowledge – between valuing knowledge as an abstract commodity transferable across situations and contexts as expressed in the curriculum and assessment regimes, and an understanding of knowledge as dynamic and contextual, constructed through a social process mediated by prior knowledge and personal and community experiences. It is this latter social view of knowledge that underpins the move towards more learner-centred practices (Trigwell & Prosser, 1996; White & Manton, 2011).

The discourse around teacher educators' pedagogy frequently implies a set of binary practices: learner-centred or teacher-centred. The situation is, however, more complex, and teacher educators are usually to be found at different stages of a trajectory of change towards more participatory practice (Murphy & Wolfenden, 2013). Each individual's trajectory will be mediated by their beliefs about learning and knowledge, their prior experiences, the kinds of knowing made possible in their institution through the availability of tools (such as OER), and conventions, rules and expectations of what can and cannot be enacted (Putnam & Borko, 2000). It is the influence of ways in which educators have taken up possibilities for OER use, on these trajectories of pedagogic change, that is the focus of this study.

OER use and impact

There is a rapidly growing body of OER (Wiley, 2016), but as yet few studies which interrogate the influence of OER on the agency of educators to enhance learning opportunities and contribute to long-term educational goals. In the Global North, from which most OER content originates, the focus of many institutional OER initiatives is on the creation of OER, their publication in repositories, and modes and tools to access OER, whilst much of the scholarly discourse about OER has been concerned with policy, business models, accessibility and modes of implementation (de los Arcos, Farrow, Perryman, Pitt & Weller, 2014; Ehlers, 2011; Shear, Means & Lundh, 2015). There is a focus on the generation of quantitative data and evidence to influence policy. An example of this is the large-scale, quantitative Open Educational Quality Initiative survey, which examined contextual and social influences on OER use across higher education and adult learning in eight European countries. It noted that in the highly digitally connected environment of Europe, critical success factors for use include institutional policies and support and, at a personal level, rewards for professionals to engage in OER adaptation and use (OPAL, 2011).

The access dimension dominates the discourse of policy and scholarship in low-income countries (Butcher, 2010; Ngugi, 2011). Previous reports of OER usage in Sub-Saharan Africa have highlighted the need for improved technology infrastructure and reduced internet access costs, alongside support for professional development to raise educators' awareness of OER and enhance their skills in utilising OER in their teaching (Okonkwo, 2012; Wright & Reju, 2012). As internet infrastructure is extended and the price of online access decreases (Bruegge et al., 2011), a growing number of local OER platforms and repositories are being established in Sub-Saharan Africa – for example, OER Africa,[4] the African Virtual University OER repository[5] and the University of South Africa institutional repository.[6] Studies from the continent do, however, indicate that there is still relatively low awareness of OER (Gunness, 2011; Hodgkinson-Williams, 2015).

Studies of OER in schools, mainly but not exclusively from the Global North, report tentatively but positively on both the quality of OER compared to conventional textbooks (Kimmons, 2015; Pitt, 2015), and improved learner attainment and engagement with open textbooks (Cartmill, 2013; Livingston & Condie, 2006; Robinson, Fischer, Wiley & Hilton, 2014). Work with educators has found that perceived quality is a key criterion for selection of resources, usually expressed as confidence in the creator or a recommendation from a trusted source (Clements & Pawlowski, 2012). There has, however, been little investigation into how or whether such open materials might support educators in developing more participatory, inclusive pedagogies. In a relatively rare OER study including a lens on educator practice, Petrides, Jimes, Middleton-Detzner, Walling and Weiss (2011) found open textbooks stimulated more interactive and collaborative classroom activities, in addition to greater classroom dialogue in American community colleges.

Studies of OER use in higher education, also mainly from the Global North, similarly focus principally on the impact on students rather than educators. Studies that include educators have reported small positive impacts on educators' practice through an enhancement of

---

4   http://www.oerafrica.org/teachered
5   http://www.avu.org/avuweb/en/faculty/avu-oer-opportunities/
6   http://uir.unisa.ac.za/handle/10500/4663

pre-existing practices associated with a more participatory approach, such as collaboration and sharing of resources (Masterman & Wild, 2011), and the use of OER is claimed to prompt positive feedback from students, leading to greater use of OER (Jhangiani, Pitt, Hendricks, Key & Lalonde, 2016; Masterman & Wild, 2011). Some innovative pedagogic models utilising OER – most notably the connectivist model (Downes, 2013) – have emerged from the plethora of Massive Open Online Courses (MOOCs) being produced globally, but such models remain outliers in the MOOC world and have yet to gain traction within formal institutional provision.

A relatively rare example of a formative exploration of the influence of OER use comes from the Teacher Education in Sub-Saharan Africa (TESSA)[7] project (Harley & Barasa, 2012). The TESSA appraisal found evidence that TESSA OER have been used in a wide range of teacher education programmes in different kinds of settings and contexts in different models and for different purposes. It identified TESSA as having:

> … [a] significant impact on the identity and practices of teacher educators and a profound impact on those of teacher-learners. It has fused theory and practice; shifted perceptions of the teacher as a "know it all" to "teacher as facilitator of learning"; and greatly enhanced the relevance of pupils' learning experiences. (Harley & Barasa, 2012, p.8)

However, in campus-based institutions, notwithstanding expressions of managerial support, the study located little evidence of TESSA being formally inscribed in curricula or in faculty statutes or guidelines. Indeed, use was often highly dependent on the activities of one or two teacher educators acting as agents of change. Greater evidence of the sustainability and embedding of TESSA OER use was found in distance learning programmes, with their collaborative planning and production of learning materials. However, there has been little new work in this area despite the call from Umar et al. (2013, p.194) to explore the link between OER adoption in the developing world "and their [practitioners'] dominant pedagogic norms and values".

It is possible that the transformational role of OER with respect to pedagogy is being limited by the way in which educators frequently draw on OER in an "atomised" way (OPAL, 2011, p.148), integrating a wide range of discrete OER from multiple sources (especially videos) into their teaching, rather than adopting an entire course or module (de los Arcos et al., 2014). Course designers report that using OER to generate entirely new programmes or modules is challenging for a variety of reasons: many resources purporting to be OER lack detailed information on licensing and usage rights; locating OER in repositories is not easy; and the variety of formats and technical information makes linking a collection of OER on a single platform challenging (Richards & Marshall, 2010; Tonks, Weston, Wiley & Barbour, 2013). Accounts of such initiatives commonly include little discussion of changes in pedagogy enabled by OER use. One exception is the AgShare[8] project in which contributing academics are reported to have become more aware of new possibilities for teaching and learning underpinned by a more interactive pedagogic approach (OER Africa & University of

---

7   http://www.tessafrica.net
8   http://www.oerafrica.org/agshare-ii

Michigan, 2012). In Malawi, a midwifery module developed with OER introduced a problem-solving-based approach in which students were able to access resources in advance of lectures. This reportedly led to greater student participation, although it is unclear whether this has been sustained (Ngalande, 2013). A recent study in British Columbia (Jhangiani et al., 2016) found faculty in teaching institutions are slightly less likely to create and adapt OER than their peers in research-focused institutions. Such hesitation could also act to limit pedagogic change.

Researching the use of open content is intrinsically problematic. As Pitt, Ebrahimi, McAndrew and Coughlan (2013) argue, the inherently open nature of the materials and courses makes it difficult for course providers to gather specific information about users, and embedding instruments to generate usage data can limit participation. A further challenge in examining the impact of OER use is identifying when educators are specifically using appropriately licensed OER, rather than merely drawing on free online resources. The OER Research Hub team tackles this by using the criterion of "adaptability" – the extent to which resources can be revised and repurposed – as an indicator of the influence of openness (de los Arcos et al., 2014). Their most recent global interrogation involved educators who engage with OER to increase the relevance of materials for their learners and who experiment with different teaching approaches. In this work, de los Arcos and colleagues point to some evidence of OER use prompting reflection on practice by educators and increased collaboration around teaching – practices congruent with the social and subjective philosophies underpinning learner-centred education. Such practices were less frequently identified in an earlier study by Beetham et al. (2012), who reported educators making use of content found online but in a manner associated with reuse or consumption rather than sharing. Implicit in many of these studies is a tension between OER as a personal tool for educators, and as an institutional tool to be employed in support of a number of objectives (ranging from access to cost saving and marketing). Pedagogic shifts are rarely mentioned explicitly as a high priority at institutional level, although this may possibly be implicit in institutional quality enhancement initiatives and/or initiatives to improve student motivation (Ives & Pringle, 2013).

Theoretical framework

Interrogation of the literature suggests that exploration of the link between OER use and pedagogic transformation has received little attention to date, and there has been little work relating OER to the global rhetoric around learner-centred practice. Conole (2008) offered a mapping of Web 2.0 tools against learner-centred approaches to illustrate the overlap in philosophical positions. In developing this work, she has suggested that OER have the potential to support more interactive, social learning experiences (Conole & Ehlers, 2010). Still, there is little published work examining educator agency with respect to pedagogic change in contexts where the use of OER has been introduced.

The OER movement is premised on the understanding that knowledge is a collective social project, and that producing OER – or, more powerfully, adapting OER and sharing these resources with a global community – offers the possibility for educators to be in dialectic engagement with the world, accessing and contributing to a global community's experiences through mutual negotiation to articulate their own position and be transformed through these interactions (Deimann & Farrow, 2013). From a sociocultural position, both formal and community perspectives are necessary for learners to be able to develop new knowledge and understand how that knowledge functions in the world. Adaptation of OER enables the generation of situational knowledge by connecting formal "school" knowledge to "community" knowledge (including indigenous knowledge), and by connecting school or classroom experiences to wider community experiences. OER thus offer epistemological and practice tools for educators, and the use of OER has the potential to support dialogue and practice in teaching and learning that is traditionally not made available through proprietary resources or conventional institutional support.

An educator engaged with OER can therefore become increasingly positioned as an agentive curriculum developer. This ontological repositioning articulates a position for educators as reflective, empowered, professional practitioners. Agency is defined here as a phenomenon which emerges in the "dialectical interaction of person and practice" (Edwards, 2015, p.779), and which is influenced by the cultural environments in which educators practise – in particular the demands exerted on teacher educators in the context of their institution and wider social world. It is past-oriented in terms of the cultural resources that educators acquire from previous experiences, but future-oriented within the cultural, material and structural possibilities of the present context (Biesta, Priestley & Robinson, 2015). Agency is thus what teacher educators do in response to problematic situations through dialogic engagement with others (peers and students) in contexts of action – their classrooms, lecture theatres and staff meetings – drawing on their beliefs, values and attributes.

This study employs this sociocultural framework to explore how teacher educators working in low-income contexts perceive that the use and adoption (including adaptation) of OER in their teaching influences their ability to achieve the agency required to move to new and more effective participatory practices. The study first identifies where practice has embraced engagement with open resources and then examines the ways in which such use has influenced and modified educators' conceptions of knowledge, knowing and learning (Cook & Brown, 1999) through attention to their descriptions of intentional teaching actions.

Methodology

This study is informed by a sociocultural approach in which meaning and experience are understood to be socially produced and reproduced. It employs an interpretative methodology (Cohen, Manion & Morrison, 2007; Habermas, 1989) to explore when and how teacher educators have used OER and how this use changed their practice with respect to teaching and learning. From this perspective, a study of teacher educators' practice cannot be understood in isolation from the teacher educators' histories of participation in the teaching endeavour and the institutional context within which they practise. Whilst contexts and structural conditions at institution level and sub-institution level will influence individual accounts of practice, institutions themselves are situated within particular national policy frameworks and structures (Bruner, 1996), and are defined by features such as their purpose, location, staff and student demographics, cultural practices, conventions, and local economic and social situations. This study is therefore not limited to either individuals or the environment, but extends across individuals, institutions and the social environment. It pays attention to the national policy context within which each institution is located, and the institutional structures – procedures, course designs and arrangements – which frame professional interactions and enable or constrain emerging practice.

The study utilised a mixed-methods approach at six teacher education institutions in the contrasting settings of Mauritius, Tanzania and Uganda. All six institutions had previously engaged with OER through at least one OER initiative (primarily the TESSA project), thereby increasing the chances of further OER use (de los Arcos et al., 2014; OPAL, 2011). Access was facilitated through existing professional relationships with teacher educators and permission to undertake the research was obtained from senior staff in each institution. Data collection took place between July 2015 and April 2016. In each institution, one member of the academic staff was invited to take on the role of local "research collaborator". A consultative briefing meeting was held for these research collaborators in July 2015 to ensure that there was a shared understanding of the aims of the research and to establish ways of working across the team. The research collaborators participated in the instrument design process and provided support for access and data collection.

Drawing on contemporary thinking, the research team rejected the idea of a rigid "insider/outsider" researcher dichotomy (McNess, Arthur & Crossley, 2013), in that the research team was neither fully one nor the other. Other than at the home institution of one member of the research team, we were all "outsiders" at the research sites in terms of racial and cultural differences. However, as fellow professional teacher educators with previous relationships with the institutions, the research team was seen as engaged in the joint enterprise of teacher education rather than as intruders. Furthermore, each team member's relational identity as a researcher (i.e. how we understood our position relative to participants) varied across institutions, mediated by previous personal interactions with the institution and the local research collaborator within the institution (Milligan, 2016). Such relationships were important to consider during the data collection process; the balance of power between researcher and participants had the potential to influence what became known in the enquiry.

Data generation and analysis

The study generated evidence from multiple sources, with data generation methods centred around interviews with key informants at the six research sites. Participating institutions varied in scale, mode of delivery, complexity and external environment, and data collection activity at each site was planned in consultation with research collaborators.

The study began with a review of relevant national-level policies in each of the three countries to better understand the context in which teacher educators in each research site were working, as well as the external opportunities and constraints which frame the educators' work and their institution's trajectory.

Following this policy analysis, a survey was designed to identify OER users at each institution. In consultation with the research collaborators at each study site, the survey was adapted slightly for each institutional context, drawing on the national and institutional policy analyses so that questions resonated with teacher educators' professional experiences in each location.

The local research collaborators used their knowledge of institutional activities to identify an initial cohort of staff to invite to participate in the study at their institution. In general, these were staff who were, or had been, involved in curriculum development work involving OER. At each institution, 10 to 12 members of staff were sent digital copies of the project information sheet and the survey by the research collaborator. These respondents did not constitute a representative sample, and the aim was not to produce an overall evaluation of OER use and impact but rather to identify staff engaged with OER who could be invited to participate in in-depth interviews. These semi-structured, thematically organised teacher educator interviews focused on the actions and decisions that the teacher educators made in relation to resources in order to explore the influence of OER use on developing knowledge and practices.

Survey response rates varied and although the research team intended to review all survey responses prior to the institution field visits, technology challenges and resource constraints meant that many surveys were collected from research collaborators during, instead of before, the field visit. On the positive side, this made for immediacy in linking the interviews directly to the survey responses.

In general, participants invited to participate in interviews were teacher educators who, from their survey responses, appeared to have drawn on specific OER (from TESSA or other OER repositories) in their teaching on more than one occasion. In light of the challenges of ICT infrastructure (particularly internet access) at these institutions, the interview respondents included those teacher educators who use OER that are not online or in digital form.

The research team aimed to select a cross-section of interviewees at each site, targeting male and female educators from different disciplinary backgrounds with varying roles and periods of service within the institution, and who had demonstrated previous engagement with OER. The aim was to interview a minimum of five academics at each institution. However, staff who had been pre-identified for interview were not always available during field visits. It was possible to interview some by Skype at a later date, but the number of academics interviewed varied across institutions, depending on what was logistically possible. A breakdown of the data collection activities and sample numbers by research site is presented in Table 1.

Table 1: Respondent numbers for data collection activities by research site

Institution/ country	Type of institution	Number of teacher educator surveys	Number of teacher educator interviews	Number of stakeholder interviews
MU1/ Mauritius	HEI focused on professional training of teachers across all phases. Offers undergraduate and postgraduate programmes, including distance education courses.	9 (4 male, 5 female)	7 (2 male, 5 female)	1 (male)
TU1/ Tanzania	Distance learning institution with over 50 000 students; approximately one-third of students studying education courses.	8 (3 male, 5 female)	5 (2 male, 3 female)	1 (male)

TU2/ Tanzania	Constituent college of an HEI established to increase the supply of graduate teachers. Campus-based provision with the recent introduction of a distance learning postgraduate programme.	10 (8 male, 2 female)	6 (4 male, 2 female)	1 (female)
UU1/ Uganda	Large campus-based institution offering a wide curriculum, including teacher education. Distance learning programmes added to the portfolio 20 years ago.	14 (7 male, 7 female)	6 (4 male, 2 female)	1 (male)
UU2/ Uganda	New campus-based university focused on vocational courses, including science, technology and education. Includes distance learning unit. Responsibility for national standards of teacher education.	7 (5 male, 2 female)	5 (3 male, 2 female)	1 (male)
UU3/ Uganda	Small institution training primary school teachers (Teachers' Certificate).	10 (7 male, 3 female)	7 (5 male, 2 female)	1 (male)
Total		58 (34 male, 24 female)	36 (20 male, 16 female)	6 (5 male, 1 female)

All interviews were conducted by members of the research team in English at the interviewee's institution or via Skype. The interviews lasted between 20 and 60 minutes; they were audio-recorded and field notes were taken during the interviews.

Analysis of the research data was undertaken by the core research team. The survey responses were analysed for patterns in OER and online resource use (a site-specific analysis was followed by cross-case analysis), paying attention to the type of resource selected and the context of practice, for example the availability of technology tools such as laptops. The interview transcripts were then analysed in two stages. The first analysis was done to identify instances of OER or other online resource use, the purpose for which it was being employed, and the rationale for selecting the resource. A second analysis was then undertaken on the descriptions of practice with these resources. For each description of use, analysis was undertaken to identify characteristics of learner-centred pedagogy drawn from the literature. A detailed coding scheme was not used as this approach has a tendency to atomise the data, isolating it from its context and limiting the understanding of relationships across different elements of the data, which is in tension with a sociocultural approach.

Study-site OER contexts

At institution MU1, there has been sporadic OER-related activity for some years, including sensitisation workshops conducted by OER Africa and COL (2014), participation in the Sankore Open Project (from 2008 onwards) (Udhin et al., 2016; Udhin & Oojorah, 2013), and use of TESSA OER in pedagogy courses (from 2010 onwards) – including an elective module, "The Creative Pedagogy Project" (Auckloo, 2011). At the institutional level, the emphasis has been on foregrounding the development of ICT and further develop staff skills in this domain. In support of this, all staff have been allocated a laptop and all classrooms are now equipped with digital projectors. MU1 leads the development of school-level curriculum materials for Mauritius and the institution has made large numbers of resources freely available in digital form. However, there is as yet no formal policy on open content, and engagement with OER has typically been at the level of individual staff action.

The first of the study sites in Tanzania (TU1) has been involved with the use of OER since 2006 through engagement in the TESSA programme, and the TESSA OER are integral to the diploma course for primary teachers (Wolfenden, 2012). More recently, there has been strong senior leadership support for the creation and use of OER, as evidenced by a collaboration with OER Africa aimed at supporting academics to publish their instructional material under an open licence (Ngugi & Butcher, 2016). Under this collaboration, all academic staff have attended workshops focused on the characteristics and properties of OER, and a draft OER policy has been developed. This is currently progressing through the institutional governance process, but appears to have had little impact on the use of OER by academics at TU1 (Muganda, Samzugi & Mallinson, 2016). Internet connectivity was reported as good by respondents, although access to laptops and desktop machines was not ubiquitous and several respondents reported having to supply their own devices.

As part of quality enhancement in teacher education, the second study site in Tanzania (TU2) has embraced the use of technology to enhance teaching and learning, including the use of OER, but there are as yet no explicit policies on either technology or OER. TU2 was involved in the second phase of TESSA activity (development of resources for the teaching of secondary science) from 2010 under the guidance of a senior institutional leader whose term of office has now expired (Stutchbury & Katabaro, 2011). Whilst other colleges which share the same university affiliation as TU2 have collaborated with external agencies in the creation and use of OER, there has been no structured cross-college engagement at TU2 itself. Internet connectivity on the campus is not reliable or comprehensive, and not all staff have their own individual institutionally supplied laptop or desktop computer. The institution is moving towards the use of Moodle as a learning management system and there is a dedicated department to support staff in sharing materials online with students.

The first and second study sites in Uganda (UU1 and UU2) have ICT policies that outline strategies for ICT use across various areas of institutional activity. At UU1, the recently revised ICT Policy makes mention of the use of OER, as does the Policy on Open and Distance Learning. Neither of these policy documents, however, extends beyond high-level support for OER; there are no targets or objectives for OER use or creation and there is no evidence of any systematic institutional support for a shift towards use of OER in teaching. At UU2, the ICT policy does not include reference to open content or open resources, and no policies were available at the third study site in Uganda (UU3). All three institutions have, however, been involved in the TESSA initiative in various ways (Wolfenden, 2012) – UU1 and UU2 since the inception of TESSA through engagement in the creation and adaptation of OER prior to use of the OER in various programmes, and UU3 through more recent (2012) use of TESSA OER. At UU1 and UU2, internet access is available across the campus, but there is limited bandwidth (staff commented on difficulties with downloading videos). At UU1, all staff have ICT hardware and there are also projectors available. There is a computer lab at UU3, but no internet connectivity, and staff provide their own hardware for offline professional use in the institution.

Sample profile

The 58 survey respondents (see Table 1) were all employed in academic roles in their institution; almost all of them were experienced teacher educators (with a mean average of 13 years' experience as a teacher educator) and included professors, senior lecturers, associate professors, lecturers, assistant lecturers and tutors. They all had "lived experience" of the reality of the school context through teaching in primary or secondary schools prior to working as a tutor or lecturer, although in several cases this experience dated back a number of years. This experience had given them familiarity with the challenges faced by teachers, which they described as useful in establishing trust with teachers and head teachers. Interviewees were selected from survey respondents who indicated a willingness to participate further in the research and who had indicated use of OER in some aspect of their practice.

Ethics

The ethical procedures followed in this study were in accordance with good practice endorsed by the British Educational Research Association and the Research on Open Educational Resources for Development project, and were agreed to by the Open University's Human Research Ethics Committee. Informed consent was sought from all participants, who were made fully aware of the research aims and methods. All institutions and participants are de-identified in this account.

Findings

The findings are discussed under three headings relating to the research question: the kinds of OER teacher educators are aware of and how they access them; how and for what purpose they use the OER; and what intended and enacted pedagogic practices are associated with OER use.

Access to and awareness of OER

In line with the findings of numerous previous studies, the critical issue for OER across all institutions in this study remains access to hardware (desktop computers, laptops and internet-enabled mobile devices) and to the internet. Access to the internet is central; without this, individual use of OER is static. Mobile phones were the dominant device for access to the internet, used by all but five of the respondents. Approximately half the sample (26 educators) accessed the internet using a desktop computer, slightly more than half used a laptop (29 educators) and a few employed a tablet computer. Access to the internet across multiple devices was common only amongst the educators in Mauritius. At both sites in Tanzania and at UU1 and UU2 in Uganda, regular access to the internet was through one or two devices only, one being a mobile phone. Thus, although institutional connectivity was not always stable or comprehensive across institutional buildings, teacher educators at these institutions had found personal solutions to access the internet. UU3 in Uganda was an outlier, with no institutional connection and 50% of respondents reporting no access of any kind to the internet. This is possibly caused by multiple intersecting factors: UU3 is a lower-status institution with no research activity in its mandate, it is the one research site situated outside a capital city (although located in a commercial city only 80 km from the capital city), and staff are on lower pay scales than those at other institutions, making it more difficult for them to afford their own internet-enabled devices and the cost of online access. It could, however, be argued that UU3 is typical of the majority of institutions training primary school teachers across the continent.

Familiarity with online resources and OER

The survey generated data on respondents' knowledge of and familiarity with different online resources, including OER. Overall, the level of awareness of different OER repositories was low and many educators' responses indicated confusion in their understanding of the characteristics and definition of OER, with some respondents listing MOOC platforms (e.g. Coursera), virtual learning environments (e.g. Moodle) and online search engines as OER. With the exception of educators at UU3, 90% of the remainder of the educators surveyed were familiar with Wikipedia and Google Scholar, with a slightly smaller number reporting familiarity with YouTube and TESSA. Slightly fewer educators (25) expressed familiarity with resources from OER Africa. Given the ubiquity of Wikipedia, Google Scholar and YouTube, and the prior collaborative work with TESSA and OER Africa at almost all the sites, these results are not unexpected. More interesting, perhaps, is that almost half of the sample (22) indicated a familiarity with OpenCourseWare offerings, although most respondents were able to give little further detail in interviews. Other OER resources mentioned included those from COL and the Khan Academy.

Familiarity with OER repositories and sites was highest at institutions where external agencies have conducted OER-specific workshops (MU1, UU1 and TU1). Interview data indicated that these workshops served to raise awareness of the range of OER available. By contrast, many educators at UU3 indicated awareness of only one source of OER – TESSA.

In summary, with regard to awareness and access, there was a wide variation in levels of awareness of different types of OER and OER repositories across institutions and survey respondents. Unsurprisingly, access to and familiarity with OER is strongly linked to educators' access to the internet and their prior participation in OER-focused activities. However, a notable feature was educators' agentive accessing of online resources through their own mobile devices rather than being limited to institutional internet provision.

Engagement with OER

Levels of engagement

Overall use of OER across the institutions was limited, but a small number of educators (five) were passionate about the use of OER, both for their own personal learning and in their teaching with students. These individuals were, however, acting autonomously, with little institutional support despite evidence of prior institution- or department-level involvement with OER. Critically, their OER activities have also not extended to integrate with their colleagues' practice. For example, at MU1, the policy environment is favourable to the use of OER, at both national and institutional level, but the student project module utilising OER initiated by one member of staff has remained very much part of her individual practice. Other colleagues were aware of this activity and several had supported teaching of the module, but there was little evidence that this had stimulated them to undertake personal innovation and move to similar activity with their own classes.

These five OER "champions" were encouraged in their use of OER by what the OER enabled them to make available to their students, the subsequent reactions of their students (greater enthusiasm and engagement) and their own personal learning gains. One educator at a distance learning institution explained that for her students, open materials offered advantages but required skills to use proficiently:

> Yes, openness, I see it as things are regularly available for use, students don't have to be there in the classroom with the instructor, everything is there. The only problem that I see with my students, my own students, for example, since they find a lot they think they can put everything they have read in their answers in responding to assignments. There's too much information and sometimes the students are not capable of synthesising and ... choosing what fits where, what fits where. But I like the openness; students can get their diplomas without difficulties we experienced in the past. (TE08)

For these champions, use of OER offered a perception that they were involved in a wider education community and that they had access to the work of a broad range of education experts, including some with whom they were familiar and admired. But even amongst this group there was modest evidence of OER adoption, although many spoke of using OER in multiple ways to meet specific learner needs, as one educator in teaching education management explained:

> ... that's the topic I am teaching – total quality management in education. What I do is borrow ideas and give examples from Tanzania. What this aspect relates to, or what they represent in a Tanzanian context, that's what I do. So the challenge is how to adopt ... to adapt the context reading from another context to a Tanzanian context, because examples and practices must be from our experiences, our students' experience, and my own experience. (TE03)

With the exception of these individual OER champions, overall use of OER was limited and group (departmental or institutional) engagement was confined to use of one OER or use of OER within a particular module or curriculum topic. In some cases, OER use has become part of the enacted curriculum. For example, at UU3, several years previously tutors were introduced to TESSA OER through a UU2 outreach programme, in which they mapped modules to the TESSA OER. UU3 tutors retained their print copies of the TESSA OER and continue to draw on the activities and ideas from these OER in lectures and classes with their students. In three institutions (MU1, UU1 and TU1), use of specific OER is reified in the specified curriculum. For example, at TU1, TESSA OER are integral to course handbooks, as instructional designers and course writers drew on the TESSA OER when creating programme materials for a pioneering distance learning diploma programme.

Factors enabling OER engagement

Beyond engagement with a specific OER initiative such as TESSA or Open Resources for English Language Teaching (ORELT),[9] there was no substantial evidence of collective engagement with OER within departments or faculties, and it was rare for one specific OER initiative to stimulate more extensive individual engagement with other OER repositories. Where there was more extended individual engagement with OER, this was found to have been stimulated by one of the following:

- An external visitor to the institution who showcased the range of OER available and examples of use.
- Study at another institution, usually abroad (the UK, New Zealand, India, South Africa and Uganda were mentioned).
- The advent of improved technology within the institution or personal acquisition of a device which enabled internet connectivity (for example, a laptop or modem).
- Support from library staff, or staff leading internal staff development sessions, such as instructional design specialists who acted as a resource for practice.

Factors constraining OER use

A number of material and discursive structures were identified which impacted directly on the agency of the teacher educators with regards to OER use. Lack of a reliable power supply; an absence of fast, consistent internet connectivity; and limited access to laptops and desktop computers were all reported to limit teacher educators' exploration of and familiarity with OER, most acutely at UU3 in Uganda. Physical conditions also inhibited teacher educators' direct use of OER with their students, as teaching rooms frequently lacked internet access or projectors to facilitate sharing and use of OER. Several respondents mentioned the large sizes of their classes (one respondent cited up to 1 000 students in a class) as deterring pedagogic experimentation and more participatory approaches.

In addition to these material structures, discursive structures also acted to constrain teacher educator exploration of OER in practice and limit the growth of confidence. For many teacher educators, being an expert in the reuse of online resources has yet to be seen as an integral part of their professional identity, which limits their agency regarding OER use. Preparation of original, "unique" resources does, however, remain integral to their professional identity – i.e. a public expression of their expertise and competence as teachers, necessary to retain authority and student respect. One respondent described in detail how she had previously shared a presentation prepared for her classes and then been very disconcerted to find it being used by someone in another university: "… that's very scary, that limits us maybe sometimes to just giving the students even those PowerPoints" (TE17). Additionally, many believed that using OER would add to their preparation time, and the absence of any visible reward for adapting, using or creating OER further deterred some from engaging in more depth with an open culture.

Many respondents found the sheer volume of available online resources daunting and were anxious for quality guidelines; without these, they doubted whether they had sufficient expertise to judge whether a resource was of appropriate quality. Several respondents mentioned that they looked for evidence that the resource originated from an academic as

---

9   www.orelt.col.org

an indicator of authenticity and quality. There were some misconceptions that resources in PDF format have higher credibility, and much scepticism that content from another context would be appropriate for their students or would be accurate: "I don't know if the material is year 1 or diploma level, is the language appropriate?" (TE25); "so many cheating [false] things are posted that are not real [accurate]" (TE04). The latter respondent attempted to be more positive, continuing "maybe it will improve and change and we'll find ourselves trusting what is being posted" (TE04). Such reservations extended to the sharing of online resources created by these educators: "I wouldn't like to share my material if I'm unsure of the quality and if someone can look at it and not learn from it" (TE14). Thus, uncertainties surrounding dimensions of quality act to inhibit both the selection and publishing of resources.

Many teacher educators felt that they lacked the various skills required to make use of individual OER in their teaching. These ranged from technical skills in uploading content to the internet (sharing) to skills needed to adapt or "restructure" OER. At the course level, several educators discussed how they felt deficient in course or instructional design competence and hence were not confident about their ability to organise materials in a way which would offer students an effective learning journey. Anxiety about copyright issues also inhibited exploitation of OER in teaching.

For some educators working in campus-based universities, their relationship with their students acted to discourage the promotion of student use of OER. Students were frequently perceived as being interested only in what they needed to know or do to pass examinations, and having little interest in exploring new ideas or participating in different kinds of learning experiences. Three educators claimed that inviting students to engage with OER within a class would distract them from the learning task, as it would "give students an opportunity to catch up on their Facebook pages" (TE09). Occasionally these teacher educators print and distribute OER to their students. They do, however, recognise that this limits the extent and type of OER that can be used, and restricts the form and extent of student interaction with OER.

Teacher educators often referred to students' limited access to technology, particularly laptops and internet connectivity, as a reason for limited OER use within their courses: "Students know they can get a lot of material they need from the open resources, but the internet connections preclude this" (TE12). This rationale was extended by some educators, who argued that an absence of internet connectivity and technical support for teachers in schools would inhibit student teachers from continuing to use OER when on their school practicum. Students' limited experience of different cultures and languages was also raised as an impediment to promoting student use of OER: "Most of the videos we find online are from the UK or that sort of thing and sometimes when the people are talking and there is an accent, an English accent, and sometimes I find that students would find it a bit difficult to follow" (TE14).

Purpose of OER use

Across the six institutions, teacher educators were found to be using OER in one of three ways: teaching *about* OER; teaching students *with* OER; and personal learning or preparation for teaching *with* OER.

These are not discrete categories as educators' practice may include one or more areas of activity. The categorisation is intended as a way of illustrating the multiple ways in which educators in this study engage with OER in their teaching practice.

Teaching about OER

In two institutions (MU1 and UU1), the study sample included teacher educators who taught formal courses with specific sessions on the forms and properties of OER. At MU1, these courses were for teachers on an in-service training programme or pre-service teachers on the diploma programme, whilst at UU1, the course was designed for university staff. At MU1, the stated aim of the in-service programme was to support teachers' use of technology in their classrooms; the lead teacher educator for the programme also wanted to "develop a culture of OER in the teaching profession" (TE06). Within the sessions, teachers were informed about open licences and key OER stakeholders and innovators, and they were also involved in creating short videos to support the teaching of a particular topic. These resources were shared within and beyond the group through a designated Facebook page. Further work arising from the digitisation of the curriculum at MU1 prompted the lead teacher educator to design and develop original OER (such as an interactive dynamic solar system). Teachers on the programme were then required to develop lesson plans to demonstrate how they would use these OER with their students. In the pre-service programme, the 45-hour module aims to highlight for teachers "how OER are important and how they can be of use to teachers in their teaching and learning" (TE2). The sessions in a multimedia lab involve supported searching for OER and assignments based on adapting an OER for a specific class and learning need.

At UU1, an educator was using OER in professional development sessions aimed at equipping staff across the institution with skills in creating resources for e-learning and distance learning. In preparation for his sessions, he identified suitable OER which might be useful to colleagues (such as COL resources) and used TESSA OER as a model structure for writing OER: "taking the methodology and grafting the content in" (TE16). He spoke eloquently about how many staff had a binary approach to OER: they either use OER in its original form or reject it outright as inappropriate. In his experience, many colleagues adopt the latter position. He suggested that this may be due to the fact that use of OER would reduce their authority, in that "students might think they have no brains of their own" (TE16) and were relying too heavily on others. He also had the impression that colleagues believed that content from another context could not be appropriate and "locked it out rather than thinking what good [they could] get out of it". He described how some of his colleagues worried that if students had access to all the knowledge in OER, there would be no need for the students to attend class. He also reported that some colleagues cited work pressure as a reason for non-engagement, and had asked about their reward for adapting and using OER. In this context he was acting as a mediator, supporting colleagues to move across boundaries of practice to a point where they would begin to engage with OER and perhaps make small adaptations. He found this a slow process, but one in which early adopters of OER could become advocates.

This educator had noticed that those colleagues who were open to working with OER could experience profound shifts in their thinking and practice. Exploring other OER gave them a quality benchmark, which sometimes caused them to feel they were doing a "substandard" job compared to their international peers and that they were using "old" methods. Staff who did engage with OER often commented on how this made their lives easier. What was covered in their teaching was now more explicit and students had easier access to the content, methods and assignments. He reported that some colleagues had moved to a flipped classroom approach and claimed to have observed more student engagement. A recent institutional review had noted that external BSc students (in distance learning mode) were achieving better learning outcomes than internal BSc students, despite lower entry requirements for those on the external programme. The university senate had asked whether examiners were being lenient on the external students, but this educator attributed their higher performance to greater use of resources (including OER), which motivated students and enabled them to engage more productively in independent learning.

Teaching students with OER

The practice of teaching with OER has been divided into three sub-categories to illustrate different levels of engagement. In reality, these are not discrete categories; the practice of teaching with OER is on a continuum of both increased use of OER and increased awareness of the characteristics and affordances of open content.

1. Using only one "named" OER in teaching

All respondents at UU3 and many at TU2 and UU2 described the use of only one "named" OER in their teaching. They had been introduced to specific OER collections, such as TESSA or ORELT, which had become core resources in their practice. Many of these educators were accessing the OER offline, in either print form (held in the library) or from CDs, and using them as a resource to inform their teaching – i.e. providing ideas for sessions and encouraging student teachers to use them, albeit often in a didactic manner which did not disturb the existing lecturer–student relationship, as this statement implies: "TESSA is activity-based approach and being activity-based approach when you actually read these materials you should be able to actually copy and then you are able to do in your teaching" (TE13). However, in all three institutions, respondents discussed how the use of these OER required increased preparation time (particularly in the initial stages of use), and how some colleagues were not prepared to devote time to this. Use of OER was thus not embedded across the institution.

2. Using multiple online resources in teaching

This practice was described by the largest group of educators, but many were unclear whether the online resources they were using were OER. Understandings of "open" were highly limited and being "open" was not often considered when selecting and using resources in the classroom. However, a small number of educators commented that recent institutional activity (at TU1 and UU1) had alerted them to the nature of different licences and they now realised they might have been using OER. Much more prevalent, particularly in TU2, was a concern regarding plagiarism and the need to acknowledge the author or publisher in both their own and their students' work. Checking the authenticity of the source was important to this group, but most were satisfied if the resource had originated from a university.

Lack of awareness of the licence did not preclude educators from adapting resources (even in cases where this may not have been permissible in terms of the resource licence) and there was much reported sharing of articles and videos directly with students through multiple channels, such as email, print and posts on Facebook and other social media platforms.

Wikipedia and Google Scholar were mentioned frequently by educators in this group. One educator offered a detailed description of how he used Wikipedia, despite many of his colleagues dismissing it as an unauthorised source. He found Wikipedia a good starting point for books and articles on particular subjects, which he then followed up: "I use Wikipedia to just provide a guide and not sources. It directs me to the sources which I then review, and cite if appropriate" (TE23).

3. Using multiple OER in teaching

This was a much smaller group, with no educators from UU3 or TU2 describing this practice. The group primarily comprised educators who were adapting materials for distance learning from multiple sources (UU2 and TU1). They described changing or modifying the material whilst trying not to amend the intended meaning of the author. They were often frustrated at their inability to adapt video to make it more appropriate for their context, and sometimes the use of the OER made considerable demands on their students – for example, students accessed resources in English, but were then expected to use these in their practice in Swahili. Many were not specifically searching for open resources but using "open" as a criterion for selection and use. One educator described her practice as "going through Google and get this article, this resource, if it's good and at the end of the day they mention it's an open resource so I might use it" (TE08). Some distance educators in this group suggested OER to students when they met for face-to-face sessions.

Educators using OER appeared to receive confirmation of the efficacy of their use from their students. One educator, an early adopter of OER, spoke passionately about how her students have developed an interest in the subject through use of varied OER and how these resources have "added life to teaching and learning environments" (TE19). Others spoke of student enjoyment, active engagement and how students became curious to learn more. Characteristic of this group of educators was the value they accorded to participating in a wider community of educators and their desire to support other educators: "I feel bad that I'm a kind of consumer of open resources rather than producing something for others" (TE20). Several described how they shared their own resources and those of their students under a Creative Commons licence that would allow future adaptation, thereby making them available for the next cohort of students: "the work [from students] is so nice that I wouldn't like it to be lost. Others can use it, not only in [here] but anywhere in the world" (TE03).

Personal learning or preparation for teaching with OER

Six educators described use of OER for their own learning or preparation of materials and/or teaching sessions rather than direct use of OER with students. The most common OER used were Wiki Educator and YouTube for exploring the speeches and work of popular scholars, engaging with contemporary thinking and finding and stimulating ideas for teaching: "I use for my own study but not for my students" (TE21) and "expanding your knowledge, your ideas about the course" (TE23). One educator (whose background included over 40 years of teaching and a journey from a diploma to a BEd and a master's degree studied through distance programmes) described exploring the physics materials from the Massachusetts Institute of Technology and Stanford University: "I just like to read what others are doing, I'm lulled by the dream of going to university to study physics" (TE5). In two of the institutions, small groups of teacher educators attempted to disseminate regularly what they had learned from such exploration, wanting to create an explicit sharing culture in their organisation. While this activity was tentative and on a small scale, it offered a promising space for shaping the community regime of competence in these institutions.

In summary, the data on OER engagement indicate differences between the institutions, but the discourse was remarkably similar across the sample and the analysis revealed many shared practices and attitudes. Most educators had only a limited understanding of the OER concept and described multiple factors which influenced, and most frequently constrained, their position and identities with respect to OER use. However, the language of "possibilities" was detected in discussions, together with a sense that OER use might support change in styles of teaching, although this was not yet feasible in their particular context. Collective engagement with OER was limited to interactions with external OER projects whilst individual commitment to OER was on a continuum from highly marginal to regular incorporation in practice. Deepening proactive use of OER was found to have been influenced by peripheral participation in other OER activities that were often external to the institution. The data showed that the educators' purpose for use of OER varied from personal learning through to support for peer educators.

Pedagogic change through OER use

The imperative to improve school pupils' productive learning requires pedagogic change in teacher training institutions in order to enhance the core skills and competencies of school teachers. Across the institutions in this study, the dominant culture of teaching was described as highly teacher-centred, characterised by lecturers "going to the classroom and telling about the topic" (TE14), although there was widespread recognition that this approach was not making opportunities available for students to develop as independent learners. One educator described the situation as follows: "so we are preparing teachers who are dependent, it's a problem. There is little emphasis on democratic opportunities for learning in schools" (TE20).

To explore shifts in pedagogic practice through OER use, the interview data were analysed against dimensions of pedagogy aligned with a more learner-centred approach. Analysis revealed three aspects of a more learner-centred pedagogic approach in these descriptions of practice with OER: engagement with multiple valued forms of knowledge; students as autonomous agents in their learning; and moving to a participatory learning culture.

Engagement with multiple valued forms of knowledge

If OER are understood as a tool for enabling changes in pedagogy, then one feature of this evolution will be teacher educators' greater confidence and competence in problematising what is valued knowledge and drawing on multiple forms of knowledge from OER to enhance student learning. In this study, institutional movement towards offering students opportunities to engage with codified knowledge, other cultural knowledge and personal knowledge was observed at multiple levels, although in most instances these shifts are modest and not yet embedded in collective practices. Educators using multiple OER, either by design or by accident, disrupt the idea that knowledge is only available to a privileged few ("building walls around the few who are prosperous" [TE12]) and directly make available different sources of knowledge to their students, as this educator explained: "I recommend resources for the students … they are given a wider panorama to broaden their perspective" (TE22). Another explains: "I tell students to read about what is happening in other countries" (TE17). Some educators articulated how such activities with OER enabled them to deepen their understanding of learning as a social practice and to draw on the knowledge brought to the learning endeavour by students.

However, engagement with knowledge from across the globe was often guarded as educators balanced their desire to extend understandings with embedded ways of participation and forms of knowledge. An educator at TU2 was introducing a new course on counselling with her students and utilising video clips from different countries to position the approach in her country within a global framework, but her choice of resources was constrained by her position that she should "use resources which are highly scaffolded and familiar to the local textbook" (TE24). Other educators also spoke about carefully selecting OER, starting with OER close to their context to counter prevailing views that OER are mainly from the USA and not appropriate to the local African context. This approach was more prevalent in the distance learning institutions, where materials (including choice of external resources) are shared and are highly visible. This hesitancy was not universal. In UU2, educators on the distance learning programme were very concerned that open resources should not be restricted to examples from Uganda, but should be varied to enable students to extend their knowledge of the world.

In the more private spaces of face-to-face lectures, educators engaged with OER could be more adventurous. For example, an educator at TU1 was compiling a set of open resources for teachers and young people to explore personal topics not previously covered in school, such as sexual risk. A few educators were encouraging their colleagues to draw on more extensive resources and directly encouraging both in-service or pre-service teachers to make use of global and local knowledge repositories to augment and challenge embedded ways of understanding knowledge. However, in some institutions or programmes, the pressure on lecturers to deliver the syllabus content acted to marginalise these activities from the enacted curriculum.

A small number of educators described the process of attuning resources to the local context and culture, drawing on shared knowledge to enhance student participation, as this educator describes:

> I borrow ideas from other countries and then I give examples from Tanzania. What this aspect relates to, or what they represent in a Tanzanian context. So the challenge is how to adopt … to adapt the content reading from another context but, because the concepts are the same, examples and practices must be from our experiences, our students' experiences and my own experience. (TE14)

Students as autonomous agents in their learning

The use of OER can challenge teacher-centred pedagogy associated with a hierarchical teacher–learner relationship, and support an understanding of teacher learning (i.e. student learning) as movement into practice – becoming a more competent and effective professional rather than being limited to the acquisition of abstract, external knowledge. Some of the teacher educators interviewed perceived learning to be more than the "conceptual–mental", concerned instead with negotiation and renegotiation of meaning in the world (Lave & Wenger, 1991). One educator spoke eloquently about his own journey:

> my own pedagogy was actually very poor ... I must say I used to be that kind of person who'd stand in front of students and talk for an hour because I copied that from my predecessor and the student would be very busy recording, recording, recording. But the first exposure was I think TESSA and then we had several seminars on OER. (TE11)

Now, although he has classes of about 100 students, he sets up opportunities for collaborative learning in which each group of students researches a topic (using some open resources) and then leads discussion on the topic. Educators at MU1 described how students are positioned in a problem-solving role in projects, working in groups to select, adapt and transform OER into a new practice for a school context – an inquiry approach which makes learning purposeful and authentic.

Currently, such innovative practices remain the result of individual efforts, hindered both by students' prior experiences in schools (as TE18 recognised: "these things are not there so they cannot just come here and start afresh, just abruptly go online and communicate their thoughts ... it should begin with our schools") and by lack of a supportive culture and practice within tertiary institutions. In general, students are not recognised as agentive and able to take on a problem-solving role, but as one educator commented, a collective approach is required: "I will not be successful alone to practise that way of learning unless the university, the whole society, is empowered to be aware of this way of learning" (TE21). The strictures of formal assessment in the study-site institutions emerged as a barrier to new forms of practice, but project activity, where available, offered a space that could be exploited for more innovative, independent activity in which the student is positioned as a thinker.

Moving to a participatory learning culture (informal and formal learning)

Coming together to understand each other's perspectives through sharing and acknowledging the agentive nature of mind was recognised by a small number of educators as critical to learning, and in particular to the professional learning of teachers. As one educator explained: "the real learning with teachers comes from when they share, they talk about it, they listen and they discuss about it" (TE2). This reconceptualisation of learning as jointly constructed and occurring with both student partners and peers was a thread in some of the interviews, particularly those with the OER champions. One educator spoke of how using OER with students "promoted team work and innovation" (TE20). Educators described how, through sharing activities such as consultation and conversation with other staff around resources (including OER), the learning situation could be reimagined. Positional leaders were rarely present in these OER activities and their lack of a shared history of participation in these activities placed them beyond the boundary of practice with OER. In their absence, hierarchies were flatter and informal leaders emerged, some of whom brokered practice across disciplinary boundaries with other educators to extend OER engagement. For example, at MU1, institutional engagement had allowed one key champion of OER to work with colleagues from the agriculture department on a project with school teachers. Such instances were, however, sparse and for many educators there were few opportunities to *jointly* develop a meaningful professional identity of knowledge and competence with OER – and hence to become productive with OER. In several institutions, the centre of expertise of OER was seen to reside in the e-learning, distance learning or ICT unit, resulting in a gap between the technical issues related to OER use and the social practice of their use in teaching. Brokering the boundaries of these different communities of practice relied on the voluntary activities of individuals and was therefore often subject to resource constraints.

Very few of the educators in this study were involved in OER networks. Those networks that were present emerged in institutions through initiatives such as TESSA, global Open Educational networks and informal groupings from study abroad, and enabled educators to interact with other educators on issues. Although difficult to maintain on a practical level, these interactions beyond the institution offered resonance and reinforcement for their identity as educators with OER competence, and they were characteristic of the OER champions.

As a qualitative study, the research presented here does not aim to draw generalisable conclusions about the impact of OER use on teacher educators' practice. Rather, the data presented aim to provide some insights into pedagogical movement shaped by OER use. Three pedagogical themes emerged, characteristic of a more learner-centred approach, from educators' discussions of their pedagogical intentions and enactment. These are influenced by the settings in which the educators practise. However, more detailed research involving observation of practice is required to understand the impact of these practices on student participation and learning.

Conclusion

This small-scale study suggests that as access to digital resources improves, educators are beginning to draw on these resources (including OER) to experiment with more interactive and participatory practices in their teaching, moving towards greater use of problem-solving activities and drawing on a wider range of knowledge sources. The innovation in practice and the transformation in pedagogy promised by OER is, however, still fragile, confined to a few converts working independently or with one or two collaborators within study-site institutions. For these "OER champions" the potential offered by OER resonates with their beliefs and values about effective teaching and their view of the kind of teacher they aspire to be. They are able to subjugate the OER to their own practice needs and speak convincingly of shifts in their practice facilitated by the use of OER. For them, OER act as a practice tool in extending their agency to move towards more participatory pedagogy. They adapt OER to fit their own and their students' learning needs in their specific setting and hold understandings of quality which are derived from contextual use (Conole & Ehlers, 2010). Uncovering such pedagogic shifts was not easy; the evidence is highly emergent and the dominant discourse around OER is focused on the processes of use, in particular issues of access (how and in what ways), rather than on the pedagogical or learning purpose of such use.

Policy initiatives at the national level have yet to be meaningfully mediated into practice at the institutions in this study and explicit institutional policy on OER is limited. Even when there is explicit institutional support for OER, use of OER is commonly fragmented and many individual teacher educators' engagement is, as yet, sporadic. For most respondents for whom OER has become part of their lived practice as teacher educators, this is the result of personal action rather than collective endeavour. Transformation occurs at a personal level and is not extended through collective action because there is typically a lack of obvious channels or mechanisms which can be leveraged to do so. Greater use of OER was generally reported in the distance learning institutions where there has historically been greater collaborative development of resources and a more embedded culture of sharing. In other institutions many educators were unaware of their colleagues' use of OER. This comment from an educator at UU1 expressing his frustration at institutional practices reflected those of colleagues at other institutions: "… there is no systematic way to introduce and sustain innovations like OER. Projects come and go, leaving only a few people engaged" (TE02).

In all institutions, structural and cultural factors acted to limit agency with OER. The demands of curriculum and assessment, professional identity, digital skills, provision of equipment and connectivity, values and weak cultures of collaboration were all important in enabling or constraining teacher educators to achieve agency with OER. These findings resonate with those of other researchers who describe similar constraints on practitioner agency with OER across sites in the Global South (Karunanayaka & Naidu, 2016; Ngugi & Butcher, 2016). Demand is currently perceived to be limited primarily by access issues, but also by issues of identity and confidence amongst teacher educators, some of whom fear losing respect if they use too many resources from other educators and who are troubled by the possibility of ridicule if they share an open resource which is perceived to be "incorrect". Those educators who are using OER have considerable cultural resources on which to draw. In their interviews, several of these educators spoke of the formative role of academic training (notably PhD study) at other institutions (usually abroad), and many were linked to external OER networks. These elements of historic identity formation influence how they respond to OER, and enhance their confidence to take risks in moving beyond conventional practice (Wolfenden, Buckler & Keraro, 2012).

Enabling educators to act in an agentive way with OER is challenging. Moving forward, attention should be given to issues of access so that educators are able to locate and view OER relatively easily and experiment with their use. This study recommends that time be made available for educators to enhance their skills in working digitally and to become familiar with principles of learning design such that these become integral dimensions of their professional identity.

Alongside these practical issues, there is a need to consider how the social and cultural context can more effectively support teacher educators to achieve agency with OER. The authors suggest that this requires a conceptualisation of agency extending across the individual and the collective (Edwards, 2015). Increasing OER use and movement towards transformational change in teacher education requires creating opportunities for collective activity with OER; currently this is absent. Participation in professional dialogue about teaching, pedagogy and content is critical. Networks of interactions within and beyond institutions need to be nurtured to enable more collaborative endeavour (including that with OER) in support of improved quality of teacher education. It is only through this engagement (i.e. relational work) that collective agency with OER – a dialectic relationship of understanding and productive activity – can be achieved. Such communities could foster the articulation of "everyday problems of practice or dilemmas of practice" (Schwen & Hara, 2003, p.4) to which OER could be brought to bear, and support renegotiation of professional identities through changed educational practices. The public sharing of modified OER would reify the practice in the community and make it accessible to others. The ways in which participation in these networks and interactions is made available to educators will be facilitated or constrained by the educators' context, and their institutional and social environment, but peer OER champions who understand what is possible in that context could play a mediating role (Macintyre, 2013).

The practices of the OER champions who participated in this study show that OER can act as a tool to enable educators to achieve professional agency, allowing them to exert judgement over and transform how they teach through using ideas and materials appropriate for their context and in line with their beliefs. The educators' trajectory with OER can thus be expressed as *access* leading to *participation* leading to *innovation* in teaching and learning (Wolfenden, 2015). It is important to note that this framework moves beyond the discourse of teacher educator and teacher deficit, which frequently underpins some OER projects and where it is assumed that better outcomes can be reached merely by making open content accessible.

Currently, there is a dissonance between the ways in which individual educators use OER and the dominant values and discourse in the study-site institutions. Coherent policy is important; it legitimises the use of OER, raises awareness of issues such as licensing and stimulates consideration of facilities, assessment and the relationship of OER creation and use with promotion policy and markers of academic esteem. Most critically, participation in policy implementation activity prompts collective engagement with OER. It is through such collective engagement that professionals are able to generate shared professional visions for education which include professional autonomy for teacher educators and move beyond the immediate demands of practice.

The educational change process is complex and the findings of this study suggest that in examining the influence of OER and ideas of openness in teacher education, it would be helpful to undertake more in-depth observations of practice over longer timeframes, to involve students and to explore more deeply the activities and characteristics of OER champions.

Acknowledgements

We wish to thank Mary Burns and Jophus Anamuah-Mensah for valuable comments received in the peer review process. Special thanks also to all our colleagues and participants at the research sites.

References

Akyeampong, K., Lussier, K., Pryor, J. & Westbrook, J. (2013). Improving teaching and learning of basic maths and reading in Africa: Does teacher preparation count? *International Journal of Educational Development, 33,* 272–282. Retrieved from http://www.sciencedirect.com/science/article/pii/S0738059312001216

Auckloo, P. (2011). Innovative teacher education: Improving classroom practices with Open Educational Resources. Paper presented at the *The International Conference on Learning, 5–8 July 2011.* Moka, Mauritius.

Bahadur, G. K. & Oogarah, D. (2013). Interactive whiteboard for primary schools in Mauritius: An effective tool or just another trend? *International Journal of Education and Development using Information and Communication Technology, 9(1),* 19–35. Retrieved from http://files.eric.ed.gov/fulltext/EJ1071348.pdf

Beetham, H., Falconer, I., McGill, L. & Littlejohn, A. (2012). *Open practices: Briefing paper.* Oxford: Jisc. Retrieved from https://oersynth.pbworks.com/w/page/51668352/OpenPracticesBriefing

Biesta, G., Priestley, M. & Robinson, S. (2015). The role of beliefs in teacher agency. *Teachers and Teaching, 21(6),* 624–640. Retrieved from http://www.tandfonline.com/doi/full/10.1080/13540602.2015.1044325

Bold, T. & Svensson, J. (2016). *Education, institutions and economic development.* The Hague: Economic Development and Institutions project. Retrieved from https://edi.opml.co.uk/wpcms/wp-content/uploads/2016/08/EDI-PF-PAPER-8.2-Svensson.pdf

Brown, J. S. & Adler, R. P. (2008). Minds on fire: Open Education, the long tail, and learning 2.0. *Educause Review, 43(1),* 16–32. Retrieved from http://er.educause.edu/articles/2008/1/minds-on-fire-open-education-the-long-tail-and-learning-20

Bruegge, C., Ido, K., Reynolds, T., Serra-Vallejo, C., Stryszowski, P. & van der Berg, R. (2011). *The relationship between local content, internet development and access prices.* Paris: Organisation for Economic Co-operation and Development, Internet and Society & United Nations Educational, Scientific and Cultural Organization. Retrieved from https://www.oecd.org/internet/ieconomy/50305352.pdf

Bruner, J. (1996). *The culture of education.* Cambridge, MA: Harvard University Press.

Butcher, N. (2010). *OER dossier: Open Education Resources and higher education.* Johannesburg: South African Institute for Distance Education. Retrieved from http://www.oerafrica.org/FTPFolder/understanding/OER%20in%20HE%20concept%20paper.pdf

Cartmill, E. T. (2013). *Viewing the use of Open Educational Resources through a community of practice lens: A case study of teachers' use of the Everything Maths and Everything Science open textbooks.* Unpublished M.Phil. Cape Town: University of Cape Town. Retrieved from https://open.uct.ac.za/handle/11427/14095

Clements, K. I. & Pawlowski, J. M. (2012). User-oriented quality for OER: Understanding teachers' views on re-use, quality, and trust. *Journal of Computer Assisted Learning, 28(1),* 4–14. Retrieved from http://onlinelibrary.wiley.com/doi/10.1111/j.1365-2729.2011.00450.x/abstract

Cohen, L., Manion, L. & Morrison, K. (2007). *Research methods in education.* London: Psychology Press. Retrieved from https://islmblogblog.files.wordpress.com/2016/05/rme-edu-helpline-blogspot-com.pdf

Conole, G. (2008). New schemas for mapping pedagogies and technologies. *Ariadne, 56.* Retrieved from http://www.ariadne.ac.uk/issue56/conole/

Conole, G. & Ehlers, U-D. (2010). Open Educational Practices: Unleashing the power of OER. *Paper presented to UNESCO Workshop on OER, May 2010*. Windhoek, Namibia. Retrieved from https://oerknowledgecloud.org/sites/oerknowledgecloud.org/files/OEP_Unleashing-the-power-of-OER.pdf

Cook, S. D. & Brown, J. S. (1999). Bridging epistemologies: The generative dance between organizational knowledge and organizational knowing. *Organization Science, 10*, 381–400. Retrieved from http://pubsonline.informs.org/doi/pdf/10.1287/orsc.10.4.381

de los Arcos, B., Farrow, R., Perryman, L-A., Pitt, R. & Weller, M. (2014). *OER evidence report 2013–2014*. Milton Keynes: OER Research Hub. Retrieved from https://oerresearchhub.files.wordpress.com/2014/11/oerrh-evidence-report-2014.pdf

Deimann, M. & Farrow, R. (2013). Rethinking OER and their use: Open Education as Bildung. *The International Review of Research in Open and Distributed Learning, 14(3)*, 344–360. Retrieved from http://www.irrodl.org/index.php/irrodl/article/view/1370/2542

Downes, S. (2013). The role of Open Educational Resources in personal learning. In R. McGreal, W. Kinuthia, S. Marshall & T. McNamara (Eds.), *Perspectives on Open and distance learning: Open Educational Resources: Innovation, research and practice* (pp. 207–221). Vancouver: Commonwealth of Learning & Athabasca University. Retrieved from https://oerknowledgecloud.org/sites/oerknowledgecloud.org/files/pub_PS_OER-IRP_web.pdf

Dyer, C., Choksi, A., Awasty, V., Iyer, U., Moyade, R., Nigam, N., Purohit, N., Shah, S. & Sheth, S. (2004). Knowledge for teacher development in India: The importance of "local knowledge" for in-service education. *International Journal of Educational Development, 24(1)*, 39–52. Retrieved from http://www.sciencedirect.com/science/article/pii/S0738059303001135

Edwards, A. (2015). Recognising and realizing teachers' professional agency. *Teachers and Teaching, 21(6)*, 779–784. Retrieved from http://www.tandfonline.com/doi/abs/10.1080/13540602.2015.1044333

Ehlers, U-D. (2011). Extending the territory: From Open Educational Resources to Open Educational Practices. *Journal of Open, Flexible and Distance Learning, 15(2)*, 1–10. Retrieved from http://www.jofdl.nz/index.php/JOFDL/article/view/64

Gonzalez, N., Moll, L. & Amanti, C. (2006). Introduction: Theorizing practice. In N. Gonzalez, L. Moll & C. Amanti (Eds.), *Funds of knowledge: Theorizing practices in households, communities, and classrooms*. Mahwah, NJ: Lawrence Erlbaum Associates.

Government of Mauritius. (2016). *Education statistics 2016*. Port Louis: Government of Mauritius. Retrieved from http://statsmauritius.govmu.org/English/Publications/Pages/Edu_Stats_Yr2016.aspx

Gunness, S. (2011). Learner-centred teaching through OER. In A. Okada (Ed.), *Open Educational Resources and social networks: Co-learning and professional development*. London: Scholio Educational Research & Publishing.

Habermas, J. (1989). *On the logic of the social sciences*. London: Heinemann.

Harley, K. & Barasa, F. S. (2012). *TESSA: Teacher education in Sub-Saharan Africa*. Formative evaluation report. Milton Keynes: The Open University. Retrieved from http://www.tessafrica.net/sites/www.tessafrica.net/files/TESSA_Formative_Evaluation_Report_October_2012.pdf

Hewlett Foundation. (2013). *Open Educational Resources: Breaking the lockbox on education (White paper)*. Menlo Park, CA: The William and Flora Hewlett Foundation. Retrieved from http://www.hewlett.org/sites/default/files/OER%20White%20Paper%20Nov%2022%202013%20Final.pdf

Hodgkinson-Williams, C. A. (2015). Open Educational Resources and pedagogical practices in African higher education: A perspective from the ROER4D project. *Keynote presentation at*

Transform 2015 Colloquium, 6–10 April 2015. Retrieved from http://transform2015.net/live/Resources/Papers/keynote1CHW.pdf

Hooker, M., Mwiyeria, E. & Verma, A. (2011). ICT competency framework for teachers in Tanzania: Teacher Development for the 21st Century (TDev21) pilot. Draft document. Dar es Salaam: Tanzania Ministry of Education and Vocational Education, World Bank and Global e-Schools and Communities Initiative. Retrieved from: https://pdfs.semanticscholar.org/54cf/59f840568981303dc65526d5b5bb44587682.pdf

Ives, C. & Pringle, M. M. (2013). Moving to Open Educational Resources at Athabasca University: A case study. *The International Review of Research in Open and Distributed Learning, 14(2).* Retrieved from http://www.irrodl.org/index.php/irrodl/article/view/1534

James, M. & Pollard, A. (2011). TLRP's ten principles for effective pedagogy: Rationale, development, evidence, argument and impact. *Research Papers in Education, 26(3),* 275–328. Retrieved from http://www.tandfonline.com/doi/abs/10.1080/02671522.2011.590007

Jhangiani, R., Pitt, R., Hendricks, C., Key, J. & Lalonde, C. (2016). *Exploring faculty use of Open Educational Resources at British Columbia post-secondary institutions.* Victoria: BCcampus. Retrieved from http://bccampus.ca/files/2016/01/BCFacultyUseOfOER_final.pdf

Karunanayaka, S. & Naidu, S. (Eds.). (2016). *Dreamweaving Open Educational Practices.* Nawala: The Open University of Sri Lanka. Retrieved from http://www.ou.ac.lk/home/images/OUSL/publications/Dreamweaving%20Open%20Educational%20Practices.pdf

Kimmons, R. (2015). OER quality and adaptation in K-12: Comparing teacher evaluations of copyright-restricted, open, and open/adapted textbooks. *The International Review of Research in Open and Distributed Learning, 16(5),* 39–57. Retrieved from http://www.irrodl.org/index.php/irrodl/article/view/2341/3405

Kunje, D. (2002). The Malawi integrated in-service teacher education programme: An experiment with mixed-mode training. *International Journal of Educational Development, 22,* 305–320. Retrieved from http://www.sciencedirect.com/science/article/pii/S0738059301000657

Lave, J. (2008). Everyday life and learning. In P. Murphy & R. McCormick (Eds.), *Knowledge and practice: Representations and identities* (pp. 3–14). London: Sage.

Lave, J. & Wenger, E. (1991). *Situated learning: Legitimate peripheral participation.* Cambridge: Cambridge University Press.

Livingston, K. & Condie, R. (2006). The impact of an online learning program on teaching and learning strategies. *Theory into Practice, 45(2),* 150–158. Retrieved from http://www.tandfonline.com/doi/abs/10.1207/s15430421tip4502_7

Macintyre, R. (2013). Open Educational partnerships and collective learning. *Journal of Interactive Media in Education, 2013(3).* Retrieved from http://jime.open.ac.uk/articles/10.5334/2013-20/

Masterman, L. & Wild, L. (2011). *JISC OER impact study: Research report.* Oxford: Jisc. Retrieved from https://weblearn.ox.ac.uk/access/content/group/ca5599e6-fd26-4203-b416-f1b96068d1cf/Research%20Project%20Reports/OER%20Projects%202011-2014/JISC%20OER%20Impact%20Study%20Research%20Report%20v1-0.pdf

McNess, E., Arthur, L. & Crossley, M. (2013). "Ethnographic dazzle" and the construction of the "Other": Revisiting dimensions of insider and outsider research for international and comparative education. *Compare: A Journal of Comparative and International Education, 45(2),* 295–316. Retrieved from http://www.tandfonline.com/doi/abs/10.1080/03057925.2013.854616

MECHR (Ministry of Education, Culture and Human Resources). (2009). *Education and human resources strategic plan 2008-2020.* Pont Fer: Government of Mauritius. Retrieved from http://planipolis.iiep.unesco.org/en/2009/education-and-human-resources-strategy-plan-2008-2020-4894

Milligan, L. (2016). Insider-outsider-inbetweener? Research positioning, participative methods and cross-cultural educational research. *Compare: A Journal of Comparative and International Education, 46(2)*, 235–250. Retrieved from http://www.tandfonline.com/doi/abs/10.1080/03057925.2014.928510

Ministry of Information and Communications Technology. (2014). *National ICT policy for Uganda 2013-2017*. Kampala: Republic of Uganda. Retrieved from https://www.ict.go.ug/sites/default/files/Resource/ICT_Policy_2014.pdf

MoEVT (Ministry of Education and Vocational Training). (2008). *In-service education and training strategy for primary school teachers 2008–2013*. Dar es Salaam: Ministry of Education and Vocational Training.

Moon, B. & Villet, C. (2016). *Reforming teacher education to promote access, equity and quality in Sub-Saharan Africa*. Vancouver: Commonwealth of Learning.

Mtebe, J. S. & Raisamo, R. (2014). Investigating perceived barriers to the use of Open Educational Resources in higher education in Tanzania. *The International Review of Research in Open and Distributed Learning, 15(2)*. Retrieved from http://www.irrodl.org/index.php/irrodl/article/view/1803/2841

Muganda, C. K., Samzugi, A. S. & Mallinson, B. J. (2016). Analytical insights on the position, challenges, and potential for promoting OER in ODeL institutions in Africa. *International Review of Research in Open and Distributed Learning, 17(4)*, 36–49. Retrieved from http://www.irrodl.org/index.php/irrodl/article/view/2465/3797

Muijs, D., Kyriakides, L., van der Werf, G., Creemers, B., Timperley, H. & Earl, L. (2014). State of the art – teacher effectiveness and professional learning. *School Effectiveness and School Improvement, 25(2)*, 231–256. Retrieved from http://www.tandfonline.com/doi/abs/10.1080/09243453.2014.885451

Murphy, P. & Wolfenden, F. (2013). Developing a pedagogy of mutuality in a capability approach – teachers' experiences of using the Open Educational Resources (OER) of the Teacher Education in Sub Saharan Africa (TESSA) programme. *International Journal of Educational Development, 33(3)*, 263–271. Retrieved from http://www.sciencedirect.com/science/article/pii/S0738059312001393

Ngalande, R. (2013). *The use of Open Educational Resources at the University of Malawi (UNIMA) - Kamuzu College of Nursing Malawi*. Zomba: University of Malawi. Retrieved from https://oerknowledgecloud.org/sites/oerknowledgecloud.org/files/OER_The_Use_ofOERs_University_Malawi.pdf

Ngugi, C. N. (2011). OER in Africa's higher education institutions. *Distance Education, 32(2)*, 277–287. Retrieved from http://www.tandfonline.com/doi/full/10.1080/01587919.2011.584853

Ngugi, C. N. & Butcher, N. (2016). Separating the rhetoric from the reality: The process of institutionalizing OER practices at African universities. *Paper presented at 8th Pan-Commonwealth Forum on Open Learning (PCF8), 27–30 November 2016*. Kuala Lumpur, Malaysia. Retrieved from http://oasis.col.org/handle/11599/2532

Nind, M., Curtin, A. & Hall, K. (2016). *Researching pedagogy*. Oxford: Bloomsbury.

OER Africa & University of Michigan. (2012). *AgShare planning and pilot project: Impact study*. Johannesburg: OER Africa.

Okonkwo, C. A. (2012). A needs assessment of ODL educators to determine their effective use of Open Educational Resources. *The International Review of Research in Open and Distributed Learning, 13(4)*, 293–309. Retrieved from http://www.irrodl.org/index.php/irrodl/article/view/1316

OPAL (Open Educational Quality Initiative). (2011). *Beyond OER: Shifting focus to Open Educational Practices – The OPAL report 2011*. Essen: University of Duisburg-Essen. Retrieved from https://oerknowledgecloud.org/content/beyond-oer-shifting-focus-open-educational-practices

Petrides, L., Jimes, C., Middleton-Detzner, C., Walling, J. & Weiss, S. (2011). Open textbook adoption and use: Implications for teachers and learners. *Open Learning, 26(1)*, 39–49. Retrieved from http://www.tandfonline.com/doi/abs/10.1080/02680513.2011.538563

Pitt, B. (2015). Exploring the impact of open textbooks around the world. *Presented at the Open Textbook Summit, 28 May 2015*. Vancouver, Canada. Retrieved from https://www.slideshare.net/BeckPitt/exploring-the-impact-of-open-textbooks-around-the-world

Pitt, R., Ebrahimi, N., McAndrew, P. & Coughlan, T. (2013). Assessing OER impact across organisations and learners: Experiences from the Bridge to Success project. *Journal of Interactive Media in Education, 2013(3)*. Retrieved from *http://jime.open.ac.uk/articles/10.5334/2013-17/*

Pryor, J., Akyeampong, A. & Westbrook, J. (2012). Rethinking teacher preparation and professional development in Africa: An analysis of the curriculum of teacher education in the teaching of early reading and mathematics. *Curriculum Journal, 23(4)*, 409–502. Retrieved from http://www.tandfonline.com/doi/abs/10.1080/09585176.2012.747725

Putnam, T. & Borko, H. (2000). What do new views of knowledge and thinking have to say about research on teacher learning? *Educational Researcher, 29(1)*, 4–15. Retrieved from https://cset.stanford.edu/publications/journal-articles/what-do-new-views-knowledge-and-thinking-have-say-about-research-teach

Richards, G. & Marshall, S. (2010). Open Educational Resources for development of university courses. In *OpenEd 2010 Proceedings, 2–4 November 2010*. Barcelona, Spain. Retrieved from https://oerknowledgecloud.org/sites/oerknowledgecloud.org/files/Richards.pdf

Robinson, T. J., Fischer, L., Wiley, D. & Hilton III, J. (2014). The impact of open textbooks on secondary science learning outcomes. *Educational Researcher, 43(7)*. Retrieved from http://journals.sagepub.com/doi/abs/10.3102/0013189X14550275

Rogoff, B. (2003). *The cultural nature of human development*. New York: Oxford University Press.

Scanlon, E., McAndrew, P. & O'Shea, T. (2015). Designing for educational technology to enhance the experience of learners in distance education: How Open Educational Resources, learning design and MOOCs are influencing learning. *Journal of Interactive Media in Education, 2015(1)*, 1–9. Retrieved from http://jime.open.ac.uk/articles/10.5334/jime.al/

Schweisfurth, M. (2013). *Learner-centred education in international perspective: Whose pedagogy for whose development?* Abingdon: Routledge.

Schwen, T. M. & Hara, N. (2003). Community of practice: A metaphor for online design? *The Information Society, 19(3)*, 257–270. Retrieved from http://www.tandfonline.com/doi/abs/10.1080/01972240309462

Shear, L., Means, B. & Lundh, P. (2015). *Research on open: OER Research Hub review and futures for research on OER*. Menlo Park, CA: SRI International.

Stutchbury, K. & Katabaro, J. (2011). TESSA secondary science: Addressing the challenges facing science teacher-education in Sub-Saharan Africa. In *DETA Conference 2011, 3–5 August 2011*. Maputo, Mozambique.

Tabulawa, R. (2003). International aid agencies, learner-centred pedagogy and political democratisation: A critique. *Comparative Education, 39(1)*, 7–26. Retrieved from http://www.tandfonline.com/doi/abs/10.1080/03050060302559

Tonks, D., Weston, S., Wiley, D. & Barbour, M. (2013). "Opening" a new kind of school: The story of the Open High School of Utah. *The International Review of Research in Open and Distributed Learning, 14(1)*, 255–271. Retrieved from http://www.irrodl.org/index.php/irrodl/article/view/1345/2419

Trigwell, K. & Prosser, M. (1996). Changing approaches to teaching: A relational perspective. *Studies in Higher Education, 21*, 275–284. Retrieved from http://www.tandfonline.com/doi/abs/10.1080/03075079612331381211?journalCode=cshe20

Udhin, W. & Oojorah, V. A. (2013). The impact of social media to empower primary school teachers – A case study of the Sankore (Mauritius) project. *Paper presented at the 2nd International Conference on Communication, Media, Technology and Design, 2–4 May 2013*. Famagusta, North Cyprus. Retrieved from http://www.cmdconf.net/2013/makale/PDF/58.pdf

Udhin, W., Goburdhun, S., Oozeerally, S., Goolamhossen, F., Peedoly, K. & Gungapersand, R. (2016). Evaluating the impact of interactive whiteboard in primary schools in Mauritius. *Paper presented at the 9th International Conference of Education, Research and Innovation. 16–18 November 2016*. Seville, Spain. Retrieved from https://library.iated.org/view/UDHIN2016EVA

Umar, A., Kodhandaraman, B. & Kanwar, A. (2013). Can Open Educational Resources thrive in closed educational systems? Some reflections on OER in developing countries. In R. McGreal, W. Kinuthia & S. Marshall (Eds.), *Perspectives on open and distance learning: Open Educational Resources: Innovation, research and practice* (pp. 193–206). Vancouver: Commonwealth of Learning and Athabasca University. Retrieved from https://oerknowledgecloud.org/sites/oerknowledgecloud.org/files/pub_PS_OER-IRP_web.pdf

UNESCO (United Nations Educational, Scientific and Cultural Organization). (2002). *Forum on the impact of open courseware for higher education in developing countries: Final report*. Paris: United Nations Educational, Scientific and Cultural Organization. Retrieved from http://unesdoc.unesco.org/images/0012/001285/128515e.pdf

UNESCO (United Nations Educational, Scientific and Cultural Organization). (2014). *Teaching and learning: Achieving quality for all: Gender summary*. Paris: United Nations Educational, Scientific and Cultural Organization. Retrieved from http://unesdoc.unesco.org/images/0022/002266/226662e.pdf

UNESCO (United Nations Educational, Scientific and Cultural Organization). (2015). *Education for all 2000–2015: Achievements and challenges*. Paris: United Nations Educational, Scientific and Cultural Organization. Retrieved from http://unesdoc.unesco.org/images/0023/002322/232205e.pdf

URT (United Republic of Tanzania). (2008). Education Sector Development Programme 2008-2017. Dar es Salaam: United Republic of Tanzania. Retrieved from http://www.globalpartnership.org/content/tanzania-education-sector-development-programme-2008-17

URT (United Republic of Tanzania). (2010a). *The Tanzania Development Vision 2025*. Dar es Salaam: United Republic of Tanzania Planning Commission. Retrieved from http://www.unesco.org/education/edurights/media/docs/061eb2eed52b8f11b09b25a8845436f19d5ae0ad.pdf

URT (United Republic of Tanzania). (2010b). *National Strategy for Growth and Reduction of Poverty (NSGRP II)*. Dar es Salaam: Ministry of Finance and Economic Affairs. Retrieved from http://www.tzonline.org/pdf/mkukutalldraft.pdf

URT (United Republic of Tanzania). (2010c). *Higher Education Development Programme 2010–2015*. Dar es Salaam: Ministry of Education and Vocational Training.

URT (United Republic of Tanzania). (2016). *National Information and Communications Policy.* Dar es Salaam: Ministry of Works, Transport and Communication. Retrieved from https://tanzict.files.wordpress.com/2016/05/national-ict-policy-proofed-final-nic-review-2.pdf

Westbrook, J., Durrani, N., Brown, R., Orr, D., Pryor, J., Boddy, J. & Salvi, F. (2014). *Pedagogy, curriculum, teaching practices and teacher education in developing countries: Education rigorous literature review.* London: Department for International Development. Retrieved from https://www.gov.uk/dfid-research-outputs/pedagogy-curriculum-teaching-practices-and-teacher-education-in-developing-countries-education-rigorous-literature-review

White, D. & Manton, M. (2011). *Open Educational Resources: The value of reuse in higher education.* Oxford: Jisc. Retrieved from https://oerknowledgecloud.org/content/open-educational-resources-value-reuse-higher-education

Wiley, D. (2016). Efficiency and effectiveness. *Keynote address at the 8th Pan-Commonwealth Forum on Open Learning (PCF8), 27–30 November 2016.* Kuala Lumpur, Malaysia. Retrieved from http://oasis.col.org/handle/11599/2697

Wolfenden, F. (2008). The TESSA OER experience: Building sustainable models of production and user implementation. *Journal of Interactive Media in Education, 2008(1).* Retrieved from http://jime.open.ac.uk/articles/10.5334/2008-3/

Wolfenden, F. (Ed.) (2012). *TESSA case studies 2010–2011.* Milton Keynes: The Open University. Retrieved from http://www.tessafrica.net/sites/www.tessafrica.net/files/files/TESSA_Case%20studies_combined_final.pdf

Wolfenden, F. (2015). TESS-India OER: Collaborative practices to improve teacher education. *Indian Journal of Teacher Education, 1(3)*, 33–48. Retrieved from http://oro.open.ac.uk/46171/

Wolfenden, F., Buckler, A. & Keraro, F. (2012). OER adaptation and reuse across cultural contexts in Sub Saharan Africa: Lessons from TESSA (Teacher Education in Sub Saharan Africa). *Journal of Interactive Media in Education, 2012(1).* Retrieved from http://doi.org/10.5334/2012-03

Wright, C. R. & Reju, S. A. (2012). Developing and deploying OERs in sub-Saharan Africa: Building on the present. *The International Review of Research in Open and Distributed Learning, 13(2)*, 181–220. Retrieved from http://www.irrodl.org/index.php/irrodl/article/view/1185/2161

How to cite this chapter

Wolfenden, F., Auckloo, P., Buckler, A. & Cullen, J. (2017). Teacher educators and OER in East Africa: Interrogating pedagogic change. In C. Hodgkinson-Williams & P. B. Arinto (Eds.), *Adoption and impact of OER in the Global South* (pp. 251–286). Retrieved from https://doi.org/10.5281/zenodo.600424

Corresponding author: Freda Wolfenden <freda.wolfenden@open.ac.uk>

Chapter 9

Factors shaping lecturers' adoption of OER at three South African universities

Glenda Cox and Henry Trotter

Summary

The research presented here focuses on understanding the obstacles, opportunities and practices associated with Open Educational Resources (OER) adoption at three South African universities. It addresses the question: Why do South African lecturers adopt – or not adopt – OER? In trying to answer this, the authors also attempt to identify which factors shape lecturers' OER adoption decisions, and how lecturers' institutional cultures influence their OER use and creation choices.

This study employed a qualitative research approach through in-depth personal interviews with 18 respondents at three different universities which together broadly represent the characteristics of South Africa's university sector. Unique analytical tools – the OER adoption pyramid and OER adoption readiness tables – were developed to help with analysing and synthesising the data.

Findings indicate that whether and how OER adoption takes place at an institution is shaped by a layered sequence of factors – infrastructural access, legal permission, conceptual awareness, technical capacity, material availability, and individual or institutional volition – which are further influenced by prevailing cultural and social variables.

This study has value and application for researchers and institutions pursuing an OER agenda, policy-makers seeking tools to assess OER readiness in institutional contexts, and funding agencies aiming to boost institutional OER engagement.

The dataset arising from this study can be accessed at:
https://www.datafirst.uct.ac.za/dataportal/index.php/catalog/555

Acronyms and abbreviations

CC   Creative Commons
CILT   Centre for Innovation in Learning and Teaching
HEI   higher education institution
IP   intellectual property
OER   Open Educational Resources
ROER4D   Research on Open Educational Resources for Development
TESSA   Teacher Education in Sub Saharan Africa
UCT   University of Cape Town
UFH   University of Fort Hare
UNISA   University of South Africa

Introduction

This study investigates lecturers' adoption or non-adoption of Open Educational Resources (OER) at three universities in South Africa, seeking to understand their motivations and practices regarding OER and the factors influencing their OER decision-making. The purpose of this study is to go beyond simply listing the various "challenges" and "barriers" to OER adoption by integrating these factors into an analytical framework that makes sense of them and allows for cross-institutional comparison.

In this chapter, we use the term OER "adoption" as an umbrella term to cover both OER "use" and OER "creation". OER *use* refers to the full gamut of activities involved in reusing, remixing, revising, retaining and redistributing other people's OER so as to incorporate them into one's teaching materials.[1] This use is made possible by the fact that those publicly available materials have been openly licensed, and can therefore be legally appropriated. OER *creation* refers to activities in which producers' teaching materials are given an open licence and shared on a digital platform or website for public consumption. These materials may be the intellectual product of one person, or include other OER that have been incorporated into them through revision or remixing. Throughout this report, we use the terms OER "contribution" and OER "sharing" synonymously with OER "creation".

Background

Since the term "Open Educational Resources" – free, openly licensed educational materials available online to anyone – was coined in 2002, scholars, funders and advocates have promoted OER as a potential answer to the numerous challenges facing higher education (Boston Consulting Group, 2013; West & Victor, 2011). It is argued that OER can reduce the cost of textbook provision (Butcher, 2011), reduce the cost of higher education (Wiley, Green & Soares, 2012), increase the accessibility of higher education to more students,[2] improve the quality of educational materials resulting from collaboration and peer scrutiny

---

1   http://opencontent.org/blog/archives/3221
2   https://www.whitehouse.gov/blog/2015/10/19/openly-licensed-educational-resources-providing-equitable-access-education-all

(Daniel, Kanwar & Uvalić-Trumbić, 2006; Orr, Rimini & Van Damme, 2015) and expand the reach, impact and brand competitiveness of different higher education institutions (HEIs) (Butcher, Hoosen & Mawoyo, 2015; Ludewig-Omollo, 2011a; Wiley & Hilton, 2009).

In pursuing these ambitions, many top-ranked HEIs globally – as well as other educational projects and initiatives – have developed platforms and repositories where lecturers can share their teaching and learning materials.[3] For instance, the Massachusetts Institute of Technology provides access to almost all of its courses and associated materials to the general public,[4] Harvard University offers several free courses online,[5] and Yale University provides free access to a number of introductory courses.[6]

The projects supporting these content-sharing initiatives can range in scale from a small group of people supported by small sums of money (Hodgkinson-Williams & Donnelly, 2010) to massive institutional projects run by large teams with long-term financial support (Abelson & Long, 2008; Carson, 2009). Some of these are sponsored by private philanthropic foundations (Atkins, Brown & Hammond, 2007), while others are supported by governments with policies advocating OER use and creation (Daniel & Uvalić-Trumbić, 2012).

The OER effort, established on a growing "culture of contribution", is no longer a nascent movement (Atkins et al., 2007), but is now said to have reached an "inflection point" where the broader changes in education, together with OER, have changed the way education can be delivered (Matkin & Cooperman, 2012). This is especially true in the Global North where many HEIs enjoy relatively robust infrastructural (electricity, hardware, connectivity) and financial resourcing, and where academics are able to engage with OER in languages – primarily English – with which they have professional familiarity (Cobo, 2013).

However, despite the infrastructural and resource capacities of many institutions in the Global North, OER adoption has yet to become a normative practice across all faculties and disciplines.[7] The reasons most commonly cited by Northern-based studies for why academics have yet to engage with OER revolve around a series of deficits. The lack of OER awareness amongst many lecturers is a barrier to adoption (Reed, 2012; Rolfe, 2012). So too is a lack of copyright permission for lecturers to share their teaching materials as OER (Fitzgerald & Hashim, 2012; Flor, 2013; Tynan & James, 2013). Additionally, many lecturers feel that there is a dearth of relevant, high-quality OER available for them to use (Clements & Pawlowski, 2012; Willems & Bossu, 2012). Moreover, some lecturers also lack the personal interest to use or create OER because they do not see its value (McGill, Falconer, Dempster, Littlejohn & Beetham, 2013; Pegler, 2012; Reed, 2012; Rolfe, 2012). This motivational deficit is influenced by lecturers' perceived lack of time to engage with OER (Allen & Seaman, 2014) and the lack of formal institutional recognition of any OER adoption activities (Jhangiani, Pitt, Hendricks, Key & Lalonde, 2016).

Hence, there appear to be a number of factors shaping OER adoption decisions amongst lecturers, though it is not clear what relationship these factors might have with each other

---

3   http://onlineuniversityrankings2010.com/2010/open-edu-top-50-university-open-courseware-collections/; https://oerqualityproject.wordpress.com/2012/10/22/directory-of-oer-repositories/; https://library.educause.edu/topics/teaching-and-learning/open-educational-resources-oer

4   http://ocw.mit.edu/

5   http://extension.harvard.edu/index.php?q=open-learning-initiative

6   http://oyc.yale.edu/

7   http://er.educause.edu/articles/2013/2/ten-years-later-why-open-educational-resources-have-not-noticeably-affected-higher-education-and-why-we-should-care

in influencing OER decision-making. Nor is it clear from the OER literature how the broader cultural and social context – the departmental and disciplinary norms and expectations that form part of a lecturer's "world" with their colleagues (both proximate and virtual) – within which lecturers operate might shape their OER choices.

This lack of clarity is mirrored in the diverse perspectives that many lecturers have concerning OER quality, a fact that demotivates adoption for some while motivating adoption for others (Hatakka, 2009; Pegler, 2012; Stacey, 2007). Regarding the use of OER, some lecturers perceive that because OER are free, they may be of poorer quality than the traditional, copyrighted educational materials sold by publishers (Boston Consulting Group, 2013). Therefore, they would prefer that OER undergo some sort of quality assurance process before they use them. By contrast, other lecturers assume that OER would typically be of good quality because the resources themselves are exposed to "diversified expertise and perspectives" (Stacey, 2007, p.11).

This complexity is compounded for lecturers who could potentially share their own teaching materials openly, but don't. According to Davis et al., many lecturers do not share their materials beyond a small, known community because they feel a "lack of confidence in the applicability of the resource" (2010, p.103). Kursun, Cagiltay and Can also note that amongst Turkish lecturers one of the main reasons for not sharing their materials as OER was "a lack of self-confidence about the quality of their course materials" (2014, p.25). In contrast to these lecturers' perceptions, Van Acker, Van Duuren, Kreijns and Vermeulen found that those who shared their materials openly did so because they believed they had value for others, an attribute that the authors identified as "knowledge self-efficacy" (2013, p.188).

Complicating these perspectives about OER quality is the lack of an associated pedagogy which is seen as a potential obstacle for many lecturers (Davis et al., 2010; Sclater, 2010). There is a concern that OER are often stand-alone content lacking facilitator or peer support and are therefore limited in their use. However, OERs' unconstrained pedagogical utility may also be seen as an enabler for use, in that many OER can be incorporated into a lecturer's teaching approach with relative ease (Santos-Hermosa, 2014). Additionally, Stacey (2007) states that learners who have access to a larger range of resources may be encouraged to further explore their fields in an autonomous and self-reliant way.

Lecturers have certain beliefs and attitudes about pedagogy and these can play an important role when they contemplate contributing, using and reusing OER. By pedagogy we mean lecturers' teaching practices, as informed by critical, reflexive engagements with learners (Waring & Evans, 2015). Users of OER can change materials to meet their needs; however, this requires "a change in pedagogical practices, and beliefs, and a move towards a more open, participatory, collaborative, creative and sharing culture" (Karunanayaka, Naidu, Dhanapala, Gonsalkorala & Ariyaratne, 2014, p.18).

Despite lecturers' diverse perceptions of OER quality and pedagogic value, many of the purported benefits inherent to OER might have their greatest impact and utility in the countries in the Global South (Bateman, 2008; Butcher, 2009; Kanwar, Balasubramanian & Umar, 2010). The fact that these materials are available online at no cost to the user would, at least theoretically, provide an incentive for resource-constrained institutions and lecturers to investigate the potential of OER adoption.

Research questions

With these insights from the literature on OER adoption in the Global North, we turn our attention to OER adoption in a Global South country. Focusing on three South African universities – the University of Cape Town (UCT), the University of Fort Hare (UFH) and the University of South Africa (UNISA) – this study seeks to understand the factors shaping lecturers' motivations and concerns regarding OER use and creation.

Primary research question:

1. Why do South African lecturers adopt – or not adopt – OER?

Subsidiary research questions:

1. Which factors shape lecturers' OER adoption decisions?
2. How does an institution's culture shape lecturers' adoption of OER?

In order to address the main research question, we review the literature on OER adoption most pertinent to our region (Africa), investigate the broad range of factors that might shape lecturers' OER adoption, and assess the role that culture might play in OER adoption decisions within that range of factors. By attending to these issues in this way, we will not only be able to answer the subsidiary questions but also use their answers to help build up towards a more comprehensive and persuasive answer to the primary question.

Literature review

This study has drawn on a relatively extensive literature that focuses on OER activity at institutions in the Global North, as discussed in the Introduction. However, we are also able to draw on pockets of research that are emerging from initiatives in the Global South that are relevant to this study.

To date, there has been a small but growing research interest in South African lecturers' adoption of OER (de Hart & Oosthuizen, 2012; Hodgkinson-Williams & Gray, 2009; Mawoyo, 2012; Percy & Van Belle, 2012; van der Merwe, 2013). Hodgkinson-Williams and Donnelly (2010) and Hodgkinson-Williams et al. (2013) provide a first glimpse of the development and push for OER activity at the UCT. Cox (2012; 2013; 2016) also examines the situation at UCT, focusing on lecturers' motivations for using and contributing OER. Lesko (2013) provides a useful overview of some of the issues involved in academics' perceptions of OER adoption, drawing on the input of survey respondents from an array of South African universities. Additionally, de Hart, Chetty and Archer (2015) share the results of a survey conducted amongst staff from UNISA at a time when the institution was developing an OER strategy (discussed in further detail below).

The research that informed this chapter is framed by three overarching concepts: structure, culture and agency. *Structure* refers to largely externally defined elements that shape individual action, such as, in this case, national and institutional infrastructure, computer and internet-related technologies, intellectual property policies and OER repositories and platforms. *Culture* includes the beliefs and norms of the (university) communities in which lecturers find themselves. *Agency* concerns the lecturers' personal capacity to choose a course of action which may or may not include OER adoption.

Structure and OER adoption

OER researchers suggest that a number of structural factors influence whether and how lecturers adopt OER, especially technological access, resource availability and legal permission.

Access

In the Global South, key infrastructure access challenges – such as insufficient technological infrastructure (Bateman, 2006; Clements & Pawlowski, 2012), low levels of internet penetration, broadband availability and electricity stability (CERI/OECD, 2007; Ngimwa, 2010) – appear to influence OER adoption and readiness at education institutions. Such access issues impact not only the institutions, but the lecturers and students themselves (whose own level of at home infrastructural access would also influence institutional and lecturer decisions about OER adoption) (Butcher, 2011; CERI/OECD, 2007; Dhanarajan & Abeydawara, 2013; Ngimwa, 2010).

Availability

Many lecturers in the Global South also worry about the availability of relevant, high-quality OER for their context (Abeywardena, Dhanarajan & Chan, 2012). Given that the development of OER is a relatively new practice, constituting just a fraction of the total number of educational materials created and used by academics globally, one can assume that there are still substantial gaps in the range of subjects covered by OER. This challenge is exacerbated for those seeking to use materials in a language where OER materials are sparse (Cobo, 2013; Zagdragchaa & Trotter, 2017).

However, there has been a proliferation of OER platforms in the Global North (as discussed above) along with a steady growth of portals in the Global South. The most relevant examples for our context, emanating from Africa, include the following initiatives:

- OER@AVU[8] – the African Virtual University's OER repository hosts a growing number of OER in English, French and Portuguese. The initial contribution of content emerged from a collective effort by "12 African universities, 146 authors and peer reviewers from 10 countries in Anglophone, Francophone and Lusophone countries"[9] to provide open materials for the university and the African public (Bateman, 2006; Diallo, Wangeci & Wright, 2012).
- OER Africa[10] – this initiative of the South African Institute for Distance Education seeks to harness African expertise to create OER that will be of benefit to educators of African-related subject areas. Much of its focus to date has been on agriculture, teacher education, and health education across multiple countries (see, for instance, Omollo, 2011a; 2011b; Welch & Glennie, 2016).

---

8   http://oer.avu.org
9   http://oer.avu.org/about
10   http://oerafrica.org/

- AfriVIP[11] – the African Veterinary Information Portal is an OER platform based at the University of Pretoria's Faculty of Veterinary Sciences (Onderstepoort campus), "enabling the sharing of its vast wealth of intellectual capital under an open license" (Haßler & Mays, 2014).
- OpenUCT[12] – UCT's Open Access and OER repository shares both research and teaching and learning resources (Czerniewicz, Cox, Hodgkinson-Williams & Willmers, 2015).
- TESSA – the Teacher Education in Sub Saharan Africa initiative is a "consortium of institutions concerned with the collaborative production of original OERs to support teacher development" (Wolfenden, 2008, n.p.). It does this by providing OER "in four languages to support school-based teacher education: English, French, Swahili (Tanzania) and Arabic (Sudan)"[13] (Murphy & Wolfenden, 2013; Thakrar, Wolfenden & Zinn, 2009).

These initiatives are also complemented by nascent national policy developments, such as South Africa's Department of Higher Education and Training's recommendation for the widespread use of OER in its *White Paper for Post-School Education and Training* (DHET, 2014) and some other smaller OER developments across the continent (Lesko, 2013).

However, it is difficult to ascertain the importance or impact of many of these initiatives as current studies suggest that the level of engagement with OER remains relatively low not only in Africa (Cox, 2016; Lesko, 2013; Samzugi & Mwinyimbegu, 2013), but across the Global South (Commonwealth of Learning, 2016; Dhanarajan & Porter, 2013; Hatakka, 2009).

But when we talk about the "availability" of OER, it is important to differentiate the fact that beyond the absolute number of OER that might be "generally" relevant to a person in a particular discipline, these OER must also be "specifically" relevant for a lecturer's anticipated use if they are to have utility. As the potential users, it is lecturers' needs that define the relevance of an OER. Additionally, assuming that lecturers can find OER that are relevant to their anticipated purposes, those OER must also meet their subjective quality standards concerning issues of accuracy, completeness and rigour. Only when all three of these criteria – relevance, utility and quality – are met, can it be said that OER are *available* to a potential user. This reminds us that, for lecturers who are developing course materials to teach their students, the "openness" of an OER is rarely more important than the practical, pedagogical concerns surrounding the relevance, utility and quality of *any* educational material.

For lecturers who are potential OER contributors, however, availability refers to the materials that they themselves have developed for their own teaching and could potentially share openly. This would include materials designed from scratch without the inclusion of any other OER, as well as those materials that are revisions of already existing OER or contain remixed components of other OER. In order to determine the availability status of their own materials, lecturers may assess them according to the same criteria that users do: asking themselves whether their materials are relevant for others and of the requisite quality to be useful. If they consider their work too context-specific or niche, or perhaps believe that

---

11   http://www.afrivip.org/
12   http://open.uct.ac.za/
13   http://www.tessafrica.net/

there are already an adequate number of similar materials available on OER platforms, they might feel that their work is not relevant as an OER.

In addition to this, while lecturers may deem the quality of their materials suitable for their own students, they may worry that other academics would view their materials as incomplete or of low quality because they do not contain all of the information or insights that would otherwise surface in their live teaching sessions. Judged by these criteria, the availability status of many lecturers' teaching materials is "unavailable", at least in their current "as is" state. Since most materials are prepared specifically for a "closed" teaching environment, the materials would require some modification before they could be shared openly. This alteration process – transitioning one's materials to a state of OER-readiness (availability) – would require time.

Permission

In addition to concerns around access and availability, HEI lecturers often also lack legal permission to share their teaching materials openly because such work product is the intellectual property of the university (Mtebe & Raisamo, 2014), or the lecturers are unsure of whether they have permission and may be "afraid of breaching intellectual property rights" (Bateman, 2006, p.9).

For OER creation, such legal permission is usually determined by institutional Intellectual Property (IP) policies. In South Africa, most universities have IP policies stating that lecturers' work product is the property of the institution, which aligns with prescriptions laid out in South Africa's Copyright Act of 2008 which grants employers default copyright ownership over employees' work-based creations.[14] At universities, this means that lecturers do not hold copyright over the teaching materials they produce and cannot, therefore, legally share these materials as OER without the permission of the institution (the copyright holder) (Mtebe & Raisamo, 2014). In some cases, it is possible to petition the university for permission to share materials as OER, but the fact that copyright is not automatically placed in the hands of the academic creator means that permission is a substantial hurdle for the majority of South African lecturers who might want to share OER. In many cases, the institution is therefore the potential agent for OER creation (the open licensing and distributing of an educational resource), rather than the individual lecturer.

In cases where lecturers possess copyright over their teaching materials, individual volition may also be influenced by institutional activities that relate to OER. Institutions can seek to promote greater OER engagement by lecturers via various mechanisms and incentives, such as providing technical staff to assist lecturers with OER adoption, resources (e.g. hardware, software, funds) for using/creating OER, recognition for OER use/creation excellence (such as an award) or pro-OER policy declarations. These support mechanisms and incentives are workplace features established specifically to enable or drive OER activity (and thus go beyond the basic provision of electricity, computers and so forth). They represent an institution's formal commitment, or lack thereof, to OER engagement, and may shape individual lecturers' volition in this regard.

---

14   http://roer4d.org/2298

Culture and OER adoption

The values, ambitions, practices and histories of educational institutions can also shape OER adoption in quite different ways. These elements help comprise the social and cultural worlds in which the lecturers operate and deal with questions regarding OER. To understand this in the South African universities we researched, we drew on the literature concerning institutional culture to help us delineate between the various governance, policy and collegial traditions at play.

Our understanding of the concept of institutional culture is defined by two approaches, both of which focus on academic organisations. McNay (1995) defines institutional culture types according to an organisation's relationship to its policies, that is: (1) how loose or tight its policy definitions are, and (2) how loose or tight its control of policy implementation is. McNay posits four institutional culture types:

1. Collegium ("laissez faire"): loose policy definition, loose control of implementation.
2. Bureaucracy: loose policy definition, tight control of implementation.
3. Enterprise: tight policy definition, loose control of implementation.
4. Corporation: tight policy definition, tight control of implementation.

This is a useful schema, but the term "culture" requires a more expansive understanding than that offered by a narrow focus on institutional policy metrics. Hence we also draw on the work of Bergquist and Pawlak (2008), which defines institutional culture types according to multiple variables, including governance style, level of members' personal autonomy, and location of members (virtual/present). Six types of academic institutional cultures are proposed – collegial, managerial, developmental, advocacy, virtual and tangible – though only the first two are relevant in this study context:

1. Collegial: decentralised governance, academic freedom, faculty contributions.
2. Managerial: bureaucracy, hierarchical, efficiency and assessment of work.

We employ "institutional culture" as a broad descriptive concept to help differentiate between complex organisational entities that are constituted by their dynamic interplay between structural (policy, etc.), social (collegial norms, etc.) and agential (level of individual autonomy, etc.) factors. How these three variables combine at any institution helps us determine the kind of institutional culture that predominates there, allowing us to ask how OER-related activity might proceed.

With this in mind, the three institutional culture types that are relevant for this study are *collegial* (decentralised power, high levels of individual autonomy), *managerial* (hierarchical, expansive policy elaboration with tight implementation) and *bureaucratic* (hierarchical, expansive policy elaboration with erratic implementation).

OER scholars acknowledge that lecturers' motivation to engage with OER may be low (Gunness, 2012; He & Wei, 2009), and may be influenced by the prevailing cultural context which includes departmental and disciplinary norms concerning the sharing of teaching materials, colleagues' awareness and knowledge of OER, colleagues' pedagogical mindsets (traditional vs. progressive, risk-averse vs. risk-taking, etc.), colleagues' level of interest in OER (whether one is part of a critical mass of OER adopters, or potentially alone in such activity), etc. (Cox, 2012; Cox & Trotter, 2016; Wolfenden, Buckler & Keraro, 2012). These are the social customs, collegial expectations and disciplinary norms that can cue the behaviour of academics concerning OER, and which academics themselves either reinforce or resist.

For some lecturers, their social and cultural context will play a key role in determining whether they develop the motivation – or volition – necessary to engage in OER activity (Ehlers, 2011; Pirkkalainen, Jokinen, Pawlowski & Richter, 2014). Others, however, may disregard these conditions and base their decisions on their values or their "personal concerns" (Cox, 2016, p.12).

Agency and OER adoption

In addition to the structural and cultural elements shaping OER adoption, lecturers' agency and activity are also shaped by their personal and institutional OER awareness, capacity and values.

Awareness

A number of researchers cite low levels of exposure to OER (Allen & Seaman, 2014) and the lack of OER awareness as a critical factor shaping lecturers' OER activity (Hatakka, 2009; Samzugi & Mwinyimbegu, 2013). Awareness of OER in this study includes an understanding that OER are teaching and learning resources that can be shared, reused and released under an open licence such as Creative Commons (CC). This is an important consideration because lecturers may share their educational materials with colleagues in an informal fashion and download resources from the internet for classroom use without any appreciation of the legal distinction between copyright-restricted educational materials and OER. This may occur in a context of acceptable "fair use" or "fair dealing" practices in which educators use a portion of copyrighted materials for illustrative purposes,[15] or it may go beyond that, stretching the limits of legal acceptability. Thus, while they may engage in downloading and sharing activities that resemble OER adoption activities, the fact that they are not consciously exchanging materials with the kind of open licensing that facilitates open content adaptation and sharing means that, strictly speaking, they are not engaged in OER adoption activity. Awareness of the principles that inform OER adoption therefore constitutes an important component of formal OER engagement and agency.

Capacity

Scholars also suggest that some educators have limited technical capacity to engage with OER (Bateman 2006; Lesko, 2013; Wolfenden et al., 2012). This type of capacity is a more focused set of skills than general computer literacy, because it requires that lecturers (or institutional assistants) possess an understanding of what differentiates OER from other educational materials as well as the technical skills to adapt (revise or remix), curate (include metadata to aid findability) and share these materials on a public platform. They must, therefore, comprehend the role of open licensing and how this impacts internet searching

---

15   Shaikh (2012). Retrieved from https://open.uct.ac.za/bitstream/handle/11427/2306/OpenUCT_Shaikh_Fair DealingInEducation_2011.pdf?sequence=1

(to find OER) as well as materials development (for open sharing of educational resources). The same goes for institutions, if they are the agents of OER creation.

Values

In addition, many of the Southern lecturers who do use OER in their teaching fail to take the next step to create and share their own OER with the rest of the world (Dhanarajan & Porter, 2013; Hattaka, 2009; Lesko, 2013). This threatens to lock them into a "culture of dependency" (Ngugi, 2011, p.284) with the North, relying on theories, concepts and solutions derived from outside of the lecturers' and students' own context. This challenge cannot be met by the efforts of scattered individuals who make the effort to contribute. As Rolfe argues, "central to sustainability is the community and growth of a critical mass of interested individuals" (2012, p.7) and, as Khanna and Basak (2013) state, an enabling OER architecture. Thus, despite the democratic and emancipatory potential of OER, which allows Southern lecturers to broadcast their intellectual and teaching expertise without the mediating influence of publishers, the rapid proliferation of OER may ironically perpetuate a "digital divide" between the South and North rather than overcome it (Smith & Casserly, 2006). Without a critical mass of Southern lecturers using and contributing OER, its potential will always remain just that: potential, never fully realised.

Methodology

This study utilised a mixed-methods approach (Cohen, Manion, Morrison & Morrison, 2007; Maxwell, 2008) to investigate the decisions that lecturers at three South African universities made in their teaching practices as relates to OER. While the sample size of 18 interviewees was relatively small in absolute numbers, respondents were drawn from three quite different universities which, together, broadly represent the characteristics found across South Africa's university sector.

Institutional research context

This study comprised workshop interactions and interviews with academics at the UCT, UFH and UNISA. In a national context of 26 public universities (and no private ones of similar size or mandate), these three possess qualities that, in their different ways, mirror a number of the qualities of the other 23, which makes them useful for comparative purposes.

UCT is a traditional,[16] urban, residential, medium-sized (26 000 students), research-intensive university with a predominantly face-to-face (contact) teaching model. It is comparatively well resourced, historically white (legally so during apartheid) and "privileged" (in South African parlance). It is defined by a *collegial* institutional culture (Czerniewicz & Brown, 2009), characterised by a decentralised power structure in which power does not flow in a top-down fashion, but rather moves laterally between faculties and allows for high levels of individual autonomy amongst the academic staff.

---

16 In South Africa, "traditional" universities offer degrees based on theoretical knowledge, while "comprehensive" universities offer a combination of academic and vocational diplomas and degrees.

UFH is a traditional, rural, residential, small (13 000 students), teaching-intensive university with a face-to-face teaching model. It is comparatively poorly resourced, historically black "African" and "underprivileged". It is defined, as shall be seen, by our interviewees' description of the institution, as having a *bureaucratic* institutional culture, characterised by a top-down power structure in which power is largely exercised by management and administrators, reducing the autonomy of individual academics. However, this power is exercised less through coherent, strategic policy implementation than by arbitrary and excessive "red tape" (from the lecturers' perspective).

UNISA is a comprehensive, dispersed, massive (over 400 000 students), teaching-intensive university with a distance (correspondence) teaching model. It is comparatively well resourced, historically multiracial and modestly privileged. It is defined by a *managerial* institutional culture (Chetty & Louw, 2012), characterised by a top-down power structure in which a relatively strong managerial class exercises power through tightly defined policies and strategies that structure lecturers' latitude and agency.

These three universities possess a broad spectrum of the differentiating qualities shared by South African universities: traditional vs. comprehensive, urban vs. rural, residential vs. dispersed, small vs. medium vs. large, teaching vs. research intensive, poorly vs. modestly vs. well resourced, collegial vs. bureaucratic vs. managerial institutional cultures, historically black/white/multiracial, and various levels of historical privilege.

Research engagement

After obtaining ethical clearance and identifying a local coordinator to facilitate research engagement at each university, we initiated the research process by carrying out OER workshops in March 2015. Each of the workshops included 12–19 participants (43 in total at the three sites) and ran for a day and a half, with the first day devoted to discussing the Open movement, opportunities afforded by OER, and how and where to find OER online. The second day covered practical elements concerning CC licensing, which, for many participants, was completely new information. Participants were also guided through a process of adapting or creating an OER and dealing with the associated technical, legal and pedagogical considerations, which provided them with practical developmental experience with OER.[17]

During the workshops we also provided space for open conversation about teaching practices, disciplinary norms, institutional IP policies, financial resources and so forth. These conversations were recorded and incorporated into our broader understanding of each university's OER context.

After completing the workshops, we conducted one-on-one, in-depth interviews with six selected lecturers at each university, chosen mainly from the workshop participants. At each university we sought to select a diverse group of respondents based on age, gender, race, position and discipline that would, cumulatively, be broadly representative of the institutional teaching staff. The interviews – comprising 50–56 semi-structured questions, depending on the answers given – lasted between 30 minutes and one hour.

---

17 To access the workshop presentations, see http://www.slideshare.net/ROER4D/openness-in-highereducation; http://www.slideshare.net/ROER4D/copyright-creative-commons-49771783; and http://www.slideshare.net/ROER4D/how-and-where-to-find-open-educational-resoures-oer.

Respondent profile

Of the 18 respondents interviewed at the three universities, 11 (61%) were female and 7 (39%) were male. One was a professor, one was an associate professor, six were senior lecturers, six were lecturers, two were postgraduate students (who were also instructors), and two were education consultants connected to a university.

Data analysis and sharing

Upon completing the research, interviews were transcribed and the resulting transcripts compiled for coding according to the concepts identified during the project proposal phase, the literature review and the transcript-processing phase. Data were then collated into themes informed by the literature review relating to the primary and subsidiary research questions (such as OER awareness, use, policies, technical skills, barriers, departmental norms, motivations, perceptions of quality, etc.), annotating them accordingly for analysis.

Interview transcripts as well as results from an accompanying survey[18] have been published[19] along with extensive metadata on the DataFirst Data Portal after undergoing a multiphased quality assurance and de-identification process. The authors and the Research on Open Educational Resources for Development (ROER4D) Curation and Dissemination team checked data files for consistency and correctness, whereafter a de-identification process was undertaken utilising an omission and revision strategy. The dataset was then reviewed by DataFirst to ensure that no overt technical errors existed and no identification of research subjects was possible, either by single or a combination of data points.

The resulting dataset, published under a CC Attribution (CC BY) licence, is comprised of 18 interview transcripts and survey data shared in Excel (.xlsx) format, along with data collection instruments, a dataset description, a project description, and a de-identification overview in PDF format.

Analytical framework

We are not the first to highlight and interrogate the multiplicity of factors shaping lecturers' OER choices, nor the motivations behind those choices. However, many studies present these factors as serialised lists (e.g. CERI/OECD, 2007; Hatakka, 2009; Pegler, 2012), as if there were a sort of equivalence between them. Prior to starting the research, this did not appear to be problematic to us. However, once we started interviewing lecturers at the three universities, three challenges to this conventional approach became clear. First, many of the factors were actually *qualitatively* different from each other, and therefore required careful and consistent delineation. Because some of the factors were within the realm of lecturers' personal control while others were less so, or were out of their control entirely, their responses to our questions made it clear that there were *categorical* differences between these factors that affected how they should be assessed. The varying degrees of control

---

18   This survey was undertaken as a component of ROER4D Sub-project 4. The resulting data are, however, not drawn on in the articulation of this chapter.

19   https://www.datafirst.uct.ac.za/dataportal/index.php/catalog/555

that lecturers had over the many factors shaping their OER adoption decisions had to be incorporated into any analysis of why they may, or may not, adopt OER.

Second, some of the factors that they mentioned were "essential" – in the sense that they had to be present for OER adoption activity to take place (in a universal sense) – while others were idiosyncratic factors that might influence one lecturer's decisions about OER, but not others (in a subjective sense). Thus, in this chapter, we use the term "factors" to discuss only those elements of OER adoption that are essential for adoption activity, while we use the term "variables" to discuss those elements that might be influential, but not essential.

Third, as became clear to us as we conducted research at the three institutions, when it comes to OER adoption in most higher education contexts, there are two potential agents of OER activity: lecturers and the institution itself. While lecturers who develop their own teaching materials may be potential users of OER in that they can incorporate external OER into their teaching materials, they can only be considered potential OER creators if they hold copyright over their teaching materials. In many instances they do not, and copyright is held by their employers, the institution. When this is the case, the institution should be regarded as the potential OER creator because only it has the legal right to license and share the educational materials openly. While the lecturers may have developed the teaching materials that are used for instruction, if copyright belongs to the institution, then the institution is the agent responsible for deciding whether the materials will be made open or not. Because of this – and the fact that our research sites had varying IP policies – we had to broaden the scope of our analysis beyond just lecturers as OER adoption decision-makers and include, where necessary, the institution as well.

To address the challenge of the points above, we developed an analytical framework, which can be described as an "OER adoption pyramid" (Trotter & Cox, 2016), based on what we found in the data. It helped us analyse OER activity in the three university research sites and provided a way for assessing the relative importance of a particular factor on lecturers' (or institutions') OER adoption activities.

OER adoption pyramid

The OER adoption pyramid framework utilises a layered analytical approach, focusing on the factors that are essential for OER activity in an institutional setting, sequenced according to the level of personal control lecturers have over them (from externally determined to internally determined). It reveals and differentiates the roles that they play in making OER activity possible. The value and flexibility of this framework will become clear through the analysis in the Findings section.

The OER adoption pyramid presented in Figure 1 consolidates the essential OER adoption factors into six categories, layered according to the level of control that individual lecturers have over them. From external to internal determination, they are: infrastructure *access*, legal *permission*, conceptual *awareness*, technical *capacity*, educational resource *availability* and personal *volition*.

Under these six terms we can locate numerous other "variables" listed in the literature and mentioned by the interviewees themselves, such as perceptions of OER quality and self-confidence. These variables – though not as determinative of OER adoption at a universal level as the six factors – can also have a powerful influence on OER decision-making by individual lecturers and institutional agents.

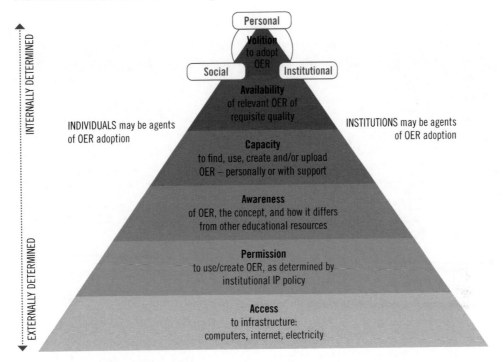

Figure 1: OER adoption pyramid

The pyramid graphically represents the categorical gradations in this external–internal spectrum of factors, and shows how the OER adoption activities of either lecturers or institutions can be assessed with it.

Access

With this in mind, the first factor determining lecturers' or institutions' engagement with OER is *access*. This refers to access to the appropriate physical infrastructure and hardware – such as electricity, internet connectivity and computer devices – necessary for engaging with digitally mediated OER. It is the OER adoption factor that lecturers have the least control over, in that it tends to be determined primarily by state resource capacity and provision (for electricity and connectivity) and institutional resource allocations (for computers).

Permission

The second factor is whether lecturers or institutions have *permission* to adopt OER. For OER use, it is the OER itself – via its licensing provisions – that determines the parameters of how it may be used (whether it can be used in part, or must be used in whole; whether it can be commercialised or not; etc.). For OER creation, it is typically the institution's IP policies that determine whether it is the lecturers (the actual developers of the teaching materials) or the institution itself which holds copyright over the teaching materials, and can therefore share them openly. This legal sharing of educational materials openly is what we call OER "creation".

Awareness

The third factor is the lecturers' or institutions' *awareness* of OER. Essentially, the relevant agent must have been exposed to the concept of OER and grasped how it differs from other types of (usually copyright-restricted) educational materials (Hatakka, 2009; Samzugi & Mwinyimbegu, 2013).

Capacity

The fourth factor is the lecturers' or institutions' *capacity*, or technical and semantic skills, for using and/or creating OER (Lesko, 2013; Wolfenden et al., 2012). This capacity can be manifest in the individual lecturer concerned or found in the form of institutional support services. This characteristic implies that a lecturer or institution enjoys the necessary technical fluency to search for, identify, use and/or create OER, or has access to support from people with those skills.

Availability

The fifth factor concerns the actual *availability* of OER for lecturers or institutions to use or share. The question of availability for a potential user is determined not only by the absolute number of OER in circulation within one's discipline, but by the *relevance* of any particular OER – in terms of content, scope, tone, level, language, format, etc. – for a specific anticipated use (*utility*), and by the *quality* of that OER as subjectively judged by the user (Abeywardena et al., 2012). As mentioned above, one can assume that there are still substantial gaps in the range of subjects covered by OER. This challenge is exacerbated for those seeking to use materials in a language where OER materials are sparse (Cobo, 2013; Zagdragchaa & Trotter, 2017). For potential OER creators, availability refers to whether the agent has – on hand – educational materials that can be shared openly. In most cases, while they may have educational materials that were developed for a specific in-class or correspondence teaching context, they would need to make some alterations to the materials (to upgrade the quality, to broaden the relevance, to establish the open permissions) before sharing them openly.

Volition

The final factor in OER adoption relates to lecturers' or institutions' motivation or *volition*: their desire or will to adopt OER. If the relevant agent enjoys the access, permission, awareness, capacity and availability necessary to engage in OER activity, then volition becomes the key factor in whether or not they will use or create OER (He & Wei, 2009; Pegler, 2012; Reed, 2012; Rolfe, 2012).

The notion of a lecturer's or institution's volition is, however, complicated because – regardless of who holds copyright over the teaching materials – individual volition is potentially shaped by both social context (departmental and disciplinary norms) and institutional structures (policies, strategies and mechanisms), while institutional volition is often shaped by its lecturers' desires and the social context that pertains across multiple sites at the university, as shown in Figure 2 (Cox, 2012; Cox & Trotter, 2016; Wolfenden et al., 2012).

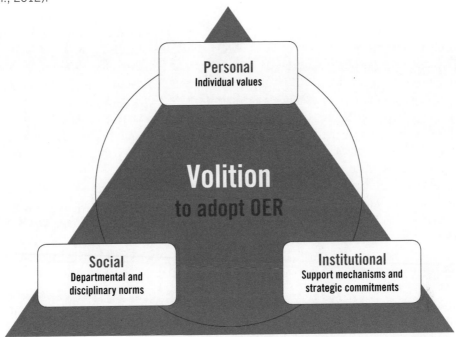

Figure 2: The final factor of the OER adoption pyramid – volition

Individual volition

At institutions where lecturers are the potential agents of OER activity, the elements shaping their individual volition are the personal, idiosyncratic, internal beliefs and practices that have bearing on whether or not they might adopt OER. These include their teaching style (i.e. interactive vs. lecture-based or materials-based), education philosophy, level of self-esteem about their own teaching materials (Beetham, Falconer, McGill & Littlejohn, 2012; Davis et al., 2010; Kursun et al., 2014; Van Acker et al., 2013), level of concern about others misusing or misinterpreting their work, etc. These are interior variables – fears, concerns, desires, aspirations – arising from within the lecturers themselves.

Institutional volition

However, in many cases, the institution possesses copyright over lecturers' teaching materials (Trotter & Cox, 2016). This means that institutional management is in fact the unit of agential analysis regarding the "creation" side of OER adoption. While lecturers have the agency to decide whether to use OER in their teaching, the institution would need to decide whether it wanted to openly license and share the teaching materials that it holds copyright over. This decision would be informed by the managerial leaders' educational philosophies (open vs. closed), strategies for the institution's engagement with students and the public, and desires for enhancing the brand of the institution. It would also be informed by the lecturers' prevailing desires and the social norms of the faculties.

Using the pyramid

The value of the OER adoption pyramid is that it enables a structured comparison of the factors involved in OER adoption at an institutional site, whether the focus is on the lecturer or the institution as the agent of analysis. It also shows that not all factors equally shape OER activity, and therefore should not be treated as such. Furthermore, as will be seen, it also generates opportunities for fruitful assessment and comparison, specifically through OER readiness tables (presented in the Findings), which clearly show which factors act as obstacles or opportunities with regard to potential OER activity at an institution.

While the OER adoption pyramid provides a generalised template for assessing OER activity (or potential activity) at a given institution, it focuses only on the six factors that we argue are necessary for OER engagement. That is, it purposefully keeps a narrow view on only those factors that should be in place for OER activity to proceed. This is a useful starting point, especially when analysing contexts where OER activity is either absent or nascent.

As mentioned above, there are many other variables which influence *how* OER opportunities are approached, understood, embraced or ignored, even if they are not essential as to *whether* OER activity may occur or not. Table 1 shows which variables are associated with each factor, allowing us to see the role they play in the broader categorical distinctions provided here.

Table 1: Variables associated with six OER adoption factors

OER adoption factors	Associated variables for OER users	Associated variables for OER creators
Volition	• Teaching style • Education philosophy • Level of self-confidence in own teaching materials • Institutional incentives and recognition • Social context: departmental, disciplinary and collegial norms concerning using OER • Cost/convenience considerations • Temporal ramifications for use	• Self-confidence in own teaching materials • Concern about others misusing or misinterpreting their work • Impact on public profile • Institutional commitment (policies, strategies) • Institutional support (technical, financial, administrative) • Institutional recognition (promotion, awards) • Social context: departmental, disciplinary and collegial norms concerning sharing one's own materials as OER, including implicit and formal recognition • Temporal ramifications for creation
Availability	• Perception of an OER's: 　– quality (accuracy, completeness, rigour) 　– relevance (in terms of epistemic perspectives, scope, language, format, localisation, etc.) 　– utility (for a specific, anticipated teaching purpose)	• Perception of one's own teaching materials': 　– quality 　– relevance 　– utility (for other educators) Brand concerns: institutions may embark on a formal quality assurance process before sharing OER so as to ensure they bolster the profile of the university

OER adoption factors	Associated variables for OER users	Associated variables for OER creators
Capacity	• Legal knowledge concerning open licensing • Technical skills to search for, identify, download and use (reuse "as is", revise, remix) OER	• Legal knowledge concerning open licensing • Technical skills to openly license one's work and upload (retain and distribute) it for public access
Awareness	• Conceptual understanding of difference between OER and other (usually copyrighted) educational materials – as well as the difference between OER use and "fair dealing"	• Conceptual understanding of difference between OER and other (usually copyrighted) educational materials
Permission	• Parameters of the OER's open licence	• IP policies (institutional) • Copyright policies (national/institutional)
Access	• Internet access • Computer access • Electricity provision	• Internet access • Computer access • Electricity provision

Validity and bias

One of the strategies used to mitigate bias was to engage in conceptual deliberation and in that process we checked each other, thereby holding each other to account. These deliberations occurred between the two main researchers and with the ROER4D Hub team. The concepts were carefully considered and distinguished. This helped to bring in some checks on any bias that may occur, which can be unchecked in qualitative research (Maxwell, 2008). Maxwell also suggests that "rich data should be collected through intensive interviews where every word is transcribed as opposed to some notes taken during the interview" (2008, p.244). In this study all interviews were transcribed.

Findings

In this section we discuss the study findings, using the OER pyramid framework to address the primary and subsidiary research questions. We profile each of the universities according to the relevant OER adoption factors, assessing their level of OER readiness per factor in the process. In this way, we are able to explain why lecturers at three South African universities adopt – or do not adopt – OER.

OER adoption profiles at three South African universities

With the OER adoption pyramid discussion in mind, we profile each of our target universities according to the six factors (access, permission, awareness, capacity, availability and volition) in order to understand how the institutions compare with each other, allowing us to grasp where the critical issues are located with regard to OER activity. Though the profiles relate to a specific time of investigation (2015) and some aspects of the descriptions will change quite rapidly, we also assume that a number of these elements will remain pertinent for some time to come. These profiles should be seen as providing "deep snapshots" of the institutions, rather than timeless renderings.

Access

During our research period, infrastructural access at the three universities coincided with the level of development characterising their geographical location, ranging from robust in urban Cape Town and Pretoria to more fragile in the rural Eastern Cape. Thus, UCT had comparatively good access, with stable, high-speed broadband and Wi-Fi on campus, computers for all staff members, many computer laboratories and terminals for student use, and reasonably stable electricity provision. Its electricity supply was, however, not uninterrupted as it suffered periodic electricity blackouts (or "load shedding", as referred to in South Africa), but at a far less disruptive rate than elsewhere in the country at the time.[20] When asked to describe the level of their access to electricity, computer hardware and internet broadband, all UCT interviewees reported good levels institutionally (on campus) and personally (at home).

By comparison, the level of access at UFH appeared low across the board: it had unstable, low-bandwidth internet connectivity – "in theory fast and stable, in practice slow and unstable", according to one lecturer – and severe electricity challenges. Lecturers reported that they sometimes faced three load-shedding sessions per day, lasting hours at a time, combined with electricity problems internal to the university. As one lecturer indicated, "Especially this year we've been without electricity for like two weeks running on campus." In addition, while academics enjoyed the use of staff computers, many students did not have their own, thus relying on the availability of computers in shared computer labs.

UNISA enjoyed a similar level of access to UCT, but with slightly less predictability in its electricity supply. This good level of access, however, pertained only to academics, as many students did not have reliable access because they live in poor, rural areas with weak infrastructural support, or in urban townships far from the UNISA satellite centres. As we will demonstrate, this discrepancy between academics enjoying good levels of access while many students do not, has an impact on the motivations that UNISA lecturers feel toward adopting OER, which they view as a largely digitally mediated (not paper-based) teaching innovation. As one lecturer shared, "these isolated communities that can only be reached really by post are going to be eliminated or marginalised [if OER are used]. So it is a serious problem and OER requires the internet".

As a point of comparison, when asked what challenges developing countries face with regards to OER use, many respondents mentioned access issues, even if they felt ambivalent about whether their own institutions conformed to the image conjured by the term "developing". This was especially true at UCT, which enjoys a relatively high level of infrastructure provision and stability, where one lecturer asserted, "We're not at all as poorly resourced as people think." Since some UCT lecturers had taught outside the metropole, they were aware of the challenges that other South African students face in this regard. As one said, "You need access to the resource in a sort of manner that's accessible at all times. I've often been in a context where you can't use it because there's a bandwidth issue."

---

20   http://mybroadband.co.za/news/energy/129998-how-cape-town-joburg-prevent-stage-1-load-shedding.html

This is the situation that UFH lecturers deal with as a norm. As one UFH lecturer responded, "if I'm talking in terms of rural areas, which is where we're working, access would be a challenge". This concern for students' varied access capacities was echoed by a UNISA lecturer who said, "We do have regions in the country where the internet access is first class, like Pretoria and Joburg and Durban and Cape Town, but if you go to other provinces like Limpopo and Eastern Cape, which are very rural, then it becomes very difficult to access internet."

In sum, these universities have varying levels of access to the technical infrastructure necessary to support online OER activity. While none of their situations is ideal, the access factor is not an insurmountable obstacle to OER adoption, even if it does influence it.

Based on this information, we can visualise the state of OER readiness for these three institutions according to this access factor for the sake of easier comparison. To do this, we differentiate between five levels of readiness corresponding with a red-to-green colour gradation: red being very low, orange being low, yellow being medium, light green being high and dark green being very high. In Table 2, we assess lecturers' readiness to both use and create OER according to their access capabilities, as well as the institutions' readiness to create OER in the same light.

Table 2: Level of institutions' OER readiness according to access factor

Access: readiness	UCT	UFH	UNISA
If lecturers are agents of OER use	▲▲	◀▶	▲▲
If lecturers are agents of OER creation	▲▲	◀▶	▲▲
If institution is agent of OER creation	▲▲	◀▶	▲▲

	very low	low	medium	high	very high
Key: Level of OER readiness	▼▼	▼	◀▶	▲	▲▲

Permission

While lecturers have the least control over the access factor discussed above, they also have relatively little control over their legal rights over the use or creation of OER. These rights are typically determined by external agents, such as the OER creator who defines the parameters of use surrounding their OER (for lecturers who want to use it) or the lecturers' institutional management which determines who "owns" locally developed teaching materials (for lecturers who want to create OER from those materials).

In contrast to most other universities in the country, UCT lecturers possess copyright on their teaching and learning materials, allowing them to transform any of their teaching resources into OER.[21] The UCT IP policy states:

> UCT automatically assigns to the author(s) the copyright, unless UCT has assigned ownership to a third party in terms of a research contract, in: scholarly and literary publications; paintings, sculptures, drawings,

---

21   http://roer4d.org/2298

graphics and photographs produced as an art form; recordings of musical performances and musical compositions; course materials, with the provision that UCT retains a perpetual, royalty-free, nonexclusive licence to use, copy and adapt such materials within UCT for the purposes of teaching and or research; and film. (UCT, 2011, p.15)

The policy goes on to clarify what this means for lecturers in terms of how they might share their work beyond the classroom, stating: "UCT supports the publication of materials under Creative Commons licences to promote the sharing of knowledge and the creation of Open Education Resources. UCT undertakes certain research projects that seek to publish the research output in terms of a Creative Commons licence" (UCT, 2011, p.15).[22] Furthermore, this opportunity is reinforced by UCT's Open Access Policy, which promotes, among other things, "the sharing of knowledge and the creation of open education resources" (UCT, 2014, p.3). This liberal policy framework is bolstered by the abiding collegial institutional culture through which academics enjoy high levels of autonomy in terms of the materials they choose to use in the classroom, including OER. UCT lecturers are therefore completely free to use and create OER.

By contrast, yet in line with most other South African universities, UFH lecturers do not have permission to share their teaching materials as they wish because the institution holds copyright.[23] As the UFH IP policy states: "The University of Fort Hare claims ownership of all intellectual property devised, made, or created by persons employed by the University in the course of their employment, whether appointed on a permanent or contract basis", which includes "works generated by computer hardware or software owned or operated by the University" and "films, videos, multimedia works, typographical arrangements, field and laboratory notebooks, and other works created with the aid of University facilities" (UFH, 2010, p.5). UFH lecturers are therefore constrained in terms of OER creation. This constraint is exacerbated by the university's bureaucratic institutional culture which often requires academics to seek permission or guidance from university management for new or innovative educational practices such as OER creation (as discussed below). At the moment, the IP policy provides the only guidance at the university concerning potential OER creation activity, which means that such sharing is forbidden. There is, however, "a certain degree of flexibility" as pertains to OER usage, as one lecturer stated. Even though UFH lecturers have their curricula "handed down to [them] pretty much", they are able to incorporate OER into their teaching so long as these resources meet the requirements of the relevant curriculum guidelines.

UNISA lecturers bear the same restrictions as their UFH counterparts in terms of copyrighted work product, with the UNISA IP policy stating: "UNISA is the owner of all IP created by members of staff within the normal courses and scope of their employment" (UNISA, 2012, p.5). However, according to UNISA's OER coordinator – a staff member overseeing the development and promotion of OER activities at the institution, and who contributed to the OER workshop we led – lecturers may petition their relevant tuition committees to allow them to share personally created teaching materials as OER. None

---

22 This does not, however, include "multiple choice tests and exam questions" or "syllabuses and curricula", which UCT retains copyright over. See http://www.rcips.uct.ac.za/rcips/ip/copyright/uct_copyright.

23 http://roer4d.org/2298

of the research participants in this study had, however, heard of this option. While this appeal mechanism does not appear to be well advertised, it does offer an opening for some lecturer-led OER creation.

Furthermore, it is technically possible that the curriculum guidelines and courseware production teams could incorporate OER into their work, though respondents admitted that they often relied on traditional teaching practices with well-known published textbooks and materials. Perhaps most crucially, however, the fact that not all students enjoy reliable access to computers or the internet means that all teaching materials must be printable and deliverable by post so that every student gets the same educational experience. Therefore, should an academic wish to use OER digitally, these resources could only be offered as "additional" or "optional" materials for the online students, and students could not be tested on material covered in those OER since the offline students would not have had access to them. This often leads to lecturers being cautious about using or sharing materials when they do not have explicit permission to do so. As more than one lecturer stated, "I just don't want to do something wrong."

UNISA's OER strategy (UNISA, 2014) envisions a time in the future when OER will be at the heart of its course design. The plan relies on the fact that the university is the owner of a large collection of "intellectual property assets" (i.e. course materials) that it can license openly and disseminate centrally. This creates an interesting opportunity for the university and its teaching staff: while the lecturers themselves do not have permission to share their teaching materials as OER, they may eventually see them incorporated into a broader OER mission under the UNISA brand. This top-down approach to IP management and OER dissemination is consistent with a managerial institutional culture context where the leadership has the mission, strategy, policy control and technical capacity to achieve this goal.

While lecturers at all of these universities are permitted to use OER in their course materials, the IP distinction revealed here – between institutions where copyright over educational materials is vested in the creators (institutional lecturers) versus the employers (the institution itself) – shows that one cannot focus solely on lecturers as the agents of OER activity. As has been seen, when it comes to OER creation/contribution, in many cases lecturers lack the legal permission necessary to make their materials open, even if they want to. In those contexts, it is the institution which is the (potential) agent of OER contribution (Table 3).

Table 3: Level of institutions' OER readiness according to permission factor

Permission: readiness	UCT	UFH	UNISA
If lecturers are agents of OER use	▲▲	▲	▲
If lecturers are agents of OER creation	▲▲	▼▼	▼▼
If institution is agent of OER creation	▼▼	▲▲	▲▲

	very low	low	medium	high	very high
Key: Level of OER readiness	▼▼	▼	◄►	▲	▲▲

Awareness

Unlike the previous factors over which lecturers have relatively little control, they do have a modicum of power over whether they are, or become, aware of OER. This outcome is certainly easier in contexts where other lecturers or managers are discussing OER publicly, raising awareness about it and so forth. But awareness of OER – along with numerous other educational innovations and trends – is obtainable by any lecturer who seeks out knowledge concerning such issues. OER is one of a number of globally current educational topics, featured in educational conference presentations, online discussion forums and pedagogically related journal articles, thus it is "out there" in online public discourse. Whether a lecturer becomes exposed to those discussions in general, and the OER concept in particular, is partially determined by their own knowledge-seeking behaviour. And certainly, if a lecturer has heard about OER but does not fully grasp it, they can easily learn more about it themselves and enhance their OER awareness and knowledge.

At UCT, all of the lecturers interviewed (n = 6) had been exposed to some extent to the concept of OER and broader discussions around "openness" (Open Access, Open Data, Open Science, open government, etc.). This is in large part due to the advocacy of institutional champions and academic units – including the library and the Centre for Innovation in Learning and Teaching (CILT)[24] – which have provided greater understanding of open practice and support for engaging with this approach. There are also institutional activities focusing on open scholarship, ranging from annual globally initiated Open Education and Open Access Week events to regular institutionally initiated workshops, seminars and training sessions concerning specific aspects of open academic practice (including OER). One lecturer, explaining how she came to learn about OER, stated, "If I hadn't attended [the Teaching with Technology] workshops [at CILT], I would never have known about [OER] or have come to some of your seminars here." Others mentioned various digital storytelling and copyright workshops attended, all of which included an OER component.

Furthermore, most of the UCT interviewees had an awareness of the OpenUCT institutional repository,[25] where both academic research outputs and OER are hosted. Thus, on the one hand, the institution itself is aware of OER (i.e. its management is aware), as shown through these awareness-raising and OER-supporting mechanisms (further demonstrated by various UCT policies and the university's signing of the Cape Town Open Education Declaration and the Berlin Open Access Declaration). On the other hand, a good proportion of the lecturers are aware of OER, developed through official activities and the casual sharing of ideas and resources that takes place between many educators. As one lecturer stated regarding her colleagues' level of OER awareness, "People have shared in the past, course links or courses that they think colleagues might be interested in doing, ya … so it's kind of just a part of the field of our work."

In the UCT context, where lecturers possess copyright over the teaching materials they create, the collegial institutional culture places the onus of OER action on individual lecturers. While university management has a working awareness of OER and supports general OER activity, the responsibility for OER action rests with individual lecturers themselves. In this sense, the institution supports OER, but does not mandate it. Thus awareness is very much

---

24   http://www.cilt.uct.ac.za/
25   https://open.uct.ac.za/

optional, and oftentimes incidental. However, the history of OER awareness-raising at UCT has not been characterised by a one-way relationship in which an "aware" management gradually develops awareness amongst its academic staff. In reality, awareness of OER at UCT was initially promoted by a small number of motivated "open champions", primarily in CILT, who not only spread awareness to other colleagues, but spent years cultivating greater awareness amongst the managerial ranks (Czerniewicz et al., 2015).[26] Sustaining this work at UCT has been challenging in the face of resource constraints and fluctuating priorities such as growing the Open Access research-oriented component of the OpenUCT repository.

By comparison, the level of OER awareness at UFH amongst participating lecturers was quite low, signified by the fact that only one participant (the study coordinator; n = 1 of 6) had heard of OER. When asked about her colleagues' awareness of OER, she stated, "Not much. They might know the word, but what it actually entails, I have my serious doubts about that." Another lecturer, when talking about herself, simply said, "I didn't know about it." It is possible that other staff members may have had knowledge of OER, but considering that a number of the workshop participants were from the Faculty of Education – a faculty one might assume to be the most knowledgeable on campus regarding OER as a teaching innovation – we did not think it likely from the indications we received from the respondents. We learned during our literature review, for instance, that there was some OER activity in the UFH Faculty of Education in 2007 and 2011 through the TESSA project (Harley & Barasa, 2012; Thakrar et al., 2009), but none of our participants from that faculty revealed that they themselves had any knowledge of OER. This lack of awareness appeared to be replicated at the institutional (managerial) level, as one respondent shared, "The institution doesn't know about OER as a whole, so it's not a big thing here. There certainly isn't any policy around it. There's certainly no making resources available for you to do these things."

With UFH's bureaucratic institutional culture and a general lack of awareness amongst both individual lecturers and management (revealed in more detail below), there is no natural group or structure at UFH to start raising awareness in a deliberate and organised manner. With little awareness amongst management, there is no official strategy or ambition towards OER, which means that the administration is unlikely to play any role in awareness-raising activities. Given that lecturers lack permission to share their teaching materials as OER, the small proportion of lecturers who are aware of OER lack any formal incentive to spend time raising awareness amongst their colleagues. While they may able to proclaim the virtues of OER use, the fact that they cannot share their own materials as OER does limit its potential appeal in terms of the overall enterprise.

At UNISA, half of the lecturers interviewed (n = 3 of 6) had at least a mild awareness of OER (less than at UCT, more than at UFH), due in large part to the awareness-raising activities of the institutional OER coordinator who organised workshops and seminars on the topic. With her high-level position in the Office of the Pro Vice-Chancellor, the OER coordinator enjoyed a solid level of institutional support in her OER campaigns.[27] This advocacy was supported by a long-term OER strategy (UNISA, 2014) adopted by the institution to promote OER. This strategy was, however, the result of high-level decision-making, and did not involve general

---

26 The CILT-based open champions were often supported with funding from donors such as the Shuttleworth Foundation and the Andrew Mellon Foundation which enabled them to promote OER within a unit, rather than as lone individuals.

27 http://www.unisa.ac.za/Default.asp?Cmd=ViewContent&ContentID=27721

staff members. The strategy calls for far-reaching changes to UNISA's business model, but because it was not yet policy, it did not appear to have been well communicated to the academics. With this in mind, the OER coordinator assumed that her colleagues had "not a clue" about OER, or, at best, their awareness was "limited". One lecturer, when asked about the level of awareness in his department, agreed: "I would just say nobody knows about it."

The majority of participants in our workshop said that they learned about OER through the UNISA OER coordinator's awareness-raising efforts (primarily through prior workshops and emails). A few also learned about OER from other colleagues who had attended prior workshops. In this managerial institutional setting, it was no surprise that much of the OER awareness-raising for individual academics had taken place through an official campaign. The management identified OER as a key priority going forward and was keen for its lecturers to understand more about it. This acknowledgement of the potential of OER might inspire more lecturers to incorporate OER into their course materials, but the fact that the institution holds copyright over teaching materials developed by staff means that this awareness would most likely not lead to academics choosing to share materials openly (as special permission would need to be obtained to do so). Indeed, the management itself would have to lead the way in deciding when and how future course materials were shared openly. Thus, lecturers' awareness of OER may be useful for increasing usage levels at UNISA, but it is management's awareness which dictates the broader strategy towards sharing those lecturers' teaching materials.

Table 4 compares the level of institutions' OER readiness according to awareness, showing high levels at UCT, low levels at UFH and medium levels at UNISA.

Table 4: Level of institutions' OER readiness according to awareness factor

Awareness: readiness	UCT	UFH	UNISA
If lecturers are agents of OER use	▲	▼▼	◄►
If lecturers are agents of OER creation	▲	▼▼	◄►
If institution is agent of OER creation	▲	◄►	▲

	very low	low	medium	high	very high
Key: Level of OER readiness	▼▼	▼	◄►	▲	▲▲

Capacity

While most interviewees stated that they were "fluent" or "highly fluent" in computer literacy (n = 17 of 18), their general technical skills did not necessarily translate into high OER-related capacity, as many were unfamiliar with the processes involved in searching for, identifying, downloading, using, creating, licensing, curating and (re)distributing OER. The presence of technology support staff on campus also did not necessarily mean that they enjoyed OER-related support, as technical staff were not always familiar with OER. The lecturers could build greater OER capacity among themselves (through online tutorials, practice and experimentation), but that would take time. Nevertheless, compared to the three factors discussed above – access, permission and awareness – lecturers have a good deal of control over this, as they themselves can develop their own OER-related capacity through online tutorials, self-practice efforts and collaboration with like-minded colleagues, though this would take time.

At UCT, technical capacity was relatively high, sometimes at a personal level, depending on a lecturer's prior level of engagement with OER, but quite certainly at an institutional level where OER experts were available for consultation and support. For instance, in the regular "Teaching with Technology" workshops that have been offered through UCT's CILT, lecturers were provided with an opportunity to develop their OER skills and given an indication of whom to call upon for support.[28] This included legal support from the university's Research Contracts and Intellectual Property Services, the IP Unit in the Law Faculty[29] and the presence on campus of the legal lead of Creative Commons South Africa,[30] who could advise on the application of CC licensing issues and copyright management of teaching materials. Thus, no UCT lecturer was without access to the necessary technical capacity to engage with OER in a meaningful manner.

This did not appear to be the case at UFH, where some respondents were worried that they might lack the appropriate technical skills to participate in OER use and creation. They were also unsure whether they would be able to find useful assistance on campus, though they assumed that technology support staff could assist. This lack of capacity for OER engagement appears to be the result of both a "traditional" teaching environment (lectures in classrooms supported by "All Rights Reserved" textbooks, and printed materials for students, etc.) and a general lack of awareness around OER (which demands slightly specialised technical knowledge).

By contrast, UNISA academics stated that they were relatively fluent technically because so much of their work was mediated by computers and the internet. Though their teaching materials were provided in printed format to students, lecturers typically interacted with students via email and class-specific online chatrooms. Thus, the environment demanded a certain level of technical ability, some of which could be transferable to OER activity. Perhaps more importantly, the OER coordinator was also available to provide assistance with certain queries, even though the position was more managerial than technical.

There does not appear to be any relationship between the type of institutional culture that predominates at these universities and the level of OER-related capacity they have (Table 5). There is no reason to assume that a collegial one, for instance, has any advantages over a bureaucratic or managerial one in terms of what OER-related skills a lecturer develops. Nor does it suggest that any of them would be more effective in terms of providing institutional assistance to lecturers for OER adoption. While these different institutional cultures shape the processes by which lecturers or institutions develop OER-related capacity, they would probably not play a determining role in their outcomes.

---

28   http://www.cilt.uct.ac.za/cilt/teaching-technology
29   http://ip-unit.org/
30   https://creativecommons.org/author/tobiascreativecommons-org/

Table 5: Level of institutions' OER readiness according to capacity factor

Capacity: readiness	UCT	UFH	UNISA
If lecturers are agents of OER use	▲	▼	◄►
If lecturers are agents of OER creation	▲	▼	◄►
If institution is agent of OER creation	▲	▼	▲

Key: Level of OER readiness

very low	low	medium	high	very high
▼▼	▼	◄►	▲	▲▲

Availability

It is impossible to know, objectively, whether there are relevant OER of the requisite quality (for a specific anticipated use) available for lecturers at these three universities without having them first conduct an exhaustive search for such materials themselves. Most have yet to do that. Most interviewees did, however, believe that there were some useful OER available to them, some of which were discovered during our workshops when we asked participants to search OER portals for content. This process was a revelation for many, as most had never searched for OER via a dedicated OER repository, meaning that they had previously struggled to determine which materials were legally open for reuse and which were closed.

Availability at UCT

All of the lecturers we interviewed at UCT (n = 6) admitted that they had yet to undertake exhaustive searches for OER themselves, but they had some awareness of what was available online. Relevance was, however, a key concern, especially in terms of the degree of appropriateness of the materials in the South African context. Since most OER come from the Global North, many said that they would only want to use OER that is localised. As one lecturer stated, "It needs to be contextualised to Africa." In addition, when asked how they perceive the quality of most OER, half said "variable", that "it ranges", while the other half said that they were not yet familiar enough with what was available online to have an opinion.

When considering whether they themselves had any educational materials that were available to share, the lecturers also expressed relevance and quality concerns. For instance, one Humanities lecturer worried that it would be difficult to express her pedagogical intent through OER:

> I teach through a notion of pedagogy of discomfort … I rely on being in class and also demonstrating to [students] moments when I feel discomfort. And to use myself, I constantly use myself as a teaching example. And that kind of stuff would … get lost. I don't think OER could adequately implement a pedagogy of discomfort and how it is imagined and thought through. It requires interaction with other people. … If something makes me uncomfortable, then boy, there's something there that has to be interrogated. I don't know how OER would deal with that!

Furthermore, when asked to what extent they were concerned about the quality of their teaching materials, they revealed that they were relatively unconcerned about the materials in terms of teaching UCT students in person, but some hesitated at the idea of making them openly available online. Encapsulating this mild caution, one lecturer shared, "I don't really have concerns. I suppose a little bit nervous in case you put something there that's not quite right, but I don't have worries necessarily."

Yet for another lecturer, making her work open would produce great anxiety because of the potential exposure and scrutiny that could result from her colleagues. She was worried about "being found out and humiliated. It's taken a long time for me to actually feel like I belong at the university, like that I'm good enough to be there". Thus, for some, it may not be a simple decision to turn their in-class teaching materials into OER because it would expose materials that were developed for a student audience to the general public, including professional colleagues whose esteem they may be anxious to maintain.

UCT's collegial institutional culture obligates lecturers to deal with these anxieties individually. This is because the university has adopted a hands-off quality assurance approach that locates responsibility over quality concerns with the individual creators. It is based on the "pride of authorship" model (Hodgkinson-Williams, 2010; Hodgkinson-Williams et al., 2013), which assumes that the concern for one's own reputation would ensure that the creator only shares materials of the highest possible quality. It also assumes that anyone employed in a teaching capacity at UCT would produce materials that are of sufficient quality for sharing. This approach is efficient and economical from the administration's perspective,[31] but for one interviewee it was not adequate. This lecturer would have preferred if there was "some process of evaluation for the production of [OER]".

Availability at UFH

Lecturers at UFH shared similar concerns regarding the relevance of OER for their particular teaching needs as users. One stated, "there's a lot of stuff that's just not applicable. Some of the stuff has snippets that are nice. [But] I seldom find things that I want to use as a whole. Because they just don't fit into what I want them for necessarily". Connecting the notion of relevance with that of quality, the lecturer went on to say, "Quality is as context demands."

Other UFH lecturers agreed and were even more pointed in their criticism of the OER they had seen. "Often there are flaws in them," one said, "so I'm very concerned about the quality of my teaching." Another equivocated, saying OER quality was "on a range ... you know, you get some really good stuff and you get some stuff that's questionable". The key reason was because "OER ... isn't peer-reviewed and there's not much in terms of quality control ... I would imagine that the perception of many academics would be that, well, it's not really an accredited space, so you know, you don't know what the quality is".

This concern about the fact that most OER is not formally peer-reviewed is shared by many others in Africa (Mawoyo & Butcher, 2012) and elsewhere (Windle, Wharrad, McCormick, Laverty & Taylor, 2010). In comparison to the peer-review process that

---

31 According to Hodgkinson-Williams (2010, p.14), materials uploaded onto UCT's former OER portal (OpenContent) were "only moderated to check for potential third-party copyright infringements. Users are encouraged to rate the items on the University's OpenContent site; this being the most democratic and inexpensive (albeit risky) QA process". That was the case when OpenContent was still running. The new OpenUCT repository (which curates both OER and Open Access content) does not have a rating or review mechanism.

characterises research article production through academic journals, most OER do not go through a similar quality assurance process, thereby reducing their comparative level of attractiveness for potential users. However, it is worth stating that, for most of the UFH respondents we spoke to (n = 5 of 6), this was a relatively hypothetical concern since most had not engaged with OER prior to the workshop. It may be possible that some of these concerns would be allayed with greater exposure to OER.

However, as potential OER creators (which, technically, they are not, since they do not hold copyright over the teaching materials that they create), UFH lecturers did not question that their work might be relevant for others. They assumed it would be, but worried about the amount of time and energy it would take to make their materials open. As one lecturer stated, "That would mean a lot of work trying to package it in a generic way that is not suited to a particular course. It's one thing to make a particular resource and make it available to your own students and spend an hour or two or three hours on it. To package it for [the public] … with a shell and all the connections that would make it generic would take 10 times the amount of time."

Regarding whether they were concerned about the quality of their own teaching materials, two lecturers said they were concerned and therefore would not want to share their work as OER just yet; two others said they were mildly concerned and would have to reassess their work with an eye to making it public before doing so; and another two said they were not concerned and would be happy to share their resources.

Availability at UNISA

Compared to their UCT and UFH colleagues, UNISA lecturers were quite positive about the potential of OER in their teaching, especially with regards to relevance. One enthused that, in her practically minded discipline which is well known for collegial sharing, "There's a whole lot of stuff available. And everybody wants to show how to do things." Others, such as one Humanities lecturer, admitted that, although there were "endless resources" in his broader field, there were "far fewer resources" on his own particular niche subject matter. He found that, because one person at Yale had provided a useful course on his topic, no one else seemed to be bothering to contribute other materials with a different perspective.

Others also wished more locally relevant materials were available. For one lecturer, the OER she found online tended to be "Northern … not so much in South Africa". Another stated similarly: "A lot of international resources, but it would be great to find something more local. … It's very difficult to find something for a South African context to refer [students] to."

Another lecturer believed that OER could provide greater opportunities to fulfil his pedagogical intent: "It can do a lot, because I mean, already there are so many things that you've got, you've got videos, you've got slides, you've got your case presentations, so you can apply to different pedagogical contexts, depending on what you want to do in class."

A similar range of responses emerged in UNISA lecturers' assessment of OER quality. One lecturer was satisfied with the OER she had engaged with because the materials came from reputable institutions: "The little bit that I've encountered has generally been quite good, especially because it's been stuff from Harvard and Yale." Others admitted that they "still have to look at it more carefully"; they "don't know. I haven't seen enough to kind of evaluate it. I'm hoping there's some kind of quality standard".

By contrast, one avid OER user suggested that there should not be an externally determined quality standard (such as would be enforced through a formal quality assurance mechanism), but rather that "that's where there's a shifting role of an academic now. It's not producing the content, but it's being able to deliberate what is good content, what is good knowledge".

For those with greater familiarity with the breadth of OER offerings, their view on OER activity was mixed. This appeared to be the case across the universities. As one UNISA lecturer stated, "Some [OER] are good, some are completely … it's not actually bad quality, it's just quality that you won't use in a university set-up. It's not material that you would integrate into a course. It may be stuff that will be for a lay person in a community."

As potential OER creators (which, again, they are technically not because they do not hold copyright over their teaching materials), UNISA lecturers did not question whether their work might be relevant for others. As distance educators with class sizes that can often be in the tens of thousands, they did not doubt the potential relevance or impact of their work. Most also felt a certain level of confidence in their materials because they are vetted by the relevant tuition committees, acting as a sort of quality assurance mechanism for all UNISA teaching materials. Yet, as would be expected, some nevertheless do feel a little anxious about the quality of their materials, especially when they think that they might be made publicly available. As one lecturer shared, "My concern is how I will be judged and reviewed. You know, the opinions and obviously peer review and the commentary you'll get afterwards."

Presumably, however, the UNISA administration (the copyright holders of the lecturers' teaching materials) feels that its lecturers have created relevant, high-quality materials that can be shared openly under the UNISA banner. Having developed an OER strategy (UNISA, 2014) with the intention of collating, quality-checking and licensing its collective teaching materials as OER, the institution's centralised approach would likely take steps to assuage any anxiety lecturers feel about the process.

Table 6 summarises the level of OER readiness at each institution when focused just on the availability factor, but in sum "availability" is a complicated OER adoption factor because it includes the perceptions of both users (lecturers) and creators (lecturers or institutions) in considering the quality, relevance and utility of potential open teaching materials.

Table 6: Level of institutions' OER readiness according to availability factor

Availability: readiness	UCT	UFH	UNISA
If lecturers are agents of OER use	▲	◄►	▲
If lecturers are agents of OER creation	▲	◄►	▲
If institution is agent of OER creation	▼	◄►	▲

	very low	low	medium	high	very high
Key: Level of OER readiness	▼▼	▼	◄►	▲	▲▲

Volition

The final factor in the OER adoption pyramid is motivation – or volition. A prominent theme in OER studies (He & Wei, 2009; Pegler, 2012; Reed, 2012; Rolfe, 2012), motivation is often invoked as a variable when analysing the dynamics around OER adoption in the Global North, since many of the other factors discussed above are often already positively met. Thus volition – at an individual and/or institutional level – is often the key to whether lecturers at well-resourced universities use or create OER. And it is the factor that lecturers (as OER agents) have the most personal control over, because volition emerges from within, even as it is influenced from without.

As discussed above, when it comes to assessing volition, it is important to determine who the agent of OER action is. For OER use, it is typically a lecturer. For OER creation, it can be either a lecturer (as at UCT) or an institution (as at UFH and UNISA). However, in either case, individual and institutional volition shapes the other, even if only one is ultimately responsible for action. This will become clearer through the analysis below.

Volition at UCT

As has been shown, UCT lecturers enjoy good access to all of the prior factors governing potential OER adoption. Thus the key factor for them in deciding whether to actually use or create OER is their individual sense of volition.

All six interviewees we spoke to at UCT said that they had used OER, but only three had done so deliberately (seeking out materials from the Khan Academy, TED Talks and MIT OpenCourseWare). The other three had happened to use materials from Wikipedia and Wikimedia Commons, though they did not explicitly understand that these were OER. In addition, two of the interviewees said that they had created OER, while four said that they had not.

Motivating variables

The reasons that UCT lecturers gave for adopting or not adopting OER were often idiosyncratic. Users said that they often found pedagogical value in OER. As one lecturer said, "when there are concepts that are difficult to explain, seeing how other people have explained it is useful, providing another perspective". Thus OER opened up a multiplicity of perspectives or voices that may have been missing, especially if their courses were based on a single textbook.

Some also believed an open approach embodied their educational values. One of the lecturers stated that they saw adopting OER "as a social responsiveness activity", which is one of UCT's key performance-assessment pillars. Others liked the fact that they "don't have to pay for the stuff". The aspect of no cost to the user was appreciated by all lecturers at UCT.

Demotivating variables

Those who had yet to use OER also provided idiosyncratic rationales for their approach towards OER. For instance, one young lecturer who said that he had not been in his department long enough to grasp what the departmental social norms or expectations were, saw this as a "mindset" problem, in that many non-user lecturers – especially "older" ones, in his estimation – had a different conception of what higher education is or should be. "I think the greatest [obstacle to OER adoption] is a traditional view of ... higher education versus a very swiftly changing picture of higher education."

This same young lecturer had a particular "mindset" when it came to OER creation. His relative youth made him feel possessive over his work. He said, "There's a lot of my own research that went [into this course material] and sometimes I really feel a bit selfish. Like I don't just want to give my brand new research away, although, you know, it is for the greater good of education." This was a person who was very interested in the Open movement, but because of his career positioning felt contradictory imperatives regarding the sharing of his work.

Another lecturer felt a tension in terms of competing values, which in this case emerged from her experience of the financial opportunities afforded by possessing full copyright over one's work.

> I'm the treasurer of our national organisation and because the university's been forced to jack up their copyright, our association gets a whopping great big cheque these days from DALRO [the Dramatic, Artistic and Literary Rights Organisation], the licensing rights [group in South Africa]. So it's actually made our association fairly wealthy. So as the treasurer I suddenly became aware of how copyright can be really a big income, you know, for our association. And also what the implications of that might mean, actually encouraging my colleagues around different South African universities to put an article from our journal into the curriculum, in order to generate income for the association.

Even though most of the resources she referenced in this statement were research outputs, the financial implications of this experience also shaped her perception surrounding the potential value of owning full copyright over her teaching materials.

Institutional culture

Because UCT lecturers work in a context characterised by a collegial institutional culture, this means that they enjoy a high degree of personal autonomy in their actions. But it also means that the norms and expectations established by their colleagues have a powerful influence on the types of activities they end up choosing to engage in. For instance, lecturers face significant peer pressure to turn out research publications on a regular basis, with this expectation forming part of the prevailing social "ethos" (Trotter, Kell, Willmers, Gray & King, 2014, p.85). This is not the case yet for the adoption of OER across the institution, but individual lecturers revealed that their social (departmental and disciplinary) context did, at times, inspire OER engagement.

One lecturer stated that, because she worked in a department with colleagues who believe in openness, "I have to actually model the practices that have been a part of the mission of the centre." She has internalised the open ethic herself and influences others she works with to do the same. "It's a two-way street," she said.

She also found inspiration in the OER that her virtual, disciplinary colleagues were creating, realising that she could create similar OER too. "For me it was, 'Oh, other people have made this and that.' And you see their resources on Twitter and you think, 'actually, I can do that'. That's a personal thing, as well as that it's supported by my colleagues." Her casual, everyday engagements with OER allowed her to gain confidence in sharing her own materials.

Institutional policy de/motivations

In addition to the interior, social and cultural influences discussed above, lecturers were asked about their views about whether an institutional policy encouraging OER adoption would influence them. Their responses ranged from dismissive to enthusiastic. Thus, one senior scholar retorted, "It would probably annoy me! It depends who wrote the policy and what the purpose is! But ya, being told what to do … unless it's aligned with what I want to do."

This sentiment was refined by another UCT lecturer who stated, "The problem with making it a policy – maybe I'm thinking in too stringent words about policy – is that if people had to do it, it would become a burden. You want it to be driven by teachers who are interested in it I think." These responses illuminate the ideals of the collegial institutional culture from which they emerge. They valorise individual interest and effort, and are premised upon the idea that internal motivation provides the strongest and most sustainable catalyst for action.

Those who imagined long-term OER contribution in their careers thought that a policy focusing on awards and recognition would be a positive feature. The perception was that this would help raise the profile of the work that otherwise goes unnoticed by the institution. However, in a context where lecturers enjoy positive policy, financial, technical and legal support – all of the structural elements necessary for engaging in OER activity – UCT lecturers did not appear to view these institutional policies and support mechanisms as "motivating" factors in their OER (or non-OER) activity. They saw them instead as "hygienic" factors (Herzberg, 1987; Pegler, 2012) that simply create the conditions necessary for *allowing* them to act on their own personal volition regarding OER, should this exist.

The OER support mechanisms in place at UCT are typically the product of hard-fought advocacy efforts by individual OER champions and initiatives that did not push for a mandate on OER activity (Czerniewicz et al., 2015; Hodgkinson-Williams et al., 2013), but were founded instead on the principle that action that stems from personal volition produces the best, most sustainable outcomes. Hence, despite the challenge of mobilising large numbers of adopters, the approach adopted at UCT appears to be consonant with the collegial nature of the institution.

Volition at UFH

In contrast to the UCT scenario, there appeared to be an almost total absence of volition regarding OER activity at UFH, mostly due to the fact that OER had never been able to move beyond the limits of the other factors relating to OER adoption, especially awareness (for lecturers and the institution) and permission (for lecturers). Without these factors being positively met, there has been little opportunity for motivation to develop at the university, among either management or lecturers.

When asked who had used OER, one interviewee said yes and five said no, but even the interviewee who answered in the affirmative had only used OER to check the quality of her own teaching materials, not to incorporate them into her teaching practice. Meanwhile, none of the interviewees had ever created OER.

Motivating variables

Most of the UFH interviewees reported that the values underpinning OER adoption aligned with their personal teaching philosophies and pedagogical interests. One lecturer imagined tapping into OER to "get perspectives other than my own". A colleague concurred, redirecting the focus of OER to providing "the students with something other than what I had been teaching them". The ease with which OER can be obtained offered a new source of potential teaching and learning materials, which was considered worth exploring. Thus, for UFH respondents, OER volition was seen as something to act upon in the future rather than something that existed prior to our workshop intervention.

Demotivating variables

All of the UFH lecturers were able to list a number of obstacles that would stand in the way of actual OER engagement (beyond the awareness and permission issues already discussed). This helped explain the current lack of volition as well as the challenge of building it going forward.

One obstacle to the development of OER volition was that of pedagogical approach, in that, as one lecturer shared, OER is "viewed as an add-on, as opposed to an integrated approach and so there is the perception that it's going to just add more work … rather than being part of the teaching itself".

Another challenge was that some lecturers worried that if they shared their teaching materials as OER, they might be misused or misconstrued by users. Though the lecturers accepted that others would be free to revise their materials if the necessary open licences were associated with those resources, they did not necessarily want to be associated with the resulting content if it misrepresented their views. One veteran lecturer stated that she had felt embarrassed by how another educator had used her presentation materials (which she had shared privately), making her think twice about releasing her teaching resources in the open with her name on them.

In addition to these challenges, it did not appear that the institution, which holds copyright over the lecturers' teaching materials, had any volition to share them as OER, at least according to the interviewees. Summing up the perspective of all of the interviewees, one said, "I don't think the university has any vision in that regard. I don't just mean absence of positive vision. It's just not something [that is on their radar]." This lack of volition is most likely due to the fact that, like most lecturers on campus, university management appeared to be similarly unaware of OER as a concept. When asked about the level of awareness administration had about OER, one said, "Little to none. Because I don't think most people know what it is."

Institutional culture

In a university with a bureaucratic institutional culture where strategies and policies are inconsistently applied (at least in the minds of the interviewees, as revealed below), UFH lecturers said that rather than waiting for strategic direction from the administration for their teaching activities, they often relied on the norms and practices determined by, primarily, colleagues within their departments or, secondarily, their disciplines.

At the departmental level, colleagues' relative lack of OER awareness did not provide inspiration or expectation for independent OER adoption. While one person in the Education

Faculty said that the level of "sharing is reasonably high" in the faculty, it was "not in an OER context, so it's an informal approach to sharing". Another colleague agreed, stating, "in my discussions with people from the Education Faculty, there's not a lot going on there".

At the disciplinary level, lecturers did not always find interest or support for OER. For instance, one lecturer stated that the Law Faculty, in which he works, "is designed around commercial economic interests. Law is generally geared towards the protection of individual proprietary interests. OER is a threat to this way of thinking".

But beyond these departmental and disciplinary concerns, the lecturers also suggested that the broader institutional mores discouraged pedagogical innovations such as OER. This stems from what one described as a "conservative academic culture", or what another called a "static group thing, where people aren't open to interrogating what their role as a teacher is, or what the role of text is … in their teaching practice". They suggest that there are "in-built institutional and philosophical constraints", essentially meaning that "change is difficult", especially with regards to a disruptive pedagogical innovation such as OER.

Furthermore, this aversion to sharing appeared to go beyond OER. As one lecturer stated, "There is I think a reluctance to just share … not until you've published it." While this assertion relates to the sharing of research outputs, it was seen by lecturers as a useful indicator of the tepid reception OER sharing would most likely also have.

Summing up the institution's challenge from a more global perspective, one lecturer suggested that the academic culture at UFH was not unique, that "a large number of lecturers or academics in developing countries would tend to … favour traditional methods of teaching rather than thinking outside the box. So it's a conceptual leap".

Institutional policy de/motivations

If none of the agents of potential OER activity have the necessary volition to engage with it, might a policy change that? In response to this question, lecturers revealed the challenges of using policy as an instrument of motivation in a bureaucratic institutional culture. Many were dubious of the value of a policy, particularly in terms of how it would be operationalised.

> No, it wouldn't [help]. Wait a minute. A policy [which says] 'this is our policy and you're now supposed to do this and this and this'? It wouldn't. If somebody in management had a vision or somebody in the university had a vision, a policy was created, that policy resulted in a support structure – an active, friendly support structure – that might influence it. But not because it's a policy on paper. In fact, probably the contrary. Because we are an institution full of policies that are either not applied or applied on a discretionary basis.

Some lecturers were concerned about the impact a policy would have on educators' own sense of volition. "My opinion is that policy breeds compliance, but doesn't build … it doesn't get the kind of approach that you want. So yes … people might become compliant and they might just put something up for the sake of it, but then I think there's a compromise of quality and a compromise of real intellectual sharing." Others were ambivalent, but thought that a policy could lead to some positive outcomes, such as a way forward for individual lecturers to share their educational materials.

While there appeared to be an overall perception that policy would add to lecturers' sense of burden, there was also the sense that it could also clarify responsibilities and provide an opening for individual action. "Enabling policies are few and far between. They're normally there to monitor and constrain. So I'd want one that was very open and brought across the point that we're in a situation where the sharing of knowledge is a positive thing."

Addressing the question of policy, we asked UFH respondents if OER volition could be somehow incentivised. Most believed that it could, though this would require awareness and vision on the part of the administration, which did not yet exist. Nonetheless, it was suggested that some measures, such as incorporating OER activity into performance assessment processes, could help. Another thought that a good incentive would involve "some sort of recognition", which could spur a sense of competitiveness between colleagues.

Others thought that the real "incentive" would be to see other colleagues adopt OER as part of their community's work practice. This could be initiated with support from the institution and maintained through collegial interaction. Once under way, it could be sustained through a community of practice which would help raise awareness through "exposure to benefits". As one lecturer stated, "If I was surrounded by adopters of OER, I would certainly be more creative in my use of same. I am not surrounded by such influences."

At UFH, the sensitivity to peer activity appeared to have a powerful impact on lecturers' sense of what they thought they should be doing as educators. While there were those who also preferred to act independently, most looked to what their peers were doing to guide their actions, which may be due to the lack of strategy and direction provided by the administration. This stands in contrast to the more individually minded behaviour of lecturers at UCT and the more managerially directed approach at UNISA, which we will now examine.

Volition at UNISA

UNISA lecturers revealed a modest level of personal motivation to engage in OER activity. This appeared to be as a result of the advocacy and training efforts of the OER coordinator, an open-minded approach to teaching methods informed by the unique challenges of correspondence-based distance education, and a solid level of institutional support. Lecturers' personal volition at this university, with its managerial institutional culture, did not, however, appear to have a major bearing on whether or not they ultimately engaged with OER. What mattered most were management's desires – or *institutional* volition. With an IP policy (UNISA, 2012) that precludes UNISA academics from sharing their teaching materials as OER, the institution itself has become responsible for OER creation, a responsibility that it has said it intends to act upon (UNISA, 2014).

When asked who had used OER, five interviewees said yes and one said no, though two of the five admitted that they had done so inadvertently, not knowing that the materials were OER at the time (it only became apparent to them during the workshop that they had used OER before). In addition, one interviewee said that he had created OER and five said that they had not. However, upon further discussion with the interviewee who said that he had created OER, we determined that, even though he had made a variety of videos open to the broader UNISA community via the university's e-learning platform, these materials were not, strictly speaking, OER, because they were not open to the public and, legally, only the university could openly license them as it held copyright over these resources.

The six interview respondents (and 17 workshop participants) we interacted with at UNISA revealed a high degree of interest in OER as it was a concept that was promoted by the institution. Our workshop was one of many that occurred during the year for staff members, raising awareness about OER and providing practical training on how to identify, use and share OER.

Motivating variables

For many interviewees, their interest in OER stemmed from the fact that the underpinning open ethic aligned with their own educational philosophies. As one stated, "Education should be free actually. So I'm not really that much concerned about sharing [i.e. not fearful to share]. I think we should share as academics so that education is provided freely to everyone." Another colleague agreed, going so far as to say that, once UNISA lecturers learned about the virtues of OER, they would need no further incentives to embrace it.

Nevertheless, others saw quite specific, implicit incentives for OER use, such as its pedagogical value. "In an OER, you can bring together several different thinkers in the field and then put them together and then expose your student to a wider range of thought."

There was also personal value for the lecturers in terms of saving time, boosting quality and raising their personal profiles amongst their peers, serving as a kind of "marketing" function.

Demotivating variables

The lecturers that we interviewed did not focus on the same kinds of demotivating variables with us as was common at the other universities. That is, since they worked in a context with a managerial institutional culture, they tended to attribute any demotivating elements to the institution and its policies, or lack thereof. We discuss those variables below.

Institutional culture

The interviewees described their context as broadly open to innovating with OER. Summing up his colleagues' interest in OER, one lecturer stated, "There's a fairly good excitement, because we know that there is potential within the online environment and there's no resistance from anyone here in our department to go online."

Nonetheless, they also recognised that there were challenges to raising the levels of interest in OER amongst academic staff. The first, and perhaps the greatest, obstacle was dealing with the legalities surrounding OER in a managerial institutional culture where lecturers do not hold copyright over their teaching materials, and where they do not always know the rules and protocols of engaging in non-traditional practices. More than one lecturer stated that they were worried about what the institutional response would be to them deviating from the usual curricular practices, while others cautioned that even though some individuals might be interested in sharing their work, many others would be hesitant due to a more cautious mindset.

> Developing country people actually think that their stuff's not good enough
> and there's a feeling around … like this deficit view of their work. And whereas

the Global North is more – I think ego, but not always ego – but it's like they've got that confidence. It's like an online confidence that they're sharing and they're like, 'I made this and I did that.' And I find even with research, African scholars are very ... they don't like to critique one another's stuff, to put themselves out there.

Institutional policy de/motivations

When asked to what extent a policy on OER would influence their choice to create and share OER, all respondents had strong, though varied, opinions. For three of them, policy was key. One lecturer stated without hesitation: "Well I'd have to abide by it, for sure. They're quite strict about policy and procedure. [After all,] we're quite disciplined as an institution." Another colleague agreed, "but [only] if we had the time and resources available". This sentiment was echoed by the most pro-OER practitioner of the group, who wanted a policy because it would place some level of responsibility with the institution. "I think if the policy can drive infrastructure change and align things up in terms of the organisational structure where money is invested, in terms of resources, then definitely. I think it would become a motivating factor for us in terms of targeting or setting ourselves targets and goals."

Though one lecturer believed that sustainable OER adoption should emerge from "one of your personal traits, to want to do something like that", she did acknowledge that "the most common answer would be an incentive" and that a "monetary incentive always encourages some sort of response". Another lecturer concurred, saying that "other" staff members (though not he himself) are heavily influenced by financial and temporal incentives, such as monetary incentives based on key performance areas and time off.

Others were more hesitant about the value of a policy if it restricted educators in any way. They preferred an environment that was enabling and encouraging rather than limiting. One of the more established lecturers dismissed the idea of a policy approach, believing that individuals would do what they wanted regardless of policy, and that individual values and mindset were more predictive of how lecturers would respond to OER.

At the time of writing, UNISA had not developed a formal OER policy, but the lecturers were aware that the university had some level of ambition for greater institution-wide OER engagement (due to the hiring of an OER coordinator and the provision of OER workshops). They were just not sure what that ambition entailed. Lecturers shared their anxiety about being in the dark regarding the administration's OER plans.

For this reason, some would prefer that the institution not only communicate clearly to the staff about OER, but take greater responsibility for promoting it. "For me the most critical thing is the institutional-driven issue. Because if it drives it, then ... everything else – the lack of skills, capacity, the capacity for academics to engage with these environments – [will be dealt with]." This idea applied not only to individual action, but seemingly to every level of the university. As one lecturer explained, operating in a policy-driven environment meant that his "department won't really do anything until they get a proper directive or policy or something from the management".

While UNISA does not yet have an OER policy, it does have an OER strategy (UNISA, 2014), which has shaped a number of activities to date. The OER strategy reveals a high level of institutional volition regarding OER use and creation, based on moral and practical grounds. According to the strategy: "OER cannot be considered as marginal, socially acceptable, nice-to-have activities. They must be integrated into mainstream institutional processes if we wish to harness the true potential of OER in our transformation process and if the shift to this paradigm is to be economically and practically sustainable" (UNISA, 2014, p.4). With this perspective in mind, management has developed a comprehensive strategic approach to the incorporation of external OER into UNISA courses, as well as the sharing of UNISA courses and course components as OER.

In addition to the OER strategy, the university has committed financial, intellectual and technical resources to this ambition. It established the position of OER coordinator in the Office of the Pro Vice-Chancellor,[32] initiated a series of workshops and training sessions to increase academics' OER literacy, signed the Paris OER Declaration and the Berlin Open Access Declaration, and formalised a collaboration with the OER Universitas (Singer & Porter, 2015) as a founding anchor partner (UNISA, 2014).

These high-level initiatives reveal that the most meaningful action regarding OER is located within the managerial strata at UNISA, where policy and other structural elements are controlled. Personal volition and cultural norms might create greater buy-in for the academics whose outputs will be marshalled for the management's ambitions, but these are not the modes of motivation that will in all likelihood scale and sustain activity at UNISA. In this context it appears that institutional volition matters most.

Table 7: Level of institutions' OER readiness according to volition factor

Volition: readiness	UCT	UFH	UNISA
If lecturers are agents of OER use	▲	▼	▲
If lecturers are agents of OER creation	▲	▼	◄►
If institution is agent of OER creation	▼▼	▼▼	▲▲

Key: Level of OER readiness

very low	low	medium	high	very high
▼▼	▼	◄►	▲	▲▲

In sum, while UNISA lecturers are the proper unit of agential analysis for OER use, this is not the case for OER creation. University management, as the copyright holder of the institution's teaching materials, fills that particular role. However, unlike UFH management, which has no apparent ambition to share its teaching materials openly beyond the university, the UNISA administration has developed an explicit plan to openly share its vast collection of content. The materials would be released under the UNISA brand, allowing it to "extend its reach and entrench itself as a major knowledge producer and distribution hub for higher education" (UNISA, 2014, p.4). While lecturers' volition regarding OER creation will likely not make a major difference in whether or how this is achieved, they will nonetheless be able to participate in a large-scale, collective OER creation process that would likely make a much more substantial contribution to OER provision than the voluntary, individualistic approach at UCT, should UNISA's OER strategy be operationalised.

---

32   These positions – of OER Coordinator and Pro Vice Chancellor – were staffed and operational at the time of research, but have since been removed, potentially affecting the institution's commitment to OER activity going forward.

Discussion

In this section, we discuss in greater detail the answers to our research questions and distil the key implications of our findings. First, we consolidate the knowledge we have gained about the factors shaping OER adoption and how their differentiation through the OER pyramid aided in our analytical work. Second, we briefly discuss the importance of identifying the proper units of agential analysis when it comes to OER use and OER creation. Third, based on the insights gained from the prior two points, we compare the three universities' levels of OER adoption readiness. Fourth, we consider the role that institutional culture plays in shaping lecturers' adoption of OER. Through these four sections, we are able to answer our two subsidiary research questions: (1) Which factors shape lecturers' OER adoption decisions? (2) How does an institution's culture shape lecturers' adoption of OER?

Lastly, bringing together all of the insights that have emerged from this research, we then answer our primary research question: Why do South African lecturers adopt – or not adopt – OER?

Factors shaping OER adoption decisions

When we began our research, we knew that OER adoption would be influenced by a number of factors and assumed that some would be more important than others at different institutions. This assumption was borne out in our research. However, as we analysed these factors in detail, it became clear that some were essential for OER activity, while others were simply sub-components within broader factor categories that influenced *how* adoption took place or not, but not *whether* it did.

Based on the data emerging from our research, we developed the OER adoption pyramid which consolidates the myriad essential OER adoption factors into six categories: access, permission, awareness, capacity, availability and volition. They are layered sequentially, moving from factors that, from the lecturers' perspective, are largely externally defined to those that are more individually determined. The pyramid visualises the relationship between these factors and highlights the fact that, ultimately, only agents who possess all six of these attributes at the same time (even if in some modified or attenuated fashion) can engage in OER activity.

We found that the pyramid offered a useful schema for analysing OER adoption activities (or their potential) at each university. It allowed us to impose a measure of order and clarity over a number of factors that had previously appeared random, idiosyncratic or even equivalent in importance. The pyramid allowed us to sequence and prioritise these factors in order to facilitate better comparability across institutions and a clearer understanding of the relationship between these various factors.

Thus, while we believe that we have identified the six essential factors determining *whether* OER adoption can happen in any HEI context, the specific factors shaping (enabling, motivating or impeding) OER adoption decisions at the three universities are discussed below according to the research questions guiding this study.

Unit of agential analysis: Lecturers or institutions?

When we initially framed our research questions, we were heavily influenced by our experiences at our home institution (UCT), with its collegial institutional culture and an IP policy that allows lecturers to hold copyright on their teaching materials. This means, regarding OER adoption decisions (for use and creation), we assumed lecturers would be the units of our agential analysis.

As we learned more about the other two research sites, we realised not only that they had different institutional cultures, but that they had IP policies which made the institution the unit of agential analysis when it came to OER creation. The implications of this realisation for us were profound in that they required assessing OER activities (and their potential at a site) from a very different perspective than we had anticipated. Having initially prioritised the agency of lecturers for both use and creation, we then broadened our scope to include institutions as potential agents of creation.

Though this made for a cumbersome analysis at times – tacking back and forth between the two agents – it clarified who was responsible for what in potential OER adoption activities and sharpened our understanding regarding what was possible at a given site.

OER adoption readiness at three South African universities

The OER adoption profiles discussed above shed light on how the six factors of the OER adoption pyramid shape OER engagement at each of the three universities examined in this study. While these profiles are intended to clarify where the obstacles and opportunities lie regarding OER use and creation for both lecturers and institutions, we can also visualise these profiles in a concrete way that allows for clearer comparative analysis. These distillations can then provide a useful shorthand for assessing each university's "OER readiness" for use and creation.

In our research, we asked a variety of questions to ascertain the level of OER readiness for each of the institutions, as discussed in detail above. However, the questions necessary to assess an institution's OER readiness according to the six factors can be reduced to those listed in Table 8. The answers to these questions not only allow us to create the OER readiness tables that follow, but also allow other researchers to conduct similar investigations at the institutions that they are interested in assessing.

Table 8: Questions to ask OER users and creators – whether lecturers or institutions – to assess OER readiness at an institution (starting from the bottom factor)

Factors	Questions for potential OER users	Questions for potential OER creators
Volition	• Do you have any desire to use OER?	• Do you have any desire to create and share your teaching materials as OER?
Availability	• Have you found OER online – of acceptable relevance, utility and quality – that you can use?	• Do you hold copyright over teaching materials – of necessary relevance and quality – that you could license and share as OER?

Factors	Questions for potential OER users	Questions for potential OER creators
Capacity	• Do you know how and where to search for and identify OER? • Do you know how the different CC licences impact the ways in which you can use an OER?	• Do you know how to license your teaching materials so that they can be shared as OER? • Do you know where (on which platforms) you can upload your materials as OER?
Awareness	• Do you have any knowledge of or experience with OER? • Do you understand how CC licences differentiate OER from traditionally copyrighted materials?	• Do you have any knowledge of or experience with OER? • Do you understand how CC licences differentiate OER from traditionally copyrighted materials?
Permission	• Do you have permission (from your curriculum committee, etc.) to use OER for teaching? • Does the desired OER allow you to use it in your specific context (e.g. no CC-ND licences on items that will be sold as course material)?	• Do you possess copyright over teaching materials that have been developed at your institution?
Access	• Do you have (stable) electricity provision? • Do you have (stable) internet connectivity? • Do you have the necessary computer hardware for OER adoption?	• Do you have (stable) electricity provision? • Do you have (stable) internet connectivity? • Do you have the necessary computer hardware for OER adoption?

With the answers to the above questions in hand, we can create colour-coded OER readiness tables showing the universities' varying levels of OER readiness according to three key elements:

- the six factors of the OER adoption pyramid;
- the potential agent of OER activity (lecturer or institution); and
- the particular focus of OER adoption (use or creation).

As above, we differentiate between five levels of readiness corresponding with a red-to-green colour gradation: red being very low, orange being low, yellow being medium, light green being high and dark green being very high. These assessments are based on the evidence discussed in the profiles above.

OER readiness if lecturers are the agents of OER use

Table 9 shows the universities' levels of OER readiness when lecturers are viewed as the agents of potential OER use. Following the layered sequence of the pyramid – examining factors moving from the base of the pyramid to the top – we see that all the universities have the necessary infrastructural access for lecturers to engage with OER use, though access at UFH is less stable than at UCT and UNISA. All provide the lecturers with good levels of permission to use OER in their coursework, with UCT and UNISA even encouraging them to do so. OER awareness amongst lecturers is quite variable, ranging from relatively high at UCT to very low at UFH and medium at UNISA. A similar profile emerges for lecturers' capacity to use OER: high at UCT, low at UFH and medium at UNISA. For availability, the levels shown are based partially on what lecturers said they believed to be the case for them, a determination which was, in many cases, hypothetical due to a lack of prior searching for OER. Thus we rated OER use availability for lecturers at UCT as high, at UFH as medium and at UNISA as high. Lastly, lecturers' volition to use OER ranged from high at UCT and UNISA to low at UFH. One of the key reasons for the low volition at UFH was low OER awareness.

Table 9: Level of OER readiness by factor if lecturers are the agents of OER use

OER adoption factor	UCT	UFH	UNISA
Volition	▲	▼	▲
Availability	▲	◄►	▲
Capacity	▲	▼	◄►
Awareness	▲	▼▼	◄►
Permission	▲▲	▲	▲
Access	▲▲	◄►	▲▲

	very low	low	medium	high	very high
Key: Level of OER readiness	▼▼	▼	◄►	▲	▲▲

The virtue of Table 9 is that it reveals, at a glance, the comparative strengths and weaknesses for each university regarding potential OER use amongst lecturers. This means that it not only provides a visual depiction of the current state of affairs at each university, but opens up possibilities for those who would seek to increase OER use at a given site through some sort of intervention. For instance, if a person, group or funder wanted to try to increase OER use at UFH, then they would do well to focus on raising lecturers' awareness, as it is very low at the institution and has knock-on effects regarding capacity and volition.

OER readiness if lecturers are the agents of OER creation

OER use is just half of potential OER adoption activities. The other half is OER creation. As has been seen, institutional IP policies govern whether lecturers are allowed to create OER or not. Thus we need to visually distinguish between lecturers' use and creation activities at each university. Table 10 shows the universities' levels of OER readiness when lecturers are viewed as the potential agents of OER creation.

It is not necessary to repeat the analysis for each factor here as we did for Table 9, but we will point out the key insights from this visualisation. The first is that, due to IP policies that vest copyright over lecturers' teaching materials in the institution, lecturers at UFH and UNISA have very low levels of permission to create OER. While lecturers at these two universities may theoretically have the possibility of appealing to university management for permission to release selected materials as OER, for the most part the IP policy represents a high legal barrier to OER creation. It also contributes to the low and middling levels of OER awareness, capacity and volition at these two universities. This stands in contrast to the situation at UCT, where lecturers hold copyright over their teaching materials and are encouraged by the administration to share them openly.

Table 10: Level of OER readiness by factor if lecturers are the agents of OER creation

OER adoption factor	UCT	UFH	UNISA
Volition	▲	▼	◄►
Availability	▲	◄►	▲
Capacity	▲	▼	◄►
Awareness	▲	▼▼	◄►
Permission	▲▲	▼▼	▼▼
Access	▲▲	◄►	▲▲

	very low	low	medium	high	very high
Key: Level of OER readiness	▼▼	▼	◄►	▲	▲▲

Secondly, despite the medium levels of awareness, capacity and volition at UNISA, the lecturers already possess teaching materials that are relatively highly "available" because they have all been through rigorous quality control processes run by their tuition committees. This gives lecturers a high degree of confidence in their materials for their own students, and for others outside the institution, if the materials were ever licensed and distributed openly.

OER readiness if institutions are agents of OER use

If we consider the institution as the agent of OER activity, a different picture emerges. For instance, what if we imagine universities as the agents of potential OER use? This is not a scenario that is discussed much above, and it is not a common activity at an institutional level, but certain HEIs globally are exploring this role (Liew, 2016; McGreal, Anderson & Conrad, 2016). However, at most universities, including those of this study, the responsibility for developing teaching materials rests with the lecturers themselves, though their decisions may be informed by institutionally mandated curriculum guidelines and committee decisions. For the most part, when talking about OER use, it is the lecturers who are the real and potential agents of activity, not the institution (hence we have not visualised this graphically as a relevant possibility).

It is, however, not inconceivable that the institution would want to make direct decisions about the teaching materials that are used in their classes, and they could conceivably demand that OER is used by lecturers. UNISA's OER strategy does encourage this, but it has not been operationalised as yet.

OER readiness if institutions are agents of OER creation

While institutions are rarely the agents of OER use, they can certainly be agents of OER creation due to the fact that many of them hold copyright over their lecturers' teaching materials. This means that, if they so desire, they can license this content openly and share it publicly. Table 11 shows the three universities' levels of OER readiness when the institution is viewed as the agent of potential OER creation.

The key insights here are that UFH and UNISA both have permission, through their IP policies, to share their lecturers' teaching materials. The institutions hold copyright over these materials, so they would be free to license that content openly. By contrast, UCT has chosen not to retain copyright over such teaching materials, rather assigning it to the individual lecturers who created it (except in the case of Massive Open Online Courses; see Czerniewicz et al., 2015). While the university holds a "perpetual, royalty-free, nonexclusive licence to use, copy and adapt such materials within UCT for the purposes of teaching and or research" (UCT, 2011, p.15), this does not allow it to share or distribute these materials beyond UCT, where the activity of open licensing pertains.

Table 11: Level of OER readiness by factor if the institution is the agent of OER creation

OER adoption factor	UCT	UFH	UNISA
Volition	▼▼	▼▼	▲▲
Availability	▼	◀▶	▲
Capacity	▲	▼	▲
Awareness	▲	▼▼	▲
Permission	▼▼	▲▲	▲▲
Access	▲▲	◀▶	▲▲

	very low	low	medium	high	very high
Key: Level of OER readiness	▼▼	▼	◀▶	▲	▲▲

In addition, the volition these institutions possess for creating OER is quite different in each case. UCT has not demonstrated any interest as an institutional entity in creating OER itself, and leaves this to individual lecturers to pursue. UFH has yet to show any interest in doing so, though it could do so in the future. UNISA has, however, revealed in multiple ways that it is very interested in using its copyright-holder status to create OER.

In sum, these OER readiness tables provide a quick, useful visualisation of the otherwise complex details that make up each institution's OER adoption pyramid profiles. In examining the three tables, we can quickly grasp where the obstacles and opportunities lie for OER use and creation between lecturers and the institutions. They also remind us that OER researchers must be mindful of who the potential agent of OER activity is when assessing OER readiness in institutional contexts.

Institutional culture and OER adoption

When we started this research, we wondered whether different cultural configurations might have an impact on OER adoption. Since we believed that there were relatively low levels of OER adoption amongst lecturers in the country, we thought this might be explained by some large-scale force, such as cultural influence. Knowing that different universities are typified by differing institutional cultures made this question seem all the more pertinent. Thus one of our research questions was: How does an institution's culture shape lecturers' adoption of OER?

To answer this, we employed the notion of institutional culture as a broad descriptive term to differentiate between complex institutional entities that are constituted by their dynamic interplay between structural (policy, etc.), social (collegial norms, etc.) and agential (level of individual autonomy, etc.) elements. How these three variables combined at any institution helped us determine what kind of institutional culture predominated there. It allowed us to understand how these different institutional cultures shaped each university's relationship with the six OER adoption factors, suggesting potential approaches for them to deal with challenges associated with the factors.

However, as shown above, the three institutional culture types that we engaged – collegial at UCT, bureaucratic at UFH and managerial at UNISA – did not possess any inherent preference for or hostility towards OER adoption. Indeed, we found culture to be an agnostic element in OER activity, and free of any predictive value regarding such adoption. However, we did find that culture had a powerful influence on how OER decisions were handled at an institution, especially with regards to the factors of permission and volition. For instance, the decision whether lecturers are granted or denied copyright over teaching materials serves to reinforce or contradict the prevailing sense of lecturers' rights vis-à-vis the institutional culture.

Thus, at UCT with its collegial institutional culture – defined by decentralised power and high levels of individual autonomy – individual lecturers are empowered to act on their own volition regarding OER. This means that the spirit of the culture aligns with the IP policy, suggesting that there will be greater sustainability for an innovation such as OER because adoption activities have been located in the space where they have the highest likelihood of success: with individual lecturers themselves. In other words, there is a crucial connection between permission (who holds copyright) and volition (who wants to act on that permission). If they are not the same agent, this creates a challenge for sustained adoption practices.

At UFH, with its bureaucratic institutional culture – defined by a top-down power structure where policies are inconsistently implemented and thus largely unsuccessful (from the lecturers' perspective) in terms of contributing to a coherent strategy – lecturers do not know whether or how they might proceed with OER adoption. They themselves do not have permission to create and share OER, but the institution (the copyright holder of their materials) has no ambition to share them as OER. This is due, in part, to the fact that few lecturers or administrators have much awareness of OER. Thus, this contradiction – of an institution (the agent) holding copyright (permission) over a vast collection of educational materials without any ambition (volition) to leverage them – remains a secondary concern to that of the simple fact that not enough people at UFH are aware of OER. If that changes, then the contradiction could be reviewed from a fresh perspective and the two parties – lecturers and management – could discuss a way forward. Nevertheless, while lack of awareness is currently the primary obstacle to OER adoption, the bureaucratic institutional culture raises general concerns about the relationship between permission and volition.

At UNISA, with its managerial institutional culture – defined by a top-down power structure that governs through tightly defined and implemented policy instruments – the management has both the permission and volition to engage in OER adoption activity. Thus, while lecturers may use OER in their course materials, they will not be responsible for turning them into OER. The institution will have to take responsibility for that, though it will likely harness the intellectual and labour resources present in the lecturers to ensure that the OER produced conform to the standards set by management. This means that, while lecturers are relieved of the opportunity to create OER themselves, they may still end up participating in a broader OER creation process. From an OER adoption perspective, this alignment promises the highest likelihood of success in a managerial institutional culture.

Why South African lecturers adopt – or do not adopt – OER

While the previous insights emerged as a result of our effort to answer a series of research questions surrounding lecturers' engagement with OER, our primary research question was: Why do South African lecturers adopt – or not adopt – OER?

To answer this, we have to deconstruct the question into its constituent parts because adoption in this study context refers to both use and creation. It will be clearer if we treat each separately, differentiating between those who have used OER versus those who have not, and those who have created versus those who have not.

a) Why do some South African lecturers use OER?

While the majority of our respondents had never purposefully sought out OER to use in their teaching, those who had did so for the following reasons (listed according to the level of personal control that they had over these factors and/or variables, moving from greater to lesser control):

- Personal values: using OER was consistent with their educational philosophies, such as the belief that all education should be free.
- Pedagogical utility: there was educational value in using OER because it provided students with additional resources to consult and multiple perspectives through which to engage an issue.
- Social norms: the use of OER was part of the departmental ethos, where colleagues discussed, shared and used OER as a matter of common practice.

In addition, some of these lecturers mentioned that the materials were free of charge and the convenience of accessing them openly online as reasons why they were drawn to them. (These variables may influence OER use, but they fall outside the list of "essential" factors that determine *whether* lecturers can use OER or not.)

b) Why do some South African lecturers not use OER?

While the majority of respondents had never purposefully sought out OER, some had found them inadvertently (usually by accessing Wikipedia or YouTube prior to having any awareness of OER as a concept). Also, while all of the respondents had permission to use OER in their teaching, the primary reason why they had not used OER was simply lack of awareness: many had never heard of it, or, if they had heard of it, did not understand what it meant.

This means that most lecturers who have not yet used OER have not *chosen* not to do so, but have rather lacked the knowledge necessary to make an informed decision about it. However, those who were aware of OER cited a number of reasons why they had yet to use such materials:

- Lack of interest: it was mentioned only by one lecturer who did not believe in the Open movement, but a sentiment likely shared by many who remain sceptical of OER.
- Pedagogical challenges: it is hard to incorporate OER into a highly interactive teaching style.
- Social norms: departmental curriculum development relies more on going through old notes and current research publications than consulting teaching resources from outside the university.
- Lack of relevance: this is a concern about resources being relevant for the African context.
- Lack of institutional support: some did not know who to contact for help.
- Lack of capacity: many did not know where to find OER, or were intimidated by the sheer number of OER to sift through.
- Lack of legal clarity: some were not sure what the institutional policy on OER use was (though this could likely have been quickly remedied through some investigation).
- Copyright concerns: a number worried about inadvertently infringing others' copyright because they did not understand the implications of various licences.

Additionally, these lecturers mentioned that "lack of time" was a big obstacle to their use of OER, though we interpreted this to mean "a lack of personal priority" (and thus comprising a subjective statement about time, not an objective one).

c) Why do some South African lecturers create OER?
Only a few respondents had actually created OER, but their reasons for doing so ranged from altruism to self-promotion to a variety of other reasons:

- Personal values: creating OER was consistent with their educational philosophies, such as the belief that all education should be free.
- Personal visibility-raising opportunities: OER sharing allowed lecturers to stake a claim to a field, demonstrating their current academic approach.
- Networking and crowdsourcing opportunities: allowed lecturers to connect with others, especially those whose work they were incorporating into their own OER.
- Pedagogical utility: it helped improve the quality of their materials because they anticipated the resources would come under heavier scrutiny than experienced in their own course settings.
- Social norms: the creation of OER was part of the departmental ethos, where colleagues discussed, used and created OER as a matter of common practice.
- Institutional incentives: financial grants were available for turning closed materials into open resources.

d) Why do some South African lecturers not create OER?
The majority of respondents had never created OER. The primary reasons why they had never created OER were due to:

- Lack of awareness: many had never heard of it, or, if they had heard of it, they did not understand what it meant.
- Lack of permission: no lecturers at UNISA or UFH have permission to share their teaching materials as OER because the university holds copyright over those materials.

This means that most non-creators have not *chosen not* to create OER, but rather that they lack the legal permission and awareness of the concept necessary to make such a decision. However, those (at UCT) who did have permission and were aware of OER cited a number of reasons why they had yet to create them:

- Lack of motivation: it is not a high priority, thus no action.
- Protective and possessive: difficult to just give away one's work.
- Lack of confidence: they expressed personal fears of embarrassment and exposure.
- Fear of misuse: they worried that others may misuse the materials.
- Pedagogical challenges: some believed that a highly interactive teaching style would be challenging to reproduce through materials that would be shared openly.
- Social ethos: their departmental norms were a key reason for not creating OER.
- Loss of revenue: disrupts potential revenue stream from copyrighted materials for lecturers.
- Materials not ready: some materials were seen as provisional, in need of testing and refinement through classroom interactions before sharing.
- Lack of legal knowledge: there were concerns about copyright and licensing.
- Lack of familiarity: they were unaware of where to find open platforms for uploading materials.

They also mentioned "lack of time", suggesting that OER creation would be a competing priority amongst many others, and that it was not yet a priority for them.

However, even with the reasons articulated here, most UCT non-creators did not see themselves as actively "choosing" not to create OER. While they did indeed have permission to create OER and were aware of the concept at some basic level, the fact that they worked in departmental or disciplinary contexts where the creation of OER was uncommon meant that they were never confronted, in any meaningful sense, with the need to make some sort of decision about whether they would create OER or not. They acknowledged that they had such a choice (at an abstract level), but the social norms and activities that defined their working environment never raised the issue of OER creation to a level that required a deliberate, conscious decision. Such an overt decision would most likely occur in a context where OER creation was the norm, where there was social pressure to do the same, and where one would have to justify non-action. Thus, it is worth keeping in mind that, for many non-creators, inactivity may result as much from OER creation being a passive "non-issue" as it does from them being hindered by various obstacles or not having the requisite volition.

In addition to the reasons given above for non-creation, lecturers at UFH and UNISA (who lack permission to contribute) suggested a few other reasons why they, or their colleagues, would not create OER, even if they had permission:

- Lack of interest: some were unpersuaded by the values of the Open movement and saw no pedagogical advantages to OER over traditional materials.
- Concern over misuse: they worried that users would misinterpret materials.
- Concern over attribution: they were concerned that authors of OER would not be properly acknowledged.
- Lack of necessity: because a number of high-powered academics have already contributed OER in their direct fields of study, further contribution feels redundant.
- Lack of incentive: institutions do not recognise OER creation in academic performance assessment for promotion purposes.
- Lack of support: sometimes there is no site of institutional support for OER creation.
- Lack of capacity: they needed more technical skills and open licensing knowledge.
- Lack of access: there was unstable internet and electricity for staff members on campus, but especially for students off campus.

In sum, we can see an important pattern emerge when it comes to OER volition when considering why lecturers use or create OER. Once all of the factors are in place for positive action, lecturers who adopt OER do so for moral, pedagogical, social, practical and self-promotional reasons. Sometimes one of these reasons is enough, but adopters usually embrace more than one. Some of these coincide with the moral, pedagogical and financial claims made by the Open movement concerning the value and utility of OER. However, as noted, the virtue of these claims has yet to be acted on by most of the adopters' colleagues.

Additionally, the question of OER volition must extend to the institutional management if it holds copyright over lecturers' teaching materials. Considering that this characterises the situation at most South African universities, it would be useful to understand more about managers' motivations (on which we can only speculate here).

Conclusion

This research project originally started with an ambition of understanding whether cultural and social contexts influenced lecturers' motivation to adopt OER at South African universities. This perspective was informed by a sense of how OER decision-making takes place in our own institutional context where individual lecturers have a great deal of freedom and autonomy in using and/or sharing OER. However, by investigating the phenomena at two South African universities besides our home institution, we learned that the cultural and social contexts were among the last issues lecturers dealt with in their OER decision-making processes. A number of other factors exerted a powerful influence on their deliberations before these cultural and social issues could even be considered, suggesting that there is perhaps a layered sequence of externally-to-internally determined factors shaping OER adoption, of which the cultural and social issues were relatively marginal. This realisation revealed a variety of crucial insights.

First, our research at three different types of HEIs revealed that the *factors influencing OER engagement* should not be understood as serial, equivocal factors, but as sequentially related factors which must all meet a certain minimum threshold at the same time for an institution to be considered "OER ready". If any of these factors – access, permission, awareness, capacity, availability or volition – fall below a critical minimum of operational acceptability, it will probably influence OER decision-making and activity at the institution.

Second, due to the different approaches to IP at the three study sites, we learned that, when it comes to OER decision-making, both lecturers and institutions may be the appropriate *units of agential analysis*. While lecturers at UCT are the agents of potential action for both OER use and creation, at UFH and UNISA the lecturers are the agents for potential OER use, while the institutions are the agents of potential OER creation. This distinction has profound implications for the kinds of strategies that might be advocated for greater OER activity in these differing contexts.

Third, the type of *institutional culture* that exists at a university will have a powerful impact on the types of options institutions have for engaging with OER. Even though institutional culture is not a readiness "factor" in the sense that access or awareness is (because OER activity can proceed under any type of institutional culture), it provides insight into the type of opportunities that exist for promoting OER activity. Thus, in a collegial context, it may be best to promote individual lecturers' agency because this coincides with the broader values of the institution. In a bureaucratic institutional culture, it may be best to grant individuals the freedom to act as agents on their own, but as members of departments and units where adoption is institutionally supported, so that a critical mass of adopters can cue broader adoption behaviour. Finally, in a managerial context, it may be best to involve high-level management in establishing guidelines and directives for activities, as this might encourage cohesion and buy-in from the primary agents of strategic action who can ensure its future sustainability.

Fourth, the *social contexts* shaping OER adoption are varied for lecturers, depending on the type of institutional culture that manifests at their universities, as well as the departmental and disciplinary norms that inform their work. While it is generally true that a positive OER environment will encourage individual activity, it does not determine that this will necessarily take place. Likewise, many individuals adopt OER in social isolation, departing from the pedagogical norms that abide in their departments or disciplines. Thus the social context is potentially an influential element of individual volition, but not necessarily a determining factor as to whether OER adoption will take place or not.

Lastly, we have learned that the "openness" of an OER is rarely more important than the practical, pedagogical concerns surrounding any educational materials' relevance and quality in terms of a specific intended use. While the ethic behind this openness may correspond with a potential user's personal educational values, it does not override the necessity that the materials meet other subjective standards of relevance, utility and quality. In this respect, for many educators OER do not comprise a special class of educational materials which are exempt from scrutiny due to their open status. Rather, like any traditional educational resource that is being considered for use, they exist in a competitive space populated by a myriad of open and closed materials which are assessed and selected according to primarily pedagogical criteria (relevance, utility and quality).

Similar thinking applies to lecturers' evaluation of their own teaching materials in terms of potentially making them open, but in this regard lecturers are typically guided by two key principles: they believe in an open educational ethic, and they find that there is pedagogical utility in going through the process of making materials open (especially in anticipating greater scrutiny, and therefore improving the quality of their work). Their motivation to create OER may also be supported by sharing a positive social environment with their colleagues, helpful institutional incentives (such as financial grants to create OER), the opportunity to network through sharing, and the chance to boost their own professional profile through sharing teaching materials.

Acknowledgements

The authors would like to thank Kerry de Hart at UNISA and Renée Coetzee at UFH for their assistance with research efforts at their institutions. We express our gratitude to Linda van Reyneveld at the University of Pretoria, Robert Schuwer at the Fontys University of Applied Science in the Netherlands, and to Kerry de Hart for their very helpful reviews of this chapter.

We would also like to extend our thanks to the wonderful network of ROER4D researchers and mentors who inspired us intellectually regarding OER adoption issues in their particular contexts, specifically Sanjaya Mishra, Batbold Zagdragchaa and David Porter. Lastly, we offer our profound thanks to Cheryl Hodgkinson-Williams and Michelle Willmers of ROER4D for their detailed review and invaluable feedback on this chapter.

References

Abelson, H. & Long, P. (2008). MIT's strategy for educational technology innovation, 1999-2003. *Proceedings of the IEEE, 96(6)*, 1012–1034. Retrieved from http://dspace.mit.edu/handle/1721.1/49866

Abeywardena, I. S., Dhanarajan, G. & Chan, C. S. (2012). Searching and locating OER: barriers to the wider adoption of OER for teaching in Asia. In *Proceedings from the Regional Symposium on Open Educational Resources: An Asian perspective on policy and practices*, 19–21 September 2012. Penang, Malaysia. Retrieved from http://oerasia.org/index.php?option=com_content&view=article&id=106&Itemid=71

Allen, I. E. & Seaman, J. (2014). *Opening the curriculum: Open Education Resources in U.S. higher education, 2014*. Babson Park, MA: Babson Survey Research Group & The William and Flora Hewlett Foundation. Retrieved from http://www.onlinelearningsurvey.com/reports/openingthecurriculum2014.pdf

Atkins, D. E., Brown, J. S. & Hammond, A. L. (2007). *A review of the Open Educational Resources (OER) movement: Achievements, challenges and new opportunities*. Menlo Park, CA: William and Flora Hewlett Foundation. Retrieved from http://www.hewlett.org/wp-content/uploads/2016/08/ReviewoftheOERMovement.pdf

Bateman, P. (2006). *The AVU Open Educational Resources (OER) architecture for higher education in Africa: Discussion paper*. Paris: Organisation for Economic Co-operation and Development. Retrieved from http://www.oecd.org/edu/ceri/38149047.pdf

Bateman, P. (2008). *Revisiting the challenges for higher education in Sub-Saharan Africa: The role of the Open Educational Resources movement*. Nairobi: OER Africa. Retrieved from http://www.oerafrica.org/system/files/7781/revisiting-challenges-web-2_0. pdf?file=1&type=node&id=7781

Beetham, H., Falconer, I., McGill, L. & Littlejohn, A. (2012). *Open practices: Briefing paper*. Oxford: Jisc. Retrieved from https://oersynth.pbworks.com/w/page/51668352/ OpenPracticesBriefing

Bergquist, W. H. & Pawlak, K. (2008). *Engaging the six cultures of the academy: Revised and expanded edition of The Four Cultures of the Academy*. San Francisco: Jossey-Bass.

Boston Consulting Group. (2013). *The Open Education Resources ecosystem: An evaluation of the OER movement's current state and its progress toward mainstream adoption*. Boston, MA: Boston Consulting Group. Retrieved from http://www.hewlett.org/sites/default/files/ The%20Open%20Educational%20Resources%20Ecosystem_1.pdf

Butcher, N. (2009). *Deconstructing OER and its potential for African higher education*. Report for OER Africa. Nairobi: OER Africa. Retrieved from http://www.oerafrica.org/system/ files/7775/butcher-deconstructing-oer-and-its-potential-african-higher-education.394e6403-89ad-48d5-8e66-13735ff9684d_0.doc?file=1&type=node&id=7775

Butcher, N. (2011). *A basic guide to Open Educational Resources (OER)*. Vancouver: Commonwealth of Learning. http://unesdoc.unesco.org/images/0021/002158/215804e.pdf

Butcher, N., Hoosen, S. & Mawoyo, M. (2015). *Open practices in higher education: Trends and possibilities for Africa*. OER Africa Report. Nairobi: OER Africa. Retrieved from http://www.oerafrica.org/system/files/9954/2015-02-13-openness-african-he-edited. docx?file=1&type=node&id=9954

Carson, S. (2009). The unwalled garden: growth of the OpenCourseWare Consortium, 2001-2008. *Open Learning: The Journal of Open, Distance and e-Learning, 24(1)*, 23–29. Retrieved from http://dx.doi.org/10.1080/02680510802627787

Centre for Educational Research and Innovation / Organisation for Economic Cooperation and Development (CERI/OECD). (2007). *Giving knowledge for free: The emergence of Open Educational Resources*. Paris: OECD. Retrieved from http://www.oecd.org/edu/ ceri/38654317.pdf

Chetty, G. & Louw, T. (2012). Managerialism or collegialism? The evolution of these approaches and perceptions thereof in higher education in South Africa. In *Proceedings of the 13th Annual International Academy of African Business and Development (IAABD) Conference* (pp. 353–367), 15–19 May 2012. Casablanca, Morocco. Retrieved from http://eprints. covenantuniversity.edu.ng/4110/1/2012-%20IAABD%20Conference%20Proceedings%20 (Page%20173-183).pdf

Clements, K. I. & Pawlowski, J. M. (2012). User-oriented quality for OER: understanding teachers' views on re-use, quality, and trust. *Journal of Computer Assisted Learning, 28(1)*, 4–14. Retrieved from http://onlinelibrary.wiley.com/doi/10.1111/j.1365-2729.2011.00450.x/ abstract

Cobo, C. (2013). Exploration of open educational resources in non-English speaking communities. *The International Review of Research in Open and Distributed Learning, 14(2)*, 106–128. Retrieved from http://www.irrodl.org/index.php/irrodl/article/view/1493

Cohen, L., Manion, L. & Morrison, K. (2007). *Research methods in education*. London: Psychology Press. Retrieved from https://islmblogblog.files.wordpress.com/2016/05/rme-edu-helpline-blogspot-com.pdf

Commonwealth of Learning (COL). (2016). *Open Educational Resources in the Commonwealth 2016*. Vancouver: Commonwealth of Learning. Retrieved from http://oasis.col.org/bitstream/handle/11599/2441/2016_Phalachandra-Abeywardena_OER-in-Commonwealth-2016.pdf?sequence=4

Cox, G. (2012). Why would you do it, ... would a student actually be interested?: Understanding the barriers and enablers to academic contribution to an OER directory. *Proceedings of Cambridge 2012*. Cambridge, UK.

Cox, G. (2013). Researching resistance to Open Education Resource contribution: An activity theory approach. Special Issue of the *Journal of e-Learning and Digital Media: Exploring the Educational Potential of Open Educational Resources, 10(2)*, 148–160. Retrieved from http://ldm.sagepub.com/content/10/2/148.short

Cox, G. (2016). *Explaining the relations between culture, structure and agency in lecturers' contribution and non-contribution to Open Educational Resources in a higher education institution*. Ph.D thesis. Cape Town: University of Cape Town. Retrieved from https://open.uct.ac.za/handle/11427/20300

Cox, G. & Trotter, H. (2016). Institutional culture and OER policy: How structure, culture, and agency mediate OER policy potential in South African universities. *The International Review of Research in Open and Distributed Learning, 17(5)*. Retrieved from https://doi.org/10.19173/irrodl.v17i5.2523

Czerniewicz, L. & Brown, C. (2009). A study of the relationship between institutional policy, organisational culture and e-learning use in four South African universities. *Computers and Education, 53*, 121–131. Retrieved from http://www.sciencedirect.com/science/article/pii/S0360131509000104

Czerniewicz, L., Cox, G., Hodgkinson-Williams, C. & Willmers, M. (2015). Open education at the University of Cape Town. In C. J. Bonk, M. M. Lee, T. C. Reeves & T. H. Reynolds (Eds.), *MOOCs and Open Education: Around the world* (pp. 53–64), New York: Routledge.

Daniel, J., Kanwar, A. & Uvalić-Trumbić, S. (2006). A tectonic shift in global higher education. *Change: The Magazine of Higher Learning, 38(4)*, 16–23. Retrieved from http://www.learntechlib.org/p/98724

Daniel, J. & Uvalić-Trumbić, S. (2012). *Fostering governmental support for Open Educational Resources internationally*. 4th Regional Policy Forum. Retrieved from http://oasis.col.org/handle/11599/1063

Davis, H. C., Carr, L., Hey, J. M. N., Howard, Y., Millard, D., Morris, D. & White, S. (2010). Bootstrapping a culture of sharing to facilitate Open Educational Resources. *IEEE Transactions on Learning Technologies, 3(2)*, 96–109. Retrieved from http://ieeexplore.ieee.org/document/5210093/?reload=true

de Hart, K., Chetty, Y. & Archer, E. (2015). Uptake of OER by staff in Distance Education in South Africa. *The International Review of Research in Open and Distributed Learning, 16(2)*, 18–45. Retrieved from http://www.irrodl.org/index.php/irrodl/article/view/2047

de Hart, K. & Oosthuizen, T. (2012). An overview of the strategic OER positioning of the only dedicated ODL University in Southern Africa. *Proceedings of the Regional Symposium on Open Educational Resources: An Asian perspective on policy and practices* (pp. 25–30). Retrieved from http://www.oerasia.org/symposium/OERAsia_Symposium_Penang_2012_Proceedings.pdf

Department of Higher Education and Training, South Africa (DHET). (2014). White Paper for Post-School Education and Training. Building an expanded, effective and integrated post-school system. Pretoria: DHET.

Dhanarajan, G. & Abeydawara, I. S. (2013). Higher education and open educational resources in Asia: an overview. In G. Dhanarajan & D. Porter (Eds.), *Open Educational Resources: An*

Asian perspective (pp. 3–18). Vancouver: Commonwealth of Learning. Retrieved from https://oerknowledgecloud.org/sites/oerknowledgecloud.org/files/pub_PS_OER_Asia_web.pdf

Dhanarajan, G. & Porter, D. (Eds.). (2013). *Open Educational Resources: An Asian perspective.* Vancouver: Commonwealth of Learning. Retrieved from https://oerknowledgecloud.org/sites/oerknowledgecloud.org/files/pub_PS_OER_Asia_web.pdf

Diallo, B., Wangeci, C. & Wright, C. R. (2012). Approaches to the production and use of OERs: The African Virtual University experience. In R. McGreal, W. Kinuthia, & S. Marshall (Eds.), *Open educational resources: Innovation, research and practice* (pp. 93i–104), Athabasca, Canada: University of Athabasca Press. Retrieved from https://oerknowledgecloud.org/sites/oerknowledgecloud.org/files/pub_PS_OER-IRP_CH7.pdf

Ehlers, U.-D. (2011). From Open Educational Resources to Open Educational Practices. *eLearning Papers,* 23. Retrieved from http://www.oerup.eu/fileadmin/_oerup/dokumente/media25161__2_.pdf

Fitzgerald, A. & Hashim, H. N. M. (2012). Enabling access to and re-use of publicly funded research data as open educational resources: a strategy for overcoming the legal barriers to data access and re-use. In *Proceedings of the Regional Symposium on Open Educational Resources: An Asian perspective on policy and practices*, 19–21 September 2012. Penang: Wawasan Open University.

Flor, A. G. (2013). Exploring the downside of open knowledge resources: The case of indigenous knowledge systems and practices in the Philippines. *Open Praxis, 5(1)*, 75–80. Retrieved from http://openpraxis.org/index.php/OpenPraxis/article/view/15

Gunness, S. (2012). Appraising the transformative power of OERs for learner-centred teaching at the University of Mauritius. *Paper presented at Cambridge 2012: Innovation and Impact - Openly Collaborating to Enhance Education, 16–18 April.* Cambridge, UK. Retrieved from https://oerknowledgecloud.org/sites/oerknowledgecloud.org/files/Appraising%20the%20transformative%20power%20of%20OERs%20for%20learner-centred%20teaching%20-%20SandhyaGunnessV2.pdf

Harley, K. & Barasa, F. S. (2012). *TESSA: Teacher education in Sub-Saharan Africa.* Formative evaluation report. Milton Keynes, UK: The Open University. Retrieved from http://www.tessafrica.net/sites/www.tessafrica.net/files/TESSA_Formative_Evaluation_Report_October_2012.pdf

Haßler, B. & Mays, T. (2014). Open Content. *The International Encyclopedia of Digital Communication and Society*, 1–11. Retrieved from http://onlinelibrary.wiley.com/doi/10.1002/9781118767771.wbiedcs154/full

Hatakka, M. (2009). Build it and they will come?: Inhibiting factors for reuse of open content in developing countries. *The Electronic Journal on Information Systems in Developing Countries, 37(5)*, 1–16. Retrieved from http://www.is.cityu.edu.hk/staff/isrobert/ejisdc/37-5.pdf

He, W. & Wei, K.-K. (2009). What drives continued knowledge sharing? An investigation of knowledge-contribution and -seeking beliefs. *Decision Support Systems, 46(4)*, 826–838.

Herzberg, F. (1987). One more time: How do you motivate employees? *Harvard Business Review, 65(5)*, 109–120.

Hodgkinson-Williams, C. (2010). Benefits and challenges of OER for higher education institutions. *Open Educational Resources (OER) Workshop for Heads of Commonwealth Universities, 28 April 2010.* Cape Town, South Africa. Retrieved from https://www.academia.edu/3042016/Benefits_and_challenges_of_OER_for_higher_education_institutions

Hodgkinson-Williams, C. & Donnelly, S. (2010). Sustaining OER at the University of Cape Town: Free, but not cheap. *OpenEd 2010 Conference, 2–4 November 2010.* Barcelona,

Spain. Retrieved from http://openaccess.uoc.edu/webapps/o2/bitstream/10609/4843/6/Hodgkinson.pdf

Hodgkinson-Williams, C. & Gray, E. (2009). Degrees of Openness: The emergence of Open Educational Resources at the University of Cape Town. *International Journal of Education and Development using ICT, 5(5)*, 1–16. Retrieved from http://ijedict.dec.uwi.edu/viewarticle.php?id=864

Hodgkinson-Williams, C., Paskevicius, M., Cox, G., Donnelly, S., Czerniewicz, L. & Lee-Pan, S. (2013). 365 days of Openness: The emergence of OER at the University of Cape Town. In R. McGreal, W. Kinuthia, S. Marshall & T. McNamara (Eds.), *Perspectives on Open and Distance Learning: Open Educational Resources: Innovation, research and practice.* Vancouver: Commonwealth of Learning and Athabasca University.Retrieved from https://oerknowledgecloud.org/sites/oerknowledgecloud.org/files/pub_PS_OER-IRP_CH3.pdf

Jhangiani, R., Pitt, R., Hendricks, C., Key, J. & Lalonde, C. (2016). *Exploring faculty use of Open Educational Resources at British Columbia post-Secondary institutions.* BCcampus Research Report. Victoria, BC: BCcampus. Retrieved from http://bccampus.ca/files/2016/01/BCFacultyUseOfOER_final.pdf

Kanwar, A., Kodhandaraman, B. & Umar, A. (2010). Towards sustainable OER: A perspective from the Global South. *Keynote presented at the Global Learn Asia Pacific conference, 18 May 2010. Penang, Malaysia,.* Retrieved from http://oasis.col.org/bitstream/handle/11599/1144/2010_Kanwar_Towards_Sustainable_OER_Transcript.pdf?sequence=1&isAllowed=y

Karunanayaka, S. P., Naidu, S., Dhanapala, T. D. T. L., Gonsalkorala, L. R. & Ariyaratne, A. (2014). From mind maps to mind sets: Shifting conceptions about OER in the Faculty of Education at the Open University of Sri Lanka. *Paper presented at the 2nd Regional Symposium on Open Educational Resources: Beyond Advocacy, Research and Policy, 24–27 June 2014.* Wawasan Open University, George Town, Malaysia. Retrieved from http://weko.wou.edu.my/?action=repository_action_common_download&item_id=369&item_no=1&attribute_id=15&file_no=1

Khanna, P. & Basak, P. C. (2013). An OER architecture framework: Need and design. *The International Review of Research in Open and Distributed Learning, 14(1)*, 65–83. Retrieved from http://www.irrodl.org/index.php/irrodl/article/view/1355/2427

Kursun, E., Cagiltay, K. & Can, G. (2014). An investigation of faculty perspectives on barriers, incentives, and benefits of the OER movement in Turkey. *The International Review of Research in Open and Distributed Learning, 15(6)*, 13–32. Retrieved from http://www.irrodl.org/index.php/irrodl/article/view/1914/3128

Lesko, I. (2013). The use and production of OER & OCW in teaching in South African higher education institutions: Case study. *Open Praxis, 5(2)*, 102–121. Retrieved from http://openpraxis.org/index.php/OpenPraxis/article/view/52

Liew, T. K. (2016). Using open educational resources for undergraduate programme development at Wawasan Open University. In F. Miao, S. Mishra & R. McGreal (Eds.), *Open Educational Resources: Policy, Costs and Transformation* (pp. 119–128). Paris: UNESCO / Vancouver: Commonwealth of Learning. Retrieved from http://oasis.col.org/bitstream/handle/11599/2306/2016_Perspectives-OER-Policy-Transformation-Costs.pdf?sequence=1&isAllowed=y

Matkin, G. W. & Cooperman, L. (2012). Beyond current concepts of OCW/OER: What you should know and why. *Proceedings of Cambridge 2012.* Cambridge, UK. Retrieved from http://presentations.ocwconsortium.org/uk2012_291_beyond_current_concepts_ocw_oer/

Mawoyo, M. (2012). *Growing an institutional health OER initiative: A case study of the University of Cape Town*. Nairobi: OER Africa. Retrieved from http://www.oerafrica.org/resource/growing-institutional-health-oer-initiative-case-study-university-cape-town

Mawoyo, M. & Butcher, N. (2012). Sharing existing teaching materials as OER: Key considerations from practice. In J. Glennie, K. Harley, N. Butcher & T. van Wyk (Eds.), *Perspectives on Open and Distance Learning: Open Educational Resources and change in higher education: Reflections from practice* (pp. 199–216). Vancouver: Commonwealth of Learning and UNESCO. Retrieved from http://oasis.col.org/handle/11599/80

Maxwell, J. A. (2008). Designing a qualitative study. In L. Bickman & D. J. Rog (Eds.), *The Sage handbook of applied social research methods*. (pp. 214–253). London: Sage. Retrieved from http://www.sagepub.com/upm-data/23772_Ch7.pdf

McGill, L., Falconer, I., Dempster, J. A., Littlejohn, A. & Beetham, H. (2013). *Journeys to Open Educational Practice: UKOER/SCORE Review final report*. London: JISC.

McGreal, R., Anderson, T. & Conrad, D. (2016). Open Educational Resources in Canada. In F. Miao, S. Mishra & R. McGreal (Eds.), *Open Educational Resources: Policy, costs and transformation* (pp. 63–76). Paris: UNESCO / Vancouver: Commonwealth of Learning. Retrieved from http://oasis.col.org/bitstream/handle/11599/2306/2016_Perspectives-OER-Policy-Transformation-Costs.pdf?sequence=1&isAllowed=y

McNay, I. (1995). From collegial academy to corporate enterprise: the changing cultures of universities. In T. Schuller (Ed.), *The Changing University?* (pp. 105–115). Buckingham, UK: Society for Research into Higher Education and Open University Press.

Mtebe, J. S. & Raisamo, R. (2014). Investigating perceived barriers to the use of open educational resources in higher education in Tanzania. *The International Review of Research in Open and Distributed Learning, 15(2)*. Retrieved from http://www.irrodl.org/index.php/irrodl/article/view/1803/2841

Murphy, P. & Wolfenden, F. (2013). Developing a pedagogy of mutuality in a capability approach - teachers' experiences of using the Open Educational Resources (OER) of the Teacher Education in Sub Saharan Africa (TESSA) programme. *International Journal of Educational Development, 33*, 263–271. Retrieved from http://www.sciencedirect.com/science/article/pii/S0738059312001393

Ngimwa, P. (2010). *OER readiness in Africa: A report submitted to the OLnet Project, August 2010*. Barcelona: OLnet. Retrieved from https://oerknowledgecloud.org/sites/oerknowledgecloud.org/files/37994804-OER-Readiness-in-Africa.pdf

Ngugi, C. N. (2011). OER in Africa's higher education institutions. *Distance Education, 32(2)*, 277–287. Retrieved from http://www.tandfonline.com/doi/full/10.1080/01587919.2011.584853

Omollo, L. K. (2011a). *Growing an institutional health OER initiative: A case study of the Kwame Nkrumah University of Science and Technology*. St. Ann Harbour, Michigan: University of Michigan and OER Africa. Retrieved from http://www.oerafrica.org/FTPFolder/Website%20Materials/Health/case_studies/2011.05%20Knust_Low_Res.pdf

Omollo, L. K. (2011b). *Growing an institutional health OER Initiative: A case study of the University of Ghana*. St. Ann Harbour, Michigan: University of Michigan and OER Africa. Retrieved from http://www.oerafrica.org/FTPFolder/Website%20Materials/Health/case_studies/2011.05.11%20UG_Low_Res.pdf

Orr, D., Rimini, M. & Van Damme, D. (2015). *Open Educational Resources: A catalyst for innovation, educational research and innovation*. Paris: OECD Publishing. Retrieved from http://dx.doi.org/10.1787/9789264247543-en

Pegler, C. (2012). Herzberg, hygiene and the motivation to reuse: towards a three-factor theory to explain motivation to share and use OER. *Journal of Interactive Media in Education, 2012(1)*. Retrieved from http://doi.org/10.5334/2012-04

Percy, T. & Van Belle, J.-P. (2012). Exploring the barriers and enablers to the use of open educational resources by university academics in Africa. *IFIP Advances in Information and Communication Technology Conference Proceedings, Vol. 378*, 112–128, 10–13 September, 2012. Hammamet, Tunisia. Retrieved from http://dl.ifip.org/db/conf/oss/oss2012/PercyB12.pdf

Pirkkalainen, H., Jokinen, J., Pawlowski, J. & Richter, T. (2014). Overcoming cultural distance in social OER environments. In S. Zvacek, M. Restivo, J. Uhomoibhi, & M. Helfert (Eds.), *CSEDU 2014: Proceedings of the 6th International Conference on Computer Supported Education*: Vol. 1 (pp. 15–24). Setúbal, Portugal: SCITEPRESS Science and Technology Publications.

Reed, P. (2012). Awareness, attitudes and participation of teaching staff towards the open content movement in one university. *Research in Learning Technology, 20(4)*. Retrieved from http://dx.doi.org/10.3402/rlt.v20i0.18520

Rolfe, V. (2012). Open Educational Resources: Staff attitudes and awareness. *Research in Learning Technology, 20(14395)*. Retrieved from https://www.dora.dmu.ac.uk/handle/2086/6188

Samzugi, A. S. & Mwinyimbegu, C. M. (2013). Accessibility of Open Educational Resources for Distance Education learners: The case of the Open University of Tanzania. *HURIA: Journal of The Open University of Tanzania, 14*, 76–88. Retrieved from https://www.ajol.info/index.php/huria/article/view/110779

Santos-Hermosa, G. (2014). ORIOLE, in the search for evidence of OER in teaching: Experiences in the use, re-use and the sharing and influence of repositories. *Qualitative Research in Education, 3(2)*. Retrieved from http://www.hipatiapress.com/hpjournals/index.php/qre/article/view/1003

Sclater, N. (2010). Open Educational Resources: Motivations, logistics and sustainability. In N. F. Ferrer & J. M. Alonso (Eds.), *Content management for E-Learning* (pp. 179–193). New York: Springer-Verlag. Retrieved from http://sclater.com/papers/OER-Motivations-Logistics-and-Sustainability-Sclater.pdf

Singer, M. & Porter, D. (2015). Exploring the process of using OER to build transnationally accredited courses within the OERu partner network: An activity theory perspective. *Presented at Open Education Global Conference, 22–24 April 2015*. Banff, Canada. Retrieved from http://conference.oeconsortium.org/2015/wp-content/uploads/2015/02/Singer_Porter_OEGlobal-2015_v1.5.pdf

Smith, M. S. & Casserly C. M. (2006). The promise of Open Educational Resources. *Change, 38(5)*, 8–17. Retrieved from http://www.hewlett.org/wp-content/uploads/2016/08/ChangeArticle.pdf

Stacey, P. (2007). Open Educational Resources in a global context. *First Monday, 12(4)*. Retrieved from http://firstmonday.org/ojs/index.php/fm/article/view/1769/1649

Thakrar, J., Zinn, D. & Wolfenden, F. (2009). Harnessing Open Educational Resources to the challenges of teacher education in Sub-Saharan Africa. *The International Review of Research in Open and Distributed Learning, 10(4)*, 1–15. Retrieved from http://www.irrodl.org/index.php/irrodl/article/view/705/1319

Trotter, H. & Cox, G. (2016). The OER Adoption Pyramid. In *Proceedings of Open Education Global 2016,* 12–14 April 2016. Krakow, Poland. Retrieved from http://open.uct.ac.za/handle/11427/18936

Trotter, H., Kell, C., Willmers, M., Gray, E. & King, T. (2014). *Seeking impact and visibility: Scholarly communication in Southern Africa.* Cape Town: African Minds. Retrieved from https://core.ac.uk/download/pdf/29051292.pdf

Tynan, B. & James R. (2013). Distance education regulatory frameworks: Readiness for openness in Southwest Pacific/South-East Asia region nations. *Open Praxis, 5(1).* Retrieved from http://openpraxis.org/index.php/OpenPraxis/article/view/31/6

University of Cape Town (UCT). (2011). *University of Cape Town Intellectual Property policy.* Cape Town: University of Cape Town. Retrieved from http://www.uct.ac.za/downloads/uct.ac.za/about/policies/intellect_property.pdf

University of Cape Town (UCT). (2014). *University of Cape Town Open Access policy.* Cape Town: University of Cape Town. Retrieved from https://www.uct.ac.za/downloads/uct.ac.za/about/policies/UCTOpenAccessPolicy.pdf

University of Fort Hare (UFH). (2010). *University of Fort Hare policy on Intellectual Property.* Alice, South Africa: University of Fort Hare. Retrieved from http://ufhgmrdc.ac.za/portals/gmrdc/downloads/policydownloads/ippolicyfinalsenateapproved2june10.pdf

University of South Africa (UNISA). (2012). *UNISA Intellectual Property policy.* Pretoria: UNISA. Retrieved from http://www.unisa.ac.za/static/corporate_web/Content/Colleges/CGS/documents/IP_Policy_app_Council_2_22.06.2012.pdf

University of South Africa (UNISA). (2014). *UNISA Open Educational Resources (OER) strategy 2014-2016.* Pretoria: UNISA. Retrieved from http://www.unisa.ac.za/contents/unisaopen/docs/OER%20Strategy%20(final)%20March%202014.pdf

Van Acker, F., Van Duuren, H., Kreijns, K. & Vermeulen, M. (2013). Why teachers share educational resources: A social exchange perspective. In R. McGreal, W. Kinuthia & S. Marshall (Eds.), *Open Educational Resources: Innovation, research and practice.* (pp. 177–192). Vancouver: Commonwealth of Learning. Retrieved from https://oerknowledgecloud.org/sites/oerknowledgecloud.org/files/pub_PS_OER-IRP_CH13.pdf

van der Merwe, A. D. (2013). Are higher education institutions positioned to reap the dividends of open education resources? The case of Durban University of Technology. *International Business & Economics Research Journal, 12(9),* 1119–1129. Retrieved from http://www.cluteinstitute.com/ojs/index.php/IBER/article/view/8057/8111

Waring, M. & Evans, C. (2015). *Understanding pedagogy: Developing a critical approach to teaching and learning.* New York: Routledge.

Welch, T. & Glennie, J. (2016). Open educational resources for early literacy in Africa: The role of the African Storybook Initiative. In F. Miao, S. Mishra & R. McGreal (Eds.), *Open Educational Resources: Policy, costs and transformation* (pp. 195–210). Paris: UNESCO / Vancouver: Commonwealth of Learning. Retrieved from http://oasis.col.org/bitstream/handle/11599/2306/2016_Perspectives-OER-Policy-Transformation-Costs.pdf?sequence=1&isAllowed=y

West, P. G. & Victor, L. (2011). *Background and action paper on OER: A background and action paper for staff of bilateral and multilateral organisations at the strategic institutional education sector level.* Menlo Park, CA: Williams and Flora Hewlett foundation. Retrieved from http://www.paulwest.org/public/Background_and_action_paper_on_OER.pdf

Wiley, D. & Hilton III, J. (2009). Openness, dynamic specialization, and the disaggregated future of higher education. *The International Review of Research in Open and Distributed Learning, 10(5).* Retrieved from http://www.irrodl.org/index.php/irrodl/article/view/768/1414

Wiley, D., Green, C. & Soares, L. (2012). *Dramatically bringing down the cost of education with OER: How Open Education Resources unlock the door to free learning.* Washington D.C.: Center for American Progress. Retrieved from http://files.eric.ed.gov/fulltext/ED535639.pdf

Willems, J. & Bossu, C. (2012). Equity considerations for open educational resources in the glocalization of education. *Distance Education, 33(2)*, 185–199. Retrieved from http://www.tandfonline.com/doi/abs/10.1080/01587919.2012.692051

Windle, R. J., Wharrad, H., McCormick, D., Laverty, H. & Taylor, M. (2010). Sharing and reuse in OER: experiences gained from open reusable learning objects in health. *Journal of Interactive Media in Education, 2010(1)*. Retrieved from http://doi.org/10.5334/2010-4

Wolfenden, F. (2008). The TESSA OER experience: Building sustainable models of production and user implementation. *Journal of Interactive Media in Education, 2008(1)*. Retrieved from http://jime.open.ac.uk/articles/10.5334/2008-3/

Wolfenden, F., Buckler, A. & Keraro, F. (2012). OER adaptation and reuse across cultural contexts in Sub Saharan Africa: Lessons from TESSA (Teacher Education in Sub Saharan Africa). *Journal of Interactive Media in Education, 2012(1)*. Retrieved from http://doi.org/10.5334/2012-03

Zagdragchaa, B. & Trotter, H. (2017). Cultural-historical factors influencing OER adoption in Mongolia's higher education sector. In C. Hodgkinson-Williams & P. B. Arinto (Eds.), *Adoption and impact of OER in the Global South* (pp. 389–424). Retrieved from https://doi.org/10.5281/zenodo.599609

How to cite this chapter

Cox, G. & Trotter, H. (2017). Factors shaping lecturers' adoption of OER at three South African universities. In C. Hodgkinson-Williams & P. B. Arinto (Eds.) *Adoption and impact of OER in the Global South* (pp. 287–347). Retrieved from https://doi.org/10.5281/zenodo.601935

Corresponding author: Glenda Cox <glenda.cox@uct.ac.za>

This work is licensed under a Creative Commons Attribution 4.0 International (CC BY 4.0) licence. It was carried out with the aid of a grant from the International Development Research Centre, Ottawa, Canada.

Chapter 10

OER in and as MOOCs

Laura Czerniewicz, Andrew Deacon, Sukaina Walji
and Michael Glover

Summary

This chapter reports on the investigation into the production and rollout of four Massive Open Online Courses (MOOCs) at the University of Cape Town (UCT) in South Africa, and on the experiences of the educators involved in their production. The overarching aim of this study is to address the question: How does MOOC-making with Open Educational Resources (OER) influence educators' Open Educational Practices (OEP)? The authors were interested to know why UCT educators wanted to make MOOCs, whether they adopted OER, whether their practices become more open after making a MOOC, and in which ways.

Drawing on Beetham et al. (2012) and Hodgkinson-Williams (2014), an analytic framework of OEP was developed comprising three dimensions: legal, pedagogical and financial. The research methodology is qualitative, using semi-structured interviews and data from MOOC discussion forums. Six MOOC lead educators were interviewed at three intervals: before their MOOCs ran, immediately after their MOOC's first run, and six to 10 months later. Transcripts were coded using OEP concepts.

The findings offer insights into the relationships between educators' motivations for making MOOCs, their MOOC design tools, the OEP that can be identified and the contradictions they experienced in making MOOCs. Despite the challenges that educators faced, they largely achieved their purposes of making MOOCs and manifested legal, pedagogical and financial dimensions of OEP. The impact on educators' open practices was observed in several subsequent projects after the MOOCs were first run. Tensions involved in making MOOCs, adopting OER and enacting OEP point to how educators could be better supported to become more open in their educational practices.

No negative experiences were attributed to the creation of OER and, indeed, MOOC-making with OER appeared to be conducive to OER adoption in general. However, more time would be needed to conclude whether these educators could become OER advocates or could function autonomously in creating and sharing OER.

The dataset arising from this study can be accessed at:
https://www.datafirst.uct.ac.za/dataportal/index.php/catalog/600

Acronyms and abbreviations

CC   Creative Commons
CILT   Centre for Innovation in Learning and Teaching
Ed4All   *Education for All: Disability, Diversity and Inclusion* (MOOC)
MedArts   *Medicine and the Arts: Humanising Healthcare* (MOOC)
Mind   *What is a Mind* (MOOC)
MOOCs   Massive Online Open Courses
OEP   Open Educational Practices
OER   Open Educational Resources
OPAL   Open Education Quality Initiative
UCR   *Understanding Clinical Research: Behind the Statistics* (MOOC)
UCT   University of Cape Town

Introduction

Massive Open Online Courses (MOOCs) are a recent and evolving form of online learning that has promised to broaden opportunities for Open Education. This study investigates whether and how the integration of Open Educational Resources (OER) in the design of MOOCs impacts upon educators' Open Educational Practices (OEP).

In 2014, the University of Cape Town (UCT) launched its first MOOC development programme, the UCT MOOCs Project. The first locally produced MOOCs were released in early 2015. UCT is a predominantly face-to-face research institution with over 28 000 students and in 2016 was ranked the top university in Africa based on the Times Higher Education World University Rankings.[1]

The African context is of particular interest in the study. UCT is located in South Africa and was the first African university to embark on a MOOC-production initiative in partnership with large international MOOC platforms. The MOOCs created at UCT all have a strong focus on Africa in terms of content; the broader study also had an interest in exploring whether an African university producing MOOCs increases regional participation in MOOCs.

UCT has a long-standing institutional commitment to supporting open scholarly activity (including OER), as is evident in its Open Access Policy.[2] The UCT MOOCs Project (2014–2017), which is the focus of this study, was an institutionally supported initiative funded by the Vice Chancellor's Strategic Fund to develop 12 MOOCs on two international MOOC platforms, Coursera[3] and FutureLearn.[4] The MOOCs were co-created by UCT's Centre for Innovation in Learning and Teaching (CILT) in collaboration with educators from different departments. The MOOCs selected for development were identified in a competitive call for proposals, in which educators applied for support and funding in order to undertake MOOC-development activities.

---

1   https://www.timeshighereducation.com/world-university-rankings/best-universities-in-africa-2016
2   http://www.uct.ac.za/downloads/uct.ac.za/about/policies/OpenUCT_Policy.pdf
3   https://www.coursera.org/
4   https://www.futurelearn.com/

The broad goals of the UCT MOOCs Project are to showcase the teaching and research excellence of UCT; give exposure to African content and knowledge; profile key postgraduate programmes and research areas aligned with the university's strategic goals; support students in academic transition; make UCT's knowledge resources globally accessible; and develop models and expertise in online learning that could be deployed in mainstream degree programmes.[5] Each individual MOOC team also had strategic goals that included the provision of open educational opportunities to engage global participants in locally generated knowledge. While not explicitly an OER creation project, the MOOC educators were invited and encouraged to release the constituent elements of each MOOC as OER (where possible) by the CILT team overseeing MOOC development – largely as a result of the prevailing institutional culture providing an enabling environment.

This study considers four of the MOOCs developed as part of the UCT MOOCs Project. These are *Medicine and the Arts: Humanising Healthcare*[6] (MedArts); *What is a Mind?*[7] (Mind); *Understanding Clinical Research: Behind the Statistics*[8] (UCR); and *Education for All: Disability, Diversity and Inclusion*[9] (Ed4All). The selection was made based on the MOOCs developed and delivered during the time period of this research project, and which were available to be considered as research sites.

MedArts is an introductory course in the emerging interdisciplinary field of the Medical Humanities. The course is presented by Associate Professor of Anthropology Susan Levine (SL)[10] of the School of African and Gender Studies, Anthropology and Linguistics at UCT, and Professor Steve Reid (SR), Head of the Primary Health Care Directorate at UCT. The six-week MedArts course is hosted on FutureLearn and has 17 presenters in addition to the two lead educators. In each week of the course, a trio of disciplinary experts is assembled from across disciplines in the health sciences, social sciences and the arts to bring their perspectives into dialogue on a healthcare topic.

Mind explores scientific and philosophical concepts pertinent to understanding our own minds. The course is presented by psychologist Professor Mark Solms (MS) of the Department of Psychology at UCT. The six-week course is hosted on FutureLearn and has a single presenter with academic assistant Aimee Dollman (AD) as host of the course. Each week a defining property of the mind is discussed from several different disciplinary perspectives.

UCR is designed to build capacity in research skills through scaffolding students' ability to read and interpret clinical data and research. The six-week course is presented by Dr Juan Klopper (JK), Head of Acute Care Surgery at UCT, and is the only course in this study hosted on the Coursera platform; it has only one presenter.

The Ed4All course is aimed at teachers and educational managers, particularly those in low-resource settings, and presents a strategy for how to integrate children with disabilities into mainstream classroom teaching. The six-week course is hosted on FutureLearn and is presented by Dr Judith McKenzie (JM), lecturer in the Disability Studies programme at UCT, and Ms Chioma Ohajunwa (CO) from the same department.

---

5   http://www.cilt.uct.ac.za/cilt/create-mooc
6   https://www.futurelearn.com/courses/medicine-and-the-arts
7   https://www.futurelearn.com/courses/what-is-a-mind
8   https://www.coursera.org/learn/clinical-research
9   https://www.futurelearn.com/courses/education-for-all
10 Initials of the lead educators and the Mind academic assistant are used in the Findings section as a code to identify respondents.

The courses studied had enrolments ranging from just over 9 000 for one run of a course (in the case of Ed4All) to nearly 35 000 participants over three runs of the course (in the case of Mind) (Table 1).

Table 1: **Enrolment overview of MOOCs examined in study**

Course	Platform	Enrolments (as of 1 June 2016)	No. of countries from which participants originate	Percentage of participants from Africa	Percentage of participants from South Africa
MedArts	FutureLearn	18 755 (3 runs)	96	20	12.5
Mind	FutureLearn	34 914 (3 runs)	126	12	7.0
UCR	Coursera	12 059 (6 runs)	91	14	3.0
Ed4All	FutureLearn	9 104 (1 run)	130	19	7.8

The rationale for this study concerns wider questions regarding how adopting OER as constituent elements of MOOCs might influence educators' practices and whether these practices become more open. While "openness" is a problematic, contested and loosely defined term (Almeida, 2017; Knox, 2013), the approach taken in this study is to focus on exploring conceptualisations of OEP, which, as Cronin (2017) suggests, is one of a number of interpretations of openness in education. Furthermore, Almeida's (2017) call for considering the value of openness in education in relation to local contexts provides a helpful approach when considering whether OER initiatives provide an opportunity to reimagine pedagogical practices. The underlying assumption of the study is that the integration of OER in an open course will lead to the transformation of the MOOC educators' teaching and learning practices. The hypothesis is that this transformation will manifest in a range of perceptions, behaviours and/or practices, and that these will align with the conceptions of OEP developed by Beetham, Falconer, McGill and Littlejohn (2012), Hodgkinson-Williams and Gray (2009) and Hodgkinson-Williams (2014). Hodgkinson-Williams (2014) offers three dimensions of openness which underpin our conceptualisation of OEP: legal, pedagogical and financial. These are expanded upon below.

This study explores Downes' (2013, p.219) assertion that: "The most obvious dimension of openness in a MOOC is the sharing of OER, but it is important to recognise that the facilitators, by participating in this network of interactions, open their instruction as well," in other words, opening up their practices. Opening up may include the open licensing of MOOC materials for reuse in a closed or other (non-MOOC) format course. While educators may not have an explicit interest in OER *per se*, creating open resources may be a means to achieve their goals. As we found, there may be other outcomes too.

This study centres on the MOOC educators and their motivations, rather than on the MOOC content or participants. While there is an interest on the part of the researchers in the concept of OER as open content, the intersection of OER and educator practices is the focus of this research. Within this context, practices are defined as "arrays of human activity that are materially mediated" and "organised around shared practical understanding" (Schatzki, 2001, p.2); practices include what educators believe as well as what they do. Given that practices and activities do not occur in isolation and can only be made sense of in practice (Engeström, 1987; Schatzki, 2001), it is necessary to describe the nature of the context in which the practices are manifest and might change. Thus, it is important to articulate the purpose of educators' practices, how the practices are mediated, contextual considerations and the kinds of tensions that arise as practices change.

The assumption is that there are likely to be linkages between the interests of educators making MOOCs aimed at diverse participants, the opportunities offered by OER and emergent OEP. While the study reports on educators' engagement with OER through various content types, levels, formats and degrees of granularity, we are particularly interested in the manifestations of OEP, focusing specifically on the legal, pedagogical and financial dimensions thereof.

OER and MOOCs are relatively new phenomena, with OER existing since the early 2000s and MOOCs for about half of that period (Hodgkinson-Williams, 2014). OEP has been recognised conceptually in the last 10 years (Andrade et al., 2011). The intersection between OER and MOOCs has, however, not received a great deal of attention, particularly from a Global South perspective. This is a serious concern given the skewed nature of OER and MOOC provision in which Global South institutions are low producers of and participants in open materials and Open Education (Czerniewicz & Naidoo, 2013). Concomitantly, Global South universities have had limited capacity to develop online courses, support more flexible forms of learning and engage in OER adoption activity. Institutions in the Global South have only recently begun to engage with MOOCs, and there is an awareness of the pedagogical and geopolitical implications of MOOCs emanating only from the developed world to be received by those in the developing world (Czerniewicz, Deacon, Small & Walji, 2014). The relative novelty of MOOCs, particularly in the context of the Global South, means that there is a need for evidence-based research to inform the educators and institutions considering MOOCs as part of their course delivery strategy or Open Education initiatives. Educators and institutions contemplating MOOC production will most likely need to consider what sort of MOOCs to create, what pedagogical approaches to adopt and what sort of knowledge is to be shared, as well as what implications MOOC production may have in the geopolitics of knowledge-sharing.

Literature review and conceptual framework

The emergence of MOOCs is a result of a convergence of distance education and the OER movement enabled by the internet and social and participatory technologies. After considering MOOCs and Open Education, and providing a broad brushstroke review of the definitions of OEP, this literature review focuses on studies pertaining to the specific dimensions of OEP considered relevant to this study, particularly the legal, pedagogical and financial dimensions.

MOOCs and Open Education

Despite the apparent relationship and similarities between the two concepts, the literature on MOOCs and OER is generally distinct. Nevertheless, the question of the nature of the relationship between them has been intriguing, and educational commentators, academics and practitioners have argued a wide range of positions regarding their relationship to one another. On the one hand, there is a view that considers MOOCs as part of or as an offshoot of Open Education (Patru & Balaji, 2016; Tingry, Boyer & Roussanaly, 2016; Weller, 2016), or as one "genre" of OER (Alevizou, 2015). On the other hand, there are those who consider MOOCs as inconsistent and distinct from OER and the open movement (Wiley, Reeves & Reynolds, 2015).

Loeckx (2016) has emphasised the fact that the first "O" in MOOC is often taken to mean that the course is "free", but it has become evident that this "free to the user" model is not financially viable. He argues further that there is an important difference between the MOOC "open-as-free" phenomenon and the openness of OER, which involves the requisite legal permissions to reuse, revise, remix, redistribute and retain educational resources. In a study analysing 49 MOOCs, Ozturk (2015) notes that:

> ... in line with the theoretical underpinnings of "OERM" [the OER movement] MOOCs initially included key features of connectivist pedagogy like autonomy, community participation, openness and diversity but the newer MOOCs, which are underpinned by financial models and informed by instructivist and cognitivist pedagogies, suggest that the "learning praxis [of] MOOCs has been commodified". (n.p. – in abstract)

Within this context, Ozturk describes an unease among some educators in the OER movement, who see the "open" in MOOC as inconsistent with the "openness" of OER.

By contrast, Piedra, Chicaiza, López and Tovar (2014, p.171) suggest viewing MOOC developments in relation to Open Education positively, in that "MOOC initiatives emphasise free access and interactive features rather than static content, [and] the dominant message is of the quantity of access rather than the openness of educational resources for use, re-use, adaptation or repurpose". Piedra et al. (2014) consider MOOCs as a move beyond open access to course content (OER) in order to access free online courses to a situation where accredited institutions are beginning to accept MOOCs and other free courses as partial credits towards formal qualifications and degrees. In this sense, MOOCs constitute the next stage in the evolution of OER. They note further that MOOCs are not open in the sense of being openly licensed and the use of content for academic credit towards a degree entails payment to MOOC providers. A similar view is taken by Patru and Balaji (2016) who, while acknowledging the desirability of openly licensed MOOCs, concede that not all MOOCs are open in the strict OER sense. At the same time, they point to limitations of OER where "OER are only part of education and as such are just one element of a MOOC (i.e. only the learning materials)" (2016, p.20). They argue that as openly accessible courses, MOOCs are an important part of Open Education.

The literature on Open Education has echoed these general divisions by focusing on either OER or MOOCs, and considerations of both in the context of Open Education are scarce (Hodgkinson-Williams, 2014; Souto-Otero et al., 2016). This apparent bifurcation appears surprising, as MOOCs claim to be concerned with widening access to education, and OER are a means of increasing access (Ebner, Lorenz, Lackner & Jemni Kinshuk, 2017). Thus the relationship between MOOCs and OER would appear to be important for achieving greater access overall (Ozturk, 2015).

The turbid nature of the relationship between OER and MOOCs extends to the research sphere. As the distinction between OER and MOOCs is becoming more "blurred" (Weller, 2016), there is uncertainty about where to position MOOC research in the current literature. OER is infrequently mentioned in the literature on MOOCs, given that the scholarship on Open Education is focused either on MOOCs or OER, as opposed to exploring relations and tensions between them (Souto-Otero et al., 2016). In a study of the evolution of OER research themes, Weller (2016) discusses whether in categorising the body of OER research, MOOCs should be considered as OER and MOOC-related research papers reclassified under OER categories. He ultimately opts to "differentiate this work from the main body of OER" (Weller, 2016, p.413). Nonetheless, in including MOOCs as part of his survey of OER literature, Weller (2016, p.414) suggests that MOOCs constitute a "particular interest or community within the overall OER field". Tingry et al. (2016) similarly choose to consider the "specificity" of MOOCs for analysis purposes while including MOOCs "implicitly" in the OER terrain.

Within the debates on whether MOOCs can or should be considered as part of the OER movement there are more pragmatic positions that present evidence for MOOCs being more closely aligned with OER. Examples of these are initiatives that encourage the use of OER content in MOOCs (Agbu, Mulder, de Vries, Tenebe & Caine, 2016; Ebner et al., 2017), and those that provide suggestions on how MOOC materials may be optimised as OER (Atenas, 2015). Noting that MOOC development has traditionally been driven by financial models that often preclude the use of OER, Ebner et al. (2017) have examined how MOOCs can be enhanced by the use of OER. In the context of German-speaking Europe (Germany, Austria, Italy and parts of Sweden), where there is an absence of "fair use" clauses for educational resources, low-fee or fee-free education systems and tight copyright restrictions, Ebner et al. have emphasised the need for OER to be incorporated into MOOCs. Two MOOC platforms have emerged to address this ambition: mooin[11] in Germany and iMooX[12] in Austria. It is a requirement that MOOCs hosted on these platforms are openly licensed (Ebner et al., 2017). The authors report that MOOCs as OER have significant advantages over fully copyrighted MOOCs, including enabling participation and cooperation with partners, increased creativity and sustainability of content, as well as increased impact. The authors suggest further that the use of OER "results in new ways of teaching" (Ebner et al., 2017, p.13) and argue that MOOCs should be openly licensed in order to enhance their impact.

From a practitioner perspective, Atenas (2015) suggests a number of technically oriented strategies for opening up MOOC content for reuse and adaptation, including openly licensing components and packaged units of the MOOC (e.g. videos, text, photographs and assignments) and hosting this content in repositories. She also suggests that MOOCs be released as openly licensed, "unguided" (meaning learners would take them in a self-paced or unsupported format) OpenCourseWare courses to allow anyone to access them without registration.

Other researchers looking ahead at the potential of MOOCs consider MOOCs incorporating OER as providing exciting opportunities for educational provision, especially in developing-world contexts (Patru & Balaji, 2016). Universities in the Global South produce only a

---

11   https://mooin.oncampus.de/
12   https://imoox.at/wbtmaster/startseite/

fraction of OER and MOOCs worldwide (Czerniewicz & Naidoo, 2013), which suggests that developing countries have been receivers and users rather than producers of OER (Nti, 2015). Arguably, both OER and MOOCs would provide opportunities for universities and academics in the Global South to rebalance skewed global networks (Nkuyubwatsi, 2013). Nkuyubwatsi (2013) has noted that MOOCs are still among the "most open" courses and that they present an opportunity to broaden access to education if interoperability and open licensing can be achieved. An African example of this intention is the National Open University of Nigeria's initiative which seeks to develop "MOOCs [which] are OER-based, so they are available for re-use and improvement by academics of other universities in Nigeria or elsewhere" (Agbu et al., 2016, p.115).

Open Educational Practices

Since at least 2007, researchers have included "practices" as a constituent aspect of the OER movement (Andrade et al., 2011; Butcher, 2011; Geser, 2007). The report of the Open Education Quality Initiative (OPAL) study, "Beyond OER: Shifting focus to open educational practices" (Andrade et al., 2011), was the first from a major study to shift the focus from making learning resources open (in the context of OER) towards "establishing OEP" with an eye to opening "learning architectures" and "transforming learning scenarios" (Ehlers, 2011, p.8). Indeed, it has been remarked that the inclusion of practices has become a global trend in discussions of OER (Conole, 2012), although what constitutes OEP is still evolving. The OPAL study conceived of OEP as nested within the broader conception of Open Education – i.e. Open Education was described as "the adoption of practices which support the (re)use and production of [OER] through institutional policies, promote innovative pedagogical models, and respect and empower learners as co-producers on their lifelong learning path" (Andrade et al., 2011, p.12). Further, OEP were described as collaborative practices of sharing openly available resources and using pedagogical practices which involve social interaction, knowledge generation, shared learning practices and peer learning (Ehlers, 2011).

The OPAL study's understanding of open practices has been critiqued for being overly focused on using or developing OER, the contention being that this understanding of OEP does not pay sufficient attention to the policies that support assessment and formal recognition of learning with OER outside formal education programmes (Murphy, 2013). Murphy proposed that OEP be defined as "policies and practices implemented by higher education institutions that support the development, use and management of OERs, and the formal assessment and accreditation of informal learning undertaken using OERs" (Murphy, 2013, p.202). Murphy's study used surveys to understand how and to what extent higher education institutions implement open educational policies and practices. Masterman (2016, p.41) makes a persuasive argument that developing an OEP conceptual framework "involves disparate sources" for OEP as there is a lack of a "holistic repertoire of practices currently observable in the field".

We approach the current study with the broader understanding of open practices in mind so as to observe how open practices play out. The overarching focus is the intersection of OER and MOOC design and their mutual impact on OEP. To investigate this interplay from the perspective of the educator requires consideration of the choices educators make as part of their work and then seeing whether and how the resulting activities establish OEP. In the literature we found two conceptualisations of openness of particular value for our purposes – namely those of Hodgkinson-Williams (2014) and Beetham et al. (2012).

Hodgkinson-Williams' (2014) dimensions of open practices are useful for distinguishing different features of open practices. Her conceptualisation of openness has the merit of drawing on and extending scholarship addressing previous understandings of openness, OER and Open Education, including the works of Okada, Mikroyannidis, Meister and Little (2012), White and Manton (2011) and Wiley.[13] In an earlier iteration, Hodgkinson-Williams and Gray (2009) conceptualised four degrees of openness in order to (1) understand the "range of openness" with important attributes associated with OER, and (2) describe OEP, or Open Pedagogy, in terms of where such practices are located along a continuum. These four degrees of openness are: social openness (on a continuum between most didactic and most participative); technological openness (proprietary interoperability or open interoperability); legal openness (on a continuum between most restrictive and most accommodating); and financial openness (less affordable versus most affordable). Hodgkinson-Williams' (2014) articulation of these conceptions widened the "social openness" category to include cultural openness and pedagogical openness, based on the argument that the original category "conflated ... too many issues under one broad label" and that these needed to be disaggregated (Hodgkinson-Williams, 2014, p.10)

With regard to reuse of OER in practice, White and Manton (2011) employed a "5D" heuristic – deciding, discovering, discerning, designing and delivering – in order to gain an understanding of how, why, when and where OER are incorporated into learning. Okada et al. (2012) expanded upon Wiley's "4Rs" framework by offering four discrete levels of reusability: "recreate content and contribute to new productions"; "adapt part of the content"; "adopt same content but adapt structure, format, interface or language"; and "adopt same content (whole, part, or combination)" (Okada et al., 2012, p.3). Each of the four levels of reusability is then sub-categorised into three ways of using OER. Okada et al. (2012) therefore enriched our understanding of the respects in which OER are reused. Hodgkinson-Williams' (2014) dimensions of openness take these notions and categories into account, providing a more comprehensive framework for understanding and describing open practices.

The five dimensions of openness which relate to the ease or difficulty of the process of adopting Open Education are:

1. Technical openness – e.g. interoperability and open formats, technical skill and resources, availability and discoverability.
2. Legal openness – e.g. open licensing knowledge and counselling.
3. Cultural openness – e.g. knowledge (on a continuum between homogeneous and diverse) and curriculum (on a continuum between institutionalised and autonomous).
4. Pedagogical openness – e.g. student demographics and types of engagement (i.e. Who is the imagined audience? Is it conventional or imagined as diverse and contextually differentiated? What pedagogical strategies are employed?).
5. Financial openness – e.g. Should OER be free or come with a modest financial price tag?

---

13 http://opencontent.org/blog/archives/2975

This study draws on three of Hodgkinson-Williams' dimensions, namely legal, pedagogical and financial. The conceptions of open practices by Beetham et al. (2012) are introduced into this framework under the pedagogical dimensions of OEP.

Legal dimensions of OEP

There are currently very few studies that explore the relationship between MOOCs and OEP. Existing studies take a strict definition of OEP as requiring adherence to Wiley's "5 Rs"[14] – the reuse, revise, remix, redistribute and retain principles which are the hallmark of OER – and thus reject MOOCs as not being open enough, since MOOCs often do not release their materials under the Creative Commons (CC) licences that facilitate "5Rs" activity (Piedra et al., 2014). Mindful of evolving global trends with changing attitudes in copyright culture and a fluid understanding of what is considered acceptable in terms of legality and copyright practice, we argue that narrow conceptions of open practices which afford primacy to the legal aspects of openness are restrictive for investigating emergent open practices of educators, especially in MOOCs. An exchange between Smith (2016) and Wiley[15] focused on whether the copyright aspect of openness needs to feature in conceptions of openness. Smith (2016) argued that it is preferable to "build up a definition [of open practices] based more on what is happening in practice, rather than preconceived theory about open", while Wiley[16] contended that in the absence of building legality into definitions of open practices, openness could be perceived as consistent with violating copyright laws and that openness which is exempt from "fair use" would have to be private as opposed to public (so as to avoid breaking the law). As researchers, our role is to observe and describe practices as they are lived in context, and we therefore take a broader view of openness. Like Smith, we do not restrict ourselves to conceptions of openness that conceive of open licensing as a necessary feature of open practices. We also consider changes in pedagogical approaches important.

The legal dimensions of OEP refer to educator engagement with OER – instances where content has been shared through legal mechanisms. This is premised on an understanding of the legal mechanisms required to adopt (including both creation and use) such openly licensed content and which fall within the ambit of copyright management. Thus, an understanding of alternative forms of licensing implies *a priori* engagement with copyright.

The OER literature pays a great deal of attention to degrees of legal openness of copyrighted content in terms of the continuum of open licensing provisions (Hilton, Wiley, Stein & Johnson, 2010; Hodgkinson-Williams & Gray, 2009), and there is some research which addresses how educators and academics engage with the legal dimensions and nuances of licensing through the adoption of OER (Cox, 2016; Davis et al., 2010; Nikoi & Armellini, 2012). However, there is a lack of evidence of such consideration in MOOC research, where the question of adapting OER in and for MOOCs and the reuse of MOOC content, specifically from the educator view, has received scant attention.

The growth of online education provision, including MOOCs, has surfaced tensions and contradictions in the institutional terrain regarding the copyright of teaching resources in general. The implications of differing institutional intellectual property policies have become

---

14   http://opencontent.org/blog/archives/2975
15   http://opencontent.org/blog/archives/4496
16   http://opencontent.org/blog/archives/4496

sites of struggle for academics[17,18] and educator associations.[19] The issues raised include ownership of forms of copyright (individual or institutional), new forms of rights (such as performance rights), as well as the implications of the evolution of partnerships with external platform providers for individual academics (Porter, 2013). The view is that commercial MOOC providers operate with restrictive copyright terms (Literat, 2015) and generally hold copyright over user-generated content (Cheverie, 2013). Even against this backdrop, it is the case that educators do sometimes retain the copyright in their teaching resources (Cox & Trotter, 2016; Klein, 2005), and that academics do sometimes have the option to make their MOOC content available as OER. It is also interesting to note that in the numerous policies that are being developed regarding online provision in universities, new forms of licensing are being included and recognised (Cate, Drooz, Hohenberg & Schulz, 2007).

Educators' awareness of copyright has generally been found to be limited or low (Duncan, Clement & Rozum, 2013; Smith et al., 2006), with confusion about copyright and licensing being reported as very common (Chen, 2014; Davis et al., 2010). A survey conducted by Reed (2012) found a distinct lack of educator clarity regarding ownership of the teaching resources they produce. In addition to a general lack of awareness of intellectual property issues, educators have also been found to be unaware of CC licences (Reed, 2012) and open licensing, describing these as hazy and "gray areas" (Cox, 2016).

It has, perhaps ironically, been the Open Access movement, along with the shift to online practice, which has brought copyright issues to the fore for many educators (Kawooya, 2007; Literat, 2015). In particular, the matter of third-party copyright has surfaced – a key consideration when educators wish to share materials beyond the context of their traditional face-to-face classrooms (Gertz, 2013), and thus become aware of the affordances of openly licensed content (Kapczynski, Chaifetz, Katz & Benkler, 2005). Through the shift online and through exposure to Open Access, educators are being reminded that they have the choice to exercise their rights as copyright holders and apply open licensing solutions to moderate the terms of use of their content, while still receiving attribution[20] (Butcher, 2011).

In light of the research reviewed, we concur with Cronin's[21] differentiation between (1) OER and legality focused definitions of open practices, and (2) broader conceptions of open practices which incorporate these OER aspects but include open pedagogies, open learning and sharing. What is clear is that however the legal aspects of OER and OEP are interpreted or positioned, they are central to research of the type undertaken in this study.

Pedagogical dimensions of OEP

For Hodgkinson-Williams (2014), the dimension of pedagogic openness includes choices about pedagogic strategies as well as deliberated strategies for facilitating student learning and assessment practices. On the other hand, Beetham et al.'s (2012) features of open practices consist of broad and typical behaviours indicative of open practices and offer illustrations of practices that align to pedagogical strategies underpinned by the need to meet the needs of diverse learners.

---

17 https://www.insidehighered.com/views/2012/06/21/essay-faculty-members-and-intellectual-property-rights
18 http://www.chronicle.com/article/aaup-sees-moocs-as-spawning/139743
19 https://www.insidehighered.com/news/2013/03/08/researchers-explore-who-taking-moocs-and-why-so-many-drop-out
20 http://www.chronicle.com/article/aaup-sees-moocs-as-spawning/139743
21 http://catherinecronin.net/research/openness-and-praxis/

Beetham et al.'s (2012) conceptions of open practices are informed by three sources. The first is the "OEP guide" (Andrade et al., 2011), which comprises a set of open practice guidelines produced by, among others, the International Council for Open and Distance Education, the Open University, the United Nations Educational, Scientific and Cultural Organization, and partnering universities in the UK and Europe. These guidelines conceive of open practices in terms of "OER usage" and "learning architecture", with each category having three levels (low, medium and high) (Andrade et al., 2011). The second source comprises Beetham's "Update on open content/practices"[22], which emerged from the UK OER programme. The third source is an OER impact study undertaken by Masterman and Wild (2011) which asks about the pedagogic, attitudinal, logistical and strategic factors conducive to uptake and sustained practice in the use of OER, and, conversely, the impediments. Based on these studies, Beetham et al.'s (2012) six indicative features of open practices offer broad and inclusive indicators of open practices that are not bound up ineluctably with open licensing constraints. These features are:

1. Opening up content to students not on campus or not formally enrolled.
2. Sharing and collaborating on content with other practitioners.
3. Reusing content in teaching contexts.
4. Using or encouraging others to use open content.
5. Making knowledge publicly accessible.
6. Teaching and learning in open contexts.

Derived from empirical studies of the open practices of educators, these features serve as useful indicators of open practices amongst educators.

We observed many of these open pedagogical practices in our study of UCT educators engaged in MOOC design, and found that these practices are better described and understood using a combination of the features of pedagogic openness from Hodgkinson-Williams and Beetham et al., explained in more detail in the Methodology section. Using their distinct features as indicators of open practices, we are able to offer a broader and more differentiated picture of how the MOOC educators' pedagogical practices and attitudes shift.

Financial dimensions of OEP

Hodgkinson-Williams (2014) refers to financial openness as a continuum in which access to learning resources is either free (most affordable) for the user, on the one end of the spectrum, or charged for (least affordable) on the other. Between these categories there are learning resources which entail a small charge, a subscription fee, an in-kind contribution or (closest to free) a registration requirement. Downes (2007) has made an in-principle argument that for a learning resource to be open it must be free to the user, whereas Thrun[23] has contended that a fee is justifiable. This dimension is tentatively explored in the context of the cost of materials and whether they should be free to the user or whether a defensible strategy of financial openness might consider affordability rather than being free of charge to be feasible. In the context of this study, we have interpreted this dimension as including discussions around MOOC business models, OER creation in MOOCs and sustainability.

---

22 https://oersynthesis.jiscinvolve.org/wp/2011/06/04/update-on-open-contentopen-practices/
23 https://pando.com/2014/05/12/a-qa-with-godfather-of-moocs-sebastian-thrun-after-he-disavowed-his-godchild/

Research questions

The overarching aim of this study is to address the question: How does MOOC-making with OER adoption influence educators' OEP?

In order to address this overarching question, we ask eight specific research questions (RQs). The first two RQs focus on the context in which the educators operate and interrogate their underlying motivations and understandings of openness. RQs 3 and 4 consider the MOOC platforms' design constraints and enabling factors, while RQs 5–7 consider the ways in which the three dimensions of openness manifest. The final RQ considers the opportunity for reuse of MOOC OER beyond the MOOC.

- RQ1. Why do educators create MOOCs?
- RQ2. How do educators understand openness in education?
- RQ3. What are the contextual dimensions which shape OEP?
- RQ4. How do MOOC design tools enable OEP?
- RQ5. How do educators understand and express copyright, licensing and the legal dimensions of openness?
- RQ6. How is pedagogical openness experienced and expressed as an OEP in MOOCs in terms of the educators' aims?
- RQ7. How is financial openness expressed?
- RQ8. How do educators use and reuse OER?

Methodology

The study employed a qualitative approach. One of the researchers, an embedded observer, interviewed the MOOC lead educators, ran focus groups and observed the process of educators creating their MOOCs. Two researchers were part of the MOOC learning design team with whom the educators collaborated in creating the MOOCs. Data were obtained through semi-structured interviews and focus group discussions with the MOOC educators and MOOC learning designers, as well as through observations of the MOOC-making process. Other sources of data included proposals submitted to the institutional MOOC Advisory Committee, monitoring and evaluation reports, promotional videos created by the educators, institutional policies and strategic plans, permission forms for MOOC content rights and artefacts of course content.

A total of 19 interviews were conducted with the MOOC lead educators, two focus groups with the MOOC learning design team and three post-course reflection sessions with the lead educators for MedArts, Mind and UCR. We interviewed the lead educators from three of the MOOCs (MedArts, Mind and UCR) at specific stages before the MOOC ran, after the first run of the MOOC and 6–10 months after the MOOC's launch. Due to time constraints, the Ed4All educators were only interviewed before the MOOC launch and once afterwards. The first interviews provided a baseline for the educators' existing practices. Similar questions were asked at each stage to enable comparison, and the responses to earlier interviews were used to further refine interview questions for later interviews. In this way, we could note changes in practices over time and ascertain where new practices or tensions might have emerged.

We also conducted focus group discussions with the lead educators after the first run of their respective MOOCs and focus groups with three members of the MOOC learning design team.

Three other respondents were members of the MOOC learning design team.

Interview and focus group data were coded using NVivo10. The initial codes were shaped by the conceptual framework through an iterative process of engaging with the data, which led to a consolidated analytical framework. Several dimensions of open practices were identified, allowing for an accurate and more differentiated picture of how educators' open practices shift in the MOOC environment.

Analytical framework

As a first step in understanding the MOOC educators' changing practices, it was informative to analyse the reasons they gave for making a MOOC. In asking this question, it was possible to clarify the MOOC educators' often implicit intentions and motivations for making MOOCs. While the immediate goal was to create an open course, the underlying reasons for creating and offering a MOOC and what they wished to achieve were not as clear. Asking this question helped to contextualise how OER and OEP might be enablers (or not) to educators' underlying objectives.

Next we used the coded transcripts to understand how the MOOC design helps, or does not help, educators achieve their objectives for the course. The term "MOOC design" is used to describe the opportunities and constraints offered by the MOOC format and platforms as a particular form of online learning, and therefore represents the tools and strategies for achieving the educators' outcomes and objectives.

The term "MOOC design" as used in this study does not refer to all tools involved in making a MOOC, but only to those that are important for the educators and which, by inference, are important in their understanding and adoption of open practices. More specifically, it includes the conceptual and licensing tools introduced by the learning designers and the tools associated with the MOOC hosting platforms.

As noted, the lead educators did not develop MOOCs or enact open practices in isolation. Learning designers co-designed the MOOCs and were equipped with licensing and conceptual tools. Licensing tools relate to the CC licences for educational resources that were suggested to lead educators by the learning designers during group discussions. These open licensing recommendations were informed by the policy environment at the university, where open licensing is encouraged.[24] Conceptual tools relate to different pedagogies as well as ways of structuring the course and presenting the materials that the learning designers bring to the MOOC creation process.

Having noted the motivation, context and tools that enable MOOC-making, we then analysed the MOOC educators' practices observed in terms of the three dimensions of openness identified in the literature and conceptual framework. These three dimensions represent three perspectives of OEP: a materials or content perspective (legal), a learner-centred perspective (pedagogical) and an institutional perspective (financial).

---

24   http://www.uct.ac.za/downloads/uct.ac.za/about/policies/OpenUCT_Policy.pdf

Hodgkinson-Williams' (2014) conception of "pedagogic openness" has been refined to account for two dimensions of the pedagogy required for teaching a diverse, global MOOC audience. The first is a communicative aspect – i.e. the communicative strategies with which educators must engage to retain the focus and attention of MOOC audiences and ensure comprehension of the content they convey. Examples of this include achieving succinctness and clarity in one's delivery, focus on the essence of an idea or concept, and heightened attention to the words and syntactic structure one employs to convey a message. Whereas traditional university lectures are 45 minutes long, MOOC educators must pare down their content delivery into a concise seven- to 12-minute video format. Achieving the communicative skills to do this is indicative of what we term "strategies of pedagogic openness". The application of such skills is contingent upon the open audience, and there is thus a sense in which one must have practical experience of teaching in this mode before one can acquire these skills.

The second aspect of strategies for pedagogic openness relates to the structuring and assessment of course content. The MOOC mode compels educators to consider the importance of selecting and arranging their learning materials in ways that facilitate learning for learners with a wide range of backgrounds and prior knowledge. Similarly, designing a range of assessments – including teacher assessment, peer assessment and self-assessment – as part of the course structure requires educators to be open to the many backgrounds and expectations of learners. Structuring courses and formulating assessment in conventional university settings is different from formulating assessment and arranging learning materials for an open, diverse and global audience. A university educator can, to a large extent, rely on assumptions about learners in the formulation of assessment, including assumptions regarding learners' language proficiency, level of education and intellectual background. The structure of courses and assessments tends to reflect these assumptions. By contrast, MOOC learners tend to be highly diverse with differing and sometimes unknown needs. Acquiring the skills to structure learning content and assess open audiences is thus an important aspect of strategies of pedagogic openness.

Three additional aspects of pedagogical openness drawn from Beetham et al. (2012) complete this study's operational definition of pedagogical openness. These are reusing OER in teaching contexts, making knowledge publicly accessible, and teaching and learning in open contexts. The first relates to how educators reuse OER that is produced as part of a MOOC. The other two aspects relate to course-level practices where educators make their knowledge publicly accessible through the MOOC and engage in teaching and learning in open networks. All of these are specific manifestations of practices, which according to Beetham et al. (2012) are catalysed by OER, and which we have reframed for a MOOC teaching and learning environment.

Finally, while financial openness has been defined quite broadly by Hodgkinson-Williams (2014) to refer to a continuum in which access to learning resources is either free or paid for, in this study we reframe this dimension to consider the cost (to the educator) of making MOOCs as well as how to ensure affordable access to MOOCs for learners who might wish to purchase a certificate. Underlying this dimension is the broader issue of the sustainability of Open Education initiatives.

The analytical framework is summarised and related to the eight research questions in Figure 1.

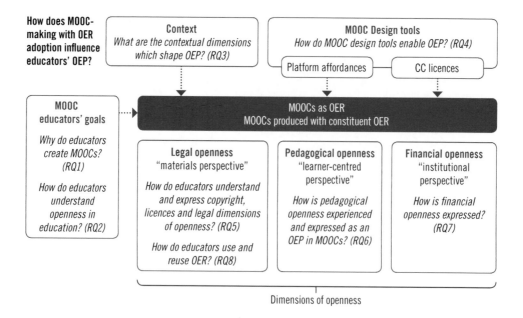

Figure 1: **Analytical framework related to the study's eight research questions**

Findings

Understanding the MOOC educators and their contexts

Why educators create MOOCs

Knowing the educators' motivations for creating MOOCs informs our understanding of educators' intentions and enables the unpacking of assumptions and choices. The motivations and objectives of individual educators emerged from an analysis of the initial proposals for funding, the promotional videos the educators created for each MOOC, and the lead educator interviews. For the MedArts and Mind educators, the objective was mainly to develop their respective disciplinary fields, while for the UCR and Ed4All educators, objectives related more to supporting flexible professional development and capacity-building. These objectives are expanded upon below in more detail.

MOOC 1: MedArts

The original MedArts proposal stated that "this MOOC is an opportunity to develop an academic project in the Medical Humanities in Africa and globally". This suggests that the educators wanted to advance the interdisciplinary field of Medical Humanities and that they saw the MOOC as a form of online learning that could help them introduce key ideas and share these in an African context. This vision is clearly articulated in the MOOC's promotional video, in which the educators describe interdisciplinarity as a way of addressing global health challenges. In the video, SR states that he is "constantly looking for new ways of addressing complex health issues like equity for social justice" and that he suspects "an interdisciplinary approach holds the key".

The MedArts lead educators saw the MOOC as a way of developing the Medical Humanities that was distinct from other activities aimed at achieving the same goal, such as writing newspaper articles, holding public lectures, writing journal articles and running a face-to-face master's course. They also felt that making MOOCs might result in research collaboration. Before the MOOC ran, they expressed reservations about whether their ambitions would be realised, but in the interviews conducted after the first run of the MOOC they considered their goals to have been achieved.

The integration of the MOOC with face-to-face classroom teaching emerged as a result of the educators' experience within online teaching. As SL remarked: "I would like our students to have access to those segments of the MOOC which could generate new interdisciplinary research projects." The role of the MOOC in promoting the interdisciplinary approach inherent in the Medical Humanities was still part of the core objective, but the MOOC experience appears to have given the educators new ways in which to enact that objective, i.e. through closer integration of the MOOC and their face-to-face teaching.

The final set of MedArts interviews was conducted six months after the MOOC was first run, during which time the MOOC had been run again. The interviews revealed that the educators now had more nuanced understandings of the field and its trajectory. SR commented that, in relation to teaching the Medical Humanities as a formal course and as a MOOC, "it's highlighted for us the lack of attention to political economy, questions around transformation, the underclass and disease and the lack of specific kinds of attention around how the arts has responded to poverty and to health crises". The MOOC experience appears to have made the MedArts educators aware of the limitations of their previous approach towards achieving their field-building objective and they partly attributed this shift in focus to the presence of many different kinds of students who participated in the MOOC. SR acknowledged that some of the learners "were doctors, nurses, healers and artists who were retired, who had a wealth of knowledge and who could then bring that back into conversations and into an environment which was not prejudiced along age lines, race lines or gender lines".

MOOC 2: Mind

The Mind lead educator, MS, had previously articulated the broad objective of growing the field of neuropsychoanalysis (Kaplan-Solms & Solms, 2000). Analysis of the initial MOOC proposal, the promotional video and the first set of interviews suggests that this was also the key focus of the Mind MOOC. In the initial proposal, MS indicated that the purpose of the MOOC was to make "technical research knowledge accessible to the general public", and that he was interested in developing a MOOC to promote "interdisciplinary and transdisciplinary research in sciences and the humanities". At the time, MS proposed a website development project with similar goals, called Talking Head, which later used MOOC material.[25]

---

25 http://talking-head.org

In the first set of interviews prior to the launch of the MOOC, he added that the MOOC aligned with his pedagogical goal, which entailed addressing the following questions: How do I speak to two different audiences at the same time? How do I make the neuroscience accessible to the psychologists, and how do I make the life of the mind accessible to neuroscientists?

In later interviews, MS reflected on how the MOOC had enabled him to reach a broader audience and that this has been important for advancing the discipline. The experience of running the MOOC strengthened his resolve to commit further time and resources to MOOC runs as well as student question-and-answer sessions, despite the time-consuming nature of the endeavour.

MOOC 3: UCR

The UCR lead educator JK's motivation for delivering the MOOC, as outlined in the initial proposal, was the desire to offer a "unitary programme for capacitating research skills [which] can contribute to reducing duplication of these types of programmes currently offered to MMed [Master of Medicine] students". The proposal indicates a desire to reach both MMed students at the university as well as those working in global healthcare settings. It also identified a longer-term, more strategic approach to influencing the way medical education is delivered in his faculty. In his proposal, he stated that the MOOC "represents an opportunity to consider and test the feasibility of certified short courses, online courses for medical education, and to build a broad research network". His personal website[26] demonstrates that this is an objective he was striving towards prior to becoming involved in MOOC-making, as he had been engaged in sharing an extensive collection of teaching resources as video OER. These efforts led to him receiving an Individual Educator Award[27] from the Open Education Consortium in 2014.

The UCR MOOC promotional video focuses heavily on the capacity-building and professional development opportunities offered in the MOOC, with the educator explaining why students need to understand medical statistics and that the course would give students "a deep sense of understanding of what is meant by the numbers and techniques mentioned in the methods and results section of research papers". In the first set of interviews prior to the MOOC launch, JK spoke of the rationale for why the MOOC was necessary, commenting that: "I have to answer those questions every day anyway, there must be lots of people out there with the exact same questions, so let's answer them in this way."

When interviewed six months after the MOOC's first run, JK was of the view that his MOOC had achieved its local aim – that of assisting junior researchers and medical students with the concepts and tools required for interpreting and undertaking clinical research. At this stage, JK also indicated that the MOOC experience had ignited an expansion of the original objective. He was not satisfied with the scope of content he was able to cover in the original MOOC and wanted to create follow-up MOOCs so that he could more adequately equip learners with the skills required to interpret and conduct clinical research. He also indicated his growing understanding that the MOOC arena had potential for financial return and could

---

26   https://www.juanklopper.com
27   http://www.oeconsortium.org/projects/open-education-awards-for-excellence/2014-winners-of-ace-awards/2014-ace-winners-individual-categories/

be part of a sustainable business model for bringing money into his unit. He did, however, state that the lack of resources to make MOOCs could be an obstruction to achieving this.

MOOC 4: Ed4All

The motivation of the Ed4All educators, JM and CO, was to enable the professional development of teachers and stakeholders working in schools to be able to foster inclusivity in schools. As stated in the promotional video, the educators' objective was to develop teachers so that "educational systems can adjust to welcome children with disabilities into schools". The initial MOOC proposal indicates that the objective was slightly broader than teacher professional development at an individual level and encompassed the inclusion of other stakeholders in the community who would need to build "partnerships across different sectors of society, especially between schools, parents, community members and disabled people's organisations".

The first interviews prior to the first MOOC run indicate that JM and CO wanted to equip educators with concepts and low-cost practical strategies to make classrooms and learning environments inclusive for disabled learners and to change attitudes: "we want to say, it doesn't take a ton of money, it doesn't take huge resources. The biggest challenge … is still attitudes" (CO). While there was a clear focus on teacher professional development, there was also an indication that the educators wanted to bring together multiple perspectives about disability and engender community-level conversation. JM stated, "My biggest hope would be that it would actually infiltrate villages and little towns … in Ghana and Nigeria and in various African and other lower- or middle-income countries."

Following the MOOC's first run, CO noted that the MOOC had gone some way towards achieving the ends she had hoped for, with associated outcomes, including people sharing stories about disability and struggles in the classroom, educators sharing reflections on their attempts to make their classrooms more inclusive, rich discussions on the topic, and even educators taking the MOOC declaring that they would try the inclusive education approach and strategies in their own schools and classrooms.

While the timeline of the study did not allow for third interviews for this MOOC, the lead educators have subsequently gone on to raise more funds for further MOOCs and online courses focused on disability and inclusion. This indicates that they see MOOCs as being an element in achieving their overall objective.

How educators understand openness in education

While the educators had specific goals relating to their rationale for offering MOOCs, it was clear that they did not explicitly equate MOOCs with openness, OER or Open Education when they planned their MOOCs. This was due less to an ideological objection to openness than to the fact that (with the exception of JK) the MOOC educators had nascent and limited understandings of "openness". Based on the initial interviews, the understanding they did have seemed to be centred around issues of access and reach, about which they were generally positive.

MOOC 1: MedArts

SR saw the openness of the MOOC encompassing "the idea that knowledge should be shared as far and as widely as possible, and not kept to a few elite" and that MOOCs were one way in which this could be achieved; so it was "the right way to go". He noted that he did not have much knowledge of MOOCs and openness before making the MOOC, and remarked that marketing would be required amongst academics to promote an understanding of openness.

MOOC 2: Mind

The Mind lead educator's assistant, AD, took the openness of the MOOC to mean that anyone could access the course and its resources on a flexible basis. Lead educator MS understood the "open" in MOOC to mean that the MOOC content "has to be open access and that everything has to be free of copyright". Furthermore, MS positioned himself as "all for open access" and remarked that "once the material is there, once it's open access, you can multiply that effect".

MOOC 3: UCR

Prior to the study, openness had long been important to UCR lead educator JK and he had a sophisticated understanding of the concept. He had already been involved in and committed to Open Education for some time and he understood "open" to mean sharing his own knowledge as he has uniquely constructed and configured it. For him, this was tied to the idea that it is better for learning if students can access multiple explications of an idea or content, as this increases the likelihood of understanding it.

MOOC 4: Ed4All

Before the Ed4All MOOC launched, lead educator CO understood openness in terms of access to the course material, sharing knowledge, acknowledging the differences among learners and producing educational content with those factors in mind. It also meant taking steps to ensure that one's content could be reused. For JM, the "open" in MOOC meant the MOOC was "basically just a free-for-all", and that you could "fit it into your own learning in a way that works for you". JM therefore saw openness in terms of content being accessible to interested learners and as a mechanism for enabling learners to participate flexibly.

Contextual dimensions shaping OEP

On investigating the contextual dimensions which shape OEP, we had initially envisioned that we would find greater variation in MOOC-making contexts that might influence OEP. The MOOC-making contexts within UCT did, however, have many similarities across disciplines. Nevertheless, the analysis reflects some differences across legal, pedagogical and financial openness dimensions, such as the fact that only one educator was seen to be engaging with financial openness.

MOOC design tools enabling three dimensions of openness

The analysis of interviews helped us identify how MOOC design tools enable OEP. These were not software or production tools. Rather, we introduced MOOC design as a bundle of tools inherent in the MOOC format which mediated, influenced and constrained the choices of the educators in this study. Furthermore, we examine how the educators engaged with the tools on offer and which tools they focused on and used, either in mainstream practice or to develop OEP in pursuit of their objectives. The "bundle" comprises three components: MOOC licensing tools, MOOC pedagogical tools and MOOC financing tools.

Experiences of legal openness, OER creation and OEP

Within the context of this study, MOOC design influenced how educators understood and expressed copyright, licences and informed the nature of legal dimensions of openness. The MOOC design tools mediated OER creation and enabled educators to make their knowledge publicly available, an indicator suggested by Beetham et al. (2012) as a form of OEP.

MOOC 1: MedArts

The MedArts lead educators were committed to openness in terms of reach and had to contend with copyright issues at the outset when two of their colleagues decided not to participate in the MOOC, citing concerns about losing control of copyright of their work if it became available beyond the confines of the traditional classroom. SR thought that his colleagues raised important issues which forced them to think about copyright and licensing in more detail. He said that he was aware of the complexities of copyright in relation to research, but not in terms of teaching. After the course had run, he acknowledged that he had not realised that copyright would be an issue, especially in terms of third-party copyright. He expressed shock when he realised that he was not able to use certain published materials (including some of his own research) in his teaching due to copyright restrictions. Despite this realisation and appreciation of the value of open licensing, the MedArts lead educators were not particularly comfortable or familiar with the specifics or nuances of the different types of CC licences and, while they had a general understanding of licensing, SL acknowledged that it was "the expert team [the MOOC design team]" that made navigating the legal issues possible.

MOOC 2: Mind

In the interviews with Mind lead educator MS and the assistant AD, it became clear that making the MOOC brought the issue of copyright to the attention of the educators from the outset. They noted restrictions experienced due to third-party copyright considerations and would have liked for more materials to be available. AD recounted how they received permission from publishers to reproduce content or use Open Access articles in their course materials.

At the beginning of the MOOC-making process, there were misunderstandings, a limited understanding of open licensing and a widely shared misconception that Open Access meant giving up one's copyright. Through working with the MOOC design team, MS was exposed to different types of open licensing and was very keen on the reuse of his materials. When he came to reflect on his experience during an interview after the first MOOC run, he said that he was unequivocally in strong support of open licensing. At the same time, he was aware of the ethics and considerations of privacy and anonymity online. He stated that he was making a MOOC in order to grow the new discipline in which he worked and to spread knowledge, and that CC licences helped him to do so.

As was the case with the MedArts educators, MS realised early on that copyright restrictions curbed the wider use of learning and intellectual resources in MOOC production and he considered restrictive copyright provisions as "antithetical" to the intellectual project.

MOOC 3: UCR

The UCR lead educator, JK, was deeply committed to making teaching resources freely available from the outset of the MOOC-making process. He expressed an aversion to the concept of access to educational resources being restricted to certain universities as well as to the notion of individual ownership, but showed no particular interest in the specifics of licensing and copyright. JK began his MOOC-making process with a strong commitment to making his educational resources "available to anyone", and was convinced of the benefits of doing so. However, as with the other educators, he was not interested in mastering the technical aspects of open licensing.

MOOC 4: Ed4All

The Ed4All educators were clear from the outset that they wanted to make their resources openly available. Despite some previous exposure to the Open Access and copyright debate, they found MOOC copyright issues complex and difficult to negotiate. While they knew about copyright, they were not familiar with the scope of open licences available and experienced copyright decision-making as a burden.

The process of making the MOOC inspired careful consideration of licensing options for the MOOC as well as discussion about the kind of licensing in the educators' future formal courses. JM noted that they had decided to openly license the Ed4All MOOC under a CC-BY licence so that even if educators wanted to reuse part of the MOOC in a paid-for course, this would still serve the core objective of offering strategies to make schools more inclusive, even in low-resource settings.

Across the four MOOCs, we found instances of educators engaging with legal openness, approaching content creation from the perspective of OER production to make resources openly available to current MOOC participants, as well as to enable reuse beyond the specific parameters of the MOOC. Two aspects affected the adoption of OER in the study: (1) an institutional policy that supports openness; and (2) learning designers who are experienced with CC licensing and can explain the benefits of open licensing to educators. Of the 21 educators involved in the four MOOCs studied, only two guest educators (in MedArts) were reluctant to utilise an open licensing approach on their own educational materials.

Although not all the MOOC educators in this study were aware of OER and associated practices, there was an enabling institutional context with regards to OEP already in place prior to the start of the MOOCs project. A number of years before the MOOCs project, the Centre for Education Technology initiated a series of open projects addressing Open Access, Open Data, Open Research and other open practices (Czerniewicz, Cox, Hodgkinson-Williams & Willmers, 2015; Deacon & WynSculley, 2009). In 2014, the university approved an Open Access Policy "for taking forward open scholarship and open education as part of a commitment to scholarly communication, e-research and digital content stewardship" (UCT, 2014, p.2). This enabling environment meant that the MOOC design team, with whom the educators in this study co-created their MOOCs, could consult people in the institution who had experience of CC licensing and intellectual property for advice. Because of this institutional open agenda, the MOOC design team were in a knowledgeable position to propose to MOOC educators that open licensing could be of value to their goals and would encourage reuse beyond the formal delivery of the MOOC. MOOC educators were given the option not to utilise open licensing, as open licensing was not a prerequisite in the MOOC-making process, nor was a specific licence proposed. However, the process of MOOC development included practical conversations about copyright management, through which the MOOC educators developed and deepened their understandings of open licensing and OER creation. Such conversations enabled educators to use and create OER in their MOOCs. Therefore, while the OER approach was not dictated, it played a role in catalysing forms of OEP mediated by the affordances of the MOOC format once it was employed in the resource-development process.

This study indicates that at least two conditions are required to support OER creation. First, educators should have a sense of the value of open licensing for achieving reach and reuse of their materials, this value being made apparent through interaction with potential and actual users. Second, it is important that, once the sense of value is established, a supporting staff member or other intermediary who is knowledgeable about copyright management and open licensing is available to assist educators who wish to explore licensing options. This is necessitated by the fact that many educators perceive the technicalities of CC licensing as beyond the ambit of their skills or labour. In all four of the MOOCs studied, the educators, while valuing the power of OER for achieving their objectives, did not wish to acquire the skills associated with open licensing and saw this as someone else's work.

While the MOOC-making process enabled OER creation and reuse, it also led to some contradictions. Even though most of the MOOC materials were OER, these materials were technically only directly accessible to those who were enrolled in the courses. This was because the OER material was contained within the MOOC and would not necessarily be persistently accessible via an Open Access repository. Therefore, these materials would not, strictly speaking, be considered OER.

It is in the interest of the Coursera and FutureLearn platforms to mitigate this apparent contradiction and make some content openly or at least easily accessible. For example, individual course pages could be opened to anyone, even if they are not enrolled in the course, and selected learning materials could be shared as OER in repositories or "on-demand". A perceived strength of using the MOOC format for the course content, as recognised by the educators, is that learning materials are presented in a context so that the embedded pedagogy, course structure and cohort of learners collectively give the learning material value for reuse and sharing. Despite the design of the MOOC platforms limiting some forms of openness, the educators can (and do) engineer other strategies for sharing, and thus adopt open practices through sharing MOOC materials to make their content and knowledge publicly available.

Another potential contradiction is that while the MOOC design requirements would seem to encourage OER adoption because the delivery mode involves non-registered students, all MOOC platform agreements make it clear that fully copyrighted materials cannot be used without permission. This was felt to be a limitation on how the educators could teach their courses. In MedArts, the educators could not set the same prescribed reading list for the MOOC as for their formal course due to copyright restrictions. They were thus compelled to find OER or Open Access literature that could be included as substitutes. One of the MedArts educators saw the lack of access to key readings in the field as reducing the "intellectual integrity" of the course, while the other lead educator considered this a limitation on the "depth" of the course.

Experience of pedagogical openness and OEP in MOOCs

The data from this study indicate that educators engaged in strategies of pedagogical openness in terms of the learning design and teaching approaches required to meet the needs of a diverse group of learners. Across the four MOOCs, the educators considered the need to structure content and assessment for a general audience and to consider the mode of delivery. Thus, the experience of making a MOOC not only exposed educators to new open pedagogical strategies, but also to feedback from MOOC participants. The feedback in the form of completed assessments, peer review, comments, discussion threads and assignments enabled the educators to witness the effect of the pedagogical strategies they employed as they taught in a distributed network and as part of a diverse community.

MOOC 1: MedArts

The MOOC-making process provided the educators with an opportunity to reflect upon their conventional educational practices. Due to the nature of MOOC design – i.e. courses structured into steps within weeks and punctuated with text, as well as co-created videos, quizzes, assignments, peer reviews and discussion prompts – and because the course would be globally accessible, the educators were induced to consider new ways of structuring their educational resources and their teaching. Lead educator SL, for example, was struck by the careful premeditated preparation that was required for producing a video in the MedArts MOOC.

When the MedArts MOOC went live with its very large number of enrolments, the lead educators had occasion to consider their own educational practices. When interviewed after the MOOC launched, SL expressed that she realised that producing crisp, carefully conceptualised videos of her lectures would allow for richer, more engaged discussion with students. This approach was considered more effective than repeatedly offering the same lecture to students in a face-to-face classroom setting who were often fatigued from a long day and struggled to muster the requisite concentration and interest. Here the flipped classroom approach using the MOOC (which involves learners engaging with materials prior to coming to class) invigorated the educator's interest in how this pedagogy could be used. SR was impressed by the formation of online learning communities and a Facebook group that was created by cancer patients who were taking the course, remarking that the community appeared to have "congealed in a more palpable way on the MOOC site, than it does in my face-to-face teaching". The MOOC's openness fostered a unique sense of community that the educators had not found possible in a traditional classroom.

MOOC 2: Mind

Communicating the ideas of their interdisciplinary fields to a diverse audience meant that the educators had to adopt different pedagogical approaches in order to be as inclusive as possible. Interviewed 10 months after the Mind MOOC launched, MS found that he was compelled to "really pare down ideas to core essential content" when communicating content because of the unknown participant profile and level of technical proficiency. He commented that this mode of teaching clarified his own thinking process and forced him to "convey really complicated material in seven-minute chunks".

MS saw the pedagogical approach he had adopted as valuable and as a means for the small number of neuropsychoanalysis specialists in the world to more effectively pool resources. He concluded that the MOOC mode of open teaching had "taught" and "encouraged" him to "use online platforms for teaching people in and about that field".

An experimental feature of Mind's open pedagogy was the "Ask Mark" videos. MOOC participants were prompted to ask the educator a question at certain points in the course; the following week he would provide answers to selected questions in a short video. This was implemented in the first two runs of the MOOC, despite the educator being disinclined to repeat the exercise due to time constraints. During a reflection session before the third run of the MOOC, however, the educator expressed an interest in fielding more questions and remarked that he really enjoyed this component. The key pedagogic openness strategies that MS acquired were more succinct delivery of content and utilisation of targeted video responses to learners' questions.

MOOC 3: UCR

In the case of the UCR MOOC, lead educator JK developed strategies of pedagogic openness which included effective ways of utilising assessment and peer review in the course, responding to learner comments and adjusting the course in response to feedback from learners. The point is not that he learned how to assess students, but rather that he adopted strategies to construct assessment tools for an open and diverse audience. He also came to see assessment as a necessary part of effective learning – particularly in an open context – and saw these strategies as relevant to his usual face-to-face teaching.

MOOC 4: Ed4All

In reflecting on different approaches required for open online teaching, in the first interview Ed4All lead educator JM observed "a gap between the person and the resources and how they actually make use of and mediate the resources", and was alerted to the necessity of bridging the access challenge. She argued that educators need to provide accessible resources so that aspiring learners can learn, and that this requires new skills on the part of educators: "there are misconceptions that you just put it up online and people can use it [but] it has to be clearly structured and it has to be done properly … there are a lot of skills involved in getting it right and doing it right".

In this instance, JM demonstrates the principle that effective open practices require more than a desire or willingness to make one's content openly available – since for open resources to be useful to potential learners, the resources must be accompanied by a pedagogical approach that enables learners to utilise resources effectively. In the interview following the first Ed4All run, CO remarked upon the substantial difference between communicating to a conventional postgraduate audience and to a MOOC audience, and argued that the latter required "a whole new set of skills". For her, the overarching point was that the open online learning environment required a new level of clarity.

Expressions of financial openness in MOOC production

As a dimension of openness, we understand an educator's manifestation of financial openness as referring to the view the educator holds about whether or how open learning should involve costs to users and how it should be funded. This dimension is particularly pertinent to MOOCs, considering the well-documented challenges of funding or achieving sustainability of Open Education initiatives in ways that also value or acknowledge the academic labour involved in creating them (Almeida, 2017).

This study revealed one case where an educator redefined his sense of openness to pragmatically understand Open Access as a system in which resources are accessible to those who cannot afford them, but involve a monetary cost to those who are able to afford access – a model implemented in the interests of longer-term sustainability.

MOOC 3: UCR

The view of UCR lead educator JK was that an economically secure learner could pay for access to the MOOC and its resources, and in doing so enable a form of cross-subsidisation which enables the continued production of learning resources. A key caveat is that learners who are unable to afford access to the MOOC must be able to secure financial aid and have the cost of obtaining a certificate (and in some cases access to the full course) covered by a third party. The openness of the MOOC is therefore contingent upon the financial standing of the learner, rather than whether it is free to all. This view is pragmatic and utilitarian. The educator considers two options: (1) financially secure learners pay for access, while financially constrained learners receive aid and thus free access; and (2) open access to all learners irrespective of their economic standing.

Within this context, option 2 means that finances for creating further learning courses are not available, while option 1 provides a sustainability model and resourcing for the creation of more learning resources.

For JK, there is a sense that his learning resources and his MOOC are open because they are accessible to those who can afford access to them as well as to those who cannot afford to pay for access. In addressing the tension between producing freely available courses and securing finances to produce such courses, he interprets open as affordable. This compromise is underpinned by the deeper value of inclusivity. Although they are not free of charge, affordable learning resources are not fully closed because there is a sense in which they are accessible.

JK's reasons for accepting a model of openness in which more affluent learners pay for access is different from Thrun's (Hodgkinson-Williams, 2014). Thrun's case for charging for access to Udacity courses hinges on the assertion that (1) paying students are more committed to the course, and (2) completion of the course is more likely when learners have paid for access to the course. The latter assertion relies on the pragmatic assumption that desirable learning occurs when a course is completed.

JK differs from the other MOOC educators who regard the question of how MOOCs are to be funded as outside of their purview. After the first run of the UCR MOOC, JK engaged with the problem of how to make future MOOCs financially sustainable. Before the MOOC was launched, he was already envisaging sustainable ways to make further MOOCs. The tension he confronts is that while MOOCs entail many benefits for learners and educators, they are expensive and the UCT MOOC Project is a funded and finite endeavour. Without a workable financial model or more funding, it would be highly challenging to undertake further MOOC development. JK referred to his inability to make additional MOOCs as a "bottleneck" and concluded that he would require external funding for further MOOC production. Eager to resolve the tension of wanting to make more MOOCs but being unable to do so under the extant financial model, JK self-financed his attendance at the 2016 Coursera conference where he met with Coursera executives to discuss funding for a follow-up course. The Coursera leadership noted that if JK could produce a course that would generate revenue from certificate sales, they would provide the initial capital to produce the MOOC.

Eleven months after the launch of the UCR MOOC, JK launched another MOOC using the initial capital provided by Coursera. For him it was important that he could secure funding for his follow-up MOOC himself. This, he argued, would constitute a "proof of concept" – namely, that an available means of locating funding for the production of MOOCs exists. Receiving funding for his MOOC from Coursera did, however, entail a compromise in terms of the openness of the course. In the UCR MOOC, entry was open to all. In his additional Coursera-funded MOOC, opting for a certificate will be compulsory, which means that learners wishing to enrol have two options: they can pay for the certificate and gain entry to the course, or they can request financial aid and gain entry. While accepting this compromise of openness-as-affordable, JK remained resolute that his MOOCs remained open, stating that if learners could not receive financial aid to access the MOOC, he would not release another MOOC under those conditions.

Educators' use and reuse of MOOC–OER beyond the MOOC

The final research question focuses on reuse of MOOC–OER beyond the formally delivered MOOC. In addressing this, we include: constituent OER available in the MOOC which can be reused in other courses or contexts, reuse of the entire MOOC (as a "pedagogically wrapped" OER) in other contexts, or cases where the MOOC teaching approach is reused in other contexts. We consider the reuse of OER or the MOOC in their entirety in other teaching contexts (or the desire to do so) as a manifestation of OEP.

Reuse in this context can have legal and/or pedagogical dimensions. Through the creation of constituent, openly licensed OER as part of the MOOCs, reuse of resources was both permitted and encouraged. It is challenging to track instances of reuse, since these permissions are granted upfront, but there were a number of examples of component reuse. In many of these cases, this was unanticipated and a surprise to the educators.

MOOC 1: MedArts

Upon release of the MedArts MOOC, lead educator SL remarked that it was important for the MedArts resources to be accessible after the MOOC run and reported that the process of making the MOOC had compelled her to start thinking about the importance of "building an archive" for the interdisciplinary field in which she was engaged. She hoped that the content of the MOOC would be reused and "replicated", noting that this was part of making content open. Specifically, SR expressed a positive view of flipped learning and noted that it would be preferable in the face-to-face classroom setting for learners to view video content before class so that discussions could start at a higher level.

Using video to communicate with learners compelled SR to reconsider the value of giving the same lecture to students approximately five times a year. To him, the accessibility and availability of the MedArts MOOC offered two benefits for students in SL's class: (1) the contents could be used in traditional face-to-face teaching to stimulate interdisciplinary research and ideas; and (2) it could be employed to spark interest in the subject amongst first-year students. Ten months after MedArts was first launched, she expressed a strong desire for the MOOC to remain available on an "open access" basis. This indicates a shift in the use of "open" vocabulary and a recognition of reuse potential. For SR, the accessibility of the MedArts MOOC was considered useful in terms of introducing people to the field of Medicine and the Arts. He reused the MOOC content numerous times and considered this a good means of increasing exposure to the field.

The MedArts MOOC was incorporated (reused) as a compulsory component of a face-to-face master's course at UCT. This exemplifies the extent to which the educators valued reuse of the MOOC materials and believed that the materials enhanced their face-to-face teaching.

MOOC 2: Mind

After the first run of the Mind MOOC, lead educator MS was of the view that reusing MOOC video lectures in his classes would be beneficial to students, as would be allowing them the autonomy to view lectures in their own time. This would be the case even when the videos were stripped of the affordances of MOOC design, such as interaction with participants and links to other resources. Lecturers would also not have to repeat lectures due to venue-size constraints. As the field progressed, he could produce new video material. He expressed a desire to use a MOOC-like format for his face-to-face teaching of larger classes by showing the video rather than repeating the same lectures in person each year. A year later, AD first used the MOOC videos in a similar way for a course for semester-abroad students. A component of the Mind MOOC was also incorporated into a formal psychiatry registrar course in the United States by one of MS's colleagues.

MS was also of the view that he would reuse his MOOC videos on his neuropsychoanalysis website so that he could reach wider audiences without having to travel to them in person. He believed that this, as well as reusing his MOOC materials more generally, would advance field-building. Later, the MOOC videos were reused in the "Talking Head" website MS initiated with similar objectives. Another important example of reuse was the "Ask Mark" videos, which were all reused by MS for a different online education project. The reuse capabilities of openly licensed material were considered a major benefit, with MS noting the potential in terms of saving time and other benefits such as linking learners to relevant texts and online sources.

MOOC 3: UCR

Prior to his involvement in MOOC-making, UCR lead educator JK was a proponent of reusing educational resources. He believed there were many positive opportunities for universities to reuse open learning materials, but that these had not been properly exploited and he regretted the fact that the university had not encouraged reuse of open learning materials more explicitly. The goal of JK's MOOC, as with those discussed above, was closely related to its reuse potential. He emphasised that having his MOOC available to students meant that he would not have to repeatedly answer the same research-related questions and that it provided affordances for students and medical professions to be better equipped with the skills necessary to interpret clinical research.

After witnessing the UCR MOOC's first run, JK noted that his MOOC had in part served his goal of equipping medical professionals and students with skills for interpreting clinical research. He remarked that he had been contacted by educators from elsewhere who had utilised the MOOC and found it very useful for teaching research and statistics. Locally, the MOOC was incorporated into a formal course offered by the Centre for Clinical Research at UCT, and the head of that unit had written to colleagues suggesting that they encourage their students to take the course. JK emphasised that he wanted his course to be reused as a formal requirement for registrars locally and was happy for the course to be reused and segmented in whatever way desired. He was impressed that his MOOC had been endorsed and reused in a variety of contexts and in that way served his aim of locally and globally equipping learners with tools to better interpret clinical research.

MOOC 4: Ed4All

As in each of the other MOOCs described, motivation around reuse of the Ed4All MOOC and its contents can be more clearly understood when it is related to the educators' objectives in creating the MOOC. For the Ed4All educators, the intention was that it would be used in low-resource learning environments and schools to shift thinking on inclusion and offer strategies for making education activities more inclusive. Reuse in such contexts was thus integral in the motivation for making the MOOC, and in its design and communications. For CO, engaging with the concept of OER and licensing their MOOC material openly as part of the MOOC-making process "forced" her to rethink and reflect on how her teaching resources related to a greater good. JM considered that it was best for all the MOOC material to be openly licensed "on principle". She also hoped to integrate part of the MOOC into her formal lecture series for physiotherapy students. For her, the ongoing accessibility of the course would also mean that learners could dip into the field and determine for themselves whether they wanted to pursue more formal study. In this way learners could be spared from paying fees for a course or degree they might not wish to study.

Having observed the MOOC's first run, CO was pleased about the fact that the materials and resources in the MOOC had been used in a number of countries. Based on comments and emails from educators, JM believed that the MOOC had made an impact on educational practices engaging children with disabilities. She desired local reuse and wanted to integrate the MOOC into a postgraduate course. She also wanted to reuse and adapt the MOOC as an introductory course for a series of European Union-funded courses for teachers working with children with disabilities. She added that she had been contacted by a Korean university for permission to use some of the resources in the MOOC. Based on what she had experienced in terms of reuse of MOOC materials, she started sharing more of her teaching resources as OER.

The Ed4All educators had their MOOC content reused in a formal face-to-face UCT course, learned that it was used in meetings and discussions in various countries, and were pleased that strategies and ideas from the course had shifted thinking among MOOC participants. JM also reflected that, in order to optimise reuse, it was better if learning materials were accompanied by a pedagogical structure.

Across all four MOOCs, the educators' enthusiasm for creating stand-alone OER was varied. Some were content with OER creation as a by-product, while others became enthusiasts and articulated the benefits of OER in and of itself. None of the educators developed negative attitudes to OER as a result of the MOOC-making experience. Each of the educators did, however, argue in some way that access to the MOOC as a whole course was more important than the reuse of constituent resource components. The MOOC topics which formed the subjects of the MOOCs in this study did not necessarily lend themselves easily to component OER creation and reuse, as these were mostly academic courses delivering conceptual ideas designed to be taught as online courses. Learning materials in such courses would require contextualisation and pedagogical scaffolding for optimal use. The objective of the educators was to offer a course with a particular goal in which they had some influence in the (re)running and updating of the course, at least initially. For some, their position changed as they received feedback, requests and invitations from learners – in some cases for the sharing and reuse of materials in different contexts.

Conclusion

This study investigated the relationships and interconnections between the making and design of MOOCs, OER and OEP. These intersections were shaped by both institutional and disciplinary contexts, as well as by the motivations of the educators who decided to create the MOOCs. We conclude with a brief overview of how MOOC-making proved to be a catalyst for both OER creation and enactment of OEP and how this study has contributed to understandings of OEP.

MOOC-making as a catalyst for OER creation

The intention to create OER was rarely expressed or perceived as important by the MOOC educators in this study. It is possible that the educators did not articulate their intentions regarding creating, licensing and delivering content using concepts such as OER due to a lack of awareness or experience of the concept, which has an accompanying vocabulary. However, the influence of the UCT MOOCs Project, the design component of the MOOC format, and the institutional context supporting openly licensed content enabled the MOOC educators to become more cognisant of the technical aspects of content licensing and the practical aspects involved in OER creation. Although not an institutional requirement, all UCT MOOCs were CC licensed, with the specific licensing provisions negotiated by the educators and the design team.

No negative experiences were attributed to the creation of OER, beyond an expressed lack of familiarity with good practice, implications of licensing choices and practicalities of creating more OER. While none of the educators resisted creating OER, it is not possible to predict how and to what extent they would create OER once the onus is on them individually. There were instances in the course of the study when educators asked about the possibility of creating OER, having been introduced to the concept while producing their MOOC. MOOC-making with OER therefore appeared to be conducive to OER adoption in general. However, with the exception of one educator who had prior experience of OER creation, more time would be needed to conclude whether these educators could become advocates or could function autonomously in creating and sharing OER.

Other creators of MOOCs on the FutureLearn and Coursera platforms have reused existing OER and released content as OER to varying degrees. The release of content as OER in other MOOCs does, however, appear relatively marginal, perhaps because it is not a default option on these platforms. Because releasing content as OER would involve additional effort in terms of capability and skills to understand licensing norms, we speculate that there is a link between the purpose of the MOOC itself and the educators' willingness and in some cases enthusiasm about releasing MOOC materials as OER.

The UCT MOOC materials were not shared in an OER or open content repository, meaning that it is not possible to run an identical course on a different platform. This is partly because none of the educators were particularly keen on this scenario, as they initially did not see their courses as being suited to this form of reuse. It was also envisaged that the MOOCs would be updated in their first few runs, making version control a concern. Additionally, agreements with the platforms used by the MOOCs in this study did not allow for the concurrent running of an identical MOOC on other platforms, and, in the case of a few materials, licences and permissions had been granted for the materials to be shared only in that MOOC format.

Understandings of OEP

Understandings of OEP tend to be contested and contextually situated. In looking at how forms of OEP were made possible in a MOOC-production environment along legal, pedagogical and financial dimensions, this study contributes to understanding how OEP developed over time in a group of MOOC educators. Conceptualisations of OEP have relied on the notion that using OER can catalyse OEP[28,29] (Armellini & Nie, 2013). While we found that this could happen in a MOOC environment where the use of OER to create MOOCs led to possibilities for strategies of pedagogical openness, we saw stronger links where OEP mediated by MOOC design in which the focus is on learner-centred pedagogical strategies led to deepening awareness and appreciation of the potential of OER in teaching and learning contexts. This concurs with findings in other contexts that OER awareness and use can arise from other forms of OEP (Cronin, 2017).

Our research suggests multiple ways in which OER, OEP and MOOCs are related from an educator's perspective. As a response to the primary research question – How does MOOC-making with OER adoption influence educators' OEP? – Figure 2 depicts some of these interconnections between the trajectory of MOOC educators adopting OEP and the processes involved in MOOC-making and OER creation. In the MOOC-mediated environment we studied, there was clear evidence of the dimensions of openness building upon one another, a factor which helped refine the conceptualisation of OEP.

---

28 http://opencontent.org/blog/archives/2975
29 https://www.edsurge.com/news/2016-08-09-open-educational-practice-unleashing-the-potential-of-oer

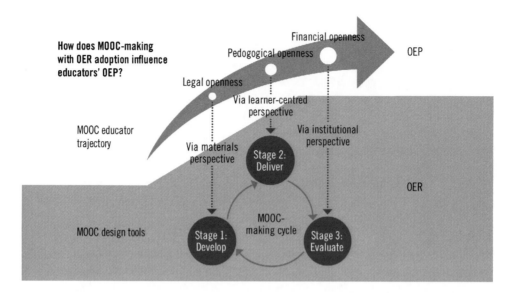

Figure 2: Schematic of possible relationships between OER, OEP and MOOC-making

The first dimension is "legal openness", marked by the acceptance of the principle of OER and the use of CC licences in the MOOC-making process. Engagement with this dimension happened at the MOOC development stage through discussions around course material development. While not the default of the MOOC format in this context, exhibiting and choosing legal openness allowed for further dimensions of OEP to become possible. That said, most of the educators in the study were not particularly ideologically committed to OER and preferred that others take the responsibility for legal compliance.

The second dimension of OEP, "pedagogical openness", was enabled by MOOC design, the opportunity to deliver the MOOC and that the MOOC environment was composed of large numbers of diverse, "non-traditional" learners who entered the space. This resulted in practices and design choices to which diverse learners responded, and this learner-centred approach impacted the way educators thought about teaching their subject or how their goal for the MOOC could be realised. At this point, we saw that educators' appreciation of the value or potential of OER became more pronounced, thus strengthening their understanding of legal openness and in some cases their enthusiasm for OER, as they saw its practical application and utility.

The third dimension of OEP, "financial openness", was exhibited by only one of the educators in this study. However, its emergence as a form of OEP is an interesting contribution to understandings of OEP as a set of goal-oriented practices that are enacted within a continuum of openness, and in which contradictions may exist but with a potential to be resolved in a particular context.

While the emergence of MOOCs may have polarised practitioners and researchers in the Open Education community, they have also enabled new perspectives on how OER and OEP might be enacted in a diverse, dynamic and evolving online environment. These dimensions help focus our gaze on different perspectives of what constitutes OEP and how these forms of OEP might be supported. The legal dimension is a "materials" perspective, and although we found OEP along this dimension, there was little active enthusiasm on the part of educators to engage with this practice. It is also likely that without support, relatively few educators would choose to share and create OER. While educators appreciated the importance and potential of open licensing of materials with respect to teaching and learning, they preferred that others take care of the practicalities.

The pedagogical dimension of OEP has a "learner-centred" perspective and was more enthusiastically enacted as educators saw the impact of the pedagogical strategies and learning designs implemented in the MOOC, especially when they were supported by learning designers. Educators responded to learners and their needs and found uses for these strategies in their formal teaching.

The financial dimension of openness, which has an "institutional" or "business model" perspective, was emergent in this study. Over time, as the MOOCs ran, one educator in particular exercised agency to develop a sustainable financial model to develop more MOOCs as well as a contextually specific and pragmatic approach to how learners might continue to be offered affordable or free learning opportunities. Outside of this study, another set of educators has since raised funding for offering follow-up MOOCs. We speculate that engagement with MOOCs, especially when they are successful or become useful for mainstream teaching (such as a flipped classroom), could lead to considerations of sustainability for continuation or enhancement, or wanting to develop more MOOCs.

Finally, while the focus of this study has been on educators in the MOOC-making process, it was found that there were two other parties that were instrumental in helping educators to achieve their goals: the experts in copyright and licensing who assisted with the complexities of permissions, and the learning designers who provided expertise and guidance, especially in assisting the educators in navigating the unfamiliar MOOC environment and new opportunities for pedagogical innovation. How these roles might enable OEP merits future investigation.

Acknowledgements

The authors wish to thank Catherine Cronin and Beck Pitt, who acted as superb peer reviewers of this chapter. Grateful thanks also to Michelle Willmers and Patricia B. Arinto for meticulous editing.

References

Agbu, J. O., Mulder, F., Vries, F. de, Tenebe, V. & Caine, A. (2016). The best of two open worlds at the National Open University of Nigeria. *Open Praxis, 8(2)*, 111–121. Retrieved from https://doi.org/10.5944/openpraxis.8.2.279

Alevizou, G. (2015). From OER to MOOCs: Critical perspectives on the historical mediation trajectories of Open Education. *International Journal of Media and Cultural Politics, 11(2)*, 203–224.

Almeida, N. (2017). Open Education Resources and rhetorical paradox in the neoliberal univers(ity). *Journal of Critical Library and Information Studies, 1(1)*, 1–19.

Andrade, A., Ehlers, U., Caine, A., Carneiro, R., Conole, G., Kairamo, A., Koskinen T., Kretschmer, T., Moe-Pryce, N., Mundin, P., Nozes, J., Reinhardt, R., Richter, T., Silva, G. & Holmberg, C. (2011). *Beyond OER: Shifting focus to Open Educational Practices.* Essen: Due-Publico. Retrieved from https://oerknowledgecloud.org/sites/oerknowledgecloud.org/files/OPAL2011.pdf

Armellini, A. & Nie, M. (2013). Open Educational Practices for curriculum enhancement. *Open Learning: The Journal of Open, Distance and e-Learning, 28(1),* 7–20. Retrieved from http://www.tandfonline.com/doi/abs/10.1080/02680513.2013.796286

Atenas, J. (2015). Model for democratisation of the contents hosted in MOOCs. *Universities and Knowledge Society Journal, 12(1),* 3–14. Retrieved from http://rusc.uoc.edu/rusc/en/index.php/rusc/article/view/v12n1-atenas.html

Beetham, H., Falconer, I., McGill, L. & Littlejohn, A. (2011). *JISC open practices: Briefing paper.* London: Jisc. Retrieved from https://oersynth.pbworks.com/w/page/51668352/OpenPracticesBriefing

Butcher, N. (2011). *A basic guide to Open Educational Resources.* Paris: Commonwealth of Learning & United Nations Educational, Scientific and Cultural Organization. Retrieved from http://unesdoc.unesco.org/images/0021/002158/215804e.pdf

Cate, B., Drooz, D., Hohenberg, P. & Schulz, K. (2007). Creating intellectual property policies and current issues in administering online courses. Presented at the *National Association of College and University Attorneys (NACUA) Annual Meeting, 7–9 November 2007.* Washington D.C., United States of America. Retrieved from https://www.insidehighered.com/sites/default/server_files/files/nacuaPDF.pdf

Chen, Y. (2014). Investigating MOOCs through blog mining. *International Review of Research in Open and Distributed Learning, 15(2).* Retrieved from http://www.irrodl.org/index.php/irrodl/article/view/1695

Cheverie, J. (2013). *Copyright challenges in a MOOC environment.* Washington, D.C.: EDUCAUSE. Retrieved from http://www.educause.edu/library/resources/copyrightchallenges-mooc-environment

Conole, G. (2012). Fostering social inclusion through Open Educational Resources (OER). *Distance Education, 33(2),* 131–134. Retrieved from https://doi.org/10.1080/01587919.2012.700563

Cox, G. (2016). *Explaining the relations between culture, structure and agency in lecturers' contribution and non-contribution to Open Educational Resources in a higher education institution.* Ph.D thesis. Cape Town: University of Cape Town. Retrieved from https://open.uct.ac.za/handle/11427/20300

Cox, G. & Trotter, H. (2016). UCT, Fort Hare or UNISA: Which university is OER ready? *Paper presented at the Teaching and Learning Conference, 30 March 2016.* Cape Town, South Africa. Retrieved from http://www.slideshare.net/ROER4D/uct-fort-hare-or-unisa-which-university-is-oer-ready

Cronin, C. (2017). Openness and praxis: Exploring the use of Open Educational Practices in higher education. *The International Review of Research in Open and Distributed Learning, 18(5).* Retrieved from http://www.irrodl.org/index.php/irrodl/article/view/3096/4301

Czerniewicz, L., Cox, G., Hodgkinson-Williams, C. A. & Willmers, M. (2015). Open Education and the open scholarship agenda: A University of Cape Town perspective. In C. Bonk, M. Lee, T. Reeves & T. Reynolds (Eds.), *MOOCs and Open Education around the world.* London: Routledge. Retrieved from http://open.uct.ac.za/handle/11427/7497

Czerniewicz, L., Deacon, A., Small, J. & Walji, S. (2014). Developing world MOOCs: A curriculum view of the MOOC landscape. *Journal of Global Literacies, Technologies, and Emerging Pedagogies, 2(3).* Retrieved from https://open.uct.ac.za/handle/11427/19562

Czerniewicz, L. & Naidoo, U. (2013). *MOOCless in Africa*. Cape Town: OpenUCT Initiative. Retrieved from https://open.uct.ac.za/handle/11427/2373

Davis, H. C., Carr, L. A., Hey, J. M. N., Howard, Y., Millard, D., Morris, D. & White, S. (2010). Bootstrapping a culture of sharing to facilitate Open Educational Resources. *IEEE Transactions on Learning Technologies, 3(2)*, 96–109. Retrieved from https://doi.org/10.1109/TLT.2009.34

Deacon, A. & WynSculley, C. (2009). Educators and the Cape Town Open Learning Declaration: Rhetorically reducing distance. *International Journal of Education and Development Using ICT, 5(5)*, 117–129.

Downes, S. (2013). The role of Open Educational Resources in personal learning. In R. McGreal, W. Kinuthia, S. Marshall & T. McNamara (Eds.), *Perspectives on Open and Distance Learning: Open Educational Resources: Innovation, research and practice* (pp. 207–221). Vancouver: Commonwealth of Learning & Athabasca University. Retrieved from https://oerknowledgecloud.org/sites/oerknowledgecloud.org/files/pub_PS_OER-IRP_web.pdf

Duncan, J., Clement, S. & Rozum, B. (2013). Teaching our faculty: Developing copyright and scholarly communication outreach programs. *Library Faculty & Staff Publications, 117*, 269–285. Retrieved from http://digitalcommons.usu.edu/cgi/viewcontent.cgi?article=1115&context=lib_pubs

Ebner, M., Lorenz, A., Lackner, E. & Jemni Kinshuk, M. (2017). How OER enhance MOOCs – A perspective from German-speaking Europe. In M. Kopp, S. Kumar, S. Schon, N. Chen & J. Spector (Eds.), *Lecture notes in educational technology* (pp. 205–220). Berlin: Springer. Retrieved from https://www.researchgate.net/profile/Martin_Ebner2/publication/306061568_How_OER_Enhances_MOOCs-A_Perspective_from_German-Speaking_Europe/links/57b1aefa08aeb2cf17c56906.pdf

Ehlers, U-D. (2011). Extending the territory: From Open Educational Resources to Open Educational Practices. *Journal of Open, Flexible, and Distance Learning, 15(2)*, 1–10. Retrieved from http://www.jofdl.nz/index.php/JOFDL/article/view/64

Engeström, Y. (1987). *Learning by expanding: An activity-theoretic approach to developmental research*. Helsinki: Orienta-Konsultit Oy.

Gertz, G. A. (2013). Copyrights in faculty-created works: How licensing can solve the academic work-for-hire dilemma. *Washington Law Review, 88*, 1465–1493. Retrieved from https://digital.law.washington.edu/dspace-law/bitstream/handle/1773.1/1316/88WLR1465.pdf?sequence=1

Geser, G. (2007). *Open Educational Practices and Resources: The OLCOS Roadmap 2012*. Salzburg: Salzburg Research Edumedia Research Group. Retrieved from http://www.olcos.org/cms/upload/docs/olcos_roadmap.pdf

Hilton III, J., Wiley, D., Stein, J. & Johnson, A. (2010). The four "R"s of openness and ALMS analysis: Frameworks for Open Educational Resources. *Open Learning, 25(1)*, 37–44. Retrieved from https://doi.org/10.1080/02680510903482132

Hodgkinson-Williams, C. (2014). Degrees of ease: Adoption of OER, open textbooks and MOOCs in the Global South. *Keynote address at the OER Asia Symposium, 24–27 June 2014*. Penang, Malaysia. Retrieved from https://www.slideshare.net/ROER4D/hodgkinson-williams-2014-oer-asia

Hodgkinson-Williams, C. & Gray, E. (2009). Degrees of openness: The emergence of Open Educational Resources at the University of Cape Town. *International Journal of Education and Development Using Information and Communication Technology, 5(5)*, 101–116.

Kapczynski, A., Chaifetz, S., Katz, Z. & Benkler, Y. (2005). Addressing global health inequities: An open licensing approach for university innovations. *Berkeley Technology Law Journal, 20(2)*, 1031–1114.

Kaplan-Solms, K. & Solms, M. (2000). *Clinical studies in neuro psychoanalysis: Introduction to a depth neuropsychology.* London: Karnac Books.

Kawooya, D. (2007). *Copyright and access to e-resources in Africa's education and research contexts: The case of selected Ugandan institutions.* Budapest: Open Society Institute. Retrieved from http://www.academia.edu/25164072/Copyright_and_Access_to_e-Resources_in_Africas_Education_and_Research_Contexts_the_case_of_selected_Ugandan_Institution

Klein, M. (2005). Protecting faculty rights in copyright ownership policies. *Presented at the 21st Annual Conference on Distance Teaching and Learning, 3–5 August 2005.* Madison, USA. Retrieved from http://studylib.net/doc/18538516/protecting-faculty-rights-in-copyright-ownership-policies

Knox, J. (2013). Five critiques of the Open Educational Resources movement. *Teaching in Higher Education, 18(8).* Retrieved from http://www.tandfonline.com/doi/abs/10.1080/1356 2517.2013.774354

Literat, I. (2015). Implications of Massive Open Online Courses for higher education: Mitigating or reifying educational inequities? *Higher Education Research & Development, 34(6),* 1164–1177. Retrieved from https://doi.org/10.1080/07294360.2015.1024624

Loeckx, J. (2016). Blurring boundaries in education: Context and impact of MOOCs. *International Review of Research in Open and Distributed Learning, 17(3).* Retrieved from http://www.irrodl.org/index.php/irrodl/article/view/2395/3687

Masterman, E. (2016). Bringing Open Educational Practice to a research-intensive university: Prospects and challenges. *The Electronic Journal of E-Learning, 14(1),* 31–42.

Masterman, L. & Wild, L. (2011). *JISC OER impact study: Research report.* Oxford: Jisc. Retrieved from https://weblearn.ox.ac.uk/access/content/group/ca5599e6-fd26-4203-b416-f1b96068d1cf/Research%20Project%20Reports/OER%20Projects%202011-2014/JISC%20OER%20Impact%20Study%20Research%20Report%20v1-0.pdf

Murphy, A. (2013). Open Educational Practices in higher education: Institutional adoption and challenges. *Distance Education, 34(2),* 201–217. Retrieved from https://doi.org/10.1080/01 587919.2013.793641

Nikoi, S. & Armellini, A. (2012). The OER mix in higher education: Purpose, process, product, and policy. *Distance Education, 33(2),* 165–184. Retrieved from https://doi.org/10.1080/01 587919.2012.697439

Nkuyubwatsi, B. (2013). Evaluation of Massive Open Online Courses (MOOCs) from the learner's perspective. *Presented at the 12th European Conference on e-Learning ECEL–2013, 30–31 October 2013.* Sophie Antipolis, France. Retrieved from http://hdl.handle.net/2381/28553

Nti, K. (2015). Supporting access to open online courses for learners of developing countries. *International Review of Research in Open and Distributed Learning, 16(4).* Retrieved from http://www.irrodl.org/index.php/irrodl/article/view/2328

Okada, A., Mikroyannidis, A., Meister, I. & Little, S. (2012). "Colearning" – collaborative networks for creating, sharing and reusing OER through social media. In *Cambridge 2012: Innovation and Impact – Openly Collaborating to Enhance Education, 16–18 April 2012.* Cambridge, United Kingdom. Retrieved from http://oro.open.ac.uk/33750/2/59B2E252.pdf

Ozturk, H. T. (2015). Examining value change in MOOCs in the scope of connectivism and Open Educational Resources movement. *The International Review of Research in Open and Distributed Learning, 16(5).* Retrieved from http://www.irrodl.org/index.php/irrodl/article/view/2027

Patru, M. & Balaji, V. (2016). *Making sense of MOOCs: A guide for policy-makers in developing countries.* Vancouver: Commonwealth of Learning. Retrieved from http://oasis.col.org/handle/11599/2356

Piedra, N., Chicaiza, J. A., López, J. & Tovar, E. (2014). An architecture based on linked data technologies for the integration and reuse of OER in MOOCs context. *Open Praxis, 6(2),* 171–187. Retrieved from https://doi.org/10.5944/openpraxis.6.2.122

Porter, J. (2013). MOOCS, "courses", and the question for faculty and student copyrights. In C. Ratcliff (Ed.), *The CCCC-IP Annual: Top Intellectual Property developments of 2012.* Urbana, IL: Conference on College Composition and Communication. Retrieved from http://www.ncte.org/library/NCTEFiles/Groups/CCCC/Committees/TopIP2012Collection.pdf

Reed, P. (2012). Awareness, attitudes and participation of teaching staff towards the open content movement in one university. *Research in Learning Technology, 20,* 1–14.

Schatzki, T. (2001). Introduction: Practice theory. In T. Schatzki, K. Cetina & E. von Savigny (Eds.), *The practice turn in contemporary theory* (pp. 1–14). London: Routledge.

Smith, M. (2016). *Feature: Open is as open does.* Cape Town: Research on Open Educational Resources for Development project. Retrieved from http://roer4d.org/wp-content/uploads/2014/01/ROER4D-Newsletter-February-March-2016.pdf

Smith, K., Tobia, R., Plutchak, T., Howell, L., Pfeiffer, S. & Fitts, M. (2006). Copyright knowledge of faculty at two academic health science campuses: Results of a survey. *Serials Review, 32(2),* 59–67.

Souto-Otero, M., dos Santos, A. I., Shields, R., Lažetić, P., Muñoz, J. C., Devaux, A., … Punie, Y. (2016). *OpenCases: Case studies on openness in education.* Sevilla: Institute for Prospective Technological Studies, Joint Research Centre, European Commission. Retrieved from http://publications.jrc.ec.europa.eu/repository/bitstream/JRC101533/jrc101533_opencases%20case%20studies%20on%20openness%20in%20education.pdf

Tingry, N., Boyer, A. & Roussanaly, A. (2016). *Open Educational Resources: A lever for digital transition of higher education?* Lorraine: Université de Lorraine. Retrieved from http://www.dtransform.eu/wp-content/uploads/2016/04/Rapport-O1A3-Version-Anglaise.pdf

UCT (University of Cape Town). (2014). *University of Cape Town Open Access policy.* Cape Town: University of Cape Town. Retrieved from https://www.uct.ac.za/downloads/uct.ac.za/about/policies/UCTOpenAccessPolicy.pdf

Weller, M. (2016). Different aspects of the emerging OER discipline. *Revista Educacao E Cultura Contemporanea, 13(31).* Retrieved from http://oro.open.ac.uk/47209/1/2321-9190-1-PB.pdf

White, D. & Manton, M. (2011). *JISC-funded OER impact study.* Oxford: Oxford University Press.

Wiley, D., Reeves, T. & Reynolds, T. (2015). The MOOC misstep and the Open Education infrastructure. In C. Bonk & M. Lee (Eds.), *MOOCs and Open Education around the world* (pp. 3–11). London: Routledge.

How to cite this chapter

Czerniewicz, L., Deacon, A., Walji, S. & Glover, M. (2017). OER in and as MOOCs. In C. Hodgkinson-Williams & P. B. Arinto (Eds.), *Adoption and impact of OER in the Global South* (pp. 349–386). Retrieved from https://doi.org/10.5281/zenodo.604414

Corresponding author: Laura Czerniewicz <laura.czerniewicz@uct.ac.za>

Section 4

South and Southeast Asia

Contents

Chapter 11

Cultural–historical factors influencing OER adoption in Mongolia's higher education sector

Batbold Zagdragchaa and Henry Trotter

Summary

The research presented here investigates the strategies and practices of educators from six public and private higher education institutions (HEIs) in Mongolia in order to understand the role of Open Educational Resources (OER) in their work. It addresses the question: Which cultural–historical factors shape OER activities in Mongolia's higher education sector? In addition, the study sets out to determine whether OER has the potential to move beyond a niche innovation advocated and funded by international donors to one that is broadly adopted, implemented and disseminated by local educators.

The study employed a sequential exploratory model in which qualitative interviews comprised the first stage of data collection, followed by quantitative surveys. The interviews were conducted with 14 participants recruited using a convenience sample from four Mongolian HEIs, two government organisations and three non-governmental organisations. In total, eight educators and six administrators were interviewed. A follow-up survey was conducted with 42 instructors and administrators at six HEIs, also recruited through convenience sampling. The study utilised Cultural Historical Activity Theory as a framework to analyse the data.

Findings indicate that despite recent efforts to promote OER by funding agencies and the government, OER awareness remains modest amongst higher education instructors and administrators. It is therefore not surprising that OER adoption rates in Mongolia are low. As a result, a culture around OER engagement has not yet emerged, with only isolated individual educators adopting OER. In contrast with many academics who often worry about the quality of OER, Mongolian educators appear to be more concerned about a particular sub-component of quality, which is relevance. In addition, many study participants expressed reservations about the potential value and utility of OER. ▶

As a country, Mongolia has developed and supported large-scale educational-resource projects, especially at the basic education level, and it may need to take a similar proactive stance regarding OER in the higher education sector if it seeks to improve the quality, relevance and cost-effectiveness of teaching content. As the first study on OER activity in Mongolia's higher education system, this research has value and application for researchers and advocates pursuing an OER agenda, for policy-makers seeking to understand how policy interventions might influence OER adoption in the national and institutional context, and for funding agencies aiming to boost educators' OER engagement more broadly.

Acronyms and abbreviations

ADB	Asian Development Bank
CC	Creative Commons
CHAT	Cultural Historical Activity Theory
DREAM IT	Development Research to Empower All Mongolians through Information and Communications Technologies
GER	gross enrolment ratio
HEI	higher education institution
ICT	information and communication technologies
IDRC	International Development Research Centre
IP	intellectual property
NGO	non-governmental organisation
NUM	National University of Mongolia
OER	Open Educational Resources
ONE	Open Network for Education
ROER4D	Research on Open Educational Resources for Development
SAP	Structural Adjustment Programme

Introduction

As the least densely populated independent country in the world – with a partially nomadic population of three million inhabiting a landmass of 1.6 million square kilometres[1] – Mongolia faces some unique challenges with regard to the provision of high-quality, cost-effective and broadly accessible higher education. These challenges are exacerbated by the increasingly globalised educational landscape where norms and standards are established in wealthy, settled (as opposed to nomadic), densely populated locales. However, the proliferation of information and communication technologies (ICT)-mediated educational innovations offers opportunities for overcoming some of those challenges.

---

1 https://www.geolounge.com/country-least-densely-populated/

Open Educational Resources (OER) represent just such an innovation (Boston Consulting Group, 2013; West & Victor, 2011) in that they are materials that are freely available – financially and legally – for anyone to use and share (Butcher, 2011); they can reduce the costs of higher education (Wiley, Green & Soares, 2012); and they can increase the number of students accessing higher education (Daniel, Kanwar & Uvalić-Trumbić, 2006; Orr, Rimini & Van Damme, 2015). However, their utility for educators is predicated on a set of pedagogical assumptions that are new and different in the Mongolian higher education sector. Their value to the system cannot be taken for granted, and thus it is worthwhile to understand what current educators and administrators think about the feasibility of OER in Mongolia. To do so, it is useful to first gain a sense of the cultural–historical context in which those OER would be utilised.

The development and current state of higher education in Mongolia

The development and expansion of formal education in Mongolia is characterised by two distinct phases: the communist era from the 1920s to 1990, and the transition phase from 1990 to the present. It is only in this current phase that OER became an innovation that Mongolian educators could engage with. The cultural and historical elements of the prior phase are, however, important to understand when assessing contemporary educators' decisions around OER, as they continue to influence the present in distinctive ways.

Higher education under Soviet influence (1920s–1990)

After three centuries under Manchu rule (i.e. Qing dynasty of China), and a decade of unsuccessful claims for independence in the 1910s, Mongolia statehood was finally recognised by its newly formed revolutionary neighbour, the Union of Soviet Socialist Republics, in 1924 (Bray, Davaa, Spaulding & Weidman, 1994). The Mongolian leadership embraced communism, leading to the development of a formal education sector that was highly influenced by the political and pedagogical ideals of the Soviet Union. According to Yano (2012, p.10): "The first Constitution, adopted in 1924, proclaimed the right of workers and their children to free and secular education, while ousting the Lama [monastery] schools. In 1933, the first unified curriculum was introduced, based on the curriculum in Soviet schools."

Thereafter, the basic education system grew to reach most members of the population, usually requiring nomadic children in distant locales to attend regional boarding schools (del Rosario, 2005). Education accounted for 14% or more of the national budget, the largest expenditure item in the government fiscus during the communist era (Bray et al., 1994). This high level of investment in education yielded impressive literacy and enrolment results. For instance, by the end of the communist era in 1990, "the adult (aged 15 and over) literacy rate was 96.5 percent, the gross enrolment ratio (GER) for basic education (primary and lower secondary, 8 years) was 98.7 percent, the GER for upper secondary education was 40.1 percent and the GER for tertiary education was 16 percent" (Yano, 2012, p.11).

Additionally, in 1942, a higher education component was established with the founding of the National University of Mongolia (NUM), which gradually expanded over the following decades and spurred the rise of a number of complementary specialist institutes (in the areas of agriculture, economics, pedagogy, etc.). The new higher education institutions (HEIs) were typically governed by their respective government ministries in a "vertical" fashion (Heyneman, 2004), meaning that "the various ministries had their own universities and produced graduates according to their development plans" (Yano, 2012, p.33). This vertical approach was different from the "horizontal" one of most Western democracies of the time, in which a single department or ministry (i.e. Education) broadly oversaw higher education activities, but allowed the HEIs themselves to flexibly respond to the needs of society and industry (Heyneman, 2004). As Weidman states:

> Mongolia was originally modelled on the Soviet system in which curricula were highly specialized and student places were determined on the basis of projected manpower needs. Universities were primarily teaching institutions, with responsibility for research and the awarding of the highest scientific degrees vested in independent institutes under the Academy of Science. (1995, p.3)

Thus, the cultural–historical foundations of Mongolia's higher education system were ideologically Marxist–Leninist, politically communist, administratively centralised, vertical and financially free to all students. However, with the fall of the Soviet Union – and the withdrawal of its economic support, amounting to a massive 30% of national gross domestic product at times (Bray et al., 1994) – Mongolians began to reappraise the viability of these foundations as the country embarked on the challenging political and economic transition which started in the early 1990s.

Higher education after the post-communist transition (1990–present)

With the formal collapse of the Soviet Union in 1991, Mongolia went through a peaceful political transition after which a multiparty system, a new constitution and a market economy were introduced. However, after decades of financial and technical reliance on the Soviet state, Mongolia remained undercapacitated to meet the new challenges it faced, and an economic crisis – characterised by rising inflation and unemployment (almost unheard of previously) and declining outputs – engulfed the country, similar to other post-communist states at the time (Bray et al., 1994).

Structural adjustment and financing

As many of the Soviet advisors and technicians departed Mongolia (Bray et al., 1994), the World Bank, along with other Western institutional brokers and funders,[2] moved in and suggested that the country embark on a series of structural adjustment programmes (SAPs) that would liberalise the economy and open it up to new investment and growth potential. According to Weidman (1995, pp.1–2), post-communist governments at the time were

---

2   Some international funders focused more on education support than the World Bank, which focused more on infrastructure and economic reform. According to Steiner-Khamsi and Stolpe (2004, p.34): "The Asian Development Bank (ADB), the Japanese International Cooperation Agency, the Soros Foundation (Mongolian Foundation for Open Society) and the Danish International Development Assistance (DANIDA) have been, thus far, the most significant contributors to education sector reform in Mongolia. The United Nations organizations, specifically the United Nations Educational, Scientific, and Cultural Organization and the United Nations Children's Fund, have contributed less on budget, but have been influential at the governmental level."

"encouraged to identify those sectors of their economies in which there are possibilities for 'cost sharing', namely, shifting greater portions of the burden of payment to the individuals who are the recipients or users of the services provided" (see also Altbach, 2004).

This included making adjustments to higher education, "a service that is both very expensive to provide and from which recipients can expect to receive significant financial benefits" (Weidman, 1995, p.6). The menu of SAP cost-sharing strategies in higher education, according to Weidman (1995), consisted of:

1. Direct cost recovery: charging student fees; eliminating student stipends.
2. Contracts and agreements with private- and public-sector agencies: sponsoring students; obtaining contracts for consulting services; paying for student internships.
3. Income-producing enterprises: renting out space; providing copying services; running bookstores; and, in Mongolia's context specifically, managing livestock herds.
4. Private contributions and endowments: soliciting gifts from alumni and donors.
5. Student employment and national service scholarships: offering work-study options; providing scholarships for national service.
6. Deferred cost recovery: taxing future earnings of graduates; taxing private-sector employers; granting student loans.
7. Expanding the private sector: opening up private HEI opportunities.

With this advice in mind, the Mongolian government quickly introduced fees for higher education students, removed most government stipends, initiated consultancy work for the universities, started managing livestock herds for income generation, offered students loans to cover the newly demanded tuition fees and opened up higher education provision to private enterprises (Weidman, 1995). However, perhaps because the government had no prior experience in this type of neoliberal "cost sharing" in the education field, its efforts led to some surprising results. For instance, the government started charging student fees at a rate meant to recover all variable (as opposed to fixed) institutional costs (such as educator salaries), something virtually unheard of even in public education contexts of developed countries where student fees were meant to cover only a portion of variable costs. As Bray et al. summed up at the time: "In the early 1990s Mongolia may have lurched from a rather extreme model of socialism to a rather extreme model of capitalism" (1994, p.41).

Massification and privatisation

As the country opened its doors to the global economy, it also opened the doors of higher learning far wider than was the case previously. In 1985 there were just eight HEIs with 24 600 students; by 1993 there were 23 new operational HEIs (Bray et al., 1994), and by 2014 there were 100 HEIs (16 state-owned, 79 private and five foreign HEI branches) with a total student enrolment of 174 000 (MECSM, 2015), primarily based in the capital city, Ulaanbaatar. Moreover, the country's higher education GER increased from 14% in 1991 to 47% in 2009.

This "massification" of higher education led to predictable logistical and infrastructural pressures, similar to those faced in other Asian and post-communist states at the time (Altbach, 2004), but it also led to increased differentiation within the sector in terms of the quality and relevance of the education offered. While graduate throughput increased, it has not always been clear whether the education students received was relevant for a modern workforce or whether the current economy could absorb these increased numbers of higher education graduates. This has led to a paradox where there were not enough *appropriately* skilled graduates in the Mongolian workforce to meet society's current needs (World Bank, 2007). Yano (2012) calls these Mongolian graduates who find themselves working in ill-suited jobs the "overeducated".

Quality and relevance

The drop in perceived and actual quality of higher education in Mongolia is hotly debated in society, and has been noticed by the funders that have, in many ways, pushed for the changes that have occurred. Thus, the Asian Development Bank (ADB), one of the most significant funders (in terms of scale and policy influence) of higher education in the country, has noted that:

> Mongolian HEIs suffer in comparison with foreign universities. Issues relating to quality of higher education include (i) proliferation of small private HEIs without quality control; (ii) weak overall system of quality assurance and accreditation; (iii) inadequate recruitment practices and supply of teaching staff; (iv) irregular application of norms for workload, contact hours, and research time; (v) inadequate monitoring of the performance of staff; (vi) lack of a national study credit and levels framework; (vii) inadequate curricula, learning materials, facilities, and equipment; (viii) low research capability and inadequate research facilities; and (ix) weak networks and partnerships with regional and international universities. (ADB, 2011a, p.3)

Gender and rural–urban imbalances

The vast economic changes that reshaped the country more broadly also exacerbated certain divisions that were becoming noticeable towards the end of the communist period. For instance, just after the beginning of the transition, Bray et al. (1994) noted that females outnumbered males in higher education, at least since the early 1990s, while the male dropout rate had increased (del Rosario, 2005). According to the Mongolian government, there were 174 000 higher education students in 2014, of whom 101 800 (59%) were female (MECSM, 2015). This "reverse gender imbalance" (Adiya, 2010) reflects, in part, education's role in Mongolian society – while it is considered very important by every family, it coexists alongside more traditional priorities of animal husbandry, which tends to be a more male-dominated occupation. Thus, this gender disparity in higher education does not signify the realisation of post-patriarchal society (Begzsuren & Dolgion, 2014), nor does it mean that males are being structurally disadvantaged in some way. Instead, it reveals that education in a country which still has a large nomadic population that makes its livelihood from livestock herding is just one of a number of priorities for families. The prestige and wealth opportunities of the nomadic lifestyle remain attractive for many, while the growing educational options offer unique possibilities, especially for females who do not enjoy the same opportunities and authority granted to males in nomadic society (Adiya, 2010).

This gender imbalance is linked to a significant rural–urban divide, in which students living in cities, especially the capital, are privileged in their access to educational opportunities. For students who live nearby to HEIs, such as those in Ulaanbaatar, it is cheaper to enrol because the institutions do not have to provide them with accommodation. Students in the cities are also better able to select the best institution according to their needs compared to their rural counterparts for whom the choices may seem opaque (Bray et al., 1994).

Language

Throughout their history, Mongolians have been practical about language issues, even though they prefer to speak their own language amongst themselves. In centuries past, when the empire of Genghis Khan spread across Eurasia, the Mongol leaders of the time did not attempt to impose their own language on the multitudes of subject populations, but rather adopted the languages of the ruled wherever they were (Chua, 2007). More recently, under Soviet influence, Russian-language textbooks (some of which had been localised to the Mongolian context) were actively used in higher education, even though the Mongolian language remained relevant in the classroom. During the transition, the government opened up opportunities for students to learn either Russian or English as their preferred second language. English emerged as the overwhelming choice for students, even though there were far fewer competent teachers of English compared to Russian at the time. The government gave policy and financial support for this choice (with aid from the donor community), also recognising in the early 2000s that English was the preeminent language of international business, education and tourism (Cohen, 2004).

Since the transition, the integration of English into education and everyday life has taken place to the extent that a form of "Mongolian English" has emerged, which "serves as a language of communication in many instances, and influences the acquisition and general use of the language in the country" (Cohen, 2004, p.15). Marzluf (2012) goes so far as to argue that a "post-socialist English" – associated with the values of transnational development, neoliberal economic policies and post-industrial educational practices – has supplanted "socialist Russian" and is now engaged in a dynamic relationship with a "fundamentalist nationalist Mongolian" which is associated with traditional, rural nomadic values. This suggests that Mongolians do not view English as a neutral linguistic tool for practical use, but are attuned to the political and social implications of embracing it as a second language. Perhaps this is most relevant for young people, especially students, who are engaging in translingual experimentation with English and Mongolian, the Roman and Cyrillic alphabets, and linguistically based forms of identity claims and performance (Dovchin, 2011, 2015; Dovchin, Sultana & Pennycook, 2015, 2016; Sultana, Dovchin & Pennycook, 2013).

Structural reform

According to the ADB, which has conducted a large-scale and influential review of the Mongolian higher education sector:

> A new 12-year education structure was introduced into schools in
> September 2008 with the aim of bringing Mongolia closer to international
> standards and norms. Tertiary education was offered in three general types
> of institutions: (i) universities with full four-year degree and postgraduate
> programs, (ii) colleges with four-year degree programs only, and (iii) technical
> and vocational schools (TVET) with two-year training programs. (2011a, p.1)

However, the rapid increase in the number of public and private HEIs since 1991 has been
largely uncontrolled. Only about half of private HEIs have been accredited, and governance,
management and financing of higher education have not kept pace with the rapid growth of
the higher education sector. This led the government to initiate a process of consolidating
public HEIs in January 2010 with the aim of concentrating educational resources in fewer,
higher-quality and better managed public HEIs (ADB, 2011b).

Governance and management

As can be seen from the discussion above, the higher education sector transformed quite
rapidly in a short period as a result of the government's responsiveness to both donors'
demands for structural adjustment as well as those of more indigenous forces, such as
Mongolians' demand for greater access to higher education. However, some features of the
communist era appeared to remain stubbornly persistent.

For instance, according to Steiner-Khamsi and Stolpe (2004), all of this "policy
borrowing" – especially in the sphere of higher education governance – was more of a
strategic mechanism to secure international funding than a genuine attempt to reshape
higher education according to the wishes of the funders. They argue that: "Once
policies were borrowed from elsewhere and funding was approved to implement them
locally, projects sailed under different objectives" (2004, p.29). The new policies were
"Mongolised" according to a locally relevant sociologic that masked administrative and
power structures which often resembled the old centralised Soviet model of operation more
closely than the new decentralised structures that were called for in the funders' policy
prescriptions. Essentially, in many cases "educational policies [were] only borrowed or
imported at a discursive level with little or limited impact on educational practice" (2004,
p.30). These authors trace the history of this policy borrowing during the first decade of
the transition and find that the policy commitments made concerning de/centralisation
"swung like a pendulum" depending on whether they were conditional for new funding
from international donors:

> In times of heightened international pressure – usually in periods preceding
> either an appraisal for or an agreement on a new loan – the Ministry of
> Education has subscribed to a comprehensive decentralization programme.
> Upon approval of international cooperation projects, however, the Ministry of
> Education has shifted its emphasis and has retained its strongly centralized
> system of planning, monitoring and governance. (Steiner-Khamsi & Stolpe,
> 2004, p.36)

The key reason they offer for this is that Mongolian officials had a different understanding from international donors as to who should govern education. For the officials, "the education system needs to be administered by state representatives rather than professionals" because, in their estimation, schools and universities are "state" institutions, not "public" ones, as the donors believe (Steiner-Khamsi & Stolpe, 2004). This has led to consistent misunderstanding between these parties regarding the best way forward for education with respect to governance, a fact which Mongolians appear to "massage" with shifting policy statements that appease donors, secure funding and allow the centralised management to largely continue functioning as it did under Soviet patronage.

Thus, under these conditions of dramatic economic change and surprising administrative resilience, the higher education sector faces a host of new challenges that it did not face prior to the transition. As a result, the cultural–historical foundations of Mongolia's higher education system have shifted in crucial ways, though the legacy of the communist era remains influential in unexpected ways. While the higher education sector was previously ideologically Marxist–Leninist, it has moved to a more neoliberal stance in line with funders' desires. Politically, it is no longer communist, but shaped by more democratic and private enterprise interests. Linguistically, it used to be influenced by the Russian language. However, English has rapidly been replacing Russian as a second language, while Mongolian remains the preferred language of interaction for students and educators. Administratively, higher education governance used to be centralised and vertical, and while there have been consistent calls for decentralisation by funders, the state has only partially acceded to this demand. Public higher education remains largely centralised, but private HEIs enjoy a degree of decentralised autonomy (which many say has resulted in a decline in quality) (Steiner-Khamsi & Stolpe, 2004). Lastly, higher education used to be free for all students under the communist regime. This is no longer the case. Indeed, of all the changes that have occurred since the transition, this has perhaps been the most dramatic, with students having to shoulder relatively high education costs, even at public HEIs.

The introduction of OER in Mongolia

It was in the context described above, from 2010 to 2014, that Mongolia hosted a series of national forums, workshops and pilot projects on OER. These activities included annual national events introducing the concept of Open Education and included educators and researchers across education sectors. The events were typically driven by international advocacy groups to help build a critical mass of support for open practice in the country and move toward the establishment of a Creative Commons Mongolia affiliate organisation, which was established in 2014.[3]

Starting in 2010, the Development Research to Empower All Mongolians through Information and Communications Technologies (DREAM IT)[4] project brought consulting expertise from Canada to Mongolia to introduce models of educational practice associated

---

3   http://creativecommons.mn/
4   DREAM IT is a project of Canada's International Development Research Centre (IDRC), which has been active as a funder in Mongolia for over 20 years, investing in information and communication technology (ICT) research through its ICT for Development programme, and more recently through its Information Networks programme. See https://www.idrc.ca/en/project/development-research-empower-all-mongolians-through-information-communication-technology.

with OER. The consulting visits were also designed to stimulate local interest in OER research projects in Mongolia, with a focus on exploring and investigating potentially transformative education strategies for the country (Baasansuren & Porter, 2013).

A national seminar on OER supported by DREAM IT and Canada's International Development Research Centre (IDRC) was held in Ulaanbaatar in October 2010. It introduced Mongolian educators and government officials to OER projects worldwide and provided opportunities for in-depth discussion about the merits and mechanics of Open Education principles and practices. In 2011, a follow-up workshop on Open Data, open government and OER was held, in which research projects funded by the IDRC through DREAM IT presented preliminary research results and demonstrated materials that each would share as OER using Creative Commons (CC) licences. Up until 2013 when it was completed, the DREAM IT project had been active in capacity-building initiatives to introduce and demonstrate a range of open practices in the Mongolian education sectors.

As a result, for example, Davalgaa.mn ("Education Wave"), a non-governmental organisation (NGO) that was funded through DREAM IT to research the development of an open training and materials development strategy for preschool teachers, presented its work at the national seminar and launched a book that it had developed separately with a publisher partner. Davalgaa made the book chapters openly available to teachers, parents and the public through its website using a CC licence.[5] It has also experimented with user-generated and CC-licensed videos produced by preschool teachers that can be viewed or downloaded from its website along with other openly licensed resources designed for preschool educators.

In 2014, the Mongolian parliament adopted a National OER Program[6] to be implemented by the Ministry of Education, Science and Culture and the Open Network for Education (ONE) Foundation of Mongolia,[7] which was established by OER activists previously involved with DREAM IT. The National OER Program has several components – including the ONE Academy for supporting open collaborative work, the development of an open university and the development of policies that allow educators to release their materials openly – to be implemented in the period 2014–2024. Initial priorities have been to localise Khan Academy[8] videos and create a Mongolian vocabulary wiki.[9] The state funding for the programme was about MNT 1 billion (USD 500 000) for 2014–2016. However, it is unclear whether the budget will support the programme after the change of political leadership as a result of the parliamentary election in June 2016.

Yet, despite this and direct action research in the preschool education sector (Davalgaa, 2013; Grunfeld & Hoon, 2013; Norjkhorloo & Porter, 2013), no significant activity has yet occurred regarding OER adoption in Mongolia's higher education sector, a fact explored in detail below. This situation is in contrast to the reported extent of OER activity in higher education in other parts of the world, including the Asian region (Dhanarajan & Porter, 2013). Thus, it remains to be seen whether OER will grow beyond its currently narrow uptake base in Mongolia's higher education sector.

---

5   http://davalgaa.mn/
6   http://bit.ly/2pX9kHv
7   http://one.mn
8   https://mn.khanacademy.org/
9   http://www.wikitoli.mn/

Research rationale and scope

This chapter reports on an exploratory research project which investigated the strategies and practices of educators from six HEIs in Mongolia in order to understand the role of OER in their work. Specifically, the chapter explores activities in academic workplace settings representing different organisational structures within the higher education domain where instructional development, teaching and learning take place. Participating institutions included four public and two private universities.

The intention of the study is to assess the cultural–historical factors that shape OER activities – and potential for further OER adoption – in Mongolia's higher education sector, in order to determine whether OER has the potential to move beyond a niche innovation advocated and funded by international donors to one that is broadly adopted, implemented and disseminated by local educators. As noted, this is the first study of OER activity in Mongolia's higher education system.

Methodology

This study used research methods, data collection strategies and interpretative frameworks that were appropriate for addressing research questions in a cultural–historical context. Because of the ability to address emergent contexts where pragmatic, grounded, iterative, interactive and flexible approaches are required, the frameworks, methodologies and approaches considered most appropriate for a study in this domain of practice included case study models (Yin, 2014), mixed methods (Creswell, 2014) and qualitative surveys (Jansen, 2010).

The study employed a sequential exploratory model (Cresswell, 2014) in which qualitative interviews comprised the first stage of data collection, followed by quantitative surveys. The interview data were reviewed and assessed and then used to refine the survey instrument that was employed.

Qualitative interviews

Qualitative interviews were conducted with 14 participants who were recruited using a sample of convenience from four Mongolian HEIs (NUM, Mongolian University of Science and Technics, Health Sciences University and Mongolian National University), two government organisations and three NGOs. A recruitment notice was sent out by email and participants volunteered to be interviewed. A total of eight educators and six administrators were interviewed for 30–40 minutes each.

A set of interview questions was developed to explore the beliefs, understandings and contexts underpinning OER use and potential in Mongolia. Based on key issues identified in a reading of the OER literature, the interview questions revolved around the following themes: **OER awareness**, as this can have a massive influence on whether OER is used or not (Allen & Seaman, 2014; Hatakka, 2009; Reed, 2012; Rolfe, 2012); **infrastructural accessibility**, because this is the foundation upon which OER activities take place (Bateman, 2006; Clements & Pawlowski, 2012; Dhanarajan & Abeydawara, 2013); **organisational culture**, as this may shape educators' choices around OER (Karunanayaka, Naidu, Dhanapala, Gonsalkorala & Ariyaratne, 2014); **institutional policy**, because this influences whether educators are allowed to engage with OER and whether they are rewarded or recognised for doing so (Cox & Trotter, 2017; Fitzgerald & Hashim, 2012; Flor, 2013; Tynan & James, 2013); **quality concerns**, because educators are reluctant to introduce new elements that might compromise the quality of their teaching (Clements & Pawlowski, 2012; Jung, Wong, Li, Baigaltugs & Belawati, 2011; Willems & Bossu, 2012); **pedagogical practices**, as these shape the type of engagement that educators may have with OER (Davis et al., 2010; Santos-Hermosa, 2014); and **OER value and utility**, as this judgement will determine whether OER become sustainable features of an education system or not (McGill, Falconer, Dempster, Littlejohn & Beetham, 2013; Pegler, 2012).

The questionnaire design process resulted in the following interview questions, listed according to their associated theme:

Awareness
What understanding of "open" practices and OER do you currently hold?
Where were you first introduced to OER: workshops, presentations or colleagues?

Access
To what degree does established technical infrastructure and support affect the potential for OER reuse in institutional settings?

Culture
What issues of organisational culture are associated with collaboration and sharing of OER among educators?

Policy
What business rules and organisational policies have been shown to directly affect OER opportunities?

Practices
What important practices and issues are entailed in the use, revision (translation), remixing, redistribution and retention[10] of OER for use in specific localised contexts in HEI settings and programmes?

Quality
What quality assurance processes and issues affect the adoption and reuse of open resources?

Value and utility
How do you see OER benefiting the Mongolian educational system, your institution or students?

---

10 http://opencontent.org/blog/archives/3251

Quantitative surveys

After assessing the responses of the qualitative interviews (n = 14), a follow-up survey was conducted with 42 instructors and administrators at six HEIs (see Appendix 1).[11] The survey was sent to 74 potential respondents representing the broader higher education sector in Mongolia, including lecturers, administrators, researchers and librarians. The survey approach was a form of convenience sampling. It followed the guidelines and process recommendations for sequential exploratory research design (Creswell, 2014), helped to elaborate, enhance and clarify the interview data, and extended understanding of the cultural–historical enablers and barriers to OER use for participants.

On the basis of the interviews – as well as through participation in a Research on Open Educational Resources for Development (ROER4D) research question harmonisation process[12] that encouraged the researcher to try to develop questions that could be compared to those from other OER surveys (CERI/OECD, 2007; Masterman & Wild, 2011; OERAsia, 2010; OER Hub, 2014) – the survey instrument was assessed, refined and ultimately implemented in September 2015. It was conducted both online (with the Google survey tool) and in paper-based format, depending on the desires of the respondents. Forty-two respondents (n = 42) completed the survey by the end of December 2015.

As shown below, questions 1–12 of the survey collected demographic and contextual data consistent with other investigations carried out as part of the ROER4D project.[13] Questions 13–34 collected data from participants about their knowledge of OER, their experiences of using OER and their experiences as developers of educational resources for use in their teaching, including any barriers they encountered. The survey also used "skip logic", which means that respondents answered questions based on their responses to previous questions. This section of the survey was deemed crucial because of its relationship to emergent themes from the interview process. The survey questions focused on obtaining data on the following items:

Interviewee demographics
1. Gender
2. Age
3. Discipline
4. Position at HEI
5. Years of teaching experience
6. Highest education qualification

---

11 http://dx.doi.org/10.5281/zenodo.815430
12 http://roer4d.org/892
13 ibid.

Internet access

7. Location of internet access
8. Devices used for internet access
9. Ownership of devices used to access the internet
10. Type of internet connection (broadband, dial-up, etc.)
11. Internet speeds available
12. Internet restrictions

Awareness of OER

13. Duration of awareness of OER concept
14. Resources you would feel free to use for teaching without worrying about copyright or licensing
15. Source of first exposure to OER concept
16. Institutional OER initiatives
17. Location of OER sources
18. Duration of awareness of alternative intellectual property (IP) mechanisms

Use of OER

19. Use of OER in teaching
20. Reasons for not using OER
21. Site of OER access
22. Use of OER "as is"
23. Use of "revised" OER
24. Frequency of combining/remixing OER
25. Assessing source of OER
26. Goals sought in using OER
27. Level of OER success
28. Reasons for lack of success
29. Reasons for success

Creating and sharing educational materials

30. Creating OER
31. Why not creating OER
32. Means of sharing OER
33. Motivations for creating OER
34. Barriers for creating OER

Data analysis

Based on the interview analysis, thematic analysis and coding (Boyatzis, 1998; Saldana, 2012) was undertaken in Excel. The semi-structured design of the interviews provided an opportunity for new topics and themes to emerge from the participant perspectives. Key findings from interview data were clustered thematically.

Quantitative data collected from closed-ended survey items were analysed using descriptive methods that report frequencies and measures of central tendency for the responses given by participants. The survey also collected data on multiple variables, including age, gender, position, discipline and experience, which might provide further opportunity to study the relationship between these various demographic variables and OER use, an analytical approach that has been found to be useful in a number of other OER survey studies (Commonwealth of Learning, 2016; de Oliveira Neto, Pete, Daryono & Cartmill, 2017; Masterman & Wild, 2011; OER Hub, 2014).

Analytical framework

This study utilised Cultural Historical Activity Theory (CHAT) (Engeström, 2001; Engeström & Sannino, 2010) as an analytical framework. Other Open researchers have noted that CHAT can provide insight into real-world activity systems in operation (including HEIs), particularly for investigations of situated practices using qualitative interviews (Trotter, Kell, Willmers, Gray & King, 2014).

CHAT provides a framework for analysing instructors' and administrators' actions towards achieving a specified *object* (goal) as mediated by *tools* (social and physical technologies), *rules* (formal policies, laws and implicit norms), *communities* and *divisions of labour*. The "CHAT triangle", as refined by Engeström (2001) (see Figure 1), visually represents the relationship between these "nodes" of the activity system, encouraging the researcher to identify "contradictions" that inhibit subjects' attainment of the object and outcome. Essentially, by ascertaining the relevant characteristics of each node in an activity system, and then assessing how they interact with each other, it is possible to find where there is a breakdown (or contradiction) in a linkage. For instance, if educators do not have access to the necessary tools (computers, internet, etc.) to use or create OER, then the linkage between the subject and tools node is "broken", creating a contradiction in the overall ecosystem. By identifying and addressing these contradictions through successive iterations, gradual progress can be made in attaining the desired object. This chapter seeks to do just that, especially by keeping in mind the cultural–historical elements that influence the character of the nodes and how they are linked.

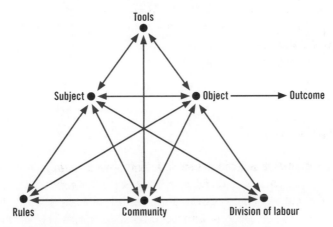

**Figure 1: Representation of an activity system in the CHAT tradition
(Source: Engeström, 2001)**

Findings

In this section, we assess the results of the interviews and surveys according to the themes identified in the literature and which structured the research instruments: awareness, access, culture, policy, practices, quality and value (utility). We do this in light of the cultural–historical elements that shape the higher education activity system with regards to OER, seeking to grasp where any contradictions or obstacles may reside in potential OER engagement.

The Mongolian higher education activity system

Before discussing the findings from the interviews and surveys, it is useful to visualise Mongolia's higher education system – with regard to OER engagement – in the context of a CHAT triangle (Figure 2). This consolidates the information from the Introduction on the cultural–historical elements shaping Mongolian higher education in general (e.g. language, finance, laws, gender, urban/rural divide, etc.), and includes the specific elements that pertain to the more recent introduction of OER to the country (e.g. OER funding, etc.). With this conceptual framework in mind, we will be able to gain better insights into the opportunities and obstacles for OER in Mongolia.

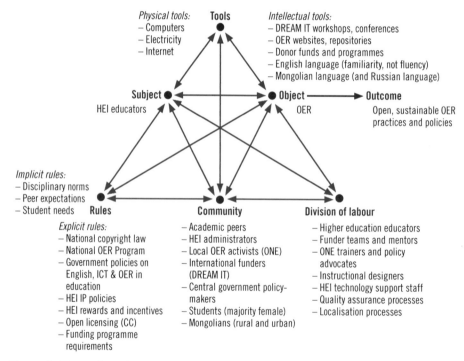

Figure 2: Mongolian higher education sector activity system as related to OER

Focused on Mongolian HEI educators who have the (hypothetical or real) object of using and/or creating OER for the purposes of developing open, sustainable OER practices and policies (as shown across the middle horizontal zone), Figure 2 shows how the various other nodes above and below mediate educator activity.

At the top of the triangle, activity related to tools are mediated by the usual physical tools that are necessary for OER access and engagement: computers, electricity and the internet. There are, however, also intellectual tools that mediate activity pertaining particularly to the Mongolian context, such as the OER awareness-raising efforts (workshops and conferences) of the donor community, growing national familiarity and use of the English language, the decline of Russian as a second language, and the continued ubiquity and relevance of Mongolian for educators and students.

Along the bottom axis, rules (implicit and formal or explicit) also mediate educator activity. The implicit rules comprise educators' disciplinary norms around OER engagement (and "openness" in general), peer expectations within a department about sharing behaviour and student desires for accessible, low-cost materials. The formal rules are those established by the central government (such as the national copyright law); the National OER Program, and various policies pertaining to the use of English, ICTs and OER in education; the institution, such as their relevant IP policies and rewards and incentive structures; alternative licensing bodies, such as CC with its open licence parameters; and donor funders, which place their own requirements on those who accept funding for OER work.

Educator activity is also mediated by the broader community in which the educators exist, comprising academic peers at their institutions (and beyond), institutional managers and administrators, international OER funders, local OER activists (such as ONE), central government policy-makers, students (the majority of whom are female) and the Mongolian public at large (which is bifurcated according to differentiated urban and rural opportunities).

Lastly, educator activity is mediated by the division of labour that exists around OER. Educators play a central role in seeking, finding, using, revising, remixing and creating OER, but they often also rely, to some extent, on international funder teams and mentors, trainers and policy advocates, instructional designers, technology support staff, as well as on quality assurance and localisation processes.

With the details of the activity system now clear, we can assess the data from the interviews and surveys to better understand how the Mongolian higher education system functions – or fails to function – in achieving desired OER goals and outcomes.

Awareness

International donors have been attempting to raise awareness around OER and openness in the country since 2010. To what extent can we say that these efforts have been successful?

In total, as depicted in Figure 3, 57% of the Mongolian educators and administrators surveyed for this study revealed that they had some level of awareness about the OER concept, while 43% said that they did not have any awareness prior to the study (Appendix 1, Q.13).

Of those who had some prior awareness, 19% had known about OER for 5–10 years, 14% had known for between two and five years, 19% had known for one to two years, and 4% had known for just less than one year (Figure 3). This suggests that there is a small core of educators and administrators who have known about OER for some time, but most would have become acquainted with the concept since 2010, perhaps partly due to the awareness-raising efforts of various donor projects. Yet, a sizeable minority had still not heard of OER prior to this study, which suggests that it is not yet a mainstream educational innovation in Mongolia.

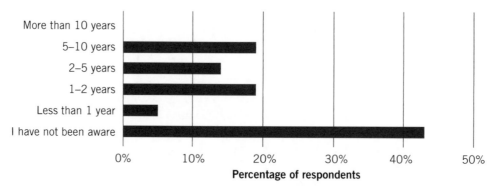

Figure 3: Period for which respondents have had knowledge of OER concept

For those who were aware of OER prior to the study (Figure 4) (Appendix 1, Q.15), 24% of respondents noted that their colleagues were the primary source of knowledge about OER, followed by 10% from academic journals and/or newspaper articles, 10% via initiatives in other institutions, 5% from initiatives within the educators' own institution and 5% from the internet.

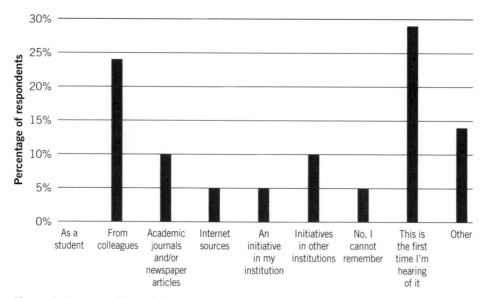

Figure 4: Sources of knowledge about OER reported by survey participants

Interview respondents also mentioned that the IDRC supported a series of seminars and workshops on OER held between 2011 and 2013, where they first became aware of OER.

To sum up the local perspective, according to the founder of the ONE Mongolia Foundation (one of the study's interviewees): "Many people know about OER, but practical use is very limited in Mongolia. We need a lot of investment to develop OER at its early stage. Several years have to be spent for awareness-raising of OER."

From a CHAT perspective, Mongolia's higher education activity system bears the traces of some mild recent donor-led OER activity which has helped raise awareness in the country. However, these workshops and programmes are just a few of many that are aimed at reforming Mongolia's education sector. They would therefore not be of the type to raise awareness to a level that permeates the entire sector. However, as the data show, educators have also gradually learned about OER through colleagues, journals and searching the internet, representing a certain measure of organic expansion of the idea. For the activity system to operate optimally in delivering OER outcomes, however, it will require a far higher level of awareness amongst educators and administrators than is currently present, as noted in research in other countries (Allen & Seaman, 2014; Hatakka, 2009; Reed, 2012; Rolfe, 2012).

Access

Access is a key educational challenge in the Global South (Bateman, 2006; Clements & Pawlowski, 2012; Dhanarajan & Abeydawara, 2013) and forms an integral component of the interview and survey questions. Essentially, are OER accessible for Mongolian educators, given the character of their infrastructural and linguistic contexts? On the CHAT triangle, this is largely covered by the top "tools" node, which distinguishes between physical and intellectual tools.

While Mongolia is still a developing country, most educators in the higher education sector appear to have access to the requisite technological infrastructure – computers, electricity and the internet – for engaging with OER. The majority (57%) of survey respondents own their own laptops, though many also use the desktop computers provided by their HEIs (Appendix 1, Q.9). Most connect to the internet at work (81%) and/or home (76%) (Appendix 1, Q.7/8) at speeds that they describe primarily as "medium" (52%) or "fast" (29–33%) (Appendix 1, Q.11). None said that there were any institutional access restrictions placed on their internet use (Appendix 1, Q.12). Thus, even though a small 9% said that they "do not have access to OER", it is not clear whether this is due to infrastructural access reasons or something else (Appendix 1, Q.20). It may be due to the intellectual tools that are also required to access OER.

As the CHAT triangle shows (Figure 2), while some of these tools pertain mostly to OER awareness (workshops, etc.), the linguistic tools – of English language familiarity (though not necessarily fluency) in a Mongolian language context that also retains the legacy of broad Russian language facility – will shape the type of access that many Mongolian educators have to OER because so many of them are based in English. With the country's move to greater English usage in higher education, this is both valuable and challenging. With Mongolians' familiarity with English, most OER are accessible to them in a basic sense. At a minimum, they are intelligible for both educators and students. However, since most OER are also developed in foreign countries – especially in Europe and North America – the concepts, examples and focus of the materials may not always be appropriate or useful for Mongolians. This suggests that, while most OER are technically and linguistically accessible in this context, they are not automatically relevant (discussed below in the Quality section) or valuable (discussed under Value and Utility).

Culture

Extending the linguistic focus more widely, culture can also have a powerful influence on whether educators adopt OER (Karunanayaka et al., 2014). On the CHAT triangle (Figure 2), this element is spread across the nodes of the bottom horizontal: rules (informal), community and division of labour.

The informal rules that mediate educator activity are those of disciplinary norms (the common practices in one's academic field), peer expectations (the social and collegial forces expressed in a department, in a faculty or by virtually-connected colleagues) and student needs (for access to low-cost, high-quality learning materials). As noted above, educators' work environment was a major factor for how many (24%) first learned about the concept of OER "from colleagues". Other educators are also key sources of information about where to look for OER, according to 29% of survey respondents, complementing another 19% who said that departmental/institutional meetings were useful for gaining OER information (Appendix 1, Q.17).

These informal rules go beyond knowledge acquisition to actual pedagogical practice. Of the 76% of survey respondents who said that they had never created and shared OER (Appendix 1, Q.30), the highest percentage of them (25%) said that they had not done so because "such sharing is not common in my discipline" (Appendix 1, Q.31). This suggests that many Mongolian educators look to their peers, both locally and internationally, to guide their activities to some extent. The fact that OER adoption is not yet a global norm[14] means that, as yet, the academic community does not provide the kind of positive pressure on Mongolians that is necessary to engage with OER at a broad level. Essentially, there is not yet a strong "culture of contribution" (Atkins, Brown & Hammond, 2007).

This notion is reinforced when assessing the activities of those in the "community" node of the CHAT triangle. The first group – international funders – played a key initial role in promoting OER, raising awareness and spurring mild uptake of OER by educators. Government policy-makers have taken this a step further with the establishment of the National OER Program (2014–2024). While much of this programme is aimed at the primary and secondary education sectors, the ONE Foundation, which is assisting in the implementation of the programme, has a broader mandate, including a focus on other higher education activity. But this diverse set of community groups is far from having a common approach to OER, even if many (rural students, male dropouts) would benefit from greater awareness and access to them. Thus, this appears to be an incipient "OER community", one that is currently more of a traditional "education community" but which is developing some nascent open-related characteristics. Building an OER ethic into this community will take some time, but the government's commitment to OER at national level gives crucial support to this possibility.

Thus, from a CHAT perspective, culture does not present an insurmountable obstacle to OER use or creation, but currently inhibits the full potential of this activity system in terms of adopting OER.

---

14 http://er.educause.edu/articles/2013/2/ten-years-later-why-open-educational-resources-have-not-noticeably-affected-higher-education-and-why-we-should-care

Policy

Focusing on the formal element of the rules node of the triangle, there are a number of relevant laws and policies that mediate (potential) OER activity. At the national level, section 17 of Mongolia's Copyright Law states that:

17.1. The author of a work created in the course of execution of his/her duties shall enjoy non-economic intangible rights.

17.2. The employer may have the exclusive rights over the exploitation of the work created as part of the exercise of official duties if not otherwise stipulated in the contract. (Government of Mongolia, 2006)

Read in the context of the education sector, this suggests that, on the one hand, educators should enjoy "non-economic intangible rights" over their teaching materials (i.e. "work created in the course of execution of his/her duties") while, on the other hand, the institution ("the employer") should enjoy sole rights over the "exploitation of the work". It is not clear how this would pertain to OER because the creation and sharing of one's teaching materials as OER entails a certain type of "exploitation" of one's own work. Yet it is likely that the "exploitation" referred to here concerns only those works where this is done for commercial purposes. This interpretation would seem to be supported based on the "non-economic" rights accorded to the creator, who, by sharing the work freely and openly as OER, is not transgressing the spirit or letter of such rights.

The government's open-mindedness regarding OER is more explicitly expressed in the Policy on ICT in Education Sector 2012–2016,[15] which, *inter alia*, plans for the following activities: "adopt creative commons license and enable open source courseware; policy support for higher education institutions that are developing open courses, enabling access to open course wares, developing distance learning infrastructure for common use" (Tuul, Banzragch & Saizmaa, 2016, p.189). These sentiments are not yet law, but they provide a positive signal for those interested in engaging with OER activities.

In addition, institutional IP policies can have more specific guidelines regarding the use or creation of OER, as they do elsewhere.[16] However, Mongolian HEIs have yet to address open licensing in their IP policies.

We did not find that OER was recognised or rewarded in the Mongolian institutional policies we reviewed. OER activity garners no special recognition for educators at this time. From a CHAT perspective, this is a significant contradiction because, of the 10 survey respondents who revealed that they had created OER in the past (Appendix 1, Q.30), this was the most important barrier to their continued creation and sharing of OER (Appendix 1, Q.34). Some 40% of these 10 respondents said the fact that there was "no reward system for staff members devoting time and energy" was "very important"; 10% said it was "important"; and none said that it was "unimportant" (Appendix 1, Q.34). This suggests that educators are very responsive to the rewards and incentives established by their employers, and that the lack of official incentive for OER activity inhibits its full potential in this system.

---

15 http://bit.ly/2pcOcBH
16 http://roer4d.org/2298

However, if an educator or HEI receives funds for an OER-related project (such as was the case with DREAM IT), there are typically requirements that certain materials be released as OER, if possible. This necessity would only comprise a small number of materials at this point, but it represents one of the few cases where some sort of official pressure is put on an educator to use or create OER.

One IP lawyer and part-time lecturer stated that universities need to take responsibility for the adoption of OER by providing greater funding for it, especially by piloting projects to see what works best:

> Students are very much interested in having learning materials of their own professors on the internet under open access. However, very few professors upload their materials. Universities have enough capacity to develop OER, but financial resources are not directed for it. Universities need to decide priority subject areas and start from pilot projects. After that, they need to research how students used these pilot OER materials.

With Mongolia's history of centralised educational governance, and educators' responsiveness to official reward policies, the rules node of the CHAT triangle is particularly important for potential OER activity. Currently, there appears to be a relatively agnostic approach to OER at the governmental level, as OER-related interventions have not happened at an institutional policy level. Some positive OER intentions are noted in one national policy document, but it will likely require greater elaboration, especially at the institutional level, to optimise OER engagement in the higher education activity system.

Quality

Another key concern in the global literature on OER concerns quality (Clements & Pawlowski, 2012; Jung et al., 2011). This was raised explicitly in the interview and survey questions, yet the primary quality concern that Mongolian educators appear to have relates to the entire higher education sector. As discussed above, with the rapid massification and privatisation of higher education following the transition, the quality standards of the sector have, in many educators' estimation, fallen sharply.

Thus they do not have the same type of concern over OER quality as expressed by educators elsewhere (Willems & Bossu, 2012). Mongolian educators who are aware of OER in many ways simply view them as more educational resources that they would consider incorporating into their teaching. They already feel largely free to download and use other educational resources, regardless of copyright (Appendix 1, Q.14), for use in the classroom, based on fair use principles and common collegial practice. The introduction of OER does not appear to radically alter the resource landscape for educators who are looking for materials which are relevant to their needs and, of course, of the requisite quality.

One educator stated: "We need to start from materials from international universities with high reputation." This was supported by 75% of the survey respondents, who said that it was either "important" or "very important" that "the materials come from a university that I respect (e.g. MIT)" (Appendix 1, Q.25). Such a provenance would act as a quality signifier to them, simplifying their search processes and reassuring them that materials are credible.

Additionally, 75% also said that it was either "important" or "very important" that, when considering using an OER, "the author has a strong reputation for their teaching (if I don't know him/her personally)" (Appendix 1, Q.25). This principle was reiterated by the 75% of respondents who said that, when looking for OER to use, they were hoping to gain "access to the best possible resources" (Appendix 1, Q.26). These sentiments suggest that quality is an important criterion for the decisions Mongolian educators make (or would make) about using OER, even if it is not their overwhelming concern when considering OER.

In the context of this study, educators' major concern about educational materials centres on the notion of local relevance. This is regardless of whether the material is open or not. With a small population living in a unique context, which was cut off from the non-Soviet world until 1990, Mongolia and its contextual concerns are not incorporated into many educational resources that are available on the internet. That reality is something Mongolian educators understand very well. Thus, they try to localise educational materials, making them relevant for their students. Of the options that survey respondents were given as to how they "revise" the OER that they use – that is, translate, summarise, rewrite, resequence or localise the materials – they were more likely to "localise" materials in their revision process for the different types of OER (videos, podcasts, images, tutorials, quizzes, etc.) used than any other activity (Appendix 1, Q.23).

While localisation is a common desire, it is not easy to undertake. As one educator stated, "the localisation process may require a lot of resources. The educators with high proficiency of English in their subject area may not be interested in localisation activities, since many of them are busy with research activities".

This calls attention to the broader sense in which the "relevance" of a resource is understood. For many educators, this means that it is available in the Mongolian language. As one lecturer at NUM stated: "Localisation of English language OER into Mongolian is important." Mongolians' familiarity with English gives them a certain level of access to English-language materials, both fully copyrighted and open, but they really only become fully accessible and relevant when they are in the language of greatest comprehension, Mongolian.

However, this perspective perhaps has more urgency in the basic education sector where English is not used as widely as in higher education. An exemplar of the externally trusted resource strategy is currently being implemented in Mongolian K-12 education, where up to 1 000 videos were identified for translation from the California-based Khan Academy platform through the Open Network for Education for Mongolia (ONE Mongolia) project. More than 500 videos have already been translated, using Mongolian audio to substitute the English voice-over (ONE Mongolia, 2016).

A similar approach was undertaken in 2012 and 2013 within a research project by Norjkhorloo and Porter (2013), where short-form videos in the Mongolian language were created on single concept lessons for use by Mongolian preschool and kindergarten teachers. The videos were released online with a CC licence accompanied by a printable textbook on a public website for use by parents, teachers or any member of the public in Mongolia (Davalgaa, 2013).

Practices

HEIs are workplace settings which typically have traditions and cultural norms that are difficult to change. The tradition of generating IP has historically been a primary driver for academics. This tradition could be perceived to be at odds with OER development, use, reuse, revision, remixing and redistribution. Using someone else's lecture notes or open textbook could be thought of as counter to the traditions of the academy. In many cases, academics author textbooks and other instructional resources as part of a relationship with publishers or vendors of educational resources. The incentive for them is compensation or a royalty stream, an approach that might need to find a substitute mechanism to foster a culture of open practices, sharing and support for OER in Mongolia.

When asked whether they ever used OER in their teaching, the majority of survey respondents (52%) said that they "never" did, 9.5% said that they "rarely" did, 29% said that they "sometimes" did, 0% said that they "often" did, and 9.5% said that they "frequently" did (Appendix 1, Q.19). Thus, there is a fairly even split between users and non-users, though the relatively low frequencies expressed suggest that it is not yet a norm. As one lecturer at NUM said: "Educators are too busy and sometimes capacity to use OER is lacking. But in general, there has been significant progress in using OER by educators and students in the last three years."

Table 1: Ways in which OER are reused by survey respondents

OER formats (Tick all that apply)	"As is" (often or always) (%)	Translate (%)	Summa- rise (%)	Rewrite (%)	Resequence (%)	Localise (%)
Textbooks	**58**	25	25	17	8	8
Images	**42**	0	17	17	8	**42**
Research articles	**42**	8	25	8	8	25
Infographics	**33**	16	8	17	0	**33**
Lesson plans	**33**	0	8	8	17	**33**
e-Books	**33**	17	8	0	17	25
Elements of a course (module/unit)	**25**	**25**	**25**	17	0	17
Videos	**25**	8	**25**	8	8	25
Lecture notes	**25**	0	17	**25**	0	25
Slide presentations (PowerPoint)	**25**	8	17	17	8	17
Datasets	**25**	17	8	8	8	17
Whole courses	17	0	**50**	17	8	8
Audio podcasts	17	8	8	17	0	**25**
Tutorials	17	0	8	17	8	**33**
Tests and quizzes	17	0	8	8	17	**33**
Top activity per format category	*11/15*	*1/15*	*3/15*	*1/15*	*0/15*	*8/15*

Note: bold numbers = highest percentage of respondents in a particular row category

Of those who said that they do use OER, the majority (50%) stated that they find resources through Google Scholar searches, followed by institutional repositories (33%) and personal websites or blogs (25%) (Appendix 1, Q.21). They also engaged with the resources in different ways depending on what format it was in. Table 1 shows the percentage of respondents who revealed the ways in which they used certain types of OER (drawn from Appendix 1, Q.22/23).

Thus, respondents showed a high proclivity for using OER "as is" (without any modification). In 11 of the 15 format categories, this comprised the top use style for respondents, especially for textbooks, images and research articles. Respondents also engaged in translation, but at a much lower level. In just one of the categories – elements of a course – does translation achieve a top use score (along with "as is" and "summarise"). This suggests that, even though many educators desire that materials be in Mongolian, the effort required to translate the materials may outweigh the benefits of having resources available in Mongolian, particularly if the students have the requisite facility with English to comprehend it.

Respondents revealed that they like to summarise OER that are whole courses, as well as elements of a course or video. These are materials that are intellectually "substantial" in that they require a significant amount of time on the part of educators who wish to engage with their contents. The educators prefer to present summarised elements of these materials rather than the unedited materials themselves, as this would likely entail temporal investments on the part of students that would be pedagogically unnecessary. However, the respondents did not appear to do much rewriting or resequencing (i.e. "remixing") with OER. Only with lecture notes did 25% of them say that they rewrote these resources.

Lastly, a high percentage of respondents engage in localisation activities with multiple formats. In eight of the 15 formats, localisation ranks as a top activity for these educators. This coincides with the localisation desires discussed above, in which interview and survey respondents said that localised materials have great value for their teaching.

In this nascent OER environment, the percentages revealed in Table 1 make sense, in that respondents are more likely to use resources "as is", followed by "localisation" and then "summarising". These are the least complex ways of reusing OER, as translation, rewriting and resequencing require extensive investments in time and, in some cases, technical and pedagogical proficiency (Okada, Mikroyannidis, Meister & Little, 2012). However, over time, as Mongolian educators become more aware of what OER are available to them, the number of educators who engage in these more complex activities may also increase.

Another activity that may increase amongst Mongolian educators is OER creation and sharing. Currently, the notion of sharing and proactive contribution to the global OER "commons" is a relatively new concept for them. As one NUM lecturer suggested: "Some educators are very cautious about sharing their educational materials. It may be they don't have sufficient understanding of a sharing culture." The survey data succinctly frame the current situation, with 76% of respondents reporting that they have *not* created or shared OER, and only 24% reporting that they have (Appendix 1, Q.30).

The 10 survey respondents who said that they have created and shared OER, did so via a number of different online platforms. Table 2 shows a list of possible distribution platforms along with the percentage of respondents who shared their teaching materials per platform (Appendix 1, Q.32).

Table 2: Platforms where respondents have shared OER

Platform	% of respondents
Personal website or blog	60
Institutional learning management system	50
Cloud-based storage (e.g. Google Drive)	50
Departmental website	30
International repository (e.g. MERLOT)	20
Image/video-based services (e.g. Flickr, PowerPoint, YouTube)	20
Institutional repository	0
Wiki site (e.g. Wikipedia, Wikieducator.org)	0

It appears that OER creators have preferred to use personal websites or blogs (60%), along with institutional learning management systems and cloud-based storage platforms (50% each). While some (30%) shared their work on departmental websites, a more modest percentage of respondents used "official" global sharing platforms such as international repositories (20%) and image/video-based services (20%), and none used a wiki site or an institutional repository (this may, however, be because these do not exist as an option).

From a CHAT perspective, these practices reveal the current state of the activity system in that the OER use and creation percentages are relatively modest with plenty of room for growth, and the particular ways in which educators use and create OER suggest an exploratory (rather than a long-term) approach to this activity. On the CHAT triangle, these practices and changes are represented on the "outcome" node. While the hoped-for outcome is sustained OER practice, which would be achieved through an optimised activity system, the current practices described above reveal that there is still some way to go until that is a reality.

Value and utility

Perhaps the most important factor in determining whether OER have a future in Mongolia is whether educators feel that they have value and utility for their teaching needs. OER will have to be as useful as conventional materials (or even more so) if they are to complement, let alone displace, the materials that educators already use. To ascertain whether OER were meeting respondents' pedagogical needs and desires, educators were asked what goals or benefits they were seeking through using OER (Appendix 1, Q.26).

Of the many possible answers they were prompted with, the three primary responses were "gaining access to the best possible resources" (75% of respondents said this was either "important" or "very important"), "promoting research and education as publicly open activities" (75%) and "outreach to disadvantaged communities" (67%). The first response refers to a desire for high-quality materials, discussed above; the second refers to a moral commitment to open educational activities; and the third refers to a desire to help overcome contemporary inequalities in Mongolia.

However, when asked how they would rate the success of their use of OER, the results were mixed, as Table 3 shows (Appendix 1, Q.27).

Table 3: Respondents' view of the success of their experience with OER

Response	% of respondents
Neutral	42
Successful	25
Not very successful	17
Not at all successful	8
Very successful	8

Only 33% of respondents who used OER thought that they had a successful or very successful experience in doing so. A sizeable minority of 25% thought it was not successful and 42% were neutral about their experience.

For OER to compete against other materials – because they, like all educational materials, are in a form of competition with each other for educators to select them – they should ideally be providing more positive results if they are to go from being a funder-driven innovation to a mainstream consideration.

For the 25% who stated that their use of OER was not successful (Appendix 1, Q.28), they revealed that "it did not enhance the quality of my teaching" (33%) and "it did not make the learning process more flexible" (33%). These responses should be treated with some caution because the absolute numbers of respondents here are low, but this does raise concern for ambitions around OER, particularly if these are common responses for other Mongolian educators beyond the scope of this project.

However, for the 33% of users who said that their experience was successful (Appendix 1, Q.29), they claimed that "it has enhanced the quality of my teaching" (50%), "it has saved me money" (25%) and "it has made the learning process more flexible" (25%). Thus, for these educators, OER satisfied quality, cost and flexibility concerns – three elements that are key for OER to remain a sustainable interest for Mongolians.

Lastly, though only 10 of the 42 survey respondents had created and shared OER, their reasons for doing so reveal some of the surprising benefits of engaging in this activity as an educator. Table 4 shows the factors motivating respondents to create OER (Appendix 1, Q.33).

Table 4: Factors motivating respondents to create OER (n = 10)

Motivating statement	% of responses
It improves the quality of my materials, knowing that other educators may use them	70
It helps other educators	60
It enhances my reputation amongst my peers	60
I have benefited from using others' educational resources, so I want to contribute also	50
I believe that teaching resources should be open	40
Other	20
It is normal practice in my discipline	0

Table 4 shows that the primary motivating factor was that it improved educators' own teaching materials because they knew that other educators might use them (70%). This encouraged the creators to improve the quality of their materials before releasing them to the public. This is a beneficial outcome for both the creator and potential users.

The next two most common responses were that "it helps other educators" (60%), an altruistic notion that taps into these educators' desire to share and connect, and "it enhances my reputation amongst my peers", a notion that taps into these same educators' self-interested desires to enhance their reputations. This is as it should be: the engagement with OER, if it is to be a successful, broad-based enterprise, needs to satisfy educator desires that are both self- and externally directed.

From a CHAT perspective, the value and utility of OER for Mongolian educators is very much an open question. This may be due to the relatively small percentages of educators who have used OER in their teaching, or who have created and shared OER with others. Perspectives regarding OER may crystalise over time, one way or another, determining whether it becomes a common, accepted and sustained innovation in the higher education space.

Conclusion and recommendations

While the OER concept is relatively new as an educational innovation, its arrival and deployment in Mongolia has a very particular history, one tied up with the radical changes that occurred after the country's transition from communism to a market economy, from Soviet patronage to international donor sponsorship, from Russian as a second language to English, from free to fee-based educational provision, and from state-controlled higher education to an increasingly massified, privatised sector.

Within this context, OER awareness-raising activities began in 2010 with a series of national forums, seminars and workshops on OER. Continued advocacy work took place, with one OER preschool research project conducted by Norjkhorloo and Porter (2013), the creation of a Mongolian Creative Commons Affiliate (2014), and the ONE Mongolia (2014) project, which introduced open practices, OER resources and training to the K-12 sector. However, to date no OER initiatives have been launched in the higher education system to provide broad-scale policy or practice strategies to guide further implementation across Mongolia's university sector.

As the Findings section reveals, the current situation in Mongolia is that open development strategies and practices are in a formative state of deployment, with low adoption rates in the education sector relative to traditional teaching approaches. A number of reasons – as illuminated in the analysis of the Mongolian education activity system – help explain this.

First, despite recent efforts to promote OER (including the establishment of a National OER Program), this study's interviews and surveys suggest that OER awareness remains modest amongst higher education educators and administrators. This relative lack of *awareness* inhibits the potential of OER in the country. Indeed, there is likely only so much that donors can do in this regard. At some point, it would seem crucial that OER become part of everyday educational practice for a larger group of instructors so that it can grow and spread across the sector in an organic manner. Because Mongolia has been highly dependent on donor organisations in education since the transition, there is every possibility that this funder-driven innovation will be ignored once the funders move on or focus on other innovations. The government, which initiated the funding for rolling out the National OER Program and ONE Mongolia project, may also alter its funding commitments as new political administrations take power, as happened in 2016. For the ideal outcome of the development of sustainable open practices and policies to be achieved (the "outcome" from the CHAT activity system), Mongolian educators will have to engage with OER in larger numbers and create communities of practice that incorporate OER into the prevailing academic culture. This takes time, and will likely take more funding from donors to ensure that such a culture can grow.

Second, a much smaller issue – but one that cannot be completely taken for granted in Mongolia's developing context – relates to infrastructural *access*. This study's data suggest that most higher education practitioners have the requisite access to computer hardware, internet connectivity and electricity to engage with OER at some level. A small percentage of respondents did, however, say that they struggled with access issues, which reminds us of how diverse the educational contexts are in this vast yet sparsely populated country. In the capital, however, where most higher education takes place, access is good.

Third, as suggested above, a *culture* around OER engagement has not yet emerged. It is a new concept, one that may have certain benefits in situations where costs are a concern for both educators and students, but the lack of awareness broadly means that it is typically only isolated individual educators who are adopting OER. Changing culture also takes time, as disciplinary norms are established globally, not just locally, and peer expectations are tied up with institutional policy, funding opportunities and pedagogical practice (as well as the kinds of results one obtains through experimenting with OER). This may be one area where donors can focus their interventions more on teams and departments and less on individuals, and more on high-level management than the mass of individual lecturers. Indeed, the peer-support programmes, as modelled at Canada's BCcampus,[17] could be useful for building a core team of OER advocates and trainers who are also higher education instructors (Porter, 2013). Even more ambitiously, the government, with donor funding and advice, could establish a sector-wide educational repository similar to the MERLOT II[18] multimedia educational resource repository developed by California State University. It is a curated repository of peer-reviewed OER learning materials that has gained the trust of higher education educators because of its reputation and peer-review processes. A similar initiative could be effective in the Mongolian context.

Fourth, the educational *policy* environment is mostly agnostic regarding OER, meaning that it leaves the choices surrounding OER adoption with individual educators. This would be fine if more educators knew about OER and had some experience with it, as they could then exercise their pedagogical freedom in assessing all types of course materials, including OER. However, in Mongolia's context of low OER awareness, government policy-makers and institutional managers can play a much greater role in enabling OER adoption by creating pro-OER policies. This is hinted at in some recent government publications, such as the Policy on ICT in Education Sector 2012–2016, but as this study's respondents suggested,

---

17 https://bccampus.ca/2014/10/09/improving-adoption-of-open-textbooks-through-faculty-advocates/
18 https://www.merlot.org/merlot/index.htm

they would be far more responsive to national- and/or institutional-level incentive policies that reward and recognise engagement with OER. For instance, the government could initiate a funding programme for OER development and sustainability that incentivises OER adoption at Mongolian universities, or a number of pilot universities could do the same within certain departments. Thus, while the national Copyright Law and various other policies appear to open the door for OER adoption for educators, a less agnostic and more explicitly supportive set of policies would be needed for robust OER engagement across the country.

Fifth, Mongolian educators are less worried about the *quality* of OER (compared to Western academics), but more concerned about a particular sub-component of quality, *relevance*. The unique cultural–historical context that Mongolians enjoy, along with the fact that most OER are developed elsewhere, makes educators desire teaching materials that are locally relevant – that is, "localised". Many already engage in localising processes with the teaching materials they have, but it takes time. If OER were more localised to the Mongolian context – which would likely mean that more Mongolians were creating and sharing OER – educators would find them very useful. Educators would also appreciate it if more OER were available in the Mongolian language, though the predominance of materials in English is not an absolute barrier to use. To deal with this, it may be useful if the government, in conjunction with international funders, embarked on a similar OER process as was done in South Africa with the independent OER producer Siyavula[19] (Goodier, 2017), which produced open textbooks for the K-12 education sector. This could be done in Mongolia – not only at the lower grade levels (where the mass benefits are obvious), but possibly with select course textbooks at the higher education level, especially in those subjects with the greatest numbers of students and/or that need to be more attuned to the local cultural and linguistic context. These could be continuously updated and revised by Mongolian academics who have an interest in keeping such materials locally relevant.

Sixth, a number of the educators and administrators interviewed and surveyed have engaged with OER-related *practices*, revealing that OER use was more common for them than OER creation. This is a common distinction (de Oliviera Neto et al., 2017), even though it is likely that if more Mongolian educators created OER, more Mongolian educators would then have locally relevant OER to use. It is therefore important to not only increase educators' range and intensity of OER use practices[20] (Okada et al., 2012), but to promote creation as well. This may likely be the key to whether OER adoption in Mongolia will become a robust, mature and sustainable activity going forward. Given that academic colleagues have often provided the greatest degree of knowledge to educators in Mongolia concerning OER, it may be useful for the OER community to initiate a "faculty fellows" programme (again modelled on the Canadian BCcampus[21]), in which peers teach peers how to think about and use OER.

Lastly, Mongolian educators have some reservations about the *value and utility* of OER. As revealed in the Findings section, while a third of respondents (33%) who had used OER were positive about their experience with them, a number (42%) were simply neutral about them and a significant minority (25%) reported negative experiences. These proportions would need to change markedly if educators are going to spread knowledge of OER to their peers, use OER again and create and share OER themselves. Given the relatively small

---

19   http://www.education.gov.za/Curriculum/LearningandTeachingSupportMaterials(LTSM)/SiyavulaTextbooks.aspx
20   http://opencontent.org/blog/archives/3251
21   https://bccampus.ca/2014/10/09/improving-adoption-of-open-textbooks-through-faculty-advocates/

sample size for this study, it may be that this does not represent the broader Mongolian educators' experience with OER, but it should raise concerns nonetheless, as this lukewarm judgement of OER – as a type of teaching material that isn't really any better than conventional teaching materials – could limit its growth and potential to a small minority of committed open advocates. The fact that Mongolian educators also feel largely free to download and use any type of educational material online (whether open or copyrighted) means that the typical value proposition made by OER advocates – that OER is "free" – may not mean much when educators are already obtaining and using desired materials for "free". This reminds us that OER compete against conventional materials in a very crowded market. It is likely that only with the creation and availability of more locally relevant materials will OER come to be associated with the value and utility that is required for sustained interest.

This research was undertaken in an effort to understand the cultural–historical factors that influence the adoption, implementation and dissemination of OER in Mongolia's higher education sector. Mongolia has shown that it can develop and support large-scale educational-resource projects (such as the ONE Mongolia project). It may need to take a similar proactive and intentional stance in the higher education sector if it seeks to improve the quality of content, and develop and sustain a population of educators and learners who are familiar and comfortable with using OER. Additionally, while certain contradictions were revealed in this activity system, most are not of the type that cannot be adjusted with greater OER awareness, official rewards and incentives for OER engagement, or continued donor funding (so that the government continues to support this innovation). The promotion of targeted training programmes along with models for compensation might provide a potential "tipping point" (Gladwell, 2002) to advance open practice and OER in Mongolia.

Acknowledgements

Heartfelt thanks are given to Atieno Adala for sharing her initial guidelines, which formed the basis of this chapter; to David Porter for his mentorship, manuscript review and efforts in assisting with the data presentation and analysis process; to Valerie Lopes for her thoughtful review of this chapter; to Alan Cliff for his attentive reading and feedback on the chapter; and to Cheryl Hodgkinson-Williams and Michelle Willmers in ROER4D for their insightful comments and guidance.

References

ADB (Asian Development Bank). (2011a). *Higher education reform project (rrp prc 43007): Sector assessment (summary): Education*. Manila: Asian Development Bank. Retrieved from https://www.adb.org/sites/default/files/linked-documents/43007-023-mon-ssa.pdf

ADB (Asian Development Bank). (2011b). *Report and recommendation of the President to the Board of Directors*. Manila: Asian Development Bank. Retrieved from https://www.adb.org/sites/default/files/project-document/61182/43007-023-mon-rrp.pdf

Adiya, E. (2010). *Gender equity in access to higher education in Mongolia*. Ph.D thesis. Pittsburgh: University of Pittsburgh. Retrieved from http://d-scholarship.pitt.edu/8631/1/enkhjargaladiya.pdf

Allen, I. E. & Seaman, J. (2014). *Opening the curriculum: Open Education Resources in U.S. higher education, 2014.* Babson Park, MA: Babson Survey Research Group and The William and Flora Hewlett Foundation. Retrieved from http://www.onlinelearningsurvey.com/reports/openingthecurriculum2014.pdf

Altbach, P. G. (2004). The past and future of Asian universities. In P. G. Altbach & T. Umakoshi (Eds.), *Asian universities: Historical perspectives and contemporary challenges* (pp. 13–32). Baltimore: Johns Hopkins University Press.

Atkins, D. E., Brown, J. S. & Hammond, A. L. (2007). *A review of the Open Educational Resources (OER) movement: Achievements, challenges and new opportunities.* Menlo Park, CA: William and Flora Hewlett Foundation. Retrieved from http://www.hewlett.org/wp-content/uploads/2016/08/ReviewoftheOERMovement.pdf

Baasansuren, B. & Porter, D. (2013). Mongolia's educational resources go into the great wide open. In H. Grunfeld & M. N. L. Hoon (Eds.), *Dream I.T.: Development research to empower all Mongolians through information technology* (pp. 47–52). Ulaanbaatar: Datacom. Retrieved from http://www.academia.edu/8335079/Mongolia_s_educational_resources_go_into_the_great_wide_open

Bateman, P. (2006). *The AVU Open Educational Resources (OER) architecture for higher education in Africa: Discussion paper.* Paris: OECD. Retrieved from http://www.oecd.org/edu/ceri/38149047.pdf

Begzsuren, T. & Dolgion, A. (2014). *Gender overview – Mongolia: A desk study.* Bern: Swiss Agency for Development and Cooperation & Independent Research Institute of Mongolia. Retrieved from https://www.eda.admin.ch/content/dam/countries/countries-content/mongolia/en/SDC-Gender-%20Overview-Mongolia-%202014-EN.pdf

Boston Consulting Group. (2013). *The Open Education Resources ecosystem: An evaluation of the OER movement's current state and its progress toward mainstream adoption.* Boston, MA: Boston Consulting Group. Retrieved from http://www.hewlett.org/sites/default/files/The%20Open%20Educational%20Resources%20Ecosystem_1.pdf

Boyatzis, R. E. (1998). *Transforming qualitative information: Thematic analysis and code development.* Thousand Oaks, CA: Sage.

Bray, M., Davaa, S., Spaulding, S. & Weidman, J. C. (1994). Transition from Socialism and the financing of higher education: The case of Mongolia. *Higher Education Policy, 7(4)*, 36–42. Retrieved from https://www.researchgate.net/publication/44818827_Transition_from_Socialism_and_the_Financing_of_Higher_Education_The_Case_of_Mongolia

Butcher, N. (2011). *A basic guide to Open Educational Resources (OER).* Vancouver: Commonwealth of Learning. Retrieved from http://unesdoc.unesco.org/images/0021/002158/215804e.pdf

CERI/OECD (Centre for Educational Research and Innovation/Organisation for Economic Cooperation and Development). (2007). *Giving knowledge for free: The emergence of Open Educational Resources.* Paris: Centre for Educational Research and Innovation & Organisation for Economic Cooperation and Development. Retrieved from http://www.oecd.org/edu/ceri/38654317.pdf

Chua, A. (2007). *Day of empire: How hyperpowers rise to global dominance – and why they fall.* New York: Doubleday.

Clements, K. I. & Pawlowski, J. M. (2012). User-oriented quality for OER: Understanding teachers' views on re-use, quality, and trust. *Journal of Computer Assisted Learning, 28(1)*, 4–14. Retrieved from http://onlinelibrary.wiley.com/doi/10.1111/j.1365-2729.2011.00450.x/abstract

Cohen, R. (2004). The current status of English education in Mongolia. *Asian EFL Journal, 6(4)*. Retrieved from http://asian-efl-journal.com/Dec_04_rc.pdf

Commonwealth of Learning (2016). *Open Educational Resources in the Commonwealth 2016.* Vancouver: Commonwealth of Learning. Retrieved from http://oasis.col.org/bitstream/handle/11599/2441/2016_Phalachandra-Abeywardena_OER-in-Commonwealth-2016.pdf?sequence=4

Cox, G. & Trotter, H. (2017). Factors shaping lecturers' adoption of OER at three South African universities. In C. Hodgkinson-Williams & P. B. Arinto (Eds), *Adoption and impact of OER in the Global South* (pp. 287–347). Retrieved from https://doi.org/10.5281/zenodo.601935

Creswell, J. W. (2014). *Research design: qualitative, quantitative, and mixed methods approaches.* Thousand Oaks, CA: Sage.

Daniel, J., Kanwar, A. & Uvalić-Trumbić, S. (2006). A tectonic shift in global higher education. *Change: The Magazine of Higher Learning, 38(4)*, 16–23. Retrieved from http://www.learntechlib.org/p/98724

Davalgaa. (2013). *Davalgaa: Expression through education.* Ulaanbaatar: Davalgaa. Retrieved from http://davalgaa.mn/

Davis, H. C., Carr, L., Hey, J. M. N., Howard, Y., Millard, D., Morris, D. & White, S. (2010). Bootstrapping a culture of sharing to facilitate Open Educational Resources. *IEEE Transactions on Learning Technologies, 3(2)*, 96–109. Retrieved from http://ieeexplore.ieee.org/document/5210093/?reload=true

del Rosario, M. (2005). *The Mongolian drop out study.* Ulaanbaatar: Mongolian Education Alliance. Retrieved from http://www.edupolicy.net/no-access/download-id/866/

de Oliveira Neto, J. D., Pete, J., Daryono & Cartmill, T. (2017). OER use in the Global South: A baseline survey of higher education instructors. In C. Hodgkinson-Williams & P. B. Arinto (Eds), *Adoption and impact of OER in the Global South* (pp. 69–118). Retrieved from https://doi.org/10.5281/zenodo.599535

Dhanarajan, G. & Abeydawara, I. S. (2013). Higher education and Open Educational Resources in Asia: An overview. In G. Dhanarajan & D. Porter (Eds.), *Open Educational Resources: An Asian perspective* (pp. 3–18). Vancouver: Commonwealth of Learning. Retrieved from https://oerknowledgecloud.org/sites/oerknowledgecloud.org/files/pub_PS_OER_Asia_web.pdf

Dhanarajan, G. & Porter, D. (Eds.). (2013). *Open Educational Resources: An Asian perspective.* Vancouver: Commonwealth of Learning. Retrieved from https://oerknowledgecloud.org/sites/oerknowledgecloud.org/files/pub_PS_OER_Asia_web.pdf

Dovchin, S. (2011). Performing identity through language: The local practices of urban youth populations in post-socialist Mongolia. *Inner Asia, 13*, 315–333. Retrieved from http://www.jstor.org/stable/24572097?seq=1#page_scan_tab_contents

Dovchin, S. (2015). Language, multiple authenticities and social media: The online language practices of university students in Mongolia. *Journal of Sociolinguistics, 19(4)*, 437–459. Retrieved from http://onlinelibrary.wiley.com/wol1/doi/10.1111/josl.12134/full

Dovchin, S., Sultana, S. & Pennycook, A. (2015). Relocalizing the translingual practices of young adults in Mongolia and Bangladesh. *Translation and Translanguaging in Multilingual Contexts, 1(1)*, 4–26. Retrieved from https://benjamins.com/#catalog/journals/ttmc.1.1.01dov/fulltext

Dovchin, S., Sultana, S. & Pennycook, A. (2016). Unequal translingual Englishes in the Asian peripheries. *Asian Englishes, 18(2)*, 92–108. Retrieved from http://dx.doi.org/10.1080/13488678.2016.1171673

Engeström, Y. (2001). Expansive learning at work: Toward an activity theoretical reconceptualization. *Journal of Education and Work, 14(1)*, 133–156. Retrieved from ftp://ftp.uwc.ac.za/users/DMS/CITI/New%20PHd%20folder/PHd%20PDF's/expansive-Engestrom_2001-1.pdf

Engeström, Y. & Sannino, A. (2010). Studies of expansive learning: Foundations, findings and future challenges. *Educational Research Review, 5,* 1–24. Retrieved from http://www.sciencedirect.com/science/article/pii/S1747938X10000035?via%3Dihub

Fitzgerald, A. & Hashim, H. N. M. (2012). Enabling access to and re-use of publicly funded research data as open educational resources: A strategy for overcoming the legal barriers to data access and re-use. In *Proceedings of the Regional Symposium on Open Educational Resources: An Asian Perspective on Policy and Practices,* 19–21 September 2012. Penang: Wawasan Open University.

Flor, A. G. (2013). Exploring the downside of open knowledge resources: The case of indigenous knowledge systems and practices in the Philippines. *Open Praxis, 5(1),* 75–80. Retrieved from http://openpraxis.org/index.php/OpenPraxis/article/view/15

Gladwell, M. (2002). *The tipping point: How little things can make a big difference.* New York: Little, Brown and Company.

Goodier, S. (2017). Tracking the money for Open Educational Resources in South African basic education: What we don't know. *International Review of Research in Open and Distributed Learning, 18(4).* Retrieved from http://dx.doi.org/10.19173/irrodl.v18i4.2990

Government of Mongolia. (2006). *Law of Mongolia on Copyright and related rights (as last amended on 19 January 2006).* Ulaanbaatar: Government of Mongolia. Retrieved from http://www.wipo.int/wipolex/en/text.jsp?file_id=203958

Grunfeld, H. & Hoon, M. N. L. (Eds.). (2013). *Dream I.T.: Development research to empower all Mongolians through information technology.* Ulaanbaatar: International Development Research Centre & Datacom. Retrieved from https://www.researchgate.net/publication/256297613_Grunfeld_H_Ng_M_Eds_2013_DREAM_IT_development_research_to_empower_all_Mongolians_through_information_communications_technology_Ulaanbaatar_Datacom

Hatakka, M. (2009). Build it and they will come?: Inhibiting factors for reuse of open content in developing countries. *The Electronic Journal on Information Systems in Developing Countries, 37(5),* 1–16. Retrieved from http://www.is.cityu.edu.hk/staff/isrobert/ejisdc/37-5.pdf

Heyneman, S. P. (2004). One step back, two steps forward: The first stage of the transition for education in Central Asia. In S. P. Heyneman & A. J. DeYong (Eds.), *The challenge of education in Central Asia.* Greenwich: Information Age Publishing.

Jansen, H. (2010). The logic of qualitative survey research and its position in the field of social research methods. *Forum Qualitative Sozialforschung / Forum: Qualitative Social Research, 11(2).* Retrieved from http://nbn-resolving.de/urn:nbn:de:0114-fqs1002110

Jung, I., Wong, T. M., Li, C., Baigaltugs, S. & Belawati, T. (2011). Quality assurance in Asian distance education: Diverse approaches and common culture. *The International Review of Research in Open and Distributed Learning, 12(6),* 63–83. Retrieved from http://www.irrodl.org/index.php/irrodl/article/view/991/1953

Karunanayaka, S. P., Naidu, S., Dhanapala, T. D. T. L., Gonsalkorala, L. R. & Ariyaratne, A. (2014). From mind maps to mind sets: Shifting conceptions about OER in the Faculty of Education at the Open University of Sri Lanka. *Paper presented at the 2nd Regional Symposium on Open Educational Resources: Beyond Advocacy, Research and Policy,* 24–27 June 2014. Wawasan Open University, Penang, Malaysia. Retrieved from http://weko.wou.edu.my/?action=repository_action_common_download&item_id=369&item_no=1&attribute_id=15&file_no=1

Marzluf, P. (2012). Words, borders, herds: Post-socialist English and nationalist language identities in Mongolia. *International Journal of the Sociology of Language, 2012(218),* 195–216. Retrieved from http://dx.doi.org/10.1515/ijsl-2012-0064

Masterman, L. & Wild, L. (2011). *JISC OER impact study: Research report.* Oxford: Jisc. Retrieved from https://weblearn.ox.ac.uk/access/content/group/ca5599e6-fd26-4203-

b416-f1b96068d1cf/Research%20Project%20Reports/OER%20Projects%202011-2014/
JISC%20OER%20Impact%20Study%20Research%20Report%20v1-0.pdf

McGill, L., Falconer, I., Dempster, J. A., Littlejohn, A. & Beetham, H. (2013). *Journeys to Open Educational Practice: UKOER/SCORE review final report.* London: Jisc. Retrieved from https://oersynth.pbworks.com/w/file/fetch/67270759/OER%20Review%20OER%20Journeys.pdf

MECSM (Ministry of Education, Culture and Science of Mongolia). (2015). Higher education statistics. Ulaanbaatar: Government of Mongolia. Retrieved from http://www.mecss.gov.mn/Дээд%20статистик

Norjkhorloo, N. & Porter, D. (2013). Exploring the use of open educational resources with teachers and parents of early-age children in Mongolia. In H. Grunfeld & M. N. L. Hoon (Eds.), *Dream I.T.: Development research to empower all Mongolians through information technology* (pp. 25–46). Ulaanbaatar: International Development Research Centre & Datacom. Retrieved from http://www.academia.edu/8335079/Mongolia_s_educational_resources_go_into_the_great_wide_open

OERAsia. (2010). *A study of the current state of play in the use of Open Educational Resources (OER) in the Asian Region (survey instrument).* Penang: Wawasan Open University. Retrieved from https://oerasia.org/images/files/OERAsia%20Survey%20Instrument.pdf

OER Hub (2014). *OER Hub survey questions.* Milton Keynes: The Open University. Retrieved from https://docs.google.com/spreadsheets/d/1fL_yf-O7OZjvH67Ue8LlfidjEXwtDQ5T0TBe-Z1GYaI/edit#gid=0

Okada, A., Mikroyannidis, A., Meister, I. & Little, S. (2012). "Colearning" – collaborative networks for creating, sharing and reusing OER through social media. In *Cambridge 2012: Innovation and impact – Openly collaborating to enhance education*, 16–18 April 2012. Cambridge, UK. Retrieved from http://oro.open.ac.uk/33750/2/59B2E252.pdf

ONE Mongolia (2014). *Open Network for Education in Mongolia.* Ulaanbaatar: ONE Mongolia. Retrieved from http://one.mn/en/

Orr, D., Rimini, M. & Van Damme, D. (2015). *Open Educational Resources: A catalyst for innovation, educational research and innovation.* Paris: OECD Publishing. Retrieved from http://dx.doi.org/10.1787/9789264247543-en

Pegler, C. (2012). Herzberg, hygiene and the motivation to reuse: Towards a three-factor theory to explain motivation to share and use OER. *Journal of Interactive Media in Education, 2012(1)*, Art.4. Retrieved from http://doi.org/10.5334/2012-04

Porter, D. A. (2013). *Exploring the practices of educators using open educational resources (OER) in the British Columbia higher education system.* Burnaby, BC: Simon Fraser University. Retrieved from http://summit.sfu.ca/item/13663

Reed, P. (2012). Awareness, attitudes and participation of teaching staff towards the open content movement in one university. *Research in Learning Technology, 20(4)*, 18250. Retrieved from http://dx.doi.org/10.3402/rlt.v20i0.18520

Rolfe, V. (2012). Open Educational Resources: Staff attitudes and awareness. *Research in Learning Technology, 20*, 14395. Retrieved from https://www.dora.dmu.ac.uk/handle/2086/6188

Saldana, J. (2012). *The coding manual for qualitative researchers.* Thousand Oaks, CA: Sage.

Santos-Hermosa, G. (2014). ORIOLE, in the search for evidence of OER in teaching: Experiences in the use, re-use and the sharing and influence of repositories. *Qualitative Research in Education, 3(2)*, 232–268. Retrieved from http://www.hipatiapress.com/hpjournals/index.php/qre/article/view/1003

Steiner-Khamsi, G. & Stolpe, I. (2004). Decentralization and recentralization reform in Mongolia: Tracing the swing of the pendulum. *Comparative Education, 40(1)*, 29–53. Retrieved from http://www.tandfonline.com/doi/abs/10.1080/0305006042000184872

Sultana, S., Dovchin, S. & Pennycook, A. (2013). Styling the periphery: Linguistic and cultural takeup in Bangladesh and Mongolia. *Journal of Sociolinguistics, 17(5)*, 687–710. Retrieved from http://onlinelibrary.wiley.com/wol1/doi/10.1111/josl.12055/full

Trotter, H., Kell, C., Willmers, M., Gray, E. & King, T. (2014). *Seeking impact and visibility: Scholarly communication in Southern Africa*. Cape Town: African Minds. Retrieved from https://core.ac.uk/download/pdf/29051292.pdf

Tuul, S., Banzragch, O. & Saizmaa, T. (2016). E-learning in Mongolian higher education. *The International Review of Research in Open and Distributed Learning, 17(2)*. Retrieved from http://www.irrodl.org/index.php/irrodl/article/view/2227/3653

Tynan, B. & James R. (2013). Distance education regulatory frameworks: Readiness for openness in Southwest Pacific/South-East Asia region nations. *Open Praxis, 5(1)*, 91–97. Retrieved from http://openpraxis.org/index.php/OpenPraxis/article/view/31/6

Weidman, J. (1995). Diversifying finance of higher education systems in the Third World: The cases of Kenya and Mongolia. *Education Policy Analysis Archives, 3(5)*. Retrieved from http://epaa.asu.edu/ojs/article/download/648/770

West, P. G. & Victor, L. (2011). *Background and action paper on OER: A background and action paper for staff of bilateral and multilateral organisations at the strategic institutional education sector level*. Babson Park, CA: William and Flora Hewlett foundation. Retrieved from http://www.paulwest.org/public/Background_and_action_paper_on_OER.pdf

Wiley, D., Green, C. & Soares, L. (2012). *Dramatically bringing down the cost of education with OER: How Open Education Resources unlock the door to free learning*. Washington, D.C.: Center for American Progress. Retrieved from http://files.eric.ed.gov/fulltext/ED535639.pdf

Willems, J. & Bossu, C. (2012). Equity considerations for open educational resources in the glocalization of education. *Distance Education, 33(2)*, 185–199. Retrieved from http://dx.doi.org/10.1080/01587919.2012.692051

World Bank (2007). *Mongolia: Building the skills for the new economy*. Report No. 40118. Washington, D.C.: World Bank. Retrieved from https://openknowledge.worldbank.org/handle/10986/7746

Yano, S. (2012). *Overeducated? The impact of higher education expansion in post-transition Mongolia*. Ph.D thesis. Washington, D.C.: University of Columbia. Retrieved from http://hdl.handle.net/10022/AC:P:13128

Yin, R. K. (2014). *Case study research: Design and methods*. Thousand Oaks, CA: Sage.

How to cite this chapter

Zagdragchaa, B. & Trotter, H. (2017). Cultural–historical factors influencing OER adoption in Mongolia's higher education sector. In C. Hodgkinson-Williams & P. B. Arinto (Eds.), *Adoption and impact of OER in the Global South* (pp. 389–424). Retrieved from https://doi.org/10.5281/zenodo.599609

Corresponding author: Batbold Zagdragchaa <batbold@npi.mn>

This work is licensed under a Creative Commons Attribution 4.0 International (CC BY 4.0) licence. It was carried out with the aid of a grant from the International Development Research Centre, Ottawa, Canada.

Chapter 12

Higher education faculty attitude, motivation and perception of quality and barriers towards OER in India

Sanjaya Mishra and Alka Singh

Summary

The premise of this study is that teachers' conceptions of the quality of Open Educational Resources (OER) and their attitudes and motivations towards using OER will influence whether and how they use and/or contribute open resources. Understanding teachers' attitudes, motivations and barriers to OER use and comparing data across institutions may help to identify the issues that influence OER uptake in India. This chapter attempts to answer the following four research questions: How are teachers' attitudes towards OER situated in the context of teaching and learning? What are teachers' motivations for using OER and sharing their work as OER? How do teachers perceive the quality of OER? What barriers to using OER do teachers perceive?

This study employed a mixed methods approach, using a survey to gather the quantitative data which form the focus of this chapter, as well as workshop engagements and interviews to collect qualitative data. The research was carried out at four universities representing the varying contexts of higher education teachers in India – one state, open university; one dual-mode university; one semi-urban university; and one multi-campus, private university – and amongst the WikiEducator India community. At each university, a three-day OER workshop took place where 30 teachers learned about OER and completed a survey. In addition to the 120 workshop participants engaged at the four universities, the survey was sent to the 107 members of the WikiEducator India community who participated in the research process. Of the total of 227 teachers who were asked to take the survey, 149 survey responses were received, of which 117 (comprised of 43% females and 57% males) were useable. A total of 28 educators from the universities were also interviewed. ▶

Despite the relatively low levels of awareness of OER demonstrated by Indian teachers prior to the research process, they were very positive about creating and sharing OER, while being slightly less enthusiastic about using externally developed materials. Many of the positive attitudes stemmed from: the sense of satisfaction obtained when others use and adapt their materials; useful feedback received from peers; increased reputational profile experienced as a result of sharing; collaborative opportunities introduced in the sharing process; and the belief that their own sharing would encourage other teachers to do the same. The teachers were mildly cautious about OER quality issues, but said that they would use OER if they were appropriate for their needs. They acknowledged a number of barriers to using and sharing OER, including a lack of understanding of intellectual property, copyright and open licensing; a lack of time; and the lack of funding, institutional incentives and support for OER activities.

The authors recommend that advocacy to raise awareness of OER in Indian universities should be a top priority, with a particular focus on teachers and senior administrators; teachers should be released from certain duties and provided with the time required to engage in OER activity; incentives in the form of awards and/ or recognition in promotion should be provided for teachers to undertake OER development; quality assurance mechanisms for OER produced should be introduced; and continuous professional development opportunities should be provided to teachers through regular workshops and training sessions on advanced information and communication technologies and OER skills.

The dataset arising from this study can be accessed at:
https://www.datafirst.uct.ac.za/dataportal/index.php/catalog/578

Acronyms and abbreviations

ATOER	Attitude Towards Open Educational Resources
CC	Creative Commons
CEMCA	Commonwealth Educational Media Centre for Asia
HEI	higher education institution
ICT	information and communication technologies
NMEICT	National Mission on Education through ICTs
OER	Open Educational Resources
ROER4D	Research on Open Educational Resources for Development
SD	standard deviation

Introduction

Higher education in India faces numerous challenges in terms of "expanding the system with equity, of improving quality while expanding the system and managing the sector efficiently and effectively" (Varghese, 2015, p.2). In order to address reform of the higher education system, the Indian government's National Knowledge Commission recommended upgrading infrastructure, improving the training of teachers, and continuous assessment of syllabi and examination systems (Pitroda, 2006). In 2008, the Commission called for a national e-content and curriculum initiative to stimulate the creation, adaptation and utilisation of Open Educational Resources (OER) by Indian higher education institutions (HEIs), and to leverage OER produced outside India (Perryman & Seal, 2016) to overcome the challenges of quality educational materials. OER are "teaching, learning and research materials in any medium, digital or otherwise, that reside in the public domain or have been released under an open license that permits no-cost access, use, adaptation and redistribution by others with no or limited restrictions. Open licensing is built within the existing framework of intellectual property rights as defined by relevant international conventions and respects the authorship of the work" (UNESCO, 2012, p.1). The types of learning materials included in the category of OER are textbooks, manuals, research papers, guides, videos, audio presentations and other online resources.

The adoption of OER has surfaced a new set of innovative teaching and learning practices, as well as presented a potentially cost-effective mechanism to improve the quality of educational offerings by optimising the use of freely available and openly licensed online resources (Daniel, Kanwar & Uvalić-Trumbić, 2009). While OER can be used by anyone, irrespective of whether they are based in a formal learning environment or not, the value proposition is particularly strong for universities that can utilise OER to improve the cost-efficiency of packaged learning materials (Wiley, Green & Soares, 2012).

Utilising OER purportedly reduces the time associated with developing courses and programmes, facilitates sharing of knowledge, preserves and disseminates indigenous knowledge, and improves educational quality at all levels (Kanwar, Kodhandaraman & Umar, 2010). For teachers and students, OER provide access to global online content that can be localised without legal restriction, introduce greater choice in terms of available learning resources and create inclusive learning communities (Butcher, 2011).

India has over 700 universities, including 17 open universities, but the use of OER in tertiary education does not appear to be widespread, despite several sporadic attempts and a number of initiatives to promote the use of OER, both nationally and institutionally. In 2013, the National Repository of Open Educational Resources[1] for K–12 educational materials was established. This activity was further bolstered, when, in 2014, the flagship project of the Ministry of Human Resource and Development, the National Mission on Education through Information Communication Technologies (NMEICT), adopted open licensing policy guidelines.[2] Institutionally, the Indira Gandhi National Open University Post Graduate Diploma in E-learning started using OER as far back as 2010 and several Indian teachers have participated in Learning4Content[3] workshops on the WikiEducator[4] platform. The Commonwealth Educational Media Centre for Asia (CEMCA) has assisted several organisations in the development of content using WikiEducator, and the Staff Training and Research Institute of Distance Education at Indira Gandhi National Open University

---

1   http://nroer.gov.in/welcome
2   http://www.sakshat.ac.in/Document/OER_Policy.pdf
3   http://wikieducator.org/Learning4Content
4   https://wikieducator.org/Main_Page

trained educators to use MediaWiki to develop self-learning materials for distance education in 2008.

Typically, OER are prepared by teachers in a specific context to assist students in their learning process. Teachers are therefore central to the production and reuse of OER. However, Petrides, Jimes, Middleton-Detzner, Walling and Weiss (2011, p.41) reported findings based on research conducted by Livingston and Condie (2006) in Scotland which indicated that student learning was tempered by "teachers' lack of expertise in fully leveraging the open resources to assist students to become more independent learners" and that "teachers lacked the technical skills to effectively integrate" new OER into their courses. Petrides et al. also expressed concerns in an open textbook project and reported that:

> ... faculty with lower comfort levels with using online technology made use of open textbooks in ways that exemplified more traditional ways of working with materials, there exists a need to build on the technology, practices and tools made possible by open textbooks to enhance teaching and learning practices. Furthermore, the research illuminates the potential importance of leveraging teachers' existing curriculum needs, teaching practices, and technological efficacy and expanding professional development to facilitate future open textbook use. (2011, p.46)

Within this context, there is a need to understand why some teachers share their work openly while others do not, and it is necessary to understand teachers' attitudes and motivations that may influence more effective use of OER. Olcott (2012) suggested that further research needs to be conducted to examine the concept of Open Educational Practices and OER issues with regard to faculty incentives and career advancement in universities. There is therefore also a need to understand how teachers' predisposition towards OER and their espoused views about pedagogical practices and innovations determine their OER practices.

Previous research indicates that teachers' conception of teaching and learning influences how they teach and engage students in the classroom (OECD, 2009; Rubin & Fernandes, 2013). The premise of this study is that teachers' conceptions of the quality of OER as well as their attitudes and motivations towards using OER will influence whether and how they use and/or contribute OER. Understanding their attitudes, motivations and barriers to OER use, and comparing data at institutional level and within a national online OER community would help to identify the issues that influence OER uptake in India. This chapter therefore critically examines a conceptual model of understanding OER adoption (encompassing both use and contribution) by teachers in universities and in WikiEducator India, presenting intertwined theoretical constructs of teachers' attitudes, motivations, perceptions of quality and barriers to uptake.

Literature review

Pegler (2012) suggests that reuse of OER can be dependent on technical, motivational and quality factors. It is therefore useful to study the aspects of attitude, motivations, perceptions of quality and barriers to uptake in terms of academic values and OER practice in India.

Attitude

Zimbardo and Leippe define attitude as: "An evaluative disposition toward some object based upon cognitions, affective reactions, behavioral intentions, and past behaviors ... that can influence cognitions, affective responses, and future intentions and behaviors" (1991, p.51).

Attitude influences an individual's choice of action and response to specific stimuli. Attitudes are latent and not directly observable, but they are revealed by actions and behaviours that are observable. In a study in the United Kingdom, Rolfe (2012) reported that new staff members had greater concerns about copyright and were more positive about using resources as a cost-saving measure, whereas longer-standing members of staff considered it difficult to adapt resources and contextualise them for their specific needs. Venkaiah (2008) reported a positive attitude among teachers towards OER in a study conducted in Indian universities. This positive attitude did not, however, result in increased use of OER in teaching and learning. Reflecting on attitudes towards OER in India in particular, Perryman and Seal suggest:

> Research into OER use and attitudes towards openness is vital in informing projects that are relevant to local contexts and which contain realistic objectives. To date, research on OER use in India has tended to focus on overviews of OER initiatives (e.g. Das, 2011), the attitudes and practices of teachers and academics (e.g. Sharma et al., 2014) and teacher educators (Perryman et al., 2015; Buckler et al., 2014; Perryman, 2013a), rather than ranging more widely. (2016, p.2)

Motivation

"To be motivated means to be moved to do something" (Ryan & Deci, 2000, p.54). The concept of motivation therefore refers to why people think and behave as they do. People do certain things to satisfy their needs, which motivates them to behave or do things in a particular way. Motivation can be intrinsic or extrinsic, and individuals can consider different factors as motivators or demotivators.

Rolfe points out that "understanding the motivations and characteristics of potential users [of OER] is important to develop strong and sustainable strategies and practices" (2012, p.10). While market positioning seems to be a key incentive amongst senior managers for adopting OER in institutional contexts, academic staff tend to view "OER in terms of educational standards and opportunities" (Nikoi & Armellini, 2012, p.173). The Centre for Educational Research and Innovation and the Organisation for Economic Cooperation and Development (CERI/OECD, 2007) examined four motivating factors in teachers' adoption of OER: (1) sharing knowledge being a basic academic value; (2) increased personal reputation in an open community; (3) being a leader in their field; and (4) there being little value in keeping a resource closed. According to Hilton and Wiley (2009), the four major motivating factors for using OER are to: (1) receive increased exposure; (2) do some good; (3) give new life to out-of-print works; and (4) improve the quality of educational resources.

Quality

OER are "useful for improving teaching quality in areas, such as providing illustrations, teaching difficult subjects, and supporting student progression" (Nikoi & Armellini, 2012, p.176). Teachers do, however, see a problem in using OER without ensured reliability or quality assurance of the open content (Richter & Ehlers, 2010). Regarding their own potential OER creation activity, many teachers fear that "their resources [are] not good enough to be shared openly and that by releasing teaching materials they [are] making themselves vulnerable to receiving overly critical feedback from their colleagues" (Brent, Gibbs & Gruszczynska, 2012, p.6). In a survey of Indian teachers, Perryman and Seal report that "78% of Indian educators indicat[ed] that they use[d] OER to compare others' teaching materials with their own in order to assess their materials' quality" (2016, p.8).

Barriers

Despite positive attitudes and motivation to use OER, teachers find it difficult to use and/or contribute OER for a variety of reasons, including a lack of supportive institutional policy, technological difficulties and poor understanding of OER. In order to have an enabling environment for OER adoption, it is necessary to reduce the real as well as perceived barriers to OER usage. Common barriers cited include "the lack of awareness about OER; the university elitism that it was not invented here so we'll use our own; faculty resistance given 'my content is king in my kingdom'; and of course the lobbying of many publishers who see the OER movement as a threat to their historical business monopoly over content" (Olcott, 2012, p.284). According to Hilton and Wiley (2009), four common obstacles to OER use and contribution are: (1) the amount of time necessary to put OER in a format that can be shared; (2) a desire to keep the resource from being seen by others; (3) few if any external reward mechanisms for creating OER; and (4) the concern that nobody will want to use the OER created.

This study is therefore based on the premise that teachers' predispositions and espoused views about OER, their motivations to use and create OER, their perceptions of the quality of OER, and the barriers they encounter while using and contributing OER could be related to actual use and contribution of OER.

Based on these assumptions, this chapter attempts to answer the following questions:
1. How are teachers' attitudes towards OER situated in the context of teaching and learning?
2. What are teachers' motivations for using OER and sharing their work as OER?
3. How do teachers perceive the quality of OER?
4. What barriers to using OER do teachers perceive?

Methodology

This study employed a mixed-methods approach in order to address the research questions. Quantitative data gathering was undertaken in the form of a survey, and qualitative data were collected in workshops and interviews.

Research site and participant selection processes

To carry out this study, four universities representing the varying contexts of higher education teachers in India were identified as study sites, based on the researchers' perception of those institutions' educators' prior awareness of OER (in turn based largely on work conducted by CEMCA). Given the previous CEMCA exposure, the researchers also had easy access to senior management in those universities, who permitted them to conduct workshops and the associated research. Research sites were comprised of:

- One state, open university: The newest open university in India at the time of research, this institution is situated in northeast India and offers only distance-education courses. The university uses printed texts as study materials, and the awareness of OER was moderate.
- One dual-mode university: This university is located in a large metropolitan city in central India, and offers both distance and face-to-face (contact) programmes. It has several regional centres across the country and operates largely in the Urdu language. The level of OER awareness is relatively low, though teachers engaged in distance teaching have been developing printed text materials for students.
- One semi-urban university: This university caters largely to students from rural areas of the southeastern part of India, and, apart from face-to-face, campus-based teaching, caters to several other educational institutions in the region that are affiliated with the university. Levels of OER awareness are extremely low.
- One multi-campus, private university: This university's main campus is located on the outskirts of a city in eastern India, but it has multiple satellite campuses in the state. It is a private university with relatively young faculty members who teach in face-to-face mode. OER awareness levels are extremely poor.

Data were also collected through an online survey from the online WikiEducator India Community, where members had been using OER for some time.

Quantitative data collection

Survey

In order to develop the survey, information on previous research in the field was gathered and a questionnaire consisting of five major parts was designed.

Part A of the questionnaire pertained to demographic details, and consisted of 16 items prepared on the basis of the Research on Open Educational Resources for Development (ROER4D) instrument harmonisation process,[5] while bearing in mind contextual aspects of the Indian higher education system.

Part B aimed to gather data and critically analyse teachers' perceptions and beliefs around sharing OER. As there was no standard attitude measurement scale available for OER, the researchers in this study created an Attitude Towards OER (ATOER) scale, which

---

5   Within ROER4D, a research question harmonisation process was initiated by the Network Hub for different sub-projects. See Trotter, H. (26 May 2014). *ROER4D Question Harmonisation Process.* ROER4D Blog. Available at http://roer4d.org/892.

was incorporated into the overall survey design.[6] Based on the input of 15 OER experts, the ATOER scale was winnowed down from 26 items to 17 after a validity and reliability test, with 13 items devoted to respondents' attitudes towards sharing OER and four items focused on their attitudes towards using OER.

Part C consisted of questions assessing motivation towards use of and contribution to OER. This section consisted of 19 items based on intrinsic and extrinsic motivation factors.

Part D dealt with perceptions of OER quality. This section contained 13 items, which focused on different criteria for defining the quality of OER.

Part E focused on barriers towards the adoption of OER. This section consisted of 18 items divided into seven sub-themes: technical barriers, personal barriers, institutional barriers, financial barriers, sociocultural barriers, linguistic barriers and legal barriers.

The questionnaire was administered in paper format as well as online. The paper-based questionnaire was circulated amongst the workshop participants in each of the four university sites on day three of the three-day workshop conducted as part of the qualitative data-gathering strategy. The particular timing for administering the survey was based on the fact that when the validity of the survey questions was tested, many respondents revealed that they were not aware of OER as a concept, meaning that they did not have well-formed attitudes or motivations regarding OER. The workshop provided an opportunity to introduce the concept of OER and the practices associated with their use. Participants were therefore able to develop or situate their feelings regarding OER into a broader set of values. A limitation of this approach is that their responses remained hypothetical, precisely because they had yet to have real experiences with OER. Thus, while exposure to OER during the workshop was crucial for many respondents in terms of being able to identify their attitudes and motivations regarding OER, for many these assertions were made without the benefit of prior experience and may not reflect how they engage with OER in the future. Given that this lack of OER awareness and experience in working with these resources is a common feature in Indian higher education, the initial assertions made by respondents in the survey represent the best approximations of their attitudes and motivations regarding OER.

The online questionnaire was created using SurveyMonkey, and the link was distributed via email to the WikiEducator India community, who had prior experience of using OER.

Qualitative data collection

Workshops

A workshop approach with supplementary interviews was adopted as the primary means of qualitative data collection. The three-day Workshop on Open Educational Resources for Development (with a fourth day for interviews) was designed to be participatory and to promote teachers' understanding of OER, while serving as a forum for data collection. Workshops were used to introduce the participants to OER, administer the questionnaire and identify participants for interviews. The following data collection strategies were implemented in the workshop:

---

6   For an exhaustive analysis of the development and utility of the ATOER scale, see Mishra, Sharma, Sharma, Singh and Thakur (2016).

- "Just-a-minute" sessions were planned to draw out teachers' positive and negative attitudes towards OER. Each session was designed to elicit an immediate response (within one minute) about their positive/negative views on OER. All participants were given five minutes to write down a statement that began with: "I am positive/negative about OER because ..." While they had sufficient time to articulate their response, only the first minute was recorded in order to gain a snapshot of perceptions about OER.

- To understand teachers' motivations for using OER, interactive question-and-answer sessions were conducted. The questions related to teachers' motivations or demotivations for adapting/contributing to OER, as well as the benefits of OER for the teaching and learning processes. This helped to create an engaging environment for participants to critically question the benefits of OER and surface why OER might be useful for them or not.

- In order to list the barriers to using and sharing educational materials, participants engaged in a snowball exercise, whereby they were given five minutes in which to write down the barriers relevant to their context. In the next stage, participants discussed the common barriers in pairs and then in groups of four, each for about five minutes, to develop consensus on a list of barriers. For logistical reasons, some groups had six members in the third level of the snowball session. The discussions were then shared and captured on a flip chart.

- To assess teachers' perceptions of OER quality, panel discussions were conducted. In each of the workshops, the research team identified four or five participants and asked them to be panellists. This was done the day before so that the panellists had time to prepare and could speak from their personal beliefs and understanding. They were also informed that their positions could be questioned by participants in the audience. During the panel discussion, a moderator (one of the research team members) asked each panellist a set of questions. In these sessions, panellists and other participants discussed issues related to definitions of quality, indicators of quality OER, the need for quality in OER, who should ensure quality in OER and other relevant topics.

Workshops were conducted with lecturers who were recruited with the help of institutional managers. The latter were contacted to assist with identifying educators who might benefit from learning more about OER and who would be willing to participate in the research process. Roughly 30 faculty members attended the workshops at each site; meaning that the survey instrument was distributed to 120 teachers in the four research locations. Managers were also requested to try to achieve equal gender representation in the staff recruited for the workshops. However, the final cohort comprised 38% females and 62% males. Only in one location did female participants outnumber the males.

In addition, the survey was distributed to the members of the WikiEducator India community, which, at the time of research, had 107 members.

The overall sample size for the study was 227 teachers: 120 from the workshops and 107 from WikiEducator India. A total of 149 survey responses was received, of which only 117 (42.7% females and 57.3% males) could be used.

Interviews

The selection of participants for the interviews was done largely on a voluntary basis, and was therefore subject to self-selection bias. The research team also specifically requested some participants to join in the interviews, based on their ability to articulate issues during the workshop. Twenty-eight participants were interviewed in the four workshops. The interview schedule was developed collaboratively with ROER4D researchers from South Africa (Cox & Trotter, 2017). However, the focus of this chapter is on the data collected from the quantitative surveys rather than the qualitative interviews.

Respondent profile

The majority (51.3%) of the 117 respondents in the study were younger than 35 years, while 37.6% were in the 36–50 age group. The number of teachers above the age of 51 was much lower, indicating that most of the teachers in the study were in the mid-career age group. Just over half (57.3%) of the respondents were male, while 42.7% were female. This gender breakdown aligns roughly with the situation at national level – according to the *All India Survey on Higher Education 2014–2015* (MHRD, 2015), about 36% of lecturers in Indian universities are female. Most of the respondents were at the level of assistant professor (60.7%), followed by associate professors (14.5%) and professors (6%). Roughly one-fifth of the respondents (18.8%) indicated that they also performed roles other than teaching, such as academic counsellor, academic administrator, assistant director, etc. These roles were mostly in the distance education institutions, and were considered academic support roles at the level of assistant professor.

Approximately half of the respondents (50.4%) were from Humanities and Social Sciences disciplines, including Education and Law, while 22.2% were from Engineering and Technology, followed by Natural Sciences (17.1%), Management and Commerce (9.4%) and Medicine and Health Sciences (0.9%). The sample therefore had representation from a wide range of disciplines.

In terms of educational qualifications, 54.7% of the respondents held a PhD, while non-PhDs comprised 37.6% and only a marginal percentage (7.7%) held MPhil degrees. Most respondents (41%) had 6–15 years of teaching experience, followed by teachers with 0–5 years (28.2%), 16–25 years (20.5%), 26–35 years (8.5%) and only 1.7% above 35 years. Roughly 70% of respondents had up to 15 years of teaching experience. In terms of modes of teaching undertaken by the respondents, 38% indicated face-to-face teaching, followed by 20% in distance teaching, and 15.8% teaching through a blended/hybrid mode of instruction. Respondents indicated that English was the dominant (97%) language of instruction, followed by Hindi (29.1%). Respondents also indicated that teaching took place in several local languages.

Of the respondents, 44% said that they had used OER prior to the workshop, though most had not known they were OER at the time, while 28% said that they had created OER (these creators were all prior users as well).

Data analysis

Both sets of survey data collected were analysed using descriptive statistics and different statistical tests for quantitative data, and the qualitative data were coded and analysed using Dedoose[7] software. However, in this chapter basic descriptive statistics are presented to provide an overview of the study.

Data sharing

The interview and survey micro data as well as instruments utilised in this study were published on the DataFirst Data Portal[8] after undergoing a multiphased quality assurance and de-identification process. The authors and the ROER4D Curation and Dissemination team checked data files for consistency and correctness, whereafter a de-identification process was undertaken utilising an omission and revision strategy.

The resulting dataset, published under a Creative Commons Attribution ShareAlike (CC BY-SA) licence, is comprised of survey data and 27 interview transcripts shared in CSV, SAS, SPSS, STATA, RTF and XSLX formats, as well as data collection instruments, a dataset description, a project description and a de-identification overview in PDF format.

Findings

In this section, we discuss the survey and interview findings as they pertain to Indian teachers' attitudes towards OER, their motivations regarding using or not using OER, their perceptions of OER quality and their perceived barriers to OER use.

Teachers' attitudes towards OER

Data on respondents' attitudes towards OER were gathered using the questionnaire and analysed as per the ATOER scale categories. Analyses of the overall means and range on the five-point ATOER scale items (1 = Strongly disagree; 2 = Disagree; 3 = Neutral; 4 = Agree; 5 = Strongly agree) indicated that respondents had a positive attitude towards OER (Mean = 4.31, Standard Deviation [SD] = 0.468). Table 1 presents data related to the 13 items in the "Sharing OER" sub-scale.

Table 1: Average of ATOER sub-scale items on "Sharing of OER"

Item statement ("Sharing of OER")	Rank	Range	Min.	Max	Mean		SD
					Statistic	Std error	
It gives me pleasure if someone adopts/adapts my educational resources.	1	3	2	5	4.65	0.04	0.52
Sharing helps me to get feedback.	2	2	3	5	4.58	0.05	0.60

---

7   http://dedoose.com/
8   https://www.datafirst.uct.ac.za/dataportal/index.php/catalog/578

Sharing of educational resources improves my professional respect.	3	4	1	5	4.54	0.05	0.62
Sharing enhances my personal and organisational reputation.	4	3	2	5	4.50	0.06	0.66
Sharing enhances my confidence as I see myself as part of a larger community.	5	3	2	5	4.46	0.05	0.58
OER increases my network and sphere of influence.	6	4	1	5	4.42	0.07	0.78
OER improves my chance of recognition at a global level.	7	4	1	5	4.41	0.06	0.74
When others use my OER, it improves my sense of achievement.	8	3	2	5	4.40	0.06	0.73
Sharing of educational resources increases my profile amongst peers and others.	9	3	2	5	4.33	0.07	0.8
OER helps to disseminate my ideas.	10	4	1	5	4.29	0.07	0.77
I believe that sharing educational materials as OER will encourage others to do so as well.	11	3	2	5	4.27	0.07	0.78
OER promotes collaboration and consortia.	12	3	2	5	4.25	0.06	0.72
As a teacher, it is my responsibility to share all educational resources created by me.	13	4	1	5	4.06	0.08	0.97

As the table reveals, the attitude scores ranged from 4.06 to 4.65, indicating that the respondents were largely positive about sharing OER (though it is worth remembering that these positive assertions were made despite most of the university respondents having little awareness of or experience with OER prior to the workshop, making many of their statements hypothetical, reflecting how they *would* feel if they had shared OER). The item with the highest mean score related to the pleasure respondents feel when someone adopts or adapts their educational resources (M = 4.65). This means that these teachers achieve a high level of satisfaction when making a contribution to their peers' educational endeavours, taking joy in knowing that their materials are valuable to others as well. This is a highly personal response, related to the sense of egotistical satisfaction that comes with knowing that others find their work useful (a validation of their materials), as well as to the sense of altruism that comes with knowing that those materials were given away for free (extending it beyond the narrower utility of a particular course).

The second-ranked response was that respondents felt that sharing educational resources helped them obtain feedback (M = 4.58), a valuable outcome if teachers are seeking to improve their materials.

The responses ranked third and fourth were that respondents felt that sharing OER may improve their professional standing (M = 4.54) and enhance their personal and institutional reputation (M = 4.50). This shows that respondents are sensitive to the potential reputational feedback loop of the sharing process.

Such (potential) activities also enhanced their confidence and made them feel like they were part of a larger community (M = 4.46). They reported that sharing OER would increase their network and sphere of influence (M = 4.42) and bring them recognition at a global level (M = 4.41).

In addition to these top-ranked responses, the teachers also indicated that sharing OER would help them feel a sense of achievement when others used their work (M = 4.40) and that it would help them disseminate their ideas (M = 4.29). They also believed that their sharing behaviour would encourage others to create and share resources as OER (M = 4.27), promoting collaboration and consortia involvement (M = 4.25). Lastly, respondents believed that sharing learning materials is part of their professional responsibility (M = 4.06).

These responses show that respondents felt positively about sharing OER as a (potential) activity. It accorded with their values regarding educational provision and coincided with many of their personal and professional desires.

This enthusiasm was moderated slightly when it came to OER use. An analysis of teachers' attitudes towards adaptation and use of OER (Table 2) shows that the participating teachers had mostly positive attitudes towards adaptation and use of OER – with means ranging from 3.72 to 4.19 – but at a slightly lower level of positivity than OER sharing.

Table 2: Average of ATOER scale items on "Adaptation and use of OER"

Item statement ("Adaptation and use of OER")	Rank	Range	Min.	Max	Mean		SD
					Statistic	Std error	
My own competencies and knowledge of OER help me to participate in or adopt OER.	1	3	2	5	4.19	0.07	0.76
I adopt OER for my teaching as they fulfil the academic requirements of my students.	2	3	2	5	4.12	0.07	0.85
I am efficient in information and communication technologies (ICT) skills needed to adopt and use OER.	3	3	2	5	4.09	0.07	0.85
I have knowledge of intellectual property rights to understand OER.	4	4	1	5	3.72	0.09	0.97

Most respondents indicated that their competencies and knowledge of OER would help them to adopt OER (M = 4.19). Teachers indicated that they use OER in delivering courses to fulfil the academic requirements of their students (M = 4.12). As OER are increasingly digital, ICT skills were considered important in the adoption of OER (M = 4.09). Teachers were not as confident about their knowledge of the intellectual property rights needed to adapt or use OER (M = 3.72).

Statistical tests were applied to gauge whether the distribution of attitude (weighted score) was the same across the "Sharing" and "Adaptation" sub-scales. Respondents were more positive about sharing OER than about adaptation and use. In order to further confirm this difference, the Mann-Whitney U Test was performed to test the hypothesis that the distribution of items was the same across categories in the sample. The result is significant at the 0.05 level (p = 0.045), which confirms that respondents agreed more strongly with sharing than with adapting OER. There was a marginal preference for sharing their own resources rather than using materials created by others.

Overall, higher education teachers in India as sampled in this study held positive attitudes towards OER. They preferred sharing their own educational materials to adapting materials prepared by others. However, the chi-square test revealed that attitudes towards OER were not significantly different between contributors and non-contributors of OER (X^2 (2, n = 114) = 1.32, p > 0.05). Similar to findings in prior research (CERI/OECD, 2007), teachers in this study indicated that they would share educational materials for the pleasure of sharing. They were also inclined to share in order to improve the reputation of their institutions as well as to build their professional image and reputation (Karunanayaka, 2012). Respondents also felt that sharing is an inherent responsibility of a teacher.

Attitudes on adaptation, however, were not as strong as attitudes towards sharing, which may be due to the fact that most of the respondents (72%) identified themselves as non-contributors of OER.

An issue that emerged from the attitudes analysis was the importance of understanding copyright and open licensing, as noted also in other studies (de Hart, Chetty & Archer, 2015; Pegler, 2012; Reed, 2012). Respondents' adaptation attitudes towards OER may also be influenced by their ability to use ICTs effectively, as revealed in earlier research (Kerres & Heinen, 2015).

Teachers' motivations regarding OER use and contribution

Higher education teachers' motivations to use and contribute OER were studied in order to identify enabling factors that encourage use, reuse, creation, sharing or adaptation of OER. Analyses of the overall mean on motivation items indicate that teachers' responses were inclined towards the positive as they largely agreed to all the items related to motivation to use and contribute OER (M = 3.97, SD = 1.166). Table 3 displays the 19 items against the Likert scale to assess respondents' motivations for using and contributing OER.

Table 3: Motivation to use and contribute OER

Item statement ("Motivation to use and contribute OER")	Rank	Range	Min.	Max	Mean		SD
					Statistic	Std error	
Sharing knowledge is a basic academic value.	1	2.00	3.00	5.00	4.70	0.04	0.49
OER will help developing countries increase access to education.	2	3.00	2.00	5.00	4.55	0.06	0.64
I believe that OER is "good" for people as it improves their learning.	3	2.00	3.00	5.00	4.53	0.05	0.56
OER gives me opportunities to learn new things.	4	3.00	2.00	5.00	4.51	0.06	0.65
OER caters to the innate desire to learn, improve and progress.	5	3.00	2.00	5.00	4.48	0.05	0.63
I like receiving comments and feedback from experts and seniors on OER I have created.	6	3.00	2.00	5.00	4.46	0.06	0.71
OER is less expensive.	7	4.00	1.00	5.00	4.40	0.06	0.72
OER saves me time.	8	3.00	2.00	5.00	4.27	0.075	0.80

I try to contribute to OER to give back to society.	9	3.00	2.00	5.00	4.25	0.06	0.67
OER provides us with opportunities for establishing new partnerships.	9	3.00	2.00	5.00	4.25	0.06	0.74
I like to be involved in peer production of OER.	11	3.00	2.00	5.00	4.22	0.06	0.70
OER improves professional image.	12	3.00	2.00	5.00	4.18	0.06	0.69
OER increases my self-confidence.	13	3.00	2.00	5.00	4.11	0.06	0.72
Technology associated with OER is easy.	14	3.00	2.00	5.00	4.10	0.07	0.78
Through OER, I can reach disadvantaged communities.	15	4.00	1.00	5.00	4.09	0.09	0.99
Involvement in OER will give me recognition.	16	3.00	2.00	5.00	4.05	0.07	0.85
I know about my intellectual property rights under Creative Commons (CC) licences.	17	4.00	1.00	5.00	3.98	0.07	0.83
Receiving appropriate credit will help me uptake OER.	18	4.00	1.00	5.00	3.95	0.09	1.04
OER provides access to the best materials and teachers.	19	4.00	1.00	5.00	3.90	0.08	0.88

While motivation can be categorised in terms of intrinsic and extrinsic factors, the statements in Table 3 can also be grouped according to their thematic principle, in order of importance: social/altruistic, learning, collaboration, cost/time/access, individual benefits, and technology and knowledge.

The most important category of factors for motivating OER use and adaptation is social and altruistic in nature. Thus, teachers asserted that sharing knowledge is a basic academic value (M = 4.70), a proposition that appears to align with the premise behind OER sharing. They strongly agreed that "OER will help developing countries increase access to education" (M = 4.55). Most believed that sharing OER is a way to "give back to society" (M = 4.25) and reach disadvantaged communities (M = 4.09). This was expressed clearly by one workshop respondent, who stated: "I am positive about OER because the poor community of people who don't have resources to afford Engineering or other courses which are of high cost can be benefitted from OER."

The next most important category of factors concerns learning. The top sentiment for respondents was that OER are "good" for people because they improve learning (M = 4.53). This means that they see OER as having a practical benefit for their work ambitions, which include helping students to learn as best they can. Most respondents also believed that OER provided them with opportunities to learn new things themselves (M = 4.51), thereby connecting the learning possibilities between their students and themselves. As one workshop attendee said, OER are "useful for learning, teaching and research purposes in various ways to enrich my knowledge". OER also cater to their innate desire to learn, improve and progress (M = 4.48). In addition, respondents revealed that they liked receiving comments and feedback from experts and seniors on their OER (M = 4.46), further reinforcing the notion that the production of OER allows them to learn and grow along with their students.

The third most important group of factors concerns collaboration. Many respondents believed that OER provides an opportunity to establish partnerships (M = 4.25) and produce materials with peers (M = 4.22). While OER does not require this, it offers opportunities in this regard which many would be keen to take advantage of.

The fourth constellation of factors revolves around cost, time and access. Most felt that OER were less expensive than traditional copyrighted materials (M = 4.40) – a crucial sentiment in resource-poor environments – while many others also thought that it saved them time (M = 4.27). As one workshop attendee said, OER "will enable the faculty to do more research in their discipline and also in ODL [Open Distance Learning] … as they will have more time". They also agreed that OER provided access to the best resources and teachers (M = 3.90), though their response showed a lower level of enthusiasm than for other items in this category. Yet, as one workshop attendee enthused: "[Because of OER], education will become more competitive and hence quality will be enhanced as now the resources will be easily accessible."

The fifth group of factors concerns the individual benefits that might accrue from using or contributing OER. Respondents were relatively positive that OER engagement would improve their professional image (M = 4.18) and even boost their sense of self-confidence (M = 4.11). They were slightly less sure that OER use and adaptation would lead to greater recognition (M = 4.05) or that such credit would lead to greater uptake of OER on their part (M = 3.95). The generally positive responses do, however, suggest that individual benefits remain an important consideration in OER motivation.

The final group of factors involves OER technology and knowledge. A number of respondents believed that the technology associated with OER was easy (M = 4.10), while others also believed that they understood their intellectual property rights under CC licences (M = 3.98), which motivates them to engage with OER.

Analysing respondents' motivations regarding the use and contribution of OER revealed that teachers were highly motivated to use, create and share OER for different academic, professional and personal purposes. They recognised that the workshops organised as part of this research project helped them become aware of how OER could be integrated into their teaching and learning experiences. This resonates with the sentiment expressed by Clements and Pawlowski (2012) that raising awareness could be successful for use and reuse of OER. Awareness and knowledge of OER emerged as a precondition for motivation to share and use OER.

When it comes to what motivates teachers to use and contribute OER, this study identified a variety of enabling factors. These were mostly intrinsic, but several extrinsic motivations appeared to play an important role in promoting the uptake of OER in India, including credit for recruitment and promotion, as well as opportunities for professional development, networking and image building. Many previous studies (Harishankar, 2012; Petrides et al., 2011; Reed, 2012; Rolfe, 2012; Terrasse, Marinova, Greller & Schwertel, 2012; Wang & Noe, 2010) have emphasised that recognition of OER contribution and use could promote OER practices in different contexts.

Perceptions of OER quality

Respondents' perceptions about the quality of OER were assessed by computing statistical measures on 13 Likert-type quality statements collected via the questionnaire and the panel discussion organised during the workshops. Table 4 shows a range of means from 3.49 to 4.46, with an average mean of 3.99 and an SD of 0.78.

Table 4: Perceptions of OER quality

Item statement ("OER and quality")	Rank	Range	Min.	Max	Mean		SD
					Statistic	Std error	
If OER are appropriate in their content I prefer to use them.	1	4.00	1.00	5.00	4.46	.06	0.71
I prefer to use OER from trustworthy sources.	2	3.00	2.00	5.00	4.37	.072	0.78
Open licensing of OER enables continuous quality improvement.	3	4.00	1.00	5.00	4.17	.08	0.89
I use trustworthy OER from reputed institutions.	4	4.00	1.00	5.00	4.09	.09	0.99
I often use OER which fulfil the pedagogical needs of the teaching and learning process.	5	3.00	2.00	5.00	4.07	.07	0.81
OER assists developing countries to have quality materials.	6	4.00	1.00	5.00	4.05	.07	0.81
OER needs localisation.	7	4.00	1.00	5.00	3.97	0.1	1.14
I don't need permission to reuse OER.	8	4.00	1.00	5.00	3.76	0.11	1.19
Lack of peer review of OER makes them susceptible to poor quality.	9	4.00	1.00	5.00	3.74	0.09	1.05
Quality of OER is questionable.	10	4.00	1.00	5.00	3.49	0.1	1.11

Overall analysis indicates that teachers were slightly cautious about OER quality. Respondents typically felt that if OER were appropriate they would use them (M = 4.46). This indicates that respondents use their own criteria for deciding what is appropriate in their context.

They also revealed a keen interest in the trustworthiness of OER sources (M = 4.37), such as those released by a reputable institution (M = 4.09). Without formal quality assurance processes governing the release of many OER, knowing that they come from reputable sources gives teachers greater confidence in them. Respondents also felt that open licensing enabled continuous quality improvement (M = 4.17), since openly licensed resources would potentially be scrutinised – and hopefully improved – by peers who use, adapt and reshare materials openly. In addition, teachers generally agreed that OER were of high quality when they support the pedagogical needs of the teachers and students (M = 4.07). And they agreed that OER would assist developing countries to obtain better-quality materials (M = 4.05), especially if they are localised (M = 3.97).

Respondents were aware that they did not need permission to use OER (M = 3.76), but were mildly concerned that the lack of peer review makes the resources susceptible to poor quality (M = 3.74). The feeling was that any educator can release their teaching materials openly online, meaning that there is plenty of room for low-quality materials to form part of the corpus of available OER. This may not be the norm, but it is a possibility that these teachers were aware of. Respondents were, however, ambivalent in their perception of whether the quality of existing OER were questionable (M = 3.49), with most expressing a "neutral" viewpoint (which makes sense given many university respondents' lack of prior OER experience before the workshops).

During the panel discussions with respondents, it was revealed that selection of the right kind of OER is important in terms of contextualisation and adaptation so as to be fit for purpose. The real measure of quality material is based on the students' learning needs and how it helps them to learn better. This perception is supported by a study by Nikoi and Armellini (2012), who posited that OER support students' progression. Teachers pointed out that OER should be student-centric and created according to the student learning level and context. The quality assurance process and indicators of quality were debated amongst some of the teachers at two levels, namely quality as end product (e.g. a high-quality textbook or video), and quality as a process (e.g. to take appropriate steps to ensure quality). It was felt that individual efforts, including self-critical evaluation, community participation, peer review and institutional quality assurance policy could positively promote the quality of OER. The discussion further surfaced the idea that the process is more important than the product, as the product can be continuously improved and contextualised due to the utilisation of open licensing.

The literature suggests that reviews by subject experts are useful to ensure quality (Hilton & Wiley, 2009). Clements, Pawlowski and Manouselis (2015) support the importance of collaborative approaches to raise the quality of OER, as was discussed by many teachers in the present study. Knox (2013) indicates that flexibility and relevance to diverse community contexts are important factors in OER quality. Many of the issues identified by the respondents with regard to quality are also covered in the *Quality Assurance Guidelines for Open Educational Resources: TIPS Framework* (Kawachi, 2014). However, the workshop participants in this study emphasised appropriateness of OER ("fit for purpose") as the foremost criterion for assessing the quality of OER, as was found in the study by Wild (2012). The trustworthiness of the source and the reputation of the organisation responsible for the OER have also been identified as quality issues (Clements & Pawlowski, 2012; Conrad, Mackintosh, McGreal, Murphy & Witthaus, 2013). The suitability of OER for teaching and learning needs (i.e. pedagogical purposes) was identified as another quality issue.

In this study teachers agreed that accountability in terms of the quality of OER rested equally with authors, editors and the institutions hosting or sharing these resources. This accords with Musunuru's (2012) study, which highlights the importance of institutional efforts to assure the quality of learning materials. While the findings of this study are consistent with existing literature with regard to perceptions around resource quality, it was also found that the perception of quality is related to whether or not an individual contributes OER. While teachers are concerned with quality and make every effort to improve their resources, those who contribute OER appear to be less fixated with quality as a factor. Those who have never contributed OER were more sceptical about the quality of OER.

Barriers to OER adoption

While the respondents in this study had a relatively positive attitude and appeared intrinsically motivated to use and adapt OER, this does not appear sufficient for mainstreaming OER in Indian HEIs, as they also indicated several barriers. The questionnaire listed 18 barriers that may affect use and contribution of OER by individual teachers in institutions. These barriers were personal, institutional, technical, legal, economic, linguistic and pedagogical, as shown in Table 5.

Table 5: Analysis and ranking of barriers to OER adoption (listed in order of weighted rank)

Barriers	Choices					Cumulative			Weighted	
	1	2	3	4	5	Score	Rank	%	Score	Rank
Lack of understanding of intellectual property, copyright and CC licensing. (Legal)	23	11	7	6	8	55	1	47.00	200	1
Current workload. (Personal)	20	13	6	5	7	51	2	43.59	187	2
Lack of recognition and reward systems for developing OER. (Institutional)	9	6	13	7	12	47	3	40.17	134	3
Lack of technological support to resolve problems. (Technical)	7	9	3	13	6	38	4	32.48	112	4
Lack of financial resources by institution to invest in OER. (Economic)	1	10	10	10	4	35	5	29.91	99	5
Lack of time. (Personal)	6	7	7	6	5	31	7	26.50	96	6
Lack of knowledge for using OER in teaching and learning process. (Pedagogical)	7	8	3	7	5	30	8	25.64	95	7
Inability to find existing OER on topics of interest. (Personal)	7	6	7	4	4	28	10	23.93	92	8
Lack of institutional policy on OER. (Legal)	3	6	9	8	7	33	6	28.21	89	9
Poor technical infrastructure. (Technical)	4	5	7	7	6	29	9	24.79	81	10
Difficulty to remix OER for specific users. (Pedagogical)	6	6	2	6	4	24	11	20.51	76	11
Lack of ICT skills required to create OER. (Technical)	4	3	7	4	4	22	12	18.80	65	12
Incompatibility of OER with my university learning management system. (Technical)	3	3	4	4	3	17	14	14.53	50	13
Unavailability of OER in native language. (Linguistic)	3	4	1	2	9	19	13	16.24	47	14
Difficulty in collaboration. (Pedagogical)	3	1	5	5	3	17	14	14.53	47	14
Inadequate bandwidth. (Technical)	1	4	4	3	4	16	15	13.68	43	15

Lack of confidence about the quality of own work. (Personal)	1	3	5	3	4	16	15	13.68	42	16
Non-user-friendly OER platforms. (Technical)	1	3	4	4	2	14	16	11.97	39	17
Other	0	1	0	0	1	2	17	1.71	5	18

Table 5 shows that the most important barrier to OER adoption, according to these respondents, is their lack of understanding of intellectual property, copyright and open licensing, the legal permissions issues surrounding OER. Mtebe and Raisamo (2014a) and Harishankar (2013) also showed that a functional understanding of CC licensing was a concern for some faculty members in terms of OER uptake.

The second highest ranked barrier to OER uptake for these respondents was their workload. They saw OER as additional work, and therefore saw current workload as a barrier to doing any additional work developing OER. In terms of high current workload and time constraints, Harishankar (2013) also found that teachers were not able to contribute due to higher work pressure. Other studies also indicated lack of time to find suitable materials as a barrier[9] (see, for example, Clements & Pawlowski, 2012; Coughlan, Pitt & McAndrew, 2013; de Hart et al., 2015; Harishankar, 2013; Hilton & Wiley, 2009; Mtebe & Raisamo, 2014b; Ossiannilsson & Creelman, 2011; Prasad & Usagawa, 2014; Prior, 2011; Rolfe, 2012).

The third most cited barrier pertains to recognition and reward. This has been cited in previous studies, such as Glennie, Harley, Butcher and van Wyk (2012), Hilton and Wiley (2009), Hylén (2006) and Rolfe (2012). While teachers seemed to be intrinsically motivated, the barriers identified indicate that their use of and contribution to OER might increase if they understood OER better, had more time to work on producing OER and received recognition for this work.

The fourth and fifth barriers identified are institutional, and relate to lack of funding and the need for increased technological support. Institutional barriers such as lack of technical support, lack of OER policy, internet bandwidth issues, as well as inadequate infrastructure in terms of labs, computers (shared or individual) and other required equipment (such as audio-video recording devices) have also been reported as barriers to OER adoption (see, for example, Coughlan et al., 2013; de Hart et al., 2015; Dhanarajan & Porter, 2013; Hylén, 2006; Mtebe & Raisamo, 2014a; 2014b).

While some respondents saw pedagogical issues and institutional policy as barriers, these were not the predominant factors identified. The other barriers mentioned by teachers related to the perceived low quality of OER and an overall lack of awareness.

Discussion

This study of higher education teachers at four institutions and the WikiEducator community in India reveals an overall positive attitude towards the uptake of OER, especially the sharing of such materials. Findings indicate that many teachers in the study sites have been using OER, whether knowingly or unknowingly, though OER adaptation activity is very limited. While

---

9 http://timreview.ca/article/271

the analysis presented thus far has focused on distinguishing the teachers' understandings of their attitudes, motivations and perceptions of quality and barriers concerning OER, we now assess those understandings based on the factors and sub-factors that emerged in the Findings discussion. These broad thematic factors are personal, institutional, economic and pedagogical. By assembling the survey results into these categories, the four research questions can be addressed in a much more nuanced way, as they allow us to compare responses across the survey elements – attitudes, motivations, quality, barriers – together.

Personal factors

A number of factors that influence teachers' perception of and engagement with OER can be described as personal, such as those relating to pleasure or satisfaction, self-development, reputation, collaboration, altruism, awareness, digital fluency and workload. Table 6 groups all the survey statements and results (drawing on Tables 1, 3, 4 and 5) regarding these personal factors in order to enable quick comparison of which elements are the most important, and how various responses in one category (attitudes, motivations, etc.) nuance the responses in other categories. Table 6 deals with personal factors as they relate to OER sharing or contributing.

Table 6: Comparison of personal factors as they relate to key survey categories regarding OER sharing (listed in order of importance according to the "Attitude" category)

Factors	Attitudes	Motivations	Quality	Barriers
Pleasure/ achievement/ self-satisfaction	Teachers experience pleasure if someone adopts/adapts their educational resources. When others use teachers' OER, it improves their sense of achievement.			Lack of confidence about the quality of own work.
Self-development	Teachers believe that sharing helps them obtain feedback.	OER gives them opportunities to learn new things. They like receiving comments and feedback from experts and seniors on OER created. OER increases their self-confidence.		
Reputation	Teachers believe that sharing educational resources: – Improves their professional respect. – Enhances their personal and organisational reputation. – Increases their network and sphere of influence. – Improves their chances of recognition at a global level. – Increases their profile amongst peers and others. – Helps to disseminate their ideas.	OER improves professional image. Involvement in OER will give me recognition.		

Collaboration/ community participation	Teachers believe that sharing educational resources: – Enhances their confidence as they perceive themselves as part of larger community. – Promotes collaboration and engagement with consortia.	OER provides us with opportunities for establishing new partnerships. I like to be involved in peer production of OER.		Difficulty in collaboration.
Altruism	Teachers believe that sharing educational materials as OER: – Will encourage others to do so as well. – Is their responsibility.	Teachers believe that: – Sharing knowledge is a basic academic value. – OER will help developing countries increase access to education. – By contributing, they give back to society. – Through OER, they can reach disadvantaged communities.	OER assist developing countries to access quality materials.	

Pleasure and achievement

As Table 6 shows, in terms of the teachers' personal attitudes towards sharing OER, they expressed a high level of satisfaction in knowing that others are using and adapting their materials. Through this action of giving, they have made a contribution to the work of their peers – and their students – thus they feel pleasure at this outcome. This coincides with their deeper educational values, and respondents indicated that they gained a sense of achievement from sharing OER.

Self-development

While these attitudes support their interest in OER sharing, it is the prospect of learning new things and obtaining feedback from experts in their fields that motivates them to engage in OER activity.

Reputation

In terms of personal reputation, teachers believe quite strongly that sharing educational materials improves their professional reputation, enhances their personal and organisational reputation, increases their network and sphere of influence, improves their chances of recognition at a global level, increases their profile amongst peers and helps to disseminate their ideas more broadly. Yet, when it comes to their actual motivations for sharing OER based on this "reputation" sub-factor, they ranked statements such as "OER improves professional image" and "Involvement in OER will give me recognition" far lower than they did others. Thus, similar to the "pleasure and achievement" sub-factor, there appears to be an interesting mismatch between the attitudes that teachers have towards sub-factors like reputation enhancement and how they believe these act as a motivation for OER activity.

Collaboration

Teachers show a solid level of positivity in sharing educational resources, which enhances their confidence as they perceive themselves to be part of a larger community. They feel that collaboration provides them with opportunities for establishing new partnerships. They ranked this at similar levels in their attitudes and in their motivations.

Altruism

Even though teachers ranked altruism statements comparatively low in terms of their attitudes (but reasonably high in absolute terms), they were the top-ranked reasons in their motivations. Teachers revealed strongly altruistic reasons for sharing OER as they believe that sharing knowledge is a basic academic value. They thus have a responsibility to share so that developing countries and disadvantaged communities will be able to increase their access to quality educational materials. They believe that by contributing OER they give back to society, and, in doing so, encourage others to also share. Table 7 deals with personal factors as they relate to OER use (drawing on Tables 2, 3, 4 and 5).

Table 7: Comparison of personal factors as they relate to key survey categories regarding OER use (listed in order of importance according to the "Attitude" category)

Factors	Attitudes	Motivations	Quality	Barriers
Digital fluency	Teachers are relatively confident about their competencies and knowledge to assist them to use or contribute OER. Teachers are confident in their use of ICT to use or adapt OER.	Technology associated with OER is easy.		Lack of ICT skills required to create OER.
Awareness of OER licensing	Teachers are not as confident about the knowledge of intellectual property rights needed to adapt or use OER.	I know about my intellectual property rights under CC licences.	Open licensing of OER enables continuous quality improvement. I don't need permission to reuse OER.	Lack of understanding of intellectual property, copyright and CC licensing.
Workload		OER saves me time.		Current workload. Lack of time.

Digital proficiency

Teachers acknowledge that they are quite confident in their use of ICT to use or adapt OER. Most consider the use of technology associated with OER as "easy" and not a barrier to the creation of OER.

Awareness of open licensing

Teachers list their prime barrier to OER adoption as their lack of understanding of intellectual property, copyright and CC licensing. Even though they appreciate that the open licensing of OER enables continuous quality improvement, they are slightly less confident about their competencies and the knowledge required to assess licensing provisions in terms of using or adapting OER.

Workload

While acknowledging that OER may save them time, two key barriers faced by teachers are current workload and lack of time.

Institutional factors

A number of factors outside of the personal also influence OER engagement, such as institutional factors. Because these are not personal, they have less relevance to attitude and relate more to the other categories of motivation, quality and barriers. As shown in Table 8 (drawing on Tables 3, 4 and 5), these include reward structures, levels of technical support, policy instruments and the reputation or quality of OER.

Table 8: Comparison of institutional factors as they relate to key survey categories (listed in order of importance according to the "Barriers" category)

Factors	Motivations	Quality	Barriers
Reward structures	Receiving appropriate credit will help them adopt OER.		Lack of recognition and reward systems for developing OER.
Technical support			Lack of technological support to resolve problems. Poor technical infrastructure. Incompatibility of OER with university learning management system. Inadequate bandwidth. Non-user-friendly OER platforms.
Policy			Lack of institutional policy on OER.
Reputation/quality assurance		They preferred to use OER from trustworthy sources. They use trustworthy OER from reputed institutions. Lack of peer review of OER makes them susceptible to poor quality. Quality of OER is questionable.	

Reward structures

Teachers concede that receiving appropriate credit would assist them to adopt OER. They ranked quite highly the current lack of recognition and reward systems for developing OER as one of the impediments to OER adoption. The need for institutional support in terms of any kind of appraisal, reward and recognition concurs with that of prior studies (Glennie et al., 2012).

Technical support

Though technical issues were not mentioned as motivators to create or use OER, teachers noted the lack of technical support to resolve problems and, to a lesser extent, the poor technical infrastructure, incompatibility of OER with their university learning management system, inadequate bandwidth or non-user-friendly OER platforms.

Policy

In the one instance that institutional policy was raised in the survey, the teachers ranked the lack of an institutional policy on OER as a modest barrier, a point that has been highlighted in other studies (Davis et al., 2010; Rolfe, 2012).

Reputation and quality of OER

Throughout the workshops and in the survey, teachers revealed that they had some concerns about OER quality, but usually stated that they preferred to use OER from "trustworthy sources" and "reputed institutions". They marginally agreed that the lack of peer review of OER made them susceptible to poor quality.

Economic factors

Another key factor that is worth distinguishing from the personal and institutional concerns is the economic aspects, as shown in Table 9 (drawing on Tables 3 and 5).

Table 9: Comparison of economic factors as they relate to key survey categories

Factor	Motivation	Barrier
Economic	OER is less expensive.	Lack of financial resources by institution to invest in OER.

Although teachers considered OER to be less expensive than traditional course materials, they point to the lack of financial investment in OER at the institutional level as a barrier.

Pedagogical factors

The last factor treated here is a pedagogical one, as shown in Table 10. (drawing on Tables 2, 3, 4 and 5).

Table 10: Comparison of pedagogical factors as they relate to key survey categories regarding OER use

Factor	Attitude	Motivation	Quality	Barriers
Pedagogical	Teachers use OER to fulfil the academic requirements of their students.	They believe that OER are "good" for people as they improve their learning. OER caters to the innate desire to learn, improve and progress. OER provides access to best materials and teachers.	If OER are appropriate in their content I prefer to use them. I often use OER which fulfil the pedagogical need of the teaching and learning process. OER needs localisation.	Lack of knowledge for using OER in teaching and learning process. Inability to find existing OER on topics of interest. Difficulty to remix OER for specific users. Unavailability of OER in native language.

Although many teachers believe that OER are valuable because they afford opportunities to learn, improve and progress, teachers make the choice about OER based on their appropriateness for their students' and their own needs. Appropriateness as a measure of quality of educational materials has been identified by Dhanarajan and Timmers (1992), Wild (2012), as well as Brent et al. (2012). Not all are convinced that OER provides access to the "best" materials, and some recognise that OER may require localisation. Many teachers admit to lacking knowledge of how to use OER in the teaching and learning process, their inability to find existing OER on topics of interest, their difficulty in remixing OER for specific users, and, to a lesser degree, the unavailability of OER in local languages. Teachers generally prefer to use OER from trustworthy sources or reputable institutions. While they acknowledge that the lack of peer review of OER may make them susceptible to poor quality, this does not seem to cast the overall quality of OER into question.

Synthesised answers to the research questions

This study set out to answer four research questions concerning Indian teachers' attitudes, motivations, perceptions of quality and barriers to OER use and adaptation. To answer these questions, the Findings section of this chapter approached the questions according to certain prime categories (attitudes, motivations, perceptions of quality and barriers), revealing how teachers responded to the various survey prompts under each category. In this section, those findings were further nuanced by analysing the otherwise categorically based responses according to various factors (personal, institutional, economic, pedagogical). With the results from these varied approaches in mind, we can now offer distilled answers to the four research questions.

(1) How are teachers' attitudes towards OER situated in the context of teaching and learning?
Despite the relatively low levels of awareness that teachers had of OER prior to the workshop, after they learned more about them and their potential in their own work, they were highly positive about creating and sharing OER, while being slightly less enthusiastic about using externally sourced materials. Many of these positive attitudes stemmed from – in order of importance – the sense of satisfaction obtained when others use and adapt their teaching materials, the useful feedback received from their peers, the reputational boost provided as a result of sharing, the chance to take advantage of collaborative opportunities opened up by sharing, and the belief that their own sharing will encourage others to do the same. Most felt they have the necessary digital proficiency to use OER and they also saw how OER could help meet their students' needs, but they did not feel confident about the knowledge of intellectual property rights or CC licensing needed to adapt or use OER. Despite this one area of concern, the teachers' largely positive attitudes to OER sharing – and, to a slightly lesser extent, OER use – offer a solid platform for building greater OER awareness and encouraging greater OER engagement in the Indian higher education sector.

(2) What are teachers' motivations for using OER and sharing their work as OER?
The motivations that Indian teachers expressed for using and sharing OER fall into a series of categories, which, in order of importance, include: social/altruistic, learning, collaboration, cost/time/access, individual benefits, and technology and knowledge.

First, the most important motivational category is social and altruistic. Teachers asserted that sharing knowledge is a basic academic value, that "OER will help developing countries increase access to education", and that sharing OER is a way to "give back to society" and reach disadvantaged communities.

Second, teachers said that OER is "good" for people as it improves their learning. Many also believed that OER provided them with opportunities to learn new things themselves, and it catered to their innate desire to learn, improve and progress. In addition, they said they like receiving comments and feedback from experts and senior colleagues on their OER work.

Third, regarding cost, time and access, many respondents believed that OER provides an opportunity to collaborate and produce materials with peers.

Fourth, most felt that OER was less expensive than traditional copyrighted materials, while many others also thought that it saved them time. They also mildly agreed that OER provided access to the best resources and teachers.

Fifth, regarding individual benefits that might accrue from using or contributing OER, teachers said that they were relatively positive that OER engagement would improve their professional image and even boost their sense of self-confidence. They were slightly less sure that OER use and adaptation would lead to greater recognition for them or that such credit would lead to greater OER uptake on their part.

Sixth, some respondents believed that the technology associated with OER was easy, while fewer believed that they understood their intellectual property rights in terms of CC licensing.

Thus, while teachers are motivated by a number of factors to share or use OER, the ones that they say are the most essential for them revolve around the social and altruistic contribution to others and learning new things themselves.

(3) How do teachers perceive the quality of OER?

Overall analysis indicates that teachers were slightly cautious about OER quality. Respondents typically felt that if OER were appropriate they would use them. This indicates that respondents use their own criteria for deciding what is appropriate in their context. They also revealed a keen interest in the trustworthiness of the sources of OER, such as those released by a reputed institution. Respondents also felt that open licensing enabled continuous quality improvement since they would potentially be scrutinised by peers who use, adapt and reshare materials openly. In addition, teachers generally agreed that OER are of high quality when they support the pedagogical needs of the teachers and students. They agreed that OER would assist developing countries to obtain better-quality materials, especially if they are localised.

Respondents were mildly concerned about the lack of peer review, which they feel makes the resources susceptible to poor quality. Nevertheless, during the workshop panel discussions, respondents said that the real measure of quality material is based on the students' learning needs and how it helps them to learn better. Teachers agreed that accountability in terms of the quality of OER rested equally with authors, editors and the institutions hosting or sharing these resources.

(4) What barriers to using OER do teachers perceive?

Respondents ranked a number of potential barriers to OER use and sharing, with their lack of understanding of intellectual property, copyright and open licensing being listed as the primary barrier. Second was the issue of the very heavy workloads experienced at their institutions. They saw OER as additional work, and therefore saw current workloads as a barrier to doing any additional work developing OER.

The third most cited barrier pertains to recognition and reward. While teachers seemed to be intrinsically motivated, the barriers identified indicate that teachers' use of and contribution to OER might increase if they understood OER better, had more time to work on producing OER and received recognition for this work.

The fourth and fifth barriers identified are institutional, and relate to lack of funding and the need for increased technological support. While some respondents also saw pedagogical issues and institutional policy as barriers, these were not the predominant factors identified. The other barriers mentioned by teachers related to the perceived low quality of OER and a lack of awareness thereof.

Conclusion and recommendations

This research indicates that most respondents feel positive about the prospects of creating OER, as well as using them. The creation and use of OER aligns with respondents' educational philosophies and professional desires, as they see the utility that OER can have for them in teaching their students, in improving their own materials (through the use of others' materials and from feedback given on their own OER), and in satisfying their wishes to help other educators with their work. The fact that the attitudes and motivations towards OER expressed were largely hypothetical, in that most respondents were revealing their feelings about situations that they had yet to personally experience, suggests that the educators do not lack the requisite feelings or motivations for engaging with OER, but that in the past they – probably like most Indian educators – lacked the awareness of OER needed to be able to act on it.

This is the first challenge for increasing OER creation and use in Indian higher education: to enhance the levels of awareness that educators have of OER so that they can act on their largely positive attitudes and motivations towards them.
Recommendation 1 is that advocacy for and awareness of OER (including open licensing) in Indian universities should be a top priority, with a particular focus on teachers and senior administrators.

The second challenge identified is that, while educators are largely positive about OER, they often lack the time to engage with OER development activities, which might entail specialised training and support, and may initially be more time consuming than their conventional educational materials development activities.
Recommendation 2 is that teachers should be released from certain duties and provided with the time required to engage in OER activity.

In addition, given the temporal constraints and demands on most educators in India's higher education system, respondents suggested that the fact that there are no rewards or recognition given for OER engagement is a barrier to OER activity. There is no signal from their institutions that OER activity is valued by the institution, thus reducing the likelihood of their engagement with OER.

Recommendation 3 is that incentives in the form of awards and/or recognition in promotion should be provided for teachers to undertake OER work.

For the uptake of OER in Indian HEIs to be promoted in a sustainable manner, a comprehensive strategy at the institutional level would be useful. At the national level, the Ministry of Human Resource and Development has adopted an open licensing policy for its flagship NMEICT project that supports content development in different subjects in higher education. However, because this is a project, its impact may be limited in terms of institutionalising OER in Indian universities. At the time of the study, only three Indian universities had an OER policy, but there was no visible OER activity in these institutions due to lack of clarity in the policies. Having appropriate policy is therefore important but not sufficient. If OER is to be mainstreamed in Indian higher education, it is important to develop an action plan with adequate funding, institutional support and policy development.

Recommendation 4 is that institutional OER policy should be developed and implemented to foster OER use.

With such recommended approaches in place, educators and institutions could shift their focus to address the more particular challenges surrounding OER, especially the need for them to be of the requisite quality and relevance. Because OER are typically not peer reviewed or quality assured by external organisations – though some are – such mechanisms could be implemented at either the institutional level (especially for the creation of OER by institutional educators) or the national level (especially for identifying high-quality OER that can be used by Indian educators). This would likely require some experimentation before arriving at a suitable and sustainable approach.

Recommendation 5 is that quality assurance mechanisms for OER produced should be developed.

Lastly, the use and creation of OER rely on a new and slightly specialised set of skills with which educators should receive continuous support, particularly at the institutional (or multi-institutional) level. This approach acknowledges that educational material development activities are always changing, responding to new needs, and that OER needs to be incorporated into the continuous development strategies that institutions develop for their educators.

Recommendation 6 is that continuous professional development opportunities should be provided to teachers through regular workshops and training sessions on advanced ICT and OER skills (finding, evaluating and remixing).

Despite the overwhelmingly positive response to OER from teachers across the study sites, the research team experienced some opposition to OER from the perspective of fostering innovation and the protection of intellectual property rights. These concerns were typically expressed by senior university managers who operated in a paradigm driven by patents and the monetisation of innovation. There was, however, a movement amongst teachers interested in supporting OER who were seeking advice and support from their institutions.

Access to knowledge resources and technology has broadened the perspectives of the teachers who participated in this study, though some concerns remain in terms of quality and, to some extent, the "not invented here" syndrome.

The results of this study can only be treated as indicative of some Indian higher education teachers' current attitudes, motivations, perceptions of quality and barriers to OER at the study sites, as the sample size is too small for a country with a large population of teachers and over 700 universities. The study can, however, be replicated in different institutions to understand the psychological determinants of teachers in those contexts. Institutions can devise better mechanisms to address barriers, motivating factors and issues of quality when they better understand their teachers' current thinking and attitudes. This would drive a more data-oriented approach towards the development of appropriate advocacy, policies and training strategies. In terms of taking the OER movement forward in India, it is important to foster a community of practice of higher education teachers interested in OER to collaborate and develop courses. While there has been substantial investment in content development through the NMEICT project, it is important to create a community of practice to revise and update locally developed online resources as part of the ongoing work of teachers and not to consistently look to central government for funding support.

These perceptions around barriers to OER uptake indicate that there is a need for training and capacity-building in order to help teachers understand the principles of OER, copyright and open licensing. Developing appropriate policy to govern the sharing of educational materials and providing technical facilities within institutions would also create enabling conditions to promote OER adoption. Providing incentives in the form of formal recognition and reward may also boost OER uptake, though it appeared that most of the teachers were intrinsically motivated of their own accord (Mishra, 2016).

Acknowledgements

The authors thank Cheryl Hodgkinson-Williams and Henry Trotter for their valuable input in the chapter development process. Special thanks are also due to Professor Madhu Parhar and Professor Venkaiah Vunnam who acted as peer reviewers of the chapter.

References

Brent, I., Gibbs, G. R. & Gruszczynska, A. K. (2012). Obstacles to creating and finding Open Educational Resources: The case of research methods in the social sciences. *Journal of Interactive Multimedia in Education, 2012(1)*. Retrieved from http://jime.open.ac.uk/articles/10.5334/2012-05/

Butcher, N. (2011). *A basic guide to Open Educational Resources*. Paris: Commonwealth of Learning & United Nations Educational, Scientific and Cultural Organization. Retrieved from http://unesdoc.unesco.org/images/0021/002158/215804e.pdf

CERI (Centre for Educational Research and Innovation) / OECD (Organisation for Economic Co-operation and Development). (2007). *Giving knowledge for free: The emergence of Open Educational Resources*. Paris: Centre for Educational Research and Innovation &

Organisation for Economic Co-operation and Development. Retrieved from http://www.oecd.
org/edu/ceri/38654317.pdf

Clements, K. I. & Pawlowski, J. M. (2012). User-oriented quality for OER: Understanding
teachers' views on re-use, quality, and trust. *Journal of Computer Assisted Learning, 28(1)*,
4–14. Retrieved from http://onlinelibrary.wiley.com/doi/10.1111/j.1365-2729.2011.00450.x/
abstract

Clements, K. I., Pawlowski, J. & Manouselis, N. (2015). Open Educational Resources
repositories literature review: Towards a comprehensive quality approaches framework.
Computers in Human Behavior, 15(B), 1098–1106. Retrieved from https://jyx.jyu.fi/dspace/
handle/123456789/46582?show=full

Conrad, D., Mackintosh, W., McGreal, R., Murphy, A. & Witthaus, G. (2013). *Report on the
assessment and accreditation of learners using OER*. Paris: Commonwealth of Learning
& UNESCO. Retrieved from http://www.pedocs.de/volltexte/2013/8404/pdf/Conrad_
etal_2013_Assessment_Accreditation_OER.pdf

Cox, G. & Trotter, H. (2017). Factors shaping lecturers' adoption of OER at three South
African universities. In C. Hodgkinson-Williams & P. B. Arinto (Eds.), *Adoption and impact
of OER in the Global South* (pp. 287–347). Retrieved from https://doi.org/10.5281/
zenodo.601935

Coughlan, T., Pitt, R. & McAndrew, P. (2013). Building open bridges: Collaborative remixing
and reuse of open educational resources across organisations. In *2013 ACM SIGCHI
Conference on Human Factors in Computing Systems 'changing perspectives' (CHI 2013)
(pp. 991–1000), 29 April–2 May 2013*. Paris, France. Retrieved from http://oro.open.
ac.uk/36473/1/B2S-CHI-2013.pdf

Daniel, J., Kanwar, A. & Uvalić-Trumbić, S. (2009). Breaking higher education's iron triangle:
Access, cost, and quality. *Change: The Magazine of Higher Learning, 41*, 30–35.
Retrieved from https://www.researchgate.net/publication/225084031_Breaking_Higher_
Education%27s_Iron_Triangle_Access_Cost_and_Quality

Davis, H. C., Carr, L., Hey, J. M. N., Howard, Y., Millard, D., Morris, D. & White, S. (2010).
Bootstrapping a culture of sharing to facilitate open educational resources. *IEEE
Transactions on Learning Technologies, 3(2)*, 96–109. Retrieved from http://ieeexplore.ieee.
org/document/5210093/?reload=true

de Hart, K., Chetty, Y. & Archer, E. (2015). Uptake of OER by staff in distance education in
South Africa. *International Review of Research in Open and Distributed Learning, 16(2)*,
18–45. Retrieved from http://www.irrodl.org/index.php/irrodl/article/view/2047

Dhanarajan, G. & Porter, D. (Eds.). (2013). *Open Educational Resources: An Asian perspective*.
Vancouver: Commonwealth of Learning. Retrieved from https://oerknowledgecloud.org/
sites/oerknowledgecloud.org/files/pub_PS_OER_Asia_web.pdf

Dhanarajan, G. & Timmers, S. (1992). Transfer and adaptation of self-instructional
materials. *Open Learning, 7(1)*, 3–11. Retrieved from http://www.tandfonline.com/doi/
abs/10.1080/0268051920070102

Glennie, J., Harley, K., Butcher, N. & van Wyk, T. V. (Eds.). (2012). *Open Educational
Resources and change in higher education: Reflections from practice*. Paris:
Commonwealth of Learning & UNESCO. Retrieved from https://oerknowledgecloud.org/
sites/oerknowledgecloud.org/files/pub_PS_OER_web.pdf

Harishankar, V. B. (2012). Tracing the trajectory of OER in India: Reflections on three initiatives.
In J. Glennie, K. Harley, N. Butcher & T. van Wyk (Eds.), *Open Educational Resources and
change in higher education: Reflections from practice* (pp. 41–56). Paris: Commonwealth
of Learning & UNESCO. Retrieved from http://oasis.col.org/handle/11599/80

Harishankar, V. B. (2013). Establishing OER practice in India: The University of Madras. In G. Dhanarajan & D. Porter (Eds.), *Open Educational Resources: An Asian perspective* (pp. 207–220). Vancouver: Commonwealth of Learning. Retrieved from http://oasis.col.org/handle/11599/23

Hilton III, J. & Wiley, D. A. (2009). The creation and use of open educational resources in Christian higher education. *Christian Higher Education, 9*, 49–59.

Hylén, J. (2006). *Open Educational Resources: Opportunities and challenges.* Paris: Organisation for Economic Co-operation and Development/Centre for Educational Research and Innovation. Retrieved from http://www.oecd.org/edu/ceri/37351085.pdf

Kanwar, A., Kodhandaraman, B. & Umar A. (2010). Toward sustainable Open Education Resources: A perspective from the Global South. *The American Journal of Distance Education, 24(2)*, 65–80. Retrieved from http://dx.doi.org/10.1080/08923641003696588

Karunanayaka, S. P. (2012). Perceptions of teachers and teacher educators on the use of Open Educational Resources in teaching and learning. *Annual Academic Sessions 2012.* Retrieved from http://digital.lib.ou.ac.lk/docs/bitstream/701300122/551/1/OU5165_000.pdf

Kawachi, P. (2014). *Quality assurance guidelines for Open Educational Resources: TIPS framework.* New Delhi: Commonwealth Media Centre for Asia. Retrieved from http://oasis.col.org/handle/11599/562

Kerres, M. & Heinen, R. (2015). Open informational ecosystems: The missing link for sharing educational resources. *The International Review of Research in Open and Distributed Learning, 16(1)*, 24–39. Retrieved from http://www.irrodl.org/index.php/irrodl/article/view/2008

Knox, J. (2013). The limitations of access alone: Moving towards open processes in education technology. *Open Praxis, 5(1)*, 21–29. Retrieved from http://www.openpraxis.org/~openprax/index.php/OpenPraxis/article/view/36

Livingston, K. & Condie, R. (2006). The impact of an online learning program on teaching and learning strategies. *Theory into Practice, 45(2)*, 150–158. Retrieved from http://www.tandfonline.com/doi/abs/10.1207/s15430421tip4502_7

MHRD (Ministry of Human Resource Development). (2015). *All India survey on higher education 2014-2015.* New Delhi: Ministry of Human Resource Development. Retrieved from http://aishe.nic.in/aishe/viewDocument.action?documentId=206

Mishra, S. (2016). Mainstreaming use and adaptation of Open Educational Resources in Indian higher education: A model. Presented at the *Pan Commonwealth Forum 8, 27–30 November 2016.* Kuala Lumpur, Malaysia. Retrieved from http://oasis.col.org/handle/11599/2671

Mishra, S., Sharma, M., Sharma, R. C., Singh, A. & Thakur, A. (2016). Development of a scale to measure faculty attitudes towards Open Educational Resources. *Open Praxis, 8(1)*, 55–69. Retrieved from http://www.openpraxis.org/index.php/OpenPraxis/article/view/236/195

Mtebe, J. S. & Raisamo, R. (2014a). Challenges and instructors' intention to adopt and use Open Educational Resources in higher education in Tanzania. *The International Review of Research in Open and Distributed Learning, 15(1)*, 249–271. Retrieved from http://www.irrodl.org/index.php/irrodl/article/view/1687

Mtebe, J. S. & Raisamo, R. (2014b). Investigating perceived barriers to the use of Open Educational Resources in higher education in Tanzania. *The International Review of Research in Open and Distributed Learning, 15(2)*, 44–66. Retrieved from http://www.irrodl.org/index.php/irrodl/article/view/1803/2882

Musunuru, K. (2012). *Open Educational Resources: A panacea for economically under privileged society in India, 2007–2011.* Rochester, NY: Social Science Research Network. Retrieved from http://ssrn.com/abstract=1932031

Nikoi, S. & Armellini, A. (2012). The OER mix in higher education: Purpose, process, product, and policy. *Distance Education, 33(2)*, 165–184. Retrieved from http://www.tandfonline.com/doi/abs/10.1080/01587919.2012.697439

OECD (Organisation for Economic Co-operation and Development). (2009). *Creating effective teaching and learning environments: First results from TALIS*. Paris: Organisation for Economic Co-operation and Development. Retrieved from https://www.oecd.org/edu/school/43023606.pdf

Olcott, D. (2012). OER perspectives: Emerging issues for universities. *Distance Education, 33(2)*, 283–290. Retrieved from http://www.tandfonline.com/doi/abs/10.1080/01587919.2012.700561

Ossiannilsson, E. & Creelman, A. (2011). Quality indicators within the use of Open Educational Resources in higher education. In A. Mendez-Vilas (Ed.), *Education in a technological world: Communicating current and emerging research and technological efforts* (pp. 372–382). Badajoz: Formatex Research Centre. Retrieved from http://www.formatex.info/ict/book/372-382.pdf

Pegler, C. (2012). Herzberg, hygiene and the motivation to reuse: Towards a three-factor theory to explain motivation to share and use OER. *Journal of Interactive Media in Education, 2012(1)*. Retrieved from http://doi.org/10.5334/2012-04

Perryman, L. A. & Seal, T. (2016). Open educational practices and attitudes to openness across India: Reporting the findings of the OER Research Hub pan-India survey. *Journal of Interactive Media in Education, 15*, 1–17. DOI: http://dx.doi.org/10.53334/jime.416

Petrides, L., Jimes, C., Middleton-Detzner, C., Walling, J. & Weiss, S. (2011). Open textbook adoption and use: Implications for teachers and learners. *Open Learning, 26(1)*, 39–49. Retrieved from http://www.tandfonline.com/doi/abs/10.1080/02680513.2011.538563

Pitroda, S. (2006). *Higher education [Recommendations]*. New Delhi: National Knowledge Commission. Retrieved from http://knowledgecommissionarchive.nic.in/downloads/recommendations/HigherEducationLetterPM.pdf

Prasad, D. & Usagawa, T. (2014). Towards development of OER derived custom-built open textbooks: A baseline survey of university teachers at the University of the South Pacific. *The International Review of Research in Open and Distributed Learning, 15(4)*, 226–247. Retrieved from http://www.irrodl.org/index.php/irrodl/article/view/1873

Prior, J. (2011). *Using online synchronous interviews to explore the workflows, barriers and benefits for practitioners involved in the creation of Open Educational Resources*. M.Phil thesis. Bristol: University of Bristol. Retrieved from https://www.academia.edu/2350007/Using_online_synchronous_interviews_to_explore_the_workflows_barriers_and_benefits_for_practitioners_involved_in_the_creation_of_Open_Educational_Resources_OER_-_ePub_version

Reed, P. (2012). Awareness, attitudes and participation of teaching staff towards the open content movement in one university. *Research in Learning Technology, 20(4)*. Retrieved from http://dx.doi.org/10.3402/rlt.v20i0.18520

Richter, T. & Ehlers, U.-D. (2010). Barriers and motivators for using Open Educational Resources in schools. *Paper presentation at Open Ed 2010: The Seventh Annual Open Education Conference*. Barcelona, Spain. Retrieved from http://hdl.handle.net/10609/4868

Rolfe, V. (2012). Open Educational Resources: Staff attitudes and awareness. *Research in Learning Technology, 20(14395)*. Retrieved from https://www.dora.dmu.ac.uk/handle/2086/6188

Rubin, B. & Fernandes, R. (2013). The teacher as leader: Effect of teaching behaviors on class community and agreement. *The International Review of Research in Open and Distributed Learning, 14(5)*. Retrieved from http://www.irrodl.org/index.php/irrodl/article/view/1510/2745

Ryan, R. M. & Deci, E. L. (2000). Intrinsic and extrinsic motivations: Classic definitions and new directions. *Contemporary Educational Psychology, 25,* 54–67. Retrieved from https://mmrg.pbworks.com/f/Ryan,+Deci+00.pdf

Terrasse, C., Marinova, B., Greller, W. & Schwertel, U. (2012). Opening up! How to take full advantage of Open Educational Resources (OER) for management education. In B. C. Rienties, P. Daly, S. Reeb-Gruber, K. Reid & P. Van den Bessche (Eds.), *Proceedings of The 19th EDINEB Conference Role of Business Education in a Chaotic World, 1–4.* Haarlem: FEBA ERD Press. Retrieved from http://dspace.ou.nl/bitstream/1820/4505/1/EDINEB2012_OER_Management_Education_OpenScout.pdf

UNESCO (United Nations Educational, Scientific and Cultural Organization). (2012). *2012 OER Paris declaration.* Paris: United Nations Educational, Scientific and Cultural Organization. Retrieved from http://www.unesco.org/new/fileadmin/MULTIMEDIA/HQ/CI/CI/pdf/Events/Paris%20OER%20Declaration_01.pdf

Varghese, N. V. (2015). *Challenges of massification of higher education in India.* New Delhi: National University of Educational Planning and Administration. Retrieved from http://www.nuepa.org/new/download/Publications/CPRHE/March_2016/CPRHE_Research%20_%20Paper-1.pdf

Venkaiah, V. (2008). *Open Educational Resources in India: A study of attitudes and perceptions of distance teachers.* Hyderabad: B.R. Ambedkar Open University. Retrieved from http://wikieducator.org/images/d/d7/PID_386.pdf

Wang, S. & Noe, R. A. (2010). Knowledge sharing: A review and directions for future research. *Human Resource Management Review, 20(2),* 115–131. Retrieved from http://www.sciencedirect.com/science/article/pii/S1053482209000904

Wild, J. (2012). *OER engagement study: Promoting OER reuse among academics (Score Fellowship Final Report).* United Kingdom: University of Oxford.

Wiley, D., Green, C. & Soares, L. (2012). *Dramatically bringing down the cost of education with OER: How Open Education Resources unlock the door to free learning.* Washington, D.C.: Center for American Progress. Retrieved from https://cdn.americanprogress.org/wp-content/uploads/issues/2012/02/pdf/open_education_resources.pdf

Zimbardo, P. G. & Leippe, M. R. (1991). *The psychology of attitude change and social influence.* Philadelphia, PA: Temple University Press.

How to cite this chapter

Mishra, S. & Singh, A. (2017). Higher education faculty attitude, motivation and perception of quality and barriers towards OER in India. In C. Hodgkinson-Williams & P. B. Arinto (Eds.), *Adoption and impact of OER in the Global South* (pp. 425–458). Retrieved from https://doi.org/10.5281/zenodo.602784

Corresponding author: Sanjaya Mishra <smishra@col.org>

This work is licensed under a Creative Commons Attribution ShareAlike 4.0 International (CC BY-SA 4.0) licence. It was carried out with the aid of a grant from the International Development Research Centre, Ottawa, Canada.

Chapter 13

Impact of integrating OER in teacher education at the Open University of Sri Lanka

Shironica P. Karunanayaka and Som Naidu

Summary

This chapter reports on a research project implemented in the Faculty of Education at the Open University of Sri Lanka (OUSL) which investigated the impact of integrating Open Educational Resources (OER) in the teaching-learning process by secondary-level student teachers in Sri Lanka. The research questions this study seeks to answer are: What are the impacts of OER integration on the use of instructional materials by teachers? What are the impacts of OER integration on teachers' pedagogical perspectives? What are the impacts of OER integration on teachers' pedagogical practices?

The study adopted a design-based research approach. An intervention programme was implemented with 230 participants who were student teachers registered in the OUSL Postgraduate Diploma in Education programme in nine OUSL centres across the nine provinces of Sri Lanka. Data were collected at multiple stages through the following quantitative and qualitative strategies: survey questionnaires, analysis of lesson plans, concept mapping, self-reflection, semi-structured interviews, focus group discussions, usage data from the learning management system and narratives in the form of "stories". While descriptive statistical methods such as percentages were used to analyse the quantitative data, the authors employed an Interpretive Phenomenological Analysis approach to analyse the qualitative data.

Findings showed that the integration of OER had a substantial impact on changing teachers' instructional resource use, pedagogical perspectives and pedagogical practices. The careful and systematic design of activities facilitated a shift from a "low" to a "high" degree of innovative use of instructional resources as well as creation of OER by teachers, while their pedagogical perspectives and practices shifted towards more constructivist, context-centric and collaborative patterns, as well as to a participatory and sharing culture, in favour of Open Educational Practices. ▶

This kind of capacity-building of teachers in the adoption of OER has the potential to strengthen the school education system in Sri Lanka. Motivating teachers through provision of further opportunities, and recognition of their initiatives through incentives and appreciation, would enhance empowerment of teachers to act as "change agents". It will also provide insights to inform recommendations for the formulation of evidence-based guidelines to support OER adoption.

Acronyms and abbreviations

CERI	Centre for Educational Research and Innovation
COL	Commonwealth of Learning
CPD	continuing professional development
DBR	Design-Based Research
EFA	Education for All
ICT	information and communication technologies
MDGs	Millennium Development Goals
MoE	Ministry of Education
OEP	Open Educational Practices
OEP-IE	OEP Impact Evaluation
OERTL	OER-integrated Teaching and Learning
OER	Open Educational Resources
OUSL	Open University of Sri Lanka
PGDE	Postgraduate Diploma in Education
ROER4D	Research for Open Educational Resources for Development
UNISA	University of South Africa

Introduction

Article 26 of the Universal Declaration of Human Rights states that: "Everyone has the right to education."[1] This notion is reinforced by various "open" concepts that have evolved in relation to teaching and learning practices under the umbrella term "Open Education", which refers to a broad range of practices to enhance accessibility, flexibility and equity in education (Souto-Otero et al., 2016). The Open Educational Resources (OER) movement has enhanced such practices of openness through promoting the legal sharing of educational resources freely online (UNESCO, 2012; Wiley & Green, 2012). OER not only offers an efficient means of sharing knowledge, but also serves as a strategic opportunity to increase the quality of education through enhancing innovations in the use and creation of teaching-learning resources, thus contributing to sustainable development[2] (OECD, 2007).

---

1   http://www.un.org/en/universal-declaration-human-rights/
2   http://www.unesco.org/new/en/communication-and-information/access-to-knowledge/open-educational-resources/

Access to reliable and useful learning resources and the cost of these resources are often identified as substantial obstacles to education and training in developing-country contexts. The increasing availability of OER helps to address these challenges by making educational resources freely accessible, thus contributing to improved cost-efficiency (UNESCO, 2012). OER also play a key role in enhancing the participatory culture of learning, creating, sharing and cooperation required by rapidly changing "knowledge societies".[3] While access to knowledge and information is vital in the transition towards knowledge societies, effective use of information and knowledge to create new knowledge is a key factor in promoting socioeconomic equity. The transformation of information into knowledge and the creation of new knowledge require innovation. Thus, the values and practices of creativity and innovation play a major part in knowledge societies. The OER movement can have a substantial influence on educational practice, not only in making educational resources easily available and accessible, but also in contributing to the continuous quality enhancement of resources through the legal mechanism of granting rights to users to revise, remix and adapt them according to contextual needs. This empowerment of users to become creators, rather than merely consumers of content, necessitates creative and innovative pedagogical thinking and practice.

In the Sri Lankan education system, OER is still a relatively novel concept. Despite the fact that the Sri Lankan general education sector has made a contribution to economic and social development in the country through several policy reforms, issues such as limited use of up-to-date instructional materials and lack of engagement in innovative pedagogical approaches by teachers are often observed in the general schooling system (NEC, 2016). Several initiatives have been implemented to address the needs of the country's education system in order to meet the challenges of the new millennium. In particular, use of information and communication technologies (ICT) has been enhanced through various projects funded by the Asian Development Bank, such as the Secondary Education Modernization Project and the Distance Education Modernization Project, while the Education for Knowledge Society Project and the Education Sector Development Framework and Programme aimed to improve the quality, relevance, effectiveness and equity of access to secondary and tertiary education, specifically in rural and disadvantaged locations (MoE, 2012; 2013). A noteworthy progressive action took place in January 2017, when the government of Sri Lanka presented the Sri Lanka Sustainable Development Bill targeting the development and implementation of a national policy on sustainable development in line with the United Nations' Sustainable Development Goals, to be implemented in parallel with the government's Sustainable Era programme.[4] This endeavour should further enhance and promote Education for Sustainable Development initiatives in the Sri Lankan education system, including the adoption of OER in teaching and learning.

Several studies conducted at the Open University of Sri Lanka (OUSL) revealed that the level of OER awareness was extremely low among practitioners, yet their preparedness and motivation to adopt the concept was quite high (Karunanayaka, 2012; Karunanayaka, Fernando & De Silva, 2013). Subsequent initiatives implemented by the Faculty of Education at OUSL have resulted in increased levels of OER adoption among practitioners, instilling

---

3   http://www.capetowndeclaration.org/read-the-declaration
4   http://bit.ly/2zS943Y

a change in thinking and practice by raising awareness and developing capacity. Previous studies have highlighted the need to establish a close partnership between researchers and practitioners in awareness-raising and capacity-building initiatives, as well as the importance of designing appropriate experiences in a systematic manner (Karunanayaka & Naidu, 2013; Karunanayaka, Naidu, Dhanapala, Gonsalkorala & Ariyaratne, 2014; Karunanayaka, Naidu, Rajendra & Ratnayake, 2015).

It is expected that the development of a culture of adopting OER among academics in Sri Lanka will have a cascading effect on enhancing the quality of teacher professional development (Karunanayaka & Naidu, 2014). This process could be facilitated by encouraging student teachers in the OUSL Faculty of Education to integrate OER in their teaching, and studying the impacts of this process. Empowering school teachers with the competencies to use, create and adapt OER in their teaching-learning process and ascertaining its impact would hopefully ensure that the benefits of this innovation do not remain confined to OUSL, but filter down to the primary and secondary school systems.

The Postgraduate Diploma in Education (PGDE) programme offered by the OUSL Faculty of Education is an in-service professional development programme for school teachers offered in three languages (Sinhala, Tamil and English) and implemented in OUSL regional and study centres throughout Sri Lanka. This chapter reports on a study that engaged a representative sample of student teachers in the OUSL PGDE programme (i.e. teachers enrolled in the programme) and investigated the impact of integrating OER in their teaching-learning process.

"Impact" is described in terms of changes that happen over time due to an intervention (OECD, 2012). Since the concept of OER was novel for school teachers in Sri Lanka, an intervention was essential to support integration of OER in their teaching and learning. The aim of this study was to investigate how and in what ways integration of OER is having an impact on instructional resource use, pedagogical practices and pedagogical perspectives of Sri Lankan school teachers.

Conceptual framework

Theory of change

When integrating OER in teaching and learning, the responsibility for finding the most appropriate materials to use (and for utilising them) in order to support effective education resides with the institutions as well as the educators responsible for the delivery of education (COL, 2011). Conceptually, using OER is similar to using any other learning resource in teaching and learning. There is, however, a difference with OER in terms of the legal permissions provided by open licensing, which allows for additional flexibility in teachers' and learners' use of resources in terms of Wiley's "5Rs"[5] – the right to reuse, revise, remix, redistribute and retain the resource.

---

5   http://opencontent.org/blog/archives/3221

Adoption of OER by educators can only be truly effective if it is driven and accompanied by a "change" in their thinking and actions. Educational change is described as a complex process comprising four broad phases: initiation, implementation, continuation and outcome (Fullan, 2007). Emphasising the fact that "change is a journey, not a blueprint", Fullan (1993, p.21) points out that, in order to deal with such complexity, the focus should not be on controlling change but on guiding it. Educators are therefore expected to be "change agents". According to Fullan's view, every stakeholder in the educational change is a change agent: "It is only by individuals taking action to alter their own environments that there is any chance for deep change" (Fullan, 1993, p.51).

In light of the fact that change efforts often focus on materials and overlook people, it has been argued that if the intended outcomes of an educational innovation are to be achieved, it is essential to have changes in actual practice along three dimensions: the possible use of new or revised materials; the possible use of new teaching approaches; and the possible alteration of beliefs (Fullan, 2007). Considering integration of OER as an educational innovation, the conceptual framework of this study was formulated based on these three dimensions. Accordingly, the current study focuses on ascertaining the impacts of OER integration in teaching and learning specifically in terms of changes in the use of instructional materials by teachers, their pedagogical practices and pedagogical perspectives. The main research questions of this study are:

1. What are the impacts of OER integration on the use of instructional materials by teachers?
2. What are the impacts of OER integration on teachers' pedagogical perspectives?
3. What are the impacts of OER integration on teachers' pedagogical practices?

Literature review

The increased availability of a wide variety of quality teaching-learning materials online in the form of OER gives teachers and learners access to educational resources in diverse formats, which can enable flexible and dynamic knowledge creation. OER can, therefore, help developing countries save money as well as course-creation time (Kanwar, Kodhandaraman & Umar, 2010). In particular, use and adaptation of OER would be a very cost-effective way to invest in curriculum development and quality teaching-learning material development at regional and national levels within the Asian context (Dhanarajan & Porter, 2013). However, while rapid progress in practices related to use and creation of OER is evident in many developed countries, there has been slow progress in OER implementation in the developing world (Hatakka, 2009). It has been suggested that to reach its full potential, a global balance is needed, where developing countries are not confined to merely being consumers of OER, but instead also producers of OER (Albright, 2005).

The potential of OER to bridge the information gap between the developed and developing world is increasingly being realised (OECD, 2007). In recent years, substantial progress with steadily growing education-development efforts has been witnessed in the developing world, particularly in areas such as teacher training, open textbooks, locally developed OER and OER policy development (Hoosen, 2012; Smith, 2013). Notable initiatives include

OERAfrica,[6] OERAsia,[7] Teacher Education in Sub-Saharan Africa,[8] Teacher Professional Development in India[9] and the eGyanKosh[10] national digital repository in India. In the Sri Lankan context, actions are currently under way to develop and implement OER policies at the provincial ministries of education (Karunanayaka & Abeywardena, 2016).

Adoption of OER and Open Educational Practices in teaching and learning

The shift of emphasis from merely having access to resources to the practice of using OER is encompassed in the concept of Open Educational Practices (OEP). Promoting OEP through the creation, use and management of OER in teaching and learning is a very challenging process (Conole & Ehlers, 2010). It not only requires a change in terms of access to OER, but also a change in the mindsets of practitioners towards a more open, participatory, creative and sharing culture.

Various studies on the adoption of OER and OEP in teaching and learning reveal that OER are increasingly being widely and actively used in the education systems of many developed as well as developing countries (de los Arcos, Farrow, Perryman, Pitt & Weller, 2014; Dhanarajan & Porter, 2013; European Commission, 2012; 2013; Hylén, van Damme, Mulder & d'Antoni, 2012; JISC, 2011; McAndrew et al., 2009; Naidu & Mishra, 2014; OPAL, 2010). The successes, challenges as well as supportive and hindering factors in the adoption of OER and OEP which these initiatives have revealed, and which are discussed below, provide useful directions on how to effectively engage in OER integration and OEP.

Challenges in the adoption of OER by educators

Despite some penetration of OER in global education systems, many studies have revealed inadequacies in the awareness and understanding of OER among faculty. Awareness and knowledge of OER among the academic community in Asia have previously been found to be very low (Dhanarajan & Abeywardena, 2013). A study on the benefits and challenges in the use of OER conducted among Organization for Economic Co-operation and Development (OECD) member countries indicates that even though the majority are active in the area of OER, mostly through specific projects or institutional initiatives, in many countries there is a lack of knowledge about OER activities among educators (Hylén et al., 2012). Similarly, two consecutive Babson OER survey reports reveal that most (>70%) faculty in the United States (US) higher education system remain unaware of OER, and adoption of OER has yet to enter the mainstream of higher education (Allen & Seaman, 2014; 2016). Teachers' appreciation of the OER concept and willingness to use these resources can, however, be seen as a positive trend. Further, a decrease in faculty concerns about permission to use or change OER and an increase in concerns about the quality of OER imply an increasing understanding of OER use (Allen & Seaman, 2014; 2016).

---

6   http://www.oerafrica.org/
7   https://oerasia.org/
8   http://www.tessafrica.net/
9   http://www.tess-india.edu.in/
10   http://egyankosh.ac.in/

According to the *OER Evidence Report 2013–2014* (de los Arcos et al., 2014), while awareness of OER and Creative Commons (CC) licensing[11] is growing, knowledge of OER repositories remains relatively low. This is a key obstacle in locating OER. Studies exploring staff attitudes toward OER found that despite limited knowledge and awareness of OER, they had positive attitudes about sharing materials[12] (Karunanayaka, 2012). This kind of sharing culture among faculty and the willingness to embrace the OER concept are promising signs that should enhance the adoption of OER.

The benefits of using, producing and sharing OER – such as open and flexible learning opportunities, increased efficiency and quality of learning resources, cost-efficiency and innovation potential – result in a systemic transformation affecting all parts of education systems (Hylén et al., 2012). Educators mainly use OER to broaden their teaching methods and the range of resources available to their students. Relevance, high quality and discoverability are therefore key requirements for educators to adopt OER (de los Arcos et al., 2015).

Despite growing evidence of the benefits of OER, there are many issues influencing OER adoption by educators. Lack of awareness of open licensing, inability to judge the quality of OER, as well as the extensive time and effort required to find relevant OER and evaluate them, are some of the common barriers to the adoption of OER identified in previous studies (Allen & Seaman, 2014; CERI/OECD, 2007; de los Arcos et al., 2014; Dhanarajan & Porter, 2013). These studies also reveal that only a small minority of educators create resources and publish them under a CC licence.

For instance, Babson surveys conducted in 2014 and 2016 found that OER was not a driving force in resource-adoption decisions by faculty in higher education systems in the US, and levels of OER use by faculty were therefore found to be low. The most significant obstacle revealed for OER adoption by faculty was the effort required to find and evaluate such materials (Allen & Seaman, 2014; 2016). Similarly, key barriers to OER use in OECD countries included lack of time and lack of a reward system (CERI/OECD, 2007).

A survey conducted on OER uptake among staff at the University of South Africa (UNISA) indicated that, despite high levels of awareness and knowledge about OER, there has not been a change in practice, mostly due to a lack of knowledge about open licensing (de Hart, Chetty & Archer, 2015). Furthermore, results of a representative survey of higher education institutions in five European countries (France, Germany, Poland, Spain and the United Kingdom [UK]) on OEP, beliefs and strategies revealed that while OER are widely used and more than 50% of higher education institutions support the use of OER, just over one-third support the development of OER (Castaño-Muñoz, Punie, Inamorato, Mitic & Morais, 2016).

Cultural obstacles to sharing or using resources developed by other teachers or institutions have been observed in several OECD case studies (CERI/OECD, 2007). There is also evidence of learners being confused by the vast range of ideas and concepts they are exposed to through a wide variety of OER (Beetham, Falconer, McGill & Littlejohn, 2012). This illustrates the need to provide careful orientation and guidance to both teachers and learners in the use of OER. However, evidence of the "viral" effects of openness has been observed, based on reports that most OER users would continue to use them and would

---

11   http://creativecommons.org/licenses/
12   http://www.researchinlearningtechnology.net/index.php/rlt/article/view/14395

recommend them to others. Many educators encourage their colleagues to use OER and are keen to make their practices more open (de los Arcos et al., 2014). These observations suggest that exposure to OER tends to lead to increased use and sharing of these resources with others.

Practices in the integration of OER in teaching and learning

Even though acceptance of OER and its integration in teaching and learning is increasingly observed in mainstream education, evidence of its impact is still "mixed" (Weller, 2014). The practices adopted by educators in integrating OER in their teaching-learning processes play a major role in the levels of impact these resources have.

Enhancing pedagogy and students' learning experiences are some of the main motivations for implementing OER integration programmes. However, it has been observed that a majority of teachers use OER to supplement traditional face-to-face instruction, rather than as core learning materials (Souto-Otero et al., 2016). Many teachers claim that using OER requires more preparation time than when using traditional materials (Bliss, Robinson, Hilton & Wiley, 2013). This could be due to the time required to adapt OER to their needs, which may be a hindering factor in the actual integration of these resources in the learning process. A study on K–12 school teachers' perceptions of the role of OER emphasised that teachers do not merely adopt OER, but adapt them to suit diverse learning needs. Mainstreaming OER is not only a matter of raising awareness, but of changing teachers' habits (de los Arcos, Farrow, Pitt, Weller & McAndrew, 2016).

Studies on OER adoption in academic practice have identified numerous challenges faced by educators, and imply the need for continuing professional development (CPD) to enhance their practices (Browne, Holding, Howelle & Rodway-Dyer, 2010; Masterman & Wild, 2011). A study on the role of OER in transforming pedagogy reveals how exposure to OER supports collaborative practices among educators (Petrides, Jimes, Middleton-Detzner & Howell, 2010). The finding that OER use encourages reflection by educators on their own practice is another important aspect that should be promoted to enhance pedagogical practice (Weller, de los Arcos, Farrow, Pitt & McAndrew, 2015). These findings have important implications for how OER could be integrated in teaching and learning, particularly in relation to the design of CPD programmes for teachers.

A study incorporating six case-study research projects around the world (in Uganda, the US, South Africa and India) conducted by the Institute for the Study of Knowledge Management in Education highlights the role of OER in supporting teacher professional development and teacher knowledge-sharing (ISKME, 2008). The case study on Curriki,[13] a wiki-based website that facilitates teachers' reuse, remixing, creation and sharing of OER, identified the need for training support in order for users to create and remix content, and emphasised the importance of promoting interaction among users. Moreover, the case study on Training Commons[14] revealed that cultural context plays an integral role in OER partnerships. The Teachers' Domain[15] case study illustrated that the transition from

---

13 http://www.iskme.org/content/curriki-facilitating-use-and-user-engagement-around-open-educational-resources

14 http://www.iskme.org/content/oer-case-study-training-commons-institute-study-knowledge-management-education

15 http://www.iskme.org/content/oer-case-study-training-commons-institute-study-knowledge-management-education

proprietary materials to OER presented complex challenges to teachers, necessitating thorough assessment of legal, pedagogical and technical aspects prior to integrating OER. The participatory approach adopted in these case studies, with the aim of continuous improvement of practices, reveals the importance of capacity-building with ongoing assessment of practices, as well as the need to document and share these practices with a wider community (ISKME, 2008). Several case studies conducted in the Asian context likewise reveal similar findings (Dhanarajan & Porter, 2013; Karunanayaka & Naidu, 2013; Naidu & Mishra, 2014). These case studies provide invaluable insights into good practices in the adoption of OER and OEP in teaching and learning.

Moving from OER to OEP

OER may increase flexibility and equal opportunity in the use of learning resources, resulting in improved accessibility and enhanced openness in education. Broadening the focus of attention beyond mere access to resources to include innovative use of resources results in OEP (Ehlers, 2011). According to Wiley's "5Rs" OER framework, users are not only permitted to make free use of materials, but also have the ability to repurpose them through improvement of existing materials and creation of new materials, as well as adopt innovative teaching practices using OER. This empowers users to engage in innovative OEP employing different degrees of openness in the usage and creation of OER.

Whereas OER focuses on resource access, OEP focuses on how openness can be practised through the use, creation and management of OER via innovative instructional methods and strategies. While a simple definition of OEP such as "a set of activities and support around the creation, use and repurposing of OER"[16] implies this idea, a broader definition provides a more holistic view of OEP as "practices which support the (re)use and production of OER through institutional policies, promote innovative pedagogical models and respect and empower learners as co-producers on their lifelong learning path" (Ehlers, 2011, p.3). Beetham et al. (2012), in a study based on outcomes of a UK OER programme, state that OEP encompass several aspects: production, management, use and reuse of OER; developing and applying open pedagogies in teaching practice; gaining access to open learning opportunities; practising open scholarship; open sharing of teaching ideas; and using open technologies.

Attempts at integrating OER and OEP in teaching-learning situations have revealed supportive as well as hindering factors. These provide insights into how to effectively engage in such processes (Carey, Davis, Ferreras & Porter, 2015; Coughlan & Perryman, 2015; Karunanayaka & Naidu, 2013; 2016; Karunanayaka et al., 2014; Karunanayaka, Naidu, Rajendra et al., 2015; Lane & van Dorp, 2011). While efficient integration of OER is supported by ICT, effective use of OER in teaching and learning can only be enhanced through adopting systematic course design processes.

---

16   http://e4innovation.com/?p=373

Various OER integration initiatives have presented frameworks for implementing OEP in different contexts, providing strategies and frameworks for consideration when designing, developing, implementing and evaluating OER. Examples include:

- The Open Educational Quality Initiative project's OEP matrix (Andrade et al., 2011), in which the link between resources and practices is captured and explained in two dimensions – openness in resource usage and creation versus openness in pedagogical models.
- The "7C" learning design framework (Conole, 2014), which presents seven elements of OEP implementation – conceptualise, capture, communicate, collaborate, consider, combine and consolidate.
- A model of "open pedagogy" (Hegarty, 2015), which discusses eight interconnected attributes – participatory technologies; people, openness and trust; innovation and creativity; sharing ideas and resources; connected community; learner generated; reflective practice; and peer review.
- A "learning engine" framework (Naidu & Karunanayaka, 2014), which functions as an effective strategy to design effective, efficient, engaging learning experiences based on innovative pedagogical models with OER as fuel for the learning engine.

These frameworks demonstrate how adoption of OER and OEP can be facilitated by creating structured enabling environments.

It is evident that enacting change towards OEP is best achieved through the strategic, systematic design of appropriate learning experiences. Designing effective, efficient and engaging learning experiences that adopt more context-centric learning approaches based on innovative pedagogical models supported by OER is identified as a viable solution to enhance a change in perspectives and practices among teachers in order to move towards OEP (Karunanayaka, Naidu & Menon, 2016; Naidu & Karunanayaka, 2014; 2015).

Methodology

The aim of this study was to investigate how and in what ways integration of OER in teaching and learning is having an impact on Sri Lankan school teachers, particularly with regard to changes in their instructional resource use, pedagogical practices and pedagogical perspectives. Ascertaining the impact of the OER integration process requires a realist understanding of causality (Maxwell, 2004), using a qualitative research approach. Hence, a Design-Based Research (DBR) approach (Reeves, 2006), which is a realist, process-oriented research approach, was adopted in this study.

DBR is a systematic and flexible methodology aimed at improving educational practices through iterative analysis, design, development and implementation. It is based on collaboration amongst researchers and practitioners in real-world settings, where researchers play the dual roles of both researchers and designers in the research process, leading to contextually sensitive design principles and theories (Wang & Hannafin, 2005). Since OER is a new concept for school teachers in Sri Lanka, it was necessary to first raise their awareness of OER and the opportunities afforded by these resources, and to build their capacity in identifying, searching, selecting and integrating OER in their teaching and learning. Next, successive action was taken to design, develop and implement solutions to authentic problems in teaching and learning through teachers' active participation in the process.

The DBR approach comprises four phases: analysis of practical problems experienced by researchers and practitioners in collaboration; designing, developing and implementing solutions as appropriate; testing and refining solutions in practice; and reflection by researchers and practitioners on authentic problems to produce design principles and enhance solution implementation (Reeves, 2006) (Figure 1).

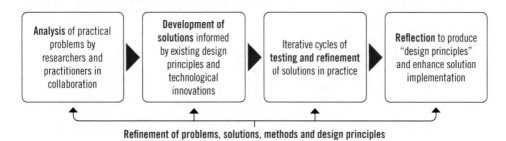

Figure 1: The four phases of Design-Based Research (source: Reeves, 2006)

Within a DBR framework, complex problems in educational practices are addressed in real-world contexts in collaboration with practitioners. Known and hypothetical design principles are then integrated with technological advances in order to render plausible solutions to these problems. Thereafter, rigorous, reflective enquiry is undertaken to test and refine innovative learning environments as well as define new design principles (Reeves, 2006). As such, DBR extends beyond the mere design and testing of interventions, and it has been claimed that DBR researchers, rather than simply "observing" interactions, are actually "causing" those same interactions (Barab & Squire, 2004). DBR is characterised as pragmatic, grounded, iterative and flexible, as well as interactive and contextual (Wang & Hannafin, 2005).

Situating the process in naturalistic contexts is identified as a core feature of DBR (Barab & Squire, 2004). DBR therefore serves as a useful approach where researchers function as designers to design solutions/strategies in collaboration with practitioners in order to improve their educational practices in real-life situations. In this study, where the goal was to ascertain the impact of OER integration in terms of changes in teachers' use of instructional resources, pedagogical thinking and pedagogical practices, DBR was considered the most desirable and appropriate research approach. Accordingly, a multiphased intervention was designed in order to support, test and refine teachers' OER integration practices in their teaching-learning process.

The intervention process

The intervention was designed and implemented in several stages utilising specific strategies in accordance with the four phases of the DBR approach.

Table 1: Strategies adopted during the intervention process in accordance with the DBR approach

Phases in the DBR approach	Intervention process		
	Intervention strategies	Purpose	Specific activities
1. Analysis of practical problems by researchers and practitioners in collaboration	• Pre-intervention survey • Orientation workshop	• Reflect on current thinking and practices in relation to use of instructional methods and materials by teachers	• Administering the pre-intervention questionnaire • Individual concept-mapping exercise • Analysis of teachers' lesson plans • Focus group discussions
2. Development of solutions informed by existing design principles and technological innovations	• Strategic and systematic design of learning experiences based on situated learning principles • Designing a series of interactive workshops for capacity-building, supporting and monitoring, reviewing and evaluation • Designing a learning management system (LMS) to support OER integration	• Capacity-building • Supporting teachers to integrate OER • Use of technology (LMS) to support teachers' integration of OER • Monitoring teachers' adoption of OER	• Designing a sequence of experiences to enhance the integration of OER and adoption of OEP among teachers • Workshop activities • LMS activities • Monitoring activities

3. Iterative cycles of testing and refinement of solutions in practice	• Capacity-building workshops • LMS to support OER adoption • Monitoring workshops • Reviewing/ evaluation	• Capacity-building and providing guidance to integrate OER • Encourage lesson planning with OER integrations and upload in LMS • Enhance sharing of OER via LMS • Monitoring, reviewing and supporting • Stimulating collaboration, cooperation, extension activities and sharing of good practices • Promoting reflective practice • Data collection	• Hands-on individual and group activities to identify/search/select OER, and planning lessons with OER integration • Providing links to OER repositories via LMS • Encouraging teachers to share OER found, reused, revised, remixed or created via LMS • Providing constructive feedback through constant communication via LMS • A competition initiated to find the most active teacher in each centre and the most active centre • Encourage extension activities at school/ centre/zonal levels • Concept-mapping exercise • Reflective journal writing • Questionnaire survey • Focus group discussions
4. Reflection to produce design principles and enhance solution implementation	• Teacher reflections • Researcher reflections	• Using teacher and researcher reflections to find solutions to authentic problems	• Compilation of "stories" by teachers and researchers based on their reflections • Creation of a weblog to share the stories of teachers' and researchers' experiences • Development of a tool to ascertain the impact of OER and OEP adoption by educators (OEP-IE Index) • Development of an enhanced framework on the use of DBR to support the adoption of OER and OEP

As summarised in Table 1, the four phases in the DBR approach were implemented in iterative cycles during the intervention process, using a number of different strategies, including specific activities that also served as systematic data-gathering techniques, both qualitative and quantitative. Details of each phase are described next.

Phase 1: Analysis of practical problems by researchers and practitioners in collaboration

In the pre-intervention phase, the existing situation with teachers in relation to the three aspects – instructional resource use, pedagogical perspectives and pedagogical practices – was analysed. The purpose was to reflect on the current thinking and practices of teachers, in order to identify the required solutions to improve the existing situation. A pre-intervention questionnaire survey, concept-mapping exercise, observation of lesson plans and focus group discussions revealed existing levels of thinking and practices related to OER, and indicated the need to raise awareness and build capacity among teachers in relation to integration of OER in their teaching.

Phase 2: Development of solutions informed by existing design principles and technological innovations

Phase 2 of the intervention involved designing effective, efficient, engaging learning experiences, as informed by existing theoretical constructs and frameworks based on situated learning principles and a constructivist approach to learning (Brown, Collins & Duguid, 1989; Duffy & Jonassen, 1991), as a solution to improve the existing condition of limited thinking and practices among teachers on integrating OER.

This phase consisted of developing two key components: designing a series of interactive workshops (two at each of the nine OUSL centres) and creating an online environment titled "OER-integrated Teaching and Learning" (OERTL) using a Moodle LMS. These two components included specific activities on capacity-building, guiding, monitoring and providing support on, as well as reviewing and evaluating, OER adoption by teachers.

The initial interaction workshops were designed to raise awareness and develop skills through intensive hands-on activities focused on identifying, searching, selecting and integrating OER in teaching practices (both individually and collaboratively), and included the following components:

- Introduction to OER and related concepts through presentations and discussions.
- Identifying OER, including understanding CC licensing.
- Searching different types of OER (subject-related resources).
- Identifying different ways of integrating OER (in terms of subject focus).
- Sharing sample learning designs (lesson plans) with integrated OER.
- Reflecting on the experience.

The OERTL online environment was organised into several sections serving different purposes, including an introduction to OER, separate sections for key subject areas with links to OER repositories, and discussion forum sections for sharing OER. Figures 2 and 3 present screenshots from the OERTL showing the introductory section with web resources to introduce the concept of OER (Figure 2), and forums to add useful OER found by participants and to share any OER created by participants (Figure 3).

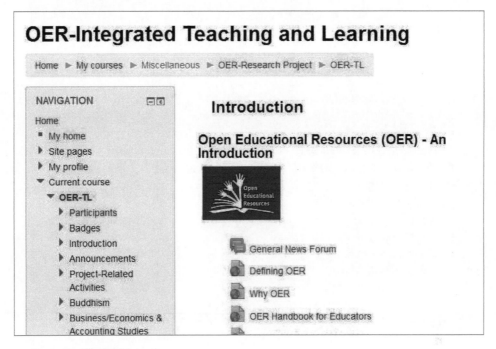

Figure 2: **The OERTL homepage**

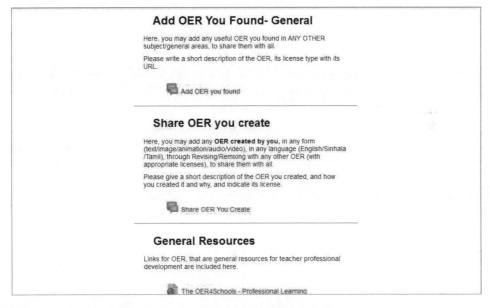

Figure 3: **Web page for adding and sharing OER in the OERTL**

As shown in the screenshots in Figures 2 and 3, OERTL was organised in a way that motivated and supported teachers not only to search, identify and integrate OER, but also to share OER with peers, upload OER-integrated lessons and concept maps and reflect on their experiences.

Phase 3: Iterative cycles of testing and refinement of solutions in practice

In Phase 3, during a series of workshops conducted at the nine OUSL centres, iterative cycles of testing and refinement of strategies in the designed learning experience occurred, together with constant interactions facilitated by the OERTL platform.

Specific activities conducted during this phase, which also supported continuous data collection, were:

- Providing hands-on individual and group activities during the workshops to identify/search/select OER and to support lesson planning with integrated OER.
- Providing subject-related links to OER repositories via the OERTL.
- Encouraging teachers to use the OERTL to share the OER found/reused/revised/ remixed/created by them.
- Providing constructive feedback during workshops and through the OERTL.
- Maintaining constant communication via the OERTL.
- Initiating a competition to find the most active teacher in each centre and the most active centre.
- Encouraging extension activities to be initiated at school/centre/zonal levels.
- Conducting the concept-mapping exercise.
- Encouraging reflective journal writing.
- Administering surveys on teachers' thinking and practices related to OER integration.
- Conducting focus group discussions on teachers' thinking and practices related to OER integration.

Phase 4: Reflection to produce design principles and enhance solution implementation

During the DBR process, researchers and practitioners engage in reflective enquiry, systematically refining the learning environment, which results in the definition of new design principles that can guide similar research and development endeavours (DBR Collective, 2003; Reeves, 2006). This occurred during the final phase in the study.

Throughout the intervention process, both teachers and researchers were encouraged to record self-reflections on their experiences and insights gained at different stages. This activity aided the discussion on finding solutions to authentic problems. Later, based on these reflections, narratives were compiled in the form of "stories". These stories were shared with all as published OER, initially as a weblog[17] and later as an edited monograph (Karunanayaka & Naidu, 2016).

The process also resulted in the development of a tool to ascertain the impact of the adoption of OER and OEP – the OEP Impact Evaluation (OEP-IE) Index (Naidu & Karunanayaka, 2017).

Development of the OEP Impact Evaluation Index

During the intervention process, the idea of a specific instrument to ascertain the impact of OER integration and OEP adoption in teaching and learning emerged. The intention was that when administered at regular intervals over a period of time, the tool could capture

---

17   https://oertlousl.wordpress.com/

behavioural shifts in the perceptions, perspectives and practices of teachers in relation to OEP. This instrument was called the Open Educational Practices Impact Evaluation Index.

The development process of the OEP-IE consisted of three phases: expert review, item analysis and pilot testing with participants.

Initially, a pool of draft items (statements) was developed based on a review of the literature by the researchers and rated under three main categories: pedagogical beliefs (PB), pedagogical practices (PP) and instructional resource use (IR), with 45 items distributed among the three categories (PB = 15, PP = 15, IR = 15). These were systematically sorted and revised during the three development phases, resulting in 42 items in three categories (PB = 15, PP = 15, IR =12) (see Naidu & Karunanayaka, 2017).

This instrument was not used to collect data from the participants during the process, but it was pilot-tested with them. Statistical analysis of reliability and validity of the instrument is yet to be undertaken.

The overall process of reflection throughout the intervention process resulted in the development of new design principles in the form of a framework on the use of DBR to support the adoption of OER and OEP (see Karunanayaka & Naidu, 2017).

Participant profile

The study participants (n = 230) were recruited by mailing an open invitation letter to student teachers registered in the OUSL PGDE programme at nine OUSL centres – Anuradhapura, Badulla, Batticaloa, Colombo, Jaffna, Kandy, Kurunegala, Matara and Ratnapura. A filtering process was undertaken on the full, final list of respondents in order to select teachers of secondary-level grades.

The following factors were also taken into consideration in the participant selection process:

- Representation from the nine provinces of the country.
- Representation from different ethnicities and language or medium of instruction (Sinhala, Tamil and English).
- Representation in gender profile, addressing any possible gender inequalities in data analysis.

The participant cohort of 230 student teachers included 152 females (66%) and 78 males (34%). The centres of Jaffna (16.5%), Batticaloa (15.7%) and Colombo (14%) had the highest number of participants. More than half (57.8%) of the participants were science graduates, with some (17.4%) holding postgraduate qualifications. A majority (75.7%) had less than five years of teaching experience, while 22.6% had 6–15 years of experience, and only 1.7% had more than 15 years of experience. The subject most of the participants were teaching was science (44.4%), with the other main subject areas being mathematics (25.6%), languages (18.6%), commerce (14.3%) and information technology (14.3%). Participants' initial proficiency in using the LMS was found to be very low: the majority (74.3%) claimed poor competency, 22.1% claimed average competence and only 3.4% claimed excellent competence (Table 2).

Table 2: Background information on participant cohort (n = 230)

Aspect	Category	Number	Percentage
Gender	Female	152	66.1
	Male	78	33.9
Academic qualification	BSc degree BA/BCom degree Other degree	133 77 20	57.8 33.5 8.7
	Postgraduate	40	17.4
Professional teaching experience	<5 years	174	75.7
	6–15 years	52	22.6
	>15 years	4	1.7
Subject area (teaching)	Science	102	44.4
	Mathematics	58	25.6
	Languages	43	18.6
	Information technology	33	14.3
	Commerce	33	14.3
	Religion	10	4.4
Proficiency in using LMS	Poor	171	74.3
	Average	51	22.1
	Excellent	8	3.4

Data collection approach

All data collection strategies and instruments were designed and prepared based on a review of relevant literature on OER and OEP after several rounds of discussion among the research team. Validation of the instruments took place through expert reviews and pilot testing, where appropriate.

A comprehensive approach to data gathering was adopted throughout the research process, with data being collected at various stages of the intervention via multiple methods. These methods were comprised of the following quantitative and qualitative strategies: survey questionnaires, analysis of lesson plans using a checklist, concept mapping, self-reflection, semi-structured interviews, focus group discussions, analysis of activity logs in the LMS and narratives in the form of "stories". Table 3 presents a summarised overview of the data collection strategies associated with each of the research questions.

Table 3: **Data collection strategies according to research questions**

Research question	Data collection strategies	Purpose
1. What are the impacts of OER integration on the use of instructional materials by teachers?	1. Survey questionnaire 2. Analysis of lesson plans using a checklist 3. Focus group discussions 4. Interviews 5. LMS records 6. Self-reflection 7. Narratives ("stories")	To capture how/in what ways and for what purposes OER are integrated in the teaching-learning materials used by teachers (pre, mid and post intervention)
2. What are the impacts of OER integration on teachers' pedagogical perspectives?	1. Survey questionnaire 2. Concept mapping 3. Focus group discussions 4. Interviews 5. Self-reflection 6. Narratives ("stories")	To capture how engagement with OER has affected pedagogical thinking/ understanding/beliefs of teachers (pre, mid and post intervention)
3. What are the impacts of OER integration on teachers' pedagogical practices?	1. Survey questionnaire 2. Analysis of lesson plans using a checklist 3. Focus group discussions 4. Interviews 5. LMS records 6. Self-reflection 7. Narratives ("stories")	To capture how/in what ways and for what purposes OER are integrated in teachers' pedagogical practices (pre, mid and post intervention)

Survey questionnaires

Questionnaires were developed to obtain information from the participants at pre-, mid- and post-intervention stages. The questionnaires consisted of closed- and open-ended questions exploring the following main topics:

- Participant background information.
- Awareness of OER and views about sharing teaching-learning resources.
- Selection and use of teaching-learning resources.
- Perceptions of openness in education, OER and related concepts and practices.

Initially, draft questionnaires were developed and pilot-tested with a small group of teachers with the same characteristics as the research participants. These were also subjected to expert review. Based on the feedback received, the items in the questionnaires were revised and refined.

The pre-intervention questionnaire was administered manually, while mid- and post-intervention questionnaires were administered electronically via the LMS.

Checklist

A checklist was prepared to review the lesson plans of participants in terms of the following categories:

- Pedagogical approach.
- Teaching-learning methods and techniques employed.
- Integration of teaching-learning resources.
- Overall comment.

Concept mapping

Participants were required to develop single-page concept maps during pre-, mid- and post-intervention stages, illustrating all concepts and practices related to OER according to their current thinking. Specific guidelines were provided addressing the following key aspects:

- Identification of key concepts and related sub-concepts (organised hierarchically).
- Connecting concepts using lines/arrows to demonstrate meaningful links.
- Providing labels to indicate relationships between connected concepts.
- Providing specific examples of concepts.

Self-reflective narratives

Participants were asked to maintain self-reflective journals throughout the intervention process following specific guidelines. They were required to write reflective notes whenever they completed a key activity, addressing the following core focus areas:

- Analysis of the importance of the activity.
- Impact of the experience on the participant and others.
- Issues arising and how these were overcome.
- Successes and failures.
- Impact of the experience on individuals.
- Whether things could have been done differently, and, if so, how?

Focus group discussions

A schedule consisting of nine questions was used to gather data through focus group discussions conducted with small groups of participants (five or six in each group, formed according to the subject taught) in each OUSL centre during pre-, mid- and post-intervention stages. The nine focus questions addressed the following key areas:

- Considerations in the selection of teaching-learning methods and instructional resources.
- Methods of integrating OER in teaching and learning.
- Challenges in OER adoption and how to overcome them.

Semi-structured interviews

Semi-structured interviews were held with selected participants (two or three from each centre) using an interview schedule consisting of questions addressing the following key areas:

- Starting points.
- Integration of OER in lessons.
- Challenges and frustrations.
- Achievements and successes.
- Good practices.
- Impact on teaching and learning.
- Future plans.

LMS records

Data on participants' LMS activity were continuously recorded and observed in order to further refine intervention activities.

Utilisation of the multiple data-gathering strategies described above helped to ensure validity through methodological triangulation (Bekhet & Zauszniewski, 2012; Morse, 1991), and helped to provide a comprehensive view of the effects of this intervention.

Data analysis methods

While descriptive statistical methods such as percentages were used to analyse quantitative data, detailed content analysis of qualitative data was the main data analysis method used to capture meaning through close engagement with content in a process of coding and interpretation. This allowed the researchers to make sense of participants' ideas, understanding, thoughts and feelings and to analyse how those changed during the course of study.

Using Interpretive Phenomenological Analysis – an approach in phenomenological psychology that is commonly used to provide insight into how a given person in a given context makes sense of a given phenomenon – helped the researchers to explore in detail participants' perceptions of the particular situations they were facing, and how they were making sense of their personal and social worlds (Smith & Osborn, 2003). This approach allowed the researchers to uncover the meaning of individual experiences based on participants' and researchers' interpretations of their "lived experiences" (Reid, Flowers & Larkin, 2005).

In addition to content analysis, concept maps were also analysed based on their morphological types (Kinchin, 2008). A concept map provides a graphical representation of an individual's structural knowledge or conceptual understanding of a particular topic, and can be used to visualise and measure the depth, breadth and organisation of their understanding (Novak & Cañas, 2008).

Narratives were analysed using a framework articulated by Rolfe, Freshwater and Jasper (2001), which presents three questions to the practitioner: "What?", "So what?" and "Now what?" "What?" describes the situation in terms of achievements, consequences, responses, feelings and problems; "So what?" describes what has been learned in terms of knowledge gained about self, relationships, models, attitudes, cultures, actions, thoughts, understanding and improvements; and "Now what?" identifies what needs to be done in order to improve future outcomes and develop learning. The emergent themes and patterns of meaning identified were used to ascertain the changes that occurred in the pedagogical beliefs and practices of participants. Narratives or stories of both practitioners and researchers were also used to explore understanding gained of particular phenomena in real-world settings.

The qualitative, "realist, process-oriented approach" (Maxwell, 2004) employed in this study relied on an understanding of the processes through which a situation occurs rather than on a comparison of situations involving the presence or absence of the presumed cause. In investigating the causal mechanisms surfaced in the multiple data-gathering approaches used throughout the intervention, causation was demonstrated through evidence of "physical causality" (Mohr, 1999), which rests on the idea of a direct physical connection in the real world, as opposed to factual causality, which is determining causality by counterfactuals.

Findings

The findings of the study are presented in response to the three research questions outlined earlier.

Impact of OER integration on the use of instructional materials by teachers

Results obtained from the pre-intervention survey of teachers' use of instructional materials (Table 4) indicated use of a range of instructional resources, from print to multimedia and online resources; print-based materials were, however, predominant (100%). Most of the teachers accessed learning material from textbooks (83%) and from the internet (73.5%), as well as from materials created by other professional bodies (65.6%) and from their academic colleagues (57.4%). The data indicate that the teachers' awareness of OER was minimal at the pre-intervention stage, with only 10% having heard the term before. Their awareness of OER was found to be focused mainly on open textbooks (4.3%), multimedia resources (1.7%) and Open Access journals (3.0%). This finding indicated a need to raise awareness of OER among the participants.

Table 4: Teachers' use of instructional materials at the pre-intervention phase

Aspect	Category	Number	Percentage
Heard of OER before	Yes	23	10.0
	No	207	90.0
Used OER before	Yes	9	3.9
	No	221	96.1
Types of OER heard of/used	Open textbooks	10	4.3
	Multimedia resources	4	1.7
	Open Access journals	7	3.0
Format of resources used as instructional materials	Print	230	100.0
	Video	63	27.4
	Audio	42	18.3
	Multimedia	57	24.8
	Online	47	20.4
Sources of instructional materials	Textbook providers	191	83.0
	Professional bodies	151	65.6
	Colleagues	132	57.4
	The internet	169	73.5

The features considered by teachers when selecting educational materials were identified based on their responses to a five-point Likert scale (ranging from "extremely" to "not at all") (Table 5). It was interesting to observe that while the majority of teachers (above 65%) were highly concerned about relevance, informative nature, easy availability, reliability, free access, reusability, cost-effectiveness, attractiveness, easy adoptability, currency of information and flexibility when selecting educational resources to be used in their teaching, a much smaller percentage (33.9%) were concerned about copyright. This suggests that the teachers were either unaware of or not sensitive to the dimensions of copyright and open licensing, compared to the other features of resources.

Table 5: Features considered by teachers when selecting instructional resources (pre intervention)

Feature	5 (Extremely)		4 (To a large extent)		3 (Somewhat)		2 (To a small extent)		1 (Not at all)		0 (No response)	
	No.	%	No.	%	No.	%	No.	%	No.	%	No.	%
Relevant	180	78.3	33	14.3	12	5.2	1	0.4	0	0	4	1.7
Informative	92	40	71	30.9	23	10	16	6.9	10	4.3	18	7.8
Copyrighted	26	11.3	52	22.6	52	22.6	36	15.7	42	18.3	69	30.0
Easily available	135	58.7	51	22.2	26	11.3	6	2.6	1	0.4	11	4.8
Reliable	117	50.9	67	29.1	24	10.4	5	2.2	1	0.4	16	7.0
Freely accessible	104	45.2	64	27.8	36	15.7	20	8.7	6	2.6	0	0
Reusable	101	43.9	54	23.5	43	18.7	12	5.2	4	1.7	16	7.0
Cost-effective	85	40.0	73	31.7	48	20.9	10	4.3	4	1.7	10	4.3
Attractive	115	50.0	66	28.7	35	15.2	2	0.9	0	0	12	5.2
Easily adoptable	104	45.2	72	31.3	32	13.9	19	8.3	1	0.4	2	0.9
Updated	112	48.7	64	27.8	40	17.4	2	0.9	3	1.3	9	3.9
Flexible	94	40.9	60	26.1	41	17.8	11	4.8	7	3.0	17	7.4

The analysis of teachers' lesson plans also showed that they depended mostly on print textbooks, teacher guides and conventional instructional materials rather than using a variety of learning resources.

After the collection of pre-intervention data, the concept of OER was introduced to the student teachers in a workshop employing the OERTL as a support mechanism. The initial effect of introducing this novel concept into teachers' use of instructional resources is exemplified by the following quotes:

> It is the first time I heard the word Open Educational Resources ... OER is a cost-effective method and easy to search relevant facts according to the subject we want.

> [We] can easily find videos, audio lectures, animations, tutorials, presentations, assignments and assessments about the lessons we wish to find.

> I can understand the meaning OER ... Now I can use useful data and information legally ... Before that I mostly used copyright data and information without permission ... now I can use free usable data sources with permission.

The statements reveal the teachers' interest in the OER concept and their motivation to adopt these resources in teaching and learning. They were highly motivated about having free access to quality educational materials that they could adopt without any legal constraint. They were also happy about the opportunities available to them to translate quality learning materials into the local languages (Sinhala and Tamil) without any restrictions.

Results of the pre-intervention and Phase 1 were useful in planning activities for Phase 2. The need for further capacity development and provision of specific guidance in OER adoption in relation to reusing, revising, remixing, redistribution and retention were identified. In terms of addressing the fact that the English language should not be a barrier for OER adoption, teachers were encouraged and motivated to create OER in local languages.

It was evident from the records in the LMS that the OERTL played a key role in facilitating teachers' access to OER related to their subject areas and their integration of these OER in their lesson plans. The forums also promoted sharing of useful resources among peers.

By mid intervention, patterns in teachers' use of instructional materials (as shown in Figure 4) had changed substantially when compared with pre-intervention data. The majority had developed competencies in searching and identifying OER, identifying CC licensing, the "5Rs", creating OER and integrating OER in their teaching practices.

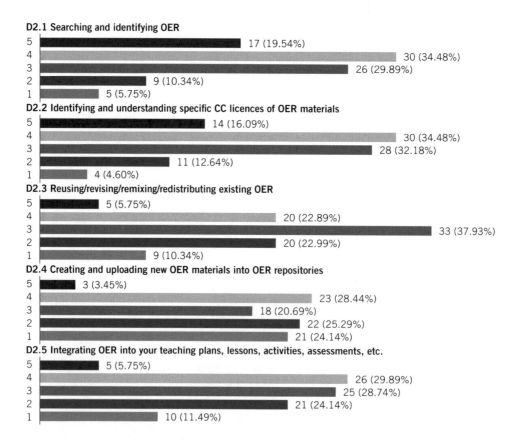

Figure 4: Types of teacher engagement with OER at mid-intervention phase (responses according to five-point Likert scale ranging from 1 "Not at all" to 5 "Extremely")

The majority of teachers (>50%) claimed they had "extremely" or to "a great extent" developed competencies in searching and identifying OER as well as identifying CC licensing. Between 30% and 35% claimed developing "extremely" or to "a great extent" competencies in the "5Rs", creating and integrating OER.

The self-reflective notes of the participants also indicated increased use of OER, despite facing several challenges in the process, such as lack of facilities, language limitations, technical issues and time constraints. The following excerpts provide a sample of participants' reflections:

> Today I found an assessment based on the lesson of "Place value of numbers".
> Actually it is a very interesting assessment and I hope children will do it freely.

> I could find the information easily using OER.

> I'm interested in OER concept. I have used some OER to my lessons.

By the end of the intervention, as indicated by the LMS records, further increased use of OER by teachers was observed. Science and technology, mathematics and information technology are the subjects where most active use was observed.

Even though the number of participants in many centres had decreased due to various challenges by the end of this stage, a majority of the participants who remained were actively engaged not only in reusing OER, but also in adaptation or revision by translating them into local languages, adapting resources to suit their contexts and even creating OER on their own. This is evident from the following excerpts from self-reflections at the post-intervention stage:

> When I use OER I modify it to local language. Some OER are [more] advanced than I expect. Thus I edit it according to my lesson.

> We were able to find interesting presentations on photosynthesis. We translated one presentation to Sinhala and used it to teach students. Sometimes we downloaded exercises and tests and made copies. Then we distributed among students.

The provision of hands-on experience during the workshops and in the utilisation of the OERTL appeared to vastly support teachers' adoption of OER. The following excerpts from self-reflections at the post-intervention stage demonstrate this:

> Workshop activities helped us to identify relevant OER and identify the nature of their licences … it helped us to gain some knowledge and practice of the "4R" concept through practical activities organised during the workshop.

> We could also access the OER site created for us … in the Moodle LMS and search for OER materials relevant to our subject areas. We could identify appropriate OER to integrate in lesson plans.

It was encouraging to see some teachers' interest grow in terms of creating their own OER in local languages, as well as in English. Exposing teachers to OER motivated them to search, select and integrate OER in lesson plans, which led to enhanced creativity and innovation in their use of instructional resources. While the teachers were highly motivated by having free access to quality educational materials which they could reuse, revise, remix and redistribute without any legal issues, they were also concerned about several challenges, as indicated in the following quotes:

> Use of OER is good opportunity for teachers to develop their teaching-learning process. But, facilities available in school is limited such as internet … If we can use computers in school this is more successful …

> It is too time-consuming a process … that searching relevant OER for integrating in the teaching process. But there are many OER …

> Because of the language problem it is difficult to integrate in the teaching-learning process. However, I'm trying to create suitable OERs in Tamil. I'll try my level best in this attempt that to create some useful resources.

Lack of adequate ICT skills was a major challenge, and many teachers required support in this area. Limited internet access and connectivity issues as well as lack of IT equipment and facilities in schools were mentioned by many teachers. Even though access to OER was free, bearing the costs of access to the internet was a challenge to individual teachers as well as schools.

Another key challenge faced by the teachers was the language issue, since OER are mostly in English. The majority of teachers were teaching in either Sinhala or Tamil, and had poor or limited English language skills.

Difficulty in finding OER for certain subjects and concerns about their quality, relevance and appropriateness in the local context were some of the other issues identified. The time needed to search and find suitable OER was a key issue due to the teachers' heavy workload. Lack of support or incentives and negative attitudes of school administration were also identified as challenges by some teachers.

Impact of OER integration on teachers' pedagogical perspectives

Teachers' initial perceptions regarding use and sharing of instructional materials were captured in the pre-intervention phase through the survey questionnaire (Table 6). Half of the participants (50.0%) believed that copyright or "ownership" of materials should be with the individual(s) who create the resource, while the next highest percentage (33%) believed it should rest with institutions. A high majority (92.2%) revealed that they share the materials they develop. A high majority (96.1%) also stated that they use learning materials developed by others.

Table 6: Teachers' perceptions regarding sharing of educational materials at pre-intervention phase

Aspect	Category	No.	Percentage
Who should copyright or "ownership" of educational materials reside with?	Individuals	115	50.0
	Institutions	76	33.0
	Publishers	29	12.6
	Not sure	30	13.0
Do you share the educational materials you develop with others?	Yes	212	92.2
	No	18	7.8
Do you use educational materials developed by others?	Yes	221	96.1
	No	9	3.9

Teachers' initial perceptions on "openness in education" were gathered via open-ended survey questions and focus group discussions, as well as through the concept-mapping exercise. As was revealed by responses to the open-ended survey questions, teachers had diverse perceptions regarding the process of freely and openly accessing educational materials developed by others, as well as providing free and open access for anyone to use the educational materials they developed. The positive and negative perceptions of the participants on these aspects (along with the reasons indicated) are presented in Table 7.

Table 7: Teachers' perceptions of the use of free and openly accessible educational materials (pre intervention)

Aspect	Associated perceptions	
	Positive	Negative
Use of freely and openly accessible educational materials, developed by others	"it will save time" "will give innovative ideas" "can get updated knowledge" "sharing knowledge"	Concerns about the "quality", "accuracy", "relevance" and "unfamiliarity of materials" "will need to modify them to suit the requirements"
Sharing educational materials developed by you (giving free and open access to any others)	"sharing is good" "it will help others" "can get feedback to improve" Feel "happy", "satisfied", "proud" and "motivated" when others use my materials	Concerns about "protecting the ownership" "how to maintain identity" "others may not realise the intended purpose of the material"

The majority of respondents were quite positive about using resources developed by others, stating that it would "save time" and provide "innovative ideas" and "updated knowledge". However, there were concerns expressed about the "quality", "accuracy", "relevance" and "unfamiliarity" of materials, as well as the need to "modify" them according to their requirements. That said, almost all participants were willing to share the materials they developed, stating that "sharing is good", "it will help others" and "can [provide] feedback to improve". While most of them felt "happy", "satisfied", "proud" and "motivated" when others used material developed by them, there were concerns about "protecting ownership" and "maintaining identity".

It was encouraging to note that even though the concept of OER was novel to the teachers, they expressed optimistic views about "openness" and its relevance to teaching and learning. Despite certain concerns about reliability, relevance and appropriateness, among others, the teachers were willing to integrate the OER concept in their teaching-learning process.

Concept mapping was used as a diagnostic tool to elicit knowledge structures and understandings of the participants, and to comprehend changes in their pedagogical perspectives. Teachers' initial pedagogical perspectives on "openness in education" were captured through qualitative analysis of the structure and content of their initial concept maps generated in the pre-intervention phase. Analysis of the knowledge structures in the concept maps indicated the occurrence of three morphological types: chains, spokes and nets (Kinchin, 2008). While the majority of morphological types were spoke structures, demonstrating limited or superficial understanding, there were some network structures, signifying a deeper understanding of the concepts. Content analysis of the concept maps revealed that even though the concept of OER was novel to the teachers, their perspectives on "sharing" and "openness" and its relevance to teaching and learning were positive and optimistic (Karunanayaka, Naidu, Kugamoorthy et al., 2015). A more detailed content analysis of these initial concept maps revealed that the majority of teachers understood the concept of openness in education as sharing of knowledge.

A majority of the teachers focused their attention on teaching-learning resources as a key concept in relation to "openness of education". While a variety of resources familiar to them (such as textbooks, video, audio, teachers' guides, research publications, laboratory instruments, electronic media, as well as many other kinds of online resources) were indicated, very few teachers mentioned OER, confirming that it is a novelty to them. Many did, however, specify factors such as availability, easy access, flexibility, cost-effectiveness, time saving, current information and information sharing as related concepts, indicating their thinking about the significance of such factors in teaching and learning.

Similarly, with regard to teaching-learning practice, teachers identified diverse associated factors, such as obtaining new information, self/independent learning, effective/innovative/creative methods, gaining attention and motivating students, as well as sharing knowledge. While acknowledging these benefits, they also identified various challenges such as lack of facilities and resources, lack of awareness, limited technical and English language skills, cost of internet connectivity, as well as concerns about the quality of materials, time spent and negative attitudes.

A detailed content analysis of the concept maps at the pre-, mid- and post-intervention stages revealed that even though the concept of OER was new to the teachers, their perspectives on "sharing" and "openness" in education and its relevance to teaching and learning were quite optimistic. Despite the fact that a majority of the initial concept maps lacked explanatory phrases and focus in the thinking (as revealed by the structural analysis) and suggested somewhat superficial knowledge on the part of participants, the perspective on sharing and openness revealed in the content analysis is indicative of an overall positive perspective on the part of the teachers.

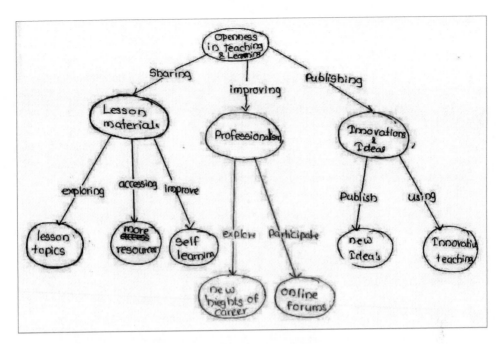

Figure 5: Pre-intervention version of a teacher's concept map

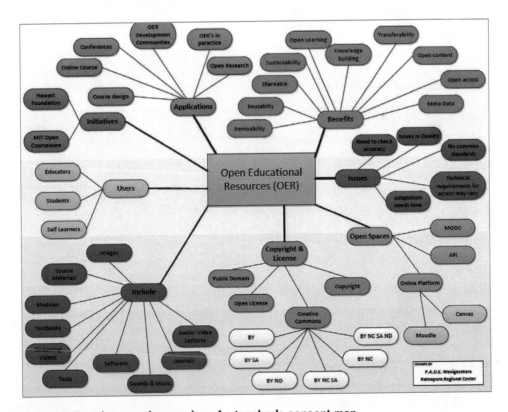

Figure 6: Post-intervention version of a teacher's concept map

Comparison of different versions of concept maps drawn by the teachers at different stages of the intervention revealed incremental developments and changes in their understandings and thinking around concepts in relation to openness in education and OER over time, as illustrated by Figures 5 and 6. For instance, at the initial stage, the concept maps were very simple and included only a few concepts and links (Figure 5), whereas the concept maps generated in the post-intervention phase were more complex, with many concepts and links depicted (Figure 6).

By the end of the intervention all participants claimed that they were prepared to face challenges and integrate the concepts of sharing and openness in their teaching and learning. The following statements from participants support this observation:

> We should update our knowledge on these concepts … and make the teaching-learning process more efficient and effective.

> As a teacher, I am eager to adapt myself towards any positive change that will reinforce my students' learning.

> Through the integration of OER … we have got the opportunity to "think out of the box" … The creation of our own OER enhanced our thinking capabilities.

These results indicated a change in the teachers' pedagogical perspectives towards more openness in education.

Impact of OER integration on teachers' pedagogical practices

Analysis of the teachers' pedagogical practices through checklist data before the intervention revealed that the majority (60%–70%) demonstrated constructive alignment between learning outcomes, activities and assessments; the use of a learner-centred pedagogic approach; opportunities for knowledge construction; a variety of learning activities; opportunities for interaction; and evidence of a sharing culture. Yet, at the same time, only a very small percentage (10%–20%) demonstrated innovative learning design and creative use of instructional resources through a variety of media types, use of technology, creation of an enjoyable learning experience, promotion of self-directed/self-regulated learning, opportunities for learner creativity, opportunities for application of knowledge, links with real-life situations, and catering to different learning styles. Further, none of the participants demonstrated use of online resources or OER. These findings affirmed the results obtained from the questionnaire survey and focus group discussions.

However, by mid intervention (as shown in Figure 4), it was evident that from an initial state of "no usage" at the pre-intervention stage, participants were gradually moving towards adopting OER through "reuse", integrating these resources in their teaching-learning methods. The gradual changes in pedagogical practice were revealed in teachers' self-reflective notes, as the following excerpts demonstrate:

> I used OER several times and one lesson plan is uploaded … Some activities are helpful to increase the efficiency of the learning process.

> I have reused OER for my lessons so far and [am] trying to remix them further.

It was observed that teachers have not only continued with searching, finding and integrating OER into their lesson plans, but also sharing them with others.

At the end of the intervention, during the evaluation workshops titled "Tell us your story: Becoming reflective practitioners" held at each of the nine OUSL centres, self-reflective narratives were written in the form of "stories" by the 85 participants who were still part of the intervention. Narrative analysis of 22 of the stories written by these teachers was conducted using thematic analysis, coding and categorisation of various aspects of the accounts (Riessman, 2005) in order to discover patterns and develop themes. These were then organised using the Rolfe et al. (2001) framework ("What?", "Now what?" and "So what?"), providing a possible causal link between ideas. This process helped to ascertain the changes that had occurred in the pedagogical thinking and practices of teachers. Specifically, it was observed that exposure to the concept of OER resulted in the development of teachers' knowledge and skills in searching, identifying and integrating OER in their teaching-learning process, and provided them with a range of new insights and some innovative practices. The identification and description of activities, self-analysis of teachers' feelings, and discussion of the effects of their actions in relation to OER integration led the teachers to consider formulating action plans for the future.

For the student teachers in this study, awareness of OER and access to a free and open pool of varied resources with legal permission to reuse, revise, remix, redistribute and retain these resources resulted in a change in their thinking and practice from traditional methods of teaching and resource use, enhancing creativity, innovative thinking and a sharing culture. There were many examples of teachers sharing OER and spreading the OER concept among their students and peer teachers through self-created booklets, handouts and awareness-raising workshops. Such changes in practices are supported by the following statements made in focus group discussions and self-reflective narratives:

> I created more than 30 OER and uploaded to [the] LMS and also searched and found more than 50 lessons to different subjects.

> We felt proud to publish a magazine on OER titled "Integrating OER in Learning Teaching Process".

> I shared my OER knowledge with my school teachers by organising a workshop.

Figure 7 shows an example of OER created by a group of participating teachers, which was shared with students and teachers at their school as well as at other schools.

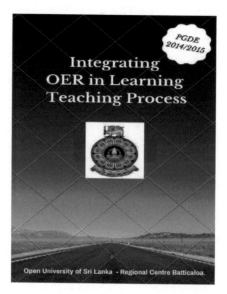

Figure 7: Example of an OER created and shared by participating teachers

These findings reveal that the teachers were challenged, encouraged and motivated to engage in the integration of OER in their future teaching-learning practice in a more productive manner.

Discussion and concluding remarks

The impact of OER integration on teachers' pedagogical practices and perspectives in this study was observed along three dimensions: their use of new or revised instructional materials, changes in their beliefs and use of new teaching approaches.

From an initial state of "no usage" or "minimal usage" of OER, participants in the study moved towards increased adoption of OER and OEP in their professional practice. Wiley's "5Rs" permissions framework associated with OER empowered teachers to move from "low" to "high" degrees of use and creation of instructional resources. Findings confirm that engagement with OER in terms of adopting the "5Rs" stimulated critical reflection among the teachers with regard to their current pedagogical practices, and also supported a shift towards a participatory and sharing culture in their practice. This included notable changes in their pedagogical practices towards a more context-centric approach. Evidence of such use, creation and management of OER via innovative pedagogical methods illustrates how the integration of OER has impacted pedagogical thinking and practices among teachers, leading to OEP.

Challenges included lack of knowledge, limited skill sets, time constraints, technical barriers and cultural obstacles. However, once introduced, teachers' appreciation and willingness to embrace OER, as well as their positive attitudes towards a sharing culture, allowed them to progressively move forward, overcoming the challenges.

This study demonstrated how a carefully structured enabling environment with strategic, systematic design of meaningful learning experiences can be used to support and facilitate the adoption of OER and OEP by teachers (see also Karunanayaka et al., 2016; Naidu & Karunanayaka, 2014; 2015). The intervention implemented during the study used several strategies to design effective, efficient, engaging learning experiences with OER integration, following tested frameworks (Ehlers, 2011; Naidu & Karunanayaka, 2014). The specific strategies of the intervention, which were designed based on situated learning principles, were constantly refined during the process based on participants' and researchers' experiences and reflections.

The process of OER integration in teaching-learning, including evaluating of its impact, was supported with the use of a design-based approach where problems were addressed by the researchers in real-world contexts in collaboration with practitioners (teachers). During this iterative process, existing design principles were integrated with technology to find possible solutions to problems related to the teaching-learning process, while researchers and practitioners engaged in reflective enquiry and defined new design principles (DBR Collective, 2003; Reeves, 2006). This process resulted in the creation of an enhanced conceptual framework in the adoption of OEP in terms of instructional resource use, pedagogical perspectives and pedagogical practices (see Karunanayaka & Naidu, 2017).

The experiences in the intervention which were based on situated learning principles included specific strategies that were designed to support teachers' move from low to high degrees of context-centric, challenging, critical, creative and collaborative thinking and practices. Altogether, these strategies contributed to changes in teachers' instructional resource use, pedagogical perspectives and pedagogical practices towards OEP.

This study has shown that careful design of OER integration is crucial for its adoption by teachers. The availability of OER helped teachers become more productive professionals. Teachers were able to engage in flexible and dynamic knowledge creation, which also provided a cost-effective way to develop and share quality teaching-learning materials.

Various inhibiting factors and challenges faced by participating teachers – similar to those identified by Hatakka (2009) and Karunanayaka and Naidu (2014) – meant that there was a decrease in the total number of active participants by the end of the intervention. However, the motivation to overcome such challenges and attempts at integrating "open" concepts in their pedagogical practices by the participants who remained active was a very prominent feature. Collaborative attempts at OER adoption, creation and sharing among teachers, with the involvement of students, was particularly noteworthy. These changes enhanced innovations in the teachers' use and creation of teaching-learning resources.

This kind of capacity-building of teachers in OER adoption has the potential to strengthen the school education system in Sri Lanka. Motivating teachers through providing further opportunities, and recognising their initiatives through incentives and appreciation, would empower teachers to act as "change agents". It would also provide insights to inform recommendations for the formulation of evidence-based guidelines to support OER adoption.

Acknowledgements

This work was carried out with the aid of a grant from the International Development Research Centre, Ottawa, Canada, through the Wawasan Open University of Penang, Malaysia. The authors wish to acknowledge the support of OUSL, contributions by the resource personnel and research assistants in the OUSL Faculty of Education and the active participation of the student teachers of the PGDE programme. Special thanks are also due to Ryhana Raheem and Cher Ping Lim, who acted as peer reviewers of this chapter.

References

Albright, P. (2005). *Internet discussion forum: Open Educational Resources, open content for higher education.* Paris: International Institute for Educational Planning & United Nations Educational, Scientific and Cultural Organization.

Allen, I. E. & Seaman, J. (2014). *Opening the curriculum: Open Education Resources in U.S. higher education, 2014.* Babson Park, MA: Babson Survey Research Group & The William and Flora Hewlett Foundation. Retrieved from http://www.onlinelearningsurvey.com/reports/openingthecurriculum2014.pdf

Allen, I. E. & Seaman, J. (2016). *Opening the textbook: Educational resources in US higher education 2015–16.* Babson Park, MA: Babson Survey Research Group. Retrieved from http://www.onlinelearningsurvey.com/reports/openingthetextbook2016.pdf

Andrade, A., Ehlers, U-D., Caine, A., Carneiro, R., Conole, G., Kairamo, A-K., Koskinen, T., Kretschmer, T., Moe-Pryce, N., Mundin, P., Nozes, J., Reinhard, R., Richter, T., Silva, G. & Holmberg, C. (2011). *Beyond OER: Shifting focus to Open Educational Practices.* Essen: Due-Publico. Retrieved from https://oerknowledgecloud.org/sites/oerknowledgecloud.org/files/OPAL2011.pdf

Barab, S. & Squire, K. (2004). Design-based research: Putting a stake in the ground. *The Journal of the Learning Sciences, 13(3)*, 1–14. Retrieved from http://www.didaktik.itn.liu.se/Texter/Barab_Squire_2004.pdf

Beetham, H., Falconer, I., McGill, L. & Littlejohn, A. (2012). *Open practices: Briefing paper.* Oxford: Jisc. Retrieved from https://oersynth.pbworks.com/w/page/51668352/OpenPracticesBriefing

Bekhet, A. K. & Zauszniewski, J. A. (2012). Methodological triangulation: An approach to understanding data. *Nurse Researcher, 20(2)*, 40–43. Retrieved from http://journals.rcni.com/doi/abs/10.7748/nr2012.11.20.2.40.c9442

Bliss, T. J., Robinson, T. J., Hilton, J. & Wiley, D. (2013). An OER COUP: College teacher and student perceptions of Open Educational Resources. *Journal of Interactive Media in Education, 2013(1)*. Retrieved from http://jime.open.ac.uk/articles/10.5334/2013-04/

Brown, J. S., Collins, A. & Duguid, P. (1989). Situated cognition and the culture of learning. *Educational Researcher, 18(1)*, 32–41. Retrieved from http://methodenpool.uni-koeln.de/situierteslernen/Situated%20Cognition%20and%20the%20Culture%20of%20Learning.htm

Browne, T., Holding, R., Howelle, A. & Rodway-Dyer, S. (2010). The challenges of OER to academic practice. *Journal of Interactive Media in Education, 2010(1)*. Retrieved from https://www-jime.open.ac.uk/articles/10.5334/2010-3/

Carey, T., Davis, A., Ferreras, S. & Porter, D. (2015). Using Open Educational Practices to support institutional strategic excellence in teaching, learning & scholarship. *Open Praxis, 7(2)*, 161–171. Retrieved from http://openpraxis.org/index.php/OpenPraxis/article/view/201

Castaño-Muñoz, J., Punie, Y., Inamorato, A., Mitic, M. & Morais, R. (2016). *How are higher education institutions dealing with openness? A survey of practices, beliefs, and strategies in five European countries.* Brussels: Publications Office of the European Commission. Retrieved from http://publications.jrc.ec.europa.eu/repository/bitstream/JRC99959/lfna27750enn.pdf

CERI/OECD (Centre for Educational Research and Innovation/Organization for Economic Cooperation and Development). (2007). *Giving knowledge for free: The emergence of Open Educational Resources.* Paris: Centre for Educational Research Innovation & Organization for Economic Co-operation and Development. Retrieved from http://www.oecd.org/edu/ceri/38654317.pdf

COL (Commonwealth of Learning). (2000). *An introduction to open and distance learning.* Burnaby: Commonwealth of Learning. Retrieved from http://oasis.col.org/bitstream/handle/11599/138/ODLIntro.pdf?sequence=1&isAllowed=y

COL (Commonwealth of Learning). (2011). *Guidelines for Open Educational Resources (OER) in higher education.* Vancouver: Commonwealth of Learning. Retrieved from http://unesdoc.unesco.org/images/0021/002136/213605e.pdf

Conole, G. (2014). The 7Cs of learning design: A new approach to rethinking design practice. In S. Bayne, C. Jones, M. de Laat, T. Ryberg & C. Sinclair (Eds.), *Proceedings of the 9th International Conference on Networked Learning* (pp. 502–509), 7–9 April 2014. Edinburgh, Scotland. Retrieved from http://www.lancaster.ac.uk/fss/organisations/netlc/past/nlc2014/abstracts/pdf/conole.pdf

Conole, G. & Ehlers, U-D. (2010). Open Educational Practices: Unleashing the power of OER. *Paper presented to UNESCO Workshop on OER, May 2010.* Windhoek, Namibia. Retrieved from https://oerknowledgecloud.org/sites/oerknowledgecloud.org/files/OEP_Unleashing-the-power-of-OER.pdf

Coughlan, T. & Perryman, L-A. (2015). Learning from the innovative open practices of three international health projects. *Open Praxis, 7(2)*, 173–189. Retrieved from http://openpraxis.org/index.php/OpenPraxis/article/view/188/152

de Hart, K., Chetty, Y. & Archer, E. (2015). Uptake of OER by staff in distance education in South Africa. *The International Review of Research in Open and Distributed Learning, 16(2)*, 18–45. Retrieved from http://www.irrodl.org/index.php/irrodl/article/view/2047

de los Arcos, B., Farrow, R., Perryman, L-A., Pitt, R. & Weller, M. (2014). *OER evidence report 2013–2014.* Milton Keynes: OER Research Hub. Retrieved from https://oerresearchhub.files.wordpress.com/2014/11/oerrh-evidence-report-2014.pdf

de los Arcos, B., Farrow, R., Pitt, R., Perryman, L-A., Weller, M. & McAndrew, P. (2015). *OER data report 2013–2015.* Milton Keynes: OER Research Hub. Retrieved from http://oerhub.net/reports/

de los Arcos, B., Farrow, R., Pitt, R., Weller, M. & McAndrew, P. (2016). Adapting the curriculum: How K-12 teachers perceive the role of Open Educational Resources. *Journal of Online Learning Research, 2(1)*, 23–40. Retrieved from http://oro.open.ac.uk/46145/

DBR (Design-Based Research) Collective. (2003). Design-based research: An emerging paradigm for educational inquiry. *Educational Researcher, 32(1)*, 5–8. Retrieved from http://www.designbasedresearch.org/reppubs/DBRC2003.pdf

Dhanarajan, G. & Porter, D. (Eds.). (2013). *Open Educational Resources: An Asian perspective.* Vancouver: Commonwealth of Learning. Retrieved from https://oerknowledgecloud.org/sites/oerknowledgecloud.org/files/pub_PS_OER_Asia_web.pdf

Dhanarajan, G. & Abeywardena, I. S. (2013). Higher education and Open Educational Resources in Asia: An overview. In G. Dhanarajan & D. Porter (Eds.), *Open Educational Resources: An Asian perspective* (pp. 3–18). Vancouver: Commonwealth of Learning. Retrieved from https://oerknowledgecloud.org/sites/oerknowledgecloud.org/files/pub_PS_OER_Asia_web.pdf

Duffy, T. M. & Jonassen, D. H. (1991). Constructivism: New implications for instructional technology? *Educational Technology, 31(5),* 7–12.

Ehlers, U-D. (2011). Extending the territory: From Open Educational Resources to Open Educational Practices. *Journal of Open, Flexible and Distance Learning, 15(2),* 1–10. Retrieved from http://www.jofdl.nz/index.php/JOFDL/article/view/64

European Commission. (2012). *Rethinking education: Investing in skills for better socio-economic outcomes.* Brussels: European Commission. Retrieved from http://eur-lex.europa.eu/procedure/EN/202132

European Commission. (2013). *"Opening up education": Innovative teaching and learning for all through new technologies and open educational resources.* Brussels: European Commission. Retrieved from http://ec.europa.eu/education/news/doc/openingcom_en.pdf

Fullan, M. (1993). *Change forces: Probing the depth of educational reform.* London: Falmer Press. Retrieved from http://files.eric.ed.gov/fulltext/ED373391.pdf

Fullan, M. (2007). *The new meaning of educational change* (4th edn.). New York, NY: Teachers College Press.

Hatakka, M. (2009). Build it and they will come?: Inhibiting factors for reuse of open content in developing countries. *The Electronic Journal on Information Systems in Developing Countries, 37(5),* 1–16. Retrieved from http://www.is.cityu.edu.hk/staff/isrobert/ejisdc/37-5.pdf

Hegarty, B. (2015). Attributes of open pedagogy: A model for using Open Educational Resources. *Educational Technology, 55(4),* 3–13. Retrieved from https://upload.wikimedia.org/wikipedia/commons/c/ca/Ed_Tech_Hegarty_2015_article_attributes_of_open_pedagogy.pdf

Hoosen, S. (2012). *Survey on government OER policies.* Paris: United Nations Educational, Scientific and Cultural Organization. Retrieved from http://www.unesco.org/fileadmin/MULTIMEDIA/HQ/CI/CI/pdf/themes/Survey_On_Government_OER_Policies.pdf

Hylén, J., Van Damme, D., Mulder, F. & D'Antoni, S. (2012). *Open Educational Resources: Analysis of responses to the OECD country questionnaire. OECD Education Working Papers, 76.* Paris: OECD Publishing. Retrieved from http://dx.doi.org/10.1787/5k990rjhvtlv-en

ISKME (Institute for the Study of Knowledge Management in Education). (2008). *Creating, doing and sustaining OER: Lessons from six Open Educational Resource projects.* Half Moon Bay, CA: Institute for the Study of Knowledge Management in Education. Retrieved from http://www.iskme.org/file?n=Lessons-From-Six-OER-Case-Studies-Creating-Doing-Sustaining-OER-Projects&id=903

Jisc. (2011). *Case studies of OER use.* Oxford: Jisc. Retrieved from http://www.webarchive.org.uk/wayback/archive/20140614115352/http://www.jisc.ac.uk/whatwedo/programmes/elearning/oer2/casestudies.aspx

Kanwar, A., Kodhandaraman, B. & Umar, A. (2010). Toward sustainable Open Education Resources: A perspective from the Global South. *The American Journal of Distance Education, 24(2),* 65–80. Retrieved from http://dx.doi.org/10.1080/08923641003696588

Karunanayaka, S. P. (2012). *Perceptions of teacher educators on the use of Open Educational Resources in teaching and learning. Research paper presented at the OUSL Annual Academic Sessions-2012, 27–28 February 2013.* Nawala, Sri Lanka. Retrieved from http://digital.lib.ou.ac.lk/docs/bitstream/701300122/551/1/OU5165_000.pdf

Karunanayaka, S. P. & Abeywardena, I. S. (2016). Advocacy, sensitization and development of OER Policy for provincial education ministries in Sri Lanka. Paper presented at the *Eighth*

Pan-Commonwealth Forum on Open Learning (PCF8), 27–30 November 2016*. Kuala Lumpur, Malaysia. Retrieved from http://oasis.col.org/handle/11599/2626

Karunanayaka, S. P., Fernando, C. & De Silva, V. (2013). Designing an online learning environment on Open Educational Resources for science education. *Asian Association of Open Universities Journal, 8(1)*, 1–11. Retrieved from http://www.emeraldinsight.com/doi/pdfplus/10.1108/AAOUJ-08-01-2013-B001

Karunanayaka, S. P. & Naidu, S. (2013). Capacity building of academic staff in the integration of ICT and OER in teacher education programs at the Open University of Sri Lanka. *Research paper presented at the Seventh Pan-Commonwealth Forum on Open Learning (PCF7), 2–6 December 2013*. Abuja, Nigeria. Retrieved from http://oasis.col.org/handle/11599/1845

Karunanayaka, S. P. & Naidu, S. (Eds.). (2014). *Integrating OER in educational practice: Practitioner stories.* Nawala: The Open University of Sri Lanka. Retrieved from http://www.ou.ac.lk/home/images/OUSL/publications/intergratingOERinEducationalPractice.pdf

Karunanayaka, S. P. & Naidu, S. (Eds.). (2016). *Dreamweaving Open Educational Practices.* Nawala: The Open University of Sri Lanka. Retrieved from http://www.ou.ac.lk/home/images/OUSL/publications/Dreamweaving%20Open%20Educational%20Practices.pdf

Karunanayaka, S. P. & Naidu, S. (2017). A design-based approach to support and nurture Open Educational Practices. *Asian Association of Open Universities Journal, 12(1)*, 1–20. Retrieved from https://doi.org/10.1108/AAOUJ-01-2017-0010

Karunanayaka, S. P., Naidu, S., Dhanapala, T. D. T. L., Gonsalkorala, L. R. & Ariyaratne, A. (2014). From mind maps to mind sets: Shifting conceptions about OER in the Faculty of Education at the Open University of Sri Lanka. *Paper presented at the 2nd Regional Symposium on Open Educational Resources: Beyond Advocacy, Research and Policy, 24–27 June 2014*. George Town, Malaysia. Retrieved from http://weko.wou.edu.my/?action=repository_action_common_download&item_id=369&item_no=1&attribute_id=15&file_no=1

Karunanayaka, S. P., Naidu, S., Kugamoorthy, S., Ariyaratne, A., Dhanapala, T. D. T .L. & Gonsalkorala, L. R. (2015). Openness in education: Teacher perspectives through concept mapping. *Research paper presented at the 29th Annual Conference of the Asian Association of Open Universities (AAOU), 30 November–2 December 2015*. Kuala Lumpur, Malaysia.

Karunanayaka, S. P., Naidu, S. & Menon, M. (2016). Transformational change at the intersections of technology, education and design at the Open University of Sri Lanka. *Paper presented at the Eighth Pan-Commonwealth Forum on Open Learning (PCF8), 27–30 November 2016*. Kuala Lumpur, Malaysia. Retrieved from http://oasis.col.org/handle/11599/2513

Karunanayaka, S. P., Naidu, S., Rajendra, J. & Ratnayake, H. (2015). From OER to OEP: Shifting practitioner perspectives and practices with innovative learning experience design. *Open Praxis, 7(4)*, 339–350. Retrieved from http://www.openpraxis.org/index.php/OpenPraxis/article/view/252

Kinchin, I. M. (2008). The qualitative analysis of concept maps: Some unforeseen consequences and emerging opportunities. *Proceedings of the Third International Conference on Concept Mapping, 22–25 September 2008*. Tallinn, Estonia & Helsinki, Finland. Retrieved from http://cmc.ihmc.us/cmc2008papers/cmc2008-p500.pdf

Lane, A. & van Dorp, C. A. (2011). Diffusion and adoption of Open Educational Resources. *eLearning Papers, 23*. Retrieved from https://oerknowledgecloud.org/sites/oerknowledgecloud.org/files/elearningpapers_2011.pdfhttp://oro.open.ac.uk/29127/1/elearningpapers_2011.pdf

Masterman, L. & Wild, L. (2011). *JISC OER impact study: Research report*. Oxford: Jisc. Retrieved from https://weblearn.ox.ac.uk/access/content/group/ca5599e6-fd26-4203-b416-

f1b96068d1cf/Research%20Project%20Reports/OER%20Projects%202011-2014/JISC%20
OER%20Impact%20Study%20Research%20Report%20v1-0.pdf

Maxwell, J. A. (2004). Causal explanation, qualitative research, and scientific inquiry in
education. *Educational Researcher, 33(3)*, 3–11. Retrieved from https://www.researchgate.
net/publication/235752514_Causal_Explanation_Qualitative_Research_and_Scientific_
Inquiry_in_Education

McAndrew, P., Santos, A., Lane, A., Godwin, S., Okada, A., Wilson, T., Connolly, T., Ferreira, G.,
Buckingham Shum, S., Bretts, J. & Webb, R. (2009). *OpenLearn Research Report 2006–
2008*. Babson Park, MA: Babson Survey Research Group & The William and Flora Hewlett
Foundation. Retrieved from http://www3.open.ac.uk/events/6/2009727_62936_o1.pdf

MoE (Ministry of Education). (2012). *The national strategic plan for the general education sector,
Education Sector Development Framework and Programme (ESDFP) – 2012–2016, Human
capital foundation for a knowledge economy: Transforming the school education system.*
Battaramulla: Policy and Planning Branch, MoE. Retrieved from http://www.moe.gov.lk/
english/images/publications/National_Strategic_Plan/National_Strategic_Plan_English.pdf

MoE (Ministry of Education). (2013). *Education First Sri Lanka*. Battaramulla: Ministry of
Education. Retrieved from http://www.moe.gov.lk/sinhala/images/publications/Education_
First_SL/Education_First_SL.pdf

Mohr, L. B. (1999). Qualitative method of impact analysis. *American Journal of
Evaluation, 20(1)*, 69–84. Retrieved from http://deepblue.lib.umich.edu/bitstream/
handle/2027.42/67113/10.1177_109821409902000106.pdf?sequence=2

Morse, J. M. (1991). *Approaches to qualitative-quantitative methodological triangulation.
Nursing Research 40(2)*, 120–123. Retrieved from https://www.researchgate.net/
publication/21153083_Approaches_to_Qualitative-Quantitative_Methodological_
Triangulation

Naidu, S. & Karunanayaka, S. P. (2014). Engines of education: Integrating OER in learning and
teaching. In S. Karunanayaka & S. Naidu (Eds.), *Integrating OER in educational practice:
Practitioner stories* (pp. 3–22). Nawala: The Open University of Sri Lanka. Retrieved from
http://www.ou.ac.lk/home/images/OUSL/publications/intergratingOERinEducationalPractice.
pdf

Naidu, S. & Karunanayaka, S. P. (2015). Impacts of OER: What difference does it make & how?
*Research paper presented at the International Conference on Distance Education (ICDE),
14–16 October 2015*. Sun City, South Africa.

Naidu, S. & Karunanayaka, S. P. (2017). Development of the Open Educational Practices Impact
Evaluation Index. Research paper presented at *OE Global 2017 Conference, 8–10 March
2017*. Cape Town, South Africa.

Naidu, S. & Mishra, S. (Eds.). (2014). *Case studies on OER-based eLearning*. Vancouver:
Commonwealth Educational Media Centre for Asia. Retrieved from http://hdl.handle.
net/11599/561

NEC (National Education Commission), Sri Lanka. (2016). *Study on curriculum development in
general education in Sri Lanka*. Nugegoda: National Education Commission. Retrieved from
http://nec.gov.lk/wp-content/uploads/2016/04/1-Final-6.pdf

Novak, J. D. & Cañas, A. J. (2008). *The theory underlying concept maps and how to construct
and use them*. Ocala, FL: Florida Institute for Human and Machine Cognition. Retrieved from
http://cmap.ihmc.us/Publications/ResearchPapers/TheoryUnderlyingConceptMaps.pdf

OECD (Organisation for Economic Co-operation and Development). (2007). *Giving knowledge for
free: The emergence of Open Educational Resources*. Paris: OECD Publishing. Retrieved from
http://dx.doi.org/10.1787/9789264032125-en

OECD (Organisation for Economic Co-operation and Development). (2012). *What is impact assessment?* Paris: Organisation for Economic Co-operation and Development. Retrieved from https://www.oecd.org/sti/inno/What-is-impact-assessment-OECDImpact.pdf

OPAL (Open Educational Quality Initiative). (2010). *OPAL OER case studies.* Retrieved from http://cloudworks.ac.uk/cloudscape/view/2085

Petrides, L., Jimes, C., Middleton-Detzner, C. & Howell, H. (2010). OER as a model for enhanced teaching and learning. In *Open Ed 2010 Proceedings, 2–4 November 2010.* Barcelona, Spain. Retrieved from http://openaccess.uoc.edu/webapps/o2/bitstream/10609/4995/6/Jimes_editat.pdf

Reeves, T. C. (2006). Design research from a technology perspective. In J. van den Akker, K. Gravemeijer, S. McKenney & N. Nieveen (Eds.), *Educational design research* (pp. 52–66). London: Routledge. Retrieved from http://www.fisme.science.uu.nl/publicaties/literatuur/EducationalDesignResearch.pdf#page=102

Reid, K., Flowers, P. & Larkin, M. (2005). Exploring lived experience: An introduction to interpretative phenomenological analysis. *The Psychologist, 18(1),* 20–23. Retrieved from http://thepsychologist.bps.org.uk/volume-18/edition-1/exploring-lived-experience

Riessman, C. K. (2005). Narrative analysis. In N. Kelly, C. Horrocks, K. Milnes, B. Roberts & D. Robinson (Eds.), *Narrative, memory & everyday life.* Huddersfield: University of Huddersfield. Retrieved from http://eprints.hud.ac.uk/4920/2/Chapter_1_-_Catherine_Kohler_Riessman.pdf

Rolfe, G., Freshwater, D. & Jasper, M. (2001). *Critical reflection in nursing and the helping professions: A user's guide.* Basingstoke: Palgrave Macmillan.

Smith, J. & Osborn, M. (2003). Interpretative phenomenological analysis. In J. A. Smith (Ed.), *Qualitative psychology: A practical guide to research methods* (pp. 51–80). London: Sage.

Smith, M. S. (2013). Open Educational Resources: Opportunities and challenges for the developing world. In M. L. Smith & K. M. A. Reilly (Eds.), *Open development: Networked innovations in international development* (pp. 129–170). Ottawa: International Development Research Centre.

Souto-Otero, M., Inamorato dos Santos, A., Shields, R., Lažetić, P., Castaño-Muñoz, J., Devaux, A., Oberheidt, S. & Punie, Y. (2016). OpenCases: Case studies on openness in education. Institute for Prospective Technological Studies, Joint Research Centre, European Commission.

UNESCO (United Nations Educational, Scientific and Cultural Organization). (2012). *2012 OER Paris Declaration.* Paris: United Nations Educational, Scientific and Cultural Organization. Retrieved from http://www.unesco.org/new/fileadmin/MULTIMEDIA/HQ/CI/CI/pdf/Events/Paris%20OER%20Declaration_01.pdf

Wang, F. & Hannafin, M. J. (2005). Design-based research and technology-enhanced learning environments. *Educational Technology Research and Development, 53(4),* 5–23. Retrieved from https://link.springer.com/article/10.1007/BF02504682

Weller, M. (2014). *The battle for open: How openness won and why it doesn't feel like victory.* London: Ubiquity Press. Retrieved from http://dx.doi.org/10.5334/bam

Weller, M., de los Arcos, B., Farrow, R., Pitt, B. & McAndrew, P. (2015). The impact of OER on teaching and learning practice. *Open Praxis, 7(4).* Retrieved from http://openpraxis.org/index.php/OpenPraxis/article/view/227

Wiley, D. & Green, C. (2012). Why openness in education? In D. G. Oblinger (Ed.), *Game changers: Education and information technologies* (pp. 81–89). Louisville, CO: Educause. Retrieved from https://net.educause.edu/ir/library/pdf/pub7203.pdf

How to cite this chapter

Karunanayaka, S. P. & Naidu, S. (2017). Impact of integrating OER in teacher education at the Open University of Sri Lanka. In C. Hodgkinson-Williams & P. B. Arinto (Eds.), *Adoption and impact of OER in the Global South* (pp. 459–498). Retrieved from https://doi.org/10.5281/zenodo.600398

Corresponding author: Shironica P. Karunanayaka <spkar@ou.ac.lk>

Chapter 14

Teacher professional learning communities: A collaborative OER adoption approach in Karnataka, India

Gurumurthy Kasinathan and Sriranjani Ranganathan

Summary

This chapter analyses collaborative Open Educational Resources (OER) adoption amongst Indian school teachers by examining the enabling and constraining techno-social, techno-pedagogical and sociocultural factors in an education context characterised by (1) low information and communication technologies (ICT) use in schools; (2) a "textbook culture" in which teachers often act as simply "content transmitters" of officially prescribed texts; and (3) diverse linguistic challenges, in which predominately English language OER may not always be relevant. The study addressed the following research question: Can a collaborative, "bottom-up" approach by teachers working together to create, adapt and share contextually appropriate resources provide a model of OER adoption?

This study adopted a mixed-methods approach – primarily through action research – in which the research team collaborated with 67 teachers and teacher educators on an OER adoption process. The team worked with the teachers between June 2013 and December 2015, utilising a combination of face-to-face workshops (19 in total), questionnaires, focus group discussions and online interactions. The participants were selected from different districts of Karnataka state, representing diverse geographic areas of the state and three subject disciplines: mathematics (26), science (18) and social science (23). The impact this collaboration had on teacher practices was compared with a Comparable group made up of 124 teachers who did not participate in the research intervention. Data analysis suggests that teachers are able to use digital methods to adopt OER and to contextualise (revise) OER to suit their needs, if given appropriate training. Their techno-social skills were advanced through greater knowledge and experience with digitally mediated collaborative OER activity. ▶

Their techno-pedagogical efficacy improved through greater networking with other colleagues and a sense of openness to having their materials adapted and revised, though teachers acknowledged that linguistic and quality challenges remained. The collaborative OER adoption approach also raised teachers' sociocultural knowledge concerning copyright and contextually relevant OER. In addition, the OER engagement processes have aided teacher professional development by building a collaborative environment with peers and introducing them to a multiplicity of educational resources.

The authors recommend that state education authorities implement a professional learning community approach to teacher professional development within in-service teacher education, implement a collaborative model for OER adoption, suggest that copyright regulations should position open licensing as the default, and implement a Free Open Source Software-based ICT programme in school education.

Acronyms and abbreviations

CCE	Continuous and Comprehensive Evaluation
COA	Collaborative OER Adoption
DIET	District Institute of Education and Training
DSERT	Directorate of School Educational, Research and Training
FOSS	Free and Open Source Software
ICT	information and communication technologies
ITfC	IT for Change
KOER	Karnataka Open Educational Resources
MHRD	Ministry of Human Resources Development
NCERT	National Council for Education Research and Training, India
OER	Open Educational Resources
PAR	participatory action research
PLC	professional learning community
RMSA	Rashtriya Madhyamika Shiksha Abhiyaan
ROER4D	Research on Open Educational Resources for Development
STF	Subject Teacher Forum
TPD	teacher professional development

Introduction

Public education in India faces a serious challenge in terms of limited curricular resources. The textbook supplied by the government through the Department of School Education for each subject is usually the sole resource at a teacher's disposal. This aligns with the approach of the education bureaucracy, which views the teacher as a "minor technician" (Scheffler, 1973) whose role is to merely transmit the content of the prescribed textbook rather than use multiple resources to explore the concept in a deeper manner with students.

Open Educational Resources (OER) can potentially enrich a learning environment of this kind. The United Nations Educational, Scientific and Cultural Organization defines OER as "teaching, learning and research materials in any medium, digital or otherwise, that reside in the public domain or have been released under an open license that permits no-cost access, use, adaptation and redistribution by others with no or limited restrictions".[1] While OER proponents may assume that the availability of free, good-quality learning materials is sufficient for OER adoption,[2] the use of open educational content in developing countries is relatively low (Hatakka, 2009). This chapter reports on an action research study on OER adoption in the public education system in the Indian state of Karnataka, which in many respects can be considered representative of the Indian national education context.

The Indian education context

India has more than 1.6 million schools, of which more than 70% are public (i.e. government) institutions (NUEPA, 2014). These government schools typically cater to children from the most marginalised sectors of Indian society as they offer free tuition as well as a range of support services, such as free textbooks, free school uniforms, lunch, bicycles and scholarships. Government schools face serious challenges in terms of the quality of education offered. The Annual Status of Education Report,[3] a nationwide study conducted by the non-governmental organisation Pratham, concludes that an unacceptably large percentage of children are unable to undertake even basic reading, writing and arithmetic. Moreover, the study also claims that around 70% of children in India do not pass Grade 10, and many of those who do, lack basic life skills and competencies.

Some reasons for the poor quality of learning in India are sociocultural. India has the largest population of illiterate adults in the world;[4] hence, many of the children who are currently attending school are first-generation schoolgoers who receive little or no support at home. Other factors impacting upon the quality of learning are pedagogical and structural, such as the limited availability of curricular resources (Kanwar, Kodhandaraman & Umar, 2010), inadequate school infrastructure and inadequate teacher professional development (TPD) (PROBE, 1998), all of which create an impoverished learning environment. When assessing the current state of Indian education, it is also important to consider the fact that universalisation of school education only received serious attention in India following the 1986 National Policy on Education.

India operates on a federal government system, with the federal (central) government functioning at the national level and provincial (state) governments operating in each of the country's 29 states. To support schools, the Indian education system has institutions established at central, state, district and block[5] levels. Education is a "concurrent subject", meaning that both central and state governments can legislate and implement education

---

1   http://www.unesco.org/new/fileadmin/MULTIMEDIA/HQ/CI/WPFD2009/English_Declaration.html
2   As discussed in the Research on Open Educational Resources for Development "Research Concepts Note", the term "adoption" is used in a comprehensive manner, and includes resource reuse, creation, revision, remixing and redistribution. The document is available at goo.gl/57tYfx.
3   http://img.asercentre.org/docs/Publications/ASER%20Reports/ASER%202014/fullaser2014mainreport_1.pdf
4   http://en.unesco.org/gem-report/allreports
5   The district is the unit of general and education administration below the state. The "block" (also known as "taluka") is the unit of education administration below the district (as per Table 1).

policy and programmes. However, in practice, the central government role is restricted to macro-policy aspects such as curricular frameworks, and actual implementation is undertaken by state governments.

Within the central government, the Ministry of Human Resources Development (MHRD) is responsible for education. The MHRD has different departments responsible for basic and higher education, which work with their corresponding departments in state governments. The state of Karnataka is the focus of this study. Its education structure is similar to other states and it has a Department of Education, which has structures/institutions at the state, district and block levels. Table 1 provides an overview of education administration and academic support structures in India.

Table 1: Overview of Indian education administration and academic support structures

Level of administration	Name of the administrative/ governing authority	Name of academic support institution	Number of institutions in India	Number in Karnataka
National	Ministry of Human Resource Development, Government of India	National Council of Educational Research and Training (NCERT)	1	N.A.
State	Department of School Education, Government of Karnataka	State Council of Educational Research and Training	29	1
District	District Education Office	District Institute of Education and Training (DIET)	Roughly 683	30
Block (taluka)	Block Education Office	Block Resource Centre	Roughly 6 000	176

Source: (NUEPA, 2015a)

Academic support institutions, such as DIET and the Block Resource Centre, are distinct from the administration institutions at each of these levels, and high levels of collaboration across institutions are required for coherent functioning. The size and complexity of the system makes coordination amongst the actors within the education system (teachers, teacher educators and education administrators) quite challenging, which has an influence on the efficiency of its overall function. Table 2 provides information on the number of schools, teachers and students in India and Karnataka in order to provide a sense of scale and the relative positioning of Karnataka in the national system.

Table 2: Number of teachers, schools and students in India and Karnataka state

	India			Karnataka state		
	Government	Private	Total	Government	Private	Total
Schools	1 180 622	498 645	1 679 267	50 934	25 780	76 714
Teachers	5 349 263	4 047 655	9 396 918	226 148	197 129	423 277
Students	135 887 920	100 080 588	235 968 508	5 065 175	5 047 563	10 112 738

Source: NUEPA (2015a; 2015b)

Linguistic diversity

The 2001 India census[6] data indicate that 13 languages are spoken by more than 10 million native speakers, 30 languages are spoken by more than a million native speakers, and 122 languages are spoken by more than 10 000 people in the country.

India is organised into states based on the language spoken and the Indian education system is also linguistically diverse. Typically, each state has one main language, spoken by the majority or at least a large percentage of its population. Invariably, many people in the border districts of any state also speak the major language of the neighbouring state. Indian education policy (Ministry of Law and Justice, 2009) requires that the state offer education with the first language of the learner as the medium of instruction. The state education system typically offers instruction in at least two languages – the official state language and English. In border areas, schools also offer the language of the neighbouring state as a medium of instruction.

In Karnataka, apart from Kannada (the state language of Karnataka) and English, government schools offer instruction in Urdu, Telugu, Tamil and Marathi languages; these are also the languages spoken in Telangana, Andhra Pradesh, Tamil Nadu and Maharashtra, respectively, which border on Karnataka state.[7] The multilingual nature of Indian society (and of the Indian education system) therefore provides a compelling context for OER adoption in multiple languages.

This chapter explores OER adoption within the Karnataka public education system in terms of techno-social, techno-pedagogical and sociocultural factors.

Techno-social factors

The term "techno" in this context refers to digital technologies, including infrastructure, devices, connectivity and software. The design and uptake of digital technologies is influenced by the social contexts in which they are utilised. At the same time, digital technologies also influence social contexts. Vespignani (2009, p.425) states: "We live in an increasingly interconnected world of techno-social systems, in which infrastructures composed of different technological layers are inter-operating within the social component that drives their use and development." The term "techno-social" in this study therefore

---

6   http://www.itu.int/en/ITU-D/Statistics/Documents/statistics/2014/ITU_Key_2005- 2014_ICT_data.xls
7   Urdu and Telugu are major languages spoken in Telangana; Telugu in Andhra Pradesh.

refers to the interrelationship between digital technologies and teachers' use thereof in OER adoption.

Reports from the International Telecommunications Union, the United Nations body responsible for global communications, reveal the poor availability of information and communication technologies (ICT) in the Global South in terms of physical access to ICT infrastructure, capacity-building for access and use, and maintenance of ICT infrastructure to enable continued access. The "Individuals Using the Internet 2005 to 2014" report[8] suggests that there is a large gap between developed and developing countries with regard to key ICT indicators. The availability of digital technologies is poor in Indian households and schools, and the lack of ICT infrastructure is a defining feature of the Indian education system (Thakur, 2014). Given the fact that OER are mostly digital in nature, poor access to ICT impacts access to OER, compromising the "free availability" feature of these resources.

Outsourced ICT implementation

The ICT@Schools programme of the government of India[9] aims to provide ICT infrastructure to all high schools in the country and has been outsourced to vendors in most states, including Karnataka. In this outsourcing model, the programme is implemented and managed by a private company which supplies the computers, sets up the labs, appoints and manages the ICT teachers, and provides the content for the ICT classes. The state of Kerala is an exception in this context, in that it chose to implement its ICT programme through the teachers in the education system.

The outsourcing model of implementation is widely regarded as a failure and state governments are open to exploring alternative models where ICT education is delivered by regular teachers. A study by the Central Institute of Educational Technology suggests that ICT use may not simply follow its provisioning. ICT integration processes therefore need to be carefully designed in order to encourage teacher use and participation (CIET, 2015).

Proprietary environment

A further limitation in developing the Indian public education system is the use of proprietary software (limited mostly to Microsoft Office applications) for generating content in the ICT@Schools programme[10] (Kasinathan, 2009b). The absence of tools for developing subject-based content has meant that creation of digital resources on the part of teachers is rare, as there is limited or no access to tools for resource creation. In response to this, India's *National Policy on Information and Communication Technology in School Education* (Department of School Education and Literacy, 2012) has recommended the establishment of a Free and Open Source (FOSS) approach and envisions that teachers will participate in the creation of digital resources.

This research investigates whether a participatory and FOSS environment where teachers collaborate in OER adoption can support teacher development and OER adoption.

---

8   http://www.itu.int/en/ITU-D/Statistics/Documents/statistics/2014/ITU_Key_2005-2014_ICT_data.xls
9   http://ictschools.gov.in/Policy/national-policy-ict-school-education-2012
10 The exception being the ICT@Schools scheme in Kerala, where the programme was implemented using open source software and applications.

Techno-pedagogical factors

"Techno-pedagogy" in this context refers to the integration of digital methods in educational processes. Mishra and Koehler (2006) suggest that knowledge of digital technologies influences and is influenced by teaching processes. The interaction between digital technologies and pedagogical processes can be termed as "techno-pedagogical". This study is concerned with two aspects – the availability and use of curricular resources in teaching, and teachers' networking for professional development. OER is digital by nature; increased techno-pedagogical knowledge may therefore have the potential to influence OER adoption in the Indian education system.

Curricular resources and OER

Content and process (curriculum and pedagogy) are generally acknowledged as the two intertwined components of learning. Eisner (1991, p.11) states: "Like the systole and diastole of the beating heart, curriculum and teaching are the most fundamental aspects … No curriculum teaches itself, it always must be mediated, and teaching is the fundamental mediator." India does, however, have what has been termed a "textbook culture" (Kumar, 1988), in that the textbook is seen as the single, definitive resource for teaching. There is therefore little focus on the use of other teaching materials and the interplay this usage may have with more advanced, effective pedagogy. In his "Origins of India's 'textbook culture'", Kumar (1988, p.452) writes:

> The second type of education system ties the teacher to the prescribed textbook. She is given no choice in the organization of curriculum, pacing, and the mode of final assessment. Textbooks are prescribed for each subject, and the teacher is expected to elucidate the text, lesson by lesson in the given order. She must ensure that children are able to write answers to questions based on any lesson in the textbook without seeing the text, for this is what they will have to do in the examination when they face one. The Indian education system is of the second type.

The textbook culture emphasises the state-published textbook as the vehicle of education, thereby "serving as a means through which the bureaucratic authority exercises its influence; it becomes the symbolic hub of the power structure that governs the teacher's daily routine" (Kumar, 1988, p.453).

The Education Department in most states supplies textbooks for all subjects free of cost to all teachers and students in government schools. This emphasis on the textbook is reinforced by the limited availability of alternative resources. Consequently, many teachers only use the textbook in their teaching. This practice informs teachers' perceptions of their role as that of being a "minor technician" (Scheffler, 1973), meaning that they merely utilise the resources and approaches made available through government channels. Scheffler (1973, p.61) writes:

> The transmission model of education coupled with the drive for increased efficiency tends to foster the view of the teacher as a minor technician within

an industrial process. The overall goals are set in advance in terms of national needs, the curricular materials pre-packaged by the disciplinary experts, the methods developed by the educational engineers, and the teachers job is just to supervise the last operational stage – the methodical insertion of pre-ordered facts into the students mind.

The "content transmitter" perspective can influence teachers in limiting their engagement with additional or alternative curricular resources and teaching methods.

Another compounding factor in addressing curriculum development is the fact that the same textbook is provided for each subject and class to all schools across the state,[11] a situation which fails to address the diverse learning needs of students. In recognition of this challenge, the National Curriculum Framework 2005 document of NCERT has emphasised the role of technology-mediated teacher development and resource-creation processes in contributing to an inclusive and contextually appropriate learning resource environment. These collaborative processes of teacher resource creation have the potential to support teachers to collectively resist the notion of the "minor technician".

Teacher networking for professional development

In India, the provision of a school within or close to every habitation is a policy requirement. The Sarva Shikshana Abhiyaan (MHRD, 2008) (or "universal education") programme of the central government, adopted by all provincial governments, requires that lower primary education facilities (grades 1–5) and upper primary schools (grades 6–8) be located within 1km and 3km of every habitation, respectively. This has resulted in the public school system being vast and dispersed. Teachers therefore seldom have contact with their peers in other schools or with other educational institutions.

It has been recommended that spaces for sharing teaching experiences be recognised as an important principle of in-service teacher education (NCFTE, 2010). There is therefore a need to study how a technology-enabled professional learning community (PLC) where teachers network virtually can support OER adoption and teacher development by reducing teacher isolation and enabling peer learning. In other words, there is a need to understand in what ways collaborative, "bottom-up" approaches by teachers working together to adopt resources can provide an effective OER adoption model, and whether such collaboration can influence TPD and teaching practices.

Sociocultural factors

The "global" OER movement is located predominantly in the geopolitical North and most OER programmes as well as OER portals for accessing resources are located in Northern institutions. Given that educational systems in the North may be more advanced in terms of institutional maturity, as well as in their methods and processes of curricular resource design and development, their resources may *prima facie* appear superior. Wholesale ("as is")

---

11 The same textbook is provided in the medium of instruction of each particular state, however many languages that may be. For instance, in Karnataka, the mathematics textbook for a class is produced in the six languages which serve as medium of instruction in different schools in the state. This does not apply to the language subject textbooks, such as English or Hindi or Kannada.

adoption of these resources can, however, pose a risk in terms of ignoring local learning contexts, strategies and abilities of learners. OER adoption of this kind also stands to further strengthen the hegemony of the North in the global educational sphere by expanding the diffusion and reach of Northern resources. If OER is to be explored as a key mechanism for addressing education needs, it is important to understand whether and how OER models that are developed within the Global South can more effectively address learners' needs in contextually appropriate ways. Given its linguistic and cultural diversity, this issue of inadequate contextually appropriate resources is of particular relevance in India.

Local language and culture

In India, most OER are developed and available in the English language, with a far smaller percentage available in the local languages of the learners. For instance, when considering Wikipedia, the most popular OER site in the world,[12] Kannada Wikipedia has around 20 000 pages – in contrast to over five million pages in English.[13] This is one example of the paucity of OER in Indian languages, relative to English.

Albright (2005, p.12) states:

> OER are cultural as much as educational, in that they give users "an insight into culture-specific methods and approaches to teaching and learning" – a practical exposure to the way that courses are "done" in another country or by another instructor. Language is clearly intertwined with culture in this dynamic. The vast majority of Open Educational Resources are in English, which is spoken by perhaps 10 per cent of the world's 6.3 billion people. Not only does the English language dominate OER provision, but English-language content tends to be based on Western learning theory. This limits the relevance and accessibility of OER materials in non-English, non-Western settings. There is a risk that language barriers and cultural differences could consign less developed countries to the role of OER consumers rather than contributors to the expansion of knowledge.

There is therefore a need to study how bottom-up OER adoption processes with teachers can aid the design and development of more culturally relevant OER in local languages. It is also important that techno-social, techno-pedagogical and sociocultural factors are not viewed in isolation, and there needs to be an acknowledgement that there may be areas of overlap between them. For instance, teacher networking can be viewed as a component of techno-pedagogical factors (in the context of peer learning) or as sociocultural factors (impacting upon teacher isolation).

Therefore, the current techno-social (limited capacities of teachers to work with ICT and lack of a FOSS environment), techno-pedagogical (textbook culture and teacher isolation) and sociocultural (lack of OER meeting local needs in local languages)[14] realities in Indian education may not be conducive to the adoption of OER in the Indian public education

---

12   https://en.wikipedia.org/wiki/List_of_most_popular_websites
13   https://en.wikipedia.org/wiki/List_of_Wikipedias
14   It should be noted that there would be many more elements within these three factors; those identified are based on the perception of the research team of their importance in the study context.

system. It was therefore deemed necessary to implement and study a programme focused on teacher capacity-building that enables teacher collaboration with regard to OER adoption.

Background to the research

The Subject Teacher Forum (STF) is an in-service TPD initiative designed and implemented by the Directorate of School Educational Research and Training[15] (DSERT) under the Rashtriya Madhyamika Shiksha Abhiyaan[16] (RMSA) scheme with support from the United Nations Children's Fund in collaboration with IT for Change (ITfC), the organisational host of this research study.

The STF was initiated in June 2011, with TPD as its primary objective. Utilising a technology-enabled PLC approach, it aims to enable teachers to utilise ICT to support professional networking and peer learning. Besides training teachers in digital methods, the STF creates subject-oriented PLCs where teachers interact with one another on mailing lists to share materials, ideas and experiences. The PLCs comprise around 12 800 mathematics, science and social science teachers from government high schools across Karnataka state.

During the STF programme implementation, the paucity of high school mathematics, science and social science contextual materials that can supplement government textbooks was noted by the teachers as well as DSERT and RMSA. There was a particularly acute need expressed by the teachers in view of the revision to the textbooks for grades 8, 9 and 10 that was carried out by DSERT during this period. Responding to this need, DSERT began the Karnataka Open Educational Resources (KOER) project in July 2013 in partnership with ITfC for a chosen subset of teachers: 67 mathematics, science and social science teachers and teacher educators who were part of the STF PLC.

The aim of the KOER project was to support these 67 teachers to collaboratively create and adopt OER to develop supplementary digital resources for the recently revised textbooks. This was implemented in a context where curricular resource development had traditionally been centralised and digital content development was outsourced. The bottom-up approach to resource creation in this project was therefore an important departure from the traditional approach.

The aim of this research was to understand in what ways such collaborative, "bottom-up" approaches by teachers working together to adopt resources can provide an effective OER adoption model and whether such collaboration influences TPD. Utilising an action research approach, ITfC worked with these 67 teachers, referred to as the Collaborative OER Adoption (COA) group, training them in digital literacy and collaborative OER adoption. It designed and conducted workshops for the COA group of teachers during the 2013/14, 2014/15 and 2015/16 academic years.[17] The research explored collaborative OER adoption by examining the enabling and constraining techno-social, techno-pedagogical and sociocultural factors to address the following research question: Can a collaborative, "bottom-up" approach by teachers working together to create, adapt and share contextually appropriate resources provide a model of OER adoption?

---

15   DSERT is part of the Education Department of the government of Karnataka (see http://DSERT.Kar.nic.in).
16   RMSA is a nationwide programme run by the government of India to support secondary education.
17   The school academic year in Karnataka begins in June and ends in March of the following year.

IT for Change

Established in 2000, ITfC has worked consistently for the innovative and effective use of ICT to promote socioeconomic change in the Global South. Intervening at the levels of both discourse and implementation, ITfC has contested dominant information society theories from the perspective of equity and social justice. It engages in research, advocacy and fieldwork in the thematic areas of development and information society, community informatics, technology governance, gender, governance and education. In the course of this work, ITfC has partnered with many regional, national and international institutions, as well as activist groups and academics.

Education is an important domain for ITfC. The organisation conducts research on its own and other programmes on integrating ICT in education and has participated in action research as well as demonstration field projects.[18] It also participates in curriculum design programmes and policy-related committees at national and state levels. The aim of ITfC is to study and build models of teacher development through integration of digital technologies, and to support government school systems to adapt the same through policy advocacy and programmatic support. The ITfC researchers in this study were visiting faculty at the Tata Institute of Social Sciences for the ICT and Education course and similar courses in other pre-service teacher education programmes.

Literature review

OER are considered to have substantial economic benefit in terms of reducing the cost of accessing learning materials (Lane, 2008) and allowing for the distribution of materials at minimal cost to the user (Wiley, Green & Soares, 2012). By opening access to freely available, globally created resources, and enabling the revision and reuse of these materials through open licensing mechanisms, OER are also seen as having the potential to address existing quality gaps (Camilleri, Ehlers & Pawlowski, 2014). The adoption of OER and their potential to expand access to and improve the quality of education is one of the key emerging issues in educational discourse today, particularly as it relates to developing countries where there is a dearth of quality learning materials (Kanwar et al., 2010). While OER offer great potential in terms of addressing quality and access issues in education, "the real challenges facing readiness to adopt OER appear to be related to socio-economic, cultural, institutional and national issues" (Ngimwa & Wilson, 2012, p.398).

These challenges need to be studied and addressed in order to enable OER adoption, particularly as there is currently a gap in reliable evidence arising from on-the-ground experiences to support the claims that OER can help countries in the Global South to address quality and cost challenges (Daniel & Uvalić-Trumbić, 2012). Hatakka (2009, p.1) comments that: "OER initiatives are very commendable and needed ... open content is not being used by educational organizations in developing countries (or rather the usage of the free resources is low)."

As the actual adoption and use of available OER by institutions in the South appears to be limited, this study seeks to understand the factors that influence the adoption of OER

---

18   http://itforchange.net/education

in the Indian context. It investigates the influence of collaborative resource creation and sharing processes on the techno-social, techno-pedagogical and sociocultural factors of the Karnataka public school education. The literature review is organised according to these three factors.

Techno-social factors

The literature review of techno-social factors presented here is focused on three central factors. Firstly, that OER are almost always digital in nature, and that teachers therefore need to acquire digital literacy skills in order to adopt OER. Secondly, proprietary technology environments can influence the capacity of teachers to create and share OER. Thirdly, participatory models can elicit greater ownership on the part of the teachers compared to outsourced models of implementing ICT programmes in schools.

Information is increasingly being created, stored and transferred in digital formats. In 2000, 75% of stored information was in analogue format (such as video cassettes); by 2007, 94% of it was digital.[19] Digital tools and resources are easy to share, but proprietisation (or digital rights management) imposes legal and technological barriers to sharing.

A study by Kasinathan (2009b) comparing the outsourcing model implemented in Karnataka with the integrated model of Kerala suggests that the outsourcing approach bypasses regular teachers, creates dependence on technology vendors to provide basic ICT literacy to students, and has led to poor ICT uptake. This outsourcing model is based on the perceived inability or unwillingness of teachers to learn to use ICTs and integrate them into their teaching. With content being developed independently without any reference to the school curriculum, teachers have largely seen ICT as irrelevant and the ICT infrastructure provided by the ICT@Schools programme is often grossly underutilised (Kasinathan, 2009b).

Users do not own proprietary digital tools, even when we "pay" for them, as we only obtain a licence for their use. Barriers to revision and redistribution of these digital artefacts are high in the case of developing countries, as the cost of the required software can be expensive in large-scale adoption in public education systems (Kasinathan, 2009b).

Techno-pedagogical factors

It has been argued that the quality of teaching practices and the quality of learning outcomes can be improved by opening up OER adoption processes for formal peer review or informal interrogation through conversations with colleagues (Petrides, Jimes, Middleton-Detzner & Howell, 2010).

In a South African study, Sapire and Reed (2011) explored whether collaborative design and redesign of materials can enhance quality while containing time and resource costs, and whether such collaboration encourages buy-in to the use of OER as well as further redesign to accommodate the needs of particular teachers and students. They concluded that "collaborative redesigning of existing materials from a range of institutions offers one solution to these challenges" (2011, p.209).

---

19 http://www.bbc.co.uk/news/technology-12419672

Paul Stacey (2013) suggests that foundation grants typically focus on establishing exemplars and cannot be relied on for sustaining ongoing operations or generating widespread adoption. Since learning materials tend to be largely financed by public expenditure (Hylén, Van Damme, Mulder & D'Antoni, 2012), it is worthwhile investigating whether collaborative resource creation can be supported by public funding to support OER development as an ongoing model of TPD within the public teacher-education system.

In a survey of 196 elementary and secondary education teachers, Rothberg (1985) found that "over 80% of teachers felt their classrooms were private worlds entered only by themselves and their students", a finding which supports previous research on teacher isolation. Teachers in this study reported that formal and informal visits to their classrooms by observers or evaluators were rare, as were their own visits to the classrooms of other teachers. There is thus a need to investigate whether virtual networks can reduce teacher isolation in the Indian education context.

Sociocultural factors

"Meaning in context: is there any other kind?" asked Mishler (1979). Ferreira (2008, p.4) states:

> ... it is yet unclear what types of learning OER may afford outside their original context. Different aspects of academic practice are inscribed in the resources being made available by OER initiatives ... This is critical for the OER movement because re-use (by teachers and learners alike) requires a double move of de-contextualization and subsequent re-contextualization under circumstances often quite distinct from the original location of the resources.

Hence, it appears naive to assume that OER can seamlessly be adopted across cultures and contexts. Translation of materials created into another language will make these materials accessible to those who speak the languages into which the materials are translated. Mere translation may, however, be inadequate, as there is often a need to recontextualise materials. As previously stated, context-appropriate education is a particular challenge in a large and diverse country such as India.

Methodology

This research adopts a mixed-methods approach (Creswell, 2014), in which lead researcher Gurumurthy Kasinathan and researcher Sriranjani Ranganathan along with other members of the ITfC research team collaborated with 67 teachers and teacher educators on an OER adoption process. The ITfC team worked with the COA teachers between June 2013 and

December 2015, utilising a combination of face-to-face workshops,[20] questionnaires, focus group discussions and online interactions.

An action research approach was considered most suitable for the study as the research team wanted to work with a group of teachers on a capacity-building programme for collaborative OER adoption while simultaneously investigating how this programme would influence specific techno-social, techno-pedagogical and sociocultural factors relating to OER adoption in the Karnataka public education system. As stated by Gilmore, Krantz and Ramirez (1986, p.161):

> Action research aims to contribute both to the practical concerns of people in an immediate problematic situation and to further the goals of Social Science simultaneously. Thus, there is a dual commitment in action research to study a system and concurrently to collaborate with members of the system in changing it in what is together regarded as a desirable direction. Accomplishing this twin goal requires the active collaboration of researcher and client, and thus it stresses the importance of co-learning as a primary aspect of the research process.

The project involved both programmatic processes (teacher capacity-building on OER adoption) and research (studying how the collaborative OER adoption processes would influence certain aspects of teachers' practices), reflecting a dual commitment to study the system as well as collaborate with teachers to transform it in terms of OER adoption.

Participant selection

The action research process adopted a criterion sampling approach (Palys, 2008) to select participants from the STF to constitute the COA group. The COA group comprised teachers in government high schools and were selected by the DIETs based on the following criteria stipulated by DSERT:

1. Participation in the PLC.
2. Subject expertise.
3. Basic familiarity with use of digital technologies.

A total of 62 teachers and five teacher-educators were selected from different districts of Karnataka, representing diverse geographic areas of the state. The 67 teachers and teacher-educators represented three subject disciplines: mathematics (26), science (18) and social science (23).

In order to determine the influence of COA processes on teachers' adoption of OER, there should ideally have been baseline data on the COA teachers prior to their participation in the teacher education programme. There was, however, a challenge in this regard: while the research process started in January 2014, the COA processes in the KOER project had

---

20 These workshops took place in the period between July 2013 and August 2015. A total of 19 workshops were held separately for mathematics, science and social science teachers in order to tailor the creation of resources by discipline.

commenced in July 2013. It was therefore not possible to conduct baseline research on the COA cohort of teachers.

In order to be able to understand the effectiveness of the COA processes, a cohort of 124 teachers, similar to the COA group but who had not been part of the STF programme, were identified as a Comparable group. The COA group and the Comparable group were thus mutually exclusive groups at the time of the study. Since the STF teacher training programme of the DSERT was ongoing during the research time frame, it was expected that the Comparable group teachers would eventually receive this training and be introduced to digital tools and methods. Hence, they have not been conceived of as a "control" group.

The selection of the teachers for the Comparable group was based on the following factors:

1. The Comparable group (like the COA teachers group) was comprised of government high school teachers from Karnataka state. The recruitment of teachers for government schools is centralised, which means that teachers from both groups have identical prerequisites for recruitment and identical processes in terms of job description, promotion, transfer, retirement, pay revision, etc. Thus, the employment contexts of both groups of teachers are identical.

2. COA teachers are from districts across the state, with rural and urban backgrounds. For the Comparable group of teachers, two districts which represented two extremes in the state (the Bengaluru Urban district and the Yadgir district) were selected. The Bengaluru Urban district is located in southern Karnataka and is predominantly urban (it includes the city of Bengaluru, the capital city of the Karnataka state), while the Yadgir district is in northern Karnataka and predominantly rural.

3. Socioeconomically, the Bengaluru Urban district is advanced, while the Yadgir district faces development challenges. The Human Development Index report of 2011[21] places Bengaluru Urban in first place in terms of development levels, while the Gulbarga district (which the Yadgir district was a part of at that time) is 29th out of 30 districts. The Raichur district, which neighbours Yadgir, is last on the list. Both districts belong to the North-east Karnataka region, which the Human Development Report identifies as the most underdeveloped region in the state. It was anticipated that selecting the Bengaluru and Yadgir districts as the location for the Comparable group of teachers would provide representation in terms of the teacher contexts across the state.

Based on these factors, it is assumed that the Comparable group of teachers could serve as the "quasi-control" group in order to provide an approximate "baseline" against which the influence of the COA processes on the COA group could be assessed. Figure 1 provides a graphical representation of the actors who participated in this study.

---

21 http://www.thehindu.com/todays-paper/karnataka-ranks-seventh-in-human-development-index/article3034473.ece

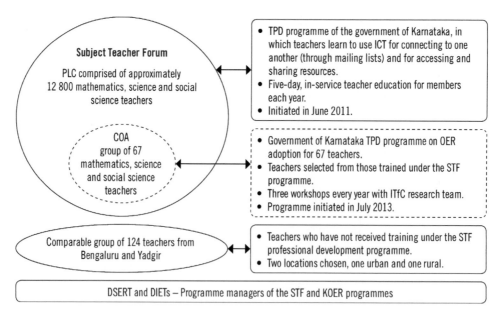

Figure 1: Graphic representation of actors and participant cohorts in the study

Parallel cycles of training and action research

The action research approach was comprised of two parts: the programmatic component of training teachers in the tools and methods required for OER adoption, and the research component studying OER adoption.

The cycles of action (STF workshops and mailing-list interactions) and reflection (individual and collective reflections of the 67 COA teachers and ITfC research team) constituting the action research process continued in an iterative manner over the two-year period of the study (January 2014–December 2015).

Programmatic teacher training component

In the programmatic component, COA teachers were trained by the ITfC team on accessing, creating and sharing OER in 19 separate workshops. Thereafter, they shared these resources via the mailing lists and uploaded resources to the KOER English and Kannada websites[22] under Creative Commons Attribution-NonCommercial-ShareAlike (CC BY-NC-SA) licences. In these workshops, COA teachers created OER in the language of their choice (some in English, some in Kannada and others in both languages) and uploaded them to the KOER websites.

The COA programme workshops were conducted in computer labs with a 1:1 teacher to computer ratio, with reasonably good internet connectivity. Some teachers also brought their personal laptops to the workshops. Subsequent to the workshops, COA teachers remained in touch with one another and the research team via mailing lists in order to

---

22 See http://karnatakaeducation.org.in/KOER/en/index.php and http://karnatakaeducation.org.in/KOER for the English and Kannada websites, respectively.

continue their OER adoption practice and participate in discussions on different issues of academic interest.

Resource materials were also shared on the KOER websites for participant access; print versions were usually not given to the participants (whereas in typical teacher training workshops, each participant would be handed a print copy of the training module at the start of training). Workshop feedback was also compiled digitally and shared with DSERT. This emphasis on the use of the digital for the design, implementation and reporting of the training programme made the systemic availability of ICT a prerequisite, thus altering the way teacher education was imagined. The programme required the maintenance of digital infrastructure in the ICT labs, which was taken care of by the DIETs, thus institutionalising technology integration at district level.

The COA teachers were trained in a variety of FOSS applications and platforms in the workshops and the agenda had a conscious emphasis on FOSS, both in terms of the theoretical implications (philosophical, pedagogical, technological and economic aspects) and practice (learning to work with FOSS applications). The use of FOSS was embedded within the COA processes based on the idea that if resources are to be adopted freely, the tools for adopting the resources should also be freely accessible.

The research team prepared a custom distribution of the Ubuntu operating system called "*Kalpavriksha*", into which more than 3 000 free and FOSS packages, including the educational software applications taught to COA teachers, were bundled. COA teachers had to pay a nominal amount (less than USD 2) for a copy of this custom installation, the amount collected was used to cover the cost of producing the DVD. The intention was to help COA teachers discriminate between the use of the word "free" as in "freedom" (to copy and reuse) rather than "gratis" (free of cost). COA teachers purchased the DVD willingly and some reported that they had redistributed it to their colleagues outside of the COA group. The custom distribution reduced installation time and effort, since all software applications bundled into the custom distribution were installed automatically along with the Ubuntu operating system. Proprietary operating systems will not allow such "free sharing" or "bundling". Appendix 1[23] provides a brief description of the FOSS tools that teachers were introduced to in the COA workshops.

This emphasis on the use of FOSS tools and processes enabled movement from the commonly used PowerPoint presentations to many other options. In a case study carried out on the STF-KOER as part of a Wawasan Open University project, Sharma (2016, p.65) states:

> The exposure to the free and open source software applications has introduced teachers to a variety of resource formats, enabling their movement from the common "power point presentations" to mind maps (using Freemind), interactive simulations (using Geogebra), text and presentations (using Libre Office), web links and video files (using RecordmyDesktop). They are also seeking and exploring multiple tools that can work on different devices and looking for convergent solutions - mobile upload of a solution to a solved problem (solved by hand), sharing recordings of broadcasts by teachers,

---

23   http://dx.doi.org/10.5281/zenodo.1036253

looking for mathematical teaching learning software for the smart phone, exploring Unicode font converters for local language typing or upgrading Geogebra from its 2D version to a 3D one.

In the typical, constrained environment of proprietary software (usually packaged with a personal computer with the Microsoft Windows operating system, Microsoft Office suite, internet Explorer/Edge and Adobe Acrobat PDF reader), the user is typically forced to limit his or her imagination to the functionalities of these applications ("What is it that I can do with the tools I have?"). In a FOSS environment, teachers often approach the issue from the perspective of "What do I want to do, and what tool will I need for this task?" They then search for the tool either in the Ubuntu software centre repository on their desktop or on the internet.

Research component: Data collection and analysis

As part of the research process, the COA teachers individually and collectively reflected on the COA processes in the workshops by responding to structured questionnaires, participating in focus group discussions and interacting via emails. While implementation and research processes were being undertaken with the COA group, these teachers were also interacting with the STF PLCs to share OER. Hence, a sample of the mailing interactions on the PLC mailing lists as well as the OER content published on the KOER websites was analysed by the research team. As a part of the research, key informant interviews were conducted with five officials from the Education Department to understand their perspectives on COA. Table 3 provides an overview of research tools used, objects of analysis and the focus of the various data collection activities.

Table 3: Overview of research tools, object of analysis and focus of data collection activity

Tools	Object of analysis	Focus of data collection activity
1. Structured questionnaire	67 COA teachers and 124 Comparable group teachers	Information about ICT use, resource adoption practices and teacher development processes
2. Focus group discussions	67 COA teachers in 10 focus group discussions	Sharing beliefs and perspectives on resources and key concepts (OER, KOER, TPD, PLC, etc.)
3. Mailing-list interactions	Emails sent to COA teachers on the PLC mailing lists	Reuse, creation, revision, remixing and redistribution of resources by teachers in PLC mailing lists
4. KOER content analysis	Select content reuse, creation, revision, remixing and redistribution by COA teachers	Creation, adaptation and sharing of resources by COA teachers on the KOER portal
5. Key informant interviews	COA teachers, teacher educators and senior department officials	Factors enabling and constraining the development of an OER model based on COA

Structured questionnaire

To assess the influence of COA processes on OER adoption and TPD, a structured questionnaire was designed and administered to COA teachers as well as the Comparable group. The questions covered different dimensions, such as demographic and professional profiles, technology habits and teachers' use of digital resources for teaching and their own learning. The demographic and professional profile component included questions on age, sex, educational qualifications and work experience.

The component on use of digital methods included questions on the following:

- Use of computers and the internet.
- Use of ICT for learning and for teaching.
- Creation, sharing, accessing and adapting learning materials in their work.
- Participation in teacher communities and forums for peer learning and sharing.

The questions on demographic profile were designed to establish if the COA and Comparable groups were similar in their basic profile and employment contexts (using statistical tests of significance). If the profiles of the two groups were found to be statistically similar based on responses to the questionnaires by the two groups, it would be possible to make inferences about the impact of COA processes on the digital habits, professional development (including adoption of OER), as well as participation in teacher communities of the COA group of teachers.

Interviewees' oral consent was obtained for the research as the culture of making interviewees sign written consent forms is not prevalent in India and individuals are usually wary of such procedures. The aims and processes of the study were discussed openly with the COA teachers in the workshops so that they were familiar with these principles before they participated in the survey and focus group discussions.

Printed versions of the structured questionnaire were provided to participants. It was administered amongst the 67 COA teachers in July 2014, and amongst the 124 Comparable group teachers in July 2014 (Bangalore Urban) and in September 2014 (Yadgir). Nineteen responses from the Comparable group were not useable; hence the number of responses considered for this group was 105. The Comparable group responses to the questionnaire serve as a proxy baseline for the project.

Responses to closed-ended questions were tabulated in a spreadsheet using the LibreOffice Calc software application. These responses were analysed using the pivot feature, which enables multivariate analysis. The information in the multivariate tables was subjected to chi-square and two-sample z-test statistical tests of significance utilising LibreOffice Calc. Chi-square tests were used when data included a distribution with two dichotomous variables, such as subject taught by teacher who was a member of the COA or Comparable group. In other cases, where the categorical variable was not dichotomous (e.g. work experience of teachers), the two-sample z-test was used. The sample size of the COA and Comparable groups for the structured questionnaire was 67 and 105 teachers, respectively. As the sample size comprised more than 30 respondents, sample variances were used as a substitute for population variances, based on the assumption that in a large sample the variances in sample and population will be similar. The z-test was selected because the sample size was larger than 30 respondents.

Focus group discussions

While the structured questionnaire attempted to identify changes in teachers' ICT habits and COA practices, 10 focus group discussions were conducted to capture teachers' experiences and expectations of the COA initiative as well as their perspectives on TPD. The focus group discussions were also used to explore the connection between the STF and COA processes. The discussions were conducted with COA teachers in periodic workshops[24] during the 2013/14, 2014/15 and 2015/16 academic years.

The first focus group discussion covered ideas for designing the collaborative KOER websites. The subsequent focus group discussions covered the following topics:

- COA teachers' experiences of COA processes and review of the collaboratively created resources.
- COA teachers' expectations of the resource repository and methods of integrating COA with the PLC.
- COA teachers' perspectives on the role of resources and COA processes on TPD.

The key ideas discussed in the focus groups are provided in Appendix 2.[25]

Focus group discussions were documented as a mind map utilising the Freemind[26] free software application. The mind map was projected during the discussions so that participants could see the points being recorded as they were discussed. These mind maps were later shared for review. Discussions were audio-recorded to support the analysis process. The record of the discussions (the mind map and audio recordings) was analysed by the research team and grouped on the basis of pre-identified themes for discussion.

Mailing-list interactions

The PLC was an important forum accessed and referred to by the COA teachers for understanding teachers' resource needs. Many COA teachers also shared their resources and experiences with the PLCs for reuse by and feedback from PLC teachers. A sample of PLC emails from the mathematics and science mailing lists, sent by the COA teachers,[27] was analysed to understand teachers' resource habits and requirements. Both mailing lists were public; members of the lists were aware that their mails could be accessed by anyone and that members of the ITfC research team were members of the lists.

The data analysis of the emails had two components: analysis of email headers (comprising select data elements such as sender, receiver, date–time, subject line, attachment status, word count and thread) for all emails on the mailing lists; a second detailed analysis of the emails was done for the three months of August 2014, February 2015 and August 2015.

In order to conduct the analysis of email headers, all emails in the mathematics–science and social science mailing lists were downloaded from the mailing lists (Google groups) into the Thunderbird free software email client. Using shell scripts and Thunderbird filter features, the emails sent by COA teachers were made available separately in defined folders so as to enable easy access and analysis. Once the data relating to headers were captured

---

24 The workshops were held separately for mathematics, science and social science teachers in order to focus on subject-specific dynamics of resource creation.
25 http://dx.doi.org/10.5281/zenodo.1036253
26 http://freemind.sourceforge.net/wiki/index.php/Main_Page
27 The mailing list for the mathematics and science teachers was mathssciencestf@googlegroups.com.

in a spreadsheet, these were analysed using LibreOffice Calc in order to obtain summary statistics on total emails sent in a month (across all months), number of mails sent by each teacher and number of mail threads.

In order to conduct the detailed mail analysis, mails of the mathematics–science sub-cohort of COA teachers sent in three selected months (August 2014, February 2015 and August 2015) were analysed. The selection of these months was based on the academic cycle – August being a "high transaction" month (after schools have opened for the academic year in June), and February being a "low transaction" month (as teachers are preoccupied with preparation for the examinations, which are usually held in March). Since the volume of the emails was very high, this analysis was not done for the social science mailing list. The following parameters were chosen for the analysis of emails:

1. Kinds of emails: This parameter indicated the nature of the email – requesting a resource, sharing a resource, providing feedback on a resource, or simply acknowledging the receipt of a resource.
2. Subject matter of emails: This parameter captured the subject of the email conversation – disciplinary subject, educational administration, larger educational issues and larger social issues.
3. Methods of sharing: This parameter captured how teachers were sharing the resources – either as an attachment, through web links or as HTML in the body of the mail.
4. Level of awareness of a resource as an OER: This parameter captured how many mails with resources were explicitly shared as OER with mention of an open licence, or shared without any explicit mention of open licensing.
5. File type of resources/files shared: This parameter ascertained the different types and formats of resources being shared (text, image, video, animations, etc.).

Actual analysis was done in a spreadsheet by recording the analytical values for the different analysis parameters for each email obtained from the email headers file. This analysis was done manually by examining each mail in the Thunderbird client.

KOER website content analysis

During the workshops, the teachers uploaded the OER that they created or accessed to the KOER website. After the workshops, some of them continued to upload content to the KOER website, while others shared the resources in emails via the PLC mailing groups. The ITfC research team uploaded the materials from the mailing lists to the KOER website.

Content analysis of the KOER website of the OER accessed and utilised by the COA group constituted an important research component. Content analysis of KOER resources had two components: first, the summary statistical data automatically provided by the MediaWiki software for KOER websites (providing data on number of pages, number of files uploaded, page views, etc.); and, secondly, the actual curricular content uploaded for mathematics, science and social science. For the first macro-statistical analysis component, both English and Kannada KOER websites were considered and listed in a tabular format and sorted using LibreOffice Calc.

The second component of data analysis, related to content analysis of the resource pages, entailed studying the mathematics and science resource pages in the English and

Kannada websites for grades 8–10. The content analysis consisted of identifying the different types of "resource units", such as concept maps, additional web links from the internet, audio segments, videos, images, text materials, simulations and animations that constitute the resource page. The social science resource pages were not included in this analysis.

Key informant interviews

In order to obtain qualitative information and perspectives relating to the aims, processes and challenges of the Education Department, interviews were conducted with five officials from the department – three senior officials from DSERT, one from the Bengaluru Urban DIET and the fifth a teacher. The discussions were intentionally kept open-ended in order to elicit the unfettered perspectives of the interviewees. The interviews addressed the following topics:

- Policies and practices relating to curriculum design and material development.
- Policies, structures and practices relating to TPD.
- Use of digital learning resources and OER.

Interviews were documented through notes taken during the process. The responses were analysed manually by clustering them according to the three themes listed above.

Findings

The impact of the COA action research process was analysed in terms of the techno-social, techno-pedagogical and sociocultural factors in the Karnataka state education system. Specific elements were chosen for analysis within each of these factors (Table 4). It is not suggested that these elements comprehensively cover all aspects of these three factors; they are, however, the elements which are considered to be most important in the context of this study.

Table 4: Elements analysed within the techno-social, techno-pedagogical and socio-cultural factors of the Karnataka state education system

Factor	Elements analysed
Techno-social	Capacity-building of COA teachers in using digital technologies Creation of a FOSS environment Systemic integration of ICT into TPD and OER adoption
Techno-pedagogical	Influence of COA processes on OER adoption Influence of KOER platform design on OER creation PLC as a site for OER adoption Impact of ICT on TPD Impact of COA processes on teacher practice Impact of COA processes on teacher networking
Sociocultural	Understanding copyright and open licensing OER to respond to teachers' and learners' contexts OER creation in the local language

Influence of COA processes on techno-social factors

Capacity-building of COA teachers in using digital technologies

The COA processes undertaken with teachers included basic digital literacy training, introduction to access and reuse of resources on the internet, creation and remixing of resources in multiple formats, and publishing on the KOER website. Training on a MediaWiki platform, which allows embedding of multiple resources, was an important component of the COA process. To understand the influence of the COA processes on use of digital technologies, data were collected from the COA group and the Comparable group of teachers through structured questionnaires.

It is necessary to assess the similarity between the COA and Comparable groups in terms of their demographic and professional profiles before using the Comparable group as a proxy baseline. The next section reports on the demographic profile and professional profile information captured through the survey process.

Demographic profile of teachers in the COA and Comparable groups

It was hypothesised that the following demographic characteristics had the potential to influence ICT and OER adoption: age, sex, educational qualifications, work experience and subject taught. If the COA and Comparable groups were found to be statistically similar in these characteristics, we could infer that they are comparable. This means that any differences between the two groups with respect to use of digital technologies could be associated with the COA processes. Other demographic variables such as religion and caste were not seen as relevant to this comparison, and were therefore not addressed in the questionnaire.

The **age variable** was sufficiently similar between the COA and Comparable groups to serve as a proxy baseline (Table 5). The use of a two-sample z-test established that the mean age was statistically similar for the two groups at a 5% significance level (p-value = 0.28).

Table 5: Age distribution of participating teacher cohort

Age (years)	Comparable	Percentage	COA	Percentage
Under 30	4	3.81	3	4.48
31–40	38	36.19	33	49.25
41–50	40	38.09	27	40.29
51 and over	19	18.09	3	4.48
Missing data	4	3.81	1	1.49
Total	105	100.00	67	100.00

Notes:
1. In order to enable easier reading of the data, the values for the Comparable group are provided first and followed by the corresponding values for the COA teachers in all tables.
2. The totals in a number of the tables are not exactly 100%. The difference of usually 0.01% is due to rounding off during the addition of the percentages, and is not an error.
3. The "Missing data" row refers to instances where respondents did not complete the associated field in the questionnaire.

Simple percentages show that the **sex composition** of the two groups differed: the Comparable group was 75% female and the COA group was 76% male (Table 6).

Table 6: Sex distribution

Sex	Comparable	Percentage	COA	Percentage
Male	26	24.76	51	76.12
Female	79	75.24	16	23.88
Total	105	100.00	67	100.00

In terms of **professional profile**, all teachers in the government schooling system were well qualified with a double qualification – one degree in a core subject area and a second degree in teacher education. The qualification parameter (highest qualification) was studied to analyse whether the Comparable group and COA group had similar levels of qualification, with educational qualifications being taken as a proxy for their investment in their professional advancement and inclination towards acquiring additional skills (Table 7). As per the chi-square test, the distribution of teachers based on their highest qualifications in the COA and Comparable groups is statistically similar, at a 5% significance level (p-value = 0.36).

Table 7: Comparison of professional qualifications

Highest degree obtained	Comparable	Percentage	COA	Percentage
Bachelor's	38	36.2	19	28.36
Master's	48	45.72	33	49.25
Masters in Education	16	15.23	15	22.39
No response	3	2.86	0	0
Total	105	100.00	67	100.00

With regard to **work experience**, both groups appeared to have similar profiles (Table 8). As per the two-sample z-test, the distribution of teachers based on mean work experience is statistically similar for the two groups at a 5% significance level (p-value = 0.51). This suggests that both groups were similar in terms of years of experience.

Table 8: Work experience comparison

Number of years work experience	Comparable	Percentage	COA	Percentage
0–5	6	5.71	3	4.48
6–10	27	25.71	22	32.84
11–15	19	18.09	6	8.96
16 and over	46	43.80	31	46.27
No response	7	6.66	5	7.46
Total	105	100.00	67	100.00

In terms of the **comparison of subjects taught**, data revealed that Comparable and COA groups taught similar subjects (Table 9). As per the chi-square test, the distribution of teachers across mathematics, science and social science subjects in the COA and Comparable groups is statistically similar at a 5% significance level (p-value = 0.85).

Table 9: Comparison of subjects taught

Subject taught	Comparable	Percentage	COA	Percentage
Mathematics	37	35.24	26	38.81
Science	32	30.48	18	26.86
Social science	36	34.29	23	34.33
Total	105	100.00	67	100.00

The data on demographic profile presented here indicate that in terms of their age, work experience, subject taught and professional qualifications, both COA and Comparable groups are statistically similar. Any difference in ICT usage habits due to these parameters can thus be ruled out.

The COA and Comparable groups are, however, different in terms of sex composition. In the overall population of government school teachers in the state, there is an equal distribution of sex. The *Secondary education in India: Progress towards universalisation* report (NUEPA, 2015b) indicates that the percentage of female teachers in Karnataka is 41.42%. The COA group had 76% male teachers, while the Comparable group had 75% female teachers. One factor that could have caused this difference is that the COA group was predominantly comprised of district-level resource personnel. Selection of district resource personnel tends to favour inclusion of male teachers due to the difficulties female teachers experience in terms of travel, accommodation, alternative child care, etc. Many female teachers tend to opt out of this role as it often involves additional responsibilities beyond regular teaching. Another factor could be that the Comparable group of teachers were from the district headquarters (Bengaluru and Yadgir town), where more female teachers tend to be appointed.

Given the fact that the two groups were similar in four out of five parameters, it was decided to use the Comparable group as a reference to analyse key parameters relating to use of ICT. The difference between the two groups with respect to sex composition is important, and the analyses and conclusions presented here should be read with this factor in mind.

ICT usage habits

The data captured on ICT usage habits include duration of computer use, internet use and ownership of a computer. Since the two groups were similar in their demographic and professional profiles, differences in ICT usage between the two groups could be associated with the participation of the COA teachers in the COA programme.

The data on ICT usage were captured in three categories to map to the programmes involved in the study, namely: less than one year (2013–2014); between one and three years (2011–2013); and more than three years (commencing prior to 2011).

The reason for this is that the STF programme had been operational since 2011 (three years prior to the start of this research study in July 2014) and COA teachers were part of the programme from 2011 to 2013. Participation in the STF PLC was one of the criteria for selection of the COA teachers. COA teachers' ICT use could therefore be related to the COA processes (less than one year), the STF programme processes (between one and three years), or before either of these two ICT training programmes was initiated. At the time of responding to the questionnaire, the Comparable group of teachers had, however, not been a part of the STF or COA programmes; their digital skills are therefore not associated with the STF and COA programmes. Differences in ICT usage could be associated with the participation of the COA teachers in the STF (one to three years) and the COA (less than one year) programmes.

Data relating to the **duration of computer and internet use** in the two groups were collected via the structured questionnaire. Findings show that 62 (92.54%) COA teachers were using computers, whereas only 12 (11.43%) Comparable teachers reported using computers. Nearly 66% of COA teachers were using computers before they joined the STF programme, compared to 3.81% of Comparable group teachers (Table 10). Approximately 18% of the COA teachers began using computers between one and three years before the commencement of the COA programme, whereas none of the Comparable group of teachers had, suggesting that participation in the STF programme has a positive co-relation with the use of computers.

Table 10: Duration of computer use

Duration of computer use	Comparable	Percentage	COA	Percentage
Less than one year	8	7.62	6	8.96
1–3 years	0	0.00	12	17.91
More than 3 years	4	3.81	44	65.67
No	93	88.57	5	7.46
Total	105	100.00	67	100.00
% of remaining teachers	**7.92** (8*100)/ (105-4-0)		**54.55** (6*100)/ (67-44-12)	

During the COA programme (less than one year), 8.96% of COA teachers began using computers, as compared to 7.62% for the Comparable group. In the one year of the COA programme, more than half the COA teachers who were not using computers began using computers (54.55%), compared to 7.92% of the Comparable group. This suggests that use of ICT is correlated with participation in the COA processes.

Sixty-one (91%) COA teachers were using the internet compared to 12 (11.43%) in the Comparable group of teachers. The COA group began with a higher internet use than the Comparable group (67.16% and 2.86%, respectively), and the increase in the number of COA teachers using the internet during the three years (which covers the period of the STF programme) is higher than that of the Comparable group (13.43% and 0.95%, respectively) (Table 11). As in the case of computer usage, about 24% of the COA teachers began using the internet either through the impact of the STF (13.43%) or the COA processes (10.45%).

Table 11: Duration of internet use

Duration of internet use	Comparable	Percentage	COA	Percentage
Less than one year	8	7.62	7	10.45
1–3 years	1	0.95	9	13.43
More than 3 years	3	2.86	45	67.16
No	93	88.57	6	8.96
Total	105	100.00	67	100.00
Percentage of remaining teachers	7.92		53.85	

In the one year of the COA programme, more than half the teachers who were not using the internet began using it (53.85%), compared to 7.92% of the Comparable group. The data presented here suggest that participation in the COA processes had a positive correlation with the use of computers and the internet.

Ownership of a personal digital device can be an indication that digital technologies are seen to be of value. In this sense, ownership of a computer or laptop by a teacher suggests that the teacher sees value in using computers. Almost 84% of COA teachers owned their own laptops or desktop computers, while only 20.9% of the Comparable group did (Figure 2).

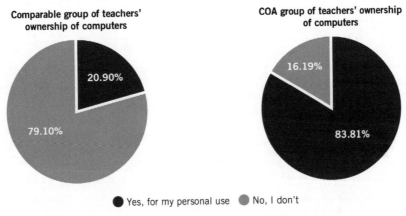

Comparable group of teachers' ownership of computers

20.90%

79.10%

COA group of teachers' ownership of computers

16.19%

83.81%

● Yes, for my personal use   ● No, I don't

Figure 2: Computer ownership amongst COA and Comparable group teachers

The COA programme team encouraged teachers to purchase personal laptops and internet connectivity, providing input on various options available and cost-feature comparisons. While the mobile phone was seen as a personal necessity by all teachers (due to compelling benefits of being able to support voice and SMS communication), this was initially not the case with computers or the internet. During the course of the COA programme, COA teachers saw the value of regularly using computers and the internet. This persuaded them to purchase devices and connectivity for their personal use. This purchasing of their own devices can be seen as a powerful proxy for self-belief in their capability to use ICT, as well as in their perception of the value of ICT to their personal and professional lives.

Overall, the data in this section indicate that the COA teachers used computers and the internet to a much greater extent than the Comparable group of teachers.

Creation of a FOSS environment

The analysis of PLC interactions on the mailing lists revealed that teachers shared useful tools that they discovered with their peers on the virtual forums. For the FOSS desktop-based tools (such as free dictionaries, Geogebra and text editors) that they were already using, COA teachers identified equivalent free tools in the mobile environment and shared these on mailing lists. Overall, COA teachers used open format documents more often (86.5%) than proprietary or closed document formats (13.5%). The frequency of the use of multiple tools to create resources in multiple formats is shown in Table 12, which lists the number of resources shared on the mailing lists by COA teachers by the format of the files. Of the 173 resources shared, 151 (87.3%) were in open formats and 22 (12.7%) in proprietary formats.

Table 12: Frequency of open and proprietary formats utilised in resources shared on mailing lists

File type	Format	File description	FOSS	Proprietary	Total
Image	JPEG		23		23
Image	PNG		1		1
Video	FLV			2	2
Geogebra	GGB		30		30
Text	EML	Mail	24		24
Text	ODT	Editable text	18		18
Text	PDF	Non-editable text	42		42
Text	HTML	Web page	13		13
Text	DOC, DOCX	Editable text (proprietary)		8	8
Text	XLS, XLSX	Spreadsheet		7	7
Text	PMD			1	1
Text	PPT, PPTX	Slide presentation		4	4
Total			151	22	173

In focus group discussions, COA teachers articulated an expectation that educational resources must be freely available (i.e. at no or low cost) and open to revision for use in the classroom. Teachers recognised that digital formats had several advantages, including accessibility, adaptability and versatility to meet multiple purposes.

Systemic integration of ICT into TPD and OER adoption

The COA programme made design choices that emphasised digital processes. COA workshops were conducted in computer labs where the programme required teachers to have a 1:1 access to computers with reasonably good internet connectivity. Teachers were required to become familiar with multiple resource creation methods, use of different software applications, and learning to publish OER on a MediaWiki platform. Workshop feedback was also compiled digitally and shared with the DSERT. This emphasis on the use of the digital for the design, implementation and reporting of the training programme made the systemic availability of ICTs a prerequisite.

The key informant interviews probed the experiences and insights of officials in the Education Department with regard to the core principles of the COA programme, including integration of digital technologies in an in-service TPD programme, use of digital technologies for OER adoption, and use of FOSS instead of proprietary software applications. The officials interviewed appreciated the benefits of using FOSS tools and the value of teachers receiving a single DVD containing the custom *Kalpavriksha* installation of the FOSS operating system containing all the software applications required. This "bundling" made software installation a simple process.

DIET personnel largely saw the integration of digital technologies in the programme as an important requirement for school education and were supportive of this. Many DIETs made special efforts to improve the ICT labs in their institutions, replacing dysfunctional hardware and boosting network connectivity. Some DIETs also identified ICT labs in other institutions (higher education institutions like engineering colleges, teacher training colleges, etc.) in order to increase their access to ICT infrastructure and allow more teachers in the districts to be trained in the STF programme, thereby growing the PLC.

In one of the key informant interviews, a DSERT officer in charge of the COA programme used an analogy to explain the importance of teacher preparation in the systemic integration of technology. He explained that in earlier ICT programmes, the department focused on providing ICT infrastructure to schools without adequately building teacher capacity to use the infrastructure for teaching activities. That approach did not work and only a small number of teachers used the infrastructure. When the STF and COA programmes focused on training teachers to use ICT, many teachers purchased personal computers, seeing the relevance and benefit of ICT for their professional development. The officer made the analogy that the department had earlier provided bicycles (i.e. computers) to schools, but did not teach people how to ride a bicycle – therefore nobody learned how to cycle. Teachers were now being taught how to cycle (i.e. how to use computers and the internet) and many were purchasing their own bicycles (i.e. devices). He suggested that while infrastructure provision and capacity-building were both required to enable the use of a technology, capacity-building was critical in terms of boosting the use of ICT by teachers, suggesting a change in the way teacher training and ICT implementation in schools could be imagined.

Techno-social challenges

Though the COA programme did influence the techno-social factors discussed above, teachers articulated several challenges and constraints in their interactions with the research team and on the mailing lists, including limited access to ICT infrastructure, nascent digital literary skills and limited time to gain technical proficiency.

Limited ICT infrastructure

The COA programme required that teachers be trained in the use of tools for accessing, creating and publishing OER on the KOER platform. Though the Education Department had provided labs, the actual number of computers was sometimes insufficient, internet connectivity was patchy and some computers were dysfunctional. Internet connectivity was particularly challenging in rural areas where connectivity was poor and bandwidth was inadequate at schools and in homes. Online resource creation processes were therefore difficult to undertake. Power outages were also quite common in many areas, which made using desktop computers a challenge. COA teachers spoke of their difficulties in using computers and finding materials online. Internet connectivity was not available in schools and most parts of the state still only had 2G[28] internet access. While the Education Department provided ICT infrastructure for the COA workshops, ongoing resource creation and adoption was impacted by these constraints.

Nascent digital literacy skills

The OER adoption process required use of the KOER online platform to host newly created or revised OER, which meant that teachers had to become proficient in the use of multiple applications (including MediaWiki) while developing the pedagogic competencies required for the revision of resources. This was seen as too complex a requirement by the teachers. They reported that imagining resources in an online format required pedagogic competencies as well as technological familiarity, which was a challenge. Though some COA teachers had a basic familiarity with ICT, some of the digital methods adopted in the programme were found to be challenging, such as editing content on the Wiki page or embedding resources in different formats (e.g. concept map, videos, images) directly on the Wiki page. Some COA teachers wanted simpler technological alternatives, such as sharing OER on the PLC mailing lists. The challenge in this context was the need to be able to imagine a hyper-linked flow of content, which was quite different from the hierarchical flow of content teachers were used to accessing in textbooks.

Limited time to gain technical proficiency

In the focus group discussions, COA teachers mentioned that the process of learning how to use ICT was complex and layered. Even if basic digital literacy was acquired, becoming proficient required devoting significant time to practice, which was seldom available. Some teachers brought with them a legacy understanding of ICT as a set of proprietary tools to be used for very specific purposes, and it took time to move to a perspective of ICT as a set of processes that could alter content and pedagogical approaches. While discussions on the mailing lists about using public applications suggested that FOSS was accepted by teachers, proprietary applications and proprietary document formats were still being used, though this was no longer the default situation.

Influence of COA processes on techno-pedagogical factors

Influence of COA processes on OER adoption

COA and Comparable group teachers were asked about their resource creation, sharing and adaptation practices in the structured questionnaire. COA teachers reported a higher percentage of material creation (88%, as opposed to 59% for the Comparable group) and material sharing (97%, as opposed to 65% for the Comparable group) (Table 13). While the

---

28   The term "2G" refers to second-generation internet. See https://en.wikipedia.org/wiki/2G.

COA teachers were chosen based on their participation in the STF programme and were already resource persons for the Education Department, this high percentage of resource creation and sharing is positively related with their participation in the COA programme.

Table 13: OER creation and sharing practices

Group	Creating learning materials	Percentage	Sharing learning materials	Percentage
Comparable	62	59.05	68	64.76
COA	59	88.06	65	97.01

Responses to the structured questionnaire indicate that COA teachers also had far greater engagement with resource adaptation than the Comparable group of teachers. Table 14 illustrates the types and frequency of OER adaptation practices of COA teachers in relation to the Comparable group of teachers.

Table 14: Types of adaptation undertaken with learning materials

Type of learning material adaptation	Comparable	Percentage	COA	Percentage
Use with own examples	70	66.67	66	98.50
Reduce or add content	65	61.90	61	91.04
Mix two or more materials	52	49.52	58	86.57
Change format (document layout)	55	52.38	52	77.61
Change sequence	58	55.24	52	77.61
Translate into another language	45	42.86	50	74.63
Use for a purpose different from original purpose	43	40.95	39	58.21

Note: The percentages in this table are all individually computed on a base of the total number of teachers in the respective groups. They do not therefore add up to 100% across the rows.

The COA teachers reported higher percentages of resource adaptation habits across different levels of OER reuse. This suggests that the COA processes had an impact on the teachers' OER adoption habits.

The level of learning-materials adaptation activity indicates an ability to engage in resource adaptation processes. COA teachers not only showed higher rates of content adaptation (e.g. including their own examples, reducing or adding content and changing the sequence of material), but also higher levels of use of sophisticated adaptation methods, such as use of materials for a different purpose from what was originally intended, and remixing two or more materials. The Comparable group teachers also adapted learning materials to meet their needs using similar practices, but undertook these less frequently than the COA group.

As indicated in Tables 13 and 14, the percentage of teachers adapting resources is greater than the percentage creating content. Teachers seemed to find it harder to create their own resource than to adapt an existing one. In the focus group discussions, some COA teachers shared their experiences in accessing and creating OER and how this helped in improving their own conceptual understanding. Such sharing encouraged other COA teachers in their OER adaptation activity.

Influence of KOER platform design on OER creation

The KOER platform was established as part of the COA programme and designed in consultation with the COA teachers in terms of form, structure and content in order to facilitate the OER creation process. The choice of the MediaWiki platform was an important pedagogic decision as it offered affordances for bottom-up OER creation. MediaWiki allows the editor to easily add text, image, audio and video content. Content can be uploaded within the MediaWiki platform or linked to other websites. Images, audio segments and videos already hosted on other platforms can also be embedded in the MediaWiki platform, meaning that they appear as if they are hosted within the MediaWiki itself. These advantages of the platform in terms of allowing remixing of different kinds of OER were raised and discussed by the COA teachers.

The COA OER development process was conceptualised in a modular way with topics (e.g. "light" or "circles") for resource creation being allocated to teams of teachers. Each topic was developed as a resource page, the template for which was developed in consultation with the teachers and refined over the course of the programme to allow for individual resource units to be shared by different teachers. The resource template had sections for content, as well as for activities and assessment, thus allowing for an integrated approach to technology, content and pedagogy. The COA teachers suggested that an online form be developed to ease the content submission process to the KOER platform.

The MediaWiki platform enabled teachers to contribute (create), edit (revise) and combine (remix) resource units[29] on any page. A web page created by a COA teacher on the KOER platform is in itself a resource to which other OER can be linked or embedded. COA teachers created the web pages required for their topics and created resource units in the form of text materials, images, audio clips, videos resources, concept maps and Geogebra simulations.[30] These resources were often created by the COA teachers using FOSS tools.

An analysis of the KOER pages pertaining to the resource topics (forming chapters in the grades 8–10 mathematics and science textbooks[31]) on the KOER platform is summarised in Table 15, which lists the resource units and states which resources have web pages, concept maps, links from the internet, audio-visual resources, lesson plans and animations. The data indicate that teachers remixed a variety of text, image and audio-visual resources for each topic on the KOER resource topic pages.

29   Resource units consist of text, images, audio and video resources, or any combinations of these.
30   See, for example, the pages on circles: http://karnatakaeducation.org.in/KOER/en/index.php/Circles.
31   Social science content was not included in this analysis.

Table 15: Overview of KOER content created by type of resource

Subject (language)	Web pages created	Concept maps	Links from the internet	Audio/ video/ image files	Text materials (lesson plans)	Animations	TOTAL
Mathematics (English)	39	24	22	18	23	8	134
Science (English)	56	21	25	23	16	4	145
Mathematics (Kannada)	42	9	7	6	5	2	71
Science (Kannada)	51	21	14	44	15	1	146
TOTAL	188	75	68	91	59	15	496

Of the 496 resources created, 146 (29.4%) were science materials in Kannada and 145 (29.2%) in English; 134 (27%) were mathematics materials in English and 71 (14.3%) in Kannada. The type of materials varied, with the most predominant being web pages (188); audio, videos and images (91); concept maps (75); links from the internet (68); lesson plans (59) and animations (15).

During the focus group discussions, teachers reviewed the KOER resource repository, both in terms of content created and adoption processes. The suggestions that emerged from these discussions include changes to the form and content of KOER, the need to build awareness of the platform and the need for coordinated district-level contributions.

The teachers suggested specific changes in terms of the form and content of the repository to make it more accessible to teachers. They felt that it would be useful to categorise resources in terms of intended use (e.g. videos of experiment demonstrations) to allow for easier user navigation. Teachers also felt that the KOER platform should make existing curricular resources created by the Education Department (textbook supplements, teacher handbooks for assessments, etc.) more accessible.

The teachers indicated that there was a need to build awareness amongst teachers and members of the state Education Department about the KOER platform. Using the STF PLC mailing list, sharing with communities through mobile services (e.g. WhatsApp), and sharing through articles and newsletters from the Education Department were suggested as possible methods of popularising the KOER platform.

For sustained OER creation, COA teachers suggested a decentralised model, comprising district-level resource groups which could regularly contribute to KOER, facilitated by DIETs in each district. They also suggested increasing the core group of resource creators through the decentralised district-level groups. The teachers further emphasised that in order to allow teachers to continue this OER process in a sustainable way, it was important for the Education Department to make resource creation a formal responsibility of teachers and to incorporate a mechanism for reviewing the quality of resources.

PLC as a site for OER adoption

COA teachers envisaged the mailing list as a way to pool resources which could be organised and uploaded to the KOER platform. The teachers felt that the PLC provided the context for resource creation by articulating resource needs and providing a forum for sharing the resources created. COA teachers saw the PLC as a significant contributing factor in their thinking on resource creation. In addition to sustaining OER creation, the teachers felt that adopting the resources shared on the mailing lists would encourage critical thinking in teachers and enhance TPD.

An analysis of the mails on the PLC provided information on the kinds of mails, subject matter of discussion and different file formats of resources shared. Table 16 provides an analysis of the mails sent on the mathematics and science PLC list in August 2014, February 2015 and August 2015.

Table 16: Number of emails addressing COA processes

COA processes	Number of emails	Percentage
Sharing resources – accessed	56	34.43
Sharing resources – created	102	62.58
Sharing resources – revised	3	1.84
Sharing resources – remixed	2	1.23
Total – resources shared	163	100.00

The number of emails containing resources created by teachers (102) is higher than the number of resources accessed elsewhere (56). This suggests that teachers are open to sharing the resources they have created. The lower number of resources accessed elsewhere could, however, also be due to limitations in internet search habits amongst teachers and a paucity of resources in the Kannada language. Since the PLC mailing list was an open forum for teachers, it was used for sharing resources as well as for discussion on various topics of interest. Most of the "other" 296 emails focused on discussions about different topics.

Impact of COA processes on TPD

Development of curricular resources is seen as an important aspect of TPD (NCTFE, 2010). This study attempted to examine whether OER adoption could provide teachers in India with additional learning materials to counter the prevailing textbook culture. Data collected from the structured questionnaire show that 63 of the 67 (94.03%) COA teachers reported using additional learning materials (other than the government-issued textbook and teacher guides), compared to 79 of the 105 (75.24%) teachers in the Comparable group.

The questionnaire also collected data on the frequency of use of additional learning materials to ascertain if the COA teachers used learning materials other than the textbook more frequently than the Comparable group (Table 17).

Table 17: Frequency of use of additional materials

Frequency of teachers' use of additional materials	Comparable	Percentage	COA	Percentage
1. Often	21	20.00	22	32.84
2. Occasionally	58	55.24	41	61.19
3. Hardly	1	0.95	1	1.49
4. Not at all	2	1.90	0	0.00
5. No response	23	21.90	3	4.48
Total	105	100.00	67	100.00

The COA teachers reported more frequent use of learning materials (32.84%) than the teachers in the Comparable group (20%).

The use of ancillary materials in addition to those traditionally prescribed by schools is an indicator of teachers' engagement with their profession and self-development. A higher percentage of additional resource use among COA teachers, many of whom are district- and state-level resource persons, suggests that engagement with curricular resources is related to TPD, considering their trajectory of development from a teacher to a resource person and trainer. Furthermore, during the focus group discussions, COA teachers questioned the dominant role that textbooks historically played in their teaching and felt that engaging with a variety of resources helped them in their own learning. Teachers could make the connection between COA processes and TPD aspects and were able to articulate their own trajectories of development as well as their aspirations.

In the focus group discussions, COA teachers expressed that resources supplementing the textbook can help to increase teachers' subject knowledge as well as student interest in a subject. They spoke of the development of new skills in terms of reading, writing, reviewing, providing feedback, considering multiple perspectives, building research capabilities, interacting with other teachers, and supporting and training fellow teachers. They articulated advantages for using resources to make teaching and learning more effective in terms of time, quality of transaction, general conceptual clarity and more engaging learning experiences. Resources in general also played a role in increasing the creativity of teachers by stimulating thinking about various options and possibilities in teaching.

The COA teachers spoke about their identity as teachers and resource creators, their capabilities as resource persons for training other teachers, self-awareness of professional development needs, possibilities for creativity and self-expression, and an increased sense of agency as they interacted with school administration and gained greater confidence.

Impact of ICT on TPD

With digital methods being centrally involved in OER adoption, it was important to investigate how enhancing ICT abilities could impact TPD. The questionnaires administered to the COA and Comparable groups captured information on the number of teachers who used ICT for their learning and teaching (Figure 3).

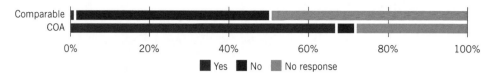

Figure 3: Use of computers and the internet to fulfil teacher professional development needs

COA teachers reported more frequent use of computers to support their development (67.16%) than teachers in the Comparable group (0.95%). Only 4.48% of COA teachers said that they did not use computers for their own development, compared to almost half of the teachers in the Comparable group (49.52%), indicating a strong relationship between the use of computers and teachers' perceptions of their need for professional development.

A starker distinction is apparent between the COA teachers use of ICT for teaching compared to teachers in the Comparable group (Figure 4).

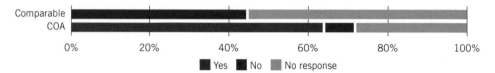

Figure 4: Use of computers by teachers for preparation and teaching

No teachers in the Comparable group used ICT for teaching, compared to 64.18% of COA teachers. The teachers in the Comparable group either explicitly indicated that they did not use computers for teaching (44.76%) or did not respond to the question (55.24%). By contrast, only 7.46% of COA teachers indicated that they did not use computers for teaching and 28.36% did not respond to the question. This suggests that there is a high level of computer use among the COA teachers in preparing for their classes and in teaching. The increased use of ICT in teaching has the potential to impact TPD by enriching teaching practices.

Impact of COA processes on teacher practice

The study did not focus on changes in teacher practice due to the COA processes, since an overall two-year period was felt to be too short to expect changes in practice. However, anecdotal evidence recounted in the focus group discussions suggests that some teachers are modifying their teaching practices, using the resources accessed and created by them or created and shared by their peers.

A few history teachers uploaded videos of students enacting different scenes from historical events, which were picked up by others on the mailing list. Many mathematics teachers shared Geogebra files which they had created and used in their classrooms for teaching different topics. One teacher reported that she had developed formative assessments based on the students using Geogebra to construct materials. Another teacher recorded a lesson using a screen-cast application of a resource on the internet for use in her classroom, where there was no internet connectivity.

Impact of COA processes on teacher networking

The research process examined how conversations around OER adoption can become an effective method of teacher development by increasing networking to counter teacher isolation. Data from the structured questionnaire provided insight into the extent of professional interaction among teachers across different contexts and helped to establish a sense of the extent to which ICT-enabled COA processes could encourage networking and peer learning.

Findings show that the number of interactions between COA and other teachers at all levels (school, taluka, district and state) was much higher than those for the Comparable group teachers (Figure 5).

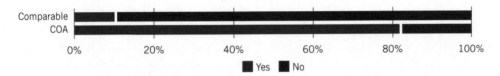

Figure 5: Extent of interaction between COA and Comparable group teachers with teachers from different districts

Just over 89% of COA teachers were in active contact with peers at block and district levels, as well as beyond their districts. In the Comparable group, just over 17% had contact of this kind with fellow teachers; the majority (82.09%) did not.

Along with exploring networking with other teachers, the study sought to ascertain if the COA teachers collaborated with other teachers to create resources. Two questions were asked: one on collaborating to create resources, and one on willingness to accept revision and modification of their resources by other teachers. In response to collaboration, 50 of the 67 (74.63%) COA teachers confirmed that they worked with others to create resources, whereas only 6 of the 105 (5.71%) Comparable group of teachers did so. These findings suggest that the COA processes supported teacher collaboration for OER creation.

A more telling finding is apparent in the teachers' responses to their willingness to accept revision and modification of the resources they created (Table 18).

Table 18: Teachers' willingness to accept revision of created materials

Response	Comparable	Percentage	COA	Percentage
Yes	8	7.62	54	80.59
No	15	14.28	6	8.96
No response	82	78.09	7	10.45
Total	105	100.00	67	100.00

Nearly 81% of COA teachers reported that they welcomed the idea of other teachers making changes to their resources; a marked difference from the only 7.62% of teachers in the Comparable group. Most telling is in fact the lack of response (78.09%) to the question of revision or a negative response (14.28%) by the Comparable group. By contrast, only seven (10.45%) of the COA teachers did not respond and only six (8.96%) said they would not be willing to have their materials modified. There seems, therefore, to be an association between the COA programme and the teachers' willingness to collaborate on OER adoption.

Techno-pedagogical challenges

Sustainability of KOER platform publishing

The publishing of resources on the KOER English and Kannada websites by teachers largely took place under the auspices of the COA workshops and was not being done on an ongoing basis by COA teachers working in their school settings or homes outside of the workshops, as was originally envisaged. Most of the edits on the wiki portal also took place on the workshop days. Teachers experienced the publishing process on the KOER platform as conceptually and technologically complex. They explained that they were unable to populate the MediaWiki website and sought more seamless methods to populate it from the mailing lists and mobile phone channels. Infrastructural challenges imposed by poor connectivity also made KOER publishing a challenging process.

Quality of OER

One of the indicators of an effective OER model is the quality of resources produced. Analysis of the materials produced and shared suggests that the materials appear to be "fit for purpose", which is typically recognised as one dimension of quality. For instance, the most commonly sought, created and shared resources on the mailing lists were question papers; question-paper pages were also the most viewed pages on the KOER platform. During the focus group discussions, COA teachers mentioned that question papers were required by all teachers in order to provide practice for their students in preparation for exams.

Some COA teachers did, however, openly express their dissatisfaction with OER that only sought to meet the basic needs of teachers, such as question papers for summative assessments. They felt that such materials reinforced existing teaching practices without a critical pedagogy approach. This sentiment expresses the view held by many teachers that the introduction of technology does not automatically lead to better pedagogical or content practices, enhanced teacher capacities or even the desire to innovate.

This dissonance can be useful in encouraging teachers to reflect upon the kind of OER that would support the progressive pedagogies required by national curricular policy, such as approaches based on constructivist learning theory.

During the focus group discussions, teachers expressed the need for credible, authentic, high-quality materials, even while acknowledging exemplars of high-quality resources amongst their group as well as in the PLC. This could be a useful point of departure to address two aspects: their sense of agency as developers of curricular materials, and their articulated need for their own development, which could facilitate the development of quality materials.

The large volume of materials shared on mailing lists and the KOER platform means that only a very small sample has been formally checked for quality assurance purposes. One of the expectations of the Education Department was that teachers would peer review the resources uploaded to the KOER platform, and use MediaWiki functionality to continually edit and revise the content. Such continuous peer editing and revision of resources is a higher-order skill not yet seen in the KOER context. Acknowledging that more formal structures are required for review processes, DSERT is considering setting up state and district resource groups of teachers and teacher educators to play the role of peer reviewing and revising OER.

Influence of COA processes on sociocultural factors

The influence of the COA processes on sociocultural factors was analysed in terms of the following: understanding of copyright and open licensing (legal aspects), and the contextual relevance of resources.

Understanding copyright and open licensing

In the public education system, textbooks and other curricular resources are largely produced by the Education Department and made available at no cost to teachers and students.

As part of the COA programme, the COA teachers were introduced to the idea of open licensing and Creative Commons, including training on how to identify openly licensed content for reuse. This was a new concept for many teachers, and their awareness of copyright issues was ascertained in the structured questionnaire (Figure 6).

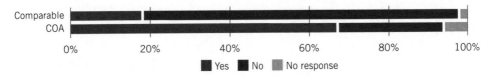

Figure 6: Teacher levels of copyright awareness

COA teachers reported higher awareness of copyright (67.16%) compared to the Comparable group (18.10%). However, even amongst COA teachers, more than one-third (32.84%) reported being unaware of copyright, despite the attention paid to copyright and open licensing during the COA workshops. It is perhaps not surprising that 80% of the Comparable group were not aware of copyright or open licensing, but it is concerning that while nearly 75% of COA teachers reported creating resources collaboratively, nearly one-third did not appear to be aware of the licensing framework that would support this collaborative OER development process.

One reason for this could be that the teachers are used to educational resources being "free" in the public education system. During the focus group discussions, it emerged that teachers found the default copyright approach counter-intuitive, especially in the context of online digital resources, since these were usually easy to download and reuse, and were mostly gratis. Full copyright stipulations on online content seemed easier for them to understand if related to paid-for content. Teachers did, however, appreciate the importance of open licensing and, as previously discussed, instinctively argued for OER for the public education system.

This brings us to an important observation about the understanding of resources in the context of the Indian education system. Throughout the study, the research team observed that both the COA and the STF PLC teachers prepared learning resources. The resources were shared on the PLC mailing lists, often with an explicit request for reuse or feedback, or even a request for the material to be shared via the KOER platform. While they did articulate objectives of reuse, revision and remixing, the teachers did not explicitly license the resources. It appeared that teachers treated the resources created by them and shared on mailing lists as self-evidently open. This sentiment is reported by Sharma (2016, p.57) in his case study on the STF-KOER programme:

> Public education in India is totally managed through state funds. State functionaries rarely engage with issues of copyright. Traditionally, publications of any kind including textbooks are funded by the state, rarely sold, even then at grossly subsidized costs and almost always covers the entire population. Educational resources are *de facto* treated as open, with states encouraged to freely share, adapt and reproduce materials developed by each other.

Sharma goes on to state that resources are traditionally also produced involving a large number of people drawn from different specialisations within the education system. Outsourcing is only for printing or logistics. In the absence of private participation, the need for an explicit statement and enforcement of legal rights (i.e. copyright) has never been recognised.

In the Research on Open Educational Resources for Development (ROER4D) "Research Concepts" document[32] it is suggested that the term "creation" in the context of OER be referred to as the production of digital teaching and learning resources that are intended from the outset to be shared openly and under some form of licence that allows reuse – teaching and learning resources that are "born open". In the case of COA teachers, the first condition ("that [they] are intended from the outset to be shared openly") is satisfied, but the second condition ("under some type of licence that allows reuse") is not; even though these specially created resources were clearly intended to be "born open". These resources have either been created from scratch, or revised from other resources shared by other teachers.

In the context of this study, resources accessed on the internet, many of which have the traditional "All rights reserved" copyright provision, have been called "explicit non-OER" and those accessed on the internet which are openly licensed have been classified as "explicit OER". "Implicit OER" was used to refer to those materials which were subject to full copyright, but were still being shared within the PLC with the intention of being shared openly.

An analysis of 163 resources shared on the STF PLC by both the COA and PLC teachers reveals that the majority (88.34%) have been sent with the implicit intent of making them OER, while only 9.82% were explicitly allocated an open licence (Table 19).

This practice presented a disjunct between legal practice (where the default copyright provision is "All rights reserved") and social practice (where any resource available online is seen as being free to download/reuse/share in the absence of an explicit copyright clause, and any resource created and shared is intended to be reused, without specifying any copyright clause) and is an issue that requires further work – not only from a research perspective, but also in terms of policy advocacy.

---

32   goo.gl/57tYfx

Table 19: Email analysis: Implicit and explicit intentions to share OER

Implicit and/or explicit intentions to share OER	Number	Percentage
Explicit non-OER	3	1.84
Implicit non-OER	0	0.00
Implicit OER	144	88.34
Explicit OER	16	9.82
Total	163	100.00

Contextual relevance of resources

OER to respond to teachers' and learners' contexts

Traditionally, material preparation and provision has been the almost exclusive responsibility of DSERT and it has been a challenge to make these materials relevant to diverse learning contexts and needs across the state.

COA teachers articulated their dynamic learning and resource needs relating to content knowledge, teaching practices and assessment techniques. This was particularly acute as their textbooks had been revised and the Continuous and Comprehensive Evaluation (CCE) had been recently introduced as an assessment method. Although immersed in a textbook culture where the only resource accessible and considered necessary is the textbook, they expressed the opinion that the new textbooks were not adequate, and that they required additional resources for subject enrichment and teaching.

Teachers also outlined the difficulties associated with enabling student learning in the face of a changing culture of learning (e.g. lower student responsiveness to teachers, reduced attention span of students) and changes in parents' expectations (e.g. many parents desire that their children should speak English fluently, though there is little or no input from home to support this – a feature in rural as well as urban government schools).

Acknowledging the changing context of their work, COA teachers were keen to create resources that could be more easily grasped by their students. High school students often had many gaps in their learning skill-sets and the recently revised textbooks were not considered to be easily understandable. To this end, a group of COA teachers came together to create foundational materials for mathematics learning and to address the learning levels of the students entering high school at Grade 8. Focusing on strengthening the science lab as a method of teaching and learning, the COA group of teachers created (from scratch) 25 Kannada video resources for demonstration of various science concepts, which formed the core resource material for a state-wide training programme. The materials in English were published on the English KOER platform and those in Kannada were published on the Kannada KOER platform.

Department officials (during the key informant interviews) appreciated the concept of teachers creating resources for themselves, since this helped them to address their local needs. They also mentioned that digital technologies could enable other teachers to have access to the "good-quality" content created by "expert" teachers, and that this was more desirable than the notion of all teachers creating OER. According to them, all teachers may not be able to, or be interested in, creating OER. They also expressed the view that easy availability of OER might encourage teachers to become lazy and not invest in making materials themselves.

Content analysis indicates that the KOER English and Kannada repositories were populated with materials that responded to these requirements through the provision of classroom activities for CCE, examination question papers, formative assessment activities and grade computation sheets. Question papers in mathematics, science and social sciences had some of the highest page views on the KOER platform.

OER creation in the local language

An important issue that arose in the focus group discussions was the relative unavailability of OER in local languages. Kannada is the state language of Karnataka, spoken by most of its six million inhabitants, and also the medium of instruction in 65% of the high schools in the state (State Project Director, 2012).

While Kannada Wikipedia was an important OER for teachers to access, the resources in Kannada Wikipedia represent a mere 0.34% of the wiki pages in English Wikipedia (Table 20), which can be seen as a proxy for the relative shortage of OER in the Kannada language. In this context, teacher creation of local-language OER becomes more important. The percentage of Kannada resources on the KOER platform as a percentage of English resources is 68%. This suggests that teachers see the COA process as being conducive to creating OER in local languages.

While Wikipedia is also a collaborative OER platform, it is interesting to see the difference in the percentage of local-language content between KOER and Wikipedia. The KOER Kannada to English content ratio is 200 times that of Wikipedia. One reason for this substantial difference could be that the COA teachers populating KOER are a coherently defined community of practising teachers creating OER to respond to their immediate professional needs. Teachers also feel a sense of ownership over the KOER platform, which has the "for the teachers, of the teachers and by the teachers" tag line.

Table 20: Breakdown of English and Kannada KOER content resources by language

Analytics category	Kannada KOER	English KOER	Ratio of Kannada to English
Web pages	3 000+	4 400+	68.18 : 100
Resource files uploaded	1 500+	2 500+	60.00 : 100
	Kannada Wikipedia	**English Wikipedia**	
Number of articles	16 500+	4.9 million+	0.34 : 100

Notes:
1. Data as at 30 September 2015.
2. KOER statistics were generated by using the "Special pages" (reports) feature of MediaWiki. The special pages can be viewed by clicking on the "Special pages" link on the KOER home page (in English[33] and in Kannada[34]). The Wikipedia data on articles in English and Kannada languages were generated from the Wikipedia "List of Wikipedia".

---

33   http://karnatakaeducation.org.in/KOER/en/index.php/Special:Statistics
34   goo.gl/tdmBm5

While the availability of local-language resources has been positively influenced by the COA processes, there are still more English OER pages than Kannada pages. One reason for this could be that technical writing is easier in the language in which teachers have studied. In Karnataka, mathematics and science teachers need to have a graduate degree in science (a Bachelor's of Science, or BSc.), which is offered in the English medium in universities across Karnataka. This may be the reason why these teachers prefer to create OER in English. Because of their bilingual competence in reading and writing English and Kannada, these teachers are able to access a wider linguistic range of OER for reuse.

Similarly, social science teachers, whose graduate degree in Humanities (Bachelor's of Arts, or BA) was usually offered in Kannada, preferred to create OER in Kannada. Consequently, OER access and reuse by the social science teachers was limited, as many were not as comfortable reading or writing in English. This pattern is also borne out in the anlaysis of the mailing-list interactions and suggests that there is a relationship between subject taught, language of interaction and language of resources created.

COA teachers mentioned that they required resources to be available in the different languages students used, and mentioned that teachers need to be able to transact in multiple languages, since in many schools students come from different linguistic backgrounds where more than one language may be spoken at home. One of the COA teachers who taught in an Urdu-medium high school translated some mathematics resources shared by other COA teachers into the Urdu language (Arabic script) and shared these on the mailing list. After Kannada and English, Urdu is the third most popular medium of instruction in government high schools across the state. This suggests that an OER adoption model embedded within the public education system has the potential to influence OER creation in local languages, making it possible for the OER model to be scaled and replicated in other states.

Critical reflections from the research

Changes to the research approach

While writing the proposal, the ITfC research team envisioned a participatory action research (PAR) methodological approach. However, it became clear that most of the COA teachers were not familiar with research methods and were trying to cope with the techno-social and techno-pedagogical challenges of OER adoption. There was therefore not adequate time and capacity in the research process to train the COA teachers on research methods. Hence, the approach was modified from PAR to action research, where the teachers participated in the COA and research processes but were not part of the research design or data analysis.

A second challenge for the research team was to define the role of the COA group of teachers and the larger PLC group of teachers in the action research. Initially, the team tried to understand the work of the PLC teachers, which included the COA teachers. Based on feedback from the ROER4D Principal Investigator as well as in an internal review workshop conducted at ITfC with one of the research advisors, it became clear that the research needed to focus on the processes of the COA group of teachers, for whom the OER adoption agenda was of central importance.

Insights from the research process

The emergence of the STF PLC as a space for OER sharing and adoption was a welcome but almost surprising outcome. While there was no benchmark for virtual interaction amongst teachers in a public education system in a developing country such as India, the poor availability of ICT infrastructure, the low competency levels of teachers in terms of adopting digital processes, and the complexity of a large public schooling system had kept expectations quite low. The high volume of emails on the PLC and the response of the COA teachers in terms of accessing these resources and publishing on the KOER platform was a gratifying outcome for the research team.

Moreover, the extent to which the COA teachers were receptive to the idea of collaborative OER adoption was a pleasing outcome. Participation in the workshops was not mandatory and many teachers had to negotiate with their school principals to be allowed to attend. Teachers would proactively share their preferences of dates for holding the workshops with the research team, indicating their willingness to attend. Besides their participation, they actively recommended additional members for inclusion in the process. In the context of a strongly hierarchical Indian education system, such active participation and inclusivity was also a pleasant surprise for the research team.

Public software

There have been several efforts to promote the use of FOSS in education. However, this has been a difficult journey as popular proprietary software is still dominant in schools. The research team explained the concept of FOSS as "public" software, suggesting that it was "owned" by all and hence open to use by all. While FOSS users needed to attribute its ownership to the creators, for all practical purposes, since they could freely use, reuse and share it, it could be seen as a "publicly owned" resource.

In the workshops, the COA teachers related the "public" term to their belonging to a "public" education system, open to all students without barriers. The schools in which they worked were "public schools", to which any child could gain access without any constraint. They appreciated that if software needed to be accessible to all in the digital society, it had to be available as a "public resource", just as universal access to education or healthcare was necessary.

Throughout the research process, the research team emphasised the fact that FOSS and OER are aligned in terms of their philosophies. FOSS offers the freedom to use, copy, modify and redistribute, similar to "5Rs" activity in the OER context.

Embedding OER adoption in the Indian public education system

While the large size of the public education system has traditionally been seen as a limitation or a weakness by the teachers, the size of the public education system in Karnataka (Table 2) helped to create a sufficient volume of interaction in the PLC.

It is possible that the networking of teachers using digital technologies can help to view the size of the system as a strength, as the large number of teachers participating in the network could be a benefit in terms of the volume of OER created and shared. Even if only a very small percentage of teachers from the public education system participate in absolute numbers, it is likely to be large enough to provide a base for OER creation and adoption.

Conclusion

In the large public education system in India, as elsewhere, teachers have traditionally been very isolated. Schools tend to be geographically dispersed and there is often only one subject teacher per subject in each school. Teachers rarely have an opportunity to meet with other teachers teaching the same subject. Traditional teacher development processes do not therefore tend to offer much scope for interaction and peer learning (Rothberg, 1985). This research project has demonstrated that virtual networks can offer opportunities for teachers to connect with one another for peer sharing and learning. Such a PLC can also be a space for OER access and adoption, which can counter the "minor technician" role usually expected of a teacher by the education bureaucracy. A collaborative OER adoption model embedded within a PLC can provide the context for the community to come together and support a systemic model of OER adoption within a public education system. A FOSS environment can also encourage teachers to freely explore and connect digital means and ends.

Teachers in this study found the creation, revision, remixing and redistribution of resources on mailing lists and the KOER platform both interesting and useful. This has made a positive impact on their digital habits and has affected the techno-social habits of certain teachers in Karnataka. It has also supported their professional development, as evidenced by their reflections on the learning that has taken place through community interaction. The nature of these discussions has enabled teachers to see the value of an online community for accessing and sharing educational resources.

Policy recommendations

The following policy recommendations have arisen from the research process:

Implement the PLC approach to TPD in in-service teacher education

The PLC model of TPD, as implemented in the STF programme, provides opportunities for self-learning, peer learning and continuous learning, which are key requirements of the National Curricular Framework for Teacher Education, 2010. Since this model utilises available resources and budgets of the education system, implementing a similar programme in other states in India would be possible. State and district-level ICT infrastructure will, however, need to be developed and maintained in order to facilitate teacher training.

Implement the COA model for OER adoption

Bringing teachers together in collaborative OER creation and sharing processes can foster the creation of contextually relevant OER, including those in Indic languages. This can provide resources that complement and supplement the textbook, currently the primary curricular resource of the teacher in the Indian education system and in many other developing countries. However, continuous peer editing and revision of resources will require that more formal structures and processes be established to ensure the quality of processes and outputs.

Copyright regulations should position open licensing as the default

One important step in promoting OER adoption would be to have a policy in which the default copyright treatment for any work would be open licensing. This would mean that legal permissions would be articulated upfront for newly created materials, which would facilitate legal reuse, revision, remixing and redistribution. Anyone who intends to prevent sharing or modification must stipulate it by explicitly stating "All rights reserved". This is a recommendation for policy, but the fact that most countries have "All rights reserved" as the default copyright expression means that this would require long-term effort at a global level.

Implement a FOSS-based ICT programme in school education

The "National Policy on ICT in School Education" (Department of School Education and Literacy, 2012) recommends the use of FOSS. India is one of a very few countries in the world that has a policy on adopting open standards (Ministry of Communications and Information Technology, 2010) for digital files in public institutions (which means that proprietary document formats are not to be used). Given the numerous advantages of the FOSS environment over a proprietary environment, these policies need to be fully implemented. Usually the apprehensions about mandating FOSS relate to perceived difficulties in implementation, and not to the concept itself. The experience in implementing FOSS in Karnataka as part of the STF programme, and earlier in Kerala (Kasinathan, 2009a), suggests that it is possible to implement a FOSS-based ICT programme in school education. Since software applications are the means by which OER can be adopted, mandating FOSS would support OER adoption by greater alignment at the philosophical and implementation levels.[35]

Possible next steps for research

A model for bottom-up collaboration in which teachers create, reuse, revise, remix and redistribute OER has been evidenced in this study. There are, however, a number of important areas that require further investigation.

1. Firstly, there is a need to study the influence of the PLC on the COA. While the COA teacher interactions with the PLC have been studied and discussed, a study of the interactions amongst the PLC teachers would be useful in terms of providing a better understanding of the COA model studied, since the COA effectiveness is partly due to it being embedded within the PLC.
2. Secondly, the actual use of the materials by teachers needs to be studied, as insight into which materials are deemed useful can help to better understand OER use with respect to TPD and student learning. This would support the further maturation and evolution of the collaborative model of OER adoption.

---

35   See http://roer4d.org/1570 for a blog by ITfC ROER4D research team member, making this argument.

3. Thirdly, scaling up the STF and PLC programmes to other states in India would help it mature as a mainstream model for OER adoption in India, which other public education systems in the Global South could explore.

Apart from these steps, it is necessary to create an awareness amongst teachers who share resources with the intention that they will be reused, revised, remixed and redistributed by others to explicitly use open licensing. This will enable the teachers who are reusing these materials as OER to operate comfortably within the boundaries of copyright law.

Acknowledgements

The authors wish to thank Mythili Ram and Rajaram S. Sharma, who provided valuable feedback in the peer review process.

References

Albright, P. (2005). *Internet discussion forum: Open Educational Resources, open content for higher education.* Paris: International Institute for Educational Planning & United Nations Educational, Scientific and Cultural Organization.

Camilleri, A. F., Ehlers, U-D. & Pawlowski, J. (2014). *State of the art review of quality issues related to Open Educational Resources (OER).* Seville: Joint Research Centre, European Commission. Retrieved from http://is.jrc.ec.europa.eu/pages/EAP/documents/201405JRC88304.pdf

CIET (Central Institute of Education Technology). (2015). *Third party evaluation of ICT@ Schools in Karnataka.* New Delhi: Central Institute of Education Technology. Retrieved from http://www.slideshare.net/GurumurthyKasinathan/ictschools-evaluation-by-ciet-ncert-karnataka2015

Creswell, J. W. (2014). *Research design: Qualitative, quantitative, and mixed methods approaches.* Thousand Oaks, CA: Sage.

Daniel, J. & Uvalić-Trumbić, S. (2012). Fostering governmental support for Open Educational Resources internationally. Presented at *6th Regional Policy Forum, 7–8 May 2012.* Muscat, Oman. Retrieved from http://oasis.col.org/bitstream/handle/11599/1064/2012_Daniel_FGSOERI_Arab_Region_Transcript.pdf?sequence=1&isAllowed=y

Department of School Education and Literacy. (2012). *National policy on information and communication technology (ICT) in school education.* New Delhi: Ministry of Human Resource Development. Retrieved from http://mhrd.gov.in/sites/upload_files/mhrd/files/upload_document/revised_policy%20document%20ofICT.pdf

Eisner, E. W. (1991). What really counts in schools. *Educational Leadership, 48(5),* 10–11. Retrieved from http://academic.wsc.edu/education/curtiss_j/eisner.htm

Ferreira, G. (2008). What about the teacher? Open Educational Resources et al. In *EADTU 2008 Conference, 18–19 September 2008.* Poitiers, France. Retrieved from http://oro.open.ac.uk/23910/2/9DA69B0B.pdf

Gilmore, T., Krantz, J. & Ramirez, R. (1986). Action based modes of inquiry and the host-researcher relationship. *Consultation, 5(3),* 160–176. Retrieved from http://www.

researchgate.net/publication/232603154_Action_Based_Modes_of_Inquiry_and_the_Host-Researcher_Relationship

Hatakka, M. (2009). Build it and they will come?: Inhibiting factors for reuse of open content in developing countries. *The Electronic Journal on Information Systems in Developing Countries, 37(5),* 1–16. Retrieved from http://www.is.cityu.edu.hk/staff/isrobert/ejisdc/37-5.pdfhttp://www.ejisdc.org/ojs2/index.php/ejisdc/article/viewFile/545/279

Hylén, J., Van Damme, D., Mulder, F. & D'Antoni, S. (2012). *Open Educational Resources: Analysis of responses to the OECD country questionnaire.* Paris: Organisation for Economic Co-operation and Development. Retrieved from http://dx.doi.org/10.1787/5k990rjhvtlv-en

Kanwar, A., Kodhandaraman, B. & Umar A. (2010). Toward sustainable Open Education Resources: A perspective from the Global South. *The American Journal of Distance Education, 24(2),* 65–80. Retrieved from http://dx.doi.org/10.1080/08923641003696588

Kasinathan, G. (2009a). *ICTs in school education – Outsourced versus integrated approach, Policy brief.* Bengaluru: IT for Change. Retrieved from http://www.itforchange.net/sites/default/files/ITfC/Policy_Brief_on_ICTs_in_School_Education_from_IT_for_Change_August_2009.pdf

Kasinathan, G. (2009b). *Computer learning programmes in schools – Moving from BOOT models to an integrated approach.* Bengaluru: IT for Change. Retrieved from http://itforchange.net/BOOT_Integrated

Kumar, K. (1988). Origins of India's "textbook culture". *Comparative Education Review 32(4),* 452–464. Retrieved from https://www.jstor.org/stable/1188251?seq=1#page_scan_tab_contents

Lane, A. (2008). Widening participation in education through Open Educational Resources. In T. Iiyoshi & M. S. V. Kumar (Eds.), *Opening up education: The collective advancement of education through open technology, open content, and open knowledge* (pp. 149–163). Cambridge: The MIT Press. Retrieved from https://mitpress.mit.edu/sites/default/files/titles/content/9780262515016_Open_Access_Edition.pdf

MHRD (Ministry of Human Resource Development). (2008). *Sarva shiksha abhiyaan.* New Delhi: Ministry of Human Resource Development. Retrieved from http://pib.nic.in/archieve/others/2008/apr/r2008042401.pdf

Ministry of Communications and Information Technology. (2010). *Policy on open standards for e-governance.* New Delhi: Ministry of Communications and Information Technology. Retrieved from http://www.gswan.gov.in/PDF/Policy%20on%20Open%20Standards%20in%20eGovernance.pdf

Ministry of Law and Justice. (2009). *Right of children to free and compulsory education Act, 2009.* New Delhi: Ministry of Law and Justice. Retrieved from http://eoc.du.ac.in/RTE%20-%20notified.pdf

Mishler, E. G. (1979). Meaning in context: Is there any other kind? *Harvard Educational Review, 49(1),* 1–19. Retrieved from http://dx.doi.org/10.17763/haer.49.1.b748n4133677245p

Mishra, P. & Koehler, M. J. (2006). Technological pedagogical content knowledge: A framework for teacher knowledge. *Teachers College Record, 108(6),* 1017–1054. Retrieved from http://one2oneheights.pbworks.com/f/MISHRA_PUNYA.pdf

NCFTE (National Council for Teacher Education). (2010). *National curricular framework for teacher education.* New Delhi: National Council for Teacher Education. Retrieved from http://ncte-india.org/ncte_new/pdf/NCFTE_2010.pdf

Ngimwa, P. & Wilson, T. (2012). An empirical investigation of the emergent issues around OER adoption in Sub-Saharan Africa. *Learning, Media and Technology, 37(4),* 398–413. Retrieved from http://dx.doi.org/10.1080/17439884.2012.685076

NUEPA (National University of Education Planning and Administration). (2014). *2013–2014 Annual report.* New Delhi: National University of Education Planning and Administration. Retrieved from http://www.nuepa.org/new/download/Publications/Annual%20Reports/Annual_Report_2013-14(English).pdf

NUEPA (National University of Education Planning and Administration). (2015a). *Elementary education in India: Progress towards UEE.* New Delhi: National University of Education Planning and Administration. Retrieved from http://dise.in/Downloads/Elementary-STRC-2014-15/All-India.pdf

NUEPA (National University of Education Planning and Administration). (2015b). *Secondary education in India: Progress towards universalisation.* New Delhi: National University of Education Planning and Administration. Retrieved from http://udise.in/Downloads/Publications/Documents/SecondaryFlash%20Statistics-2014-15.pdf

Palys, T. (2008). Purposive sampling. In L. M. Given (Ed.), *The Sage encyclopedia of qualitative research methods* (pp. 697–698). Los Angeles, CA: Sage.

Petrides, L., Jimes, C., Middleton-Detzner, C. & Howell, H. (2010). OER as a model for enhanced teaching and learning. In *Open Ed 2010 Proceedings, 2–4 November 2010.* Barcelona, Spain. Retrieved from http://openaccess.uoc.edu/webapps/o2/bitstream/10609/4995/6/Jimes_editat.pdf

PROBE (Public Report on Basic Education). (1998). *Public report on basic education.* New Delhi: Oxford University Press. Retrieved from http://www.educationforallinindia.com/public_report_basic_education_india-1998_probe.pdf

Rothberg, R. A. (1985). *Improving school climate and reducing teacher isolation [Abstract].* Retrieved from http://eric.ed.gov/?id=ED270855

Sapire, I. & Reed, Y. (2011). Collaborative design and use of Open Educational Resources: A case study of a mathematics teacher education project in South Africa. *Distance Education for Empowerment and Development in Africa, 32(2),* 195–211. Retrieved from http://dx.doi.org/10.1080/01587919.2011.584847

Scheffler, I. (1973). *Reason and teaching.* London: Routledge & Kegan Paul.

Sharma, R. (2016). Subject teacher forums and the Karnataka Open Educational Resources programme – A case study. In G. Dhanarajan (Ed.), *Vignettes of selected Asian experience.* Penang: WOU Press.

Stacey, P. (2013). Government support for Open Educational Resources: Policy, funding, and strategies. *The International Review of Research in Open and Distributed Learning, 14(2).* Retrieved from http://www.irrodl.org/index.php/irrodl/article/view/1537/2481

State Project Director. (2012). *Education in Karnataka State, 2011–12: A state-level and district–wise analytical report.* Karnataka: State Project Director, Sarva Shiksha Abhiyan. Retrieved from http://ssakarnataka.gov.in/pdfs/data/2011-12_analytical_report.pdf

Thakur, G. K. (2014). ICT and digital divide in Indian school system. *International Journal of Interdisciplinary and Multidisciplinary Studies (IJIMS), 2(2),* 34–38. Retrieved from http://www.ijims.com/uploads/f90404702bff04fca837D6.pdf

Vespignani, A. (2009). Predicting the behaviour of techno-social systems. *Science, 325,* 425–428. Retrieved from https://www.researchgate.net/publication/26692140_Predicting_the_Behavior_of_Techno-Social_Systems

Wiley, D., Green, C. & Soares, L. (2012). *Dramatically bringing down the cost of education with OER: How Open Education Resources unlock the door to free learning.* Washington, D.C.: Center for American Progress. Retrieved from http://files.eric.ed.gov/fulltext/ED535639.pdf

How to cite this chapter

Kasinathan, G. & Ranganathan, S. (2017). Teacher professional learning communities: A collaborative OER adoption approach in Karnataka, India. In C. Hodgkinson-Williams & P. B. Arinto (Eds.), *Adoption and impact of OER in the Global South* (pp. 499–548). Retrieved from https://doi.org/10.5281/zenodo.601180

Corresponding author: Gurumurthy Kasinathan <guru@itforchange.net>

Chapter 15

An early stage impact study of localised OER in Afghanistan

Lauryn Oates, Letha Kay Goger, Jamshid Hashimi and Mubaraka Farahmand

Summary

This study evaluates a group of Afghan teachers' use of Open Educational Resources (OER) from the Darakht-e Danesh Library (DDL) – a digital library comprised of educational materials in English, Dari and Pashto – investigating whether these resources enabled improvements in teaching practice and led to improved subject knowledge. Conducted with secondary-school teachers in Parwan, Afghanistan, who accessed the DDL over a four-week period in 2016, the study asked the following research questions: To what extent did teachers in this study access and use OER in the DDL? Did access and use of OER in the DDL enhance teachers' subject-area content knowledge? Did access and use of DDL resources enhance teachers' instructional practices? To what extent did teachers' understanding of OER and its value change?

The study utilised quantitative and qualitative methods to examine the behaviour and practices of 51 teachers in rural Afghanistan, all of whom were teaching at the secondary level or affiliated with a local teacher training college. The study collected data from server logs, pre- and post-treatment questionnaires, lesson plan analyses, teacher interviews and classroom observation. A purposive sampling technique was utilised to select the teachers, drawing from educational institutions with which the Canadian Women for Women in Afghanistan non-governmental organisation had previously interacted. ▶

Findings indicate that when the DDL was used by teachers, the OER accessed positively impacted teachers' knowledge and helped them in lesson preparation. On average, the 33 teachers who visited the lab at least three times downloaded 12 OER each over the course of the study. However, a number of teachers did not download or use any OER, and many more preferred to continue using only the traditional textbook to prepare their lesson plans even after exposure to the DDL. Furthermore, while teachers found the OER helpful in creating assessment activities for their students, there was no observed improvement in teacher understanding and use of formative or summative assessment. Lastly, there was limited understanding among the teachers of the exact meaning of "open", with most viewing OER as learning materials obtained from the internet, libraries or simply from outside of their school. Teachers made little reference to licensing or to the accessibility characteristics of OER. Thus, while teachers who used OER appeared to benefit from these resources, the concept was new to them, representing a disruption to the familiar way of preparing and delivering lessons.

For further diffusion of OER as an innovation in teachers' learning and practice, concerted action will be required to build the collection of OER available in Afghan languages, provide support in how teachers might integrate OER into their teaching, and ensure connectivity in the context of limited internet access in rural areas and a teacher population with widely varying levels of proficiency in using digital technology.

The dataset arising from this study can be accessed at:
https://www.datafirst.uct.ac.za/dataportal/index.php/catalog/622

Acronyms and abbreviations

CW4WAfghan	Canadian Women for Women in Afghanistan
DDL	Darakht-e Danesh Library
ICT	information and communication technologies
NGO	non-governmental organisation
OER	Open Educational Resources
TESSA	Teacher Education in Sub-Saharan Africa
TESS-India	Teacher Education through School Based Support in India

Introduction

Background

Since the Taliban regime ended in late 2001, the basic education system in Afghanistan has experienced a rebirth with millions of girls returning to school or enrolling for the first time, new teacher colleges opening in every province and ongoing efforts to reform the curricula. There are, however, still substantive challenges. With the devastating impact to the nation's economy and infrastructure of a war that raged continuously since 1978, and the presence of an ongoing Taliban insurgency that has singled out the education sector for violent attack due to Taliban opposition to secular and girls' education, Afghanistan is a difficult environment in which to teach and learn.

Afghan teachers contend with a daunting lack of resources. Most schools do not have libraries or science laboratories, many students go without textbooks, and teachers have little material to help them work through a new curriculum that many struggle to understand. The school curriculum is also acknowledged to be in need of further development (Georgescu, 2008). Afghan textbooks, although updated several times in the post-Taliban period, are considered to be riddled with errors, poorly sequenced and of generally low quality (Tani, 2014).[1] At the secondary level, in particular, there are extreme textbook shortages and no teachers' guides (Nazari et al., 2016). A study of teacher education in Afghanistan (Nicholson, 2013) found that even in Kabul, the largest urban centre in the country, students often lacked access to textbooks, textbooks were not distributed in a timely manner and teacher guidebooks were often not distributed to teachers – a finding echoed by Bethke (2012).

Additionally, despite greatly increased enrolment and thousands of schools being constructed or rebuilt, the majority of Afghan teachers are not formally qualified to teach because they have not met the minimum qualifications, which is two years of training at a teachers' college. Unqualified teachers may not be knowledgeable about their assigned subject area or competent with pedagogy, including assessment of student performance. They may use traditional, didactic teaching practices and rely on student textbooks to guide their lesson planning and assessment practices. Teacher morale is often low due to poor teacher compensation, challenging work environments and limited intrinsic interest in the profession. Weak teaching capacity coupled with a lack of resources and other delivery challenges such as minimal instructional time (classes typically are 30 minutes in length) have resulted in many Afghan pupils being unable to read by the time they enter the upper primary school level (Grades 4–6). One study found that, depending upon the province, 25–50% of Grade 6 students in Afghanistan could not read, and 20% fewer Afghan students in government schools were able to answer basic comprehension questions by Grade 6 when compared to Grade 4 students in Iran (ACER, 2013). This situation puts students at an extreme disadvantage by the time they enter secondary school.

Open Educational Resources and the Darakht-e Danesh Library

There are many contributing factors to the current education crisis in Afghanistan, but one that has been particularly neglected in discussions about the situation is the lack of good teaching and learning material available in Afghan languages.[2] The publishing sector in general, and the educational publishing sector in particular, is weak and lacks diversity

---

1　See, for example, https://iwpr.net/global-voices/afghanistan-new-textbooks-baffle-teachers.
2　Afghanistan's two official languages are Dari (Afghan Farsi) and Pashto. However, there are at least 42 languages spoken today in Afghanistan, although many are in danger of falling out of use. Of these languages, 35 are indigenous to Afghanistan, highlighting the richness of linguistic diversity in a small geographic area. However, only four languages spoken in Afghanistan are considered to be standardised and institutional, while five are developing, 20 are vigorous, five are in trouble and seven are dying. Languages such as Inku, Mogholi, Pahlavani and Parya already have no known speakers; Wotapuri-Katarqalai is now categorised as extinct; and Domari, Prmuri and Tirahi are considered nearly extinct (Simons & Fennig, 2017).

of content, relying primarily on imported books. Non-governmental organisations (NGOs) working in the education sector have produced training materials and other resources for teachers, but they tend not to disseminate their materials beyond their own project beneficiaries, and there is a limited culture of sharing materials openly within the education sector. It is therefore difficult to find quality teacher resources in Afghan languages for educational use.

The global Open Educational Resources (OER) movement has made large collections of materials available to educators free of charge and without certain copyright restrictions, providing teachers with direct access to valuable sources of knowledge as well as new teaching tools and pedagogical approaches. However, teachers in the developing world who speak languages other than English are largely excluded from taking advantage of this wealth of free information. This is particularly the case in Central Asia, as languages from this region have little representation in digital libraries (Oates, 2009), including libraries with openly accessible materials. It was in consideration of these challenges in the education context that the Darakht-e Danesh ("Knowledge Tree") Library (DDL) for educators in Afghanistan was established in 2014 by the Canadian Women for Women in Afghanistan (CW4WAfghan) NGO.[3]

The long-term goal of the DDL is to contribute to the improvement of the quality of basic education in Afghanistan and to improve student learning outcomes in Afghan classrooms. It is envisioned that increased access to a growing collection of OER will improve both teachers' subject knowledge and teaching practice. Furthermore, in developing the DDL, it was hypothesised that the OER approach may offer a potential solution to some of the education-quality challenges in Afghanistan if OER is developed in local languages and if the technology to deliver resources is adapted to respond to the infrastructure challenges, such as limited electricity and poor internet access.

The DDL is a digital educational resource collection for teachers, providing relevant subject information, lesson plans, games, experiments and books in over 30 subject-area categories ranging from biology to fine arts. The DDL housed around 2 000 resources at the time of writing (with new resources being added daily). The DDL uses an innovative, interactive, user-friendly, multilingual, custom-designed web platform, and provides a service in the three languages used in Afghanistan's public school system (Dari, Pashto and English). The DDL is Afghanistan's first OER initiative, serving as an independent source of knowledge, information and pedagogical tools for Afghan teachers, with the aim of addressing the extreme lack of educational materials for teachers in Afghanistan who have very limited access to relevant and high-quality educational resources.

Users are also encouraged to contribute their own content by submitting it to the site. To date, however, most content has been produced by the DDL team, drawing from various OER available in English and translating them into Dari and Pashto. Translations are carried out by DDL's team of volunteers – bilingual Afghans around the world who contribute to developing the collection by giving their time to work on translations. Translations and submissions are reviewed by DDL's full-time multilingual editor, who approves final versions for publication after making any revisions and checking the translation against the original.

---

3   The library and background information about its creation can be viewed at www.darakhtdanesh.org and www. ddl.af.

Edited versions are shared with the volunteer to support their continued development. If a translation requires minor revisions, it is sent back to the volunteer for further work. In cases where a translation is of poor quality, it is not used and the volunteer is not assigned more work. The library also sources existing educational materials in Dari and Pashto by formally seeking permission from the creators to include them in the collection. Material submitted by users is checked by the editor to ensure it meets the library's development standards.

Several different access models have been employed to make the DDL accessible to educators in Afghanistan, the overwhelming majority of whom do not have access to the internet to discover and use the DDL independently. The DDL can be downloaded as an application that is useable offline on a feature phone, smart phone or tablet. It can also be installed in a networked computer lab using one computer configured as a server with the other computers as clients, allowing the library to be accessed offline (however, in order to synchronise the collection and to send usage data to the main DDL server, the server computer must occasionally be connected to the internet via a 3G or 4G connection).

As staff members of the CW4WAfghan NGO that founded the digital library and engaged in ongoing work to expand the DDL in terms of both its content and reach to more users in Afghanistan, the authors have an inherent interest in better understanding the impact of the OER the DDL have developed or adapted through translation and localisation, and the platform through which they are disseminated, to guide forthcoming efforts. It is also the authors' hope that this chapter will contribute to filling the gap created by the lack of research to date on the value of localised OER in developing country contexts.

Literature review and theoretical framework

This study considers three levels of impact from teachers' use of OER: access and use, knowledge and practice, and understanding of OER. For access and use, we sought to understand the frequency with which the teachers in the study made use of OER, considering the DDL useability and relevance for the target users, while also considering their level of awareness and acceptance of OER (addressing research question 1). For impact on knowledge and practice, we sought to understand whether use of OER in the DDL impacted teachers' knowledge of subjects taught and their practice as teachers, such as the content they plan to deliver in a lesson and the teaching methods used to deliver and assess the lessons (addressing research questions 2 and 3). In order to probe teachers' understanding of OER, we sought to better understand whether teacher perceptions of "open" and its value, along with what constitutes OER, changed during the course of the study (research question 4).

We consulted literature on local-language OER initiatives in comparable environments – the extent of which is quite limited[4] – in addition to literature on the value of OER for increasing subject expertise and instructional practice, and literature relevant to OER uptake.

---

4 Most of the outputs here are produced by the Teacher Education in Sub-Saharan Africa (TESSA) and Teacher Education through School Based Support in India (TESS-India) projects of UK Open University, and the South African initiative advancing community-based open education, Siyavula.

This study aims to contribute to the "emerging framework for localisation to ensure more equitable and sustainable OER development and use" (Buckler, Perryman, Seal & Musafir, 2014, p.222), and to understand how increased access to localised open content may impact teachers' subject knowledge and teaching practice in Afghanistan. Open content offers many educational opportunities and has the potential to advance key development and human rights goals in all contexts. However, as Hatakka (2009) explains, there are primary inhibiting factors for OER reuse in localised contexts in developing countries. In Afghanistan, these inhibiting factors are language, relevance, access, technical resources, quality and intellectual property. In a podcast, Wiley (2007) discusses how the process of localisation addresses these inhibitors through "the tailoring of content by locals for locals using appropriate, sustainable technologies".

Measuring OER uptake and use

De Hart, Chetty and Archer (2015) discuss the various phases of uptake through which individuals and institutions progress when integrating OER into their practice. Following Rogers' (2003) five stages of innovation diffusion, they frame OER adoption within the following "stages": (1) knowledge (awareness); (2) persuasion (interest); (3) decision (evaluation/benefit); (4) implementation (trial); and (5) confirmation (adoption). These phases serve as a useful framework to identify where teachers are positioned in their use of OER for teaching and learning, and we apply this framework to interpret our own findings. The pace at which individuals progress through these stages varies, depending upon the level of localisation and the relevance of content, local support, technology available, institutional and cultural practices, teacher access to resources, and prior knowledge of OER. Ascertaining which stage an individual teacher is at can help determine the respective importance of these variables on uptake.

Localisation as a factor of use

Drawing on the TESSA and TESS-India experiences – OER collections developed for East Africa and India, respectively – Buckler et al. (2014) emphasise the role of localisation in making OER relevant and useful for the educational reform aspirations of developing countries, in contrast to transferring OER from the developed world to the developing world where it may have limited uptake and impact.

The TESS-India experience also highlights the cultural and institutional shifts required to overcome teachers' negative perceptions of the value of OER. As others have found, "dumping content onto a server isn't the most effective way to encourage fast learning" and "the best way to spread content is with locally created content".[5] The importance of content rooted in the cultural and geographic contexts in which teachers teach is further discussed by Jimes, Weiss and Keep (2013), who show that teachers view content created by local field experts and scholars as more useful and reliable than textbooks created by governments or for-profit publishing companies. As Wenger has emphasised (in opposition to passively consuming the work of others), "in order to engage in practice, we must be alive in a world where we can act and interact" (1998, p.51).

---

5   https://opensource.com/education/14/8/crowdsourcing-open-education-africa

Castells (2000, p.31) makes a further argument that can be applied to the case for localisation, contending that sites of use should be proximate to sites of innovation if the goal is sustainable change; in such a context, "users and doers may become the same". Innovations made elsewhere and imported into an environment are unlikely to spur new innovations or nurture communities of practice that can improve and adapt a tool to suit their needs.

User language and accessibility

One of the areas of impact this study has considered is OER access and, within that context, the availability of OER in the language best understood by users. At the DDL, we emphasise language accessibility as the pre-eminent feature required for OER uptake by Afghan teachers and have concentrated our efforts on localising the DDL collection according to user language. In general, multilingual digital platforms are understudied, remaining "a bit of an enigma" (Diekema, 2012, p.10) – particularly as regards multilingual digital libraries in the developing world. While the theme of accessibility is prevalent within the OER literature, language as a criterion of accessibility is undersupported in practice and underresearched, with very few OER collections supporting multiple languages, alphabets or scripts (West & Victor, 2011). The literature review validates that there is little precedent to draw upon when assessing the potential of local-language OER as a feature of accessibility.

Budzise-Weaver, Chen and Mitchell's (2012) case study of four multilingual digital libraries offered relevant lessons for the DDL, as they explore the potential for crowdsourcing content, for collaboration, and consider what design is appropriate for multilingual information systems, as does Leinonen, Purma, Põldoja and Toikkanen's (2010) work. Other studies affirm the lack of attention to the issue of multilingualism in OER repositories and digital libraries. Amiel (2013), for example, points to the lack of multilingual interfaces and metadata, and how this restricts use of these sites in other languages. Amiel (2013, p.132) also discusses how language is a neglected problem in the discourse on remixing, revision and adaptation of OER,[6] and notes how language revision "involves a substantial amount of thought into the process of localisation".

The notion that OER "travels well" (meaning that the resource can be easily transferred to different cultural and linguistic contexts) is also useful in supporting localisation, where users can take a resource and easily translate, adapt and/or recontextualise it to meet local needs (Petrides & Jimes, 2008). Since much of the DDL collection consists of OER that were originally in English and then translated into Dari and/or Pashto, we identify and select for translation resources that travel well, although sometimes content is adapted in other ways to suit Afghan audiences (such as by adding further graphics or explanatory notes for unfamiliar terms). Jimes et al. (2013) also discuss how localisation of OER can extend beyond the ability to translate and modify content for classroom needs, to providing a means to create formats that are useable in diverse local contexts. This impact study attempts to be a useful test to determine the useability and relevance of DDL OER, as localised OER.

In addition to the focus on delivery format, translation and localisation, there is a great need for more research on strategies that support *original* content creation for local use, particularly in cases where local languages are used. For instance, Buckler et al. (2014)

---

6   The degree of openness of an educational resource is often determined with reference to the "5Rs": the extent to which users are free to retain, reuse, revise, remix and redistribute educational materials. See https://opencontent.org/blog/archives/3221.

call for more research to illuminate strategies of localisation, adaptation and *production* of OER by the user community. Although this study does not cover production of OER by the study participants, some of the OER in the collection are the creations of Afghan teachers who submitted their resources.

Value of OER for increasing subject expertise and improving instructional practice

Numerous factors contribute to teacher effectiveness, but the importance of subject knowledge and its impact on a teacher's ability to organise and use content effectively for student learning is key (Hattie, 2012). While research on the impact of subject knowledge on teacher effectiveness is largely confined to the United States, Metzler and Woessmann (2010), in a primary school study in rural Peru, observed that teacher knowledge of a subject resulted in a statistically significant impact on student achievement, and is a relevant factor in overall teacher quality and student achievement. Related to this, Misra (2014) explains how the TESS-India project is working towards improving the quality of teaching practice in India by making available OER that provide an opportunity for deepening content knowledge and trying new instructional approaches.

This study is an early-stage evaluation of the use of an Afghan digital library's resources by its small group of users over a short period of time, investigating whether the OER accessed via the DDL enabled teachers' use of educational content in their teaching practice and whether this content positively impacted educators' subject knowledge and pedagogical practice. To evaluate the effectiveness of the resources in the early stages of the library's development, this study asked the following research questions:

1. To what extent did teachers in this study access and use OER in the DDL?
2. Did access and use of OER in the DDL enhance teachers' subject-area content knowledge?
3. Did access and use of DDL resources enhance teachers' instructional practices?
4. To what extent did teachers' understanding of OER and its value change?

With this study, we hope to contribute to the literature some findings on the impact of OER from a context that has not previously been studied, but where challenges to teacher education exist that OER may be particularly well suited to address.

Methodology

This study primarily used quantitative methods and one qualitative process. Given that this is not a longitudinal or long-term project, and remaining cognisant of the challenges inherent in isolating causality of learning outcomes (Halai, 2004), the study collected a variety of data obtained from server logs, pre- and post-treatment questionnaires, lesson plan analyses, teacher interviews and classroom observation – all of which were conducted to understand what impact, if any, OER had on teacher practice and teachers' subject knowledge. This section describes the participants, followed by an explanation of the methods used, sources and the process for analysis.

The methodological approach employed in this study was designed in collaboration with OER research experts who mentored the DDL staff based in Kabul and assisted in the design of the instruments.[7] The Kabul team travelled to the study sites in Parwan to collect the data between March and June 2016.

Participants

This study examined the behaviour and practices of a group of secondary school teachers in Parwan, a rural province of Afghanistan, who accessed the DDL over a four-week period in April/May 2016. Respondents included 24 females and 27 males (51 participants in total), all from the same rural province and all teaching at the secondary level or affiliated with the local teacher training college. Of these, 25 were university graduates (with a bachelor's degree), two had postgraduate degrees, 23 had graduated with a two-year teacher college certification and one had a high school diploma.[8] Twenty teachers had 6–10 years of teaching experience, 13 had taught for 2–5 years, 12 had taught for more than 20 years, and six had taught for 11–15 years. Thus, there was a range of educational levels, as well as a range of experience in teaching.

Methods

A purposive sampling technique was utilised to select the teachers, drawing from educational institutions where CW4WAfghan had previously worked[9] and where the security situation was stable enough to allow access to the schools. Schools included a girls' high school (22 teachers), a boys' high school (20 teachers) and a teacher college (nine teachers who were also lecturers at the college). The teachers were interviewed and given a pre-treatment questionnaire to collect relevant basic demographic information about them (such as number of years teaching) and to probe their level of experience with digital devices, their current teaching practices, as well as their beliefs about and awareness of OER. Samples of their lesson plans were also collected prior to their exposure to the DDL. The teachers then participated in a workshop in which they were taught how to register an account on the DDL, search the library, save learning materials and share their own materials. There was no specific instruction given on how to integrate the learning materials into their teaching practice. This was left to the teachers to determine so that the researchers could observe their practice and how they chose to use the OER (if at all) in a more natural way.

The teachers were then given access to the DDL through several means at three physical sites that were selected because they were the only locations where teachers could regularly

---

7   Consulting experts were Letha Kay Goger, an OER digital librarian and adjunct faculty in the School of Education at Fresno Pacific University, California, and Mythili Gowtham, an open learning and OER researcher from the Indira Gandhi National Open University, New Delhi.

8   This particular group of teachers had higher educational attainment levels than is typically seen in rural areas of Afghanistan. This is attributable to Parwan's proximity to the capital, Kabul, and a longer history of access to public education than many other areas.

9   This training, known as the Fanoos ("lantern") Teacher Training Program, consisted of basic teacher training covering both subject content and pedagogy, and was delivered for unqualified in-service teachers (teachers who do not have a teacher college diploma or any previous formal training as teachers). Teachers who completed the training were certified as qualified teachers by the Ministry of Education. The programme has been running since 2008, and has trained approximately 1 000 teachers annually, covering six Afghan provinces to date.

access computers: the computer lab in the local teachers' college and the labs in two public schools where the DDL was installed on an offline local network because there was no internet connection in the labs. Teachers made up to 15 visits each to the labs during the four-week period of the study, which was tracked by their log-in data. The offline DDL was also loaded onto teachers' mobile devices, enabling them to access the library from their mobile devices. In addition, two tablets pre-loaded with the DDL were placed in one of the school's libraries, where they could be signed out like books.

Data sources

Data on the teachers' use of the DDL library were collected during the approximately four weeks of lab time logged by teachers. Data from 18 teachers who visited fewer than three times were excluded as it was felt that fewer than three visits would be insufficient exposure to OER to measure changes in awareness, practice and knowledge. The total sample size for assessing DDL use was therefore 33 participants. Data were collected in three stages: before teacher training and use of the library, while the teachers were using the library and after they had used the library regularly (visiting at least three times). Table 1 shows the relationship between data collection processes and the types of impact that the data were designed to illuminate.

Table 1: Types of impact measured and data collection instruments

Type of impact examined	Instrument	Period administered
ACCESS and USE: Increased awareness and use of OER in DDL via a variety of access points and pathways **Research question 1:** *To what extent did teachers in this study access and use OER in the DDL?*	Post-treatment questionnaire	Post-treatment
	Server-log data	During and post-treatment
KNOWLEDGE and PRACTICE: Enhanced teacher subject-area content knowledge and improved teaching methods **Research questions 2 and 3:** *Did access and use of OER in the DDL enhance teachers' subject-area content knowledge and/or teacher instructional practice?*	Pre-treatment lesson plan rubric	Pre-treatment
	Pre-treatment questionnaire	Pre-treatment
	Post-treatment lesson plan rubric	Post-treatment
	Post-treatment questionnaire	Post-treatment
	Classroom observation rubric	Post-treatment
OPEN EDUCATION: Increased teacher understanding of OER and improved perception of its value **Research question 4:** *To what extent did teachers' understanding of OER and its value change?*	Pre-treatment questionnaire	Pre-treatment
	Post-treatment questionnaire	Post-treatment
	Server-log data	Post-treatment questionnaire

After teachers in the study accessed the DDL over the four-week period, the research team once again collected lesson plans from the 33 teachers as a proxy to measure teacher growth in subject knowledge, teaching effectiveness and use of OER. The post-treatment lesson plan took the same form as the pre-treatment lesson plan assessment, asking teachers to plan a lesson in their subject area addressing the four questions below. The teachers' answers to each of the four questions would indicate changes in specific aspects of teaching practice (aspects identified as indicators of change in teaching practice are indicated in brackets).

1. What resources and materials will be used in teaching? (subject knowledge, OER use, teaching practice)
2. What teaching method will be used to cover the topic? (teaching practice, OER use, subject knowledge)
3. What activities will be used to build student understanding or skills? (teaching practice, OER use)
4. How will student understanding be assessed during the lesson? (teaching practice, subject knowledge)

To assess whether their lesson design effectiveness with regard to the four questions improved, regressed or remained the same, each teacher's pre-treatment and post-treatment lesson plans were scored using a rubric[10] administered by a trained teacher educator.

After the lesson plan assessment, participant teachers were observed teaching in their classrooms. Observations were conducted by CW4WAfghan teacher educators. Each observation was logged in a rubric designed to identify the depth of the teachers' subject knowledge and presentation skills, effectiveness of teaching methods and activities, and the level of OER integration in their teaching. The classroom observation rubric identified teachers as "beginning", "emerging" or "effective" in terms of the following six criteria (aspects identified as indicators of change in teaching practice are indicated in brackets):

1. Learning objectives are discussed in the beginning of the session. (subject knowledge, teaching effectiveness)
2. Introduction of the topic is made clear and interesting. (subject knowledge, teaching effectiveness)
3. Examples, case studies or demonstrations are used to explain the topic. (subject knowledge, teaching effectiveness, OER use)
4. Teaching materials like slides, pictures and handouts are used to explain topic. (teaching effectiveness, OER use)
5. Effective teaching methods and activities are used to deliver and reinforce learning. (teaching effectiveness, OER use)
6. Supplementary teaching materials (OER) are used to explain the topic. (subject knowledge, teaching practice, OER use)

---

10 The pre-intervention scoring rubric, post-training scoring rubric, teacher classroom observation rubric as well as other research instruments can be accessed as part of the published dataset arising from this study at https://www.datafirst.uct.ac.za/dataportal/index.php/catalog/622.

The research team administered a post-treatment questionnaire with the same questions as the pre-treatment questionnaire, and interviewed the teachers to identify self-reported differences in their teaching practice and perception of OER before and after using the OER in the DDL. The pre- and post-treatment questionnaires asked those who used the library to consider their knowledge and skill levels before and after accessing the OER in the library. Specifically, the teachers were asked to report on their experience of using OER and the value added to their teaching, if any; changes in their knowledge as a result of using OER, if any; sharing of resources; their understanding of the concept of OER and openness; and any change in their teaching practices following use of the DDL. Background data on the following aspects were collected: sex, age, location, teaching level, subjects taught and number of years of teaching experience.

Following implementation of the questionnaire, interviews were also conducted with some of the teachers' students to determine whether and how (from the student perspective) the exposure to OER impacted on the teachers' practice in the classroom. Only the students of teachers who used the DDL at least six times were interviewed, reducing the number of student interviews to 22 out of the original planned sample of 50. However, because the students were reluctant to openly discuss their teachers' performance, this dataset was excluded from the data analysis.

Data analysis

Data collected in the field through the eight data collection instruments (see Table 1) were analysed in addition to demographic data. These data included languages spoken and taught, teaching level, sex, subject(s) taught, age and location, as well as usage data, including number of visits, sessions, views and downloads of OER in the DDL.

The data collected were entered and cleaned in a customised online database. The data were tabulated and analysed according to their relevance to the three types of impact listed above: access and use, knowledge and practice, and understanding of openness. Different data collection instruments were developed to address these different impacts, with some instruments addressing more than one type of impact (see Table 1). Based on our theoretical framework assumption that impact is reflected in the various stages of uptake (specifically Rogers' [2003] five stages of innovation uptake), the data were analysed to understand the impact of the DDL, using primarily percentage and frequency distributions and disaggregation by variables. From the data, we looked for evidence of impact on teacher subject-area knowledge and teaching practices, such as shifts in instruction.

Data sharing

The quantitative micro data as well as instruments utilised in this study have been published on the DataFirst Data Portal[11] after undergoing a multiphased quality assurance and de-identification process. The research team and the Research on Open Educational Resources for Development (ROER4D) Curation and Dissemination team checked data files for consistency and correctness, whereafter a de-identification process was undertaken utilising an omission strategy.

---

11 https://www.datafirst.uct.ac.za/dataportal/index.php/catalog/622

The resulting dataset, published under a Creative Commons Attribution (CC BY) licence, is comprised of seven quantitative data files shared in CSV format, as well as data collection instruments, a dataset description, a project description and a de-identification overview in PDF.

Findings

As stated, this study examines whether OER accessed by school teachers via the DDL enables teachers' use of supplementary educational content in their teaching practice and whether this content positively impacts upon teachers' subject knowledge and pedagogical practice. While the study engaged only a small number of respondents, several datasets were generated to provide numerous angles from which to assess the teachers' experiences in interacting with OER, their responses to OER, and, ultimately, the extent to which they use OER in their teaching and how this affects their practice as teachers.

Teacher use of OER

During the four-week study period, teacher use of OER in DDL increased. On average, the 33 teachers who visited the lab at least three times downloaded 12 OER each over the course of the study. Ten of 18 teachers in the girls' high school downloaded resources, including one teacher who downloaded 23 OER and one teacher who downloaded only one. At the boys' high school, all teachers except for two downloaded OER, including a teacher who downloaded 52 OER and two teachers who downloaded only two OER. The large number of teachers from the girls' high school who did not download any materials (and did not sign in to the library more than once) may be attributed to the fact that women have reduced mobility and increased family burdens that could have prevented them from coming to the lab as frequently as male teachers. At the teacher training college, all nine participants downloaded OER, ranging from 32 resources to one. The high rates of access and use by teacher educators at the teacher training college – many of whom also teach in local schools – suggest that this particular group of teachers is more invested in searching for and using OER.

Most teachers said they had a good experience using OER in the DDL (84% rated the experience as "good", "very good" or "excellent"). However, many teachers continued to rely on the student textbook to prepare lessons. This was despite the fact that 40 respondents stated that they were able to easily discover OER in the library, and 42 stated that they could successfully access resources in the repository; 49 participants stated that they could easily read the content (in terms of font, format, colour). This contradiction may suggest that OER are a deviation from entrenched practices and some teachers chose not to use OER despite having access, perhaps because they are accustomed to using textbooks as the primary information source by which to prepare a lesson. While 20 teachers reported that they used both OER and the textbook, and eight said they mainly used OER from the DDL to design their lesson plan effectively, 23 said they did not use any OER and relied solely on a textbook when preparing their lesson plan. There was no significant variation found in teachers' use of OER versus the textbook by age, sex, level of education, years of teaching experience or level of comfort using information and communication technologies (ICTs).

Although this study was not designed to measure levels of teacher comfort with ICT, the pre-treatment questionnaire included ICT-related questions as a foundation for understanding teacher practice with technology. It was found that almost all of the teachers in the study owned at least one digital device. However, of those who did own a digital device, less than half (22) had internet access on their device. Of these 22, three said their internet speed was very slow, 15 said it was good or slow, and four said it was very good. Only four participants had email addresses.

All respondents were asked about their level of comfort in using digital devices. The group was split down the middle: six said they were very comfortable and 19 comfortable, while 14 said they were not very comfortable and nine said they were not at all comfortable using digital devices. Respondents were also asked about the frequency of their use of their digital devices (Table 2). Overall, this group of teachers reported a diversity of experiences and comfort levels in using technology, which demonstrates the gradual penetration of technology among teachers, albeit with limitations such as restricted or slow internet access.

Table 2: Teachers' self-reported frequency of digital device use

Device	Use frequently	Use occasionally	Use rarely	Never use
Desktop computer	9	18	4	17
Laptop	5	15	5	23
Mobile telephone	15	8	4	20

The teachers were also asked to rate their experience of using OER in the DDL. Table 3 presents feedback in response to specific criteria in the post-treatment questionnaire. Overall, teachers found the OER relevant: half of the teachers said the OER sometimes met their needs, a smaller portion said the OER always met their needs (32%), while 18% said that the OER never met their needs.

Table 3: Teacher ratings of OER effectiveness in the DDL

Area of application	Always	Sometimes	Never	Total
OER in the DDL generally provided me with more current content than I previously had.	15 (29%)	28 (55%)	8 (16%)	51
The OER I consulted in the DDL extended my knowledge of the topic.	19 (37%)	26 (51%)	6 (12%)	51
The content in the OER I consulted adequately covered my learning and teaching needs in terms of knowledge, skills and conception of the subject.	18 (35%)	24 (47%)	9 (18%)	51
The OER helped me prepare lesson plans.	15 (29%)	23 (45%)	13 (25%)	51
The OER were helpful in creating classroom activities.	18 (35%)	24 (47%)	9 (18%)	51
The OER were helpful in creating assessment activities for my students.	13 (25%)	26 (51%)	12 (24%)	51

Impact of OER on teacher subject knowledge

When it came to expanding teachers' knowledge of a topic, 67% of teachers (34 of 51) said they could identify new topics in the DDL that were suitable for teaching or learning about their subject of interest. When asked if they could relate the new topic(s) in the DDL with the curriculum they taught, 70% (36 of 51) said they could.

The data in Table 3 reflect how teachers perceived the value of OER in the DDL for extending their knowledge on topics taught and helping in lesson preparation. In total, 88% of the teachers indicated that OER in the DDL either sometimes or always extended their knowledge of the topic taught, and 82% of the teachers indicated that OER consulted in the DDL adequately covered their teaching and learning needs in terms of building their knowledge, conceptual understanding and skills on a topic. Increased teacher subject knowledge is also reflected in the improved lesson plans developed post-treatment (74%) and in classroom activities (82%). A total of 76% of teachers indicated that OER were helpful in creating assessment activities for their students, but no improvement in teacher understanding or use of formative or summative assessment of student learning was observed in their pre- and post-treatment lesson plans and during the classroom observation.

Impact of OER on teaching practice

Overall, it was found that exposure to OER in the DDL among the sample of teachers led to improved competencies that are reflective of effective teaching practice.

Lesson plans

Changes to teaching practice were assessed from the scores assigned to the teachers' lesson plan designs before and after DDL training and exposure to OER. Based on the lesson plan rubric, teachers were scored as "effective", "emerging" or "beginner" in key elements of lesson design (Table 4).

Table 4: Change in teacher lesson-design effectiveness (pre- and post-DDL training and access)

Lesson plan area of design	Teacher effectiveness level		
What content or skills will the students learn?	Effective	Emerging	Beginner
Pre-treatment and DDL access	16	15	20
Post-treatment	22	14	15
Change	+6	-1	-5
What resources and materials will be used in teaching?	Effective	Emerging	Beginner
Pre-treatment and DDL access	10	24	17
Post-treatment	18	27	6
Change	+8	+3	-11

What teaching method will be used to cover the topic?	Effective	Emerging	Beginner
Pre-treatment and DDL access	15	18	18
Post-treatment	18	24	9
Change	+3	+6	-9

What activities will be used to build student understanding or skills?	Effective	Emerging	Beginner
Pre-treatment and DDL access	5	15	31
Post-treatment	8	17	26
Change	+3	+2	-5

How will student understanding be assessed during the lesson?	Effective	Emerging	Beginner
Pre-treatment and DDL access	9	21	21
Post-treatment	8	21	22
Change	-1	0	+1

The biggest improvement in lesson design was seen in how teachers responded to the question, "What resources and materials will be used in teaching?" Ten teachers scored as "effective" in the pre-treatment rubric and 18 teachers scored as "effective" in the post-treatment rubric; 17 teachers scored as "beginner" in the pre-treatment rubric and only six teachers scored as "beginner" in the post-treatment rubric. It was only with regard to the question on assessment ("How will student understanding be assessed during the lesson?") that no improvement before and after exposure to the DDL was observed. This aligns with the data drawn from the questionnaires and classroom observation, which also suggest that participants struggled with how to assess (or measure) learning in their students. This is a critical area in instructional design where most Afghan teachers need additional support. Overall, there was general improvement in competencies for designing lessons after teachers used OER in the DDL.

Classroom observations

There was no opportunity to do pre-treatment observation of teachers in the classroom, but teachers were observed delivering lessons in the classroom post-treatment by the CW4WAfghan teacher trainers (the same individuals who scored their lesson plans). The trainers scored teachers (n = 33) against the six competencies outlined in Table 5.

Observation of classroom teaching practice during the study revealed that the largest number of teachers were "beginners" when it came to using teaching materials like slides, pictures and handouts to explain the topic (competency 4) and using supplemental (OER) materials to explain the topic (competency 6). This may suggest that, for the lesson being observed, teachers had not yet accessed OER that specifically supported instruction of the topic, or that they had not yet developed the instructional strategies for integrating a variety of teaching materials into the lesson. At the same time, the relatively high number of teachers demonstrating instructional competency in competencies 1, 2, 3 and 5 may reflect the educational and experience levels of teachers in the study (many teachers had a bachelor's degree or a two-year teaching certificate, which is a comparatively high proportion relative to the overall teaching population in the country).

Table 5: Classroom observation results

Competency area	Effective (%)	Emerging (%)	Beginner (%)
1. Learning objectives are discussed at the beginning of the session.	61	6	33
2. Introduction of topic is made clear.	61	15	24
3. Examples, case studies, demonstrations are used to explain the topic.	61	18	21
4. Teaching materials like slides, pictures and handouts are used to explain the topic.	36	24	40
5. Variety of teaching methods and activities are used to deliver the topic.	52	21	27
6. Supplementary materials (OER) are used to explain the topic.	27	33	40

The teachers' improved skills in instructional practice planning after exposure to the DDL was evidenced in improved lesson plan design. It is not clear whether this improvement is due to exposure to OER lesson models in the DDL, the general benefit of the DDL professional training, review or the use of the lesson plan template in creating lesson plans. The research team assumes that a combination of these factors led to improved lesson design and instructional practice.

Impact on awareness of OER

This section examines the teachers' level of awareness and use of OER before and after the DDL training, including their understanding of the qualities and values of openness in terms of educational resources that are open. In the pre-treatment questionnaire, 22 of the teachers said they had used OER before their participation in the study (a context in which they had guided access to OER). However, other responses in the questionnaire demonstrated little familiarity with OER and much confusion about what constitutes OER. Most teachers had some idea that OER generally had to do with information that was online and many respondents assumed that OER had to do with the internet, with libraries, books or information. For example, one teacher responded: "OER means having the internet where we can find any information about anything." Another responded: "OER refers to TV, media, radio, Facebook, Twitter, digital library." Many also specified that they thought OER were specifically resources from *outside* the school: "OER is information other than school books and the information is from the internet" and "OER are books from outside of the school like magazines, newspapers and material from the internet". This perception may relate to Afghanistan's context where schools typically have minimal learning resources besides official textbooks and other kinds of learning materials would, therefore, necessarily have to come from outside of the school.

Several teachers used the word "free" in their responses, but only in one case did a teacher refer to a characteristic of OER that relates to its licensing: "OER means accessing the topics that are not restricted and are free." Several responses also suggested that teachers associated OER with diversifying teaching methods. For instance, one teacher said: "OER is educational trips, doing experiments, showing simulations, playing movies related to the topics, and using the internet and computers." Another responded: "I think OER includes lessons, books, and materials for teaching like a book and board to teach with." Overall, it was found that OER is largely an unfamiliar concept for these teachers, although they were able to reference some characteristics of OER, such as information that is free, often online and can help teachers diversify their pedagogical practice.

Following training and use of the DDL, teachers were asked about their previous use of OER retrospectively (now that they might have a better understanding of the concept). Of those teachers who said they had previously used OER, the topics and resources they had looked up previously included resources for language learning, computers, full-text materials (such as Rumi's works), Islamic content, family education and topics related to the subjects they taught, including logarithmic equations, atomic physics, letter recognition, inventions of the Wright brothers, Afghan history, blood circulation and texts on speaking, listening and writing. While some accessed videos, most consulted text documents in Microsoft Word or PDF. When asked about the original source of these resources, most simply said they came from the internet or from a Google search, while some said they had come from a CD, library or books. One said she had used an Iranian website, and two said they had previously used the DDL.

Following training, most teachers (76%) said they were willing to share resources found in the DDL with other teachers, and that OER helped them initiate collaboration among students (78%), while somewhat fewer (66%) said OER would help them work collaboratively with other teachers. In total, 60% of the teachers reported that they were aware of how OER in the DDL were licensed, but their grasp of copyright and licensing was unclear.

Generally, the data from the post-treatment questionnaire, post-treatment lesson plans and classroom observations indicate that teachers found OER in the DDL to be relevant, applicable to their classrooms, and able to extend their knowledge of the topics they are teaching. Since teachers' exposure to OER and DDL prior to this study was quite limited, this trend in responses indicates an expected shift from level 1 (*awareness*), to level 2 (*interest*), and level 3 (*evaluation of benefit*), and even venturing to level 4 (*trial and implementation*) in de Hart et al.'s (2015) uptake scale. It also suggests that the localised OER in DDL will be well received by teachers across Afghanistan and may hold potential for positive impact on teacher practice.

Discussion

The study considered impact in three areas: access and use, knowledge and practice, and teacher understanding of the qualities and value of openness. Below, we outline what the findings illuminated for each of these types of impact in the context of teachers' use of OER in the DDL. In addition, the study considered OER as an innovation, and applied Rogers' (2003) stages of innovation diffusion to identify which phase the teachers were at in terms of their adoption of OER, as a change to their normal practice, drawing on de Hart et al.'s (2015) application of this framework to OER adoption. This was considered a relevant and appropriate conceptual framework for this study, given that the introduction of the DDL and open educational content for expanding educators' subject knowledge and teaching practice can be viewed as a "disruptor" and may require a significant shift in thought and practice for many educators who teach in conditions of highly limited access to knowledge resources beyond the government-provided textbooks.

Diffusion of OER among Afghan teachers

Rogers' (2003) theory of diffusion of innovation is useful in enhancing our understanding of the sample of Parwan province teachers' uptake of OER. Based on teacher self-evaluation questionnaires following the study, and the level of OER use in lesson plans and observed teaching sessions within a relatively short period of time, over 50% of the teachers in the study clearly moved from "awareness" to "interest" to "evaluation" in the course of this exposure to OER. Another 25% moved a step further to "implementation", with the remaining 25% demonstrating minimal interest (based on them remaining "beginners" when their post-treatment lesson plans were assessed, and the fact that they made no use of OER in their lesson). This seeming lack of interest could be the result of inexperience or discomfort with technology, the inability to discover OER that supported their teaching, social factors, lack of accessibility to the DDL when visiting the lab, or a combination of factors not yet known or yet to be understood. However, the portion of teachers willing to "implement" OER so soon after their first exposure conveys a positive message in terms of OER uptake and, given the relative newness of using technology-enabled content for learning and teaching, suggests that increased future uptake is likely and may yield positive results in improved teaching.

Some teachers in the study remained resistant to using OER, preferring to depend solely on traditional textbooks. This may be due to the emphasis placed on the textbook in developing countries, where it is often seen as the curriculum and teachers have limited time to seek out, explore and apply other learning resources in their teaching. This is particularly relevant in situations where a large portion of teachers are unqualified or underqualified, and where the state may exert pressure on teachers to work solely with the textbook, rather than trusting them to identify third-party content to teach lessons in the curriculum. Further, the use of high-stakes exams, like Afghanistan's national school-leaving exam, the Kankor, places significant pressure on teachers to teach to the exam and not deviate from the content of the textbook.

Measures required for increased teacher access and use

The need to find ways to make educational material accessible to Afghan teachers and students, and the potential that OER and ICT tools offer in this regard, is clear. To realise the potential of OER to transform educational practice, educators must have consistent and appropriate access to OER in the format best suited for their locale, as well as access to technologies which can be drawn upon or used for innovation under the circumstances. Internet connectivity and limited bandwidth are acute challenges outside of Kabul and in Parwan province where this study was conducted. Installing an offline version of the DDL on decentralised servers worked well, but required staff to periodically connect their personal devices to acquire new acquisitions and updates to the library made since installation. With the exception of occasional power outages that blocked usage of the labs where the DDL was installed, the system worked well, but required repeated visits and improvisation on the part of DDL technical team members to develop a functioning system.

The findings have provided valuable guidance to the DDL team in terms of further developing the library collection to ensure access to relevant resources. Teachers made it clear that they had a need for more resources in all subjects and that they needed to be able to find topics that suited the curriculum they were working with. The data also showed teachers' continuing reliance on textbooks and, by extension, the importance for DDL resources to be findable with reference to the topics in government textbooks. At the same time, teachers wanted access to information on subjects outside of the curriculum, like philosophy and sports, as well as professional development materials, in addition to resources like lesson plans. In some instances it was found that there was a reluctance among some teachers to prepare lessons using any resources other than the government textbook. The DDL will therefore need to consider activities that can support teachers in learning how to integrate OER into lesson preparation and diversify their information sources.

Quality, localised OER for increasing teacher knowledge and practice

In a young digital library like the DDL, it is not surprising that teachers indicated a need for more content in their subject area, language and instructional level. At the same time, the fact that 66% of the teachers consider that OER in the early-stage DDL provided them with more current subject knowledge than they previously had reflects the dearth of educational resources available to teachers in Afghanistan, and how OER can fill this gap. The adaptation and increased localisation of content into mother-tongue languages to ensure cultural or geographical relevance, improved technical access, and content that reflects 21st-century knowledge and skills will increase the amount of useful educational material in the library for teaching and learning.

OER that model effective instructional methods across core subject areas would be useful. Although there was evidence of modest improvement in the increased use of a variety of OER and instructional methods and activities over the course of the study by the teachers, there continues to be considerable room for growth. Teachers who used the DDL made notable efforts to integrate additional resources and instructional activities into their classrooms, but many teachers' lesson plans were not always aligned to meeting instructional objectives, perhaps because of lack of appropriate resources, the need for additional subject knowledge or factors this study could not determine.

Related to this, one finding stands out as informative: the need to support teachers in their ability to assess student knowledge and skills as a result of their teaching strategies. Within the study, teacher lesson plan designs, post-treatment questionnaire responses and classroom observations all demonstrated a propensity toward "delivering" content rather than engaging students in learning activities and measuring understanding or growth through formative assessment in the instructional session. Curating OER that assists teachers in building formative assessment into their teaching strategies in the DDL could improve teacher effectiveness in terms of the goal of more learner-centred education.

The study's findings suggest that building teacher subject knowledge, integrating a variety of instructional practices and including multiple opportunities for assessing student learning are all critical for effective teaching and learning. As both the quantity and quality of localised OER available to Afghan teachers increases (especially OER that include teaching practices based on student inquiry, critical thinking and problem-based learning), opportunities for teachers to build learner-centred education will grow.

Increasing teacher understanding of "openness"

The concept of openness was largely misunderstood by teachers prior to the intervention, with the concept most often being interpreted as content not provided by the government or resources that are freely available on the internet. The findings of this study clearly demonstrate the need for additional work with teachers to improve their understanding of the value of OER for accessing relevant content created by other educators, and for sharing their own collaborative development of localised content with other educators. At the same time, introducing the concept of OER to rural Afghan teachers is challenging in that framing a description of OER in terms of comparison with "non-open" resources cannot be done as easily as this might be done in other contexts, as intellectual property is poorly understood. In the Afghan context, it appears that OER are not replacing traditionally copyrighted materials; rather, they are supplementing the traditional textbook as the sole learning material teachers typically utilise. Explaining how OER are different from other educational resources is challenging when teachers have little access to either.

Looking ahead

Teachers shared varied and specific recommendations when invited to give suggestions for improving the DDL. Many asked for more resources in their subject, more resources for higher grade levels, resources to be mapped against the Afghan curriculum, pictures and audiovisual resources, resources for teaching student teachers and for an audience of university students, more Pashto resources, resources for new subjects or subjects not in the Afghan curriculum (like sports, psychology and philosophy), as well as information on technology. Several suggestions related to accessibility, such as the need to ensure that the DDL remains accessible offline for teachers, while others asked for internet access or for the DDL to be installed in schools.

More widespread OER adoption, and its consequent impacts, will be realised over a longer timespan than the period observed in this study. That said, the level of teacher receptiveness to OER displayed in the study was highly encouraging, and the teachers' feedback is informative in terms of ongoing development of the DDL, providing guidance on what to prioritise in further development of the collection and what conditions must be in place to facilitate access and impact. In a short window of time, many teachers accepted and adopted OER in their teaching practice, and for those who did, we were able to record an impact on knowledge and practice. Going forward, we hypothesise that the pace at which individuals progress through the stages of OER uptake will vary dramatically, based upon level of localisation and relevance of content, local support structures, available technology, institutional and cultural practices, teacher access to resources, prior knowledge of OER (including an understanding of intellectual property) and the DDL, as well as the willingness (and confidence) of individual teachers to move away from relying primarily on the traditional textbook to build their lessons.

In asking what more can be done to amplify the impact of OER in Afghanistan, our analysis suggests that increased use of OER for both professional learning and teaching will be bolstered by fostering a local community of practice. Further work may consider how to continue to support and encourage the creation, adaptation and reuse of teacher-created content within the Afghan context. Practice with using OER, including OER creation, can be integrated into ongoing teacher training efforts as one means of further diffusing adoption. In addition, continued development of the DDL collection will need to consider the demands of teachers in terms of the content and support they require – taking into consideration diversified subject matter, format, form and language – to enable further uptake. Access continues to be a key concern, requiring strategies to enable access for teachers within their communities through flexible technical solutions that are responsive to the specific contextual challenges of rural Afghanistan.

Conclusion

This study drew on the experiences of a group of teachers in a particular rural context for whom regular access to OER in their own language was facilitated via the DDL in order to assess whether OER would enable their use of ancillary educational content in their teaching practice. We also asked whether this content would positively impact the educators' subject knowledge and pedagogical practice, and probed the extent to which the teachers could easily use and access the OER, and their understanding of openness. We found impact in terms of utility and relevance for the teachers in helping them make gains in their subject understanding and lesson preparation, and while the teachers had many suggestions for how to make the digital library's OER more useable, a large proportion were able to find and use OER from the library's small collection and apply these resources, registering an improvement in their teaching. While the study could not measure the rate of adoption, given the modest size and scope of the DDL collection, this finding still suggests that there is great potential benefit in amplifying the utilisation of OER in Afghanistan if resources are invested in localising materials, expanding their availability and enabling access to the necessary technologies. Further development of OER could also address areas of particular weakness among Afghan teachers whose practice did not seem to be impacted by their use of OER in the study, such as subject knowledge and use of effective assessment practices, or teachers who opted to continue using only the textbook to plan lessons despite having access to relevant OER and finding it easy to use the DDL.

From the perspective of the adoption of an innovation, OER represents a disruption to a long-held reliance on government-issued textbooks as the main source from which to extract information taught to students, particularly for teachers who lack formal training. A majority of teachers in the study were quick to move through Rogers' (2003) first three stages of innovation diffusion, with a smaller number willing to apply OER in their practice (the implementation stage). This suggests that OER can be assimilated into teaching practice in Afghanistan and that teachers find value in it for supporting their classroom objectives.

This study provides an initial glimpse into Afghan teachers' current awareness of OER, their reactions to a specific directed experience of using OER, and how the experience affected their teaching in terms of impact on their subject knowledge and practice. It is our hope that this initial investigation into localised OER use in a rural Afghan province will assist in providing targeted direction on areas for further investigation and investment in order to enable OER to address the significant and urgent challenges facing the basic education sector in Afghanistan.

Acknowledgements

The authors wish to thank Rebecca Miller and Sacha Innes who acted as peer reviewers of this chapter.

References

ACER (Australian Council for Educational Research). (2013). *Monitoring educational development in Afghanistan: Technical proposal to extend development and implementation of MED program to grade 3 trial phase in 2014.* Sydney: Australian Council for Educational Research.

Amiel, T. (2013). Identifying barriers to the remix of translated Open Educational Resources. *The International Review of Research in Open and Distributed Learning, 14(1),* 126–144. Retrieved from http://www.irrodl.org/index.php/irrodl/article/view/1351/2428

Bethke, L. (2012). *Education joint sector review 1391/2012.* Kabul: Islamic Republic of Afghanistan. Retrieved from http://anafae.af/wp-content/uploads/2016/09/Primary-and-Secondary-Schooling-Sub-Sector-Report.pdf

Buckler, A., Perryman, L., Seal, T. & Musafir, S. (2014). The role of OER localisation in building a knowledge partnership for development: Insights from the TESSA and TESS-India teacher education projects. *Open Praxis, 6(3),* 221–233. Retrieved from http://dx.doi.org/10.5944/openpraxis.6.3.136

Budzise-Weaver, T., Chen, J. & Mitchell, M. (2012). Collaboration and crowdsourcing: The cases of multilingual digital libraries. *Electronic Librarian, 30(2),* 220–232. Retrieved from https://www.semanticscholar.org/paper/Collaboration-and-Crowdsourcing-The-Cases-of-Multi-Budzise-Weaver-Chen/f913edc4ddb89414ba91f787f9e8e73097e3572d

Castells, M. (2000). *The rise of the network society – Volume I: The information age, economy, society and culture* (2nd edn.). Malden, MA: Blackwell Publishing.

de Hart, K., Chetty, Y. & Archer, E. (2015). Uptake of OER by staff in distance education in South Africa. *The International Review of Research in Open and Distributed Learning, 16(2),* 18–45. Retrieved from http://www.irrodl.org/index.php/irrodl/article/view/2047

Diekema, A. (2012). Multilinguality in the digital library: A review. *The Electronic Library, 30(2),* 165–181. Retrieved from http://dx.doi.org/10.1108/02640471211221313

Georgescu, D. (2008). Primary and secondary curriculum development in Afghanistan. *Prospects, 37,* 427–448. Retrieved from https://link.springer.com/article/10.1007/s11125-008-9058-x

Halai, A. (2004). Action research to study classroom impact: Is it possible? *Educational Action Research, 12(4),* 515–534. Retrieved from http://dx.doi.org/10.1080/09650790400200266

Hatakka, M. (2009). Build it and they will come?: Inhibiting factors for reuse of open content in developing countries. *The Electronic Journal on Information Systems in Developing Countries, 37(5),* 1–16. Retrieved from http://www.is.cityu.edu.hk/staff/isrobert/ejisdc/37-5.pdf

Hattie, J. (2012). *Visible learning for teachers: Maximizing impact on learning.* London: Routledge.

Jimes, C., Weiss, S. & Keep, R. (2013). Addressing the local in localization: A case study of open textbook adoption by three South African teachers. *Journal of Asynchronous Learning Networks, 17(2),* 73–86. Retrieved from http://eric.ed.gov/?id=EJ1018301

Leinonen, T., Purma, J., Põldoja, H. & Toikkanen, T. (2010). Information architecture and design solutions scaffolding authoring of Open Educational Resources. *IEEE Transactions* on Learning Technologies, *3(2)*, 116–128. Retrieved from https://pdfs.semanticscholar.org/6158/e47439895992c9dceb4d14e98c813e0fbb94.pdf

Metzler, J. & Woessmann, L. (2010). *The impact of teacher subject knowledge on student achievement: Evidence from within-teacher within-student variation.* Bonn: Bonn Institute for the Study of Labor (IZA). Retrieved from http://ftp.iza.org/dp4999.pdf

Misra, P. K. (2014). Online training of teachers using OER: Promises and potential strategies. *Open Praxis, 6(4)*, 380. Retrieved from http://www.learntechlib.org/d/150752

Nazari, N., Rose, A., Oates, L., Hashimi, J., Shakir, O. & Siddiqi, B. (2016). *Technical assessment of selected offices within the Afghan Ministry of Education for textbook development and distribution.* Kabul: United States Agency for International Development (USAID). Retrieved from http://pdf.usaid.gov/pdf_docs/PA00M4W5.pdf

Nicholson, S. (2013). *A study of teacher and school administration personnel training programs in Afghanistan.* Kabul: War Child Canada. Retrieved from http://www.alseproject.com/uploads/4/7/7/3/47739169/130224_wcc_study_teacher___sch_admin_training_afghanistan.pdf

Oates, L. (2009). Coming up short in the OER movement: African language OERs. *Access to Knowledge: A Course Journal, 1(2)*. Retrieved from http://web.stanford.edu/group/ojs3/cgi-bin/ojs/index.php/a2k/article/view/449

Petrides, L. & Jimes, C. (2008). "Travel Well" Open Educational Resources: A presentation of ongoing research. *Presentation at iSummit 2008, 29 July–1 August 2008.* Sapporo, Japan.

Rogers, E. M. (2003). *Diffusion of innovations* (5th edn.). New York: Free Press.

Simons, G. F. & Fennig, C. D. (Eds.). (2017). *Ethnologue: Languages of the world* (20th edn.). Dallas, TX: SIL International. Retrieved from http://www.ethnologue.com

Tani, W. B. (2014). *Textbook analysis in Afghanistan: Comparison of mathematics' textbooks of grades 7–9.* M.Phil in Education thesis. Karlstads: Karlstads University.

Wenger, E. (1998). *Communities of practice: Learning, meaning and identity.* Cambridge: Cambridge University Press.

West, P. G. & Victor, L. (2011). *Background and action paper on OER: A background and action paper for staff of bilateral and multilateral organisations at the strategic institutional education sector level.* Menlo Park, CA: Williams and Flora Hewlett foundation. Retrieved from http://www.paulwest.org/public/Background_and_action_paper_on_OER.pdf

Wiley, D. (2007). *Openness, localization, and the future of learning objects* [Audio podcast]. Retrieved from http://opencontent.org/presentations/bcnet07/

How to cite this chapter

Oates, L., Goger, L. K., Hashimi, J. & Farahmand, M. (2017) An early stage impact study of localised OER in Afghanistan. In C. Hodgkinson-Williams & P. B. Arinto (Eds.), *Adoption and impact of OER in the Global South* (pp. 549–573). Retrieved from https://doi.org/10.5281/zenodo.600441

Corresponding author: Lauryn Oates <programsdirector@cw4wafghan.ca>

Section 5
Conclusion and recommendations

Contents

Chapter 16

OER and OEP in the Global South: Implications and recommendations for social inclusion

Patricia B. Arinto, Cheryl Hodgkinson-Williams and Henry Trotter

Acronyms and abbreviations

DDL   Darakht-e Danesh Library
HEI   higher education institution
IP   intellectual property
MOOC   Massive Open Online Course
NGO   non-governmental organisation
OEP   Open Educational Practices
OER   Open Educational Resources
ROER4D   Research on Open Educational Resources for Development

Introduction

The Research on Open Educational Resources for Development (ROER4D) project was undertaken to provide a better understanding of the uptake of Open Educational Resources (OER) and their impact on education in the Global South. The 18 sub-projects that comprise the larger project investigated the extent of OER adoption by educators and students; the factors influencing OER adoption; and the impact of OER adoption on access to educational resources, the quality of teaching and learning, and some of the costs of education provision in 21 countries in South America, Sub-Saharan Africa, and South and Southeast Asia.

The findings of each of the sub-projects are discussed in the various chapters comprising this volume, and a meta-synthesis of these findings is presented in Chapter 2. Using a social realist lens, the meta-synthesis provides a comparative analysis of OER use, adaptation and creation across the research sites, and identifies the structural, cultural and agential factors that enable and constrain these Open Educational Practices (OEP). It points out disjunctures in adoption processes in the countries and institutions studied, and draws insights regarding the extent to which OER adoption can expand access to educational materials, enhance the quality of educational resources and educators' pedagogical perspectives and practices, and improve the affordability and sustainability of education in the Global South.

This concluding chapter explores the implications of the main research findings presented in the meta-synthesis for the attainment of social inclusion, which lies at the heart of the Open Education movement. The Paris OER Declaration of 2012[1] explicitly calls upon states to "[p]romote and use OER to … contribut[e] to *social inclusion*, gender equity and special needs education [and i]mprove both cost-efficiency and quality of teaching and learning outcomes"[2] (emphasis added). The Ljubljana OER Action Plan of 2017[3] likewise recognises that, "[t]oward the realization of inclusive Knowledge Societies … [OER] support quality education that is equitable, inclusive, open and participatory". Understanding how OER, OEP and Open Education more generally, can help to achieve social inclusion is particularly critical in the Global South where increased demand, lack of resources and high costs limit the capacity of education systems to provide accessible, relevant, high-quality and affordable education. This chapter aims to contribute to this understanding the

---

1   http://www.unesco.org/new/fileadmin/MULTIMEDIA/HQ/CI/WPFD2009/English_Declaration.html
2   http://www.unesco.org/new/fileadmin/MULTIMEDIA/HQ/CI/CI/pdf/Events/English_Paris_OER_Declaration.pdf
3   https://en.unesco.org/sites/default/files/ljubljana_oer_action_plan_2017.pdf

potential of OER and their accompanying OEP through a critical exploration of the ROER4D findings in terms of whether and how OER adoption promotes equitable access, participatory education and empowerment of teachers and students, and thus helps to achieve social inclusion. The chapter begins with a brief overview of the relationship between OER and social inclusion, details the implications of ROER4D's findings as they pertain to social inclusion, and concludes with recommendations for advocacy, policy, practice and further research in OER and OEP in the Global South.

Social inclusion

Social inclusion refers to "the process of improving the terms for individuals and groups to take part in society ... It ensures that people have a voice in decisions which affect their lives and that they enjoy equal access to markets, services and political, social and physical spaces".[4] The process assumes that people face some level of social "exclusion" – a complex reality that may be influenced by factors of "socio-economic status, culture (including indigenous cultures), linguistic group, religion, geography (rural and remote/ isolated), gender, sexual orientation, age (including youth and old age), physical and mental health/ability, and status with regard to unemployment, homelessness and incarceration" (Gidley, Hampson, Wheeler & Bereded-Samuel, 2010, p.1).

OER advocates have approached the relationship between OER and social inclusion in different ways. Bliss and Smith write that in the early days of the open movement, "much of our attention focused on OER's usefulness at providing knowledge in its original form to those who otherwise might not have access. The implicit goal was to equalize access to disadvantaged and advantaged peoples of the world – in MIT's [Massachusetts Institute of Technology] language to create 'a shared intellectual Common'" (2017, p.15).

OER proponents then expanded their understanding of social inclusion to incorporate notions of participation (Lane, 2012) and social justice (Jhangiani, 2017), especially in contexts shaped by cultural and/or linguistic marginalisation (Bradley & Vigmo, 2014). Critiquing any approach that would appear to be based on a "top-down" provision of educational resources by educational elites to others (Perryman & Coughlan, 2013), Richter and McPherson (2012, p.202) argue that "just providing those resources as a contextualized 'give-away' cannot lead to reach the aim of educational justice throughout the world ... [and] ... that when implementing learning in foreign contexts, not taking the cultural context of the targeted learners into consideration can lead to their frustration and finally to a general denial of participation". Thus, educators are encouraged to become "public-facing" so as to meet the needs of the communities that they are serving with their materials development (Perryman & Coughlan, 2013).

More recently, OER scholars have suggested that "studies into the activities and competences of self-direction are needed" (Knox, 2013, p.830), meaning that it is time to collapse the boundary separating learner and educator, and between materials-user and materials-creator. Social inclusion means empowering educators and students to be the creators of their own materials and knowledge, not just recipients or adapters of others'

---

4   http://www.worldbank.org/en/topic/socialdevelopment/brief/social-inclusion

work. A similar sentiment animates those who encourage the historically and persistently excluded from knowledge production (Jhangiani & Biswas-Diener, 2017), such as scholars in the Global South, to transcend the demeaning and exclusionary situation where "data gathering and application happen in the colony, while theorising happens in the metropole" (Connell, 2007, p.ix).

The ROER4D project understanding of social inclusion is informed by these varied approaches, though we find their differences to be of degree rather than type. Gidley et al.'s (2010) discussion of "degrees" of social inclusion is especially useful in understanding the dynamics of OER and social inclusion. Arguing that inclusion is not a binary outcome – i.e. you are either included or not – they propose "a nested schema regarding degrees of inclusion" where "the narrowest interpretation pertains to the neoliberal notion of social inclusion as access; a broader interpretation regards the social justice idea of social inclusion as participation; whilst the widest interpretation involves the human potential lens of social inclusion as empowerment" (Gidley et al., 2010, p.2).

The most basic form of social inclusion is access to resources. Gidley et al. suggest that this is connected to neoliberal ideology, which sees access as being about "investing in human capital and improving the skills shortages for the primary purpose of economic growth as part of a nationalist agenda to build the nation's economy in order to better perform in a competitive global market" (2010, p.2). It is an instrumentalist approach, seeing people as having certain deficits (in skills, etc.) that should be overcome with greater access, leading to social capital and opportunities for individuals, as well as expanded economic growth for their societies.

A more expansive form of social inclusion includes notions of participation which are connected to principles of social justice. This addresses issues of "human rights, egalitarianism of opportunity, human dignity, and fairness for all" (Gidley et al., 2010, p.4) by enabling individuals' participation "in the key activities of the society in which they live" (Saunders, Naidoo & Griffiths, 2007, p.17) beyond mere employment. Higher education can help to achieve this degree of social inclusion by promoting social responsibility and community engagement, for example through participatory action research, service learning and other forms of university–community partnerships.

The highest level of social inclusion is empowerment of individuals to reach their full potential based on the principle that each person is complex and multidimensional, and that difference and diversity are strengths to be leveraged and enhanced rather than ignored or suppressed. In education, this degree of social inclusion is realised through an emphasis on dialogue, multiculturalism, personal empowerment, lifelong learning and social transformation. In this context, "education can be understood as transformative" (Gidley et al., 2010, p.5), fostering one's dignity and generativity.

OER and OEP: Implications for social inclusion

In this section, we discuss the findings of the ROER4D sub-project studies regarding OER engagement in the Global South in terms of the degrees of social inclusion.

In general, the ROER4D studies found variable access to and engagement with OER in the research sites in South America, Sub-Saharan Africa, and South and Southeast Asia. Of the three forms of engagement with OER – namely, using OER "as is", adapting OER and creating OER – the most frequently cited by research participants was the use of OER "as is". The second most frequently reported activity was creation of OER. Compared to these two forms of OER engagement, there were fewer reports of OER adaptation (which includes localisation and translation).

The discussion below explores the factors that account for the extent of OER use, adaptation and creation observed in the ROER4D studies in order to draw insights into how social inclusion through OER and OEP can be achieved in the Global South.

Factors influencing access to educational materials through OER use

OER are considered to be a means for making educational content more accessible to educators and students, especially in economically depressed regions where textbooks and other learning resources are scarce and/or costly. However, findings from the ROER4D studies suggest that access to OER in the Global South countries studied is uneven. In their survey of educators and students in nine countries in South America, Sub-Saharan Africa, and South and Southeast Asia, de Oliveira Neto, Pete, Daryono and Cartmill (Chapter 3) found that while a little more than half (51%) of educators and almost two-fifths (39%) of students said that they had used OER at least once, as many as a quarter of the educators and slightly more than a quarter of the students said they had never used OER, and slightly less than a quarter (24%) of the educators and more than a third (35%) of the students said they were not sure whether they had used OER. The ROER4D studies suggest that educators' and students' level of access to OER is an important factor in whether and to what extent they use OER. Access to OER in turn is shaped by OER awareness, technological infrastructure and OER availability.

OER awareness refers to familiarity with OER as a concept and an understanding of how OER are different from other types of (non-open) educational materials. In the ROER4D studies, lack of OER awareness was apparent in the fact that many educators and students signified uncertainty regarding whether they had used OER. Cox and Trotter (Chapter 9) and Kasinathan and Ranganathan (Chapter 14) note that this uncertainty stems in part from a lack of understanding of the legal restrictions of copyright, which is exacerbated by the ease with which online materials may be downloaded free of charge, regardless of their associated licence. In some cases, educators engage in what is arguably too liberal an application of the principle of "fair use", which permits use of copyrighted material without permission from the copyright holder for non-commercial and restricted use in the classroom and for other "transformative" purposes (such as critique). In general, there was a low level of familiarity with open licensing among the research participants and the range of permissions this allows. Thus, while many educators and students might inadvertently use OER (because the item they downloaded from the internet happened to have an open licence), their deliberate use of such resources is limited.

Although online access to OER is optimal to ensure maximum reusability, some OER used by ROER4D research participants were available as print copies in institutional libraries (Adala, 2017) or as government-supplied textbooks (Goodier, Chapter 7). To be able to access online OER, one must have a digital device and a stable internet connection, which in turn requires reliable electricity provision. In the ROER4D studies, access to computers and other digital devices (such as mobile phones) and to the internet was not a problem for most of the educators in higher education and less so amongst school teachers. However, many students, especially in rural and economically depressed communities, lacked even basic connectivity. This had a constraining effect not only on the students' use of digital resources, but also on the educators' pedagogical decisions to use digital materials in their teaching. For example, Cox and Trotter (Chapter 9) found that lecturers at a distance education university in South Africa worried about the lack of connectivity for their rural students, and thus limited the amount of digital materials they incorporated into their teaching. In their study of OER adoption in six institutions in East Africa, Wolfenden, Auckloo, Buckler and Cullen (Chapter 8) referred to inadequate access to laptops and desktop computers and lack of internet connectivity as factors that restricted teacher educators' exploration of OER, particularly in rural higher education institutions (HEIs). The inadequate technical infrastructure is also one reason for the low level of digital literacy, which in some instances is the main factor limiting access to and use of digital resources, including OER. It is this multidimensional digital divide that validates Willems and Bossu's contention that, "while equity reasons often underpin the provision of OER, challenges continue to be experienced by some in accessing open digital materials for learning" (2012, p.185).

Another important access factor is the availability of suitable OER. While the quantity of available OER is growing, this is not necessarily of value to educators, who often find the vast number of online resources overwhelming, as Wolfenden et al. (Chapter 8) observe. Added to this is the question of the appropriateness of the available OER for an educator's or student's specific use. Several of the ROER4D sub-projects found that educators and students use online materials based on their perceived relevance, regardless of whether they are openly licensed. A key aspect of relevance is language. Most of the globally available OER are in English, which means that they need to be translated for use in contexts where the medium of instruction is different, such as Swahili in Tanzania (Wolfenden et al., Chapter 8), Dari and Pashto in Afghanistan (Oates, Goger, Hashimi & Farahmand, Chapter 15), Urdu in Pakistan (Waqar, Shams, Malik, Ahsan ul Haq & Raza, 2017), and Tamil and Sinhala in Sri Lanka (Karunanayaka & Naidu, Chapter 13).

In sum, while OER can help to address the problem of inadequate educational resources, access to OER in the Global South is constrained by lack of awareness and understanding of OER, poor connectivity and limited access to computers, and the unavailability of relevant and/or useable OER. Since access is a prerequisite for OER adoption, these factors also limit educators' and students' adaptation and creation of OER, activities which represent higher degrees of engagement with OER and, more generally, participation in knowledge production. We discuss this aspect of the relationship between OER adoption and social inclusion in the next section.

Factors shaping participation through OER adaptation

Beyond providing access to educational resources, the power of OER as a means for achieving social inclusion lies in its potential to transform teaching into a more participatory process. In particular, adapting OER (for example by translating it into a local language, customising it to suit a particular set of students or combining several OER to make a new resource) broadens an educator's understanding of what teaching entails beyond "delivering" instruction, encourages reflection on how to engage students more, and promotes collaboration with other educators as well as with students. However, the ROER4D studies indicate limited adaptation of OER by educators and students. In the cross-regional survey (de Oliveira et al., Chapter 3), only 18% of educators and 6% of students reported having participated in adapting or modifying OER at least once. Educators and students generally use OER "as is" (verbatim), which is the most basic form of reuse, equivalent to simply "copying" content. The factors that account for this relatively low degree of participation in OER-based practice include technical skills (including fluency in English), pedagogical practices, institutional policies and support mechanisms.

Adaptation of OER requires a range of technical skills, including translation, multimedia proficiency and instructional design. As mentioned, there is a predominance of OER in English and translating these resources poses a challenge for those whose native language is not English. Oates et al. (Chapter 15) describe how OER in English are translated into Dari and Pashto by volunteer translators for the Darakht-e Danesh Library (DDL) in Afghanistan. Translation also takes time, which could be a barrier to OER adoption by educators, as Zagdragchaa and Trotter (Chapter 11) point out in their study of OER adoption practices in Mongolia. Educators in the East African teacher education institutions studied by Wolfenden et al. (Chapter 8) said that using OER adds to their preparation time, as it requires careful assessment of the quality of resources as well as restructuring of content to align it with particular learning objectives. These activities also require instructional design skills which the educators often do not have.

Pedagogic orientations and practices, which include educators' beliefs about the nature of knowledge, conceptions of learning, teaching perspectives and professional identities, also account for educators' attitudes to and practice of adapting OER. Among school teachers in Afghanistan, Oates et al. (Chapter 15) observed the "entrenched practice" of relying on the textbook in preparing lessons despite the availability of a variety of OER that they could easily access from the DDL. Wolfenden et al. (Chapter 8) noted the perception of some teacher educators in campus-based universities in East Africa that using OER in the classroom would distract students from the learning task, and it would not be appreciated by students, who are thought to be interested only in passing examinations and reluctant to explore new ideas or try out new learning experiences.

Institutional policies and the corresponding support mechanisms also influence whether and how OER are used by educators. In many cases, due to lack of OER awareness in the first instance, a policy mandating the use of OER could propel educators to use such resources. For example, policy guides for shifting from use of proprietary textbooks and materials to OER-based course packages have recently been enacted in distance education institutions in Malaysia (Menon, Phalachandra, Emmanuel & Kee, 2017) and the Philippines (Bonito, Reyes, Serrano, Ramos & Orias, 2017). At one South African university, the institution's Open Access policy encourages (but does not require) educators to use, adapt, create and share their educational materials as OER. This approach is useful in "collegial" institutional cultures where educators enjoy a high degree of personal autonomy in their pedagogical decisions (Cox & Trotter, Chapter 9). Educators also value policies dealing with rewards and incentives which officially recognise educators for their adoption of OER. For example, educators at four Indian HEIs identified the lack of a recognition and reward system as a major obstacle to OER development (Mishra & Singh, Chapter 12), and half of 42 Mongolian university educators surveyed said that the lack of a reward system for OER adoption was an important factor in their decision-making on this issue (Zagdragchaa & Trotter, Chapter 11).

Aside from incentives, educators across several research sites referred to the need for skills training, administrative and technical support, and tools and resources for OER-based teaching and learning. In the ROER4D studies in India (Kasinathan & Ranganathan, Chapter 14; Mishra & Singh, Chapter 12) and Sri Lanka (Karunanayaka & Naidu, Chapter 13), skills development was provided through workshops for educators and course developers. In the sub-projects in India (Kasinathan & Ranganathan, Chapter 14), Colombia (Sáenz, Hernandez & Hernández, Chapter 5) and Afghanistan (Oates et al., Chapter 15), technical support in curating and circulating OER developed by school teachers was provided by non-governmental organisations (NGOs). Educators at a South African university who were involved in the development and delivery of Massive Open Online Courses (MOOCs) with OER as component elements appreciated working with instructional designers in designing the different elements of the MOOCs and navigating the intricacies of copyright management (Czerniewicz, Deacon, Glover & Walji, Chapter 10). In these examples, educators had access to technical support in developing derivative (adapted) as well as original materials, in applying the relevant licences to enable sharing and reuse of materials, and in uploading resources to a project or institutional OER platform where they could be accessed by colleagues within and beyond their respective institutions.

It should be noted that most of the educators who participated in the ROER4D studies worked in environments where there were few institutional support mechanisms for OER adoption, including use of existing OER and development of derivative and/or new OER. Most of the institutions featured in ROER4D sub-project studies did not have OER-specific policies, which meant that any potential OER activity within these institutions would be governed by national copyright legislation and institutional intellectual property (IP) policies, which might be agnostic about OER use but antithetical to OER creation (including production of derivative work) due to the fact that, in many countries, legislation grants employers copyright over works created by employees in the course of their official duties. This includes teaching materials created by educators, which means that educators technically do not have the right to openly share their teaching materials unless these rights are ceded to them by their institutions. On the positive side, some of the HEIs in the ROER4D studies have drafted policies that either grant copyright of teaching materials to the educator who created them (allowing them to share their materials as OER) or that commit the institution to managing and sharing the teaching materials of its educators under an institutional banner (Cox & Trotter, Chapter 9).

In sum, the participation factors discussed here shed light on the challenges involved in going beyond use of OER "as is" to engaging with OER in more dynamic ways to improve the quality of instruction (and the quality of the educational resources themselves) to foster participatory learning. The theoretical and empirical literature points to the need for educator training, policy and technical support, as well as cultures of collaboration as components of the more durable types of social and institutional arrangements that can bolster and sustain OEP, especially OER adaptation. ROER4D findings, however, show that educators and students participated in OER adaptation activities far less frequently than in the other types of OER adoption activities (use and creation of OER). As discussed in the next section, while OER creation ranked lower as an activity than OER use "as is", it was still more prevalent than OER adaptation, a practice that requires pedagogical clarity (allowing educators to see exactly how they can integrate OER into their teaching), technical capacity (to revise and remix OER and then to reshare the new OER openly) and a supportive social and institutional environment (to sustain open, collaborative instructional materials development).

Factors empowering educators and students through OER creation

A more expansive form of social inclusion is empowerment, which is best exemplified through OER creation. This activity was less prevalent among ROER4D research participants than OER use, but more common than OER adaptation. In the cross-regional survey (de Oliveira et al., Chapter 3), 23% of educators and 9% of students stated that they had created OER at least once. Based on the findings from the ROER4D studies, the factors that promote OER creation include opportunities afforded by (typically externally funded) OER projects, collaboration with colleagues and students, and agential factors related to personal motivation and the desire to assert an epistemic stance.

The ROER4D sub-projects that employed participatory action research or design-based research methodologies demonstrated the role that funded OER projects can play in providing educators (particularly in rural communities) with opportunities to engage in OER creation. In Colombia, 22 teachers in six rural schools, who were equipped with the necessary skills and resources and supported by a community of practice composed of peers and experienced facilitators, created 16 OER for use in different subject areas (Sáenz et al., Chapter 5). The research-led interaction took the teachers from a point of relative "disempowerment" with regard to developing their own teaching materials, to a position where they were creating a broad array of OER to be shared openly. Projects like these counter the sense of disempowerment that comes from being on the wrong side of the digital divide. They can also be instrumental in the formation of professional development networks where collaborative OER creation can flourish, as shown in the sub-project in India where school teachers created 25 original demonstration videos in the local Kannada language, which formed the core resource material for a statewide training programme (Kasinathan & Ranganathan, Chapter 14). Even among university faculty, collaborative creation of materials is relatively rare and usually takes place in experimental contexts, such as the launch of an institutionally funded MOOC initiative at one South African university (Czerniewicz et al., Chapter 10).

It would seem that attitudes towards collaboration and sharing are informed by the educator's professional community. In higher education especially, this community consists of a discipline-based department that exerts a strong influence on educators' teaching practices as well as attitudes to knowledge-building and -sharing. As interviews at South African universities revealed, educators were sensitive not only to general disciplinary norms but also to departmental cultures where peer pressure can shape their teaching choices, sometimes leading to OER adoption (Cox & Trotter, Chapter 9). Thus, for example, lecturers at a South African distance education university who already enjoyed high levels of intra-departmental sharing, thought that it made sense to share learning resources beyond their departmental contexts. However, when the opposite was the case – i.e. when colleagues were not in the habit of sharing teaching materials (due to a lack of confidence or anxiety about others "stealing" their ideas) – respondents were less enthusiastic about OEP.

A few educators who were early OER adopters and who observed that teaching with OER made learning more enjoyable and engaging for students, also described sharing (with an open licence) materials created by their students aside from their own work (Wolfenden et al., Chapter 8). Embracing a learner-centred pedagogy to the point of encouraging students to become co-creators of OER is deeply empowering for all concerned, disrupting the power dynamics traditionally associated with the transmissive educator–student relationship. It should be noted, however, that this was a very nascent phenomenon in the ROER4D research sites. For the most part, such open co-creation is not happening (Westermann Juárez & Venegas Muggli, Chapter 6), as educators are constrained by conventional teaching approaches, culturally informed notions of the educator–student relationship, over-reliance on the traditional textbook and a modest familiarity with OEP.

Personal motivation, especially the desire to enhance one's reputation, underpins some educators' practice of creating and sharing teaching materials as OER. In some cases, such as at one South African university (Cox & Trotter, Chapter 9), educators may receive official recognition for their OER contributions (in this case, an award given at a public ceremony). In most other instances, recognition comes in the form of feedback from users of the content who offer words of praise and gratitude and then share the resource with their colleagues. Mishra and Singh (Chapter 12) report that most of the Indian university educators in their study equated sharing educational resources with improving their professional stature, enhancing their personal reputation and boosting their institutional standing. While this self-promotional facet of OER creation is rarely discussed in the open movement, it forms an important element in the diverse mix of reasons that individuals have for engaging in OEP.

Another form of motivation for creating and sharing OER is personal fulfilment and confidence. Educators across the ROER4D research sites said that they experienced a great deal of satisfaction from sharing their materials openly. It addressed a deeply held desire concerning what type of educator they wanted to be and how they imagined themselves at their most effective, as evidenced in the results of an attitudinal survey of Indian university lecturers (Mishra & Singh, Chapter 12). In many ways, such motivation is personally defined, as ROER4D researchers also met many educators who said that they would not get the same sense of fulfilment out of openly sharing their materials because they were concerned about quality and the potentially critical assessment they might receive from colleagues. For those who were able to produce materials that they believed reflected well on themselves and could also be of real value to others, the act of sharing materials openly was a gratifying one.

Finally, creation and sharing of OER can be a way of asserting an epistemic stance, or one's own unique (individual or collective) perspective of knowledge. This is vital for people from marginalised communities whose histories and knowledge have been sidelined or suppressed by colonial or hegemonic powers. The internet as a communication platform, and OER as an educational resource that can be freely shared, provide an opportunity for educators in the Global South to contribute their own ideas, give voice to their own perspectives and participate in a global conversation. For the school teachers participating in ROER4D sub-project studies, such epistemic assertiveness represented a new level of agency characterised by a greater sense of accountability and a widening of their sphere of influence (Sáenz et al., Chapter 5). Likewise, for university educators, the offering of MOOCs provided an opportunity to assert alternative epistemic perspectives on a global scale, though it involved both personal and institutional reputational risks (Czerniewicz et al., Chapter 10). By contributing original OER and/or MOOCs, educators were offering knowledge to the world in their own unique voices and through their own "theory from the South" (Comaroff & Comaroff, 2012), engaging in a dynamic conversation with hegemonic epistemic perspectives while strengthening their sense of self-identity.

In sum, the ROER4D studies show that OER creation as a form of empowerment for educators and students from the Global South is fostered by professional development, membership in a community of practice and personal qualities and motivations related to personal histories as well as professional identities. There are a number of legal and technical challenges to OER creation, including complex licensing processes and IP policies that grant copyright over teaching materials to employers. For those educators who do create their own instructional materials, they have a ready supply of content that could be shared as OER, as long as the legal and technical requirements are dealt with and they have the confidence and desire to do so. For some, this process of sharing is imperative in order to ensure that voices from the South are broadcast to the world – particularly to others in similar contexts who need high-quality, locally relevant materials. However, for the time being, OER creation remains the exception rather than the rule.

Figure 1 provides a summary overview of the factors that influence each of the three forms of OER engagement – OER use, adaptation and creation – and the associated levels of social inclusion, with factors ordered from least socially inclusive (at the bottom of each list) to most.

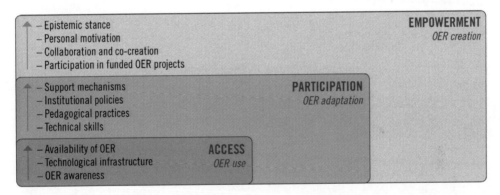

Figure 1: Levels of social inclusion through OER use, adaptation and creation, with the structural, cultural and agential factors that impact on each type of OER engagement

We posit that these three forms of OER adoption comprising the Open Education cycle (described in Chapter 2) contribute to the achievement of social inclusion in the following ways:

- OER use in general and OER use "as is" widen access to educational materials and to education more broadly.
- OER adaptation fosters participatory pedagogy, which encourages learner-centred teaching, extends the range of localised OER available to students and deepens learner engagement.
- OER creation empowers educators and students to contribute to knowledge production.

Recommendations

Based on our analysis of the findings from the ROER4D studies in 21 countries in South America, Sub-Saharan Africa, and South and Southeast Asia, we propose the following recommendations to ensure equitable access to OER, active adaptation of OER to suit local contexts, and creation and sharing of openly licensed teaching and learning resources showcasing local knowledge in relevant languages.

Advocacy

Recommendations for cultural interventions by intergovernmental agencies, NGOs, donor and research agencies include:

- Creating awareness of OER and how these legally reusable materials are different from other types of materials available on the internet.
- Engaging with policy-makers, particularly at state/provincial and institutional levels, to deliberate research findings and the value propositions of OER.
- Initiating projects where intergovernmental agencies, NGOs and donor and research agencies support initial research, implement an OER adaptation and/ or creation project, and developmentally monitor both processes using user-focused evaluation.[5]

Policy

Recommendations for structural interventions by government agencies and policy-makers include:

- Providing an enabling infrastructure, including a reliable power supply and hardware and connectivity, especially in underserved areas.
- Developing a favourable policy environment for OER creation, particularly as relates to legal permission for educators to share materials they create in the course of their work.
- Developing local platforms or portals where educators and students can host and share local content and practices (depending on the size of the country and the number of languages spoken, there could be one or several of these portals).
- Engaging with internet service providers for zero-rate access[6] to these platforms.
- Providing support to educators, particularly as relates to technical proficiency, open licensing and learning design.
- Allocating time, rewards and recognition for the adaptation and creation of OER.

---

5   The user-focused evaluation used in the ROER4D project was based on the work of Patton (2008), which was customised for International Development Research Centre projects by Ramirez and Brodhead (2013).

6   "Zero-rate access" refers to the provision of free internet access to specified educational sites, as implemented in South Africa in 2017 by internet service providers (see https://www.mtnblog.co.za/mtn-zero-rates-access-to-online-curriculum-for-university-students/).

Practice

Recommendations for transforming institutional culture and developing agency include:
- Promoting teacher professional development in OER adoption, including critical digital literacy, participatory pedagogy and instructional design.
- Building professional learning networks and local communities of practice.
- Developing local-language and curriculum-aligned OER in order to have sufficient collections of OER that could be easily used by educators and students alike.
- Encouraging a culture of sharing within disciplines and departments.
- Encouraging educators to co-create OER with students.

Further research

Recommendations for further research (topically) include:
- Use and adaptation of OER by basic education students.
- Creation, use and adaptation of OER by informal learners.
- Uptake of OER originally created in the Global South.
- Provincial collaborative teacher professional development networks supporting OER adoption in schools.
- School-based collaborative teacher professional support for OER adoption.
- Institutional policies enabling OER creation, especially copyright permission but also reward and recognition.
- Extent of OER reuse within institutional learning management systems and portals.
- Cost-effectiveness of OER adoption in the Global South.
- Textbook practices and OER adoption in the Global South.

Conclusion

The relationship between OEP (OER use, adaptation and creation) and the degrees of social inclusion (access, participation and empowerment) should be understood not as a hard set of findings, but as an emergent and provisional set of understandings around how engaging with OER, and OEP more generally, may lead to varied social inclusion outcomes. The three-tiered nested schema presented in Figure 1 is valuable for thinking through these concepts and identifying where there may be critical disjunctures in OEP across the Global South. A key insight is that while equitable access remains a challenge in the Global South and should be addressed, it is in the realms of individual and community participation and empowerment that future OER interventions hold their greatest promise and will yield their largest gains. It is in those areas that broader inclusivity can be achieved and sustained.

Acknowledgements

The authors would like to thank Michelle Willmers for her detailed review of this chapter.

References

Adala, A. (2017). Assessing the impact of OER availability on the emergence of Open Educational Practices in Sub-Saharan Africa: The case of an ICT-integrated multinational teacher education programme in mathematics and science. Unpublished ROER4D report to the International Development Research Centre.

Bliss, T. J. & Smith, M. (2017). A brief history of Open Educational Resources. In R. S. Jhangiani & R. Biswas-Diener (Eds.), *Open: The philosophy and practices that are revolutionizing education and science* (pp. 9–27). London: Ubiquity Press. Retrieved from https://doi.org/10.5334/bbc.b

Bonito, S., Reyes, C., Serrano, J., Ramos, R. & Orias, C. (2017). Impact of OER on cost and quality of course materials in postgraduate distance education courses in the Philippines. Unpublished ROER4D report to the International Development Research Centre.

Bradley, L. & Vigmo, S. (2014). *Open Educational Resources (OER) in less used languages: A state of the art report.* Brussels: LangOER project. Retrieved from http://files.eun.org/langoer/10%20WP2%20study.compressed%20(1).pdf

Comaroff, J. & Comaroff, J. L. (2012). Theory from the South: Or, how Euro-America is evolving toward Africa. *Anthropological Forum, 22(2),* 113–131.

Connell, R. (2007). *Southern theory: The global dynamics of knowledge in social science.* Cambridge: Polity.

Cox, G. & Trotter, H. (2017). Factors shaping lecturers' adoption of OER at three South African universities. In C. Hodgkinson-Williams & P. B. Arinto (Eds.), *Adoption and impact of OER in the Global South* (pp. 287–347). Retrieved from https://doi.org/10.5281/zenodo.601935

Czerniewicz, L., Deacon, A., Glover, M. & Walji, S. (2017). OER in and as MOOCs. In C. Hodgkinson-Williams & P. B. Arinto (Eds.), *Adoption and impact of OER in the Global South* (pp. 349–386). Retrieved from https://doi.org/10.5281/zenodo.604414

de Oliveira Neto, J. D., Pete, J., Daryono & Cartmill, T. (2017). OER use in the Global South: A baseline survey of higher education instructors. In C. Hodgkinson-Williams & P. B. Arinto (Eds.), *Adoption and impact of OER in the Global South* (pp. 69–118). Retrieved from https://doi.org/10.5281/zenodo.599535

Gidley, J., Hampson, G., Wheeler, L. & Bereded-Samuel, E. (2010). Social inclusion: Context, theory and practice. *The Australasian Journal of University-Community Engagement, 5(1),* 6–36. Retrieved from https://researchbank.rmit.edu.au/view/rmit:4909

Goodier, S. (2017). Tracking the money for Open Educational Resources in South African basic education: What we don't know. *The International Review of Research in Open and Distributed Learning, 18(4).* Retrieved from http://dx.doi.org/10.19173/irrodl.v18i4.2990

Jhangiani, R. S. (2017, March 30). *Serving social justice and pedagogical innovation through Open Educational Practices* [Video file]. Retrieved from http://hdl.handle.net/1808/24718

Jhangiani, R. S. & Biswas-Diener, R. (Eds.). (2017). *Open: The philosophy and practices that are revolutionizing education and science.* London: Ubiquity Press. Retrieved from https://www.ubiquitypress.com/site/books/10.5334/bbc/

Karunanayaka, S. & Naidu, S. (2017). Impact of integrating OER in teacher education at the Open University of Sri Lanka. In C. Hodgkinson-Williams & P. B. Arinto (Eds.), *Adoption and* impact of OER in the Global South (pp. 459–498). Retrieved from https://doi.org/10.5281/zenodo.600398

Kasinathan, G. & Ranganathan, S. (2017). Teacher professional learning communities: A collaborative OER adoption approach in Karnataka, India. In C. Hodgkinson-Williams & P. B. Arinto (Eds.), *Adoption and impact of OER in the Global South* (pp. 499–548). Retrieved from https://doi.org/10.5281/zenodo.601180

Knox, J. (2013). Five critiques of the Open Educational Resources movement. *Teaching in Higher Education, 18(8)*. Retrieved from http://www.tandfonline.com/doi/abs/10.1080/13562517.2013.774354

Lane, A. (2012). A review of the role of national policy and institutional mission in European distance teaching universities with respect to widening participation in higher education study through Open Educational Resources. *Distance Education, 33(2)*, 136–150.

Menon, M., Phalachandra, B., Emmanuel, J. & Kee, C. L. (2017). A study on the processes of OER integration for course development. Unpublished ROER4D report to the International Development Research Centre.

Mishra, S. & Singh, A. (2017). Higher education faculty attitude, motivation and perception of quality and barriers towards OER in India. In C. Hodgkinson-Williams & P. B. Arinto (Eds.), *Adoption and impact of OER in the Global South* (pp. 425–458). Retrieved from https://doi.org/10.5281/zenodo.602784

Oates, L., Goger, L. K., Hashimi, J. & Farahmand, M. (2017). An early stage impact study of localised OER in Afghanistan. In C. Hodgkinson-Williams & P. B. Arinto (Eds.), *Adoption and impact of OER in the Global South* (pp. 549–573). Retrieved from https://doi.org/10.5281/zenodo.600441

Patton, M. Q. (2008). *Utilization-focused evaluation*. Thousand Oaks, CA: Sage.

Perryman, L–A. & Coughlan, T. (2013). The realities of "reaching out": Enacting the public-facing open scholar role with existing online communities. *Journal of Interactive Media in Education (3)*, p.Art. 21. DOI: http://doi.org/10.5334/2013-21

Ramirez, R. & Brodhead, D. (2013). *Utilization focused evaluation: A primer for evaluators*. Penang: Southbound. Retrieved from https://evaluationinpractice.files.wordpress.com/2013/04/ufeenglishprimer.pdf

Richter, T. & McPherson, M. (2012). Open Educational Resources: Education for the world? *Distance Education, 33(2)*, 201–219.

Sáenz, M. P., Hernandez, U. & Hernández, Y. M. (2017). Co-creation of OER by teachers and teacher educators in Colombia. In C. Hodgkinson-Williams & P. B. Arinto (Eds.), *Adoption and impact of OER in the Global South* (pp. 143–185). Retrieved from https://doi.org/10.5281/zenodo.604384

Saunders, P., Naidoo, Y. & Griffiths, M. (2007). *Towards new indicators of disadvantage: Deprivation and social exclusion in Australia*. Sydney: Social Policy Research Centre. Retrieved from https://www.sprc.unsw.edu.au/media/SPRCFile/Report12_07_Deprivation_and_exclusion_in_Australia.pdf

Waqar, Y., Shams, S., Malik, N., Ahsan ul Haq, M. & Raza, S. M. M. (2017). An exploratory case study: Enabling and inhibiting factors and extent of use of OER in Pakistan. Unpublished ROER4D report to the International Development Research Centre.

Westermann Juárez, W. & Venegas Muggli, J. I. (2017). Effectiveness of OER use in first-year higher education students' mathematical course performance: A case study. In C. Hodgkinson-Williams & P. B. Arinto (Eds.), *Adoption and impact of OER in the Global South* (pp. 187–229). Retrieved from https://doi.org/10.5281/zenodo.601203

Willems, J. & Bossu, C. (2012). Equity considerations for Open Educational Resources in the glocalization of education. *Distance Education, 33(2)*, 185–199.

Wolfenden, F., Auckloo, P., Buckler, A. & Cullen, J. (2017). Teacher educators and OER in East Africa: Interrogating pedagogic change. In C. Hodgkinson-Williams & P. B. Arinto (Eds.), *Adoption and impact of OER in the Global South* (pp. 251–286). Retrieved from https://doi.org/10.5281/zenodo.600424

Zagdragchaa, B. & Trotter, H. (2017). Cultural-historical factors influencing OER adoption in Mongolia's higher education sector. In C. Hodgkinson-Williams & P. B. Arinto (Eds.), *Adoption and impact of OER in the Global South* (pp. 389–424). Retrieved from https://doi.org/10.5281/zenodo.599609

How to cite this chapter

Arinto, P. B., Hodgkinson-Williams, C. & Trotter, H. (2017). OER and OEP in the Global South: Implications and recommendations for social inclusion. In C. Hodgkinson-Williams & P. B. Arinto (Eds.), *Adoption and impact of OER in the Global South* (pp. 577–592). Retrieved from https://doi.org/10.5281/zenodo.1043829

Corresponding author: Patricia B. Arinto <patricia.arinto@gmail.com>